INTERNATIONAL ECONOMIC LAW AND GOVERNANCE

International Economic Law and Governance

Essays in Honour of Mitsuo Matsushita

Edited by
JULIEN CHAISSE
and
TSAI-YU LIN

OXFORD
UNIVERSITY PRESS

OXFORD
UNIVERSITY PRESS

Great Clarendon Street, Oxford, OX2 6DP,
United Kingdom

Oxford University Press is a department of the University of Oxford.
It furthers the University's objective of excellence in research, scholarship,
and education by publishing worldwide. Oxford is a registered trade mark of
Oxford University Press in the UK and in certain other countries

First published 2016

Published in the United States of America by Oxford University Press
198 Madison Avenue, New York, NY 10016, United States of America

British Library Cataloguing in Publication Data
Data available

ISBN 978–0–19–877825–7

Cover image: Shinagawa: departure of a Daimyo, in later editions called Sunrise, No.2 from the series '53 Stations of the Tokaido' ('Tokaido gojusan tsugi no uchi'), pub. by Hoeido, 1833 (oban size, yoko-e - horizontal format, colour woodblock print), Hiroshige, Ando or Utagawa (1797–1858).

Professor Mitsuo Matsushita

Foreword

'Liber amicorum' to celebrate Mitsuo Matsushita's contributions to international economic law

Chang-fa Lo

Professor Mitsuo Matsushita is one of the most respected leading figures in international economic law (IEL). His meritorious services, including being one of the founding members of the Appellate Body of the World Trade Organization from 1995 to 2000, have been well recognized throughout the world. His great writings, including so many widely circulated books and articles in the fields of international trade, competition law, and investment law, have been considered as widely influential. His educational services, including his professorship at Tokyo University and visiting professorships at Harvard Law School, Michigan Law School, Columbia Law School, Monash University in Australia, and at the College of Europe in Bruges, Belgium, have been deeply appreciated by his students and by these educational institutions themselves.

He is so immensely respected in the Asia-Pacific region and beyond, not only because of his leading role in IEL, but also because of his upright character in handling things, his warmness in treating friends, and his willingness in helping younger scholars. He was the founding chairperson of Asia WTO Research Network (AWRN) and continued to lead the group for almost ten years (from 2004 to 2013). It is because of Professor Matsushita that our colleagues in Asia-Pacific region in the field of IEL have a permanent platform to engage in regular and exciting academic exchanges.

For all these reasons, Members of AWRN decided to make a joint effort to publish a Festschrift in honour of Professor Matsushita, in order to express their sincere gratitude for the inspiration he is to all of us and to celebrate his contributions to IEL. Professors Julien Chaisse and Tsai-yu Lin have been kind enough to take on the role of inviting Professor Matsushita's former colleagues, friends, students, and admirers to submit their chapters on the main theme of 'International Economic Law and Governance', in which Professor Matsushita has played such an important role in shaping the rules and in engaging in operating the mechanism. Julien and Tsai-yu, together with their team, also spent much time and effort in editing the book. It is because of them that we have the book that reflects Professor Matsushita's great contribution so well. I should also thank authors of the chapters in the book for having contributed to the joint work.

I hope that the high quality of this book properly reflects our appreciation to Professor Matsushita for having guided us by his great personality and scholarly achievement.

Chang-fa Lo
Chairperson, AWRN

Contents

PART III ISSUES IN THE POLICY- AND LAW-MAKING PROCESS

Table of Cases

Note: WTO and GATT cases are indexed according to their common abbreviated names (where these are in use in the text), with the full name in parentheses. Where Panel and Appellate Body hearings of the same case are listed separately the Panel hearing appears first.
n = footnote.

INTERNATIONAL CASES

WTO Dispute Settlement Body

GATT Panels

REGIONAL CASES

ECJ/CJEU (European Court of Justice/Court of Justice of the European Union) (cases in number order)

European Court of Human Rights (ECtHR)

European Commission

NAFTA

NATIONAL CASES

Canada

India

United States

List of Contributors

Frederick M Abbott is Edward Ball Eminent Scholar Professor of International Law at Florida State University College of Law. He has served as expert consultant for numerous international and regional organizations, governments and nongovernmental organizations, mainly in the fields of intellectual property, public health, trade, competition and sustainable development. He recently served as a member of the Expert Advisory Group (EAG) to the UN Secretary General's High Level Panel on Access to Medicines. Professor Abbott is published widely in the fields of international intellectual property rights law, public health, international economic and competition law and international law. Books include *International Intellectual Property in an Integrated World Economy*, 3rd edn 2015 (with T Cottier and F Gurry), *Emerging Markets and the World Patent Order*, ed. with Carlos M Correa and Peter Drahos (2013), and *Global Pharmaceutical Policy* (2009) (with G Dukes). He is Co-Chair of the Committee on Global Health Law of the International Law Association, having served as Rapporteur for the Committee on International Trade Law from the inception of its work in 1993 to its conclusion in 2014. He is consultant to the World Health Organization, the United Nations Development Program and other multilateral institutions. Professor Abbott is on the editorial board of the Journal of International Economic Law (Oxford). He regularly serves as panelist for the WIPO Arbitration and Mediation Center. He has served as counsel to governments in WTO dispute settlement proceedings, and in national court proceedings. Professor Abbott is Co-Director of the Executive Course on Intellectual Property, Diplomacy and Global Public Health for the Global Health Programme of the Graduate Institute, Geneva. He is a graduate of the Yale Law School and the University of California, Berkeley.

Dukgeun Ahn is Professor of International Trade Law and Policy. Professor Ahn has taught at various universities including Singapore National University, University of Hong Kong, University of Barcelona in Spain, World Trade Institute in Switzerland and the KDI School of Public Policy and Management in Korea. In addition, he has advised several developing country governments, international organizations as well as various Korean ministries on trade law and policy issues such as World Trade Organization (WTO) disputes, trade negotiation and trade policy making. Professor Ahn is currently working as a Commissioner of the Korea Trade Commission and served as a Member of National Economic Advisory Council. He is also listed as a panellist candidate for the WTO dispute settlement as well as the Korea–US FTA and Korea–EU FTA. He received Award by the Minister of Commerce, Industry and Energy of Republic of Korea, 2004; Award by the Prime Minister of Republic of Korea, 2005; Simdang Academic Excellence Award, Korea Association of International Trade Law, 2012; and Award by the Minister of the Interior, 2015. He works as an editorial board member for many academic journals, including Journal of International Economic Law (Oxford University Press) and International Trade Law (Quarterly Journal of Ministry of Justice). Professor Ahn holds both PhD in Economics and JD (Member of New York Bar) from the University of Michigan, Ann Arbor.

R Rajesh Babu is an Associate Professor of Law at the Indian Institute of Management (IIM) Calcutta, India and the Editor-in-Chief of the IIM Calcutta journal *Decision* published by Springer. Before joining IIM Calcutta, Dr Babu served as Senior Legal Officer (2002–2009) in the Asian-African Legal Consultative Organization (AALCO), a New Delhi Headquartered intergovernmental organization. He obtained his PhD from the Jawaharlal Nehru University (JNU), New Delhi. He has received scholarship from the Hague Academy of International Law, The Hague and the Graduate Institute (IHEID), Geneva. He has published several articles in international and national journals in the area of WTO law, dispute settlement, etc. His current research and areas of interest include international economic law, constitutional law, international adjudication, property rights, investment, and higher education policy. Dr Rajesh Babu has been the Guest Editor of the *Journal of Risk Research* and manuscript (book) reviewer for Routledge and Oxford University Press. His recent book is *Remedies under the WTO Legal System* (Martinus Nijhoff). His forthcoming co-edited book is *Management Education in India: Perspectives and Practices* (Springer 2016).

Raj Bhala joined the KU Law faculty in 2003 as the Rice Distinguished Professor, the highest university-level professorship at KU. He received the 2011 Woodyard International Educator Award, a university-wide award granted to one faculty member for outstanding contributions to internationalization efforts, the 2010 Moreau Award for advising and counselling students, and a 2008 Kemper Award for Teaching Excellence. He has worked in 28 countries and played in another 19 countries. Bhala is a member of the United Kingdom's Royal Society for Asian Affairs, the Council on Foreign Relations, the American Law Institute, the Fellowship of Catholic Scholars, and the All India Law Teacher's Congress. The Indian Society of International Law has conferred on him Life Membership. Bhala's scholarly reputation in international trade is global, based in part on a sustained, prolific publication record. That record includes a treatise, *Modern GATT Law*, now in its two-volume second edition, and *International Trade Law*, a two-volume textbook in its fourth edition. Both books are widely acclaimed for their substance and style. His newest book, *TPP Objectively*, is the first comprehensive analysis of the law, economics, and national security of the Trans Pacific Partnership. It breaks new ground in it being the first to argue for women's and LGBTQ rights in free trade agreements. Bhala's record also includes more than three dozen provocative articles, including eight major pieces on the Doha Round of multilateral trade negotiations, several works on poor countries, and a trilogy on stare decisis. Bhala's articles have appeared in The International Lawyer, the most widely circulated international law review, five times. Bhala's energy and enthusiasm extend to Islamic Law. He is the first non-Muslim American law professor to write a comprehensive textbook in the field, *Understanding Islamic Law Shari'a*, now in its second edition. This highly praised, widely used work covers in an accessible manner the religion, history and law of Islam. Bhala is honored and humbled to teach Islamic Law to United States Special Operations Forces. Bhala's eagerness to pioneer new fields in the American legal academy extends to India. He is under contract to write the first textbook on the business laws of modern India. Bhala practised international banking law at the Federal Reserve Bank of New York, which twice granted him the President's Award for Excellence. At the New York Fed, he represented the United States in international wire transfer negotiations at the United Nations Commission on International Trade Law (UNCITRAL), dealt with legal issues in the largest financial market in the world (foreign exchange), and was actively involved in international banking law enforcement, including the infamous scandal involving the Bank of Credit and Commerce International (BCCI). His UNCITRAL work earned him a Letter of Commendation from the State Department. Bhala earned a law degree from Harvard, was a Marshall Scholar in England where he obtained Master's degrees from LSE and Oxford, and holds a Bachelor's degree from Duke, where he was an Angier B. Duke Scholar. He loves marathon and half-marathon running, and studying Shakespeare and Hindi.

Chios Carmody is Associate Professor at Western University Faculty of Law in London, Ontario, Canada. He currently teaches courses in Contracts, International Trade Law and International Business Transactions. Since 2002 he has been Canadian National Director of the Canada-United States Law Institute. Professor Carmody has been a Visiting Professor at Université Montpellier, Visiting Adjunct Professor at Georgetown University Law Center and Emile Noël Fellow at the Jean Monnet Center for International & Regional Economic Law & Justice, NYU Law School. His current work focuses on developing a theory of WTO law as the reflection of a theory of law in general.

Julien Chaisse is an award-winning specialist in international economic law with particular expertise in the regulation and economics of foreign investment. His research also covers other relevant fields, such as WTO law, international taxation, and the law of natural resources. Before joining the CUHK Law Faculty in 2009, Professor Chaisse served in the Ministry of Foreign Affairs of France, and started his academic career in Europe. Professor Chaisse has authored a broad body of well-regarded and widely-cited articles on topics ranging from the rise of sovereign wealth funds, the regulation of foreign investment, and decision-making challenges facing the WTO, which have been published in the top refereed journals of international law. In recognition of his outstanding scholarly achievements, Professor Chaisse received the CUHK Research Excellence Award in 2012, and was appointed Director of the Center for Financial Regulation and Economic Development of our Faculty since 2013. In addition to scholarly work, Professor Chaisse has wide experience as a practitioner, and is engaged as expert, counsel, and arbitrator in transnational dispute settlement.

Won-mog Choi is a professor of Ewha Law School, Ewha Women's University at Seoul and director of the WTO Law Center at Seoul. He was the President of the Korea Society of International Economic Law and is the Editor-in-Chief of the *Korean Journal of International and Comparative Law* (Brill). Professor Choi is a member of the Editorial Board of many journals including the *Journal of International Economic Law (Oxford)*, the *Law and Development Review*, *Indian Journal of International Economic Law*, *Journal of Korea Trade*, and the *Beijing Law Review*. He was a visiting professor or professorial fellow to National University of Singapore, Hong Kong University, University of New South Wales at Sydney, and Southwest University of Political Science and Law of China. He has been a member of the New York Bar since 1999. He received his legal education in South Korea (Seoul National University, LLB and MPA) and the United States (Georgetown Law, LLM and SJD). Prior to joining faculty of Ewha, he worked for the Foreign Ministry of South Korea as a diplomat and legal officer in charge of numerous trade issues. After he joined academia, Won-mog has been providing law and policy advice to most of the trade negotiations in which South Korea has been participating so far. He is also the chairman of the Korean society of Overseas Resources Development and the president of Korea ABS forum. He is widely recognized as a renowned columnist in South Korea, contributing columns on the topics of trade and foreign affairs regularly in major newspapers in South Korea. Among his numerous academic writings, his writings on the topic of like products in WTO Agreement and his research on FTA issues are widely recognized as authoritative, and the outcome of these researches was recently collected in the *Max Planck Encyclopedia of Public International Law*.

William J Davey is the Guy Raymond Jones Chair Emeritus at the University of Illinois College of Law, where he has taught courses in international trade law, European Union law, international business transactions, and corporate/securities law since 1984. From 1995–1999, he was on leave and served as the director of the Legal Affairs Division of the World Trade Organization. He has served on several WTO dispute settlement panels, including cases involving Brazil, Canada, the European Union, South Korea, Japan, Pakistan and Ukraine, and the United States. He retired in August 2008 but continues to teach international trade law. In 2007, the University of Berne conferred an honorary doctor of laws degree on Professor Davey, inter alia, 'for his fundamental work in the development and evolution of the World Trade Organization's dispute settlement system'. In 2004, he received the University of Illinois' Distinguished Faculty Award for International Achievement. Professor Davey is the author of *Legal Problems of International Economic Relations; Non-discrimination in the World Trade Organization: The Rules and Exceptions; European Union Law; Enforcing World Trade Rules: Essays on WTO Dispute Settlement and GATT Obligations; Pine & Swine: Canada–United States Trade Dispute Settlement*; and *Handbook of WTO/GATT Dispute Settlement*, as well as the editor of *The Future of International Economic Law*. He has also written many articles and book chapters on various international trade law issues. Professor Davey is associate editor of *The Journal of International Economic Law* (Oxford) and co-general editor of the Cambridge International Trade and Economic Law book series.

Claus-Dieter Ehlermann is one of the leading authorities on international trade, European competition and European Union administrative law. He has represented governments before the WTO dispute settlement body, and he has been retained as advisor to certain governments, industry federations and undertakings involved in WTO disputes. Professor Dr Ehlermann has been engaged to submit an expert opinion in the context of NAFTA litigation. Professor Dr Ehlermann has also acted as an Arbitrator under Article 21.3(c) of the Dispute Settlement Understanding of the WTO. With regard to EC law, Professor Dr Ehlermann has represented companies in EC competition law matters, assisting companies in merger control procedures, State aid and international arbitration proceedings. On the regulatory side, Professor Dr Ehlermann has advised major companies in Europe and the United States on the impact of current and pending EU legislation. Professor Dr Ehlermann was a member of the Appellate Body of the World Trade Organization in Geneva from December 1995 through 2001, serving as chairman during the last year of his mandate. Prior to his service on the WTO Appellate Body, Professor Dr Ehlermann held several senior positions with the European Commission. He was Director-General of the Directorate-General for Competition (1990–1995), Spokesman and Special Adviser for Institutional Questions of President Jacques Delors (1987–1990) and Director-General of the Legal Service of the European Commission (1977–1987). Professor Dr Ehlermann is considered to be one of the leading academic thinkers on EC law and has published widely. He was chair of EC Law at the European University Institute (Florence).

Yuka Fukunaga is Professor of International Economic Law, School of Social Sciences, Waseda University (Tokyo). She has published a number of articles in books and journals including the *Journal of International Economic Law* and the *Journal of International Dispute Settlement*. She has also presented papers at major conferences including meetings of the Society of International Economic Law and the American Society of International Law. Attorney-at-law in New York; former Assistant Legal Counsel, Permanent Court of Arbitration (PCA) (The Hague); former Intern, World Trade Organization (WTO)

Appellate Body Secretariat (Geneva); former Visiting Professor, Far Eastern Federal University (Vladivostok); former Visiting Fellow, Graduate Institute of International and Development Studies (Geneva); former Visiting Professorial Fellow, Georgetown Law Center (Washington, DC). She has received LLD and LLM from the Graduate Schools for Law and Politics, University of Tokyo, and LLM from the School of Law, University of California, Berkeley (sponsored by Fulbright). She has recently published a book, entitled *Securing Compliance with International Economic Agreements and Dispute Settlement: The Role and Limits of the WTO Dispute Settlement and Investment Arbitration* (Japanese).

David A Gantz is Emeritus Director of the International Trade and Business Law Program at the University of Arizona, James E. Rogers College of Law. He also serves as Associate Director of the National Law Center for Inter-American Free Trade. He has taught courses in international trade law, international environmental law, NAFTA and Other Regional Trade Agreements, public international law, international business transactions, international investment and technology transfer, European Union law and the United States legal system. He is faculty adviser to the Arizona Journal of International and Comparative Law. David is a graduate of Harvard College (AB 1964) and Stanford Law School (JD 1967, JSM 1970). After two years with the United States Agency for International Development law reform project in Costa Rica and a year as a law clerk with Judge Charles M Merrill of the United States Court of Appeals for the 9th Circuit, he spent seven years with the Office of the Legal Adviser, United States Department of State. At the State Department, he was the chief lawyer responsible for Inter-American affairs. Subsequently, he practised international trade and corporate law in Washington, DC He is a member of the Ohio and District of Columbia bars, and is admitted to practise before the Court of International Trade, the Court of Appeals for the Federal Circuit and the United States Supreme Court, among others. He joined the Rogers College of Law faculty in 1993. He was a visiting professor at the George Washington University Law School during the 2003–2004 academic year and at American University during the fall 2009 semester. From 1981–1993, David was an adjunct professor of law at the Georgetown University Law Center. He has served as a binational panelist under the trade dispute resolution provisions of Chapters 19 and 20 of NAFTA, as a NAFTA Chapter 11 arbitrator, and as an expert witness in other trade and investment disputes. He has also served as the United States judge on the Administrative Tribunal of the Organization of American States. David has written extensively on NAFTA customs and trade law issues, NAFTA and WTO dispute resolution, foreign bribery and other international trade, investment and environmental law matters, including NAFTA and western hemisphere free trade and treatise, regional trade agreements: law, policy and practice and liberalizing international trade after Doha: multilateral, plurilateral, regional, and unilateral initiatives.

Bernard M Hoekman is a Professor at the Robert Schuman Centre for Advanced Studies, European University Institute in Florence, Italy and Director, Global Economics in the Schuman Centre's Global Governance Programme. Prior positions include Director of the International Trade Department and Research Manager in the Development Research Group of the World Bank; and economist in the GATT Secretariat. A graduate of the Erasmus University Rotterdam, he obtained his PhD in Economics from the University of Michigan. He is a CEPR Research Fellow where he co-directs the Trade Policy Research Network and a senior associate of the Economic Research Forum for the Arab countries, Iran and Turkey. His research focuses on trade and development, the global trade order, services trade and investment and regulatory cooperation.

Tomoko Ishikawa is an Associate Professor at the Graduate School of International Development, Nagoya University. She received an LLM from the University of Tokyo, a second LLM from the University of Cambridge, and earned her PhD in public international law from University College London (UCL). She is a member of the Legal Advisory Committee of the Energy Charter Treaty. Her professional experiences include serving as a Judge at Tokyo District Court and holding the position of Deputy Director at the International Legal Affairs Bureau of the Ministry of Foreign Affairs of Japan, where she worked on bilateral/trilateral investment treaties, Free Trade Agreements and WTO dispute settlement. Her publications include: 'Provisional Application of Treaties at the Crossroads between International and Domestic Law' (2016) 31(2) *ICSID Review*; 'Keeping Interpretation in Investment Treaty Arbitration "on Track": The Role of State Parties' in J Kalicki and A Joubin-Bret (eds), *Reshaping the Investor-State Dispute Settlement System: Journeys for the 21st Century* (Brill/Nijhoff 2015); 'The Principle of Effective Interpretation in the World Trade Organization and Investment Arbitration: Difference in Parameters?' (2015) 8(2) *Contemporary Asia Arbitration Journal*; 'International Sovereign Debt and Investment Treaty Arbitration: *Ambiente Ufficio S.p.A. and others v. Argentina*' *Rivista Dell'Arbitrato* (Issue 2/2014), 'Collective Action Clauses in Sovereign Bond Contracts and Investment Treaty Arbitration—an Approach to Reconcile the Irreconcilable' (2014) 4(2) *Accounting, Economics and Law: A Convivium*; 'The Role of International Environmental Principles in Investment Treaty Arbitration: Precautionary and Polluter Pays Principles and Partial Compensation' in FR Jacur et al (eds), *Natural Resources Grabbing: An International Law Perspective* (Brill/Nijhoff 2014); 'Third Party Participation in Investment Treaty Arbitration' (2010) 59(2) *International and Comparative Law Quarterly*.

Meredith Kolsky Lewis is Professor of Law and Vice Dean for International and Graduate Programs at the SUNY Buffalo Law School, where she directs the Cross-Border Legal Studies Center. She also maintains an appointment at the Victoria University of Wellington Law School. Lewis's research focuses on international economic law, with a particular emphasis on international trade law, free trade agreements and the WTO. Lewis is Co-Executive Vice President and a founding member of the Society of International Economic Law; co-rapporteur of the International Law Association's Committee on Sustainable Development and the Green Economy in International Trade Law; and a member of the Asian WTO Research Network. Lewis received her BA from Northwestern University and her JD and MSFS degrees from Georgetown University. Prior to entering academia, she practised international trade and litigation in the Washington DC and Tokyo offices of Shearman & Sterling LLP.

Julio A Lacarte Muró is a career Uruguayan diplomat who has been involved with the GATT/WTO trading system since its inception. He served as Deputy Executive Secretary of the GATT in 1947–1948. He returned to the GATT as Uruguay's Permanent Representative in 1961–1966 and 1982–1992, during which periods he served as Chairman of the Council, the Contracting Parties and the Uruguay Round negotiating groups on dispute settlement and institutional questions. In 1995, Mr Lacarte was selected as the first chairman of the WTO Appellate Body. He has also served as the Deputy Director of the International Trade and Balance-of-Payments Division of the United Nations and as the Director of Economic Cooperation among Developing Countries of UNCTAD. He has also been Uruguay's Ambassador to several countries, including the European Communities, India, Japan, the United States and Thailand. Mr Lacarte has been a professor at the International Association of Comparative Law and at the University of Comparative Law at Strasbourg University.

Jaemin Lee is currently Professor of Law at School of Law, Seoul National University in Seoul, Korea. He also serves as Associate Dean for Academic Affairs of the law school. His major areas of research include international trade law, international investment law, and public international law. Upon graduation from College of Law, Seoul National University in 1992, he joined the South Korean Ministry of Foreign Affairs and Trade as a career foreign service officer. His post in the ministry included a deputy directorship of the Treaties Division and the North American Trade Division. Between 2001 and 2004, he also practised law with Willkie Farr & Gallagher LLP (Washington, DC office) as an associate attorney of the firm's international trade group. Between 2004 and 2013, he taught international law, international investment law, and international trade law at School of Law, Hanyang University in Seoul, Korea. He is a member of the American Society of International Law, American Bar Association, Washington Foreign Law Society, Korean Society of International Law, and the Korean Society of International Economic Law. He is also the Editor-in-Chief of the Seoul International Law Journal, and the Managing Editor of the Journal of East Asia and International Law.

Chin Leng Lim is Professor of Law, a Member of Court and a Member of Senate at the University of Hong Kong. Outside the university he practises as a barrister from Keating Chambers, 15 Essex Street, London and serves as a member of the HKSAR's Committee for Pacific Economic Cooperation, tasked to advise the Commerce Secretary. He is a Visiting Professor at King's College London, was recently the inaugural Lionel A. Sheridan Visiting Professor at the National University of Singapore and a Visiting Scholar-in-Residence at WTO Headquarters. His latest books include *Alternative Visions of the International Law on Foreign Investment* (Cambridge University Press 2016), *Trans-Pacific Partnership* (Cambridge University Press 2012), edited with Elms and Low, and *International Economic Law after the Global Crisis* (Cambridge University Press 2015), edited with Mercurio.

Tsai-yu Lin is a professor at National Taiwan University (NTU) College of Law and the Director of its Asian Center for WTO & International Health Law and Policy (ACWH). Professor Lin has actively published books and articles in the areas of WTO laws, international investment law, and international health law. She is also the executive secretary of Asian WTO Research Network (AWRN); commissioner of Taiwan's International Trade Commission; a senior member of Editorial Committees of the *Asian Journal of WTO & International Health Law and Policy* and the *Contemporary Asia Arbitration Journal*; and a member of the Indicative List of Governmental and Non-Governmental Panelists for resolving WTO disputes. Professor Lin currently advises Taiwan's Government on trade and related health law and policy issues.

Chang-fa Lo has been Justice of the Constitutional Court of the ROC (Taiwan) since October 2011. Prior to his current judicial position, he was the Chair Professor and Lifetime Distinguished Professor at National Taiwan University (NTU); Dean of NTU College of Law; Director of Asian Center for WTO and International Health Law and Policy of NTU College of Law (ACWH); Director of Center for Ethics, Law and Society in Biomedicine and Technology of NTU; Commissioner of Taiwan's Fair Trade Commission; Commissioner of Taiwan's International Trade Commission; and legal advisor for Taiwan's GATT/WTO accession negotiations. In his capacity as the Director of ACWH, Professor Lo launched two English journals, namely, the *Asian Journal of WTO and International Health Law and Policy* and the *Contemporary Asia Arbitration Journal* (CAA) in 2006 and 2008, respectively. In his tenure as Dean of NTU College of Law, he also launched an English journal, the *NTU Law Review*. Prior to his teaching career, he practised law in Taipei. He received his SJD degree from Harvard University Law School in 1989. He was appointed by the WTO as a panelist for *DS332 Brazil—Measures Affecting Imports of Retreaded Tyre* in 2006, *DS468 Ukraine—Definitive Safeguard Measures on Certain Passenger Cars* in 2014, and as a member of the Permanent Group of Experts under the ASCM in 2008. He has also been the chairman of the AWRN since 2013. He is the author of 12 books, editor of four books, and has authored about 100 journal papers and book chapters.

Petros C Mavroidis is Edwin B. Parket Professor at Columbia Law School (New York City), and Professor of Law at the University of Neuchatel (Switzerland). He was chief reporter for the American Law Institute on the project 'Principles of International trade Law: the WTO', and was on leave at the European University Institute, in Florence until 2016.

Bryan Mercurio is Professor and Vice Chancellor's Outstanding Fellow of the Faculty of Law at the Chinese University of Hong Kong (CUHK), having served as Associate Dean (Research) from 2010–2014. Specializing in international economic law, Professor Mercurio is a leading expert in the intersection between trade law and intellectual property rights. His work also frequently deals with free trade agreements, dispute settlement and increasingly international investment law. Professor Mercurio is the author of one of the most widely used case books on WTO law (2nd edn, Hart Publishing 2012, with S Lester and A Davies) and editor of the leading collection on bilateral and regional trade agreements (2nd edn, Cambridge University Press 2016, with S Lester and L Bartels). Professor Mercurio previously worked in government, taught in the faculty of law at the University of New South Wales (UNSW) and as visitor at universities in Australia and North America. He has held visiting positions at a number of institutions in Asia, Europe and the United States and is currently a Professorial Visiting Fellow at UNSW and Senior Fellow at the Melbourne Law School.

Junji Nakagawa is a Professor of International Economic Law at the Institute of Social Science (ISS), University of Tokyo. He received his BA, MA and PhD, all in law, from the University of Tokyo, and worked for the Tokyo Institute of Technology as Associate Professor of Law before joining the ISS in 1995. He has an extensive research and teaching experience in North America, Asia, South Africa, and Europe. His latest visiting appointment has been as a Visiting Professor at the Free University of Berlin. He has served on the University of Tokyo's Division of International Planning as its Director, and has been in charge of drafting the Long-term Internationalization Plan of the University since 2010. He was one of the founding members of SIEL and has been a co-Treasurer since 2015. His latest books include *WTO: Beyond Trade Liberalization* (Iwanami Publishing 2013); *Transparency in International Trade and Investment Dispute Settlement* (Routledge 2013); *International Harmonization of Economic Regulation* (Routledge 2011); and *Multilateralism and Regionalism in Global Economic Governance: Finance, Trade and Investment* (Routledge, 2011). His recent articles include 'China's Industrial Policy and the WTO Law' in Chin Leng Lim and Bryan Mercurio (eds), *International Economic Law after the Global Crisis* (Cambridge University Press 2015), and 'The Emerging Rules on State Capitalism and Their Implications for China's Use of SOEs' in Lisa Toohey, Colin B Picker and Jonathan Greenacre (eds), *China in the International Economic Order* (Cambridge University Press 2015).

Laura Nielsen received her PhD from the University of Copenhagen and her LLM in International Trade Law from the University of Arizona. She is on the WTO indicative list for panelists, and serves as an editor of the *Asian Journal of WTO and International Health Law and Policy*. Finally, she was formerly with the Danish Mission to the WTO in 2002, and a visiting scholar in the WTO in 2006.

Luke Nottage specializes in international arbitration, contract law, consumer product safety law and corporate governance, with a particular interest in Japan and the Asia-Pacific region. He is Professor of Comparative and Transnational Business Law at Sydney Law School, founding Co-Director of the Australian Network for Japanese Law (ANJeL) and Associate Director of the Centre for Asian and Pacific Law at the University of Sydney. Luke is also a Director of Japanese Law Links Pty Ltd. His current major research project (2014–2016) is an ARC Discovery Project on foreign investment dispute resolution. Luke studied at Kyoto University (LLM) and Victoria University of Wellington (BCA, LLB, PhD), and first taught at the latter and then Kyushu University Law Faculty, before arriving at the University of Sydney in 2001. He has held fellowships at other leading institutions in Japan and Australia as well as Germany, Italy, and Canada. Luke's publications include *Product Safety and Liability Law in Japan*, *Corporate Governance in the 21st Century: Japan's Gradual Transformation*, *International Arbitration in Australia*, *Foreign Investment and Dispute Resolution Law and Practice in Asia*, *Consumer Law and Policy in Australia and New Zealand*, *Asia-Pacific Disaster Management*, and eight other books. Luke has also published over a hundred chapters and refereed articles, mainly in English and Japanese. He has held or retains executive roles in the Australia-Japan Society (NSW), the Law Council of Australia, the Australian Centre for International Commercial Arbitration, and the Asia-Pacific Forum for International Arbitration. Luke has contributed to several looseleaf commentaries; has consulted for law firms world-wide, ASEAN, the European Community, the OECD, the UNDP and the Japanese government; and has made numerous public Submissions to the Australian government, especially on arbitration and consumer law reform. Luke is a founding member of the ACICA Arbitration Rules committee and on the panel of arbitrators for BAC, JCAA, KCAB, KLRCA, SCIA, and TAI.

Shin-yi Peng is a professor of law at National Tsing Hua University (NTHU). She is currently serving as Commissioner of the National Communications Commission (NCC), the Executive Yuan, Taiwan. Prior to that she was the Director of Institute of Law for Science and Technology at NTHU and was also Deputy Director of NTHU's Research Center for Humanities and Social Sciences. Before joining the NTHU, Professor Peng has taught at the JD programme in University of Wisconsin Law School, where she received her SJD degree. A Member of the New York Bar, she was an intern at George, Hull, Porter & Kohli in Seattle, Washington. Her current research focuses on telecommunications law, spectrum management, trade in services, and WTO dispute settlement. She has been a Visiting Fellow at Georgetown University Law Center's Institute of International Economic Law, and a Visiting Professor at the Faculty of Law of Maastricht University. Professor Peng actively publishes articles in Asia, the United States, and Europe. She is also a frequent speaker at various international conferences, including the conferences organized by the WTO Headquarters in Geneva, the Society of International Economic Law (SIEL), and the American Society of International Law. Professor Peng has received a number of awards including Outstanding Research Award from the National Science Council of Taiwan. She is also the Case Author of the 6th ELSA Moot Court Competition on WTO Law (Case Title: 'Teleland–Measures Affecting Telecommunications Service'). She serves in an advisory and consultative capacity to the Ministry of Economic Affairs in Taiwan, advising the Government on trade law and policy issues ranging from goods and services to investment, RTAs (especially Chapters of Telecommunications and Electronic Commerce), and other social regulatory issues. She is a member of the Indicative List of Governmental and Non-Governmental Panelists for resolving WTO disputes.

In July 2012, Professor Peng was elected as a member of the Executive Council of the SIEL—the largest society of international economic lawyers in the world.

Ernst-Ulrich Petersmann is an Emeritus Professor of International and European Law at the European University Institute (Florence) and a former head of its Law Department. He was legal advisor in the German Ministry of Economic Affairs, GATT and the WTO, and representative of Germany in numerous European and UN institutions. He acquired his *doctor iuris utriusque* (*summa cum laude*) at Heidelberg University in 1976 and taught international and European law at numerous universities in Germany, Switzerland, Italy, the USA, China, India, and Singapore. Professor Petersmann has published 30 books and more than 300 articles, book contributions and book reviews. His most recent monograph is on *Multilevel Constitutionalism for Multilevel Governance of Public Goods—Methodology Problems in International Law* (Hart Publishing 2016).

R V Anuradha is a founding Partner at Clarus Law Associates, New Delhi. She heads the Firm's practice in International Trade Law and Policy. She graduated from the National Law School of India University in Bangalore (1995), and has advanced degrees in international economic law and law and development from the University of London (1996), and the New York University School of Law (2002). Prior to establishing Clarus Law Associates, she was a partner at the law firm of Amarchand Mangaldas. Anuradha has been regularly ranked by Chambers and Partners and International Who's Who of Trade and Customs Lawyers as a leading practitioner in her field. She is a member of the Asia WTO Research Network—a network of academics and practitioners working on WTO law and policy in the Asian region. Anuradha advises the Government of India and the private sector on various matters arising under the WTO and Free Trade Agreements, including disputes arising under such agreements. She has also undertaken studies on trade law and policy for Centre for WTO Studies—IIFT, the World Bank, and export promotion associations in India. She also teaches at training programmes on trade law and policy at the Centre for WTO Studies—IIFT, and at various law schools in India.

Frieder Roessler served as Executive Director of the ACWL from its inception in 2001 until July 2012. In this capacity, he played a significant role in establishing and developing the ACWL. Since stepping down from his position as Executive Director, he has continued to serve in a part-time capacity with particular involvement in the ACWL's training programmes. Mr Roessler was educated in Germany, Switzerland, and the United States. After completing his legal training in Germany, he worked for the World Bank and then for the GATT and the World Trade Organization. In 1989, he was appointed Director of Legal Affairs, a post which he held until 1995. Mr Roessler's main task at the GATT and the WTO was to advise dispute settlement panels and to prepare drafts of their reports or supervise their preparation by his staff. He was also closely involved in the legal aspects of the Uruguay Round negotiations and participated in the legal drafting process at the end of the Round. After leaving the WTO, Mr Roessler joined the faculty of law of Georgetown University in Washington, DC. He has also been an adjunct professor at the Jean Moulin University of Lyon and at Paris and taught at the universities of St Gallen in Switzerland and of Minnesota in the United States.

Thomas J Schoenbaum is Harold S. Shefelman Distinguished Professor of Law at George Washington University. Prior to joining George Washington University Law School, Professor Schoenbaum taught at the law schools of the University of North Carolina, Tulane University, and the University of Georgia. At Tulane he served as associate dean and at Georgia he was executive director of the Dean Rusk Center of International and Comparative Law. He is also a Fellow at GW's Center for Law, Economics & Finance (C-LEAF). He has practised law extensively as special counsel for several law firms and has litigated corporate, environmental, and admiralty cases in the federal courts. Professor Schoenbaum has received six Fulbright awards and has held teaching posts in many countries, including Germany, Belgium, the United Kingdom, South Africa, Austria, Russia, and Japan. He has served as visiting fellow at St John's College, Oxford and as principal fellow of the Lauterpacht Research Centre of International Law at Cambridge. Professor Schoenbaum specializes in international commercial and environmental law. He is the author of many articles and books, including *The World Trade Organization: Law, Policy and Practice, Admiralty and Maritime Law* and *Environmental Policy Law*. He is currently working on new books in the areas of international environmental law and international business transactions.

Yasuhei Taniguchi is a Professor Emeritus of Kyoto University in Japan and currently Of Counsel to Matsuo & Kosugi in Tokyo. He has taught not only at Kyoto University for 39 years but also at other universities in Japan as well as in the United States (such as Harvard, Stanford, Berkeley, NYU, Michigan, etc.), Hong Kong, Australia (Melbourne, etc.) and Europe (Paris XII). He served as a member of the Appellate Body of the WTO (2000–2007, Chairman 2005–2006), Vice-President of International Association of Procedural Law (1995–2007), President of Japan Association of Civil Procedure (1992–1995) and Judge of Singapore International Commercial Court (2015–). He has been active in the arbitration related works including investment arbitration. His more than 50 published works in Western languages include: *The Obligation to Mitigate Damages* in Dossiers IV of the ICC Institute of World Business Law, *Understanding the Concept of Prima Facie Proof in WTO Dispute Settlement*, The WTO: Governance, Dispute Settlement & Developing Countries, WTO Dispute Resolution as Arbitration, in 52 *Japanese Yearbook of International Law* 904, and *La responsabilité civile et la charge de la preuve au Japon* in Mélange Chabas.

Joel P Trachtman is a Professor of International Law at the Fletcher School of Tufts University. His recent books include *The Tools of Argument: How the Best Lawyers Think, Argue, and Win*; *The Future of International Law: Global Government*; *The International Law of Economic Migration: Toward the Fourth Freedom*; *Ruling the World: Constitutionalism, International Law, and Global Governance*; *Developing Countries in the WTO Legal System*; *The Economic Structure of International Law*; and *International Law and International Politics*. He has consulted for the United Nations, the OECD, APEC, the World Bank, the Organization of American States, and the United States Agency for International Development. Trachtman has served on the Boards of the *American Journal of International Law*, the *European Journal of International Law*, the *Journal of International Economic Law*, the *Cambridge Review of International Affairs*, and the *Singapore Yearbook of International Law*. He is a member of the bar of the State of New York. From 1998–2001, he was Academic Dean of The Fletcher School, and during 2000 and 2001, he served as Dean *ad interim*. In 2002, he was a Manley O. Hudson Visiting Professor of Law, and in 2004 he was Nomura Visiting Professor of International Financial Systems, at Harvard Law School. He graduated in 1980 from Harvard Law School, where he served as Editor-in-Chief of the *Harvard International Law Journal*. His undergraduate education was at the London School of Economics and Columbia College.

Rolf H Weber holds a chair for Private, Economic and European Law at the University of Zurich since 1995 and has been a practising attorney admitted to the bar in Zurich and Switzerland since 1978. He is a founder and director of the European Law Institute (EIZ), the founder of the previous the Center for Information and Communication Law (ZIK), now replaced by the Center for Information Technology, Society, and Law at the University of Zurich (ITSL), as well as the publisher of the ZIK-book series and the EIZ-book series. Professor Weber is also a Member of the University Research Priority Program 'Financial Market Regulation' and contributed as Judge to several Moot Courts on WTO Law. Additionally, Rolf H Weber is a member of the editorial board of several Swiss and international legal periodicals.

Ines Willemyns is a PhD researcher at the Leuven Centre for Global Governance Studies (GGS) and the Institute of International Law at the KU Leuven. She is conducting her doctoral research on regulatory cooperation in trade in services at the multilateral and plurilateral level. More generally, she conducts research on various aspects of International Economic Law, WTO Law, and International Trade Law. She has obtained her Master of Laws from the KU Leuven in 2014 and her LLM in International Economic Law and Policy (IELPO) at the University of Barcelona in 2015. Ines wrote her thesis for the IELPO LLM on the topic: 'Disciplines on state-owned enterprises in WTO Law and the new Free Trade Agreements: TPP, TTIP and TiSA'.

Jan Wouters is Jean Monnet Chair *ad personam*, Full Professor of International Law and International Organizations, and founding Director of the Institute for International Law and of the Leuven Centre for Global Governance Studies, an interdisciplinary centre of excellence, at the University of Leuven. He studied law and philosophy at Antwerp University, obtained an LLM at Yale University and was Visiting Researcher at Harvard University. As Visiting Professor at Sciences Po (Paris), Luiss University (Rome) and the College of Europe (Bruges) he teaches EU external relations law. As Adjunct Professor at Columbia University he teaches comparative EU-US perspectives on international human rights law. He is a Member of the Royal Academy of Belgium for Sciences and Arts, is President of the United Nations Association Flanders Belgium, and practises law as Of Counsel at Linklaters, Brussels. He is Editor of the *International Encyclopedia of Intergovernmental Organizations*, Deputy Director of the *Revue belge de droit international*, and an editorial board member in ten other international journals. He has published widely on international and EU law, international organizations and global governance. His recent books include *The European Union and Multilateral Governance* (2012), *International Prosecutors* (2012), *Informal International Lawmaking* (2012), *Private Standards and Global Governance* (2012), *China, the European Union and Global Governance* (2012), *The EU's Role in Global Governance* (2013), *National Human Rights Institutions in Europe* (2013), *The Law of EU External Relations* (2013, 2nd edn 2015), *China, the EU and the Developing World* (2015), *Global Governance of Labour Rights* (2015), *Global Governance Through Trade: EU Policies and Approaches* (2015), *The Contribution of International and Supranational Courts to the Rule of Law* (2015), *Global Governance and Democracy: A Multidisciplinary Analysis* (2015), and *Armed Conflicts and the Law* (2016). Apart from his participation in international scientific networks, he advises various international organizations and governments, trains international officials and is often asked to comment international events in the media. He is coordinator of a large-scale FP7 Programme FRAME, 'Fostering Human Rights Among European (External and Internal) Policies', and of the InBev-Baillet Latour EU China Chair, at the University of Leuven.

Chien-huei Wu is currently Associate Research Professor in Institute of European and American Studies, Academia Sinica, Taipei, Taiwan and coordinated the EU thematic study group in that Institute during the period of 2013 to 2015. Before pursuing his doctoral degree in European University Institute at Florence, he worked for the Ministry of Justice in Taiwan as a district attorney during the period of 2001 to 2005. His research interests cover EU external relations law and international economic law. He follows closely EU–China and EU–ASEAN relations and pays particular attention to comparative regionalism and WTO–IMF linkage. He is the author of 'WTO and the Greater China: Economic Integration and Dispute Resolution' and various articles. He has been visiting fellow/professor to World Trade Institute, University of Bern, University of Cologne, University of Passau, and Georgetown University, and lectured in various institutions.

1

Introduction: A *Liber Amicorum* to Celebrate Mitsuo Matsushita's Contributions to International Economic Law

Julien Chaisse and Tsai-yu Lin

This *Liber Amicorum* represents the collaborative and creative endeavours of thirty-five contributors, who are all special colleagues—friends and disciples—to honour Mitsuo Matsushita, a figure who has gained international respect for dedicating his long and splendid career to the field of international economic law. The idea of this book came from the members of the Asian WTO Research Network (AWRN) after Mitsuo Matsushita stepped down from his post as the founder of the AWRN in 2014.

Mitsuo Matsushita served as the founding member of the WTO Appellate Body from 1995 to 2000. In his distinguished academic career, Mitsuo Matsushita has held professorships at Sophia University and Tokyo University. He has been a Visiting Professor at Harvard University, Georgetown University, the University of Michigan, Columbia University, and at the College of Europe in Bruges, Belgium. Mitsuo Matsushita is also an outstanding jurist—all contributors have used his textbook[1] to prepare their own lectures, and learned a lot from his articles.

Through the numerous publications covering international trade, competition, and investment law, Mitsuo Matsushita has distinguished himself as a forerunner of the governance of international economic relationships and has considerably developed the discipline. It is impossible to summarize Mitsuo Matsushita's scholarship in the present introduction but a number of his publications that have had a direct impact on the chapters, messages, and structure of this book can be briefly remembered.

Of course, Mitsuo Matsushita has analysed the operation of the WTO's dispute settlement system over recent years. His analysis concludes that the system has been relatively successful in resolving disputes, especially considering that the parties involved are sovereign states and that the WTO has only limited enforcement

[1] See Mitsuo Matsushita and others, *The World Trade Organization: Law, Practice, and Policy* (2nd edn, OUP 2006).

powers. However, one consequence of that success is that WTO Members are bringing more cases involving more complex issues to the system for resolution.[2] The result is that the WTO dispute settlement system has recently been—and continues to be—under considerable strain, which justifies a number of reforms that would reduce the burden on the WTO Dispute Settlement Body (DSB).[3]

At a rather early stage, Mitsuo Matsushita's scholarship has addressed governance of international trade where the WTO should share with other international organizations and nation states that are Members.[4] It is important for the WTO to establish efficient working relationships with other international organizations that deal with related matters. Examples of such organizations are, inter alia, the UNCTAD (United Nations Conference on Trade and Development), the WIPO (World Intellectual Property Organization), the ILO (International Labour Organization), the ITU (International Telecommunications Union) and the OECD (Organization for Economic Co-operation and Development). Mitsuo Matsushita observes that only an efficient and friendly co-operation between the WTO and these international organizations can ensure a good governance of international trade.[5]

However, it is worth noting that there are possible conflicts and inconsistencies between a WTO agreement and other international agreements, between the WTO and its Members' domestic jurisdictions, and among WTO agreements. In the case of genetically modified organisms (GMOs), for instance, the Cartagena Protocol provides that a Member of the Protocol can take a measure to prohibit the use and import of GMOs according to the 'precautionary principle' in the absence of solid scientific evidence regarding GMOs' harm to human life and health. In contrast, the Agreement on the Application of Sanitary and Phytosanitary Measures allows the precautionary principle only in a limited way. Therefore, whatever is allowed under the Cartagena Protocol may not be allowed under the SPS Agreement. Allowing a Member's reliance on the Cartagena Protocol to justify its measures incompatible with the obligations of the WTO agreement would allow such a Member to circumvent the WTO disciplines. They would also be changing the rights and obligations of WTO Members without any negotiation and amendment. On this view, Mitsuo Matsushita suggests that some thought should be given to address these issues, otherwise WTO Members will be deprived of stability and predictability of the consequences of their activities, and this is harmful to the liberal trade order in international trade.

[2] See Mitsuo Matsushita, 'The Sutherland Report and its Discussion of Dispute Settlement Reforms' (2005) 8(3) J Intl Econ L 623, 623–29.

[3] See Mitsuo Matsushita, 'Transparency, *Amicus Curiae* Briefs and Third Party Rights' (2004) 5(2) J World Inv & Trade 329, 329–30.

[4] See e.g., Mitsuo Matsushita, 'Governance of International Trade under World Trade Organization Agreements: Relationships between World Trade Organization Agreements and Other Trade Agreements' (2004) 38(2) J World Trade 185, 185–210.

[5] See e.g., Mitsuo Matsushita and Julien Chaisse, 'Maintaining the WTO's Supremacy in the International Trade Order: A Proposal to Refine and Revise the Role of the Trade Policy Review Mechanism' (2013) 16(1) J Intl Econ L 9, 9–36.

Mitsuo Matsushita underlines that clear rules on the relationship between WTO disciplines and free trade agreements (FTAs) should be firmly established. In the face of emerging challenges from the stalemate of the Doha Development Agenda (DDA), which has again been evidenced at the Tenth WTO Ministerial Conference in Nairobi, 2015, and the spread of FTAs and recent mega-FTAs, such as the Transpacific Partnership Agreement (TPP), Transatlantic Trade and Investment Partnership (TTIP), and the Regional Comprehensive Economic Partnership (RCEP), the WTO could try to establish an 'FTA network' in which FTA officials are frequently convening and discussing trade rules and other matters with the view to convergence. Mitsuo Matsushita put forward that this would create more harmonized and co-ordinated rules and activities among FTAs, as well as a more harmonized relationship between FTAs and the WTO. This is a 'soft law' approach.[6] The WTO can play such a role through activities of the Trade Policy Review Mechanism (TPRM) and the Committee of Regional Trade Agreements.

Mitsuo Matsushita notably considered two important issues concerning the application of GATT Article XXIV, i.e. the interpretation of 'substantially all' and trade remedies. Article XXIV:8 provides that 'substantially all of trade' must be liberalized if an FTA is qualified for exemption. But it remains unclear whether or not the meaning of 'substantially all' should include qualitative as well as quantitative features. As Mitsuo Matsushita notes, the 'substantially all' requirement originally entails an FTA's completion so that benefits of trade among inside parties are maximized.[7] Article XXIV is premised upon the idea that integration of markets will promote economic developments of the participants of an FTA and ultimately benefit the whole world trading system.

Mitsuo Matsushita suggests that assumptions need to be reconsidered and a more realistic set of rules should be incorporated into the WTO system with a view to accommodating some existing FTA agreements. Article XXIV:8 exempts certain measures from the obligation to liberalize, such as Articles XI, XII, XIII, XIV, XV, and XX. However, trade remedies (for example, anti-dumping, countervailing duties, and safeguards) are not enumerated as an exempted category. One concern that has arisen is whether trade remedies can be applied within an FTA.[8] On the basis of the liberal interpretation, as long as substantially all of the internal trade of the FTA remains open, Members of the WTO who are also members of an FTA can apply trade remedy measures. In spite of this, according to Mitsuo Matsushita, an application of a trade remedy measure within an FTA may have a significant impact on internal trade, and this would deprive the trade remedy measures of legitimacy based on this justification.

[6] See Mitsuo Matsushita, 'A View on Future Roles of The WTO: Should There be More Soft Law in The WTO?' (2014) 17(3) J Intl Econ L 701, 701–15. See also Matsushita and Chaisse (n 5).

[7] See Mitsuo Matsushita, 'Governance of International Trade under WTO Agreements Relationships between WTO Agreements and Other Trade Agreements' (2004) 38(2) J World Trade 185.

[8] See Mitsuo Matsushita, 'Some International and Domestic Antidumping Issues' (2010) 5(2) Asian J WTO & Intl Health L & Policy 249, 249–68.

Mitsuo Matsushita particularly put forward that the WTO must seek ways to ease the tension between the multilateral trading system and FTAs.[9] Importantly, legal principles of the WTO and FTAs should be firmly established, and WTO negotiators should come up with clear rules on the relationship between WTO disciplines and FTAs.

Mitsuo Matsushita also put forward a new notion that the WTO should play a new role to reconcile various FTAs in the future.[10] That is, given the stalemate of the DDA and the spread of FTAs and recent mega-FTAs, such as the TPP, TTIP, and the RCEP, the role of the WTO in the governance of the international trade order has a new horizon. FTAs are basically fragmentary. Rules and activities of FTAs need to be co-ordinated and their rules should be operated in such a way that they do not interfere with each other and do not unduly erect barriers to outside parties.

This volume is a fitting tribute to Mitsuo Matsushita's impressive work. The authors are distinguished and the chapters will be of interest to those working in the field of international economic law and elsewhere. The editors consider that the scholarship of Mitsuo Matsushita should be appropriately reflected in the outstanding contributions. In honour of Mitsuo Matsushita's intellectual contributions, the scholarly work brought together in this volume reflects on the current state of international economic law and its future.

With the advent of the WTO and a rich body of jurisprudence under its dispute settlement mechanism, international economic order has substantially evolved. Against the background of an increasing economic interdependence, the question of appropriate means and institutions for the regulation and governance of international economic relations arises. Nation states have for long—and successfully—claimed to be the proper and sovereign forum for determining a country's international economic policies. Increasingly, supranational and non-governmental actors are moving to the front stage. New forms of multilateral and global policymaking have been emerging. They involve states and national administrations (often horizontally interacting with their counterparts abroad), key international organizations, international conferences, multinational enterprises, and a wide range of transnational pressure groups and NGOs, all of which claim their share in exercising power and influence on international and domestic policymaking. In short, national governments are increasingly integrated into a multi-layered system of local, national, regional, and global levels of governance.

We face the challenge of finding new, accountable, and appropriate structures that are able to cope with globalization. Trade regulation is at the forefront of this process. WTO law has moved to the centre stage in the development of international law. It spearheads what we increasingly call global law: principles or rules which are no longer restricted to delimiting spheres of influence (co-existence),

[9] See Mitsuo Matsushita, 'Regionalism and the Disciplines of the WTO: Analysis of Some Legal Aspects under Article XXIV of the GATT' (2005) 13 Asia Pac L Rev 191.

[10] See Mitsuo Matsushita, 'A View on Future Roles of the WTO: Should There Be More Soft Law in the WTO?' (2014) 17 J Intl Econ L 701, 701–15.

or bringing about co-operation, but actually entailing elements of integration as trade law is being partly or fully harmonized. International trade law not only involves principles and rules delimiting national sovereignty (negative integration) but also increasingly describes rules that nations should enact (positive integration).

The international economic legal order has rapidly progressed with global economic integration. To reflect on more recent questions and diverse issues, the contributors in this volume evaluate the transformations and the legalization of international economic relations, with a focus on dispute resolution. Their works span a broad spectrum of contemporary international economic regulations: WTO law, law of regional integration, investment law, competition law, economics and politics of trade, international dispute resolution, and inter-regime co-ordination. Some of the themes that are very significant in Mitsuo Matsushita's scholarship are also closely examined, such as the rise of the soft law mechanism in international economic regulation, the role of the WTO and dispute settlement, and the specific regimes applicable to important economic fields. Among these, competition, subsidies, anti-dumping, intellectual property, natural resources, and investment are notable topics.

In order to analyse and illuminate the evolution and current challenges faced by the international economic governance, the *Liber Amicorum* for Mitsuo Matsushita covers three main themes. Part I provides a comprehensive and critical analysis of the rule-based international dispute settlement mechanisms; Part II investigates the normative influences to and from WTO law; and Part III focuses on policy- and law-making issues.

The WTO celebrated its twentieth anniversary in 2015 and has proved to be very successful in strengthening the contours of the international economic order and promoting reforms in a number of Member countries. One can find abundant literature on amendments made by different countries and sectors because of the law or the Organization or the Dispute Settlement Body (DSB) decisions. Almost all of the 490-plus trade disputes that have arisen since 1995 have been resolved in accordance with WTO law.[11]

Given the legacy of a power-driven foreign policy, it is evident that the rule of law in international trade regulation is not as mature as in traditional areas of domestic law. We observed the impact of market power in the context of ensuring compliance with the DSB's decisions. We observed the shortcomings in the protection of individual rights by denying direct effect, it being a vital element of the rule of law, properly speaking. We observed the traditions of deference exercised by domestic courts in foreign affairs, to the extent they are given jurisdiction at all. Much remains to be done, in particular in the light of emerging constitutional doctrines. Nevertheless, it is appropriate to state that the WTO system is already based on the rule of law, not only in terms of substantive law but also in

[11] See World Trade Organization, Dispute Settlement Body Annual Report, WT/DSB/64, 26 November 2014.

terms of procedural rules. While negotiations still largely follow politics and diplomatic traditions, the Understanding on Rules and Procedures Governing the Settlement of Disputes (DSU) provides for fair procedures in the administration of justice. The same pattern seems to drive international arbitration in the context of investor–state disputes. Indeed, one of the key features of investment protection consists of allowing foreign investors to challenge the host governments' actions before an international arbitral court. The ability of foreign investors to bring their disputes to independent arbitrators provides an extra guarantee that domestic authorities live up to their international obligations, thus ensuring a favourable and stable investment climate in the host country. Part I explores the two most successful systems of international economic dispute settlement. Relevant chapters provide a deeper evaluation of the WTO's dispute settlement system, the function of the Appellate Body, treaty interpretation, and WTO jurisprudence. In addition, the limitation and reform of investor–state arbitration are analysed.

The discussion of explicit and implicit exceptions, which has been an important topic in Mitsuo Matsushita's scholarship, shows that the law of the WTO does not operate in isolation. It is closely intertwined with other, equally legitimate, policy goals. Such goals not only form part of domestic law; they can also be found in international law in general and in treaty law in particular. Some norms of international law may be concurring with international trade regulation in mutual support. Others may create tensions or even conflicts.

The issues arising when interfacing WTO law and other areas of international law are therefore dealt with in Part II on 'normative influences to and from WTO law'. The relationship of WTO law and other areas of international law primarily emerged, as a practical and political issue, in the context of multilateral environmental agreements. It forms part of the 'trade and ...' problems.

More recently, the debate has prominently gained momentum in relation to trade and human rights. Given the significance of human rights as guiding principles of international economic law, the quest for coherence has induced what we today call a constitutional debate in international trade law. In Part II, contributions discuss inter-regime co-ordination and cross-cutting issues between WTO and general international law, health law, environmental law, financial law, and investment law.

As the WTO celebrated its twentieth year of existence, many emerging issues and challenges obligate the WTO to build better and more responsive global trading surroundings. We take a look at what is ahead for the multilateral trade system. Part III looks at the most salient issues concerning the 2020 world economy: questions such as the ever-more-complex trade and investment agreements landscape; consumer protection and the generation of public goods; the role of trade in promoting inclusive business; reinvigorating manufacturing—new industrial policy and the trade system. Issues to be discussed include trade remedies (subsidies, countervailing measures, and anti-dumping); natural resources; patents and access to medicine; sanitary and phytosanitary measures; and trade and competition policy. These issues not only involve industry protection and international competition, but also concern states' right to regulate health and natural resource matters and to achieve a balance with trade interests.[12]

Furthermore, the WTO—for the time being—does not allow for variable geometry and membership, except for some plurilateral trade agreements that remain in force. The structure of the WTO reflects the consensus of 1994 that all countries alike should have equal rights and obligations, subject only to provisions on special and differential treatment for developing and least-developed countries. New Members may be obliged in their Protocol of Accession to join particular plurilateral agreements. The legal structure of the WTO, however, does not exclude a return to a more extensive variable geometry in the future. Thus, it is conceivable to introduce new and controversial disciplines to investment and competition (anti-trust law), just to name two, in the form of plurilateral agreements.

Recent developments show an increasing recourse to preferential trade in South East Asia. For many years, Japan and Singapore were the only major powers exclusively operating on the global system. The rise of the People's Republic of China as the dominant economic power of the region in the twenty-first century induces countries to join forces with a view to enhancing future bargaining powers vis-à-vis China. The process of regional integration within a system of global multilateralism raises major conceptual and legal policy issues. On the one hand, it is believed by some commentators that regional trading blocs are beneficial for, and complementary to, the multilateral and non-discriminatory system of the WTO. Here, regional trade agreements are seen to reinforce the global trading system rather than putting its integrity and stability at risk.

On the other hand, regionalism is considered by other analysts as a major threat to a co-operative and multilateral world economic order, as reflected in the Bretton Woods institutions. The multitude of preferential arrangements results in a complex web of rules of origin and a spaghetti bowl which renders trade more cumbersome. Accordingly, the creation of regional trading blocs is opposed and strict legal requirements are sought. Contributions in Part III explore insightful systemic issues from the perspective of trade law governance. The potential impacts that the new plurilateral agreements and free trade agreements (such as TTIP, CETA, and TPP) would impose on the future WTO are also covered.

This project would not have got off the stage of a wonderful idea were it not for the charismatic energy and determination of Chang-fa Lo, who is now continuing the work initiated by Mitsuo Matsushita as Chairman of the Asia WTO research Network.

Thanks must also be extended to Mr Dini Sejko, PhD Cand at CUHK law, who acted as 'Project Manager', Winnie Jo-Mei Ma, Honorary Assistant Professor of Law, Bond University, who was the 'editorial proofreader', and Ching-Fu Lin, Assistant Professor at National Tsing Hua University, as 'executive editor'. The editors also express their gratitude to the many members of the National Taiwan

[12] See e.g., Mitsuo Matsushita, 'Competition Law and Policy in the Context of the WTO System' (1995) 44 DePaul L Rev 1097, 1097–118. See also Mitsuo Matsushita, 'International Co-operation in the Enforcement of Competition Policy' (2002) 1 Wash U Global Stud L Rev 463, 463–76.

University (NTU) College of Law Asian Center for WTO & International Health Law (ACWH), who have played an important role in bringing this volume to fruition as assistant editors, namely Yi-Nung Liao, Chia-chi Chen, Yi-Tzu Chen, Yi-Hsin Chen, Yi-ying Chiang, Cheng-Kai Wang, Mao-wei (David) Lo, Yu-An Chen, Nai-Fang Wong, Helen Hai-ning Huang, Hsin-hua Wang, Tzu-Fan Chang, and Mengke Cheng.

Finally, the editors wish to thank Oxford University Press for publishing this exceptional volume and for the support shown from the very outset, which allows us to pay a due tribute to the gigantic contribution Mitsuo Matsushita has made to international economic law.

PART I

RULES-BASED INTERNATIONAL DISPUTE SETTLEMENT

2

The WTO Dispute Settlement System: Dealing with Success

*William J Davey**

I. The WTO Dispute Settlement System: Dealing with Success

Throughout his long career, Professor Matsushita was unquestionably the leading Japanese academic in the field of international trade law. His active involvement in this field culminated in his service as one of the initial members of the World Trade Organization's Appellate Body, where he played an influential role in the development of the WTO dispute settlement system as we know it today. It thus seems appropriate in this volume honouring him that we take a close look at how this system, which he was so instrumental in shaping, has operated in practice. Accordingly, this chapter commences with an overview of the operation of the WTO dispute settlement system over the past twenty years. It concludes that the system has been relatively successful in resolving disputes, especially considering that the parties involved are sovereign states and that the WTO has only limited enforcement powers. However, one consequence of that success is that WTO Members are bringing more cases involving more complex issues to the system for resolution. The result is that the WTO dispute settlement system has recently been, and continues to be, under considerable strain. The resources of the WTO Secretariat, which provides staff support to WTO dispute settlement panels, and the Appellate Body, which hears appeals from panel decisions, have been stretched to the point where cases are delayed essentially because of staffing shortages. Since the negotiation side of the WTO seems to be dysfunctional, the likelihood is that in the future WTO Members will want to bring even more cases into the dispute settlement system, thereby exacerbating an already difficult situation. The chapter concludes by examining a number of changes that might be made to the system that would help to ease the current problems, speed up the overall process of WTO dispute settlement, and ensure that the system will continue to be as successful over the next twenty years as it has been in the past.

* Guy Raymond Jones Chair in Law Emeritus, University of Illinois College of Law.

II. The Record of WTO Dispute Settlement: 1995–2015

At various points over the past ten years, I have examined the WTO dispute settlement system and attempted to evaluate the extent to which it can be considered to have been a success.[1] Essentially, this has involved (i) analysing how the system has evolved over time—it is a much different system today than it was in its very early years; and (ii) assessing how it has performed in terms of the results of the individual cases. In this section, I consider these issues from the perspective of 2015. Before doing that, however, it is useful to recall the key characteristics of the WTO system that make it unique in international state-to-state dispute settlement. First, the WTO system has exclusive jurisdiction over disputes between its Members involving the WTO rules and agreements.[2] Second, it has compulsory jurisdiction over WTO Members in such disputes. So long as the complaining Member wishes to pursue the matter, the respondent may not block the process, which may ultimately end in the complainant taking retaliatory action against the respondent if it does not comply with its WTO obligations.[3] Third, the system has both initial and appellate instances, both of which are supported by separate staffs, which helps to ensure the high quality of the decisions. Fourth, the system establishes deadlines for the completion of the various stages of dispute settlement, and while they are often not achieved, their existence helps pressure actors in the system to try to achieve relatively timely decisions.[4] Finally, the continuous monitoring by the Dispute Settlement Body (DSB) of decided cases pending compliance is unique and helps to ensure that WTO rules are ultimately respected.[5] These improvements over the GATT dispute settlement system have helped to ensure the continuing success of the WTO system of multilateral trade dispute settlement.[6]

[1] William J Davey, 'The WTO and Rules-based Dispute Settlement: Historical Evolution, Operational Success and Future Challenges' (2014) 17 J Intl Econ L 679; William J Davey, *The WTO Dispute Settlement System at 18: Effective at Controlling the Major Players?* (2013) EUI Working Paper RSCAS 2013/29 http://cadmus.eui.eu/bitstream/handle/1814/26794/RSCAS_2013_29.pdf?sequence=1 accessed 19 March 2016; William J Davey, 'WTO Dispute Settlement: Promise Fulfilled?' in Inge Govaere, Reinhard Quick, and Marco Bronckers (eds), *Trade and Competition Law in the EU and Beyond* (Edward Elgar 2011) 194–203; William J Davey, 'Compliance Problems in WTO Dispute Settlement' (2009) 42(1) Cornell Intl LJ 119; William J Davey, 'The WTO Dispute Settlement System: The First Ten Years' (2005) 8(1) J Intl Econ L 17.

[2] Understanding on Rules and Procedures Governing the Settlement of Disputes, art 23, 15 April 1994, Marrakesh Agreement Establishing the World Trade Organization, Annex 2, 1869 UNTS 401, 33 ILM 1226 (DSU).

[3] After sixty days of failed consultations, the complaining party may request the establishment of a panel: DSU art 4.7. The panel must be established at the second DSB meeting at which it is requested, DSU art 6.1, and will be composed by the Director-General of the WTO if one of the parties so requests after twenty days of unsuccessful attempts by the parties to agree on panellists: DSU art 8.7. The panel report may be appealed to an Appellate Body, and roughly two-thirds are. The reports of the panel (as issued, or as modified on appeal) and the Appellate Body must be adopted by the DSB so long as one Member so requests: DSU arts 16, 17.14. If the respondent fails to bring the contested measure into conformity with its obligations within a reasonable period of time, DSU art 21, the complaining Member can take retaliatory action: DSU, art 22.

[4] DSU arts 12.8, 12.9, 17.5, 20, 21.4.

[5] DSU art 21.6.

[6] For an analysis of the problems of the GATT dispute settlement system, see generally William J Davey, 'Dispute Settlement in GATT' (1987) 11(1) Fordham Intl LJ 51.

A. The evolution of the WTO dispute settlement

The history of WTO dispute settlement can be usefully divided into four phases. While the dividing line between the phases is not as distinct as I make it out to be in the following analysis, I think it is nonetheless useful to approach the history of dispute settlement in this way.

Initially, in the 1990s, the WTO dispute settlement system was characterized by (i) extensive use, particularly by the United States and the European Union; (ii) the re-appearance of the many unresolved cases that bedevilled GATT dispute settlement—in some instances the same cases were brought to the WTO (for example, *EC—Bananas III*[7] and *EC—Hormones*[8]), and in some cases similar issues were presented (for example, *US—Shrimp*[9] raised issues similar to *US—Tuna*[10]); and (iii) the emergence of the Appellate Body as an activist tribunal that imposed its particular viewpoint on the interpretation of WTO agreements.[11] From its early days, the Appellate Body evinced a tendency to respect WTO Member discretion in applying legitimate health and environmental regulations, so long as they were not inappropriately discriminatory and respected procedural requirements. At the same time, the Appellate Body generally strictly enforced WTO rules on trade remedies and other trade restrictions.[12] As an initial member of the Appellate Body, Professor Matsushita was especially influential in this regard. Despite the large number of very controversial cases brought into the WTO dispute settlement system during this period, it was viewed generally as very successful. Initially, there were concerns that the major WTO Members might not 'accept' losing.[13] But although there were tense moments in the early years as to whether the major Members would accept the rules and results of WTO dispute settlement (particularly in the *Bananas* case, which involved the United States and the European Union[14]), the system survived and flourished. Indeed, during the 1998–1999 Understanding on Rules and Procedures Governing the Settlement of Disputes (DSU) Review process, all participating Members indicated their general satisfaction with the system.[15]

After this initial period, the next few years (the early 2000s) were marked by a significant increase in the use of the WTO dispute settlement system by the advanced

[7] Further information (full citation, history, summary, etc) on individual cases can be found on the WTO website under Dispute Settlement: Chronological List of Disputes by entering the dispute number, which in the case of *EC—Bananas III* is DS27, <https://www.wto.org/english/tratop_e/dispu_e/dispu_status_e.htm> accessed 4 March 2016.

[8] ibid WT/DS26. [9] ibid WT/DS58.

[10] GATT DS/21 & 29 (unadopted GATT panel reports).

[11] Davey, 'The First Ten Years' (n 1) 17–23. [12] ibid 21–23.

[13] The leading GATT dispute settlement scholar, Professor Robert Hudec, shared those concerns. Robert E Hudec, 'The New WTO Dispute Settlement Procedure: An Overview of the First Three Years' (1999) 8(1) Minn J Global Trade 1, 11–15.

[14] John H Jackson, William J Davey, and Alan O Sykes, *Legal Problems of International Economic Relations* (6th edn, West 2013) 371–72; Dispute Settlement Body, *Minutes of Meeting: Held in the Centre William Rappard on 25, 28 and 29 January and 1 February 1999*, WT/DSB/M/54, 20 April 1999, 1–35.

[15] Davey, 'The First Ten Years' (n 1) 23.

developing countries. Of particular note were the challenges brought by Brazil to US cotton subsidies and EU sugar subsidies. While the United States and the European Union remained major users of the system, they no longer dominated as they had in the earlier time period. Also during this period, there was a noticeable reduction in the number of cases brought, probably due in part to better case selection, as from this period forward the percentage of consultation requests leading to panel proceedings increased. As to the subject matter of disputes, there were increasing numbers of cases involving trade remedies and subsidies. While there were concerns that the drop-off in consultation requests reflected some dissatisfaction with the system, in fact panels and the Appellate Body were busy throughout this period.[16]

The third period (essentially the last years of the first decade of the twenty-first century) was particularly noteworthy, as the United States became an ever-more-frequent respondent, as there were numerous challenges to its use of trade remedies. Many of these challenges involved 'zeroing', a method of calculating anti-dumping duties that inflated dumping margins. The United States lost almost all of these challenges to its trade remedies, but over time (sometimes quite an extended time), it generally complied with the decisions.[17]

The last of the four periods is the recent past, and in particular the first half of the second decade of the new century. This period was noteworthy for the increased involvement of China as a respondent and complainant, generally in cases involving the United States, the European Union, and Japan.[18] During this period, the number of cases rebounded somewhat. Perhaps the most telling development during the period was the fact that the volume of cases was such that the resources of the Secretariat were unable to keep pace, and a significant number of panel cases were resolved only after much delay. While this was due in part to the Secretariat resources consumed in handling the massive and never-ending Boeing-Airbus subsidy disputes, it was also due to the fact that WTO Members were bringing ever-more-complex cases to the system for resolution.[19] This resulted in part from the fact that the Doha Round negotiations are going nowhere as of this writing, but it was also due to the fact that the WTO Membership views the dispute settlement system as one clear positive of the WTO. Indeed, while there have been negotiations over reform of the DSU on and off since 1998, the fact that Members have never agreed on any changes is generally thought to be due to the fact that the system, while not perfect, is perfectly functional. Thus, in a way, the system has become a victim of its own success. In order to appreciate that success

[16] See generally ibid 24–25.

[17] Davey, *The WTO Dispute Settlement System at 18* (n 1) 5–7.

[18] ibid 5.

[19] The delays, the growth in dispute complexity, and the rebound in the number of cases, among other issues, are outlined in detail in Director-General Robert Azevedo's speech to the WTO Dispute Settlement Body in September 2014, which is reproduced in the Appellate Body's Annual Report for 2014 in Annex 2, *Appellate Body Annual Report for 2014*, WT/AB/24, 3 July 2015, 86–91. An indication of the growth in complexity is that the substantive part of panel reports grew from an average of 49 pages in the 1996–2000 period to an average of 183 pages in the 2010–2014 period (excluding the reports in the so-called Boeing-Airbus subsidy disputes), ibid 88.

more fully, I turn now to a consideration of how effectively the system has in fact resolved disputes between WTO Members.

B. Assessing the results of the WTO dispute settlement system

When I assessed the results of the WTO dispute settlement system after ten years of operation, I concluded that roughly half of the consultation requests led to a mutually satisfactory resolution of the dispute.[20] Almost all of the remaining cases resulted in panel/Appellate Body reports. Of those that required implementation, roughly eighty per cent of them had been implemented at the time the study was completed.[21] Looking at the system from the perspective of twenty years on, this record has, if anything, improved. At the most recent DSB meeting prior to this writing (20 July 2015), there were only five cases on the surveillance agenda in respect of which the reasonable period of time for implementation had expired. Of those, four were very old cases, three of which had been partially settled. The fifth was more recent, but involved the same parties and issues as a case where reports were adopted in March 2015. While there were three other cases in respect of which a Member complained that there had not been full implementation, the Member concerned had elected not to pursue the matter under Article 21.5 of the DSU.[22] Thus, since there have been over 200 adopted panel reports to date (or around 175, if Article 21.5 actions are excluded), one could argue that there is a success rate of over ninety-five per cent.

Such a high number must be taken with a large pinch of salt, however. In studying the results of individual cases more carefully, I have found that in trade

[20] Davey, 'The First Ten Years' (n 1) 45–49. In many cases, no settlement was notified, but an examination of the underlying dispute and/or contact with trade officials involved in the dispute led me to conclude that many cases where no settlement had been notified had in fact been satisfactorily resolved. Sometimes parties had formally settled but not reported, sometimes the underlying measure (usually a trade remedy measure) had expired or an investigation had been closed without action, and sometimes there were other indicia of resolution. For a more detailed analysis of the results and timing of the settlements (or other disposition), see William J Davey, 'Evaluating WTO Dispute Settlement: What Results Have Been Achieved through Consultations and Implementation of Panel Reports?' in Y Taniguchi, A Yanovich, and J Bohanes (eds), *The WTO in the Twenty-first Century: Dispute Settlement, Negotiations and Regionalism in Asia* (CUP 2007) 98, 102–08.

[21] Davey, 'The First Ten Years' (n 1) 47.

[22] See the agenda contained in WTO/AIR/DSB/13, 10 July 2015 <https://www.wto.org/english/news_e/news15_e/dsb_agenda_20jul15_e.pdf> accessed 8 August 2015. The partially settled cases and their current status were: *United States—Section 110(5) of the US Copyright Act*, WT/DS160/24/Add.126, 10 July 2015; *United States—Anti-dumping Measures on Certain Hot-rolled Steel Products from Japan*, WT/DS184/15/ADD.151, 10 July 2015; *European Communities—Measures Affecting the Approval and Marketing of Biotech Products*, WT/DS291/37/ADD.89, 10 July 2015. The completely unsettled matter is *United States—Section 211 Omnibus Appropriations Act of 1998*, WT/DS176/11/Add.151, 10 July 2015. The fifth matter is *United States—Anti-dumping Measures on Certain Shrimp from Viet Nam*, WT/DS404/11/Add.37, 10 July 2015, with the related case being *US—Shrimp II (Viet Nam)* (DS429), in which the reports were adopted on 22 April 2015. The three other matters raised were *US—Offset Act (Byrd Amendment)* (DS217); *Thailand—Cigarettes (Philippines)* (DS371); and *China—Electronic Payment Services* (DS413).

remedy cases, the prevailing party often gets little real relief. For example, in safeguard cases, it is often true that the safeguard had expired or was about to expire by its own terms before the reasonable period of time for compliance had expired.[23] In anti-dumping cases, the investigating authorities often recalculated duties or re-assessed the injury determination, with the result that there was no real change as a result of the WTO case.[24] Moreover, it must be admitted that complainants often choose for a variety of reasons not to pursue a matter further, even though they believe that they have not achieved complete vindication of their rights.

Finally, and perhaps most significantly, it must be recognized that compliance often occurs after the expiration of the reasonable period of time therefor. I found, for example, that roughly sixty per cent of the cases are implemented within the reasonable period of time (or relatively soon after its expiration). The remaining cases often take much longer before implementation is achieved.[25] Probably the best-known example is the *EC—Bananas* case, where the reasonable period of time expired on 31 December 1998, but compliance was agreed only in November 2012.[26] The negative impact of this lack of prompt compliance is compounded by the fact that panel reports are often issued many months after the deadlines established in the DSU.[27] As noted above, in the past couple of years this problem has become much, much worse, as panels often commence their work months after they have been composed because of a lack of available Secretariat staff to provide support.

C. Summary

Overall, the record of WTO dispute settlement must be judged quite positively. It is noteworthy that in the realm of state-to-state dispute settlement, the WTO system has been very active (as noted, so active as to outstrip the WTO's ability to service the current caseload) and the results of the system have largely been respected. There were legitimate fears when it was created that the major powers would not accept adverse decisions, but in fact they have. While they may drag their feet, in some cases for years, they have ultimately complied, or reached settlements that the complaining parties have accepted (explicitly or implicitly by deciding not to bring a further WTO challenge). In turning to the second part of this chapter, this summary suggests that the focus should be on improving the timeliness of the system and of compliance.

[23] Davey, 'Evaluating WTO Dispute Resolution' (n 20) 110. [24] ibid 110–11.

[25] ibid 112–16.

[26] See 'Historic signing ends 20 years of EU–Latin American banana disputes' (*WTO: 2012 NEWS ITEMS*, 8 November 2012) <https://www.wto.org/english/news_e/news12_e/disp_08nov12_e.htm> accessed 4 March 2016.

[27] William J Davey, 'Expediting the Panel Process in WTO Dispute Settlement' in Merit E Janow, Victoria Donaldson, and Alan Yanovich (eds), *The WTO: Governance, Dispute Settlement and Developing Countries* (Juris Publishing 2008) 409, 415–21.

III. Improving WTO Dispute Settlement Procedures

In considering how to improve timeliness and compliance, I would suggest a number of possible actions. As mentioned earlier, the WTO Membership in general seems satisfied with the operation and overall performance of the system. As a consequence, there is no groundswell of support for change. Certain action is needed and, in fact, some useful action has already occurred recently. As noted above, while the number of WTO disputes has not accelerated in recent years, the complexity of those cases brought to the dispute settlement has certainly grown. The result has been an inability of the WTO Secretariat to staff panels. This particular problem may be on its way to a solution, since the WTO Director-General announced in September 2014 that he was making additional staff positions available to the dispute settlement function.[28] While it will take some time for the new personnel to learn the arcane world of WTO dispute settlement, within a year or two the capacity of the system should have increased significantly. However, even before the staff shortages became so severe, there were problems with timeliness—both in processing cases and in achieving compliance/settlement. Since it seems to me that ultimately the system must act to improve its timeliness in these two areas, I offer some specific suggestions on how to do so.[29]

A. Speeding up the panel process

There are two ways in which the panel process could be speeded up without sacrificing the quality of panel reports. First, the WTO should implement a system of full-time panellists. Second, specific changes should be made to the current panel timetable found in the DSU.

1. *Permanent panel body*

During the Doha dispute settlement negotiations, the European Union proposed the creation of a permanent panel body, from which all panels would be drawn.[30] Essentially, the European Union proposed that a group of twenty or so individuals would constitute the panel body and would staff all WTO panels.

[28] *Appellate Body Annual Report for 2014* (n 19).

[29] It should also be noted that the WTO Secretariat has tried to come up with ways to make the dispute settlement process more efficient within the framework of the existing DSU rules, which can only be changed by WTO Members. These efforts are described in Bureau of National Affairs, 'WTO Members Quietly Adopt Reforms to Dispute Proceedings' (*International Trade Daily*, 2012). However, while some of these reforms have been useful in reducing the number of pages to be translated in reports (e.g. through using short executive summaries of party arguments) and improving the effectiveness of the panel process (e.g. through improvement in the use of questions to parties by panels), it is my impression that they have not fundamentally addressed the problems of delay.

[30] For a thorough discussion of the permanent panel body proposal, see Dispute Settlement Body, *Contribution of the European Communities and its Member States to the Improvement of the*

There are a number of advantages to such a proposal. First, there would be significant time savings, as parties often spend many weeks in the panel selection process, only to resort in the end to appointment to the Director-General in most cases. In the first ten years of WTO dispute settlement, the median time for composition of a panel was eight weeks.[31] With a permanent panel body, the selection process would be automatic and could be accomplished within a week or so after the DSB established a panel. In addition, since such panellists would be required to be available, the several weeks now lost to scheduling delays would also be avoided. Moreover, with a panel body, the panellists would likely know each other well and be able to establish an effective working relationship immediately, which is often not the case at present. Second, there would be other significant advantages not related to saving time. For example, a permanent panel body would allow for the standardization of panel working procedures and the effective implementation of such reforms as increased use of preliminary rulings and remands, which seem to have wide support, and provisional remedies, which may gain such support over time. Ad hoc panels would simply be less able to handle such procedures in a timely and effective way. In addition, currently most panellists serve only once or twice. Yet as cases become more complex, particularly in respect of procedural aspects and the evaluation of evidence, experience is ever more necessary. Over time, one could expect the overall quality of panel reports and proceedings to increase with a permanent panel body as panellists become more experienced. Consistency of approach and results would be more easily achievable.[32]

The principal objections to the European Union proposal seem to have been concerns over cost, the loss of party control of panellist selection, and a potential lack of expertise. The cost concerns seem insignificant, a matter of only a few million dollars. Given the importance of the WTO dispute settlement system to the functioning of the multilateral trading system, the clear improvement that a permanent panel body would make in the dispute settlement system would be

WTO Dispute Settlement Understanding: Communication from the European Communities, TN/DS/W/1, 13 March 2002 and William J Davey, 'A Permanent Panel Body for WTO Dispute Settlement: Desirable or Practical?' in Daniel L M Kennedy and James D Southwick (eds), *The Political Economy of International Trade Law: Essays in Honor of Professor Robert E Hudec* (CUP 2002) 496–527; William J Davey, 'Mini-symposium on a WTO Permanent Panel Body' (2003) 6(1) J Intl Econ L 171, 181–235 (papers by Cottier, Davey, and Shoyer; comments by Bourgeois, Cartland, Chang, Wasesha, Lacarte, and Roessler); Debra P Steger, *Establishment of a Dispute Tribunal in the WTO, in Trade and Development Symposium: Perspectives on the Multilateral Trading System, International Centre for Trade and Sustainable Development (ICTSD)* (2012) <http://ssrn.com/abstract=2065448 > accessed 4 March 2016.

[31] Davey, 'Expediting the Panel Process in WTO Dispute Settlement' (n 27) 416.

[32] Other advantages that have been cited include increased legitimacy (assuming that members of the permanent panel body did not have the governmental affiliations that some believe raise conflict of interest problems today), broader geographic diversity of panellists (assuming that the United States, the European Union, and China would have nationals on the body), and a reduction of WTO Secretariat influence (assuming that the permanent panel body had its own staff), William J Davey, 'The Case for a WTO Permanent Panel Body' (2003) 6(1) J Intl Econ L 177, 180–82.

well worth such a small investment. The concern over party control seems to be based on erroneous assumptions about how the WTO system works in practice. In recent years, the Director-General has appointed most or some of the members of most panels. In any event, the members would retain control through appointing the members of the permanent panel body. As to the concern about expertise, panels are always able to seek outside expertise. Moreover, a selection system could probably be devised such that panellists for a specific case would have certain expertise.[33]

Overall, I believe that the creation of a permanent panel body would be a positive step forward for the WTO dispute settlement system. In this chapter, I focus on the time-saving aspects of such a change, but as noted above, there are clear additional benefits as well, particularly relating to improvement in the quality of reports.

2. *Panel scheduling*

Briefing

At the moment, the DSU Appendix 3 guidelines provide for up to six weeks for the filing of the complainant's first written submission and up to three weeks thereafter for the respondent's submission. Although in my experience most complainants have insisted on the six-week period, there is no justification for it. They should know what their case is about and they largely control the timing of the proceeding through establishment and composition. Allowing them six weeks to prepare their initial submission is totally unnecessary. Beyond that, it is unfair to the respondent, who should have relatively more time to prepare a response, since it does not know exactly what the arguments will be. Complainants should be required to file their briefs within, at most, two weeks of panel composition, and respondents should be given three or four weeks to respond. This would save several weeks compared to the current practice. The opposition to this proposal seems to be based on a desire by complainants not to forego the strategic advantage they now have. But since that advantage is unfair, this change is clearly a very easy and fair way to save several weeks.[34] In this regard, it is noteworthy that the Appellate Body requires that the written submission supporting the appeal must be filed on the same day as the appeal.[35]

Interim Review

The interim review requirement adds a minimum of five weeks to the time needed to complete a panel report.[36] The interim view stage does have some value, as it allows for the correction of factual misunderstandings and ensures that panels

[33] ibid 182–86.

[34] Davey, 'Expediting the Panel Process in WTO Dispute Settlement' (n 27) 423.

[35] Appellate Body, *Working Procedures for Appellate Review*, WT/AB/WP/6, 16 August 2010, para 21(1).

[36] DSU art 15, Appendix 3.

address all arguments considered to be important by the parties.[37] Nonetheless, its elimination would be an easy way to save five weeks. Moreover, to the extent that there are factual misunderstandings, the parties will still receive the report before it is circulated to the Membership at large. That would mean that there would be time in the weeks while the report is being translated for the parties to be permitted to ask for 'correction' of the report.

Adoption/Appeal of Panel Reports

Perhaps the best example of unnecessary time in the DSU process is the sixty days provided for adoption of the panel report or appeal in lieu thereof.[38] That time could easily be reduced to thirty days. While governments that have lost a case claim that they need all of the time to decide whether to appeal because of the need to consult with interested parties and deal with complex inter-agency decision making, the reality is that they know the result of the case when they receive the final report, which is weeks before it is circulated to the Membership at large, and could (indeed, should) start any necessary decision making at that time. Moreover, since the Appellate Body report must be adopted, a period of two weeks should suffice for those who wish to speak at the relevant meeting to prepare their remarks.[39]

3. *Summary of time frame changes*

Making all of these suggested changes could save a lot of time, especially if a permanent panel system is adopted. Table 2.1 recapitulates the changes in the basic panel/Appellate Body stage:

Table 2.1 Changes in the basic panel/Appellate Body stage

Panel composition	6 weeks
Panel briefing	3 weeks
Panel report preparation	
Scheduling	2 weeks
Interim report	5 weeks
Panel report adoption	4 weeks
AB report adoption	2 weeks
Total	22 weeks

Thus, the current time taken by cases from establishment to adoption could be reduced by five months.

[37] Davey, 'Expediting the Panel Process in WTO Dispute Settlement' (n 27) 424.
[38] DSU art 16.
[39] Davey, 'Expediting the Panel Process in WTO Dispute Settlement' (n 27) 425–26.

I would add one further thought. Newcomers to WTO dispute settlement often find that the panel reports are extremely long, and often wonder if all that verbiage is necessary. I tend to think that reports could be shorter, but the ethos of report drafting must change. I mention this only in passing, however, because I think that, if anything, the standard approach of the Appellate Body to reviewing panel reports more or less ensures that they will be very long. Unlike many appellate courts, the Appellate Body gets into the minutia of panel reasoning and insists that panels must have considered every conceivable argument in respect of an issue. Given that approach, panels will likely always write a lot more than might really be necessary to decide a given case.

B. Improving compliance

In considering how to improve the timeliness of compliance, two changes would be useful. First, the period which losing parties are given to bring their non-conforming measures into compliance with their WTO obligations could be standardized and shortened. Second, it would be possible to devise more effective remedies for non-compliance, which would be expected to improve compliance.

1. *The reasonable period of time for implementation*

In each dispute, it is necessary to set a reasonable period of time for compliance.[40] If the parties cannot agree on such a period, it is set by arbitration (which has traditionally been done by a member of the Appellate Body). In that regard, the DSU specifies that the reasonable period of time for implementation should normally not exceed fifteen months.[41] Unfortunately, the major players in the early WTO cases insisted on fifteen months for implementation (*US—Gasoline*; *Japan—Alcohol Taxes*, *Canada—Periodicals*, *EC—Bananas*, and *EC—Hormones*).[42] This probably had the effect of ensuring that longer periods for implementation would become the norm than otherwise might have been the case. In any event, while the average has fallen to nine months or so, and it is now clearly accepted that the fifteen months period referred to as a guide for arbitration is not to be viewed as a minimum or standard time, the periods are still too long.[43] Under the standard approach to setting the period, the focus is on the length of the legislative process, which rewards complex systems. It seems to me that having a complex legislative system is fine and perhaps even admirable, but should not give a violator a reward by lengthening the penalty-free period during which it is able to inflict damage on

[40] DSU art 21. While art 21.1 of the DSU requires 'prompt compliance', art 21.3 provides that if it is impracticable to comply immediately, the Member concerned shall have a reasonable period of time in which to comply. Members virtually always claim that immediate compliance is impracticable if the contested measure is still in effect.

[41] DSU art 21.3(c).

[42] WT/DS2, WT/DS8, WT/DS31, WT/DS27, and WT/DS26, respectively (see n 7).

[43] Davey, 'Expediting the Panel Process in WTO Dispute Settlement' (n 27) 419–20.

others. The reasonable period of time should be capped at a level lower than fifteen months, if necessary with some leeway for developing countries in special circumstances. A period of six or nine months should be sufficient and could be adopted in all cases.[44] Some Members will have difficulty complying on time in some cases, but the fact that they will become subject to suspension of concessions or other remedy should have a salutary effect in focusing their efforts on implementation.

2. *Improving remedies*

Under the DSU, if a responding Member fails to bring its challenged measure into conformity with its WTO obligations within the reasonable period of time for compliance, the prevailing Member may ask for compensation.[45] If compensation cannot be agreed within thirty days of the expiration of the reasonable period of time, then the prevailing Member may request the DSB for authority to suspend concessions owed to the defaulting Member (i.e. authority to take retaliatory action).[46] The DSB is required to grant such a request absent a consensus to the contrary.[47] If there is a dispute over the level of retaliation, it is referred to arbitration by the original panel.[48] If there is a dispute over whether the challenged measure has been brought into conformity, the matter is referred to the original panel.[49]

Since compensation is almost never agreed upon, the basic remedy for noncompliance in a WTO proceeding is retaliation. As detailed below, there are a number of serious problems with reliance on retaliation as the only remedy, and there have been many ideas on how the systems of remedies in WTO dispute settlement could be usefully improved.[50] Indeed, improving remedies through the use of financial compensation is one of the topics on which Professor Matsushita has made important contributions.[51]

In considering how to improve remedies in the WTO system, it is important to recall that the existing remedies are prospective—whether in the form of compensation or retaliation. In addition, it is important to consider their two principal

[44] ibid 426–28.

[45] See generally William J Davey, 'Sanctions in the WTO: Problems and Solutions' in Chad P Bown and Joost Pauwelyn (eds), *The Law, Economics and Politics of Retaliation in WTO Dispute Settlement* (CUP 2010) 360–72. DSU art 22.2.

[46] ibid. [47] DSU art 22.6.

[48] ibid. The arbitrator's decision is final and the DSB is to authorize retaliation on the basis of its report, DSU art 22.7.

[49] DSU art 21.5. There is some ambiguity in the relationship of this provision and the provisions of art 22. This gave rise to serious problems in the *Bananas* case, where the United States claim a right to retaliation before completion of any art 21.5 procedure (see n 14). This ambiguity needs to be clarified, but how to do so is beyond the scope of this chapter. At the moment, standard practice is to have art 21.5 procedure precede art 22 arbitration and authorization. However, because of the uncertainty caused by the DSU's ambiguity, it is often the case that both proceedings are started simultaneously and art 22 arbitration is suspended pending completion of art 21.5 proceeding.

[50] See generally Chad P Bown and Joost Pauwelyn (eds), *The Law, Economics and Politics of Retaliation in WTO Dispute Settlement* (CUP 2010).

[51] Mitsuo Matsushita, 'The Sutherland Report and Its Discussion of Dispute Settlement Reforms' (2005) 8(3) J Intl Econ L 623, 624–25.

aims: to restore the balance of concessions that was upset when one Member violated its obligations (a temporary aim, since compliance is the preferred result); and to give that Member an incentive to comply. The current problem with achieving the first aim—rebalancing—is that if retaliation is authorized, rebalancing takes place at a lower level of trade liberalization than had been agreed to. It would be desirable if a remedy could be devised that would not lead to less liberalization overall. In that regard, one might consider monetary payments or requiring the payment of compensation through a reduction in other tariffs or trade restrictions maintained by the non-complying Member.[52]

In respect of the second aim—incentive to comply—there are two issues: timing and level of compensation or retaliation. At present, because remedies are prospective, there is an incentive for the defaulting Member to delay the time at which point they might be implemented, such as by seeking a long reasonable period of time for compliance and then forcing the prevailing Member to go through an Article 21.5 panel (and Appellate Body) proceeding. Moreover, if the threat of retaliation does not work, it is possible that the actual existence of retaliation will become viewed as the status quo and a long-term solution, even though the WTO rules in theory require compliance.

While retaliation seems to work when threatened by a large country against a smaller one, and has worked as between two large countries, it may not be an effective remedy for a small country (even if it can target sensitive, large-country sectors such as intellectual property rights holders). Moreover, the *EC—Bananas* and *EC—Hormones* cases[53] show that it is not always effective between large players. Its inefficacy and the unfavourable position in which it leaves developing countries may soon combine to create a serious credibility problem for the system that must be confronted.

In light of the existing compliance problems noted above and the need to craft a more effective remedy for the typical WTO Member, I believe that some form of monetary remedy should be available in WTO dispute settlement, a position that has also been endorsed by Professor Matsushita.[54] While the precise details of such a remedy would need to be worked out, the following offers some general guidelines:[55]

1. *Choice of remedy/differential treatment.* The normal WTO remedy is retaliation in the sector where the violation occurred, subject to the possibility of retaliation in other sectors if the inadequacy of same-sector retaliation is shown.[56] The possibility of a monetary remedy should be similarly available, i.e. when same-sector retaliation would be inadequate. This would effectively allow smaller countries to demand monetary compensation, while the United States and the European Union would usually not be able to do

[52] See Joost Pauwelyn, 'Enforcement and Countermeasures in the WTO' (2000) 94(2) Am J Intl L 335.

[53] WT/DS27 and WT/DS26 (see n 7).

[54] Matsushita, 'The Sutherland Report' (n 51).

[55] Davey, 'Sanctions in the WTO: Problems and Solutions' (n 45) 365–68.

[56] DSU art 22.3.

so, and would never be able to do so vis-à-vis smaller countries. As such, there would probably be no need for special and differential treatment to govern the right to compensation.[57]

2. *Enforceability of compensation*. If the enforceability of an award of compensation is thought to be in doubt, it could be agreed in the WTO that Article 22 arbitral awards are enforceable under the New York Convention on the Recognition and Enforcement of Foreign Arbitral Awards, which on the face of it seems to apply to awards against governments.
3. *Increased levels of nullification and impairment*. It is appropriate to maintain the link between the level of nullification and trade flows.[58] But the current approach should be modified so that the trade effect is measured from an earlier point in time than the expiration of the reasonable period of time for compliance.[59] In addition, in the event that the defaulting country does not bring its measure into conformity with WTO rules, the level of permitted retaliation/compensation should be increased annually on the theory that a continued failure to implement is in itself a justification for concluding that the original level of nullification has increased, with the result that the permitted level of retaliation would also increase.[60] These changes would result in an increased incentive to comply within the reasonable period of time, since they would significantly increase the consequences of not doing so. The fact that the cost of non-compliance would increase over time would reduce the likelihood that countries would view compensation as a permanent settlement of the matter.[61]

[57] The situation where a poor country was required to pay compensation could also be avoided or moderated by having a rule that adjusted the level of compensation set under normal procedures in light of the relative GNP per capita of the country in question with a standard GNP per capita or, possibly, the GNP per capita of the prevailing country.

[58] DSU art 22.4 (level of retaliation should be equivalent to level of nullification or impairment).

[59] For example, if the trade effect is measured from adoption of the original report(s), then the trade effects of the non-conforming behaviour during the reasonable period of time for implementation and during any art 21.5 or art 22.6 proceedings would be calculated and the level of permitted retaliation would take that time into account. Suppose in a given case that the trade effects were 100 per month and were level throughout the pendency of the case and thereafter, then if the reasonable period of time was six months, the arbitration report under art 22.6 was issued five months after the expiration of the reasonable period of time and the authority to retaliate was granted one month later, there would be a right to retaliate in an additional amount of 1,200. This would need to be allocated over time—one could allocate it over the first year of retaliation (so retaliation would be at a level of 200 per month) or adopt some other method. Compared to the present system, it would make non-compliance more costly.

[60] This increase would need to be calculated in light of the level of retaliation calculated as described in note 59. Thus, under the facts set out there, the increase in retaliation would be from a base of 200.

[61] The possibility that the payment of compensation would be viewed as giving wealthy countries a way to 'buy out' of their WTO obligations, particularly in respect of poor countries, was a major concern of the authors of the so-called Sutherland Report in their discussion of DSU reform proposals, Peter Sutherland and others, *The Future of the WTO: Report by the Consultative Board to the Director-General Supachai Panitchpakdi* (WTO 2004) 54 <https://www.wto.org/english/res_e/publications_e/future_wto_e.htm> accessed 4 March 2016. A provision that increases the compensation due over time would make this less likely to occur.

4. *Reparations.* The standard international law remedy is reparations.[62] To adopt such a rule for WTO violations would represent a major change in approach and should be considered only after the foregoing reforms have been tried and found to be inadequate. In this regard, it is worth noting that the proposal to increase levels of nullification contains an element of reparations, but it would be owed only in the event of failure to comply within the reasonable period of time, as opposed to being owed in all cases and at the level of actual damage.

The adoption of the proposal outlined above should result in higher levels of retaliation/compensation, which hopefully would improve the WTO dispute settlement system's compliance record by greatly encouraging timely compliance. But even if these changes do not improve compliance, they would provide some relief for countries harmed by WTO rule violations, since they would be able to claim compensation. Since both compensation and rebalancing are appropriate goals of retaliation, the changes will certainly result in some improvement compared to the current situation.

IV. Conclusion

The WTO dispute settlement system has been relatively successful in resolving disputes between its Members. One consequence of that success is that WTO Members are bringing more cases involving more complex issues to the system for resolution. The result is that the WTO dispute settlement system has recently been, and continues to be, under considerable strain. This has exacerbated already existing problems of delays in the processing of cases and in achieving compliance with WTO rulings. Ultimately, Members and their constituencies are likely to become ever more frustrated with such delays so as to put the system's reputation for success in jeopardy. That future can be avoided if the WTO acts now to take action to cut delays in the panel process and improve remedies for non-compliance. Doing so will ensure the continued success of the system that Professor Matsushita played a major role in setting up.

[62] See James Crawford, *The International Law Commission's Articles on State Responsibility: Introduction, Text And Commentaries* (CUP 2006) 201–06 (noting that art 31(1) of the International Law Commission's Articles on State Responsibility provides: 'The responsible State is under an obligation to make full reparation for the injury caused by the internationally wrongful act').

3

The Dispute Settlement System of the WTO: A Bright Picture with a Few Dark Spots

*Claus-Dieter Ehlermann**

Even in the very first years of its existence, the Dispute Settlement Understanding (DSU) was qualified as the 'jewel in the crown' of the WTO. Several Director-Generals of the WTO have used this expression, notably Pascal Lamy. Academic publications frequently refer to it, most recently Michael Trebilcock in his Robert Hudec Public Lecture in Bern.[1]

However, today, the qualification 'jewel in the crown' seems to be used less often than in the past; perhaps because the DSU is no longer a novelty, but a familiar part of the WTO, perhaps to avoid quarrels with the critics of the WTO jurisprudence, critics who do not agree with certain reports on the use of trade defence instruments. Pure speculation may even lead to the assumption that less praise for the DSU attenuates psychologically the appalling lack of equilibrium between the judicial and the political branches of the WTO.

The lack of equilibrium is obvious: on the one hand, the highly efficient DSU, with its panels and the Appellate Body, adopting reports, if necessary by a majority of two to one; on the other hand, a ministerial conference composed of 161 Member States, operating in practice only by consensus. On the first point, it is useful to recall two sentences of the so-called Sutherland Report of 2005. First: 'The current WTO dispute settlement procedures … are to be admired and are a very significant step forward in the general system of rules-based international diplomacy.' And second: 'By most accounts, and most measures, the operation of the dispute settlement system in the WTO has been a remarkable success.' To which James Bacchus, a former Chairman of the Appellate Body, adds: 'Today, WTO law is seen worldwide as one of the main sources of international law. In

* Professor Dr Claus-Dieter Ehlermann is a former chair of the WTO Appellate Body and a Senior Counsel at WilmerHale, Brussels.

[1] Michael Trebilcock, 'Between Theories of Trade and Development: The Future of the World Trading System' (2014) University of Toronto Law Working Paper Series No 2014-10 <http://ssrn.com/abstract=2473158> accessed 5 March 2016.

fact, WTO dispute settlement may well have produced more new international law in the form of international jurisprudence in the past two decades than all the other proliferating sources of international law combined.'[2]

However, the lack of equilibrium between the judicial and the political branches of the WTO are dangerous. I stressed this while I was still a Member of the Appellate Body. The concern has been expressed most powerfully in the Farewell Speech of former Appellate Body Member David Unterhalter. It is worthwhile to read Unterhalter's full text. I will however just quote three key sentences:

> Adjudication is robust when it lives in a dynamic relationship with legislative competence. If too much rests upon dispute settlement, the system gets out of kilter, and the atrophy of one part of the system ultimately takes hold of everything else.... [I]t is important to recognize that the system is fragile: its success depends upon its utility to the membership; and it will develop only if the WTO project as a whole does so.[3]

The consequences of the weakness of political decision making on the DSU might differ. But everybody will agree that this weakness has major consequences for Regional Trade Agreements (RTAs). The number and importance of RTAs has dramatically increased, inter alia because of the incapacity of the WTO to decide politically. The fate of the Doha Round and the latest blockage of the draft Bali package are a vivid demonstration of this incapacity.

The current debates on the Comprehensive Economic and Trade Agreement (CETA) between the European Union and Canada and the Transatlantic Trade and Investment Partnership (TTIP) between the European Union and the United States, still under negotiation, have led me to reflect about the risks which the more and more refined dispute settlement mechanisms of RTAs present for the DSU. Fortunately, my initial fears seem to be unjustified. On the one hand, modern FTAs of the European Union demonstrate that the European Union takes great care to respect the DSU, as well as the findings of panels and the Appellate Body. Thus, for instance, the European Commission's latest textual proposal for a legal text on the 'Dispute Settlement (Government to Government)' chapter of the TTIP states that recourse to the dispute settlement provisions under the FTA is without prejudice to any action in the WTO framework, including dispute settlement action, and includes a typical fork-in-the-road provision, preventing a party to the FTA from seeking redress for the breach of a substantially equivalent obligation under both the TTIP and the WTO Agreement in both fora. Moreover, an arbitration panel established under the TTIP is obliged to take into account relevant interpretations in the adopted panel and Appellate Body reports. The Commission also recently proposed a new Investment Court System that should replace the existing investor-to-state dispute settlement (ISDS) mechanism in all ongoing and future European

[2] James Bacchus, 'Not in Clinical Isolation' in Gabrielle Marceau (ed), *A History of Law and Lawyers in the GATT/WTO: The Development of the Rule of Law in the Multilateral Trading System* (CUP 2015) 507.

[3] 'Farewell speech of Appellate Body Member David Unterhalter' (World Trade Organization 2014) <https://www.wto.org/english/tratop_e/dispu_e/unterhalterspeech_e.htm> accessed 5 March 2016.

Union investment negotiations, including in the context of the TTIP. In addressing concerns of trade unions and civil society about the existing ISDS mechanism, this new model envisages inter alia that judgments would be made by publicly appointed judges with high qualifications, comparable to those required for the members of permanent international courts such as the WTO Appellate Body, as well as a new permanent Appeal Tribunal operating on principles similar to those of the Appellate Body.

More generally, a recent study of the WTO shows that RTA partners continue to be frequent users of the DSU to resolve their trade disputes, including those that could have been brought under the mechanisms established in their RTAs.[4]

Academic literature has identified a host of reasons that explain the attractions the DSU offers compared with similar mechanisms of RTAs. Some authors go so far as to plead for the use of WTO panels and the Appellate Body to settle disputes arising under RTAs—an apparent analogy with the possibility offered through 'enhanced co-operation' in the European Union. Such a system of '*Organleihe*' would certainly be desirable, but is highly unlikely to be accepted by at least some major Members of the WTO.

On the other hand, recently, the Appellate Body has stated in *Peru—Agricultural Products*[5] that while two parties can settle a dispute on a given issue bilaterally, they cannot give up their rights to pursue WTO dispute settlement proceedings on a permanent basis, for instance by means of an FTA dispute settlement provision. This seems to rule out the enforceability in WTO dispute settlement of clauses that give to an FTA dispute settlement mechanism exclusive jurisdiction or even fork-in-the-road provisions, to the extent they relate to rights and obligations that the FTA parties have under the WTO covered agreements. In other words, in *Peru—Agricultural Products* the Appellate Body seems to have clarified that such dispute settlement provisions in FTAs would not necessarily represent 'legal impediments' (as referred in the *Mexico—Soft Drinks*[6] dispute) that may prevent WTO adjudicators from exercising jurisdiction.

While competition with RTAs and their dispute settlement is not a threat for the WTO, increased workload risks becoming so, at least for the Appellate Body. The problem is described in a communication entitled 'The workload of the Appellate Body', reproduced in the Appellate Body's Annual Report for 2013. The number of *parties* involved, and *claims* raised, in an average WTO dispute has more than doubled since the early years of the WTO. Disputes involving more than one *complainant* have become a frequent occurrence. The number of *third* parties has also increased, to slightly less than ten on average per dispute. The number of *issues*

[4] Claude Chase and others, 'Mapping of Dispute Settlement Mechanisms in Regional Trade Agreements—Innovative or Variations on a Theme?' (2013) WTO Economic Research and Statistics Division Staff Working Paper No ERSD-2013-07 <https://www.wto.org/english/res_e/reser_e/ersd201307_e.pdf> accessed 5 October 2015.

[5] Appellate Body Report, *Peru—Additional Duty on Imports of Certain Agricultural Products*, WT/DS457/AB/R, adopted 31 July 2015.

[6] Appellate Body Report, *Mexico—Tax Measures on Soft Drinks and Other Beverages*, WT/DS308/AB/R, adopted 24 March 2006.

raised is, in many cases, between ten and twenty. The increased workload of panels is reflected in the workload of the Appellate Body. Appeals involve more *participants* and *third participants*, as well as a higher number of *issues*. All this has been compounded by an increase in the factual complexity of disputes and is reflected in longer panel and Appellate Body reports. As the 2014 chair of the Appellate Body Ricardo Ramírez-Hernández stated in the foreword to the Appellate Body's Annual Report for 2014, although that year was 'trendsetting' in terms of complexity of appeals and number of panel reports appealed, this is just the tip of the iceberg, and the upward trend of dispute settlement activity will continue for the next several years.

There is nothing abnormal in this evolution. It is rather a confirmation of the success of WTO dispute settlement. However, it raises problems, in particular for the Appellate Body, because of the ninety-day deadline and the very small number of seven Members. I have been, and remain, a passionate defender of the ninety-day deadline, while I see reasons for the increase of the number of seven. I am, however, worried about the possible consequences of the actual situation. These consequences are described—I believe for the first time—in a paper by Ricardo Ramírez and Kaarlo Castren.[7] They include (i) a concentration on issues that are central to the dispute and a relative neglect for other issues; (ii) a shortage of time for the search of consensus among the three Members who decide the appeal; (iii) an impossibility to 'complete the analysis'; and (iv) an even more deferential attitude towards panels.

There is no magic tool to solve the workload problem for the Appellate Body. In the immediate future, the most appropriate technique seems to be a staggering of appeals, which pre-supposes a staggering of panel reports. But some remedy to the workload problem is inevitable to avoid negative effects on the quality of Appellate Body reports.

Finally, I would like to point to a threat for the Appellate Body that has increased recently and is seriously undermining its credibility. I am referring to the denaturation of the selection process of Appellate Body Members. To submit the candidates for Appellate Body membership to a process of scrutiny that resembles the selection of judges of the Supreme Court of the USA is highly detrimental for the independence—and the outside appearance of independence—of the Appellate Body, in particular in combination with the shortness of the mandate of Appellate Body Members. I have always criticized the shortness of this mandate. The possibility to prolong the first mandate of four years by a second mandate, also of four years, does not improve the situation. On the contrary, in a certain sense, it makes it worse.

In sum, twenty years of dispute settlement in the WTO offer a bright picture, with also a few dark spots.

[7] Ricardo Ramírez-Hernández and Kaarlo Castren, 'Will the Increased Workload of WTO Panels and the Appellate Body Change How WTO Disputes are Adjudicated?' in Gabrielle Marceau (ed), *A History of Law and Lawyers in the GATT/WTO: The Development of the Rule of Law in the Multilateral Trading System* (CUP 2015) 616.

4

The Scope of Regulatory Autonomy of WTO Members under Article III:4 of the GATT: A Critical Analysis of the Jurisprudence of the WTO Appellate Body

*Frieder Roessler**

Professor Matsushita is an expert in both domestic and international economic law and has written impressive papers touching upon the potential conflicts between the two. As a member of the WTO Appellate Body he was involved in a number of appeals that touched upon the right of the Members of the WTO to impose internal measures affecting the sale of domestic and imported products. After Professor Matsushita's departure from the Appellate Body in March 2000, the Appellate Body issued a number of rulings defining the scope of the regulatory autonomy of Members under the national-treatment provisions of the General Agreement on Tariffs and Trade 1994 (GATT) and the Agreement on Technical Barriers to Trade (TBT Agreement). Given Professor Matsushita's interest in the relationship between international trade law and domestic regulations, I would like to contribute to this *Liber Amicorum* a brief analysis of these rulings.

Article III:4 of GATT requires the Members of the WTO to accord imported products treatment no less favourable than that accorded to like domestic products. Article 2.1 of the TBT Agreement imposes the same obligation in respect of technical regulations. In a series of cases, the Appellate Body has ruled in essence that imported and domestic products are 'like products' within the meaning of Article III:4 of the GATT if they directly compete in the market, and that the imported product is accorded 'less favourable treatment' within the meaning of that provision if it is accorded less favourable competitive opportunities.[1]

* Formerly Director of the Legal Affairs Division of the GATT (1989–1994), Visiting Professor at the Georgetown University Law Center (1995–1998) and Executive Director of the Advisory Centre on WTO Law (2001–2013).

[1] For a detailed review of this case law, see Frieder Roessler, 'Beyond the Ostensible—A Tribute to Professor Robert Hudec's Insights on the Determination of the Likeness of Products under the National Treatment Provisions of the General Agreement on Tariffs and Trade' (2003) 37(4) J World Trade 771.

In *EC—Asbestos* the Appellate Body explained:

As products that are in a competitive relationship in the marketplace could be affected through treatment of *imports* 'less favourable' than the treatment accorded to *domestic* products, it follows that the word 'like' in Article III:4 is to be interpreted to apply to products that are in such a competitive relationship. Thus, a determination of 'likeness' under Article III:4 is, fundamentally, a determination about the nature and extent of a competitive relationship between and among products.[2]

Regulations that distinguish between different types of products and accord one of them less favourable treatment are typically adopted precisely because the market does not make the distinction that the regulator considers necessary. For instance, if a government prohibits the use of rubbish bags that cannot be easily incinerated, it presumably does so because the public purchasing such bags does not take into account how difficult it is to dispose of them. In practice, many, if not most, regulations are consequently applied to competing products and prohibit the placing on the market of one of them. Many, if not most, regulations are thus likely to be inconsistent with Article III:4 according to the Appellate Body's jurisprudence.

This is a surprising result because, according to Article III:1, the scope of application of the whole of Article III is confined to regulations applied 'so as to afford protection'. In the view of the Appellate Body, Article III:4 itself is an expression of the principle set forth in Article III:1. It argues that, 'if there is "less favourable treatment" of the group of "like" imported products, there is, conversely, "protection" of the group of "like" domestic products'.[3] However, Article III:1 does not refer to measures whose application protects domestic production. It refers to measure applied 'so as to' protect domestic production. 'So as to' means 'with the aim and effect'. The objective of Article III:1 is therefore achieved only with an interpretation of Article III:4 that takes into account not only the effect of the regulatory distinction, but also its aim. Put differently, Article III is not intended to apply to all regulations that have a, possibly incidental, protective effect; it applies only to regulations that are aimed to produce such effects.

The GATT panel in *US—Malt Beverages* explained the pitfalls of likeness determinations that fail to take into account the aim of the regulatory distinction as follows:

The purpose of Article III is not to prevent contracting parties from differentiating between different product categories for policy purposes unrelated to the protection of domestic production... Once products are designated as like products, a regulatory differentiation, e.g. for standardization or environmental purposes, becomes inconsistent with Article III even if the regulation is not 'applied ... so as to afford protection to domestic production'. In the view of the panel, it is therefore imperative that the like product determination in the context of Article III be made in such a way that it does not unnecessarily infringe upon the regulatory authority and domestic policy options of contracting parties....

[2] Appellate Body Report, *European Communities—Measures Affecting Asbestos and Asbestos-containing Products* (*EC—Asbestos*), WT/DS135/AB/R, 12 March 2001, para 99.

[3] ibid para 100.

Consequently, in determining whether two products subject to different treatment are like products, it is necessary to consider whether such product differentiation is being made 'so as to afford protection'.[4]

Some regulations making product distinctions for legitimate purposes might be justifiable under one of the public policy exceptions set out in Article XX of the GATT. However, the ten policy goals listed in Article XX do not comprise the immense realm of legitimate policy goals pursued through internal regulations. The policy goals listed in Article XX are largely identical to the policy goals listed in the general exceptions clause of the 1929 League of Nations Convention on the Abolition of Import and Export Prohibitions Restrictions.[5] Article XX was thus drafted with policy objectives in mind that can only be realized by discriminating between products as to their origin or destination, in particular policy goals that can only be achieved through import or export restrictions. Thus, the protection of human health can require import restriction on products carrying diseases. That policy goal is included in both the League of Nations convention and Article XX. Conversely, the harmonization of technical standards does not require measures discriminating between products as to their origin or destination. That policy goal is included in neither the League of Nations convention nor Article XX. In any case, given the brief, exhaustive list of policy purposes included in Article XX, it is obvious that the drafters had never intended this provision to be the sole legal basis for justifying internal regulations that distinguish between groups of products competing in the domestic market solely on the basis of their physical characteristics and accord one of them less favourable treatment.

Contrary to a common misconception, Article XX is thus not a list of important societal values of the Members of the WTO, and the ten policy goals listed in this provision do not comprise all legitimate policy goals that Members pursue through measures covered by Article III. The drafters of the GATT therefore obviously assumed that the legitimacy of a distinction between products with different physical characteristics would be taken into account under Article III, and that a need to invoke Article XX would arise only in respect of internal regulations that distinguished between products as to their origin or destination. The drafters of the TBT Agreement similarly assumed that technical regulations that distinguish products with different characteristics for legitimate policy reasons would not be found to violate that Agreement's national treatment requirement because they did not include any public policy exception similar to Article XX in that Agreement.

There is thus a range of perfectly legitimate internal regulations that are not applied 'so as to afford protection' but are nevertheless not justifiable under Article

[4] Report of the Penal, *United States—Measures Affecting Alcoholic and Malt Beverages* (*US—Malt Beverages*), GATT BISD (39th Supp), 19 June 1992, 293–94. I explained the rationale for this ruling further in Frieder Roessler, 'Diverging Domestic Policies and Multilateral Trade Integration' in Jagdish N Bhagwati and Robert E Hudec (eds), *Fair Trade and Harmonization: Prerequisites for Free Trade? Volume 2: Legal Analysis* (MIT Press 1996) 21–56.

[5] Art 4, 1929 League of Nations Convention on the Abolition of Import and Export Prohibitions Restrictions.

XX. This includes all regulations that distinguish between competing products for the purpose of harmonizing standards, improving the efficiency of production, reducing transaction costs for consumers, or preventing deceptive practices.[6] The Appellate Body's market-oriented approach renders all of them inconsistent with Article III:4, makes Article III:1 inoperative in the context of Article III:4, and gives Article XX a function that it cannot fulfil. If transposed to Article 2.1 of the TBT Agreement, the consequences are even more far-reaching because of the lack of a public policy exception.

In *Japan—Alcoholic Beverages*, the United States appealed the finding of the panel that likeness can be determined purely on the basis of physical characteristics, consumer uses, and tariff classification, without considering whether the regulatory distinctions are made so as to afford protection to domestic production. The United States suggested that the Appellate Body follow instead the 'aims-and-effects' approach adopted by the GATT panel in *US—Malt Beverages*.[7] The Appellate Body reacted with complete silence. There is in its legal analysis not a word evaluating the United States' argument.

In *EC—Bananas*, the Appellate Body sharply rejected an initiative of the panel to inquire into the purpose of the measure at issue before finding it inconsistent with Article III:4. It ruled that 'Article III:4 does *not* specifically refer to Article III:1. Therefore, a determination of whether there has been a violation of Article III:4 does *not* require a separate consideration of whether a measure "afford[s] protection to domestic production".'[8] It is true that Article III:2 distinguishes between internal charges on 'like' and directly competitive products and refers to Article III:1 only in respect of the latter, while Article III:4 makes no distinction between 'like' and directly competitive products and contains no explicit reference to Article III:1. However, the lack of reference to Article III:1 in Article III:4 cannot be decisive because Article III:1 unambiguously defines the object and purpose of the whole of Article III and therefore also implicitly addresses the issue of likeness under Article III:4.

In *EC—Asbestos* there was another attempt to make the Appellate Body change its approach to likeness determinations, this time by the European Union. The European Union explained:

> If non-commercial considerations may only be considered at the Article XX stage of the analysis, then the list of policy purposes for which regulators may distinguish between products is unduly limited to the categories listed in Article XX.[9]

Again, there was absolutely no evaluation of the European Union's arguments reflected in the Appellate Body's report. One member of the Division wrote in a separate opinion: 'The necessity or appropriateness of adopting a "fundamentally"

[6] Art XX(d) of the GATT mentions 'regulations ... relating to ... the prevention of deceptive practices'. However, this provision can only be invoked to justify measures to secure compliance with such regulations, not the regulations themselves.

[7] *US—Malt Beverages* (n 4) 206.

[8] Appellate Body Report, *European Communities—Regime for the Importation, Sale and Distribution of Bananas*, WT/DS27/AB/R, 9 September 1997, paras 215–16.

[9] *EC—Asbestos* (n 2) para 37.

economic interpretation of the "likeness" of products under Article III:4 of the GATT 1994 does not appear to me to be free from substantial doubt ...'.[10] However, the member did not explain whether these doubts were related to the problems to which the European Union had alerted the Division.

And so two important Members of WTO asked the Appellate Body to refrain from adopting an interpretation of Article III:4 that, in their view, unduly curtails their regulatory autonomy and the Appellate Body does not evaluate their concerns with one word. And a panel's concern about this interpretation is dismissed by the Appellate Body without any substantive evaluation of the issue. I said to myself that, one day, a perfectly legitimate regulation will come before the Appellate Body that does not fall under one of the sub-paragraphs of Article XX and the Appellate Body will then be forced to either declare it illegal or change its jurisprudence. Or a case will arise under the national treatment provisions of the TBT Agreement that will put the Appellate Body before the same choice.

This happened sooner that I thought. In the *US—Clove Cigarettes* case, the panel found that the interpretation of Article 2.1 of the *TBT Agreement* should *not* be approached primarily from a competition-oriented perspective, but that the weighing of the evidence relating to the 'likeness' criteria should be influenced by the fact that the regulation at issue had the purpose of regulating flavoured cigarettes for public health reasons.[11] The Appellate Body did not budge, insisting that an interpretation of the concept of 'likeness' under the TBT Agreement must also be based on the competitive relationship between and among the products. However, it did not exclude a consideration of the policy purpose of the regulation altogether. It ruled that:

> the context and object and purpose of the *TBT Agreement* weigh in favour of reading the 'treatment no less favourable' requirement of Article 2.1 as prohibiting both *de jure* and *de facto* discrimination against imported products, while at the same time permitting detrimental impact on competitive opportunities for imports that stems exclusively from legitimate regulatory distinctions.[12]

If a panel has to examine whether the purpose of the regulatory distinction is legitimate, does it not have to examine its aim? And if it must examine its impact on imported products, does it not also have to examine its effect? Did the Appellate Body not introduce into Article 2.1 the 'aims-and-effects' test in disguise? I believe it did, and I presume there was a sigh of relief among the Members of the WTO.

I found it somewhat strange that the Appellate Body concluded that the place to conduct the inquiry into the purpose and effect of the regulatory distinction was not the concept of likeness but the concept of no-less-favourable treatment. Whether two products that are not identical should nevertheless be considered to be alike depends on the relevance of the differences between them and that, in turn, varies with

[10] ibid para 154.

[11] Panel Report, *United States—Measures Affecting the Production and Sale of Clove Cigarettes* (*US—Clove Cigarettes*), WT/DS406/R, 2 September 2011, para 7.119.

[12] Appellate Body Report, *US—Clove Cigarettes*, WT/DS406/AB/R, 4 April 2012, para 157.

the purpose and consequence of the regulatory distinction between them. The likeness determination therefore seems to be the natural place to take the legitimacy and the impact of the regulatory distinction into account. Moreover, both under GATT and WTO jurisprudence, the approach to likeness varied over the years, while the assessment of the treatment of products has consistently been limited to an assessment of the competitive opportunities accorded to them. That approach was originally adopted in 1958 by the GATT panel in *Italy—Agricultural Machinery*[13] and had since then been followed, without exception or variation, by all GATT and WTO panels and the Appellate Body in respect of all agreements. The Appellate Body thus preserved the consistency of its jurisprudence on likeness at the expense of changing the well-established jurisprudence on no-less-favourable treatment.

Be that as it may, the Appellate Body avoided, under Article 2.1 of the TBT Agreement, the unfortunate consequences of the exclusively market-based approach under Article III:4 of the GATT. The next step, I thought, would be to extend the novel interpretation of the no-less-favourable treatment concept to Article III:4 of the GATT. Then the scope of regulatory autonomy would not be narrower under the GATT than under the TBT Agreement. Technical regulations must meet the requirements of both the TBT Agreement and the GATT, and, in respect to such regulations, Members are consequently free to invoke their rights under either agreement. It therefore does not make sense to permit under the TBT Agreement regulations imposed for *any* legitimate policy purpose but permit under the GATT only those serving the few purposes listed in Article XX. If that were the case, Members adversely affected by a technical regulation serving a legitimate purpose not listed in Article XX could obtain a withdrawal of the regulation by invoking their rights under the GATT, rather than the TBT Agreement. That would nullify the practical effect of the Appellate Body's interpretation of Article 2.1 of the TBT Agreement, which would not be permitted by the Appellate Body.

So I thought. But I was to be surprised.

In *EC—Seal Products*, the panel found that the legal standard that the Appellate Body had developed for Article 2.1 of the TBT Agreement did not equally apply to Article III:4 of the GATT. The European Union appealed. It explained that this could lead to a situation where, under Article 2.1 of the TBT Agreement, a technical regulation that has a detrimental impact on imports would be permitted if such detrimental impact stems from a legitimate regulatory distinction, while, under the GATT, the same technical regulation would be permitted only if its objective falls within one of the subparagraphs of Article XX. As a consequence, complainants would have a strong incentive not to invoke Article 2.1 of the TBT Agreement and, instead, to bring claims under the GATT, even if the measure at issue qualified as a technical regulation.[14]

[13] Report of the Panel, *Italian Discrimination against Imported Agricultural Machinery*, L/833-7S/60, GATT BISD (7th Supp), 23 October 1958, 63–64.

[14] Appellate Body Report, *European Communities—Measures Prohibiting the Importation and Marketing of Seal Products* (*EC—Seal Products*), WT/DS400/AB/R, WT7DS401/AB/R, 25 November 2013, para 2.183.

The Appellate Body responded that the European Union perceived a legal imbalance that did not exist. It stated:

> under the TBT Agreement, the balance between the desire to avoid creating unnecessary obstacles to international trade under the fifth recital, and the recognition of Members' right to regulate under the sixth recital, is not, in principle, different from the balance set out in the GATT 1994, where obligations such as national treatment in Article III are qualified by the general exceptions provision of Article XX.[15]

It noted, but did not address, the difference in the range of policy goals that may be pursued under the TBT Agreement and the GATT. Instead, it called the practical relevance of that difference into question, stating that:

> the European Union has not pointed to any concrete examples of a legitimate objective that could factor into an analysis under Article 2.1 of the TBT Agreement, but would not fall within the scope of Article XX of the GATT 1994.[16]

I found this statement surprising. First of all, the European Union *did* provide examples to illustrate its concerns, among them regulations whose objective is to provide origin information to consumers, an objective that clearly falls outside the scope of Article XX.[17] The Appellate Body dealt with such a regulation in *US—COOL*, and hence was fully aware of that example. In that case, the complainants invoked both Article 2.1 of the TBT Agreement and Article III:4 of the GATT, and the panel, having found the measure to be inconsistent with the TBT Agreement, exercised judicial economy with respect to the claims under the GATT. However, suppose the complainants had invoked only their rights under the GATT, then the COOL regulation would have had to be declared to be inconsistent with the GATT simply because it distinguishes products competing in the market. This would have been an absurd result.

A simple glance at the notifications of technical regulations made by Members to the TBT Committee could have provided the Appellate Body with further examples. These notifications include regulations designed to provide consumers with information on the net content of pre-packaged products,[18] to harmonize the technical standards for tractors and the machinery towed by them,[19] and to ensure that consumers are informed of the presence of aromas in wine products.[20] All these measures distinguish between groups of competing products, treat one group less favourably than the other, and serve a purpose not listed in Article XX.

[15] ibid para 5.127. [16] ibid para 5.128.

[17] European Commission Submission to the WTO, Other Appellant Submission by the European Union in European Communities—Measures Prohibiting the Importation and Marketing of Seal Products, 29 January 2014, para 307. The illustrative list of objectives listed in this submission was not included in the Appellate Body's summary of the European Union's arguments.

[18] Committee on Technical Barriers to Trade, Notification—Mexico, G/TBT/N/MEX/217, 20 September 2011.

[19] Committee on Technical Barriers to Trade, Notification—Ukraine, G/TBT/N/UKR/62, 26 September 2011.

[20] Committee on Technical Barriers to Trade, Notification—European Union, G/TBT/N/EEC/404, 20 September 2011.

The Appellate Body's refusal to interpret Article III:4 of the GATT in harmony with Article 2.1 of the TBT Agreement makes all of them subject to challenge under the GATT.

The Appellate Body concludes its examination by asserting that:

> our interpretation of the legal standards under Articles I:1 and III:4 of the GATT 1994, and Article 2.1 of the TBT Agreement, is based on the text of those provisions, as understood in their context, and in the light of the object and purpose of the agreements in which they appear, as is our mandate. If there is a perceived imbalance in the existing rights and obligations under the TBT Agreement and the GATT 1994, the authority rests with the Members of the WTO to address that imbalance.[21]

This is a most unfortunate statement. The discrepancy in the scope of regulatory autonomy under the TBT Agreement and the GATT is the result of interpretative choices made by the Appellate Body. There is no principle of interpretation that prevents the Appellate Body from addressing this discrepancy by adopting the interpretation proposed by the European Union. By ruling otherwise, the current Appellate Body effectively ruled that a future Appellate Body, perhaps composed of different members, that examines the same issue in another case could not adopt a different interpretation because it would be exceeding its mandate. I ask myself whether the Division acted within its mandate under the Dispute Settlement Understanding (DSU) and in accordance with the Appellate Body's internal collegiality rules when it declared that no interpretation other than the one it adopted to resolve the case before it could be adopted in any future case. Whatever the answer to this question, it was no doubt unwise for the Appellate Body, and hardly in its institutional interests, to cast its own interpretative authority into fetters.

The European Union's arguments implied that the Appellate Body, with its exclusively market-based approach to the interpretation of Article III:4, had manoeuvred itself into a dead-end street. The Appellate Body defends itself against that accusation by denying the existence and relevance of the problem and its competence to resolve it. It begins by claiming that the scope of regulatory autonomy was 'in principle' the same under the TBT Agreement and the GATT, which is legally incorrect. It then suggests that the imbalance perceived by the European Union would not have any practical relevance, which is factually incorrect. And, finally, it declares that if Members nevertheless perceived an imbalance, only they could address it, which is institutionally untenable. There is no recognition of the problem, no evaluation of different avenues to solve the problem, and no ruling on the problem. The reader is left with the impression that the Appellate Body adjudicated in this most unfortunate case not a dispute between the European Union and other Members, but a conflict between the European Union and itself, and that the European Union had no fair hearing because the Appellate Body was the judge and the accused at the same time.

[21] *EC—Seal Products* (n 14) para 5.129.

What will the Appellate Body do if the issue arises again in a future case? Would it then declare a perfectly legitimate domestic regulation to be inconsistent with WTO law merely because it distinguishes between products for reasons not listed in Article XX? That is possible, but unlikely. The Appellate Body has the right to change its jurisprudence (and has done so frequently, albeit not explicitly),[22] and it is not legally bound by the reasoning supporting earlier rulings. However, in this case, the Appellate Body would not only be expected to explain the need for a change but also why it now considers the new interpretation to be consistent with the accepted principles of interpretation and its mandate. The Appellate Body may therefore seek to avoid the issue. It might, for instance, compensate its narrow interpretation of Article III with an interpretation of the sub-paragraphs of Article XX sufficiently broad to cover all legitimate regulations that come before it. However, Article XX is a general exception that can in principle be invoked in respect of any provision of the GATT. The broadened interpretation could therefore be invoked not only in respect of internal regulations but also in respect of import restrictions, customs tariffs, and other measures imposed at the border, and it would therefore have unintended side effects. Correcting the narrow interpretation of Article III through a permissive interpretation of Article XX would therefore weaken the international trade order generally. I therefore hope that the Appellate Body will not follow a path of least resistance, but reconsider its interpretation of Article III:4 and harmonize the scope of the Member's regulatory autonomy under the national treatment provisions of the TBT Agreement and the GATT.

[22] See Frieder Roessler, 'Changes in the Jurisprudence of the WTO Appellate Body during the Past Twenty Years' J Intl Trade Law Poly (forthcoming).

5

How to Reconcile Health Law and Economic Law with Human Rights? Looking for Hercules in the WTO Appellate Body

Ernst-Ulrich Petersmann

I. The Challenge of Judicial Administration of Justice

I met Mitsuo the first time in the late 1980s during my work as GATT legal counsellor when—at the invitation of the Japanese Fair Trade Centre—I gave lectures at Tokyo on GATT dispute settlement rulings challenging Japanese trade restrictions aimed at protecting non-economic public interests. Since the 1990s, we co-operated annually in the context of the International Law Association's Trade Law Committee, for which I served as rapporteur (1993–1999) and chairman (2000–2014). In view of Mitsuo's work as a member of the WTO Appellate Body (AB), this contribution in honour of Mitsuo discusses methodological questions of 'judicial administration of justice' related to the five pending WTO disputes challenging Australia's legislation on plain-packaging of cigarettes. Are the complainants right that Australia's legislation unjustifiably encumbers the trademarks and other intellectual property rights of tobacco producers and creates unnecessary obstacles to international trade? The pertinent WTO rules (notably in Articles III and IX GATT, Article 2 TBT Agreement, Articles 2, 3, 15, 16, 22, and 24 TRIPS Agreement) do not specifically answer these legal claims. Are advocates of legal positivism right that WTO judges have discretion in interpreting the relevant WTO rules and deciding this dispute? Is this judicial discretion confirmed by the fact that WTO dispute settlement bodies have so far hardly ever applied the customary law requirement of interpreting international treaties and settling related disputes 'in conformity with principles of justice', including also 'human rights and fundamental freedoms for all'?[1] What are 'the basic principles and ... objectives underlying this multilateral trading system' (Preamble of the WTO Agreement) and justifying it vis-à-vis

[1] This citation from the Preamble of the Vienna Convention on the Law of Treaties (VCLT) reflects the 'integration principle' in art 31:3(c) of the VCLT.

citizens as 'democratic principals' of all governance agents? Is the American legal philosopher Dworkin right that in 'hard cases'—where the applicable legal rules do not specifically answer the disputed legal questions—it 'remains the judge's duty ... to discover what the rights of the parties are, not to invent new rights retrospectively'?[2] As Dworkin requests judges to act like Hercules in clarifying the law on the basis of a theory that 'best fits' and justifies the applicable rules and principles through constructive interpretations protecting equal rights of citizens rather than judicial discretion and utilitarian policies, why does the extensive WTO jurisprudence on methods of treaty interpretation not reveal a theory of justice vis-à-vis citizens as the constitutional and democratic agents of justice? Should the WTO follow the example of the World Bank and other UN institutions by recognizing that the development objectives pursued by UN and WTO institutions not only aim at promoting economic growth, but also broadly defined 'human development' in conformity with transnational rule of law and the human rights obligations of all WTO Member States, as I have argued since my appointment as first 'legal officer' ever employed by the GATT in 1981? As the World Bank achieved this change in legal interpretation and legal practices at the initiative of its Legal Counsel I. Shihata in the 1990s without formal amendment of the World Bank agreement, how do we explain the lack of a corresponding leadership by WTO lawyers and judges?[3]

Judicial disputes tend to arise if the parties interpret the applicable rules in conflicting ways and request the judge to apply and clarify the law by administrating justice leading to a legally binding judgment. Dworkin's rejection of 'judicial discretion' seems to be confirmed by the explicit WTO mandate that the 'dispute settlement system of the WTO ... serves to preserve the rights and obligations of Members under the covered agreements, and to clarify the existing provisions of those agreements in accordance with customary rules of interpretation of public international law' (Article 3 Dispute Settlement Understanding (DSU)). Independent adjudication aims at rules-based interpretation and legally binding adjudication based on impartial judicial reasoning. As no legal system can specifically answer all future legal questions concerning the interpretation of legal rules and principles, the multilevel GATT/WTO system also cannot be based only on legislation, administration, and 'member-driven WTO governance' without judicial rule-clarification 'providing security and predictability to the multilateral trading system' (Article 3 DSU). As a global 'aggregate public good' (PG), the WTO trading system is composed of local, national, regional, and global jurisdictions that must act coherently in order to reduce transaction costs and protect legal security. WTO law regulates (sub)national, regional, and global rulemaking and protects 'access to justice' at (sub)national, regional, and WTO levels of trade

[2] Ronald Dworkin, *Taking Rights Seriously* (Duckworth 1977) 81.

[3] For an answer, see Ernst-Ulrich Petersmann, 'The Establishment of a GATT Office of Legal Affairs and the Limits of "Public Reason" in the GATT/WTO Dispute Settlement System' in Gabrielle Marceau (ed), *A History of Law and Lawyers in the GATT/WTO. The Development of the Rule of Law in the Multilateral Trading System* (CUP 2015) 182–207.

governance as a precondition for multilevel rule of law.[4] Yet, due to the 'executive dominance' in WTO governance and the diplomatic self-interests in limiting legal, judicial, and democratic accountability for WTO violations, the judicial remedies prescribed by WTO law for the benefit of citizens are not effectively protected inside most WTO Member States.

The main lesson from more than 2,500 years of legal and political experiences—for example, since the ancient Constitutions of Greek, Roman, and other Italian city republics—with collective protection of PGs (*res publica*) remains the need for limiting abuses of power through 'republican constitutionalism' empowering citizens to hold abuses of public and private power legally, judicially, and democratically accountable. Modern democratic constitutionalism and multilevel governance of international PGs confirm that:

1. the capability of democratic self-government is limited by the 'public reason' of government agents and citizens as 'democratic principals';
2. independent and impartial judicial administration of justice is of constitutional importance—also in multilevel health and trade governance—for institutionalizing 'public reason' and clarifying 'principles of justice' justifying law and governance vis-à-vis citizens; and
3. rights-based trade and investment agreements enabling citizens to hold governments legally, democratically, and judicially accountable for welfare-reducing violations of transnational rule of law (for example, among European countries) have proven more effective than economic integration agreements based on authoritarian top-down regulation without effective judicial remedies for citizens.[5]

This chapter argues that, just as health governance derives its legitimacy from protecting the 'enjoyment of the highest attainable standard of health (as) one of the fundamental rights of every human being' (WHO Constitution) that can be enforced by citizens in domestic courts, the effectiveness and legitimacy of multilevel trade governance is likewise dependent on treating producers, investors, traders, and consumers, civil society and democratic parliaments as legal subjects—rather than mere objects—of WTO law, as required by the human rights obligations of WTO Members and the WTO commitments to protect 'access to justice' at national, regional, and WTO levels of governance. Even though human rights and general consumer welfare are nowhere mentioned in WTO law and remain neglected by rulers inside many WTO Member countries, the legitimacy of multilevel trade governance depends less on utilitarian claims by trade diplomats (for example, of protecting 'Kaldor-Hicks efficiency' rather than

[4] On WTO rules protecting individual access to judicial remedies in domestic courts, and the refusal by many governments to offer citizens effective legal and judicial remedies in domestic courts against arbitrary violation of GATT/WTO rules, see Ernst-Ulrich Petersmann, *The GATT/WTO Dispute Settlement System* (Kluwer 1997) 19ff, 233ff.

[5] Cf Ernst-Ulrich Petersmann, *International Economic Law in the 21st Century. Constitutional Pluralism and Multilevel Governance of Interdependent Public Goods* (Hart 2012) 145ff.

'Pareto optimality' of trade rules) than on democratic and judicial protection of equal rights of citizens and respect for the WTO requirements of 'providing security and predictability to the multilateral trading system' (Article 3 DSU) for the benefit of citizens as the ultimate subjects and sources of legitimacy of all legal systems.

II. Health Law, Economic Law, and Human Rights Law: Fragmentation and Integration of International Law

All human societies depend on legal rules in order to co-ordinate autonomous actions (for example, through private law), provide public goods (for example, through public law), and hold abuses of power legally accountable (for example, through tort law, criminal law, and constitutional law). Like human beings, also legal systems—for example, in the sense of primary rules of conduct and secondary rules of recognition, change, and adjudication—tend to evolve through dialectic experiences of governance. Due to the existential human need for producing, trading, and consuming goods and services necessary for human development, economic law belongs to the oldest areas of national and international legal regulation. Health and human rights matters were mainly regulated through domestic law up to World War II. Multilateral health and human rights law (HRL) developed only after the war in the context of the United Nations (UN), the World Health Organization (WHO), and regional organizations. Apart from multiple non-binding resolutions, strategies, and codes of practice, the WHO has negotiated only three health agreements: the International Health Regulations, the Framework Convention on Tobacco Control (FCTC), and the Health Nomenclature Regulations.[6] HRL is now based on hundreds of UN and regional human rights conventions, related protocols, non-binding human rights resolutions, national constitutions, and multilevel jurisprudence. International economic law (IEL) dynamically evolves on the basis of thousands of international monetary, trade, financial, investment, transport, taxation, and other agreements and related jurisprudence. Arguably, in a world composed of some 200 sovereign states and hundreds of international organizations with scarce resources confronting unlimited demand by more than seven billion citizens, the fragmented evolution of multilevel economic, health, and HRL in response to the diverse priorities and democratic preferences of countries and citizens is inevitable. Yet, are the ubiquity of 'governance failures' and 'market failures' in multilevel economic, health, and human rights governance—as illustrated by the unnecessary poverty of some two billion people without effective access to protection of human rights, public health, water, sanitation, and adequate food, or by the death of more than six million people per year due to the consumption of toxic tobacco products—likewise inevitable? The answer to this question depends on the human capacities

[6] Cf Lawrence O Gostin, *Global Health Law* (Harvard University Press 2014) chs 3–4.

for 'public reason' enabling multilevel regulation of 'market failures' and of 'governance failures' so as to protect human rights and welfare for all.

Similar to the disagreement among evolutionary biologists on whether the physical world of appearances and its underlying 'laws' evolve into increasing order or chaos, and to disagreements among religions as to the extent to which god created man in his own image (i.e. as being capable of 'enlightenment' of the 'human condition'), also anthropologists and lawyers disagree on whether the reasonable human capacities to control human emotions and 'basic instincts' enable people to limit and 'civilize' the power-oriented 'fragmentation' of national and international legal systems. Can the human efforts at preventing conflicts, since the ancient Constitutions of Athens and Rome some 2,500 years ago, through 'republican virtue politics', 'constitutional mind-sets', self-imposed 'hand-tying' (following Ulysses' advice upon approaching the island of the sirens), 'moral imperatives', and 'constitutional contracts' succeed in transforming antagonistic legal fragmentation into peaceful co-operation beyond city republics and constitutional democracies? 'Realists' and 'radical pluralists' emphasize the inevitable conflicts among competing legal regimes:

- conflicts resulting from diverse, *internal value assumptions of legal actors* justifying the legal coherence, validity, and hierarchy of national and international 'self-contained legal regimes' from different legal perspectives, such as different basic norms ('*Grundnorm*') and legal preconceptions ('*Vorverständnis*') in terms of Kelsen's legal theory of the structures ('*Stufenbau*') of national and international legal orders deriving their respective legitimacy from a presumed, national, or international 'foundational norm';
- conflicts due to interest-driven, *strategic self-interests of legal actors* and of institutional biases of specialized legal regimes (for example, of trade law, investment law, intellectual property law, environmental law, UN HRL, UN Security Council regulations), whose interest-driven legal priorities and conflicting legal claims and value premises often collide;
- inherent inter-regime conflicts resulting from their '*autopoietic dynamic of social differentiations*' following the particular rationality of social subsystems (such as the economy, security protection, internet regulation) and related, functionally oriented conflict rules and remedies.[7]

The prevailing 'Westphalian conceptions' of 'international law among sovereign states' and their prioritization of rights of rulers over rights of citizens confirm that much of the 'banality of evil' condoned by UN and WTO diplomats[8] is due

[7] For an analysis of these 'three versions of radical pluralism' (Kelsen's legal orders based on competing 'foundational norms', Koskenniemi's imperial international law regimes, and Luhmann's autopoietic social systems), see Kaarlo Tuori, 'Transnational Law: On Legal Hybrids and Perspectivism' in Miguel Maduro and others (eds), *Transnational Law. Rethinking European Law and Legal Thinking* (CUP 2014) 9, 30–37.

[8] On Arendt's controversial psychoanalysis of Eichmann, one of the many thoughtless administrators of Hitler's holocaust, see Hannah Arendt, *Eichmann in Jerusalem: A Report on the Banality of Evil* (Penguin 1963).

to their 'path-dependent fast thinking' (rather than reasonable 'slow thinking'), opportunistic 'diplomatic mind-sets' (rather than 'constitutional mind-sets'), and 'thinking with outdated mental models'.[9] My own studies of legal fragmentation of HRL[10] and IEL[11] proceed from the recognition of human rights and other 'constitutional principles of justice' by all UN Member States and the customary law requirement—as codified in the VCLT (Preamble and Article 31)—of interpreting international treaties and settling related disputes 'in conformity with principles of justice', including also 'human rights and fundamental freedoms for all'. Contrary to authoritarian 'Westphalian claims' (for example, by Thomas Hobbes) that citizens remain in a constant war of everyone against everybody else unless they transfer absolute powers enabling monarchs and diplomats to impose justice and social peace top-down, constitutional democracies have empirically proven capable of protecting human rights, public health, and social welfare through mutually beneficial co-operation among citizens inside and among democracies. Hence, similar to citizen-oriented 'social contract theories' (for example, from Locke, Rousseau, and Kant up to Rawls) justifying constitutional democracies, also modern international law must be justified in terms of protecting human rights and the welfare of all citizens.[12] The more globalization transforms *national PGs* into *transnational 'aggregate PGs'* that no single government can protect unilaterally, the more national Constitutions become 'partial constitutions' that can protect international PGs only through multilevel governance institutions based on international law and judicial protection of rule of law.

HRL and constitutional law require reconciling and 'integrating' fragmented national and international legal regimes, their respective 'basic norms', particular interests and systemic rationalities by connecting and 'balancing' their underlying 'general principles' of law and justice through democratic law-making and multilevel adjudication promoting legal coherence based on 'public reason'. The traditional distinctions and 'binary logic' of national and international law categories are progressively transformed by the emergence of 'transnational law' and 'multi-valued legal reasoning' balancing and reconciling competing legal values and legal regimes, for instance by respecting 'margins of appreciation' and 'judicial comity' (for example, based on '*solange*' doctrines among national and European courts), mutually 'consistent interpretations' of national and international rules of law, or 'equivalent protection' and 'reciprocal recognition' principles. Notably in European law, the progressive 'constitutionalization' of IEL has promoted an international 'integration law' deriving its moral and democratic legitimacy from national, European, and UN HRL and multilevel constitutionalism limiting abuses

[9] For a criticism of these three principles of 'diplomatic thinking', see World Bank Group, *World Development Report 2015: Mind, Society and Brain* (World Bank 2015).

[10] Cf Ernst-Ulrich Petersmann, 'Human Rights and International Economic Law' (2012) 4(2) Trade, L & Dev 283–314.

[11] Cf Ernst-Ulrich Petersmann, '"Fragmentation" and "Judicialization" of International Law as Dialectic Strategies for Reforming International Economic Law' (2013) 5(2) Trade, L & Dev 209–55.

[12] Cf Petersmann, *International Economic Law in the 21st Century* (n 5).

of public and private powers. The changes in 'legal systems' (for example, their 'rules of recognition'), regulatory tasks (for example, of international PGs), legal orders (for example, due to 'transnational law'), and legal phenomena (for example, due to globalization) may not change 'the nature' of law and legal actors. They require, however, reviewing and adapting path-dependent theories of law and legal interpretation.

III. Justice in Robes: Can 'Forum Shopping' and 'Rules Shopping' Prejudge the Outcome of Tobacco Control Litigation?

Dworkin's book on *Justice in Robes* begins with the story of US Supreme Court Justice Oliver Wendell Holmes, who responded to the greeting by a friend—'Do justice, Justice'—by stating: 'That is not my job.'[13] Also today, many members of international trade and investment tribunals will deny that a judge's moral convictions should bear on his/her judgments on what the law is. Yet, traditional definitions of 'legal positivism' and of 'law' (for example, in terms of authoritative issuance and enforcement of legal rules as social facts) may no longer be clearly separable from 'natural law' theories due to the incorporation of 'principles of justice' and 'inalienable human rights' into national and international legal systems and the constitutional mandates of courts of justice to 'administer justice'. Judicial justifications of court decisions—so that citizens understand and accept rules as legitimate and voluntarily comply with law—may challenge traditional distinctions between 'legal positivism' (focusing on the 'law in the books') and sociological conceptions of law (focusing on the 'law in action' and the dynamic interactions between rules and legal practices). The disagreements in American jurisprudence—for instance, over whether statutory interpretations should be guided by (i) a 'textualist approach' (as advocated by Justice Scalia); (ii) an 'archaeological approach' focusing on the legislative history and intent (as advocated by Judge Posner); or by (iii) a 'present-minded approach' focusing on the current legal and social context (as advocated by Aleinikoff)—are largely disregarded by international courts in view of their focus on the need for 'dynamic interpretation' taking into account the changing context of international law and relations.[14] Questions of textual, historic, and 'functional interpretation' and adjudication are often also influenced by more general philosophies of hermeneutics, such as Gadamer's claim that interpretation is always a dialectic, creative search for a common understanding among interpreters directed not only

[13] Ronald Dworkin, *Justice in Robes* (Harvard University Press 2006) 1ff.

[14] Cf the contributions by José E Alvarez, 'What are International Judges for? The Main Functions of International Adjudication', and by Chester Brown, 'Inherent Powers in International Adjudication' in Cesare P Romano and others (eds), *The Oxford Handbook of International Adjudication* (OUP 2014) 158ff, 828ff.

at discovering traditional truths (for example, as reflected in textual provisions, legislative expectations, and current policies), but taking into account also the current perspectives of interpreters criticizing illegitimate traditions that arbitrarily neglected legitimate interests (for example, human rights to hold governments accountable for their Westphalian power politics).[15]

A. HRL as constitutional constraint of the 'rules of recognition'

Most governments and many economic actors perceive IEL from a consequentialist (for example, utilitarian) rather than deontological (for example, human rights) perspective as an instrument for enhancing 'national interests' and economic welfare (usually defined in terms of 'Kaldor-Hicks efficiency' justifying government discretion to distribute the 'gains from trade' and neglecting 'Pareto efficiency' of trade policies in terms of maximizing general consumer welfare and individual economic benefits). UN HRL and the WHO Constitution, by contrast, recognize not only the 'enjoyment of the highest attainable standard of health (as) one of the fundamental rights of every human being', but also that 'the health of all peoples is fundamental to the attainment of peace and security and is dependent on the fullest cooperation of individuals and States' (Preamble, WHO Constitution). Since the UN Charter and the Universal Declaration of Human Rights (UDHR), all UN Member States have repeated in numerous UN instruments time and again that:

- 'recognition of the inherent dignity and the equal and inalienable rights of all members of the human family is the foundation of freedom, justice and peace in the world'; and
- 'it is essential, if man is not to be compelled to have recourse, as a last resort, to rebellion against tyranny and oppression, that human rights should be protected by the rule of law' (Preamble of the UDHR).

Hence, the 'rules of recognition' of international law (as defined in Article 38 of the ICJ Statute) must be construed as limiting legal claims of 'Westphalian rulers' and their diplomats whenever they are inconsistent with the human rights obligations of UN Member States and other 'general principles of law' as 'foundation of justice' and rule of law.[16] In view of the universal recognition of 'inalienable' human rights based on a 'jus cogens' core, WTO judges should justify their legal interpretations of WTO rules vis-à-vis governments and citizens not only in terms of consequentialist policy conceptions (for example, 'nullification or impairment of trade benefits'), but also as explicitly recalled in the Preamble of the VCLT, they should decide 'in conformity with principles of justice', including 'human rights and fundamental freedoms for all' (for example, in balancing trademark rights

[15] Cf Hans-Georg Gadamer, *Truth and Method* (Seabury 1975); William N Eskridge, 'Gadamer/Statutory Interpretation' (1990) 90(3) Colum L Rev 609ff.

[16] Cf Ernst-Ulrich Petersmann, 'Need for a New Philosophy of International Economic Law and Adjudication' (2014) 17(3) J Int Econ L 639ff.

with health rights in the WTO disputes over tobacco control measures), with due respect for 'constitutional pluralism' in justifying 'law as integrity' (Dworkin) in the multilevel WTO legal and dispute settlement system.[17] For instance, the GATT/WTO distinctions between 'violation complaints', 'non-violation complaints', and 'situation complaints' (cf Articles XXIII GATT and GATS) are based on complementary principles of distributive justice, corrective justice, commutative justice, and equity. The WTO guarantees of individual access to judicial remedies in domestic courts and of access to WTO dispute settlement bodies also reflect principles of individual and collective 'constitutional justice'.[18] If the 'rules of recognition' (for example, the 'general principles of law recognised by civilised nations' and 'international custom as evidence of a general practice accepted as law') are construed in conformity with the 'inalienable' human rights of citizens and their democratic institutions and 'courts of justice', the WTO objective of 'sustainable development' should be construed—like the 'development' objectives of the Word Bank—as referring not only to economic growth, but also to promotion of human rights, rule of law, and other 'principles of justice' protecting human capacities, social welfare, and democratic consent of citizens.[19]

B. HRL as constitutional restraint of forum shopping and rules shopping

The WHO dispute settlement provisions for recourse to the International Court of Justice (ICJ) or to international arbitration have hardly ever been used so far. Tobacco industries and tobacco-exporting countries prefer challenging public health protection measures in *non-health fora*—such as *WTO* and *investment dispute settlement proceedings*—in the hope that their institutional choice might influence the 'balancing' of health and non-health concerns; for instance, if trade and investment tribunals neglect HRL and WHO law. Also *national dispute settlement proceedings* (for example, in less-developed countries) risk being biased by the powerful resources and lobbying of tobacco industries, the lack of constitutional guarantees (for example, in US federal law) of human and constitutional rights to high levels of public health protection, or by the non-participation of some countries (like Argentina and the United States) in the WHO FCTC. In view of the global nature of the tobacco epidemic and of the social injustices caused by 'business as usual', national and international courts must co-operate in the dozens of pending disputes—in national and international courts, arbitral tribunals, and other

[17] On deontological, consequentialist, and virtue-centred, normative justifications of law, including a theory of judging ('virtue jurisprudence') based on (i) judicial temperance; (ii) judicial courage; (iii) judicial temperament; (iv) judicial intelligence; (v) judicial wisdom; and (vi) justice, see Lawrence B Solum, 'Virtue Jurisprudence: A Virtue-Centered Theory of Judging' (2003) 34 Metaphilosophy 178ff.

[18] Cf Petersmann, *The GATT/WTO Dispute Settlement System* (n 4) 135ff, 233ff.

[19] Cf Petersmann, *International Economic Law in the 21st Century* (n 5) 374ff; Philipp Dann, *The Law of Development Cooperation: A Comparative Analysis of the World Bank, the EU and Germany* (CUP 2013).

dispute settlement bodies[20]—so as to protect the legal coherence of multilevel health governance and of administration of justice in tobacco control disputes at national and international levels.

In the disputes over tobacco control measures, judges are requested to review the extent to which governments are justified in restricting economic rights (for example, freedoms of commercial expression, investor rights, and intellectual property rights owned by tobacco companies) on grounds of health protection and related health rights.[21] Should the judicial 'balancing' of intellectual property rights invoked by tobacco companies (for example, trademarks protected under the TRIPS Agreement) with human rights to health protection differ depending on whether tobacco disputes are litigated in national or international courts, WTO dispute settlement bodies, or investment arbitration? Do the diverse legal contexts, procedures, and applicable law in these jurisdictions require different kinds of 'judicial balancing', depending on whether the reconciliation of economic rights with health rights is regulated in treaty 'objectives' (for example, Article 7 TRIPS Agreement), treaty 'principles' (Article 8 TRIPS Agreement), or general treaty provisions (for example, Article 2 TBT Agreement) rather than in exception clauses (for example, Article XX GATT)? Can powerful tobacco companies pre-judge tobacco litigation through 'forum shopping' and 'rules shopping' to the detriment of public health protection (for example, in less-developed countries without independent judiciaries)? Do the inherent powers and duties of judges ('justices') justify judicial balancing of trademark rights with the human right to health protection even if, as in a WTO dispute, the defendant state invokes the state duty to protect public health rather than human rights?

Trade and investment courts too often ignore the customary law requirement that 'disputes concerning treaties, like other international disputes, should be settled … in conformity with the principles of justice and international law', including also 'respect for, and observance of, human rights and fundamental freedoms for all' (Preamble, VCLT). Arguably, the WHO FCTC offers a quasi-universal framework for 'balancing' health rights with the economic rights of tobacco producers, which is also supported in national and international health jurisprudence based on the following legal principles.

1. Protection of public health as a human right and 'constitutional principle' has a higher 'legal weight' than intellectual property rights (for example, trademarks as 'negative rights') provided the following 'optimisation requirements' are respected:

[20] For more details of the cases briefly discussed below, see the references in the website 'Tobacco Control Laws: Explore Tobacco Control Legislation and Litigation from Around the World' <www.tobaccocontrollaws.org/litigation/decisions> accessed 20 June 2015.

[21] For an overview and discussion of national and international tobacco litigation, see Ernst-Ulrich Petersmann, 'How to Reconcile Health Law and Economic Law with Human Rights? Administration of Justice in Tobacco Control Disputes' (2015) 10(1) Asian J WTO & Intl Health L & Policy 27–78.

a) the health protection measure regulating economic rights contributes (significantly) to the protection of public health; and
b) it regulates economic rights in non-discriminatory and proportionate ways (for example, without 'creating unnecessary obstacles to international trade'; cf Article 2 TBT Agreement, Article 20 TRIPS).

2. As states have legal rights/duties to pursue a high level of health protection through complex, interacting measures producing synergies (like the FCTC), the 'consistent interpretation' requirement (Article 31:3 VCLT) justifies a legal presumption that FCTC-conforming restrictions are legally also justifiable in other legal regimes (for example, WTO and WIPO law, regional and national legal systems).

In *US—Clove Cigarettes*, the Appellate Body noted: 'The balance set out in the preamble of the TBT Agreement between, on the one hand, the desire to avoid creating unnecessary obstacles to international trade and, on the other hand, the recognition of Members' right to regulate, is not, in principle, different from the balance, set out in the GATT 1994, where obligations such as national treatment in Article III are qualified by the general exceptions provision of Article XX.'[22] Hence, as sovereign rights 'to protect public health' and 'promote the public interest in sectors of vital importance to socio-economic development' are recognized in numerous WTO provisions (such as Article 8 TRIPS Agreement), the WTO treaty objectives of ensuring 'a balance of rights and obligations' (Article 7 TRIPS Agreement) and 'security and predictability in the multilateral trading system' require comprehensive legal and judicial balancing in legal and judicial interpretations of WTO rules. The 'balancing' of WTO market access and *economic regulations* with sovereign rights of WTO Members to protect *non-economic PGs* may depend more on 'principles of justice' (like transparency, non-discrimination, suitability, necessity, and proportionality of governmental restrictions of economic rights) than on whether WTO rules protect non-economic PGs through 'general exceptions' (like Articles XX GATT, XIV GATS) or general 'principles' and 'objectives' (cf Articles 7–8 TRIPS Agreement, the preambles of the WTO and TBT Agreements). The legal requirements to interpret WTO rules in conformity with other legal obligations of WTO Members (for example, global WHO health law) limit judicial review and may justify judicial deference (for example, towards national legal restrictions of smoking and their judicial justification by human health protection as a 'higher value' than the trademarks of cigarette producers). They promote coherence of WTO and UN law and, thereby, also 'security and predictability' in the multilateral trading system (Article 3 DSU), for instance by justifying legal presumptions that limitations of trademarks by national legislation on 'plain packaging of cigarettes' may not be 'unjustifiable' (in terms of Article 20 TRIPS) to the extent they comply with the WHO FCTC accepted by more than

[22] Appellate Body Report, *United States—Measures Affecting the Production and Sale of Clove Cigarettes*, WT/DS406/AB/R, 4 April 2012, para 96.

170 countries.[23] The customary 'integration', 'consistent interpretation', and judicial comity requirements must not be rendered ineffective by the fact that no UN treaty has the same membership as WTO agreements. Legitimate legal, democratic, and judicial 'balancing' of economic and non-economic rules must remain justifiable by an inclusive 'reasonable equilibrium' rather than merely by 'instrumental rationality' of diplomats and economists. The criteria of reasonableness and their respective weight may differ depending on the concrete circumstances (for example, in WTO disputes among members that have accepted the same UN and WTO legal obligations for promoting 'sustainable development').

IV. The WTO Appellate Body as Exemplar of 'Public Reason' in International Trade Law? Looking for Hercules

According to the 'general rule of interpretation' codified in Article 31:1 VCLT, a 'treaty shall be interpreted in good faith in accordance with the ordinary meaning to be given to the terms of the treaty in their context and in the light of its object and purpose'. The Appellate Body emphasizes that '(i)nterpretation pursuant to the customary rules codified in Article 31 of the (VCLT) is ultimately a holistic exercise that should not be mechanically subdivided into rigid components';[24] the 'interpretative exercise is engaged so as to yield an interpretation that is harmonious and coherent and fits comfortably in the treaty as a whole so as to render the treaty provision legally effective'.[25] The customary law requirement of interpreting treaties and settling related disputes 'in conformity with the principles of justice and international law' (Preamble, VCLT) is consistent with Dworkin's theory of 'law as integrity' explaining why a reading of the 'black letter rules' may not enable the 'best understanding' unless the interpreter also explores the 'principles' underlying the rules in order to justify why a certain interpretation 'fits best' with the objectives of the legal system concerned.[26] Yet justice, human rights, democracy, and rule of law—like many provisions of IEL (for example, on national treatment, subsidies, and 'dumping')—are 'interpretive legal concepts' which people share even though they often disagree about the criteria for interpreting and applying the legal terms. GATT/WTO jurisprudence has hardly ever referred to 'principles of justice'; due to its 'Member-driven' focus on rights and obligations among governments, it has neglected justifying GATT/WTO rules vis-à-vis producers, investors, traders, consumers, and other citizens as main economic actors and 'democratic principals' in the world trading system. At the request by many governments (including

[23] Cf Tania Voon and others (eds), *Public Health and Plain Packaging of Cigarettes. Legal Issues* (Elgar 2012).

[24] Appellate Body Report, *European Communities—Customs Classification of Frozen Boneless Chicken Cuts*, WT/DS269/AB/R, 12 September 2005, para 176.

[25] Appellate Body Report, *United States—Continued Existence and Application of Zeroing Methodology*, WT/DS350/AB/R, 4 February 2009, para 268.

[26] Cf Dworkin, *Justice in Robes* (n 13) 22ff.

EU and US governments), domestic courts in many WTO Member countries deny citizens rights to invoke and enforce WTO rules in domestic courts. As a result, multilevel trade governance in the WTO remains 'disconnected' with citizens as primary 'agents of justice' with 'inalienable' human rights. Compared with the rights-based, citizen-oriented structures of trade law among the thirty-one Member States of the European Economic Area (EEA), this intergovernmental 'disfranchisement' of citizens in WTO legal practices runs counter to the explicit WTO legal requirements to protect individual access to justice also in domestic legal systems inside WTO Members, for instance in the field of GATT (cf Article X), the WTO Anti-dumping Agreement (cf Article 13), the WTO Agreement on Customs Valuation (cf Article 11), the Agreement on Pre-shipment Inspection (cf Article 4), the Agreement on Subsidies and Countervailing Measures (cf Article 23), the General Agreement on Trade in Services (cf Article VI GATS), the Agreement on Trade-related Intellectual Property Rights (cf Articles 41–50, 59 TRIPS), and the Agreement on Government Procurement (cf Article XX).

A. The WTO legal and dispute settlement system remains based on authoritarian benevolence rather than on 'constitutional justice'

What are the systemic implications of the explicit recognition of a 'multilateral trading *system*' and WTO 'dispute settlement *system*' (cf Article 3 DSU) for 'systemic interpretation' of WTO rules by WTO dispute settlement bodies? From a citizen perspective, HRL requires democracies to enhance consumer welfare and protection of human rights through trade liberalization and regulation (for example, of toxic tobacco products), even without reciprocity by foreign rulers. For the same reasons, the customary and treaty requirements of 'consistent interpretation'—as recognized, inter alia, in Article XVI:4 WTO Agreement, Article 3 DSU, and in the numerous WTO guarantees of access to domestic courts—can justify interpreting domestic trade rules in conformity with GATT/WTO obligations for the benefit of domestic citizens even without reciprocity by foreign jurisdictions. Yet, such 'citizen perspectives' tend to be ignored in WTO practices dominated by diplomats interested in avoiding legal and judicial accountability for their foreign policy discretion and in protecting the 'Westphalian *status quo*' of diplomatic privileges (for example, due to veto powers of hegemonic states) and immunities (for example, due to outdated 'act of state' doctrines).

In GATT/WTO rule-making and in the almost 500 WTO dispute settlement proceedings since 1995, trade diplomats have limited the 'interpretative legal community' to essentially WTO governments and WTO institutions; apart from the exceptional participation of *amici curiae* and technical experts, citizens and non-governmental organizations are prevented from actively participating in WTO rule-making and WTO dispute settlement proceedings. National parliaments tend to 'rubberstamp' WTO agreements without influencing the content of WTO rules, and citizens are excluded from WTO law-making processes. Similar to Thomas Hobbes' justification of 'absolute monarchical powers' for authoritarian top-down governance by claims of alleged incapacity of human beings to maintain peace and social order (*homo homini lupus est*), UN and WTO diplomats continue to invoke 'state sovereignty' as justification for their treatment of citizens as mere objects, rather than legal subjects of UN and WTO law. This limitation of the legal, democratic, and judicial accountability of trade politicians vis-à-vis citizens lacks democratic legitimacy in view of the fact that rights-based, citizen-driven trade governance has proven to be much more effective and legally accountable in customs unions and free trade agreements among European states than GATT/WTO governance driven by 'rent-seeking' interest groups to the detriment of consumer welfare and human rights (which are nowhere mentioned in WTO law). Even though WTO law prescribes legal protection of individual access to justice also in *domestic legal systems* inside WTO Members, the pertinent WTO rules only exceptionally protect *individual rights* to invoke and enforce WTO rules in domestic courts (for example, pursuant to Article XX WTO Agreement on Government Procurement) or *individual access* to international arbitration (as provided for in Article 4 of the WTO Agreement on Pre-shipment Inspection). WTO law recognizes (for example, in the Preamble of the WTO Agreement and in the DSU) the 'systemic nature' of WTO law, its 'dispute settlement system', and 'basic principles ... underlying this multilateral trading system'. Yet the 'executive dominance' in WTO governance and WTO jurisprudence one-sidedly prioritizes rights of governments over rights of citizens. It remains rare that—such as in the almost twenty WTO dispute settlement proceedings that challenged the protectionist 'zeroing practices' of EC and US anti-dumping authorities in their calculations of anti-dumping duties—the WTO Appellate Body interpreted the WTO requirement of 'fair price comparisons' from the perspective of the reasonable interests of economic actors rather than—as advocated by trade bureaucrats and WTO panels—from the perspective of EC and US governmental claims that governments had not intended to limit their sovereign right to apply discriminatory 'zeroing methodologies' by concluding the WTO Agreement on Anti-dumping.[27]

Empirical studies of the 'constitutional principles' underlying common market and competition rules in federal states (for example, the United States, Switzerland, and Germany) and among European democracies suggest that 'equal freedoms' of citizens offer the most convincing 'first principle of justice' (as explained in Kantian and Rawlsian theories of justice) for multilevel, judicial protection of equal rights and non-discriminatory conditions of competition in the mutually beneficial division of labour among producers, investors, traders, and consumers.[28]

[27] Cf Sungjoon Cho, 'Global Constitutional Lawmaking' (2010) 31 U Pa J Intl L 621–78.

[28] Cf Petersmann, *International Economic Law in the 21st Century* (n 5) ch I; Ernst-Ulrich Petersmann, *Constitutional Functions and Constitutional Problems of International Economic Law* (Fribourg University Press 1991). The diverse judicial interpretations of civil, political, economic, and social human rights (e.g. as universally agreed in UN human rights law) as 'negative freedoms from' disproportionate governance restrictions, or as 'positive freedoms to' individual self-determination and self-realization, reflect divergent conceptions of liberty rights, human dignity, and of citizens as authors and addressees of constitutional democracies; cf Petersmann, *International Economic Law in the 21st Century* (n 5) 172ff (distinguishing four concepts of liberty).

As GATT/WTO jurisprudence has so far failed to justify the multilevel GATT/WTO guarantees of equal freedoms and non-discriminatory conditions in terms of 'constitutional justice' as suggested by Dworkin's 'adjudicative principle of integrity', does the absence of a Dworkinian 'Hercules' among WTO judges—and the lack of a coherent conception of justice and fairness vis-à-vis citizens in WTO governance—entail a risk of judicial neglect for the human right to health in the pending WTO disputes challenging Australia's tobacco control legislation?

If, as suggested in section III above, the human rights obligations of all UN and WTO Member States are recognized as constitutional restraints of the 'rules of recognition' as well as of 'forum shopping' and 'rules shopping', then national and international judges should interpret multilevel trade regulation (for example, in WTO law and the WHO FCTC) in conformity with the constitutional objectives of protecting equal rights of citizens, rule-of-law, and its underlying constitutional principles of justice. Just as national and regional common market, competition, and free trade rules among constitutional democracies are construed by national and European courts in conformity with the human rights obligations of governments, so must the GATT/WTO legal, dispute settlement, and trading system be construed in conformity with UN HRL and the WHO FCTC, rather than only in terms of Hobbesian power politics and Kaldor-Hicks efficiency. As the legal and 'dispute settlement system of the WTO is a central element in providing security and predictability to the multilateral trading system' (Article 3:2 DSU) and requires 'each Member (to) ensure the conformity of its laws, regulations and administrative procedures with its obligations' under WTO law (Article XVI:4 WTO Agreement), national, regional, and WTO dispute settlement bodies should give priority to governmental duties to protect human rights over utilitarian principles of welfare economics (for example, including trademarks as 'negative rights' promoting 'fair competition'). As rightly emphasized by European courts in their interpretation of European trade rules:

> the fact that certain provisions of the Treaty are formally addressed to the Member States does not prevent rights from being conferred at the same time on any individual who has an interest in compliance with the obligations thus laid down.[29]

The more globalization transforms *national* into *international* PGs (like the global division of labour), the more national democratic legislation becomes substituted by international agreements for the collective supply of international PGs. Their democratic legitimacy and control depend not only on parliamentary ratification. Even more important than the *ex post* parliamentary approval of agreements negotiated among government executives is that international 'PGs agreements' protect equal freedoms and rights enabling citizens to hold governments legally, democratically, and judicially accountable vis-à-vis citizens as 'democratic principals' of all governance agents. As explained by Dworkin, '(l)aw as integrity asks judges

[29] Cf Case 43/75 *Defrenne v Sabena* [1976] ECR 455, para 31; Case C-281/98 *Angonese* [2000] ECR I-4139.

to assume, so far as this is possible, that the law is structured by a coherent set of principles about justice and fairness and procedural due process, and it asks them to enforce these in the fresh cases that come before them, so that each person's situation is fair and just according to the same standards'.[30] 'Hobbesian interpretations' of multilevel UN and WTO governance are inconsistent with HRL in the twenty-first century, as rightly emphasized in the '*Kadi*-jurisprudence' of the Court of Justice of the EU (CJEU) recognizing that UN Security Council regulations and their implementation inside the European Union also remain constitutionally restrained by 'inalienable' human rights, even if alleged foreign terrorists like Mr Kadi invoke such rights.[31]

B. Multilevel judicial governance of the world trading system can contribute to 'constitutionalizing' WTO law for the benefit of citizens

The historical evolution of constitutional democracies confirms the much older 'republican experience' that collective protection of PGs—and the effectiveness of republican 'civic virtues' (for example, in struggles for decolonization) and of agreed 'principles of justice' (for example, in the 1776 US Declaration of Independence, the 1948 UDHR)—depend on the constant transformation of republican rights of citizens into constitutional, legislative, administrative, and international rules, their judicial protection and institutionalization of 'public reason' so that citizens can invoke and enforce their constitutional rights vis-à-vis multilevel governance institutions and voluntarily comply with rules that citizens recognize as legitimate. Struggles by citizens for 'common markets' inside federal states and European trade law illustrate how rights-based interpretations of trade and competition rules and their decentralized enforcement by self-interested citizens have limited 'market failures' as well as 'governance failures' and promoted consumer welfare and rule of law. Similar to the decentralized enforcement of international commercial law through multilevel judicial protection of economic freedoms (like freedom of contract, property rights, mutually agreed arbitration), 'cosmopolitan interpretations' of the now more than 3,000 international investment agreements—i.e. as protecting individual investor rights and their decentralized enforcement through investor–state arbitration—have improved judicial remedies and legal accountability of governments in international investment law more effectively than power-oriented 'Westphalian methods' of diplomatic protection and inter-state disputes in the ICJ. The transformation of European economic and human rights treaties among states into 'constitutional instruments' protecting human and other

[30] Ronald Dworkin, *Law's Empire* (Harvard University Press 1986) 225, 243. Even though Dworkin developed this legal methodology for national legal systems, the methodology is legally applicable also for international treaty interpretation 'in conformity with principles of justice' and the human rights obligations of states (cf Preamble and art 31 VCLT).

[31] Cf Matej Avbelj and others (eds), *Kadi on Trial: A Multifaceted Analysis of the Kadi Trial* (Routledge 2014).

fundamental rights of citizens beyond state borders through multilevel legislation, administration, and adjudication illustrates that functionally limited, multilevel constitutional protection of transnational PGs is a 'realistic utopia' if citizens, democratic governments, and courts of justice insist on transforming principles of justice into international rules and institutions.

1. Need for clarifying the 'constitutional functions' of IEL

If IEL is construed from a democratic citizen perspective as deriving its legitimacy from protecting 'constitutional justice' rather than only 'state sovereignty' and 'Kaldor-Hicks efficiency', then multilevel trade governance must prioritize the equal freedoms and human rights of citizens, for instance by judicial 'balancing' of whether governmental protection of health rights (for example, to breathe air free from toxic tobacco smoke) justifies related restrictions of economic rights (like trademarks of tobacco companies). In their task of interpreting and reconciling health law, economic law, and human rights in mutually coherent ways, judges must distinguish 'rules' (based on 'if-then-commands' determining the outcome of the dispute) and 'principles' (characterized by a dimension of weight that must be optimized in a more-or-less fashion) as sub-categories of legal norms.[32] A rule with a limited scope of application (like the human right to health protection) and a principle representing the same value (like health protection as a more general governmental duty) may co-exist as overlapping legal norms. Alleged conflicts among rules are resolved by determining their respective scope of application (for example, of trademarks as merely 'negative rights'). Collisions among principles are resolved by favouring the principle that weighs more in the dispute (for example, health protection), while optimizing the competing principle to the extent that its simultaneous application is legally and factually possible (for example, by limiting only certain uses of intellectual property to the extent necessary for health protection).

2. Need for clarifying the 'constitutional functions' of courts of justice

'Constitutional conceptions' of IEL emphasize the 'constitutional functions' of courts of justice to protect equal rights of citizens. Diverging interpretations of WTO legal obligations by national, regional, and WTO dispute settlement bodies—such as diverging interpretations of human rights obligations—call for 'judicial dialogues', rather than for arbitrary disregard by domestic courts of WTO obligations and WTO dispute settlement rulings at the request of trade diplomats. Diverse national jurisprudence can induce private and public litigants to struggle for the 'best legal interpretation' and, thereby, contribute to institutionalizing 'public reason' in WTO jurisprudence. Unconvincing national court decisions can be limited and corrected, for instance, through 'preliminary rulings' by the CJEU

[32] Robert Alexy, *A Theory of Constitutional Rights* (OUP 2002).

inside the European Union and 'advisory opinions' by the EFTA Court inside the EEA. If national and European courts would apply the 'consistent interpretation' requirements of WTO law, judicial comity and judicial dialogues could also influence the reasoning of WTO dispute settlement findings and, in co-operation with domestic courts, protect transnational rule of law in multilevel trade governance for the benefit of citizens.

In contrast to the comprehensive WTO jurisprudence on reciprocal rights and obligations among WTO Members, the WTO obligations of governments 'in providing security and predictability to the multilateral trading system' and individual 'access to justice' for the benefit of citizens and non-governmental economic actors continue to be neglected. They should be respected and protected by national and regional courts challenging diplomatic privileges and claims to prioritize rights of governments over rights of citizens. Arguably, just as health law and the WHO FCTC give priority to the human right to health and justify non-discriminatory restrictions of tobacco trade and related intellectual property rights, multilevel judicial governance of international trade must respect the 'margins of appreciation' of each WTO Member in limiting toxic tobacco consumption for the benefit of citizens and their human rights. WTO judges should recognize that state-centred and utilitarian justifications of WTO rules derive their ultimate legitimacy from 'constitutional justice' and respect for the human rights of citizens as democratic 'agents of justice' of all multilevel governance institutions, including the WTO. In view of the limited effectiveness of UN and WTO law in reducing unnecessary poverty and abuses of power inside so many UN and WTO Member States, multilevel judicial co-operation and protection of the domestic 'conformity of laws, regulations and administrative procedures' with WTO obligations (cf Article XVI: 4 WTO) can help citizens to protect themselves against the manifest injustices of 'tobacco trade as usual'. Multilevel judicial protection of WTO guarantees of equal freedoms, non-discriminatory conditions of competition, and transnational rule of law in international trade can enhance 'public reason' and 'democratic capabilities' bottom-up[33] by empowering citizens to assume their 'republican responsibilities' for collective supply of international PGs like 'the optimal use of the world's resources in accordance with the objective of sustainable development' (Preamble, WTO).[34] State-centred 'Westphalian conceptions' of WTO law—by treating citizens as mere objects rather than legal subjects and depriving citizens of effective judicial remedies—serve the self-interests of politicians in avoiding legal and judicial accountability for illegal trade restrictions that tax domestic citizens and redistribute domestic income in favour of rent-seeking interest groups (for example, European banana trading companies that successfully lobbied for illegal EU import restrictions from 1991 to 2012, redistributing

[33] On the idea of public reason as a 'collective capability', see Erin I Kelly, 'Public Reason as a Collective Capability' (2012) 43 Rutgers L J 295–316.

[34] On the need for empowering 'human resources' for piecemeal reforms of manifest injustices rather than focusing only on ideal conceptions of 'just rules' for 'just societies', see Amartya Sen, *The Idea of Justice* (Harvard University Press 2009).

billions of dollars as in a banana republic). Prioritizing the human right to health protection and the corresponding governmental duties to restrict consumption of toxic tobacco products offers a better interpretation of the WTO trade, intellectual property, and health protection rules in view of its coherence with international health law and the human rights obligations of all WTO Members and the reasonable, human needs of citizens. Professor Matsushita's recent proposal of creating 'a group comprising a small number of experts (perhaps ten members or so) to review reports of the Appellate Body regularly and occasionally to publish review reports' could also help to induce more inclusive 'public reason' into the WTO 'diplomats jurisprudence'.[35]

[35] Cf Mitsuo Matsushita, 'Reflections on the Functioning of the Appellate Body' in Gabrielle Marceau (ed), *A History of Law and Lawyers in the GATT/WTO. The Development of the Rule of Law in the Multilateral Trading System* (CUP 2015) 547ff; Petersmann, 'The Establishment of a GATT Office of Legal Affairs' (n 3) 182ff.

6

The WTO Jurisprudence of Article XX(g) and the Conservation of Natural Resources

*Joel P Trachtman**

Professor Matsushita has played a leading role, as a member of the Appellate Body and as a scholar, in advancing the WTO jurisprudence of Article XX(g) of GATT. Article XX(g) permits WTO Member States an exception for violations of other GATT provisions in connection with measures relating to the conservation of exhaustible natural resources, provided that the conditions in Article XX(g) itself, and in the chapeau of Article XX, are met. In the very first case in which the Appellate Body considered Article XX(g), Professor Matsushita was a member of the Appellate Body division that decided the landmark *US—Gasoline* case.[1] He has also contributed important scholarship on some of the recent Appellate Body decisions relating to China's measures restricting exports of certain natural resources.[2] This chapter offers a comment on the recent developments in the *China—Rare Earths* decision of the Appellate Body.[3]

In the recent WTO case involving Chinese restrictions on exports of rare earths, China conceded that its export quotas violated Article XI of GATT 1994, so the remaining question was whether they could be excepted under Article XX(g). In order to qualify for an exception under Article XX(g), the relevant measure must (i) relate to the conservation of exhaustible natural resources; (ii) be made effective in conjunction with restrictions on domestic production or consumption; and (iii) satisfy the requirement of the chapeau of Article XX to the effect that it not be

* Professor of International Law, The Fletcher School of Law and Diplomacy, Tufts University, Medford, Massachusetts, USA.

[1] Appellate Body Report, *United States—Standards for Reformulated and Conventional Gasoline*, WT/DS2/AB/R, adopted 20 May 1996 (*US—Gasoline*).

[2] Mitsuo Matsushita, 'Export Controls of Natural Resources and the WTO/GATT' (2011) 6(2) Asian J WTO & Intl Health L & Policy 281–312; Mitsuo Matsushita, 'Export Control of Natural Resources: WTO Panel Ruling on the Chinese Export Restrictions of Natural Resources' (2011) 3(2) Trade, L & Dev 267–95; Mitsuo Matsushita, 'A Note on the Appellate Body Report in the Chinese Minerals Export Restriction Case' (2012) 4(2) Trade, L & Dev 400–20.

[3] Appellate Body Report, *China—Measures Related to the Exportation of Rare Earths, Tungsten, and Molybdenum*, WT/DS431,432,433/AB/R, adopted 29 August 2014 (*China—Rare Earths, Appellate Report*).

applied as arbitrary or unjustifiable discrimination, or as a disguised restriction on trade. The burden of proof for each of these parameters is on the respondent. The panel found that China did not meet this burden of proof as to any of rare earths, tungsten, or molybdenum.[4]

China appealed two sets of intermediate findings in the panel's analysis of whether China's export quotas on rare earths, tungsten, and molybdenum were justified pursuant to Article XX(g).[5]

- First, China argued that the Panel erred in its interpretation and application of Article XX(g) of the GATT 1994 in finding that China's export quotas on rare earths and tungsten do not 'relate to' conservation within the meaning of Article XX(g).
- Second, China argued that the Panel erred in finding that China's export quotas on rare earths, tungsten, and molybdenum are not 'made effective in conjunction with' domestic restrictions under Article XX(g).

In this chapter, I review the reasoning of the panel and of the Appellate Body in these two areas.

I. 'Relating to'

As to the 'relating to' prong of the Article XX(g) test in connection with rare earths and tungsten, China only appealed the panel's rejection of one of its six arguments: the argument that China's export quota on rare earths and tungsten sends a signal to foreign consumers of rare earth products to diversify their sources of supply and/or find substitutes for these products that they import from China. If this 'signal' induces foreign consumers to diversify, China's argument goes, then China's export quota can be said to 'relate to' conservation.

At the outset of our discussion of the 'related to' prong, it is worth noting that the subparagraphs of Article XX use varying language to connect a national measure to the particular types of policy goals listed in each subparagraph. So, for example, Articles XX (a), (b), and (d) use 'necessary', while Article XX (c), (e), and (g) use 'relating to'. WTO jurisprudence, beginning with the *Gasoline* case in which Professor Matsushita served as a member of the Appellate Body division, has used an *effet utile* approach to interpretation to give significant meaning to the difference between these terms.[6] Necessity is thought to require that there is not

[4] The panel determined that the rare earths, tungsten, and molybdenum, were exhaustible natural resources. Panel Report, *China—Measures Related to the Exportation of Rare Earths, Tungsten, and Molybdenum* (*China—Rare Earths, Panel Report*), WT/DS431,432,433/R, 13 December 2013, para 7.250.

[5] China did not appeal the panel's finding, made on an *arguendo* basis, that the export *duties* at issue are not justified by either subparagraph (b) or the chapeau of art XX of the GATT 1994. Because of the limited scope of China's appeal, even if China had won its appeal, it would still have lost the case.

[6] *US—Gasoline* (n 1) 16–18.

a less restrictive means to achieve the chosen goal,[7] while 'relating to' is a kind of suitability test or means–ends rationality test, asking simply whether the measure is a suitable tool to achieve the specified goal.

Perhaps there was some thought given by negotiators of the original GATT to these different connecting words. But there is a certain degree of overlap between these subparagraphs, and it is not clear that the distinctions make sense.[8] For example, why would human life face a *tougher* necessity threshold for use as a basis for exception under Article XX(b) than conservation of exhaustible natural resources under Article XX(g)? Indeed, in the case at hand, China defended its quotas under Article XX(g), but defended its export duties, which arguably had the same purpose, under Article XX(b) (presumably because the export duties could not meet the 'made effective in conjunction with domestic restrictions' requirement of Article XX(g)). This constitutes yet another puzzle presented by the narrow context-based *effet utile* approach to interpretation.

Under the 'relating to' test, there must be 'a close and genuine relationship of ends and means' between that measure and the conservation objective.[9] Earlier jurisprudence,[10] now superseded,[11] had stated that the national measure sought to be defended under Article XX(g) must be 'primarily aimed at' conservation. Even in the *Gasoline* case, in which the Appellate Body relied on the 'primarily aimed at' test, the Appellate Body only did so because all the parties had accepted that formulation.[12] In applying that test in the *Gasoline* case, the Appellate Body stated that it was satisfied because there was a 'substantial relationship' between the measure at issue and the conservation purpose, 'the baseline establishment rules cannot be regarded as merely incidentally or inadvertently aimed at the conservation of clean air in the United States for the purposes of Article XX(g)'. This test seems less demanding than 'primarily aimed at'.

There are three types of evidence that can be considered in connection with the 'related to' analysis under Article XX(g): (i) statements of legislative intent; (ii) objective analysis of the design and structure in order to determine intent or likely effect; and (iii) evidence of actual effects.

Most of the panel's analysis of the extent to which China's export quota relates to conservation focused on legislative intent, and the panel found that, according

[7] In addition, the Appellate Body has developed a complex balancing test for determining 'necessity'.

[8] But see *US—Gasoline* (n 1) 18.

[9] Appellate Body Report, *United States—Import Prohibition of Certain Shrimp and Shrimp Products* (*US—Shrimp*), WT/DS58/AB/R, adopted 6 November 1998, para 136.

[10] *US—Gasoline* (n 1); Report of the Panel, *Canada—Measures Affecting Exports of Unprocessed Herring and Salmon*, L/6268, adopted 22 March 1988, GATT BISD 35S/98.

[11] *US—Shrimp* (n 9), Appellate Body Report, *China—Measures Related to the Exportation of Various Raw Materials* (*China—Raw Materials*), WT/DS394/AB/R, WT/DS395/AB/R, WT/DS398/AB/R, 30 January 2012.

[12] *US—Gasoline* (n 1) 18–19. The Appellate Body observed that 'the phrase "primarily aimed at" is not itself treaty language and was not designed as a simple litmus test for inclusion or exclusion from Article XX(g)'.

to statements of legislative intent, China's goal for this legislation was primarily industrial policy.[13]

The Appellate Body conceded that 'the text of Article XX(g) does not prescribe a specific analytical framework for assessing whether a measure satisfies the component requirements of that provision'. But it continued that 'all the same, we observe that, in past disputes, the Appellate Body has emphasized the importance of the design and structure of the challenged measure to a proper assessment of whether a measure satisfies the requirements of Article XX(g)'.[14]

The panel based its decision that China's export quotas do not 'relate to conservation' on the panel's view that, while the quotas would induce conservation on the part of foreign consumers, it would also send a 'perverse signal' of lower prices in the domestic market, inducing reduced conservation by domestic consumers. The panel's statement on application of Article XX(g) is worth quoting at length:

> The Panel takes note of China's indication that various rare earth recycling projects, efforts to modify industrial designs of downstream products so that they use less rare earths, and developments of rare earth substitutes are under way. The Panel acknowledges that these efforts may go a long way towards furthering what all involved in this dispute recognize is China's bona fide conservation policy. Nevertheless, our consideration of the design and architecture of China's export quota on rare earths does not convince us that the export quota is designed in such a way as to ensure that domestic demand is not stimulated by low prices. There does not appear to be any mechanism to ensure that the export quota is set at such a level that, in combination with the extraction and/or production caps, no perverse incentives will be sent to domestic consumers.[15]

The design and structure of an export quota in this context ensure that they will result in a reduction of foreign consumption in an amount greater than the increase in domestic consumption.[16] Thus, in the most basic sense, there is no doubt that China's production quota, considered alone, has the effect of reducing output.

It is not clear that the panel or the Appellate Body accepted this basic theoretical result. The panel focused on the extent to which the foreign price signals were offset by 'perverse' domestic signals of reduced prices leading to increased domestic consumption. But as noted above, the design and structure only result in a partial offset, not a full negation of the conservation signal. So, it is necessary to consider why the panel and Appellate Body determined that this reduction in output is not enough to consider the Chinese export quotas as 'relating to' conservation.

Assuming that the panel and the Appellate Body did not recognize that the perverse signal only partially offset the conservation effect, they made a basic error of economics. If the definition of 'related to' is limited to a simple question of whether

[13] *China—Rare Earths, Panel Report* (n 4) paras 7.400–7.4006.

[14] *China—Rare Earths, Appellate Report* (n 3) para 5.96.

[15] *China—Rare Earths, Panel Report* (n 4) para 7.448.

[16] See the economic explanation of this proposition developed by Eric Bond in Eric Bond and Joel Trachtman, 'China—Rare Earths: Export Restrictions and The Limits of Textual Interpretation' (2016) 15(2) World Trade Rev 189–209.

the measure's design and structure are consistent with a reduction of output, then China's export quota was related to conservation.

If, on the other hand, the panel and Appellate Body did recognize that the design and structure of China's measure necessarily cause a reduction of output, then they must have determined (i) that the mixed nature of the legislative intent was sufficient to find that China had not shown that its measure 'related to' conservation; and/or (ii) that the design and structure somehow showed insufficient contribution to conservation to satisfy the 'related to' criterion. Determination (i) is similar to a 'primarily aimed at' test, which test, as noted above, appears to have been superseded. Determination (ii) requires some assessment of effects. That is, if the design and structure are insufficient to show that China's measure did not relate to conservation, then it must have been the subjective aim or the magnitude of effects that formed the basis for the panel's finding.

China argued under Article XX(g), that its measure made a 'contribution' to the conservation of natural resources, borrowing the 'contribution' concept from Article XX(b) jurisprudence, where, indeed, the contribution is permitted to be relatively small. The Appellate Body's analysis under Article XX(b) in *Brazil—Tyres* seems to require only a finding of a theoretical 'material' contribution to the achievement of the regulatory goal.[17] However, the Appellate Body in *Rare Earths* insisted on a formal separation of concepts:

> In the light of the different connecting words used, we consider that a mixing of the different tests under Article XX(b) and Article XX(g), absent of context, would result in an approach that ignores the important distinctions between the various subparagraphs of Article XX.[18]

Here, one might have taken a different approach, based on the object and purpose of the treaty, recognizing that while the connecting words are different, the substantive concept and purpose—that the national measure must be authentic enough to make a measurable contribution to the purported goal—is similar. Indeed, if a theoretical contribution is sufficient under the more demanding 'necessity' connector, why would it not suffice under the 'relating to' connector? Again, context, object, and purpose would counsel a less hermetically (and hermeneutically) sealed approach to these different subparagraphs. Excessive formalism can result in the erection of linguistic or jurisprudential structures that may not have been intended by the drafters and, more importantly, may fail to encompass the substantive nuance of real-life situations. If 'related to' were understood to be consistent with some material contribution to conservation, as discussed above, China's measure would have qualified.

[17] Appellate Body Report, *Brazil—Measures Affecting Imports of Retreaded Tyres*, WT/DS332/AB/R, adopted 17 December 2007. See Chad P Bown and Joel P Trachtman, 'Brazil—Measures Affecting Imports of Retreaded Tyres: A Balancing Act' (2009) 8 (Special Issue 1) World Trade Rev 85.

[18] *China—Rare Earths, Appellate Report* (n 3) para 5.116.

The Appellate Body observed that focus on 'design and structure' allows the panel to go beyond the text of the domestic measure, and even beyond nominal intent, which seems necessary to a substantive analysis, but then it agreed with the panel, and with prior jurisprudence, that it is not necessary to determine the empirical effects of the measure.[19] It is true, as the Appellate Body pointed out in *US—Gasoline*, that the empirical determination of effects is fraught with difficulties, not least of which are that no effects might be observed immediately.[20] China complained that the panel excluded evidence of effects. Indeed, the panel made the following statement:

> There is therefore no need for the Panel to decide, in quantitative or qualitative terms, precisely what level of contribution a challenged measure has made to the conservation objective. Instead, the Panel looks at the nature of the challenged measures to determine whether, as a matter of design and architecture, they assist, support or further the goal of conservation.[21]

Thus, a narrow approach to 'design and structure' would support China's contention that its measure relates to conservation. In order to find that China's measure did not relate to conservation, the panel would have had to consider that evidence of stated intent somehow negated this aspect of the design and structure, or that the magnitude of the conservation effect was insufficient. But the panel declined to consider evidence of actual effects.

China argued that it was an error to exclude evidence of actual effects, in cases where a respondent could not successfully show that its measure had the requisite design and structure.[22] However, the Appellate Body disagreed with China's characterization of the panel's findings.[23] The panel merely found that assessment of actual effects was not necessary in this case, not that it is precluded. The Appellate Body stated that panels are not precluded from examining actual effects. But it did so without abandoning the focus on design and structure: 'in any event, where the design and structure of a challenged measure clearly illustrate the absence of a nexus between that measure and the conservation objective, it would be difficult to attribute the evidence of positive effects on conservation to that measure'.[24] This is the familiar social science precept that without a theory of causation, we cannot attribute causation to correlated events.

Thus, the Appellate Body concluded that the panel did not err by focusing on design and structure. However, note that the predicate of the Appellate Body's statement is questionable: as discussed above, it is difficult to agree that the design and structure of China's export quotas 'clearly illustrate the absence of a nexus' with the conservation objective.

[19] ibid para 5.98. [20] *US—Gasoline* (n 1) 20.

[21] *China—Rare Earths, Panel Report* (n 4) para 7.379, referring to *Shrimp Appellate Body Report* (n 9) para 141.

[22] China's appellant's submission, para 155, citing *China—Rare Earths, Appellate Report* (n 3).

[23] *China—Rare Earths, Appellate Report* (n 3) para 5.108. [24] ibid para 5.113.

The panel examined design and structure, finding that there is some reduction of foreign consumption, but that the 'perverse incentives' expand domestic consumption. As discussed above, this is definitely true in theory and we would expect it to be true in practice. But the panel never evaluated the magnitude of the foreign reduction, or the magnitude of the effect of the perverse incentives. Note the language of the panel's statement quoted above: China must ensure that no perverse incentives are sent. However, in order to 'relate to' conservation, should it not be enough if the effects of the perverse incentives are less than the effects of the conservation incentives? Or if there is a tougher test, then it would be necessary to compare the foreign reduction with the perverse incentives. If actual effects are not examined, then all the panel has to support a determination that the Chinese measure does not relate to conservation is speculation about the relative magnitudes of the effects.

The Appellate Body simply approved the panel's reasoning in this context.[25] The Appellate Body went so far as to state that 'we also consider that the Panel did not, as suggested by China, find that export quotas can send effective conservation signals to foreign users'.[26] This statement does not seem to comport with what the panel actually said ('the Panel accepts that export quotas do or at least can send conservation-related signals to foreign users'[27]), or with economic theory.

The Appellate Body stated that 'uncertainty regarding the levels of the export and production quotas led the Panel to highlight its concern about the absence of "any mechanism to ensure that the export quota is set at such a level that, in combination with the extraction and/or production caps, no perverse incentives will be sent to domestic consumers" '.[28] Again, this seems too high a burden to set in connection with the 'related to' test: Article XX(g) does not require purity.

As discussed above, as a matter of design and structure, the export restriction policy is 'related to' conservation in the narrow sense of reducing the total extraction of the resource, but the effects of the policy could be related to other policy goals, such as industrial policy or development policy.

As noted above, the panel found that the non-conservation goals expressed in the legislation prevented an inference of a conservation purpose, and found that the primary goal of China's export quota was industrial policy.[29] Is it possible to have a non-conservation primary goal, and still be 'related to' conservation? Recall that the Appellate Body has moved beyond the requirement, expressed in *US—Gasoline*, that a measure be 'primarily aimed at' conservation in order to satisfy the 'related to' criterion.[30] But what if the measure is primarily aimed at non-conservation goals? The panel seems to suggest that under these circumstances, a measure cannot be 'related to' conservation.

[25] ibid para 5.156. [26] ibid para 5.160.

[27] *China—Rare Earths, Panel Report* (n 4) paras 7.725, 7.443.

[28] *China—Rare Earths, Appellate Report* (n 3) para 5.159, citing *China—Rare Earths, Panel Report* (n 4) para 7.448.

[29] *China—Rare Earths, Panel Report* (n 4) paras 7.398–7.403.

[30] *China—Rare Earths, Appellate Report* (n 3), para 355, citing *US—Shrimp* (n 9), para 136.

II. Made Effective in Conjunction with Domestic Restrictions

China's other claim of error in connection with the panel's decision regarding Article XX(g) of GATT 1994 had to do with the panel's statements to the effect that Article XX(g) includes a requirement of 'even-handedness' as between national measures to conserve natural resources that otherwise violate GATT on the one hand, and restrictions on domestic production or consumption on the other hand. This concept exceeds the ordinary meaning of Article XX(g), which simply refers to measures 'made effective in conjunction with restrictions on domestic production or consumption'.

The Appellate Body found that even-handedness is not a separate requirement, but is a shorthand way that has been used to describe the requirement in Article XX(g) that the measure be made effective in conjunction with domestic restrictions.[31] The panel did not express with perfect clarity whether it did consider even-handedness as a separate requirement, so the Appellate Body held that 'the Panel erred to the extent that it found that "even-handedness" is a separate requirement that must be fulfilled in addition to the condition that a measure be "made effective in conjunction with restrictions on domestic production or consumption" '.[32]

Examining the question of whether the panel erred in its application of this prong, the Appellate Body simply held that the restrictions on domestic production or consumption must be 'real',[33] but need not be 'evenly distributed'.[34]

Here, one might observe that China, along with the Appellate Body, has identified an important avenue for evasion of what one might infer from the context was the object and purpose of Article XX(g): to ensure authenticity of concern for conservation by ensuring that the major burden of the conservation is not imposed on foreign interests. It is arguable, however, that the 'made effective in conjunction with' language has the object and purpose of requiring even-handedness. So this is an example of a textualist interpretation leaving an important substantive gap in the WTO object to restrain unjustified protectionism.

The Appellate Body highlighted this concern, noting that 'it would be difficult to conceive of a measure that would impose a significantly more onerous burden on foreign consumers or producers and that could still be shown to satisfy all of the requirements of Article XX(g)'.[35] When put that way, it does sound like a requirement of even-handedness. In any event, this avenue of potential avoidance is not very wide, because the chapeau of Article XX would be likely to deny an exception to measures that constitute a means of arbitrary or unjustifiable discrimination, so long as the chapeau is understood as addressing the measure, and not just the way in which the measure is applied.

[31] *China—Rare Earths, Appellate Report* (n 3) para 5.124. [32] ibid para 5.127.
[33] ibid para 5.132. [34] ibid para 5.134. [35] ibid.

In the absence of further guidance under Article XX(g), the requirement of non-discrimination under the chapeau seems the natural rule for evaluating the extent to which domestic regulations act in conjunction with export policies.

China also challenged the panel's finding that the 'made effective in conjunction with' requirement is to be evaluated, again, based only on structure and design, and not on actual effects. So, here, although the Appellate Body upheld the panel's reasoning on the basis that the panel never stated that it was *precluded* from examining actual effects, it appears that examination of effects will rarely, if ever, be appropriate. The Appellate Body referred to its earlier response to China's claim regarding 'relating to', stating, puzzlingly, that 'the legal characterization of a measure cannot be contingent upon the occurrence of subsequent events'.[36]

This language is striking, because the plain language of Article XX(g)—asking whether a measure relates to conservation of exhaustible natural resources and whether it is made effective in conjunction with domestic restrictions on production or consumption—would ordinarily be understood as asking whether the measure actually conserves natural resources and whether domestic production or consumption is actually restricted. Here, the Appellate Body seems to have added words of limitation that are not contained in Article XX(g), reading into the text words of limitation that are not there. This language first appeared in the *Gasoline* Appellate Body Report, in which the Appellate Body seemed to suggest that a respondent would not be required to show actual conservation effects of its measures as a condition for use of the Article XX(g) exception. It seems appropriate in that context, given the fact that conservation effects may take some time to appear. However, it does not seem appropriate to exclude evidence that might be offered by a respondent that its measure had measurable conservation effects.

This counter-textual approach is especially striking when so closely juxtaposed with the Appellate Body and panel's exaltation of textualism over object and purpose in the context of its analysis of the availability of Article XX to except China's export duties.

III. Conclusion

The WTO Agreement may be understood as a state-contingent contract containing obligations and exceptions, each dependent on findings of particular facts. The exceptions contained in Article XX of GATT may be understood as designed to provide a mechanism for relaxing WTO obligations where specified reasons apply and specified conditions are met. This serves to preserve WTO obligations, while ensuring that compliance with these obligations is not excessively costly in terms of other values, such as conservation of exhaustible natural resources.

Export quotas will not generally be economically efficient mechanisms for conservation of exhaustible natural resources. However, this does not necessarily

[36] ibid para 5.138.

mean that they cannot, under any circumstances, 'relate to' conservation within the meaning of Article XX(g). While China's export quota on rare earths could not meet the requirements of the Article XX chapeau, the Appellate Body confirmed the panel's approach to Article XX(g) in a way that makes it unclear how this defence will operate in the future.

First, while the Appellate Body confirmed the panel's finding that the structure and design of China's quota do not 'relate to' conservation, it did not deal with the fact that the structure and design of China's measure, in economic terms, will reduce output. While the narrow reduction of output may be insufficient to 'relate to' conservation, neither the panel nor the Appellate Body explains how China's measure failed to meet the test. Perhaps the problem was that China's measure was primarily addressed to industrial policy purposes. Perhaps the problem was that China's measure failed to provide sufficient benefits in terms of conservation. If the problem was the latter, it would have been appropriate for the panel to allow China to present evidence of the extent of conservation effects.

Second, while the Appellate Body found that the 'made effective in conjunction with domestic restrictions' prong of the Article XX(g) test does not require even-handedness, it did not provide guidance to future panels as to how to compare the magnitude of domestic restrictions to the magnitude of measures sought to be justified under Article XX(g). The Appellate Body also accepted the panel's determination not to examine empirical evidence offered by China of the conservation effects of its domestic measures compared to the conservation effects of its export quota.

7

Balancing Investment Protection and Other Public Policy Goals: Lessons from WTO Jurisprudence

*Yasuhei Taniguchi** *and Tomoko Ishikawa***

I. Introduction

International economic law is a particular area of international law that offers more active dispute settlement mechanisms than any other area: the World Trade Organization (WTO) dispute settlement system and investment arbitration. If the success of these mechanisms is defined by the number of cases received by its forums, they would be regarded as highly successful indeed. As of the date of writing, the WTO Appellate Body and panels have produced 125 and 209 reports, respectively.[1] For investment arbitration, according to the UNCTAD World Investment Report 2015, the total number of known investment arbitration cases is 608.[2] As of the end of 2015, the International Centre for the Settlement of Investment Disputes (ICSID) had registered 549 cases under the ICSID Convention and Additional Facility Rules.[3]

* Professor Emeritus, Kyoto University, Japan. Member, Appellate Body (2000–2007).

** Associate Professor, Nagoya University, Japan.

[1] See 'Total Reports and Awards Circulated Each Year' <http://www.worldtradelaw.net> accessed 7 April 2016. For a detailed statistical analysis of WTO dispute settlement, see K Leitner and S Lester, 'WTO Dispute Settlement 1995–2015—A Statistical Analysis' (2016) J Intl Econ L. In 2014, the WTO Director-General Roberto Azevêdo stated that:

> [t]here is no question that the WTO's dispute settlement system has been a success. The numbers tell their own story about how valued it has become: In just under 20 years since the system came into being, 482 requests for consultation have been received ... in 68 years the International Court of Justice has received 162 cases.

DG Roberto Azevêdo, 'Azevêdo Says Success of WTO Dispute Settlement Brings Urgent Challenges' (*WTO News*, 26 September 2014) <https://www.wto.org/english/news_e/spra_e/spra32_e.htm> accessed 7 April 2016.

[2] UNCTAD, 'World Investment Report 2015: Reforming International Investment Governance' (June 2015) xi <http://unctad.org/en/PublicationsLibrary/wir2015_en.pdf> accessed 7 April 2016.

[3] ICSID, 'The ICSID Caseload—Statistics (*Issue*, 2015-1)' <https://icsid.worldbank.org/apps/ICSIDWEB/resources/Documents/ICSID%20Web%20Stats%202016-1%20(English)%20final.pdf> accessed 7 April 2016.

On the other hand, if the success of a dispute settlement mechanism is measured by reference to trust and support in the system, there is a notable difference between the two. The WTO Appellate Body is described as 'an international tribunal of historic achievement',[4] not only because of the volume of its cases, but also due to the wide support and trust it has received from the WTO member states. Certainly, the WTO dispute settlement system is not free from criticism,[5] and the reports of panels and the Appellate Body for particular cases are frequently subject to critical discussions in the Dispute Settlement Body (DSB).[6] Nevertheless, as noted over a decade ago:

> There are … a number of viewpoints expressed by governments and non-government observers that suggest a general sense of satisfaction with the dispute settlement system. That has led to the suggestion that there does not exist a strong political incentive to reform the system. Indeed, … an important underlying concern is, or should be, to not 'do any harm' to the existing system since it has so many valuable attributes.[7]

The fundamental reform of the dispute settlement system is not on the Doha agenda.[8] The system is also widely recognized by scholars as an efficient and legitimate state–state dispute settlement forum.[9]

In contrast, investment arbitration has increasingly faced severe criticism and scepticism, leading to the withdrawal from the ICSID Convention[10] and termination of international investment agreements (IIAs) by several countries.[11]

[4] Isabelle Van Damme, *Treaty Interpretation by the WTO Appellate Body* (OUP 2009) 3, citing James Bacchus, 'WTO Appellate Body Roundtable' (2005) 99 Am Socy Intl L Proceedings 175.

[5] e.g. for criticisms of its alleged 'judicial activism', see Richard H Steinberg, 'Judicial Lawmaking at the WTO: Discursive, Constitutional, and Political Constraints' (2004) 98(2) Am J Intl L 247; John Ragosta and others, 'WTO Dispute Settlement: The System is Flawed and Must be Fixed' (2003) 37(3) Intl Lawyer 697; José E Álvarez, 'The WTO as Linkage Machine' (2002) 96(1) Am J Intl L 146.

[6] Steinberg (n 5) 266: 'A member dissatisfied with a particular decision, or judicial lawmaking in general, is likely to signal disapproval—typically through a diplomatic statement at a DSB meeting. Such pronouncements may be harsh.' Of course, this does not affect the adoption of such reports under the reverse consensus rule (DSU art 17.14). See also Junji Nakagawa, *Transparency in International Trade and Investment Dispute Settlement* (Routledge 2013) 54.

[7] Report by the Consultative Board to the former Director-General Supachai Panitchpakdi, *The Future of the WTO: Addressing Institutional Challenges in the New Millennium* (2004) para 254 <https://www.wto.org/english/thewto_e/10anniv_e/future_wto_e.htm> accessed 7 April 2016.

[8] *Doha Ministerial Declaration*, WT/MIN(01)/DEC/1, adopted 14 November 2001, para 30: 'We agree to negotiations on improvements and clarifications of the Dispute Settlement Understanding …'

[9] e.g. Nicholas DiMascio and Joost Pauwelyn, 'Nondiscrimination in Trade and Investment Treaties: Worlds Apart or Two Sides of the Same Coin?' (2008) 102 Am J Intl L 48, 53: '[t]he WTO dispute settlement mechanism—in particular, the WTO Appellate Body—garnered legitimacy and efficiency as a mechanism for the settlement of state-to-state trade disputes'; Alberto Álvarez-Jiménez, 'The WTO Appellate Body Decision-making Process: A Perfect Model for International Adjudication?' (2009) 12(2) J Intl Econ L 289, 331: 'the design and practice of the AB has created a decision-making process that is unique in the world in the quality of the outcomes that it produces. Much care should be taken when attempting to reform the institution….'

[10] They include Bolivia (denunciation effective November 2007), Ecuador (denunciation effective January 2010), and Venezuela (denunciation effective July 2012).

[11] e.g. it is reported that South Africa has served notices of termination of Bilateral Investment Treaties (BITs) on approximately thirteen states. See Jackwell Feris, 'Challenging the Status

Recent discussions about investor-to-state dispute settlement (ISDS), in particular investment arbitration, in the context of the negotiation of the Transatlantic Trade and Investment Partnership (TTIP) most vividly demonstrate this point, as concerns and call for the fundamental reform of ISDS are raised in both the European Union and the United States, the two major economic blocs. For example, in May 2015, the European Economic and Social Committee adopted the 'Opinion on Investor Protection and Investor to State Dispute Settlement in EU Trade and Investment Agreements with Third Countries', in which it expressed its concern over investment arbitration that '[i]n some prominent cases it has become a lobbying tool where the very threat of litigation creates a regulatory chill which inhibits legislators pursuing legitimate public interest policies'.[12] Notably, in the United States, eminent law and economics scholars issued a letter to the US Congress expressing concerns that investment arbitration 'weakens the rule of law by removing the procedural protections of the legal system and using a system of adjudication with limited accountability and review'. The letter further requested that Congress 'ensure(s) ISDS is excluded from upcoming trade agreements'.[13] The European Commission has proposed an Investment Court System,[14] which is included in the text of the TTIP as well as the EU–Viet Nam Free Trade Agreement. In light of these concerns and developments, it is not an exaggeration to state that the future of investment arbitration is precarious.

In the background of this setting lies the fact that investment arbitration tribunals actually review government actions taken in the public interest. Investor–state disputes have evolved from traditional expropriation cases to conflicts arising out of regulatory interference with various aspects of the investment, and therefore they are now considered as 'regulatory disputes within the public law sphere'.[15]

Quo—South Africa's Termination of its Bilateral Trade Agreements' (2014) <https://www.dlapiper.com/ja/japan/insights/publications/2014/12/international-arbitration-newsletter-q4-2014/challenging-the-status-quo/> accessed 7 April 2016.

[12] Opinion of the European Economic and Social Committee, see *Investor Protection and Investor to State Dispute Settlement in EU Trade and Investment Agreements with Third Countries*, REX/411, adopted 27 May 2015 <http://www.eesc.europa.eu/?i=portal.en.rex-opinions.35922> accessed 7 April 2016, paras 1.7 and 1.21. See also European Commission, Commission Staff Working Document, 'Report: Online Public Consultation on Investment Protection and Investor-to-State Dispute Settlement (ISDS) in the Transatlantic Trade and Investment Partnership Agreement (TTIP)' (13 January 2015) <http://trade.ec.europa.eu/doclib/docs/2015/january/tradoc_153044.pdf> accessed 7 April 2016; European Commission, Concept Paper 'Investment in TTIP and Beyond—The Path for Reform' (2015) <http://trade.ec.europa.eu/doclib/docs/2015/may/tradoc_153408.PDF> accessed 7 April 2016.

[13] Letter from Professor Judith Resnik and others (30 April 2015) <http://www.washingtonpost.com/r/2010-2019/WashingtonPost/2015/04/30/Editorial-Opinion/Graphics/oppose_ISDS_Letter.pdf> accessed 7 April 2016.

[14] European Commission, Press release, 'EU Finalises Proposal for Investment Protection and Court System for TTIP' (12 November 2015) <http://europa.eu/rapid/press-release_IP-15-6059_en.htm> accessed 7 April 2016.

[15] Benedict Kingsbury and others, 'The Emergence of Global Administrative Law' (2005) 68 L Contemp Probs 15, 36–37. See also Gus Van Harten, *Investment Treaty Arbitration and Public Law* (OUP 2007) ch I; Robin F Hansen, 'Parallel Proceedings in Investor–State Treaty

Moreover, the fact that investment treaty arbitration is the combination of a variety of different investment treaties and arbitral tribunals raises concern over the lack of legal certainty and predictability in the dispute settlement system. This has given rise to scepticism over legal certainty and judicial self-restraint in investment arbitration, which are 'both key to the operation of a trusted international judicial system'.[16] The following remarks by the EU Trade Commissioner summarize these concerns well: 'I want the rule of law, not the rule of lawyers. I want to ensure fair treatment for EU investors abroad, but not at the expense of governments' right to regulate.'[17]

Indeed, various proposals for the reform of ISDS have been made, including institutional and structural reform proposals.[18] The purpose of this chapter is not to add another reform proposal, but rather to examine, in light of the different levels of acceptance of legitimacy between the WTO Appellate Body and investment arbitration, the possibility that WTO jurisprudence provides guidance for use by investment arbitration tribunals to address these concerns. The analysis is structured as follows.

Arbitration: Responses for Treaty-Drafters, Arbitrators and Parties' (2010) 73(4) Modern L Rev 523. Burke-White and Staden provide a definition of public law arbitrations as 'arbitrations for which the critical issue on which the outcome turns to be whether the state has the power and legal ability to undertake regulation in the public interest'. William W Burke-White and Andreas von Staden, 'Private Litigation in a Public Law Sphere: The Standard of Review in Investor–State Arbitrations' (2010) 35 Yale J Intl L 285 (note 7).

[16] Duncan French, 'Treaty Interpretation and the Incorporation of Extraneous Legal Rules' (2006) 55(2) Intl Comp LQ 281, 283. Howse identifies three elements in legitimacy in the adjudication: fair procedures; coherence and integrity in legal interpretation; and institutional sensitivity. Robert Howse, 'Adjudicative Legitimacy and Treaty Interpretation in International Trade Law: The Early Years of the WTO' in J H H Weiler (ed), *The EU, The WTO and The NAFTA: Towards a Common Law of International Trade* (OUP 2000) 35–70. See also Barnali Choudhury, 'Recapturing Public Power: Is Investment Arbitration's Engagement of the Public Interest Contributing to the Democratic Deficit?' (2008) 41 Vand J Transnatl L 775.

[17] Blog Post by Cecilia Malmström, 'Investments in TTIP and Beyond—Towards an International Investment Court' (*European Commission Blog*, 5 May 2015) <http://ec.europa.eu/commission/2014-2019/malmstrom/blog/investments-ttip-and-beyond-towards-international-investment-court_en> accessed 7 April 2016. See also the letter from Resnik and others (n 13): 'Although ISDS tribunals are not empowered to order injunctive relief, the threat and expense of ISDS proceedings have forced nations to abandon important public policies.' On 'the rule of lawyers', Van Harten also points out that 'investment treaty arbitration does not incorporate conventional safeguards of judicial independence such as secure judicial tenure, objective methods of appointment of judges to specific cases, and restrictions on outside remuneration by the judge'. See Gus Van Harten, 'Arbitrator Behaviour in Asymmetrical Adjudication: An Empirical Study of Investment Treaty Arbitration' (2012) 50(1) Osgoode Hall LJ 211, 218.

[18] UNCTAD, 'Reform of Investor–State Dispute Settlement: In Search of a Roadmap' (2013) <http://unctad.org/en/PublicationsLibrary/webdiaepcb2013d4_en.pdf> accessed 7 April 2016. This report examines the following five paths for reform: (a) promoting alternative dispute resolution; (b) tailoring the existing system through individual IIAs; (c) limiting investor access to ISDS; (d) introducing an appeals facility; and (e) creating a standing international investment court. See also UNTAD, 'Taking Stock of IIA Reform' (2016) <http://unctad.org/en/PublicationsLibrary/webdiaepcb2016d1_en.pdf> accessed 7 April 2016. It should also be noted that the UNCITRAL Rules on Transparency in Treaty-based Investor–State Arbitration came into effect on 1 April 2014, and the Convention on Transparency in Treaty-based Investor–State Arbitration was adopted by the United Nations General Assembly on 10 December 2014 (opened for signature on 17 March 2015).

Section II demonstrates that, despite various differences between the WTO dispute settlement system and investment arbitration, they have a commonality in their function: they both provide judicial review of government actions that affect international economic activities in light of obligations under international law. This also means that they face the same normative issue of balance between the need to respect sovereign regulatory power and the need for effective implementation of such obligations. In WTO disputes, the issue of balance manifests itself in a particularly serious and dynamic manner in the assessment of the general exceptions contained in Article XX of the General Agreement on Tariffs and Trade (GATT) and Article XIV of the General Agreement on Trade in Services (GATS), and the Appellate Body has developed and clarified its approach to address this issue. The analysis herein argues that when assessing whether the government's measure at issue constitutes a breach of certain investment protection obligations, investment arbitration tribunals do consider the same elements as those considered by the Appellate Body in the context of GATT Article XX and GATS Article XIV. This provides a theoretical basis for the relevance of the WTO jurisprudence on the general exceptions to the interpretation and application of these substantive obligations.

Section III demonstrates the benefits of referring to WTO jurisprudence in investment arbitration. First, the text observes that the real source of concern over investment arbitration lies not in actual 'pro-investor bias' in the outcome of disputes but in the lack of clear and coherent reasoning as to the balancing between public interests and investment protection. In contrast, behind the support of the WTO dispute settlement system there is the Appellate Body's continuous effort to achieve coherence and integrity in legal interpretation, and the institutional sensitivity it has developed since its creation.[19] Furthermore, there is wide acknowledgement that the criteria established by the WTO Appellate Body demonstrate appropriate deference to the states' sovereign power to regulate for legitimate public interests. Therefore, consistent reliance on these criteria by investment arbitration tribunals, wherever appropriate, will not only provide a more solid reasoning based on consistent criteria, but will also help to address the concern, misplaced in many cases, over their 'pro-investor bias'.

Section IV describes the deferential approach of the WTO Appellate Body in the application of general exception clauses and concludes the chapter by examining how this approach may actually inform the interpretation of investment protection obligations by investment arbitration tribunals.

This chapter does not propose the 'borrowing' of the interpretation of specific provisions, an activity that would be subject to the textual and contextual differences between the two regimes. Nor does it deny the possibility that a measure that can be justified under GATT Article XX constitutes a breach of investment treaty obligations, and vice versa. This is indeed possible where the obligations in question

[19] It is widely accepted that de facto precedence exists in the WTO dispute settlement system. Cf Van Damme argues that a more appropriate terminology than the term 'precedent' is 'the idea of a *jurisprudence constante*'. Van Damme (n 4) 198.

are different,[20] and even where the obligation appears to be the same (for example, national treatment), the textual and contextual differences between the agreements may well justify different outcomes.[21] Instead, this chapter focuses on the approach of the Appellate Body in interpreting the components of general exceptions clauses. This is because it is through this approach that its 'grand vision'[22] towards sensitivity to Member States' rights to regulate has been demonstrated, which forms the basis of the wide acceptance of its legitimacy.

II. Different Systems, Shared Features

While international trade law and investment law often deal with the same activities[23] and closely related issues,[24] the WTO law regime and investment law regime[25] are distinct in many respects, making it impossible to treat them as constituting a single legal order. Such differences include, inter alia, the background of their development,[26] the structure and design of their dispute settlement

[20] Kurtz emphasizes the difference between the relative standards of treatment (such as GATT art III) and 'strong, absolute protections, especially on guarantees of full compensation in the event of expropriation'. Jürgen Kurtz, 'The Use and Abuse of WTO Law in Investor–State Arbitration: Competition and its Discontents' (2009) 20(3) Eur J Intl L 749, 755.

[21] 'Like products' in GATT is evidently not the same question as whether foreign and domestic investors are in 'like circumstances'. See Roger P Alford, 'The Convergence of International Trade and Investment Arbitration' (2014) 12(1) Santa Clara J Intl L 35.

[22] Here, the term 'grand vision' refers to the mindset of tribunals, against the background of which norms are interpreted and applied. See Marcos A Orellana, 'Science, Risk and Uncertainty: Public Health Measures and Investment Disciplines' in Philippe Kahn and Thomas Waelde (eds), *New Aspects of International Investment Law* (Brill 2007) 671–790.

[23] e.g. supply of services through a commercial presence covered by GATS (mode 3) normally involves foreign direct investment. It is reported that '[a]round half of world trade today takes place between affiliates of multinational enterprises, which trade intermediate goods and services.' European Commission, 'Communication from the Commission to the Council, The European Parliament', The European Economic and Social Committee and the Committee of the Regions—Towards a Comprehensive European International Investment Policy COM (2010) 343 Final (7 July 2010) 3 <http://trade.ec.europa.eu/doclib/docs/2011/may/tradoc_147884.pdf> accessed 7 April 2016. For the impact of the WTO rules on investment, see e.g., Debra P Steger, 'International Trade and Investment: Towards a Common Regime?' in Roberto Echandi and Pierre Sauvé (eds), *Prospects in International Investment Law and Policy* (CUP 2013) 156–65.

[24] e.g. trade flow in many cases immediately raises the question of investment protection. Gaetan Verhoosel, 'The Use of Investor–State Arbitration under Bilateral Investment Treaties to Seek Relief for Breaches of WTO Law' (2003) 6(2) J Intl Econ L 493.

[25] A definition of the concept 'regime' is provided by Krasner as follows: 'implicit or explicit principles, norms, rules and decision-making procedures around which actor expectations converge in a given issue-area'. Stephen D Krasner, 'Structural Causes and Regime Consequences: Regimes as Intervening Variables' in Stephen D Krasner (ed), *International Regimes* (Cornell University Press 1983) 1.

[26] See DiMascio and Pauwelyn (n 9) 51–53; Tomer Broude, 'Investment and Trade: the "Lottie and Lisa" of International Economic Law?' in Roberto Echandi and Pierre Sauvé (eds), *Prospects in International Investment Law and Policy* (CUP 2013) 139–55. See also Panel Report, *Canada—Administration of the Foreign Investment Review Act*, GATT Doc. L/5504–30S/140, adopted 7 February 1984, para 5.9: 'The purpose of Article III:4 is not to protect the interests of the foreign investor but to ensure that goods originating in any other contracting party benefit from treatment no less favourable than domestic goods.'

mechanisms,[27] the actors in the dispute settlement mechanism,[28] their processes, and the substantive obligations encompassed.[29] On the last point, the following statement of a GATT panel is suggestive: '[t]he purpose of Article III:4 is not to protect the interests of the foreign investor but to ensure that goods originating in any other contracting party benefit from treatment no less favourable than domestic goods'.[30] Likewise, DiMascio and Pauwelyn observe that while the trade regime is 'overall welfare, efficiency, liberalization, state-to-state exchanges of market access, and trade opportunities—not individual rights', the traditional investment regime is 'about individual rights, not state-to-state exchanges of market opportunities'.[31]

On the other hand, in his recent work on the relations between the WTO and investment law, Kurtz identifies the 'five convergence factors' that push these two fields of law together, including, inter alia, the jurisdictional overlap between the two systems and cross-fertilization of jurisprudence.[32] He then presents 'the metaphor of a double helix' to describe the relations between the two fields of law, according to which trade and investment law 'are partly constituted by, and will increasingly cohere, around that unifying core.'[33] The scope of this chapter is limited to the examination of how and when WTO jurisprudence may inform investment arbitration tribunals in interpreting investment law obligations, and this focus highlights the following common features between the two regimes. First, in both WTO law and international investment law, there are issues of possible conflicts between treaty obligations and governmental right to regulate for public interests, such as the protection of human rights and the environment.[34] This underscores the need for a proper balance between some loss of 'policy space' at the national level and the advantages of participation in the regime by undertaking certain international obligations.[35] Second, they both provide for international dispute

[27] e.g. investment treaty arbitration is 'non-reciprocal in that investors can sue states under an investment treaty but cannot themselves be sued by states'. Van Harten, 'Arbitrator Behaviour in Asymmetrical Adjudication' (n 17) 218. This may well affect the absence of political and legal filters 'against improper or incautions invocation of legal rights' in investment arbitration. See Kurtz, 'The Use and Abuse of WTO Law in Investor–State Arbitration' (n 20) 757.

[28] While the WTO dispute settlement is reserved for states, private investors have standing against a host state. At the same time, it should be noted that in both regimes it is the private parties who are 'the eventual beneficiaries of the standards of protection under both discipline'. See Anastasios Gourgourinis, 'Reviewing the Administration of Domestic Regulation in WTO and Investment Protection Law: The International Minimum Standard of Treatment of Aliens as "One Standard to Rule Them All"?' (2011) 8(3) Transnatl Disp Management 4. See also Panel Report, *United States—Sections 301–310 of the Trade Act of 1974*, WT/DS152/R, 22 December 1999, para 7.77.

[29] An important exception is the norm of non-discrimination. See Alford (n 21) 40–41.

[30] *Canada—Administration of the Foreign Investment Review Act* (n 26) para 5.9.

[31] DiMascio and Pauwelyn (n 9) 54 and 56. Therefore the WTO law does not concern obligations against unlawful expropriation, denial of justice, fair and equitable treatment of already-established investment, the guarantee of full protection and security. See Alford (n 21) 40.

[32] Jürgen Kurtz, *The WTO and International Investment Law: Converging Systems* (CUP 2016) 10–20.

[33] ibid 24.

[34] Broude aptly observes that 'the "trade and ..." problem' is 'mirrored by the "investment and ..." problem'. Broude (n 26) 9.

[35] For the WTO regime, see Report by the Consultative Board (n 7) para 143.

settlement forums that review and evaluate domestic governmental practices in light of the state's international law obligations.[36] It means that these forums face the same question of where their judicial review of government actions becomes an excessive intrusion into sovereign regulatory power of the state.[37] In WTO jurisprudence, this balancing has been most extensively discussed in the context of the exceptions contained in the GATT and the GATS. In this respect, it should be noted that, in the recent *EC—Seal Products* case, the Appellate Body confirmed that a determination of 'likeness' under Article III:4 of the GATT is generally based on competitiveness,[38] and thereby arguably rejected the 'aims-and-effects test' that examines domestic regulatory objectives and the regulation's effect on imports in the determination.[39]

Burke-White and von Staden, having argued the 'public-law' nature of investment treaty arbitration, observe that:

> Similar public law or even quasi-constitutional disputes have already become relatively common within the framework of the WTO based on the exceptions contained in the General Agreement on Tariffs and Trade (GATT) and the General Agreement on Trade in Services (GATS).[40]

Certainly, many investment treaties, including the North American Free Trade Agreement (NAFTA) Chapter 11, do not include GATT XX- or GATS XIV-type general exception clauses. This does not mean, however, that investment arbitration tribunals do not conduct a balancing exercise. Rather, in investment treaty arbitration, the issue of balance between competing interests is primarily sought in the assessment of whether the government's measure at issue constitutes a breach of investment protection obligations (as opposed to the assessment of whether the breach can be justified by exceptions).[41] It is argued that the balancing under general exception clauses is particularly pertinent to the interpretation of the fair and equitable standard of treatment (FET) and indirect expropriation, for the following reasons. Examination of the compatibility of the measure in question with these obligations requires the consideration of the effect of the measure, the objective of the measure, the application of the proportionality principle, and the principle of

[36] Gourgourinis (n 28) 1. See also Alford (n 21) 37: 'They both use international tribunals as the vehicle for dispute settlement, thereby allowing for judicial review of sovereign state violations of international law.'

[37] Steven P Croley and John H Jackson, 'WTO Dispute Procedures, Standard of Review, and Deference to National Governments' (1996) 90(2) Am J Intl L 193; John H Jackson, 'Sovereignty—Modern: A New Approach to an Outdated Concept' (2003) 97 Am J Intl L 782; Gisele Kapterian, 'A Critique of the WTO Jurisprudence on "Necessity" ' (2009) 59 Intl Comp LQ 89.

[38] Appellate Body Report, *European Communities—Measures Prohibiting the Importation and Marketing of Seal Products* (*EC—Seal Products*), WT/DS400/AB/R, WT/DS401/AB/R, 22 May 2014, paras 5.79–5.82.

[39] DiMascio and Pauwelyn (n 9) 65.

[40] Burke-White and von Staden (n 15) 292.

[41] Appellate Body Report, *Thailand—Customs and Fiscal Measures on Cigarettes from the Philippines*, WT/DS371/AB/R, 17 June 2011, para 173: 'an analysis of whether a measure infringes an obligation necessarily precedes, and is distinct from, the "further and separate" assessment of whether such measure is otherwise justified'.

legitimate expectations. Except for the principle of legitimate expectations,[42] these elements for consideration are common with those considered in the examination of GATT Article XX and GATS Article XIV. While the differences between obligation clauses and exceptions such that the burden of proving an exception rests on the party invoking it[43] may have practical implications, they do not affect the correspondence of the elements for consideration described above. Legum and Petculescu observe that:

> [T]here appears to be general congruence between the exception to GATT Article XX and the FET standard. Since it is difficult to imagine a measure that would be a violation of the FET standard and that would not also be viewed as arbitrary under GATT XX, it does not seem that this Article generally brings anything to the existing limitations under the FET standard in international customary law.[44]

They therefore conclude that 'a "general exception" clause similar to GATT Article XX appears not to be particularly well suited to the investment law regime',[45] casting doubt over the recent and increasing tendency to incorporate general exception clauses modelled on the GATT Article XX or GATS Article XIV in international investment agreements.[46] Lévesque generally supports this view by stating that 'general exceptions have a limited role to play in international investment law. I will go as far as to say that there is a risk that such provisions could reduce rather than improve this balance.'[47] The (arguably) limited utility of incorporating general exception clauses into investment treaties does not, however, suggest the limited utility

[42] For the reluctance of the Appellate Body to accept legitimate expectations as a stand-alone principle of treaty interpretation, see Van Damme (n 4) 65–68 and 100–01. See also Barton Legum and Ioana Petculescu, 'GATT Article XX and International Investment Law' in Roberto Echandi and Pierre Sauvé (eds) (n 26) 340, 356. On the other hand, Gourgourinis argues that the examination of the chapeau of art XX is heavily 'influenced by the disciplines of the grandfathered Article X GATT 1994', which consist of largely the same concepts as those considered in the application of the principle of legitimate expectations, such as legal security, stability of the legal and business framework, treatment in an even-handed and just manner, etc. Gourgourinis (n 28) 20–21.

[43] For the importance of exceptions in interpretation and application, see Asif H Qureshi, *Interpreting WTO Agreements: Problems and Perspectives* (CUP 2006) ch 4; Peter Van den Bossche and Werner Zdouc, *The Law and Policy of the World Trade Organization: Text, Cases and Materials* (3rd edn, CUP 2013) 546–47.

[44] Legum and Petculescu (n 42) 355–56. With respect to expropriation, they also argue that 'GATT Article XX largely corresponds to the existing police powers exception ... and so would add little other than the benefit of codification to this discipline' (ibid 362).

[45] ibid 362.

[46] Also there are investment treaties that directly incorporate WTO exceptions by reference to GATT art XX and GATS art XIV, e.g. ASEAN, Australia–New Zealand Free Trade Area Agreement, ch 15, art 1(2).

[47] Céline Lévesque, 'The Inclusion of GATT Article XX Exceptions in IIAs: A Potentially Risky Policy' in Roberto Echandi and Pierre Sauvé (eds) (n 26) 370. In contrast, Newcombe argues that even if general exceptions are implicitly included in the elements for consideration in investment arbitration, it does not necessarily make general exceptions irrelevant in the context of IIAs, as they may 'act as a safety net against overly broad interpretations (by arbitral tribunals)'. Andrew Newcombe, 'General Exceptions in International Investment Agreements' in Marie-Claire Cordonier Segger, Markus W Gehring, and Andrew Newcombe (eds), *Sustainable Development in World Investment Law* (Wolters Kluwer 2011) 370. Kurtz also supports the incorporation of targeted and tailored exceptions—as opposed to an uncritical transplantation—into investment treaties that would allow

of WTO jurisprudence on this issue for the interpretation and application of investment treaties. Quite the contrary, given that examination of whether the measure in question constitutes indirect expropriation or a breach of the FET standard requires a similar balancing exercise to that required in the assessment of general exception clauses, the WTO case law in the context of exception clauses may indeed provide guidance for the interpretation and application of these substantive obligations.

Having demonstrated the theoretical basis for sharing the approach, a question to follow is the benefits to investment arbitration of seeking guidance within WTO jurisprudence. This text asserts that reliance on the approach on how to find the balance adopted by the WTO Appellate Body—with or without explicit reference—will enhance the legitimacy of investment arbitration, as explained in section II.

III. Benefits of Reference to WTO Jurisprudence in Theory

As noted in section I, a point of difference between the WTO dispute settlement system and investment arbitration is the degree of acceptance of its legitimacy. Certainly, the careful structure of the WTO dispute settlement system—in particular, the appeal mechanism, which 'allows a space for deliberation and critique with respect to the panel ruling'[48]—is clearly a major reason for the wide acceptance and support of the system by Member States, as well as scholars.[49] However, equally significant elements are the Appellate Body's continuous effort to achieve coherence and integrity in legal interpretation,[50] and the institutional sensitivity it has developed since its creation.

On the former, the effort for a coherent jurisprudence by the Appellate Body has been reinforced by de facto *stare decisis*,[51] which is explained by the Appellate Body in the *US—Stainless Steel* case as follows:

> [T]he legal interpretation embodied in adopted panel and Appellate Body reports becomes part and parcel of the *acquis* of the WTO dispute settlement system. Ensuring

the freedom of states to regulate for public policy. Kurtz, *The WTO and International Investment Law* (n 32) ch 5.

[48] Howse (n 16) 44.

[49] With this respect, Kuijper observes that '[t]he DSB's real function lies in the debate that follows after the adoption of a panel report ... [t]he debate gives the opportunity to the losing party to let off steam and voice its disappointment'. Pieter-Jan Kuijper, 'WTO Institutional Issues' in Daniel Bethlehem and others (eds), *The Oxford Handbook of International Trade Law* (OUP 2009) 122.

[50] Howse (n 16) 52.

[51] John H Jackson, 'The Case of the World Trade Organization' (2008) 84(3) Intl Aff 437: 'this author thinks that the WTO is not very far below the *stare decisis* top rung of the precedent ladder'. Steinberg (n 5) 254:

> On occasion, the Appellate Body has reached decisions that seem inconsistent with precedent ... However, in general, previous decisions and doctrine are so highly persuasive in WTO jurisprudence, and their use is so central to the discourse of dispute settlement, that it may be said that the WTO observes de facto *stare decisis*.

See also Robert Howse and Efraim Chalamish, 'The Use and Abuse of WTO Law in Investor-State Arbitration: A Reply to Jürgen Kurtz' (2010) 20(4) Eur J Intl L 1087.

'security and predictability' in the dispute settlement system, as contemplated in Article 3.2 of the Dispute Settlement Understandings (DSU), implies that, absent cogent reasons, an adjudicatory body will resolve the same legal question in the same way in a subsequent case.[52]

The fact that the Appellate Body decides by Divisions, rather than in full, has not prevented the achievement of coherence in its case law.[53] Professor Matsushita, in his recent work, clearly explains this point, referring to the 'exchange of views' set out in Rule 4.1 of the Working Procedures for Appellate Review:

> Although in the WTO jurisprudence stare decisis is not recognised, the Appellate Body strives to maintain consistency between a ruling in an appeal and that in subsequent appeals involving the same issue. One way to promote this consistency is to maintain collegiality among members of the Appellate Body and, for this purpose, the exchange of views which occurs in respect of each case is useful.[54]

In addition, Kurtz observes that, in the rare cases where divergent rulings arise, the Appellate Body has offered 'appropriate room for flexibility' for vertical inter-judicial dialogue which 'could conceivably lead to increases in levels of jurisprudential quality, with both WTO panellists and Appellate Body members enhancing their authority and legitimacy in the eyes of states parties'.[55]

The concept of precedence in WTO jurisprudence is 'centrally important to the effectiveness of the WTO dispute settlement procedure goals of security and predictability'.[56] Importantly, predictability 'can lead governments ... to refrain from ... expensive activity if their chances are not very great'.[57]

On the latter point, as early as 2000, Howse observed that in contrast with GATT panels that failed to display institutional sensitivity, in the decision making of the WTO Appellate Body 'we can see a contrasting trend towards institutional sensitivity emerging, although perhaps not as consistently as would be desirable from the perspective of legitimacy'.[58] Later, in 2004, the Consultative Board to the former Director-General Supachai Panitchpakdi acknowledged in its report

[52] Appellate Body Report, *United States—Final Anti-dumping Measures on Stainless Steel from Mexico*, WT/DS344/AB/R, 30 April 2008, para 160. See also Panel Report, *China—Measures Related to the Exportation of Rare Earths, Tungsten, and Molybdenum* (*China—Rare Earths*), WT/DS431-3/R, 26 March 2014.

[53] Álvarez-Jiménez (n 9). See Appellate Body, *Working Procedures for Appellate Review*, WT/AB/WP/6, 16 August 2010, r 4 (Collegiality).

[54] Mitsuo Matsushita, 'Reflections on the Functioning of the Appellate Body' in Gabrielle Marceau (ed), *A History of Law and Lawyers in the GATT/WTO: The Development of the Rule of Law in the Multilateral Trading System* (CUP 2015) 552. It should be noted that Professor Matsushita then proceeds to identify an issue in the present practice of 'exchange': while collegiality would not be maintained if views expressed by other Appellate Body members are not taken into account by a division handling a case, if such views have any bearing on the deliberation of the division, 'those four members should have a chance to hear the claims and arguments of the disputing parties at the oral hearings and get a first-hand impression of the parties' claims' (ibid 552–53).

[55] Kurtz, *The WTO and International Investment Law* (n 32) 237–38.

[56] Report by the Consultative Board (n 7) para 232.

[57] ibid para 224.

[58] Howse (n 16) 64.

that: 'the Appellate Body, from the very beginning of its existence, has indicated through statements in its reports that it is quite cognizant of the need for deference to Members'.[59] Specifically regarding general exception clauses, Marceau observed, in 2006, that:

> Through a new interpretation of exception provisions, our appellate body has managed to operationalize these exception provisions so as to provide members with policy space to administer non-WTO concerns, as long as the invocation of non-WTO concerns are not disguised protectionism.[60]

It is therefore safely concluded that there is wide recognition of the continuous effort of the Appellate Body to respect the policy space for Member States to protect public interests.

This is in contrast to the distrust in investment arbitration described above, which results from the concern that tribunals have failed to develop a consistent and reasoned approach towards interpretation, and have not demonstrated sufficient deference to the sovereign right to regulate.[61] This has led to concerns over the legitimacy of investment arbitration, such that 'the lack of familiarity with national context and the lack of public law experience of ICSID tribunals can undermine those tribunals' perceived legitimacy.'[62] In terms of treaty interpretation, the legitimacy concern is expressed as the concern that investment arbitration tribunals interpret and apply investment treaties in a particular manner to justify personal views of the arbitrators as to the role and function of investment treaties.[63]

On the other hand, in most cases, it is in fact not the actual 'bias in favour of investors' on the part of investment arbitration tribunals, but the lack of consistent reasoning that sufficiently demonstrates their deferential approach that lies behind such concerns. It is aptly observed that:

> The most persistent and troubling adjudicatory flaw is not … a crude pro-investor bias. The real concern lies in the choice of hermeneutics and especially the stubborn tendency to preference outcome over process in reasoning (as is often naturally the case in commercial arbitration). Those practices are problematic for several reasons, not least the obvious failure

[59] Report by the Consultative Board (n 7) para 130.

[60] Gabrielle Marceau, 'The WTO is NOT a Closed Box' (2006) 100 Am Socy Intl L Proceedings 29, 30.

[61] Kurtz observes that '[o]ne of the most striking differences between the two systems (the WTO and investment arbitration) turns on the question of express flexibilities for public regulation', *The WTO and International Investment Law* (n 32) 281.

[62] Burke-White and von Staden (n 15) 332.

[63] Jürgen Kurtz, 'Adjudging the Exceptional at International Investment Law: Security, Public Order and Financial Crisis' (2010) 59 Intl Comp LQ 325, 350; Kurtz, *The WTO and International Investment Law* (n 32) 5. Solanes and Jouravlev also observe that the expansive interpretation of foreign investor rights 'is the result of decisions, which do not relate their content to either state practice, or the internal national law of sets of representative States. It is, rather, a circular evolution that takes place on its own, resulting from the decisions themselves.' Miguel Solanes and Andrei Jouravlev, *Revisiting Privatization, Foreign Investment, International Arbitration, and Water* (United Nations Publications 2007) 68.

of many arbitral tribunals to follow the interpretative taxonomy mandated by the Vienna Convention on the Law of Treaties (VCLT).[64]

Indeed, statistics by UNCTAD and ICSID on the outcomes of the known cases of investment arbitration indicate that a larger number of cases were decided in favour of the host state than those in favour of investors. For example, the UNCTAD World Investment Report 2015 states that:

> Out of these (405 concluded cases), 36 per cent (144 cases) were decided in favour of the State (all claims dismissed either on jurisdictional grounds or on the merits), and 27 per cent (111 cases) ended in favour of the investor (monetary compensation awarded). Approximately 26 per cent of cases (105) were settled and 9 per cent of claims (37) discontinued for reasons other than settlement (or for unknown reasons). In the remaining 2 per cent (8 cases), a treaty breach was found but no monetary compensation was awarded to the investor.[65]

Nevertheless, without the clear expression of 'public law sensibilities' by investment arbitration tribunals, the outcomes, however fair they may be, are insufficient to address the distrust of investment arbitration as a whole.

These considerations support the instant proposition that incorporating the approach developed by the WTO Appellate Body in investment arbitration will help investment arbitration tribunals to address the 'legitimacy concern' of investment arbitration. Section IV demonstrates the 'deferential approach' by the WTO Appellate Body by assessing its jurisprudence on GATT XX and GATS XIV, and examines the implications of this approach on the interpretation of the fair and equitable standard of treatment and indirect expropriation. While WTO jurisprudence on SPS and TBT Agreements may also provide useful guidance, the examination of this chapter is limited to the general exception clauses. In addition, this text focuses on the recognition of the right of the Member States to determine the level of protection and its impact on the interpretation of the term 'necessary' (GATT Article XX(a)(b)(d) and GATS Article XIV(a) to (c)).

[64] Jürgen Kurtz, 'The Shifting Landscape of International Investment Law and Its Commentary' (2012) 106(3) Am J Intl L 686, 688. Review article for Kenneth J Vandevelde, *Bilateral Investment Treaties: History, Policy, and Interpretation* (OUP 2010); Jeswald W Salacuse, *The Law of Investment Treaties* (OUP 2010); and Stephan W Schill (ed), *International Investment Law and Comparative Public Law* (OUP 2010).

[65] UNCTAD, 'World Investment Report 2015' (n 2) 116. According to the ICSID statistic, the ratio is as follows: Award upholding claims in part or in full (46%); Award dismissing all claims (28%); Award declining jurisdiction (25%); Award deciding that the claims are manifestly without legal merit (1%). ICSID, 'The ICSID Caseload' (n 3) 14. It should be noted, however, that these statistics may also have different implications, as illustrated by the following reading of the UNCTAD report result: 'despite the oft-heard refrain that "states 'win' more often than they lose," it is the investors that have actually won most of the time: 72 per cent of the decisions on jurisdiction, and 60 per cent of cases decided on the merits'. Howard Mann, 'ISDS: Who Wins More, Investors or States?' (June 2015) <http://www.iisd.org/itn/wp-content/uploads/2015/06/itn-breaking-news-june-2015-isds-who-wins-more-investors-or-state.pdf> accessed 7 April 2016.

IV. Benefits of Reference to WTO Jurisprudence in Application

Deference to the state's policy space has been consistently found in the jurisprudence of the Appellate Body on GATT XX and GATS XIV. The fact that reliance on GATT XX has actually resulted in limited success does not alter the existence of such deference, because (otherwise) GATT-inconsistent measures that clearly meet the requirements of Article XX seldom go to WTO dispute settlement.[66] It is observed that this fact 'does not indicate that Article XX plays only a marginal role in allowing WTO members to adopt or maintain otherwise GATT-inconsistent measures to promote or protect societal values. Rather, the opposite is true.'[67]

This deferential approach finds its reflection in various elements of the assessment of general exceptions. It is arguably found in the Appellate Body's expression on the standard of review in the WTO context.[68] In *EC—Hormones*, it stated that the applicable standard of review applicable to all WTO agreements with regard to factual issues[69] 'is neither "de novo review" nor "total deference", but rather the "objective assessment of the facts" '.[70] This expression is admittedly far from a clear legal doctrine on the standard of review,[71] yet the rejection of 'total' deference suggests that deference is not excluded in 'objective assessment' within the meaning of Article 11 DSU.[72]

[66] Van den Bossche and Zdouc (n 43) 553. See also Report by the Consultative Board (n 7) para 223:

> less than half the complaints actually go on to a panel process. The remaining cases undoubtedly include a number of complaints that are settled, but also some complaints that are merely dropped or otherwise disposed of.

[67] Van den Bossche and Zdouc (n 43) 553.

[68] It is, however, observed that 'a principled legal doctrine on the standard of review in the WTO context has not yet been formulated.' Kapterian (n 37) 98.

[69] The Appellate Body noted that the Anti-dumping Agreement was indeed the only WTO text explicitly prescribing a particular standard of review, yet this standard was specific to the Agreement. G Axel Desmedt, 'Hormones: "Objective Assessment" and (or as) Standard of Review' (1998) 1(4) J Intl Econ L 695, 696.

[70] Appellate Body Report, *European Community—Measures Concerning Meat and Meat Products (Hormones)* (*EC—Hormones*), WT/DS26/AB/R, WT/DS48/AB/R, 16 January 1998, para 117.

[71] Kapterian (n 37) 98. In this regard, Burke-White and von Staden propose the importation of a standard of review based on the margin of appreciation, arguing that it 'would better align with the character of both public law disputes and investor–state arbitral tribunals, thereby enhancing much needed perceptions of legitimacy in the ICSID system'. Burke-White and von Staden (n 15) 286–87. See also Choudhury (n 16) 823–27. In contrast, Kurtz argues that, given the different institutional context of different legal regimes, considerable caution should be exercised in relying on the standards of review developed by European courts in investment arbitration. Kurtz, 'Adjudging the Exceptional at International Investment Law' (n 63) 367–68.

[72] See e.g., *China—Rare Earths* (n 52) para 7.145: 'Panels and the Appellate Body have examined both the "design" and "structure" of a challenged measure to decide whether its "objective" is the protection of life and health, generally showing a degree of deference to Members' policies designed to "protect human, animal or plant life or health".' See Desmedt (n 69) 698. Croley and Jackson observe that the language of DSU art 3.2 ('Recommendations and rulings of the DSB cannot add to or diminish the rights and obligations provided in the covered agreements') 'could be interpreted as a constraint on the standard of review, but possibly not to the extent of art 17.6 of the Anti-dumping Agreement'. Croley and Jackson (n 37) 200.

Naturally, the question of where the standard is to be found between the two extremes—'de novo review' and 'total deference'—needs to be clarified through the adjudication of particular cases. Subsection IV.A will examine the Appellate Body's approach on the right of the Member States to determine the level of protection and its impact on the interpretation of the term 'necessary', to demonstrate the deferential approach by the Appellate Body with regard to the regulatory autonomy of national authorities.

A. The right of the Member States to determine the level of protection and the 'necessity' requirement

The ten exceptions under GATT Article XX all require the relationship between public policy objectives and GATT-inconsistent measures by different terms ('necessary' (a, b, d); 'relating to' (c, e); 'imposed for' (f); 'undertaken in pursuance of' (h); and 'essential to' (j)). As noted by the Appellate Body in *US—Gasoline*, it is reasonably assumed that, with respect to each and every category, a different kind or degree of connection or relationship between the measure and the state policy is required.[73] Of these, the term 'necessary' suggests a relatively strict degree of connection,[74] yet in this respect, the Appellate Body's 'move away' from the rigid interpretation of 'necessary' by GATT panels is particularly significant. The *United States—Section 337* panel adopted the interpretation that the measure is only 'necessary' if it is the least possible derogation from the GATT, by stating that 'in cases where a measure consistent with other GATT provisions is not reasonably available, a contracting party is bound to use, among the measures reasonably available to it, that which entails the least degree of inconsistency with other GATT provisions'.[75] In applying this test, the panel did not examine whether the alleged alternative measures could achieve the level of protection (enforcement) desired by the United States.[76] This approach, which was followed by subsequent GATT panels,[77]

[73] Appellate Body Report, *United States—Standards for Reformulated and Conventional Gasoline* (*US—Gasoline*), WT/DS2/AB/R, 29 April 1996, 18.

[74] In *Korea—Beef*, the Appellate Body distinguished 'necessary' in art XX(d) from 'the more flexible "relating to" standard of Article XX(g)'. Appellate Body Report, *Korea—Various Measures on Beef* (*Korea—Beef*), WT/DS161/AB/R, WT/DS169/AB/R, 10 January 2001, paras 161–62 (including fn 104). Cf Professor Matsushita observes that art XX(b) does not require the 'even-handedness' principle required in art XX(g), i.e. the requirement that measures controlling international trade of products for the purpose of conserving exhaustible natural resources be made in conjunction with restrictions on domestic production or consumption of those natural resources. Mitsuo Matsushita, 'Export Control of Natural Resources—WTO Panel Ruling on the Chinese Export Restrictions of Natural Resources' (2011) 3(2) Trade, L & Dev 267.

[75] Panel Report, *United States—Section 337 of the Tariff Act of 1930*, L/6439–36S/345, 7 November, 1989, para 5.26.

[76] ibid para 5.33. See also Kapterian (n 37) 101.

[77] e.g. Report of the Panel, *United States—Measures Affecting Alcoholic and Malt Beverages* (*US—Malt Beverages*), BISD 39S/206, 19 June 1992, para 5.52; and Report of the Panel, *Thailand—Restrictions on Importation of and Internal Taxes on Cigarettes* (*Thailand—Cigarettes*), BISD 37S/200, 7 November 1990, para 223. Also, the panel in the *Tuna-Dolphin* case concluded that the contested US measures would not meet the requirement of necessity set out in art XX(b) as '[t]he

does not pay due regard to the right of Member States to choose their level of protection.[78]

The Appellate Body departed from this 'trade trumps' approach and moved towards a more deferential approach in assessing the 'necessity' requirement. First, it adopted the principle that a Member State is entitled to choose its own level of protection according to its own circumstances in pursuing legitimate public policy goals, even in the absence of the provisions that presume such rights of Member States.[79] Implicit recognition of this deferential approach is found in the first Appellate Body report in *US—Gasoline*, in which it stated:

> WTO Members have a large measure of autonomy to determine their own policies on the environment (including its relationship with trade), their environmental objectives and the environmental legislation they enact and implement.[80]

When interpreting the term 'necessary' in Article XX(d) in *Korea—Beef*, the Appellate Body recognized the right of Member States 'to determine for themselves the level of enforcement of their WTO-consistent laws and regulations'.[81] In subsequent cases, the Appellate Body has clearly acknowledged the right of the Member States to determine the level of protection of certain public interests listed in GATT Article XX or GATS Article XIV that they consider appropriate (for example, *EC—Asbestos* (on GATT Article XX(b)[82]), *US—Gambling* (on GATS Article XIV(a)[83]), *Dominican Republic—Cigarettes* (on GATT Article XX(d)),[84] *Brazil—Tyres* (on GATT Article XX(b)),[85] and *EC—Seal Products* (on GATT Article XX(a))).[86]

United States had not demonstrated ... that it had exhausted all options reasonably available to it to pursue its dolphin protection objectives'. Panel Report, *United States—Restrictions on Imports of Tuna*, DS21/R–39S/155, 3 September 1991, para 5.28. See Thomas J Schoenbaum, 'International Trade and Protection of the Environment: The Continuing Search for Reconciliation' (1997) 91(2) Am J Intl L 268.

[78] Kapterian (n 37) 102.

[79] e.g. art 5.6 of the SPS Agreement; art 2.2 of the TBT Agreement. See also Appellate Body Report, *Australia—Measures Affecting Importation of Salmon* (*Australia—Salmon*), WT/DS18/AB/R, 20 October 1998, paras 199–204; Joanne Scott, *The WTO Agreement on Sanitary and Phytosanitary Measures* (OUP 2007) 35–38.

[80] *US—Gasoline* (n 73) 30.

[81] *Korea—Beef* (n 74) para 176.

[82] Appellate Body Report, *European Communities—Measures Affecting Asbestos and Products Containing Asbestos* (*EC—Asbestos*), WT/DS135/AB/R, 12 March 2001, para 168: 'it is undisputed that WTO Members have the right to determine the level of protection of health that they consider appropriate in a given situation'.

[83] Appellate Body Report, *United States—Measures Affecting the Cross-border Supply of Gambling and Betting Services* (*US—Gambling*), WT/DS285/AB/R, 7 April 2005, para 308: 'a "reasonably available" alternative measure must be a measure that would preserve for the responding Member its right to achieve its desired level of protection with respect to the objective pursued under paragraph (a) of Article XIV'.

[84] Appellate Body Report, *Dominican Republic—Measures Affecting the Importation and Internal Sale of Cigarettes*, WT/DS302/AB/R, 25 April 2005, para 70.

[85] Appellate Body Report, *Brazil—Measures Affecting Imports of Retreaded Tyres* (*Brazil—Tyres*), WT/DS332/AB/R, 3 December 2007, para 156.

[86] *EC—Seal Products* (n 38) para 5.200.

This principle gives significant flexibility to the interpretation of the term 'necessary', because it is understood not to require a government to compromise the full achievement of its desired level of protection.[87] In *Korea—Beef*, the Appellate Body assessed whether alternative measures would secure the same—*desired*—level of protection as the actual measure.[88] It is observed that this approach is not the standard cost–benefit analysis, because it 'does not involve balancing the achievement of the underlying goal of the measure against the trade costs', and 'the only alternatives that are eligible for consideration are those that achieve the same amount of the underlying goal'.[89] Regan summarizes the Appellate Body's approach in *Korea—Beef* as follows:

> If there is no less trade-restrictive way to achieve the chosen level of protection without unreasonable administrative/enforcement cost, the actual measure is legal, period. There is no logical space left for cost–benefit balancing with the underlying goal.[90]

In *EC—Asbestos*, the Appellate Body developed this new prong of the necessity test by acknowledging that a risk assessment, which forms the basis of the determination of the level of protection 'that they consider appropriate in a given situation',[91] may be evaluated either in quantitative (i.e. is it regarded as socially acceptable) or qualitative (i.e. how likely is it) terms.[92] In the context of the SPS Agreement, the Appellate Body had already made it clear that risk assessment should take into account qualitative elements as well as quantitative information,[93] and in this case, it applied the same approach to GATT Article XX(b).[94] This approach allows greater leeway for regulatory policy of the Member States, because the public perception of risk is wider than that of experts, and reflects a number of legitimate concerns.

The Appellate Body in *Brazil—Tyres* furthered this deferential approach in the assessment of the 'necessary' test on several accounts. First, it introduced the concept of 'material contribution', by stating, inter alia, that: 'a panel might conclude that an import ban is necessary on the basis of a demonstration that the import ban at issue is apt to produce a material contribution to the achievement of its objective'.[95] This concept is explained by the Appellate Body as follows: 'a contribution exists when there is a genuine relationship of ends and means between the

[87] Jan Neumann and Elizabeth Türk, 'Necessity Revisited: Proportionality in World Trade Organization Law after *Korea—Beef*, *EC—Asbestos*, and *EC—Sardines*' (2003) 37(1) J World Trade 199, 208–09.

[88] *Korea—Beef* (n 74) para 180.

[89] Donald H Regan, 'The Meaning of "Necessary" in GATT Article XX and GATS Article XIV: The Myth of Cost–Benefit Balancing' (2007) 6(3) World Trade Rev 347, 349. He describes the Appellate Body's approach as follows: 'the actual measure is "necessary" if every alternative measure that achieves the same level of the ultimate goal at lesser trade cost entails unreasonable administrative/ enforcement cost'. ibid 349.

[90] ibid 351–52.

[91] *EC—Asbestos* (n 82) para 180.

[92] ibid paras 167–68. The Appellate Body also clearly stated that there would be no reasonably available alternative if the suggested alternative measures could not achieve the chosen level of health protection (ibid para 174). See also Patricia Birnie and others, *International Law & the Environment* (3rd edn, OUP 2009) 774.

[93] *EC—Hormones* (n 70) paras 187, 194; *Australia—Salmon, Appellate Report* (n 79) para 124.

[94] *EC—Asbestos* (n 82) para 167: '... as with the SPS Agreement, there is no requirement under Article XX(b) of the GATT 1994 to quantify, as such, the risk to human life or health'.

[95] *Brazil—Tyres* (n 85) para 151.

objective pursued and the measure at issue', and for the measure to be characterized as necessary, 'its contribution to the achievement of the objective must be material, not merely marginal or insignificant, especially if the measure at issue is as trade restrictive as an import ban'.[96] Second, the Appellate Body rejected the idea that 'an import ban, or another trade-restrictive measure, the contribution of which is not immediately observable, cannot be justified under Article XX(b)'.[97] Even where a single measure in isolation is insufficient to materially contribute to the stated objective, it may still do '[a]s a key component of a comprehensive policy (comprising a multiplicity of interacting measures)', because certain complex public health or environmental problems may be tackled only with such comprehensive policy.[98] On this approach, Van Damme observes that:

> The generality of parts of the Appellate Body's analysis demonstrates its intention to guarantee the negative integration that the WTO covered agreements aim to achieve and to allow WTO Members the necessary policy space to react to new global problems, left untouched by WTO law. It signalled that individual measures would be tested against the background of these more general policies.[99]

Third, the Appellate Body accepted the qualitative hypothesis adopted by the panel that the import ban would increase the demand for domestically re-treaded tyres and a higher production of such tyres would result in waste reduction, at least in the short term.[100] Fourth, the Appellate Body acknowledged the relevance of Member States' level of economic development and available resources in the assessment of the existence/absence of reasonably available alternatives, by stating that:

> [T]he capacity of a country to implement remedial measures that would be particularly costly, or would require advanced technologies, may be relevant to the assessment of whether such measures or practices are reasonably available alternatives to a preventive measure, such as the Import Ban, which does not involve 'prohibitive costs or substantial technical difficulties'.[101]

[96] ibid para 210.

[97] ibid para 151. Certain flexibility in the interpretation of the terms 'to secure compliance' under art XX(d) is found in *Mexico—Soft Drinks*, where the Appellate Body stated that: 'a measure can be said to be designed "to secure compliance" even if the measure cannot be guaranteed to achieve its result with absolute certainty.' Appellate Body Report, *Mexico—Tax Measures on Soft Drinks and other Beverages*, WT/DS308/AB/R, 6 March 2006, para 74.

[98] *Brazil—Tyres* (n 85) paras 210, 151. This approach has been followed by, e.g., Panel Report, *China—Measures Related to the Exportation of Various Raw Materials*, WT/DS394/R, WT/DS395/R, WT/DS398/R, 5 July 2011, paras 7.374–7.376, 7.484, 7.517. See also J Craig Barker and Isabelle Van Damme, 'Appellate Body Report, *Brazil— Measures Affecting Imports of Retreaded Tyres*, Adopted on 17 December 2007' (2008) 57(3) Intl Comp LQ 710, 714–15.

[99] Van Damme (n 4) 299.

[100] *Brazil—Tyres* (n 85) para 153. The Appellate Body, however, noted quantitative estimates of the reduction of waste tyres that would result from the import ban would have strengthened the foundation of the panel's findings (ibid).

[101] *Brazil—Tyres* (n 85) para 171. See Kevin R Gray, 'Measures Affecting Imports of Retreaded Tyres' (2008) 102(3) Am J Intl L 610, 613 and 616. It should also be noted that the panel in *EC—Asbestos* also stated that the identification of reasonable alternatives is to be undertaken in the light of economic and administrative realities of the relevant state (*EC—Asbestos* (n 82) para 207). See Jan McDonald, 'Tr(e)ading Cautiously: Precaution in WTO Decision Making' in Elizabeth Fisher

Overall, it has been observed that the reasoning of the Appellate Body in this case 'demonstrated a concerted effort to take account of the complexity of regulatory environments.'[102]

This approach was endorsed by the recent Appellate Body report in *EC—Seal Products* in the context of GATT Article XX(a), in which the Appellate Body noted 'that the panel in *US—Gambling* underscored that Members have the right to determine the level of protection that they consider appropriate, which suggests that Members may set different levels of protection even when responding to similar interests of moral concern'.[103] On the concept of 'material contribution' that the Appellate Body introduced in *Brazil—Tyres*, it stated that a measure's contribution is 'only one component of the necessity calculus under Article XX', and adopted a flexible 'holistic necessity analysis', which involves a consideration of potential alternative measures, 'the nature, quantity, and quality of evidence, and whether a panel's analysis is performed in quantitative or qualitative terms'.[104] On this basis, the Appellate Body rejected the contention of Canada and Norway that 'the Panel was required to apply a standard of "materiality" as a generally applicable predetermined threshold in its contribution analysis'.[105]

Certainly, the Appellate Body's approach in interpreting general exception clauses is not free from criticism. For example, some argue that the Appellate Body's approach to examine the 'value-judging aspect',[106] i.e. the relative importance of non-protectionist goals of the contested measure,[107] is 'a serious intrusion' on the Members' regulatory autonomy.[108] However, given that the concept of public purpose is 'not subject to effective reexamination by other states',[109] the

and others (eds), *Implementing the Precautionary Principle: Perspectives and Prospects* (Edward Elgar 2006) 160–81.

102 Kapterian (n 37) 114. On the other hand, he points out that this reasoning 'may be argued to fall foul of consistency with the treaty text as this lower threshold diminishes the distinctions between the ten sub-clauses of article XX.' ibid. Gray also observes that the Appellate Body's decision 'arguably broadens the scope of Article XX by showing some deference to the nontrade policy objectives of WTO members and a greater appreciation of the complexity of environmental problems and the associated need for a comprehensive response involving a variety of measures.' Gray (n 101) 616.

103 *EC—Seal Products* (n 38) para 5.200.

104 ibid para 5.215.

105 ibid para 5.216. Other recent cases include *China—Publications*, in which the panel, while concluding that the measure at issue not 'necessary' within the meaning of art XX(a) due to the availability of a less trade-respective alternative measure proposed by the United States (this conclusion was upheld by the Appellate Body), began its analysis of the necessity requirement by acknowledging that 'the US proposal would allow China to achieve its desired high level of protection of public morals'. Panel Report, *China—Measures Affecting Trading Rights and Distribution Services for Certain Publications and Audiovisual Entertainment Products*, WT/DS363/R, 12 August 2009, para 7.894.

106 Kapterian (n 37) 110.

107 *Korea—Beef* (n 74) para 162: '[t]he more vital or important [the] common interests or values' pursued, the easier it would be to accept as 'necessary' measures designed to achieve those ends. See also *EC—Asbestos* (n 82) para 172; *US—Gambling* (n 83) para 306.

108 Regan (n 89) 349; Neumann and Türk (n 87) 214. For a contrasting view, see DiMascio and Pauwelyn (n 9) 87.

109 American Law Institute (ed), *Restatement (Third) of the Foreign Relations Law of the United States* (1987) vol 2, 200, s 712, cmt (e). This difficulty was recognized as early as 1961 in Harvard Draft Article No 12, 18 February 1961: 'it is extremely difficult to conceive of a situation where an

examination of the value of the stated goals of the contested measure is inevitable. For the purposes of this chapter, it should be noted that this is even more so in the context of investment treaties, which typically do not include an exhaustive list of legitimate objectives equivalent to GATT Article XX or GATS Article XIV, and therefore it is nearly always possible for the host state to claim the existence of some public purpose.

The overview of the case law of the Appellate Body on general exception clauses, therefore, demonstrates that it has fairly consistently endorsed and practised the principle of deference to national governments in both fact-finding of the case and interpreting general exception clauses. Indeed, it is observed that '[g]eneral claims of a bias towards a free trade agenda ... often are not sufficiently substantiated'.[110]

On this basis, subsection IV.B examines how WTO jurisprudence in this context actually informs investment arbitration tribunals in the interpretation of the FET standard and indirect expropriation.

B. Implications for investment arbitration

As noted above, there is general congruence between the general exceptions in the WTO and the FET standard and indirect expropriation in investment treaties, in that both require the examination of the quantitative considerations (the effect of the measure) against qualitative considerations (the purpose and context of the measure)[111] in the assessment of proportionality. In investment arbitration, the proportionality principle was introduced into investment treaty arbitration[112] by the *Tecmed v Mexico* tribunal in the context of indirect expropriation in the following terms: 'there must be a reasonable relationship of proportionality between the change or weight imposed to [sic] the foreign investor and the aim sought to be realized by any expropriatory measure'.[113] The tribunal found that, in this case, there was no 'serious urgent situation, crisis, need or social emergency' that could be 'weighed against the deprivation or neutralisation of the economic or commercial value of the Claimant's investment', and concluded accordingly that the measures amounted to expropriation. The endorsement of the proportionality principle has then been followed by subsequent cases, including *Azrix v Argentina*,[114] *LG&E*

international tribunal would undertake to review a state's determination of what is a dominating public purpose except in a situation so flagrant that the procedure involves a manifest denial of procedural justice'.

110 Van Damme (n 4) 302.

111 Francesco Costamagna, 'Legitimate Regulation vs Regulatory Expropriation in Pubic Infrastructure Investments after Azurix' (2007) 4(2) Transnatl Disp Management.

112 It should be noted that relevant investment treaty (Spain–Mexico BIT) did not contain any requirement of proportionality.

113 *Tecnicas Medioambientales TECMED SA v Mexico*, ICSID Case No ARB (AF)/00/2, Award (29 May 2003), para 122. The tribunal referred to the following ECtHR cases: *Matos e Silva Lda v Portugal* (1997) 24 EHRR 573; *Mellacher v Austria* (1989) 12 EHRR 391; *Pressos Compania Naviera SA v Belgium* (1996) 21 EHRR 301; *James v UK* (1986) 8 EHRR 123.

114 *Azurix Corp v Argentine Republic*, ICSID Case No ARB/01/12, Award (14 July 2006), paras 311–12.

v Argentina,[115] *Deutsche Bank v Sri Lanka*,[116] and *Occidental v Ecuador*,[117] in the context of both indirect expropriation and the FET standard.

It is often argued that the proportionality principle in a broad sense consists of the following three sub-principles: suitability, necessity, and proportionality *stricto sensu*.[118] Of these sub-principles, the suitability test, which requires that the means must be suitable to achieve its legitimate objectives, is 'of secondary importance since it concerns only the relationship between the end and the means',[119] and in many cases will be subsumed by the requirement of public purpose.[120] The necessity test is generally understood to require that, if another means is less restrictive, yet capable of producing the same result, such means should be adopted. It comprises two questions: (i) whether there are less restrictive alternative measures; and (ii) whether the alternative measures are equally effective in achieving the pursued objective.[121] Yet it is unclear how strictly the existence and effectiveness of the 'less restrictive alternatives' should be assessed. The essence of proportionality *stricto sensu* is a balancing between the measure's objectives and adverse consequences on the affected investor's interest.[122] It may well provide an assessment framework, but this should not mean that the tribunals can freely conduct a general balancing test.[123]

Here, it is argued that the deferential approach of the WTO Appellate Body on the necessity requirement provides helpful guidance with investment arbitration tribunals in the assessment of the second element of the proportionality principle—that is, necessity—which is understood in the form of a sliding scale

[115] *LG&E Energy Corp, LG&E Capital Corp and LG&E International Inc v Argentine Republic*, ICSID Case No ARB/02/1, Decision on Liability (3 October 2006), para 195.

[116] *Deutsche Bank AG v Democratic Socialist Republic of Sri Lanka*, ICSID Case No ARB/09/2, Award (31 October 2012), para 522.

[117] *Occidental Petroleum Corporation and Occidental Exploration and Production Company v The Republic of Ecuador* (*Occidental v Ecuador*), ICSID Case No ARB/06/11, Award (5 October 2012), paras 404–08, 427, 452.

[118] Jürgen Schwarze, *European Administrative Law* (rev edn, Sweet & Maxwell 2006) 854–60; Takis Tridimas, 'Proportionality in Community Law: Searching for the Appropriate Standard of Scrutiny' in Evelyn Ellis (ed), *The Principle of Proportionality in the Laws of Europe* (OUP 1999) 65, 68; Yutaka Arai-Takahashi, *The Margin of Appreciation Doctrine and the Principle of Proportionality in the Jurisprudence of the ECHR* (OUP 2002) 192; Harry Woolf and Jeffrey L Jowell, *De Smith, Woolf & Jowell's Principles of Judicial Review* (Sweet & Maxwell 1999) 504–06; Neumann and Türk (n 87) 203 ('[t]he ECJ proportionality test consists of three steps: effectiveness, necessity and proportionality *strictu sensu*').

[119] Schwarze (n 118) 855–56.

[120] The suitability may also be challenged on the ground that the proposed measure is impossible to apply in practice, e.g. Case C-331/88, *Fedesa* [1990] ECR I-4023.

[121] Federico Ortino, *Basic Legal Instruments for the Liberalisation of Trade: A Comparative Analysis of EC and WTO Law* (OUP 2004) 471.

[122] Proportionality *stricto sensu* does not demand the strict necessity but demands that 'the means does not have excessive restrictive effects on the applicant's interests, comparing with the interest pursued by it'. Han Xiuli, 'The Application of the Principle of Proportionality in *Tecmed v Mexico*' (2007) 6(3) Chinese J Intl L 635, 637.

[123] Neumann and Türk argue that a general balancing of constitutional values needs democratic legitimacy and therefore 'the WTO is not ready for classical proportionality from an institutional perspective'. Neumann and Türk (n 87) 232–33.

from the strictest to the most flexible test. This chapter does not aim to provide a comprehensive analysis of the application of the proportionality principle by investment arbitration tribunals; nor does it aim to second-guess the outcome of particular cases or criticize the conclusions reached by investment arbitration tribunals. The aim of the analysis in this section is more modest and limited: to provide a few examples of the reasoning of investment arbitration tribunals on the proportionality principle, and to examine how the Appellate Body's approach, had it been consulted, could have guided investment arbitration tribunals in applying the proportionality principle in a manner that is more flexible, nuanced, and deferential to the host state's regulatory power than in present case law. In doing so, the following analysis focuses on certain elements of the necessity test that reflect the deferential approach identified in subsection IV.A: the recognition that there is no reasonably available alternative if the suggested alternative measure may not achieve the *chosen* level of protection; the qualitative risk assessment; the assessment of the contested measure against the background of these more general policies; the acknowledgment of the relevance of Member States' levels of economic development; and available resources in the assessment of the existence/absence of reasonably available alternatives.

In *Tecmed v Mexico*, the relevant issue was whether the refusal to renew the permit to operate a landfill of hazardous industrial waste for reasons related to environmental concerns (in particular) amounted to indirect expropriation. The tribunal answered this question in the affirmative, applying the proportionality principle. In the application of the principle, the tribunal appears to have adopted the strict necessity test, according to which a measure is only proportional if there are *no* measures that impair investment less, by requiring the 'availability of measures which cause less of a burden for the investor' as a necessary element of proportionality.[124]

In the more recent *Occidental v Ecuador* case, the relevant measure was the termination of the relevant contract by the host state in response to the claimant's violation of Ecuadorian law. The tribunal applied the proportionality principle in the following way: it first identified several options as alternatives to the contested measure, and concluded, without any comparison between the measure and such alternatives, that the termination was not a proportionate response to the claimant's violation of domestic law, 'the Respondent's argument that there was really no option but to terminate is unsound and it is not accepted'.[125] Notably, with respect to one such alternative, the tribunal stated

[124] Anne K Hoffmann, 'Indirect Expropriation' in August Reinisch (ed), *Standards of Investment Protection* (OUP 2008) 151, 164. Cf Newcombe and Paradell argue that the tribunal's reference to a 'reasonable relationship of proportionality' between legitimate government aim and the measure in question (para 122) indicates that '[t]his standard appears to lie somewhere between the requirement that there be a plausible basis for the measure and the requirement that the measure be the least restrictive necessary in order to meet the objectives of the government'. Andrew Newcombe and Lluís Paradell, *Law and Practice of Investment Treaties: Standards of Treatment* (Kluwer Law International 2009) 365.

[125] *Occidental v Ecuador* (n 117) para 436.

that '[n]o doubt this option was viewed by the Respondent as unpalatable and unrealistic, but as a matter of logic such an option did exist'.[126]

It is argued here that the brusque approach to the proportionality principle by these tribunals would have changed by incorporating WTO jurisprudence in the necessity test. Taking into account the elements developed by the Appellate Body in this context, such as the recognition of the right of states to determine the level of protection and the acknowledgment of the relevance of states' levels of economic development and available resources, would have guided them towards reasoning (even if the conclusion is the same) that demonstrates greater sensitivity and deference to the decisions of the host state.

Also, in applying the proportionality principle, the *Tecmed* tribunal did not bring the environmental issue to centre-stage on the finding that the true reason for refusing to renew the permit was the 'socio-political' circumstances surrounding the landfill (i.e. the opposition by the local community), rather than the environmental and public health concerns. As noted, the qualitative risk assessment endorsed by the Appellate Body in the application of the necessity test considers social and political choices of what is an acceptable level of risk.[127] This approach, if incorporated by the tribunal, would have brought changes to its blatant rejection of the relevance of environmental issues.

Moreover, there are considerations that suggest that investment arbitration tribunals should be even more sensitive to sovereign regulatory power than the WTO adjudicatory bodies. First, while the WTO general exception clauses have exhaustive lists of general public policy exceptions with linking words such as 'necessary', under most investment treaties, the necessity test has been employed as an operative element of the proportionality principle applied to judge the legality of a measure without an exception clause. It follows that investment arbitration tribunals may take into account any legitimate policy objective, which gives the tribunals more flexibility in applying the proportionality principle. Second, as DiMascio and Pauwelyn point out, investments have a broader impact on economy and society of the host state than trade, because the former introduces 'the producer or the production process' in the host country's economy and social fabric.[128] This means that more extensive regulation may be required for investments than trade, which

[126] ibid para 435.

[127] On the qualitative risk assessment, see e.g., Elizabeth Fisher, 'Is the Precautionary Principle Justiciable?' (2001) 13 J Envtl L 315; Nicolas De Sadeleer, *Environmental Principles: From Political Slogans to Legal Rules* (OUP 2002) 190; Nicolas De Sadeleer, 'The Precautionary Principle in European Community Health and Environmental Law: Sword or Shield for the Nordic Countries?' in Niclolas De Sadeleer (ed), *Implementing the Precautionary Principle: Approaches from the Nordic Countries, EU and USA* (Earthscan Publications Ltd 2007) 10, 19; European Commission, 'Communication from the Commission on the Precautionary Principle' (Communication) COM(2000) 1, para 5:

> [d]ecision-makers need to be aware of the degree of uncertainty attached to the results of the evaluation of the available scientific information. Judging what is an 'acceptable' level of risk for society is an eminently political responsibility. Decision-makers faced with an unacceptable risk, scientific uncertainty and public concerns have a duty to find answers. Therefore, all these factors have to be taken into consideration.

[128] DiMascio and Pauwelyn (n 9) 57.

warrants 'more deference to the regulating state in investor–state disputes than in trade disputes'.[129]

Given these considerations, when applying—where relevant—the proportionality principle, investment arbitration tribunals should refer to the Appellate Body's deferential approach as the initial guidance in the assessment of the necessity test as a component of the principle.[130] The tribunal should then proceed to the examination of the existence/absence of the alleged breach of the FET standard or indirect expropriation, taking into account the specific circumstances of the case—in particular, the impact of the foreign investments at issue on the public interests of the host state. This approach allows investment arbitration tribunals to depart from the strict application of the necessity test, which forms an important element of consideration in the assessment framework of proportionality.

V. Conclusion

Reference to WTO jurisprudence has not been uncommon in investment arbitration. Indeed, tribunals have frequently referred to GATT/WTO case law, in particular when interpreting national treatment provisions and 'security exception' clauses.[131] However, the reference is limited to the context of interpretation of specific terms, the utility of which is subject to many conditions. This is demonstrated in the divergent views of such tribunals on, for example, whether or not to accept the relevance of the GATT/WTO interpretation of 'like products' in

[129] ibid 58.

[130] Although outside the context of the proportionality principle and as obiter dictum, a NAFTA tribunal referred to the right of states to determine the level of protection in the recent *Bilcon v Canada* award. See *William Ralph Clayton and others v Canada*, UNCITRAL, Award on Jurisdiction and Liability (17 March 2015) para 598. See also *Chemtura Corporation v Canada*, UNCITRAL, Award (2 August 2010) para 153.

[131] See e.g., *SD Myers, Inc v Canada*, UNCITRAL, Partial Award (13 November 2000) paras 244–46; *Occidental Exploration and Production Company v Ecuador*, LCIA Case No UN3467, Final Award (1 July 2004) paras 174–76; *Corn Products International, Inc v Mexico*, ICSID Case No ARB(AF)/04/1, Decision on Responsibility (15 January 2008) para 121; *Cargill, Incorporated v Mexico*, ICSID Case No ARB(AF)/05/2, Award (18 September 2009) para 193; *Sergei Paushok, CJSC Golden East Company and CJSC Vostokneftegaz Company v Mongolia* (*Paushok v Mongolia*), UNCITRAL, Award on Jurisdiction and Liability (28 April 2011) para 315 (on national treatment); *Continental Casualty Company v Argentina*, ICSID Case No ARB/03/9, Award (5 September 2008) paras 192–95. For references to the WTO jurisprudence in other contexts, see e.g., *Marvin Roy Feldman Karpa v Mexico*, ICSID Case No ARB(AF)/99/1, Award (16 December 2002) para 177 (on the question of burden of proof); *Methanex Corporation v United States*, UNCITRAL, Decision of the Tribunal on Petitions from Third Persons to Intervene as Amici Curiae (15 January 2001) paras 31–33 and *United Parcel Service v Canada*, UNCITRAL, Decision on Petitions for Intervention and Participation as Amici Curiae (17 October 2001) para 64 (on the acceptance of *amicus curiae*). For a detailed analysis of the security exception clause in the Argentina–US BIT with reference to the interpretation of the term 'necessary' in arts XX(a), (b), and (d) of the GATT, see Kurtz, 'Adjudging the Exceptional at International Investment Law' (n 63); Burke-White and von Staden (n 15) 323–29.

GATT Article III:4 in the interpretation of 'like circumstances' in national treatment provisions of the relevant investment treaties.[132]

The approach adopted in this chapter is to look beyond specific treaty provisions, by focusing on the deferential approach adopted by the WTO Appellate Body in seeking balance between the need to respect sovereign regulatory power and the need for effective implementation of international trade obligations. The chapter first described the criticisms of investment arbitration, which is contrasted with the overall support for the WTO dispute settlement system. It demonstrated that whereas behind the support of the WTO dispute settlement system there are the Appellate Body's continuous effort to achieve coherence and integrity in legal interpretation, and the institutional sensitivity it has developed since its creation, in the background of criticism of investment arbitration there is the concern over the legal uncertainty in investment arbitration, and the fear that investment arbitration may result in too much encroachment upon domestic regulatory power. It also demonstrated the commonalities between the two regimes, that they both face the same normative question of how much interference by the adjudicating bodies should be permitted when reviewing government actions, in light of the obligations under international economic law. This provides a theoretical basis for investment arbitration tribunals to seek guidance in the Appellate Body's deferential approach in appropriate circumstances. This chapter focused on the proportionality analysis as an area of examination where the balance is most vividly materialized, and argued that by consulting such deferential approach as the starting point of the analysis, investment arbitration tribunals may alleviate the concerns over the alleged 'bias' in favour of investors. To address increasing concerns over the system, there is urgent need for investment arbitration tribunals to explicitly demonstrate their deferential approach in the reasoning of each decision in a coherent manner. A practical, effective, and persuasive way for investment arbitration tribunals to do so is to depart from the strict necessity test to the assessment framework of proportionality that the means do not have excessive restrictive effects on the investments, making explicit reference to WTO jurisprudence, which does provide helpful guidance on this balancing. While this chapter limits its examination to the Appellate Body's approach in interpreting general exception clauses, there are other contexts where WTO jurisprudence may provide useful guidance for investment arbitration—for example, openness towards international norms outside the

[132] e.g. in *Occidental v Ecuador*, the tribunal rejected such relevance by emphasizing that the nature of the national treatment at issue in this case was different from that covered by GATT art III:4, and stating, inter alia, that: 'the reference to "in like situations" used in the Treaty seems to be different from that to "like products" in the GATT/WTO. The "situation" can relate to all exporters that share such condition, while the "product" necessarily relates to competitive and substitutable products.' *Occidental v Ecuador* (n 117) paras 175–76. By contrast, in *Paushok v Mongolia*, the tribunal, while noting the textual difference, concluded that 'before concluding to discrimination in the present case, the sectors covered should relate to competitive and substitutable products, an expression regularly used in WTO/GATT cases', distinguishing *Occidental v Ecuador. Paushok v Mongolia* (n 131) paras 313–15.

WTO agreements (such as the precautionary principle and the principle of sustainable development) demonstrated by panels and the Appellate Body—which are left for further research. It is hoped that this chapter provides an analysis that suggests the possibility of effective 'normative sharing' between the WTO dispute settlement system and investment arbitration, as a way to address ever-growing concern over investment arbitration.

8

Trade Law and the Vienna Treaty Convention's Systemic Integration Clause

Chin Leng Lim

I. Introduction

Professor Mitsuo Matsushita has shown an abiding interest in the systemic problems faced by the multilateral trading system. I recall his interventions on GATT Article XX and, in particular, his keen interest in the challenges posed by regional trade agreements (RTAs). He has spoken often about the RTA problem during events held by the Asia WTO Research Network over the past decade. This tribute to him discusses Article 31(1)(3)(c) of the Vienna Convention on the Law of Treaties (VCLT),[1] or the 'systemic integration clause',[2] in light of his concerns.

Article 31(3)(c) has been discussed in the WTO jurisprudence. Panels and the Appellate Body have occasionally had to address questions about the integration of the WTO legal order with WTO Members' other international legal obligations.[3] But—with some notable exceptions—it is an issue that could benefit from greater attention still. Such benign neglect may be questioned, since this clause could provide a broader approach to external norms than Article XX's General Exceptions Clause in resolving conflicts between WTO and non-WTO treaties, and between WTO treaty norms and a whole range of non-treaty-derived norms.[4] The utility of the clause in dealing with conflicts between WTO and RTA rules has been a subject of special neglect.[5]

[1] The Vienna Convention on the Law of Treaties (VCLT), 1155 UNTS 331, 8 ILM 679 (1969).

[2] Campbell McLachlan, 'The Principle of Systemic Integration and Article 31(3)(c) of the Vienna Convention' (2005) 54 Intl Comp LQ 279.

[3] Appellate Body Report, *United States—Definitive Antidumping and Countervailing Duties on Certain Products from China* (*US—Definitive Antidumping and Countervailing Duties*), WT/DS379/AB/R, adopted 25 March 2011, paras 307–08, 311–13; Appellate Body Report, *European Communities and Certain Member States—Measures Affecting Trade in Large Civil Aircraft* (*EC—Large Civil Aircraft*), WT/DS316/AB/R, adopted 1 June 2011, paras 841, 844–47, 849, 851.

[4] The notable exception I have in mind is Joost Pauwelyn, *Conflict of Norms in Public International Law* (CUP 2003) 253–74.

[5] RTAs have been the subject of voluminous literature. On the proliferation of RTAs, see e.g., The Warwick Commission, *The Multilateral Trade Regime: Which Way Forward?—The Report of the First Warwick Commission* (University of Warwick 2007) 45, 51–53; Peter Sutherland and others, *The Future*

The Vienna Convention's 'systemic integration clause', as we shall call it, read together with the Appellate Body's famous pronouncement in *US—Gasoline* that the GATT is not to be read in clinical isolation from public international law,[6] deserves close attention as the multilateral trading system continues to grapple with non-trade regulatory issues and the increasing complexity of the WTO's interrelationship with RTAs.

However, while the existence and applicability of the systemic integration clause in the WTO *acquis* has been acknowledged and upheld by the Appellate Body, the full manner in which it could be 'operationalized', to borrow Philippe Sands' terminology,[7] remains a matter of conjecture. Part of that difficulty lies as I have said in an incomplete exploration of the clause itself in the trade literature, but it also lies in the clause's very narrow application thus far in the WTO's case law.

II. Trade Law's Recent Problems

Going back roughly ten years, there were two academic debates that had proceeded alongside each other, in relative isolation. Trade lawyers were struggling to come to grips with the systemic effects of the proliferation of RTAs, while the WTO dispute settlement system had begun to prove itself a successful arbiter not only of trade disputes but also of trade-related disputes. However, the RTA problem is not a 'trade-related' problem. Rather, it is purely a difficulty with the design of the global trading system itself and it was until recently considered to have posed a systemic threat to the multilateral system. It did not, at

of the WTO: Addressing Institutional Challenges in the New Millennium (Report by the Consultative Board to Director-General Supachai Panitchpakdi, World Trade Organization 2004) paras 103, 104; *World Trade Report 2011* (World Trade Organization 2011). For the scholarship on WTO regulation, see Sungjoon Cho, 'Breaking the Barrier between Regionalism and Multilateralism: A New Perspective on Trade Regionalism' (2001) 42 Harv Intl LJ 435–52; Frederick M Abbott, 'A New Dominant Trade Species Emerges' in William J Davey and John Jackson, *The Future of International Economic Law* (OUP 2008), 133; Leon Trakman, 'The Proliferation of FTAs: Bane or Beauty?' (2008) 42 J World Trade 367. The subject of WTO and RTA norm conflicts have focused on issues concerning trade remedies, safeguard action, and jurisdictional conflicts between WTO and RTA disputes settlement ('systemic issues'). For a brief description of these issues, see C L Lim, 'Some Lessons from Past FTA Disputes' in C L Lim and Magret Liang, *Economic Diplomacy* (Institute of Policy Studies—World Scientific 2012) 185, 189–95. On jurisdictional conflicts, see Henry Gao and C L Lim, 'Saving the WTO from the Risk of Irrelevance' (2008) 11 J Intl Econ L 899. For WTO–RTA norm conflicts, see C L Lim and Henry Gao, 'The Politics of Competing Jurisdictional Claims in WTO and RTA Disputes: The Role of Private International Law Analogies' in Tomer Broude and others (eds), *The Politics of International Economic Law* (CUP 2011) 282. On the manner in which the systemic issues have been put aside for now in current attempts by the WTO to increase surveillance and knowledge of RTAs, see Jo-ann Crawford and C L Lim, 'Cast Light and Evil Will Go Away: The Transparency Mechanism for Regional Trade Agreements Three Years After' (2011) 45 J World Trade 375.

[6] Appellate Body Report, *United States—Standards for Reformulated and Conventional Gasoline* (*US—Gasoline*), WT/DS2/AB/R, adopted 20 May 1996, 17.

[7] Philippe Sands, 'Treaties, Custom and the Cross-fertilisation of International Law' (1999) 1 Yale Hum Rts Dev LJ 85; quoted in McLachlan (n 2) 281.

least primarily, pose a problem about the intersection of trade and other 'related' norms—for example, environmental and conservational norms, labour standards, and so on.[8]

Some of us have looked to the success of the dispute settlement system in light of the threat posed by RTAs and asked if the WTO could be 'saved' by extending the reach of the dispute settlement system to include the settlement of RTA disputes.[9] Clashes between WTO and RTA dispute settlement had by then emerged. This is not to say that we had not noticed a larger problem too; namely, the relationship of the dispute settlement system to other 'non-trade' tribunals, which concerned the allocation of jurisdictional competence against the background of a fragmented public international legal order.[10]

At around the same time, public international law scholars had done considerable work on ways to ameliorate the larger problem of fragmentation and this, as we know, eventually culminated in a widely cited International Law Commission (ILC) report on the subject.[11] But coming back to trade law scholarship, the questions posed by RTAs was not always viewed by trade lawyers as a part of the larger debate about fragmentation. Our writings often did not go far enough to discuss the extent to which the trade systemic issue posed by RTAs and the wider governance issue posed by environmental and other challenges in trade dispute settlement could both be framed together as common treaty interpretative problems. This tribute to Mitsuo Matsushita aims to fill that gap by explicitly addressing both issues in a common treaty interpretative light.

After all, both trade law and much of public international law today are treaty-driven in content.[12] RTAs themselves are progressively building upon and advancing a common body of global trade law principles, a common public trade law.[13] However, to date we have largely only focused on the architectural issues of accommodating RTAs within the global trading order, and on the challenges to the multilateral system posed by the existence of treaty obligations which exist outside of the WTO's own set of covered agreements. This has been a narrow way of conceiving and framing the issue. International lawyers have long debated the shortcomings of formalism in understanding radical international

[8] See the articles in Jose E Alvarez, 'Symposium: The Boundaries of the WTO' (2002) 96 Am J Intl L 1.

[9] Gao and Lim (n 5).

[10] C L Lim, 'Free Trade Agreements in Asia and Some Common Legal Problems' in Yasuhei Taniguchi, and others (eds), *The WTO in the Twenty-First Century: Dispute Settlement, Negotiations, and Regionalism in Asia* (CUP 2007) 434, 452; C L Lim and Bryan Mercurio (eds), *International Economic Law after the Global Crisis: A Tale of Fragmented Disciplines* (CUP 2015).

[11] Rep of the Intl Law Comm'n, 58d Sess, 1 May–9 June and 3 July–11 August 2006, UN Doc A/CN,4/L.702, 18 July 2006.

[12] See, however, C L Lim, 'The Strange Vitality of Custom in the International Protection of Property and Contracts' in Curtis A Bradley (ed), *Custom's Future* (CUP 2016) 205.

[13] McLachlan (n 2) 282, citing Higgins' view of international law as a process of authoritative decision making. See further, Rosalyn Higgins, *Problems and Process: International Law and How We Use It* (OUP 1994) 3–6; Myres S McDougal and Harold D Lasswell, 'The Identification and Appraisal of Diverse Systems of Public Order' (1959) 53 Am J Intl L 1, 5; Michael Reisman and others, 'McDougal's Jurisprudence: Utility, Influence, Controversy' (1985) 79 Am Socy Intl L 266.

legal developments. An alternative to formalism is to view the emergence of new rules—in this case new RTA rules—as a process of incremental law-making without over-emphasizing the sources of those rules or nature of the specific treaty frameworks to which they belong. In other words, we should focus on the stock of trade rules and trade rule-making as a larger process of norm-making than the impression given by a singular focus on the sustenance of the WTO regulatory structure.

To be sure, this is not to give up on the value of a cohesive multilateral system, rendered most efficient by the operation of the MFN rule. It is merely to recognize that the pendulum swings between bilateral and multilateral initiatives over time. It has been observed on more than one occasion that RTAs proliferate when multilateral talks degenerate. The present era of mega-Free Trade Agreements (mega-FTAs) in the form of the Trans-Pacific Partnership (TPP), Regional Comprehensive Economic Partnership (RCEP), and Transatlantic Trade and Investment Partnership (TTIP) talks reveals only the latest manifestation of such an ebb and flow. There is a real risk, however, that a Geneva-centric view might fail to fully capture and reflect the evolving *practice* of international trade law, the wants of businesses, and the policies of governments.[14] If this is so, it could become even more important to determine how non-WTO trade norms may be read compatibly with WTO norms.

III. The 'Systemic Integration' Clause in Article 31(3)(c) of the Vienna Treaties Convention

The VCLT's rule on treaty interpretation has a secure place in the jurisprudence of WTO dispute settlement proceedings. The rule is expressed in a body of principles contained in Articles 31 and 32. These principles have been accepted within the WTO's corpus of panel and Appellate Body reports as being reflective of customary international law,[15] reflecting the position taken in the public international law field. That the principles are custom is shown through the example of the United States, which treats the VCLT principles as being so despite not itself being party to the VCLT.[16]

[14] See further, C L Lim, 'Overcoming the Geneva Impasse: How Regional Trade Agreements Can Help Global Trade' (2015) 6 OMFIF Bulletin 12.

[15] *US—Gasoline* (n 6) 17; Appellate Body Report, *India—Patent Protection for Pharmaceutical and Agricultural Chemical Products* (*India—Patents*), WT/DS50/AB/R, adopted 16 January 1998, para 46; Appellate Body Report, *Argentina—Measures Affecting Imports of Footwear Textiles, Apparel and Other Items*, WT/DS56/AB/R, WT/DS56/AB/R/Corr. 1, adopted 22 April 1998, para 42; *United States—Countervailing Duties on Certain Corrosion-resistant Carbon Steel Flat Products from Germany* (*US—Carbon Steel*), WT/DS213/AB/R, WT/DS213/AB/R/Corr. 1, adopted 19 December 2002, paras 61–62; Appellate Body Report, *United States—Continued Existence And Application of Zeroing Methodology*, WT/DS350/AB/R, adopted 19 February 2009, para 268. For scholarly commentary, see James Cameron and Kevin R Gray, 'Principles of International Law in the WTO Dispute Settlement Body' (2001) 51 Intl Comp LQ 248, 252–56.

[16] See Richard K Gardiner, *International Law* (Longman 2003) 83–84.

As such, WTO panels and the Appellate Body have built up a jurisprudence on treaty interpretation regardless of whether a WTO Member is party to the VCLT. It would not be going too far to say that WTO practice has itself contributed to the development of the rules on treaty interpretation.[17]

The question which this chapter poses to the reader has to do with one rule of interpretation in particular; namely, the rule under Article 31(3)(c) of the VCLT—often termed the 'systemic integration clause'. That clause requires (the operative word being 'shall') 'account' to be taken, 'together with the context', of 'any relevant rules of international law applicable in the relations between the parties'. Thus conceived, two sovereign states, A and B, engaged in a dispute governed by Treaty X shall require account to be taken by the tribunal of other relevant international law rules, including treaty and customary rules, which are applicable to the two states in their relations with each other. Therefore, in interpreting Treaty X in the context of the dispute between A and B, the question which normally arises is whether, and if so how, account should be taken of Treaty Y or Treaty Z to which A and B are also party, or of a customary international law rule which applies to A and B.

This is how the systemic integration clause is viewed today. It was not always so. In fact, the systemic integration clause was not previously viewed to have been concerned with systemic integration at all. Rather, it was viewed as an expression of the doctrine of inter-temporal law such that the words in a treaty might usefully be taken to have been used in the sense they bore under the rules of international law in existence at the time the treaty was made, but without ignoring the fact that it may be equally useful to have regard to the current state of the law.[18] Viewed in this light, it is today the equivalent of an amphibian tank despatched to do battle in the desert.[19] There had also been some doubt about what 'international law' means exactly in Article 31(3)(c), but the clause is now thought to extend to general principles of law,[20] general or customary international law,[21] and even general principles of treaty interpretation.[22] It was Sir Ian Sinclair who considered that it could extend to other applicable treaties too,[23] and this view seems to have taken hold in the practice of tribunals, including the practice of the WTO Appellate Body.[24]

[17] Anthony Aust, *Modern Treaty Law and Practice* (3rd edn, CUP 2013) 207.

[18] Ian Sinclair, *The Vienna Convention on the Law of Treaties* (2nd edn, Manchester University Press 1984) 138–40; ibid 216 and the works cited therein; Gardiner (n 16) 89. Cf Anthony D'Amato, 'International Law, Intertemporal Problems' in Rudolf Bernhardt, *Encyclopedia of Pubic International Law* (North-Holland 1992) 1234–36.

[19] This image is not mine, but was conjured in relation to UCC 2-207 by Professors White and Summers; James J White and Robert S Summers, *Uniform Commercial Code* (5th edn, Thomson Reuters 2002) 54.

[20] See the cases cited by Pauwelyn (n 4) 255; including *Golder v UK* (1975) Series A no 18, 14; *Espahanian v Bank Tejarat* (1983 I) 2 Iran–US CTR 157 (which could have been a reference to custom); and footnote 157 in Appellate Body Report, *United States—Import Prohibition of Certain Shrimp and Shrimp Products* (*US—Shrimp*), WT/DS58/AB/R, adopted 6 November 1998, 62.

[21] In Sands' seminal article he appears to treat the reference to 'international law' as a reference to custom; Sands (n 7) 8, 11.

[22] Gardiner (n 16) 90.

[23] Sinclair (n 18) 119; Pauwelyn (n 4) 255.

[24] See the discussion in section VI, below.

This last issue about whether the systemic integration clause refers to other treaty law is an especially important point for when we come to consider the relationship between the WTO's treaties and RTAs, below.

Explicit writing on Article 31(3)(c) as a 'systemic integration' clause probably began with Philippe Sands QC. Other writers—McLachlan, Pauwelyn, and Marceau among them[25]—adopted and developed the point further. The rationale for viewing Article 31(3)(c) in this manner—as a systemic integration rule—is that no treaty exists in a vacuum. Each treaty is instead only a part of the larger international legal system. Perhaps the most obvious illustration is that the rule that treaties are binding on their parties arises from the general international law doctrine of *pacta sunt servanda*. According to this reasoning, treaty construction should therefore provide for the relationship between the individual treaty under consideration and other rules in the system to which it is logically connected through a common system of public international law.[26]

IV. The Structure of the Vienna Convention's Provisions on Treaty Interpretation

It was once upon a time questioned whether treaty interpretation could be reduced to rules. That debate was resolved during the Vienna Conference. The structure and content of the VCLT's provisions on treaty interpretation are today most familiar to our readers, as they are to all students of international law. However, it may still be useful to revisit the relevant provisions, briefly. Putting aside a fourth paragraph on words of special meaning in a treaty,[27] for that need not concern us, I shall refer to the first three paragraphs of Article 31 of the VCLT in the common manner as the 'basic rule' (paragraph 1), the 'internal context' rule (paragraph 2), and the 'external context' or 'subsequent conduct' rule (paragraph 3).

A. The basic rule

Article 31, paragraph 1, states the basic rule that a treaty 'shall be interpreted in good faith in accordance with the ordinary meaning to be given to the terms of the treaty in their context and in the light of its object and purpose'. Notwithstanding the order of the terms 'good faith', 'ordinary meaning', 'context', and 'object and purpose', one starts with the ordinary meaning.[28] It has been emphasized often in

[25] Gabrielle Marceau, 'Conflicts of Norms and Conflicts of Jurisdictions, the Relationship between the WTO Agreement and MEAs and Other Treaties' (2001) 35 J World Trade 1081, 1087. Pauwelyn's views are discussed further below.

[26] McLachlan (n 2) 280.

[27] VCLT art 31(4): 'A special meaning shall be given to a term if it is established that the parties so intended', cf Marrakesh Agreement Establishing the World Trade Organization, 15 April 1994, 1867 UNTS 154, Explanatory Notes; Gardiner (n 16) 85.

[28] Aust (n 17) 209; Lord McNair, *Law of Treaties* (OUP 1961) 365; Gerald Fitzmaurice, 'Law and Procedure of the International Court of Justice 1951–4: Treaty Interpretation and Other

the WTO context,[29] that the ordinary meaning of the terms is the 'centre point', around which the other aspects of the interpretative process 'must revolve like satellites'.[30] However, dictionary definitions are only 'important guides'. They are not 'dispositive statements' in this regard.[31]

But let us say the ordinary meaning of the terms leads to a meaning that could not, when the terms are interpreted in good faith, have been intended. Then in such a case the principle of good faith would take priority, and a meaning that could not have been intended should be abandoned.[32] As for the object and purpose of the treaty, it plays merely a confirmatory role in practice, in the same way that Article 32, which provides for supplementary means of interpretation, operates.[33]

B. 'Internal' context

The word 'context' in paragraph 1, much like the reference to the 'object and purpose' of the treaty, is a reminder that the treaty words cannot be construed in the

Treaty Points' (1957) 33 Brit YB Intl L 203, 204–08. This, it would appear was Sir Humphrey Waldock's own view, see his *Third Report on the Law of Treaties*, [1964] II YB Intl L Comm'n 5, UN Doc A/CN.4/167 and Add 1–3, 52–53, and accompanying commentary therein, discussed in Edward Slavko Yambrusic, *Treaty Interpretation: Theory and Reality* (University Press of America 1987) 172–75. The United States Government argued this view in a Note Verbale in response to the Special Rapporteur, Sir Humphrey's, 1966 Draft, declaring that the concept of the 'ordinary meaning' is 'the centre point about which the other aspects of the process of interpretation must revolve like satellites'; United States, *Note Verbale, Comments on the Final Draft Articles to the Law of Treaties Prepared by the International Law Commission (United States)*, 6 October 1967, UN Doc A/6827/Add.2, 5; UN Secretary-General, *Analytical Compilation of Comments and Observations Made in 1966 and 1967 with respect to the Final Draft Articles on the Law of Treaties: Working Paper Prepared by the Secretariat*, UN Doc A/CONF 39/5, Vol I and II, 10 February 1968, 204; Yambrusic (ibid) 206.

[29] Appellate Body Report, *Japan—Taxes on Alcoholic Beverages* (*Japan—Alcoholic Beverages*), WT/DS8/AB/R, WT/DS10/AB/R, WT/DS11/AB/R, adopted 1 November 1996, 105; Appellate Body Report, *European Community—Measures Concerning Meat and Meat Products (Hormones)*, WT/DS26/AB/R, WT/DS48/AB/R, adopted 13 February 1998, para 181; *India—Patents* (n 15) para 45; *US—Shrimp* (n 20) para 114; Appellate Body Report, *United States—Final Countervailing Duty Determination with Respect to Certain Softwood Lumber from Canada*, WT/DS257/AB/R, adopted 17 February 2004, paras 58–59; *United States—Measures Affecting the Cross-border Supply of Gambling and Betting Services* (*US—Gambling*), WT/DS285/AB/R, WT/DS285/AB/R/Corr. 1, adopted 20 April 2005, n 191.

[30] *Comments on the Final Draft Articles to the Law of Treaties Prepared by the International Law Commission (United States)* (n 28) 5.

[31] Appellate Body Report, *United States—Continued Dumping and Subsidy Offset Act of 2000*, WT/DS217/AB/R, WT DS/234/AB/R, adopted 27 January 2003, para 248; Appellate Body Report, *European Communities—Customs Classification of Frozen Boneless Chicken Cuts* (*EC—Chicken Cuts*), WT/DS269/AB/R, WT/DS286/AB/R; WT/DS269/AB/R/Corr 1, WT/DS286/AB/R/Corr 1, adopted 27 September 2005, paras 175–76; *US—Gambling* (n 29) paras 164, 166.

[32] Aust (n 17) 208–09.

[33] ibid 209, 217. For the contrary view that the *travaux preparatoires*, rather than being supplementary and confirmatory, ought to have been given equal importance of place with consideration of the plain meaning of the treaty, see Waldock and Rosenne in 872nd Meeting, [1966] I YB Intl L Comm'n 198, UN Doc A/CN.4/186 and Addenda; A/CN.4 L.107, L.115, paras 27, 33; and Verdross' view that the treaty interpretation is a unified process, 872nd Meeting (n 33) para 38; discussed in Yambrusic (n 28) 200.

abstract but must make sense within the context in which those words occur. There are two kinds of context.

The view taken by the VCLT, in paragraph 2 of Article 31, is that the terms of the treaty—including its preamble and annexes—form a part of the 'internal' context of the treaty.[34] Paragraph 2 then goes on to define this internal context to include any 'agreement' relating to the treaty which was made by all the parties in connection with the treaty, such as a Protocol of Signature for example, and any 'instrument' made by only some of the parties in that regard which is accepted by the other parties to be related to the treaty.[35]

C. Subsequent conduct or 'external' context

Paragraph 3 of Article 31 goes on to define the 'external context'. There are three further sub-paragraphs—(a), (b), and (c). Article 31(3)(a) requires subsequent agreements between the parties to be taken into account 'together with the context' of the treaty.[36] Article 31(3)(b) requires subsequent conduct which establishes the agreement of the parties to be taken into similar account (Article 31(3)(b)).[37] Finally, Article 31(3)(c)— what we have called the 'systemic integration clause'—requires such relevant and applicable rules of international law between the parties to be taken into similar account.[38]

V. Article 31 Viewed in Logical Sequence

It has been said that Article 31 of the VCLT arranges the several factors in a logical sequence, but is not intended to reflect a hierarchical ordering. In sum, one looks first to the treaty text, including its preamble and annexes, in search of the intent of the treaty parties. Intent is a factor, as we have said, in the event that the literal interpretation of the words leads to absurdity. In such a case, the words would have to be construed in good faith instead in order to avoid that absurd result. Thereafter, subsequent agreements, conduct establishing such agreement, and relevant and

[34] For examples of using the 'internal' text as context, see *US—Carbon Steel* (n 15) para 69; *EC—Chicken Cuts* (n 31) paras 193–94.

[35] Aust (n 17) 210–12. See *US—Gambling* (n 29) para 175; *EC—Chicken Cuts* (n 31) para 195.

[36] Appellate Body Report, *European Communities—Regime for the Importation, Sale and Distribution of Bananas*, WT/DS27/AB/RW2/ECU, WT/DS27/AB/RW/USA, WT/DS27/AB/RW2/ECU/Corr 1, WT/DS27/AB/RW/USA/ Corr 1, adopted 11 December 2008, paras 383, 390–91; Appellate Body Report, *United States—Measures Affecting the Production and Sale of Clove Cigarettes*, WT/DS406/AB/R, 24 April 2012, paras 257–58, 260, 267; Appellate Body Report, *United States—Measures Concerning the Importation, Marketing and Sale of Tuna and Tuna Products*, WT/DS381/AB/R, 13 June 2012, paras 371–72.

[37] See *Japan—Alcoholic Beverages* (n 29) 106; Appellate Body Report, *Chile—Price Band System and Safeguard Measures Relating to Certain Agricultural Products*, WT/DS207/AB/R, WT/DS207/AB/R/Corr 1, paras 213–14; and especially *EC—Chicken Cuts* (n 31) paras 255, 259, 265–66, 271–73.

[38] See further, below.

applicable rules of international law are also taken into account. Other factors are subsidiary only, such as the object and purpose of the treaty, and supplementary means of interpretation such as *travaux preparatoires*.

This largely reflects how trade lawyers also view the application of the VCLT; the usual formula being that one must interpret the treaty words 'in their ordinary meaning in their context'—i.e. in respect of both the internal context under paragraph 2 of Article 31, and the external context under paragraph 3—'and in light of the object and purpose' of the particular agreement.[39]

Yet the application of the VCLT has been fairly limited when viewed against the backdrop of the kinds of systemic problems that the WTO system has faced in recent years. Without seeking to be comprehensive, three illustrations should suffice to show this point. I have deliberately chosen them because they are so familiar to us.

VI. Three Illustrative Problems

A. The GATT Article XX illustration

Article XX of the General Agreement on Trade and Tariffs (GATT) has had a long and interesting history, well-known to students of the GATT–WTO. The famous pre-WTO GATT *Tuna—Dolphin I* and *Thai—Cigarettes* disputes were first encounters with a need to integrate trade rules with other rules in international economic law and the wider public international law order.

Viewed historically, from the perspective of the concern of trade regulation with trade liberalization coming out of the Second World War, non-trade factors could easily have been used to mask protectionist measures. Unsurprisingly, this concern featured especially strongly in the early panel disputes under GATT 1947. A restrictive view was taken towards the interpretation of Article XX. In *Tuna—Dolphin I*, this narrow view focussed on the interpretation of the word 'necessary' in Article XX(b)'s general exception for measures 'necessary to protect human, animal or plant life or health'. The panel required the exhaustion of all options reasonably available. In *Thai—Cigarettes* and *US—Alcohol*, the panels similarly adopted the view that the measures must be 'least trade restrictive' in order to qualify for the general exception. An equally restrictive approach had been taken to measures which are 'primarily aimed' at conservation, under Article XX(g), in *Tuna—Dolphin I* and *Tuna—Dolphin II*.[40] Against that

[39] *US—Shrimp* (n 20) para 114; Appellate Body Report, *Argentina—Safeguard Measures on Imports of Footwear*, WT/DS121/AB/R, adopted 12 January 2000, para 91; and also Appellate Body Report, *United States—Definitive Safeguard Measures on Imports of Circular Welded Carbon Quality Line Pipe from Korea*, WT/DS202/AB/R, adopted 8 March 2002, para 251, where the importance of the context and object and purpose of the treaty were emphasized in a situation where the terms of a provision did not convey one certain meaning.

[40] See David A Wirth, 'The Role of Science in the Uruguay Round and NAFTA Trade Disciplines' (1994) 27 Cornell Intl LJ 817; Jeffrey L Dunoff, 'Institutional Misfits: The GATT, the ICJ and Trade–Environment Disputes' (1994) 15 Mich J Intl L 1043.

background, the WTO Appellate Body's subsequent *Shrimp–Turtle* ruling was a breakthrough.[41]

Today, our view of Article XX continues to evolve. Trade lawyers might take their cue from the debate in international investment law, where the absence of a general exceptions clause in investment treaties has caused commentators to search for other ways to build in such exceptions through an interpretative route instead. Virtue may have been born out of necessity, but virtue it is once we appreciate that neither international trade law nor international investment law can exist in clinical isolation from the international legal order.[42] Put crudely, if neither has a true basis in what we think of as the international legal order, then the legitimacy of international trade regulation and international investment law ought to be subjected to a higher and more searching degree of scrutiny as bodies of extra-international legal rules. Notwithstanding the deficiencies of the international legal order, the day may yet come when serious debate takes place about the desirability of oversight by a superior tribunal such as the International Court of Justice. Until then, we should assume that trade dispute bodies, including the Appellate Body of the WTO, take seriously their role in applying the general rules of public international law, including the general rules of treaty interpretation.

In that regard, one could ask if the categories listed in Article XX are exhaustive when viewed against the wider landscape of trade law's integration into the public international law system. For most experienced trade lawyers, it would be impractical and unnecessary to suggest that they are not. It would be impractical because Article XX works reasonably well, and it would be unnecessary because the interpretation of Article XX, as we have seen, has already witnessed dynamic change, evolution, and adaptation over time. We are not perfect, but we learn. In *Shrimp–Turtle*, for example, the Appellate Body chose to construe Article XX in light of the preamble of the Marrakesh/WTO Agreement.[43]

The only point which is raised here for discussion is whether the basis for account to be taken of other non-GATT obligations lies solely in Article XX itself, or whether it is not the public international law rules of treaty interpretation which ultimately guide and shape the way in which non-GATT, and even non-WTO, treaty and other rules of international law ought to be taken into account in the interpretation of the GATT and other similar trade treaty instruments.

In the WTO's case law, we have only—barely—touched on this issue. One example consists of the passing acknowledgements in two related cases—*China—Raw Materials* and *China—Rare Earths*—of the doctrine of permanent sovereignty over natural resources.[44] Unlike *Shrimp–Turtle*'s reference to the principle

[41] *US—Shrimp* (n 20).

[42] *US—Gasoline* (n 6) 17.

[43] *US—Shrimp* (n 20) para 129.

[44] The *applicability* of this doctrine as a customary doctrine had been acknowledged by the panel in the earlier *Raw Materials* case, although China's argument was ultimately rejected under a proper interpretation of China's treaty commitments; see Panel Report, *China—Measures Related to the Exportation of Various Raw Materials*, WT/DS394/R, WT/DS395/R, WT/DS/398/R, 5 July 2011, paras 6.35, 7.157, 7.265, 7.356, 7.381–7.383, 7.407. The Appellate Body does not appear to have addressed these arguments. See also, Sonia E Rolland, 'China—Raw Materials: WTO Rules on

of sustainable development in the Marrakesh Agreement, the permanent sovereignty doctrine receives no explicit mention in any WTO treaty text. The dynamism of the Appellate Body's shaping, and re-shaping, of Article XX leaves more questions than answers when it invokes the role of 'reasoned judgments in confronting the endless and ever-changing ebb and flow of real facts in real cases in the real world',[45] or the 'contemporary concerns of the community of nations about the protection and conservation of the environment'.[46]

I believe the missing factor in explaining such Appellate Body decisions lies in the need for greater, explicit reliance on Article 31(3)(c)'s systemic integration clause. We also need better examples of the need to account for systemic integration in trade law's approach to treaty interpretation, and now turn to a second illustration.

B. Safeguards and the parallelism doctrine

This is sometimes seen to be a part of a larger, vexed issue; namely, whether GATT Article XXIV, which permits the formation of RTAs, can excuse other GATT violations; for example, by assuming that Article XXIV requires the removal not only of duties but also 'other restrictive regulations of trade' (ORRs) as a pre-condition to the formation of an RTA. This could be read to include the need to remove trade remedy and emergency safeguard action.

However, it is the 'MFN problem' in respect of the exclusion of RTA partners from safeguard action that is particularly well known, and I shall focus on it in this chapter. The Appellate Body has consistently applied the doctrine of parallelism whereby WTO Members cannot be excluded from the application of safeguards where they have been included in an adverse safeguards investigation. But because the removal of ORRs is a matter concerning the interpretation of GATT Article XXIV, it is widely viewed as a systemic issue in relation to which practical-minded Geneva hands will quietly counsel a Member-driven solution, as opposed to having a solution imposed by the Appellate Body.

But say an RTA forbids emergency safeguards from being applied. This in fact would be WTO-plus. Should panels and the Appellate Body ignore such treaty behaviour outside the WTO when interpreting Article XXIV's potential regulation of safeguard action between the members of an RTA?

In a passage that in retrospect came close to acknowledging the treaty interpretative issues raised by the extra-WTO treaty behaviour of WTO Members, one panel had concluded that:

Chinese Natural resources Export Dispute' (2012) 16(21) Insights <http://www.asil.org/insights/volume/16/issue/21/china-raw-materials-wto-rules-chinese-natural-resources-export-dispute> accessed 7 March 2016. See further, Panel Report, *China—Measures Related to the Exportation of Rare Earths, Tungsten, and Molybdenum*, WT/DS431/R, WT/DS432/R, WT/DS433/R, 26 March 2014, para 7.457 *et seq*.

[45] *Japan—Alcoholic Beverages* (n 29) 14.

[46] *US—Shrimp* (n 20) para 129. For this author's earlier criticisms, see C L Lim, 'Law and Diplomacy in World Trade Disputes' (2001) 6 Singapore J Intl Comp L 436, 472.

[i]t is a matter of fact that many agreements establishing free-trade areas or customs unions allow for the possibility to impose safeguard measures on intra-regional trade, while few regional integration agreements explicitly prohibit the imposition of intra-regional safeguard measures once the formation of such an integration area is completed.[47]

But if this is so, the analysis either misses the point or does not go far enough. What is important, from the viewpoint of an Article 31(3)(c) analysis, is the establishment of a relevant and applicable rule of international law between the parties.

The gap in analysis shown in our two illustrations thus far has since been remedied as panels and the Appellate Body have come to better grips with the systemic integration clause in Article 31(3)(c). This has, in turn, revealed some of the clause's true complexity in its special application to the GATT multilateral context.

C. Dispute settlement under regional trade agreements

My final illustration is of a broader approach towards the need to better 'integrate' the WTO regime with the large number of RTAs that exist today. A well-known difficulty has had to do with the relationship between RTA and WTO dispute settlement arrangements.

For the most part, RTA draftsmen and treaty parties generally ensure that RTAs are not only consistent with the WTO's permission to enter into RTAs under GATT Article XXIV and GATS Article V, but also that in RTAs concluded after 1994 there are express saving provisions which provide for the preservation of WTO rights. In the case of the need to align the dispute settlement provisions under the WTO and various RTAs, one principal device has been the resort to an *electa una via clause* in the RTA itself. Well-known examples may be found in NAFTA Article 2005.6 and Article 1 of MERCOSUR's Olivos Protocol.[48]

However, difficulties have emerged. For example, in the *Argentina—Poultry* and *Mexico—Soft Drinks* cases,[49] a question arose about the proper relationship between RTA dispute settlement provisions and WTO dispute settlement. In each case, notwithstanding parallel proceedings in the *Argentina—Poultry* case and Mexico's attempt to initiate NAFTA dispute proceedings in *Mexico—Soft Drinks*,[50] WTO dispute settlement was successfully commenced in Geneva.

Some trade lawyers have gravitated towards general principles of international law in the search for a solution to the *lis pendens* problem. Thus it is said that the principle that 'the later treaty applies', or that 'the more specific treaty applies' may be used to resolve the situation. However, we only need to pause and ask where such canons come from and it is immediately clear that a solution is being sought

[47] Panel Report, *Argentina—Safeguard Measures on Imports of Footwear*, WT/DS121/R, 25 June 1999, para 8.96.

[48] See e.g., Gao and Lim (n 5) 907; Lim and Gao (n 5) 282, 290.

[49] Panel Report, *Argentina—Definitive Anti-dumping Duties on Poultry from Brazil*, WT/DS241/R, 22 April 2003; Appellate Body Report, *Mexico—Tax Measures on Soft Drinks and Other Beverages* (*Mexico—Soft Drinks*), WT/DS308/AB/R, 6 March 2006.

[50] Lim and Gao (n 5) 295.

from the international law canons of treaty construction. It prompts the thought that we might go further still and take actual account of other principles of treaty interpretation. This is where Article 31(3)(c)'s role emerges.

It is important to frame the scenario clearly to appreciate how far, at least in principle, the systemic integration clause could go. Coming back to the *Argentina—Poultry* and *Mexico—Soft Drinks* scenarios, neither situation was viewed through the lens of Article 31(3)(c). Instead, the issue in *Argentina—Poultry* had to do with the fact that the Olivos Protocol, which would have precluded recourse to WTO dispute settlement, had not been ratified by Brazil. According to the panel, there was therefore no conflict with an RTA rule, which in this case would have allocated jurisdictional competence between RTA and WTO dispute settlement. In the *Mexico—Soft Drinks* case, the Appellate Body focused largely on whether panels and the Appellate Body had the power to stay jurisdiction in favour of an RTA tribunal and concluded that they did not. In both situations, Article 31(3)(c) could have played a useful role.

The argument would go something like this. In the *Argentina—Poultry* scenario (and also in the *Mexico—Soft Drinks* scenario), it must be noticed that there is at least doubt about the ability of panels and the Appellate Body to apply RTA rules as such, since panels and the Appellate Body are confined to the application of the WTO-covered agreements only. Unless account taken of such RTA rules is seen as a part of the application of the customary rules of treaty interpretation of public international law (for example, Article 31(3)(c)'s systemic integration clause).[51] In interpreting the Dispute Settlement Understanding (DSU) provisions which the Appellate Body had relied upon in *Mexico—Soft Drinks*, some account (how much is a question we will come back to) should be taken of the fact that WTO Members have gone on to create multiple RTA dispute settlement regimes. That is the gravamen of the matter. Taken further, this could mean that the DSU provisions which in *Mexico—Soft Drinks* were said to prevent the Appellate body from staying a dispute in favour of RTA dispute settlement should be read in such a way as to be congruent with the existence of RTA dispute settlement rules.

This is likely to be seen as a far-reaching proposition for many trade lawyers. Yet our own picture of the practice of WTO law is, I believe, moving apace, and theoretical questions which once seemed far away now draw near.

VII. A Growing Understanding of Article 31(3)(c) of the Vienna Treaties Convention

When scholarly writing on Article 31(3)(c)'s application in WTO law first began, there was hardly a useful case to rely on. The question, while not entirely theoretical,

[51] Understanding on Rules and Procedures Governing the Settlement of Disputes, Marrakesh Agreement Establishing the World Trade Organization, Annex 2, 1869 U.N.T.S. 401, art 3(2). See further, Gao and Lim (n 5) 911.

called for speculation. Gabrielle Marceau was among the first trade lawyers to explore the issue specifically from the perspective of WTO law.[52] In the same vein, Professor Joost Pauwelyn had cited *US—Shrimp*'s resort to general principles of law (of good faith and *abuse de droit*) without any express reference to Article 31(3)(c).[53] There had certainly been no account taken of non-WTO treaties. One question may have been whether Article 31(3)(c)'s reference to 'international law' points the interpreter to other treaty norms, such as RTA treaty rules, although for Marceau and Pauwelyn there was no reason at all to limit the term 'international law' to any specific formal legal source.

This has since been confirmed by the Appellate Body, in *US—Antidumping and Countervailing Duties (China)*, wherein China had invoked the International Law Commission's Draft Articles on State Responsibility for Internationally Wrongful Acts.[54] The United States objected to this resort to Article 31(3)(c) of the VCLT. The Appellate Body nonetheless applied the systemic integration clause in Article 31(3)(c). It confirmed that the reference in Article 31(3)(c) to 'international law' refers also to other applicable treaties, indeed to all the sources of international law listed in Article 38(1) of the Statute of the International Court of Justice.[55] The Appellate Body explained that by 'relevant' rules of international law, the clause refers to other rules of international law that concern the same subject matter as the WTO treaty terms being interpreted.[56] In ascertaining the 'applicability' to the parties of the ILC's Draft Articles on State Responsibility, the Appellate Body reasoned that the articles in question reflect customary international law.

The question we end up with, when pursued logically, is whether RTA rules being non-WTO treaty rules can also be taken into account in the interpretation of WTO treaty texts. Is that not another possible means to a solution to the increasingly serious problem of RTA–WTO conflicts? At one level, WTO Members entering into an RTA wish to establish exclusive rights and obligations between themselves which are exempted from the most-favoured-nation obligation under Article 1 of the GATT. However, there could arise situations in which the RTA parties clearly intended to clarify the meaning of WTO treaty terms. This is no mere theoretical possibility, and may even be desirable. As the Appellate Body had put it in *EC—Large Civil Aircraft*, discussed further below, a 'delicate balance' must be struck in approaching such questions.

In *EC—Large Civil Aircraft*,[57] the Appellate Body emphasized that the chapeau of Article 31(3)(c) ascribes the weight to be given to such other rules of international law. These shall only be 'taken into account'.[58] The question in that dispute

[52] See Marceau (n 25).

[53] *US—Shrimp* (n 20) para 158 in n 157; Pauwelyn (n 4) 255, 256.

[54] Panel Report, *United States—Definitive Anti-dumping and Countervailing Duties on Certain Products from China*, WT/DS379/R, 24 August 2009, Annex C, Executive Summary of the Second Written Submission of China.

[55] *US—Definitive Antidumping and Countervailing Duties* (n 3). This broad approach had also been Marceau's view, Marceau (n 25) 1087.

[56] ibid. [57] *EC—Large Civil Aircraft* (n 3).

[58] I discuss this question of 'weight' further in Lim, 'The Strange Vitality of Custom in the International Protection of Property and Contracts' (n 12).

had to do with whether a separate agreement between the parties ought to be taken account of in that manner.[59] But a more complex issue also emerged for the first time. Does the reference in Article 31(3)(c) to 'the parties' refer only to the parties to the dispute, or to all WTO Members?[60] The problem goes something like this. An agreement between the parties to the dispute does not apply to all the WTO Members, but the WTO treaty term being interpreted does. Having expressed, without further explaining, the need for caution the Appellate Body declared that:[61]

> Article 31(3)(c) of the Vienna Convention is considered an expression of the 'principle of systemic integration' which, in the words of the ILC, seeks to ensure that 'international obligations are interpreted by reference to their normative environment' in a manner that gives 'coherence and meaningfulness' to the process of legal interpretation.

The answer, according to the Appellate Body, lies ultimately in striking 'a delicate balance' between 'on the one hand, taking due account of an individual WTO Member's international obligations and, on the other hand, ensuring a consistent and harmonious approach to the interpretation of WTO law among all WTO Members'.[62]

One can imagine in such a case that as between the two disputing parties, a clarification of a WTO norm in their RTA conduct would apply to them, but the position is less clear as to whether even a large pattern of such clarifications in several RTAs would necessarily affect disputing parties who have issued no such clarification of WTO norms in their RTAs or at all. There is one possible way out. While Article 31(3)(a) is a different provision of the Vienna Convention on the Law of Treaties, it may be thought that Article 31(3)(c) should in such situations be guided also by the view taken towards Article 31(3)(a). Article 31(3)(a) applies instead in situations in which the disputing parties have themselves made such a clarification in an agreement between themselves. An application of Article 31(3)(c) in similar vein would not be inconsistent with that. However, in a situation where only Article 31(3)(c) applies (i.e. where the two disputing parties have not made such a clarification), the application of the views expressed in other RTAs may not be so easily applicable.

A GATT panel has dealt with the converse situation, where the agreement of all GATT Contracting Parties was required for the application of Article 31(3)(a). As Pauwelyn has observed, this view, which had been taken by the GATT panel in *US—Tuna*, has already been criticized by Mavroidis and Palmeter.[63] Mavroidis and Palmeter argue that in an Article 31(3)(c) case, the agreement of the two parties would suffice and an application of Article 31(3)(a) which is inconsistent with Article 31(3)(c) should also be avoided.[64]

[59] *EC—Large Civil Aircraft* (n 3) para 841. [60] ibid para 844.

[61] ibid para 845. [62] ibid.

[63] Panel Report, *United States—Restrictions on Imports of Tuna*, DS29/R, 16 June 1994, unadopted, para 5.19. The point concerned the non-adoption of the Convention on the International Trade in Endangered Species (CITES) by all GATT Contracting Parties.

[64] David Palmeter and Petros Mavroidis, *Dispute Settlement in the WTO: Practice and Procedure* (Kluwer 1999) 57.

VIII. Distinguishing the Three Scenarios

Thus, even for writers who have counselled the view that WTO obligations should be read alongside other treaty obligations, there is often a high degree of caution expressed about how far this view of Article 31(3)(c) should go. This is in line with what other commentators in the broader international economic law field think. The most common refrain is that the rule is only one of treaty interpretation. Or, as Pauwelyn puts it:[65]

> 'outside rules' to be referred to pursuant to Article 31(3)(c) can only assist in giving meaning to the terms used in, for example, the WTO treaty; they cannot change or overrule those terms. As Sands noted, 'under 31(3)(c), the treaty being interpreted retains the primary role. The customary norm [to be referred to under Article 31(3)(c)] has a secondary role, in the sense that there can be no question of the customary norm displacing the treaty norm, either partly or wholly.'

The scenarios I have outlined above have deliberately included the example of direct conflicts between WTO norms and RTA norms, but I have also arranged them along an imaginary spectrum according to their presumed level of intrusiveness in upsetting the balance of rights and obligations between WTO Members, and in the balance struck between trade and non-trade concerns in the WTO treaty texts. Along this imaginary line, the Article XX issue is probably the least controversial as an example of an area in which account of non-WTO treaty rules should be taken. It is not difficult to imagine why. The interpretation of an Article XX clause is premised upon a general exception that the GATT already provides to the application of other GATT rules. Put simply, the very premise of GATT Article XX is that taking other non-trade concerns into account, concerns that are likely to be regulated under other international treaties, does not automatically conflict with non-GATT–WTO norms.

The safeguards exemption issue in our second illustration is more challenging. Assuming that an RTA allows safeguard action to be applied against an RTA member, the argument that the RTA member should be exempted because GATT Article XXIV requires the elimination of ORRs is not strong. There is no clear conflict with a WTO norm, and it is debatable whether the RTA rule is even 'relevant'. At best, there is only an interpretative issue about whether Article XXIV permits RTA members to take safeguard action against each other notwithstanding its reference to the elimination of ORRs. Modifying that scenario, let us imagine instead an RTA that expressly prohibits safeguard action against other RTA members. What would be the objection to the exemption of those members from safeguard action? As things stand, the objection is based on the WTO rule that emergency safeguard action should be non-discriminatory. Requiring weight to be accorded to the exemption of RTA members in the interpretation of the WTO

[65] Pauwelyn (n 4) 254.

Safeguards Agreement's non-discrimination requirement would allow an RTA to affect the rights of other non-RTA WTO parties to non-discriminatory treatment. In the language of Article 31(3)(c), the issue concerns not the 'relevance' of the RTA in the interpretation of WTO safeguards law, but the 'applicability' of the RTA to the situation where not all WTO Members have signed up to an extra-WTO prohibition of the application of safeguard measures. In such a case, a delicate balance would need to be struck, in the language of the Appellate Body in *EC—Large Civil Aircraft*, between 'taking due account of an individual WTO Member's international obligations and … ensuring a consistent and harmonious approach to the interpretation of WTO law among all WTO Members'.[66]

We require a yet better example, one in which the RTA obligation does not stand accused of blatantly contradicting a WTO right but which—unlike the Article XX scenario in our first illustration—still demonstrates some degree of tension between WTO and RTA norms. Article 31(3)(c) is after all only a rule of interpretation and, at the end of the day, an interpretation which flies in the face of the text is not an interpretation at all but a call to reform. The Safeguard Agreement's requirement that safeguards should be applied on a most-favoured-nation basis is at least textually clear.

So we come to the final analysis of our third illustration. According to the WTO Appellate Body in *Mexico—Soft Drinks*,[67] allowing an RTA to prohibit recourse to WTO dispute settlement is a deprivation of a WTO right, since every WTO Member has the right to commence a dispute under the WTO dispute settlement system. Thus, prohibiting a dispute that has been brought to RTA dispute settlement from being litigated or re-litigated in Geneva would be tantamount to the removal of that right of access to Geneva justice. However, it may be objected that the party whose rights are said to be deprived has also entered freely into a further treaty commitment to subject disputes to a specialized dispute settlement regime outside Geneva. One may question the wisdom or desirability of doing so, especially the desirability of a fragmented international trade dispute settlement regime.[68] But where two WTO Members have freely chosen such a course of action, without affecting the rights of other WTO Members, it would be difficult to understand the view that such extra-WTO RTA dispute settlement commitments ought not to be taken into account of at all when construing a WTO Member's right of access to Geneva justice.

IX. The Structure and Context of WTO Norms

In sum, the manner in which Article 31(3)(c) may be used, and in which its employment may be optimal, depends upon the substantive WTO norm, and the competing non-WTO norm.

[66] *EC—Large Civil Aircraft* (n 3) para 845.

[67] *Mexico—Soft Drinks* (n 49) paras 52–53.

[68] See Gao and Lim (n 5).

Mavroidis and Palmeter, whom I referred to earlier, consider that other 'applicable' treaties could include such treaties (for example, RTAs) to which two or more WTO Members are party, but does not require that all other WTO Members should also be party to that treaty.[69] In contrast, Pauwelyn appears to favour the view that for a treaty to be taken into account under Article 31(3)(c), it should reflect the common intention of all the parties to the relevant WTO agreement,[70] unless the RTA norm is to be 'directly' applied by the WTO panel or Appellate Body.[71]

Again, it would seem that such questions are best answered not in the abstract, but by looking at the facts and the context. Let us first take the higher threshold of a common intention of all WTO Members, which Pauwelyn suggests is a pre-requisite for applying Article 31(3)(c). In the case of our first scenario above, involving GATT Article XX, it is, for the reasons already given, easy to say that it is, in fact, the common intention of the parties that non-WTO rules should be taken into account in the interpretation of GATT Article XX. The situation might be different in the case of the exemption of RTA members from safeguard action, as it is likely to be difficult to show that WTO Members intended that RTAs that preclude safeguard measures should be taken into account in the interpretation of the GATT and the Safeguards Agreement. As for WTO–RTA dispute settlement conflicts, as I have said, the question is whether it would affect other WTO Members if two parties have chosen to say by treaty that RTA disputes which overlap with their existing WTO commitments should be brought to dispute resolution elsewhere other than in Geneva.

Even if the lower threshold advocated by Mavroidis and Palmer were to be adopted (namely that even if a treaty applying only to the disputing parties ought to be taken into account), one would still have to apply that view within the specific facts and the context of the interpretative question that arises. Adopting the lower threshold need not change the interpretative outcome. There is no reason to think that the lower threshold would necessarily overcome the view that just because two or more WTO Members have agreed to exempt each other from safeguard action that would necessarily resolve the problem. That issue has to do, instead, with the fact that other WTO Members would be discriminated against.

X. Conclusion

In this tribute to Matsushita, I have chosen to discuss the scope for the systemic integration of WTO and RTA norms through Article 31(3)(c) of the VCLT. I have

69 Mavroidis and Palmeter (n 64) 57; discussed further in Pauwelyn (n 4) 259.

70 Pauwelyn, (n 4) 261–62.

71 ibid 263; see further, on the application by WTO panels and the Appellate Body of RTA treaty rules, Gao and Lim (n 5).

used the integration of non-trade norms under GATT Article XX as a useful comparison.

So far as the VCLT is concerned, Article 31(1) accepts that sometimes treaty words cannot mean what they suggest upon their literal reading. Moreover, treaty words cannot be read in the abstract. Rather, under Articles 31(1) and (2), they ought to be read in the context in which they appear, for words often have shades of meaning.[72] Article 31(2) then defines such context to include the terms—including the preamble and annexes—*and* any agreement relating to the treaty that was made by all the parties in connection with the treaty, and any instrument made by some that is accepted by others to be related to the treaty.

But it is sub-paragraphs (a), (b), and (c) of Article 31(3), which deal with subsequent agreements between the parties, subsequent conduct establishing the agreement of the parties, and other relevant and applicable rules of international law, which may be relevant to the kinds of problems we have discussed. There is an overlap at least of functions between Article 31(3)(c)'s systemic integration clause and Articles 31(2) and 31(3)(a) and (b) in providing concurrent tools of treaty interpretation for the integration of WTO and RTA norms and for determining the relevance of non-trade treaties to the interpretation of WTO norms.

Because the 'RTA problem' has often been discussed as an issue that will ultimately require the intervention of WTO Members, it is often thought that panels and the Appellate Body should exercise caution and avoid activist interpretations of WTO treaty commitments. The argument in this chapter is that panels and the Appellate Body have a *duty*, not just a discretion, to apply the rules of treaty interpretation. As RTAs have reluctantly or otherwise become accepted as a part of the landscape of international trade regulation, the time has come to devote as much attention to the interpretative issue which RTAs raise as we have previously devoted to the design and architectural aspects of the RTA problem. The two issues, seemingly disparate, are conjoined.

[72] Gardiner (n 16) 85.

9

When Popular Decisions Rest on Shaky Foundations: Systemic Implications of Selected WTO Appellate Body Trade Remedies Jurisprudence

*Meredith Kolsky Lewis**

I. Introduction

When former Appellate Body member Professor Mitsuo Matsushita gives general remarks at a conference, he often recounts, in highly amusing detail, a story about when, early in the history of the WTO, he and fellow Appellate Body members were called upon to consider the appeal in the *Japan—Alcoholic Beverages* case.[1] At issue in that case was, inter alia, whether vodka and shochu (a Japanese alcohol) are 'like products' pursuant to the first sentence of GATT Article III:2. Professor Matsushita humorously explains that the seven Appellate Body members felt compelled to 'do a little field work', and arranged a taste test for themselves to compare vodka and shochu.[2] While this tale may or may not reflect the actual actions of the Appellate Body members, it could be understood to include an implicit suggestion that 'real-world' context and experience are relevant to determining likeness.

* It is my great pleasure to contribute this chapter in honour of my mentor and friend, Professor Mitsuo Matsushita. Professor Matsushita has expressed interest in and been supportive of my scholarship since our first meeting at a 2006 conference in Australia. We have had many interesting discussions over the years, but have particularly shared an interest in the applicability of economic principles to issues arising in WTO dispute settlement, and in disputes with popular outcomes but for which we may not have agreed with the reasoning. I therefore felt the focus of this chapter would be fitting as a tribute to Matsushita-sensei.

[1] Appellate Body Report, *Japan—Taxes on Alcoholic Beverages* (*Japan—Alcoholic Beverages*), WT/DS8, 10, 11/AB/R, 4 October 1996. *Japan—Alcoholic Beverages* was only the second appeal to be heard by the Appellate Body.

[2] The Appellate Body hears appeals in divisions of three, but all seven members consult and discuss each appeal. Thus while Professor Matsushita was not on the division assigned to the *Japan—Alcoholic Beverages* dispute, he would have participated in discussions regarding the issues in the dispute.

We see a similar message—this time documented explicitly in an Appellate Body report—in the *European Communities—Measures Concerning Meat and Meat Products (Hormones)* dispute.[3] In discussing how to assess the risk to humans of treating cattle with growth hormones, the Appellate Body wrote one of the most famous lines in WTO jurisprudence: 'It is essential to bear in mind that the risk that is to be evaluated in a risk assessment under Article 5.1 [of the Agreement on the Application of Sanitary and Phytosanitary Measures] is not only risk ascertainable in a science laboratory operating under strictly controlled conditions, but also risk in human societies as they actually exist, in other words, the actual potential for adverse effects on human health in the real world where people live and work and die.'[4] Although Justice Feliciano has indicated publicly that he penned this line, Professor Matsushita also participated on this division and I am therefore taking the liberty of inferring his agreement with the sentiment.[5]

The instinct to look to the real world for context of course also finds support in the WTO Dispute Settlement Understanding (DSU). Article 3.2 indicates that the dispute settlement system 'serves to preserve the rights and obligations of Members under the covered agreements, and to clarify the existing provisions of those agreements in accordance with customary rules of interpretation of public international law'.[6] The Appellate Body made clear in its first appeal that 'customary rules of interpretation of public international law' included Articles 31 and 32 of the Vienna Convention on the Law of Treaties (VCLT),[7] explaining that the 'general rule of interpretation [in VCLT Article 31] has attained the status of a rule of customary or general international law. As such, it forms part of the "customary rules of interpretation of public international law"' which the Appellate Body has been directed to apply.[8] Article 31(1) provides that: 'A treaty shall be interpreted in good faith in accordance with the ordinary meaning to be given to the terms of the treaty in their context and in the light of its object and purpose.'[9]

In practice, particularly in certain trade remedies cases, the Appellate Body has not been consistent in applying Article 31 of the VCLT and considering the context of the relevant treaty text in light of its object and purpose, and has instead either been overly mechanistic in its textual interpretation or has

[3] Appellate Body Report, *European Communities—Measures Concerning Meat and Meat Products (Hormones)* (*EC—Hormones*), WT/DS/26, 48/AB/R, 16 January 1998.

[4] ibid 72.

[5] The Appellate Body division responsible for the *EC—Hormones* case consisted of Justice Feliciano (presiding), Claus-Dieter Ehlermann, and Professor Matsushita.

[6] DSU 15 April 1994, 1869 UNTS 401, art 3.2.

[7] Vienna Convention on the Law of Treaties (VCLT), 23 May 1969, 1155 UNTS 331.

[8] Appellate Body Report, *United States—Standards for Reformulated and Conventional Gasoline*, WT/DS2/AB/R, 29 April 1996, 17 (footnote omitted). The Appellate Body similarly indicated the applicability of VCLT art 32 in *Japan—Alcoholic Beverages* (n 1) 10 ('[t]here can be no doubt that Article 32 of the *Vienna Convention*, dealing with the role of supplementary means of interpretation, has also attained the same status'), and of the provisions of VCLT art 33 in a series of later cases. See Isabelle Van Damme, 'Treaty Interpretation by the WTO Appellate Body' (2010) 21 Eur J Intl L 605, 608 n 4.

[9] VCLT art 31(1).

strayed from the text, seemingly in favour of an outcome-based result. Section I of this chapter will discuss the appropriate role context should play in interpreting the WTO agreements. Sections II to IV will critique aspects of the Appellate Body's jurisprudence in the zeroing cases, the 1916 Act dispute, and the early safeguards cases, as generating interpretive difficulties by failing to give enough attention to real-world context and object and purpose.[10] Section V will explore possible reasons for these departures by the Appellate Body from a contextualized textual analysis, and identify some systemic implications of these decisions.

II. How Should the Covered Agreements be Interpreted?

The DSU provides guidance as to how the dispute settlement panels and Appellate Body should approach interpreting the covered agreements. Of particular relevance are Articles 3.2, 11, and 19.2, which address, inter alia, how treaty interpretation and reviews of domestic conduct should be conducted.

A. Context and object and purpose

As noted above, Article 3.2 requires reference to Articles 31 and 32 of the VCLT to ensure provisions are clarified in accordance with public international law rules of treaty interpretation, and Article 19.2 cautions that 'the panel and Appellate Body cannot add to or diminish the rights and obligations provided for in the covered agreements'.[11]

In adjudicating in accordance with the VCLT, the drafting history of the VCLT emphasizes a preference for a textual, rather than a teleological, approach to treaty interpretation.[12] However, 'textual' does not mean that the words of the text are of sole relevance. Indeed, Article 31 of the VCLT additionally requires consideration of context and the terms' object and purpose. Article 31 provides:

1. A treaty shall be interpreted in good faith in accordance with the ordinary meaning to be given to the terms of the treaty *in their context* and in the light of its object and purpose.
2. *The context* for the purpose of the interpretation of a treaty *shall comprise*, in addition to the text, including its preamble and annexes:
   (a) any agreement relating to the treaty which was made between all the parties in connection with the conclusion of the treaty;

[10] Because this chapter aims to provide a macro-level critique, the cases are summarized briefly, rather than described in detail.

[11] DSU art 19.2.

[12] Michael Lennard, 'Navigating by the Stars: Interpreting the WTO Agreements' (2002) 5 J Intl Econ L 17, 20–22.

(b) any instrument which was made by one or more parties in connection with the conclusion of the treaty and accepted by the other parties as an instrument related to the treaty.

3. There shall be taken into account, together with the *context*:

(a) any subsequent agreement between the parties regarding the interpretation of the treaty or the application of its provisions;

(b) any subsequent practice in the application of the treaty which establishes the agreement of the parties regarding its interpretation;

(c) any relevant rules of international law applicable in the relations between the parties. [emphasis added]

Thus while WTO treaty analysis must begin with the actual text, '[t]his is only a starting point. The reference to the object and purpose and the context confirms that interpretation is not well served if it does not consider other elements besides the text of the treaty.'[13]

The Appellate Body has considered context and object and purpose in a variety of cases[14] but it has not done so consistently. For example, in *EC—Chicken Cuts*, the Appellate Body, in interpreting the meaning of 'salted' in the European Communities' tariff schedule, considered context under both Article 31(1) and 31(2). Its analysis pursuant to VCLT Article 31(2) was particularly extensive, spanning nearly fifty paragraphs.[15] With respect to Article 31(1), the Appellate Body approved of the panel's determination that 'factual context' is a part of the ordinary meaning.[16] This suggests an intent to interpret 'ordinary meaning' with reference to context rather than solely the dictionary definition.[17] The Appellate Body also characterized the treaty interpretation process as a 'holistic exercise that should not be mechanically subdivided into rigid components'.[18]

In contrast to its focus on context and taking a holistic approach thereto in *EC—Chicken Cuts*, the Appellate Body has in other cases, particularly certain trade remedies disputes, seemed either to assess context in an overly mechanistic way[19] or to ignore the VCLT altogether.

[13] Van Damme (n 8) 620. [14] ibid 622.

[15] Appellate Body Report, *European Communities—Customs Classification of Frozen Boneless Chicken Cuts* (*EC—Chicken Cuts*), WT/DS269, 286/AB/R, September 2005, paras 188–235.

[16] ibid para 187.

[17] Van Damme (n 8) 626.

[18] *EC—Chicken Cuts* (n 15) para 176. Even in *EC—Chicken Cuts*, however, the Appellate Body examined 'context' completely separate from 'object and purpose', see Henrik Horn and Robert L Howse, 'European Communities—Customs Classification of Frozen Boneless Chicken Cuts' (2008) 7 World Trade Rev 9, 15. A more holistic approach to context would not assess these two elements entirely separately.

[19] See e.g., Federico Ortino, 'Treaty Interpretation and the WTO Appellate Body Report in US—Gambling: A Critique' (2006) 9 J Intl Econ L 117, 131 (critiquing Appellate Body's assessment of context as being overly mechanistic); Lennard (n 12) 23 (analysis should involve a holistic approach, rather than being conducted robotically).

B. Standard of review

In addition to taking into account context and object and purpose, the panels and Appellate Body also need to determine the appropriate standard of review to apply in assessing the measures they are reviewing. DSU Article 11 provides the following general guidance[20] on the standard of review to be applied in reviewing a Member's measure: 'a panel should make an objective assessment of the matter before it, including an objective assessment of the facts of the case and the applicability of and conformity with the relevant covered agreements'.

The Appellate Body has stated that the appropriate standard under Article 11 'must be considered in light of the obligations of the particular covered agreement at issue in order to derive the more specific contours of the appropriate standard of review'.[21] Ross Becroft has argued that 'where there has been a prior national-level process, such as in trade remedy matters, this approach should result in a more deferential standard being applied'.[22] However, the Appellate Body has not applied a more deferential standard of review in trade remedies cases, but has instead repeatedly criticized panels in such cases for failing to conduct a sufficiently rigorous review of the underlying evidence.[23] Furthermore, the Appellate Body has essentially ignored the more deferential standard of review required by the Anti-dumping Agreement.[24]

The following sections elaborate upon the concerns described in this introduction.

III. The Zeroing Cases

As many readers will know, the WTO dispute settlement system has addressed the permissibility of zeroing, a methodology used in calculating anti-dumping duties, on numerous occasions.[25] These cases have generated significant controversy because of the level of disagreement between the panels and Appellate Body on the merits, and because it took many years and lost cases before the United States largely ceased the practice of zeroing.[26] This section will focus on the former.

[20] As will be discussed below, the Anti-dumping Agreement contains its own agreement-specific standard of review provision, art 17.6(ii).

[21] Appellate Body Report, *United States—Countervailing Duty Investigation on Dynamic Random Access Memory Semiconductors (DRAMS) from Korea*, WT/DS296/AB/R, 27 June 2006, para 184.

[22] Ross Becroft, 'The WTO Standard of Review: A Means to Strengthen the Trading System' in Susy Frankel and Meredith Kolsky Lewis (eds), *Trade Agreements at the Crossroads* (Routledge 2014) 70.

[23] ibid 70–71.

[24] Agreement on Implementation of Article VI of the General Agreement on Tariffs and Trade 1994 (Anti-dumping Agreement), 15 April 1994, 1868 UNTS 201, art 17.6(ii).

[25] For the purposes of this chapter, no understanding of zeroing is required. For an explanation of the methodology and different contexts in which it has been challenged, see Meredith Kolsky Lewis, 'Dissent as Dialectic: Horizontal and Vertical Disagreement in WTO Dispute Settlement' (2012) 48 Stan J Intl L 1, 18–19.

[26] The US change in policy was reported in the Federal Register in 2012. See Antidumping Proceedings: Calculation of the Weighted-Average Dumping Margin and Assessment Rate in Certain Antidumping Duty Proceedings; Final Modification, 77 Fed Reg 8101 (14 February 2012).

On the surface, the zeroing cases might appear straightforward and to raise no cause for concern. The Appellate Body has never found any use of zeroing to be permissible, and, following an early case involving the European Union,[27] the United States has been the sole respondent in the many separate disputes challenging zeroing in a host of contexts. Zeroing is widely reviled as a practice, as its use will almost always result in higher anti-dumping margins. However, these cases merit attention because the reasoning applied therein raises a number of concerns. While the Appellate Body has never upheld the use of zeroing, several dispute settlement panels determined that at least some forms of zeroing were permissible, and two panels so found even *after* the Appellate Body had found such zeroing to be impermissible in earlier disputes.[28] Eventually the Appellate Body encouraged panels, in the name of security and predictability, to stop fighting this fight, and panels indeed began following the Appellate Body's decisions.[29] However, the initial level of disagreement between the panels and the Appellate Body was, and remains, unprecedented.[30]

The Anti-dumping Agreement contemplates three ways to compare prices, and in which zeroing could therefore theoretically be used:

> [T]he existence of margins of dumping during the investigation phase shall normally be established on the basis of a comparison of a weighted average normal value with a weighted average of prices of all comparable export transactions or by a comparison of normal value and export prices on a transaction-to-transaction basis. A normal value established on a weighted average basis may be compared to prices of individual export transactions [under certain elaborated conditions]....[31]

From the earliest cases, there was primarily agreement that Article 2.4.2 prohibited zeroing in the weighted average to weighted average (WA–WA) context. The disagreement centred over whether the above provision also prohibited zeroing when transactions were compared to transactions (T–T) or a weighted average was compared to separate transactions (WA–T). In the four cases leading up to the Appellate Body signalling that the debate should end, eleven of twelve panellists found zeroing in the T–T and/or W–T context to be permissible, while the divisions of the Appellate Body unanimously found in each case that such zeroing was impermissible.[32]

Before turning to the merits, it bears noting that the Anti-dumping Agreement requires a more deferential standard of review than DSU Article 11. Article 17.6(ii)

See also Sungjoon Cho, 'No More Zeroing? The United States Changes its Antidumping Policy to Comply with the WTO' (9 March 2012) 16(8) Am Socy Intl L Insights.

[27] Appellate Body Report, *European Communities—Anti-dumping Duties on Cotton-type Bed Linen from India*, WT/DS141/AB/R, 1 March 2001.

[28] See Panel Report, *United States—Measures Relating to Zeroing and Sunset Reviews* (*US—Zeroing (Japan)*), WT/DS322/R, 20 September 2006; Panel Report, *United States—Final Anti-dumping Measures on Stainless Steel from Mexico* (*US—Stainless Steel (Mexico)*), WT/DS344/R, 20 December 2007.

[29] Appellate Body Report, *United States—Final Anti-dumping Measures on Stainless Steel from Mexico*, WT/DS344/AB/R, 30 April 2008, para 160.

[30] See Lewis (n 25) 19–21.

[31] Anti-dumping Agreement, art 2.4.2.

[32] For a discussion of these cases and the level of disagreement, see Lewis (n 25) 19–22.

provides: 'the panel shall interpret the relevant provisions of the Agreement in accordance with customary rules of interpretation of public international law. Where the panel finds that a relevant provision of the Agreement admits of more than one permissible interpretation, the panel shall find the authorities' measure to be in conformity with the Agreement if it rests upon one of those permissible interpretations.'[33]

Thus the Anti-dumping Agreement contemplates that there may be provisions that could be subject to more than one permissible interpretation. In such a case, the adjudicators should defer to the interpretation of the domestic authorities, if it is based on one of the permissible interpretations.[34] Some have argued that Article 17.6(ii) was intended to require deference akin to the so-called *Chevron* deference that US courts apply in administrative law cases.[35] This narrative would be consistent with the understanding, expressed by several scholars, that Article 17.6(ii) of the Anti-dumping Agreement was drafted by the United States in order to imbed precisely this type of deference.[36] While others have rejected the notion that Article 17.6(ii) was intended to build Chevron-style deference into the Agreement per se,[37] it is difficult to argue with the proposition that Article 17.6(ii) requires some level of deference.[38]

Without delving into the arguments made by the panels and Appellate Body, the fact that four panels in a row (each of which featured one or more panellists with extensive trade remedies experience) read Article 2.4.2 to permit the zeroing methodology at issue, would seem like strong evidence either that (a) the panels had the only correct interpretation; or (b) there were two permissible interpretations. As to the former, the panels in the later two disputes identified flaws in the reasoning of the Appellate Body in the two earlier disputes,[39] including noting that the Appellate Body's reading of Article 2.4.2 as prohibiting zeroing in all instances would render the WA–WA and WA–T methodologies the same and

[33] Anti-dumping Agreement, art 17.6(ii).

[34] See Van Damme (n 8) 609.

[35] *Chevron USA, Inc v Natural Resources Defense Council, Inc*, 467 US 837 (1984). In *Chevron*, the Supreme Court held that in interpreting statutes that mandate agency action, courts should give deference to the implementing agencies' interpretations of said statutes unless those interpretations are unreasonable.

[36] See e.g., Roger P Alford, 'Reflections on US—Zeroing: A Study in Judicial Overreaching by the WTO Appellate Body' (2006) 45 Colum J Transnatl L 196, 200–02.

[37] See e.g., Sungjoon Cho, 'The World Trade Constitutional Court' (2009) Faculty Scholarship Paper No 182, 27 <http://scholarship.kentlaw.iit.edu/fac_schol/182> accessed 7 March 2016; Carlos Manuel Vázquez, 'Judicial Review in the United States and in the WTO: Some Similarities and Differences' (2004) 36 Geo Wash Intl L Rev 587, 603–04; Steven P Croley and John H Jackson, 'WTO Dispute Procedures, Standards of Review, and Deference to National Governments' (1996) 90 Am J Intl L 193, 205–06.

[38] See e.g., Andrew T Guzman, 'Determining the Appropriate Standard of Review in WTO Disputes' (2009) 42 Cornell Intl LJ 45, 75 ('Article 17.6 of the AD Agreement reflects the decision of the member states that panels should refrain from aggressive review of anti-dumping measures').

[39] The Appellate Body's decision in the Appellate Body Report, *United States—Laws, Regulations and Methodology for Calculating Dumping Margins ('Zeroing')* (*US—Zeroing (EC)*), WT/DS294/AB/R, 18 April 2006 dispute was particularly deficient, relying largely on its own prior reports, rather than conducting a VCLT analysis of the Anti-dumping Agreement.

thus render the third sentence inutile.[40] In the *US—Zeroing (Japan)* appeal, the Appellate Body disagreed with this assessment but did little to clarify its own analysis.[41] With respect to the latter, the Appellate Body rejected the notion that the large number of panellists' readings of Article 2.4.2 could be correct; it has never found multiple permissible interpretations of the Anti-dumping Agreement, and has effectively read Article 17.6(ii) out of the Agreement.[42] Isabelle Van Damme has commented that rather than looking for permissible interpretations, '[t]he Appellate Body seeks the "proper" or "correct" interpretation, not any "permissible" interpretation.... A right interpretation is not the same as a possible interpretation; and a possible interpretation is not the same as the better or best answer to an interpretive problem.'[43]

Although WTO Members are probably pleased with the Appellate Body's zeroing jurisprudence, they should instead have some concerns. Particularly in its early zeroing decisions, the Appellate Body did not base its decisions on a clearly textual VCLT analysis, but instead relied on the concept of 'the product as a whole' (as the only acceptable basis for assessing dumping, rather than looking at individual transactions), which does not appear in the Anti-dumping Agreement but was instead an argument raised in the European Communities' written submissions.[44] This non-textual and non-contextual approach runs afoul of DSU Article 3.2 and erodes security and predictability.

The Appellate Body's failure to give effect to Article 17.6(ii) of the ADA similarly reflects a blinkered approach that has disregarded context and object and purpose. The Anti-dumping Agreement is the only WTO agreement to have a separate standard of review, and it is a notably deferential standard. Reading this standard out of the Agreement is inappropriate, even if applying it would mean fewer measures were struck down. That is the bargain Members struck in their negotiations, and the Appellate Body should not disregard it. Doing so arguably violates DSU Article 19.2 by diminishing Members' rights under the covered agreements.

Finally, the Appellate Body's approach in the zeroing decisions discussed above may complicate the Organization's efforts to complete future agreements. The Rules negotiations in the Doha Round have included efforts by the United States to make it explicit that zeroing is permitted.[45] Even if the United States backs

[40] *US—Zeroing (Japan)* (n 28) paras 7.136–7.143.

[41] See Tania Voon, 'The End of Zeroing? Reflections Following the WTO Appellate Body's Latest Missive' (2007) 34 Legal Issues Econ Integration 211, 225.

[42] In some instances it has declined to accept that there was more than one permissible interpretation of the treaty text; in others, it has simply ignored art 17.6(ii). See Van Damme (n 8) 610. See also Voon (n 41) 219 (art 17.6(ii) has arguably been rendered a dead letter).

[43] Van Damme (n 8) 610.

[44] See Lewis (n 25) 37.

[45] These efforts began early in the zeroing saga. In the 2007 draft chairperson's text relating to anti-dumping and subsidies, provisions were included specifying the permissibility of zeroing in a number of contexts. See WTO, Negotiating Group on Rules, *Draft Consolidated Chair Texts of the AD and SCM Agreements*, TN/RL/W/213, 30 November 2007. The United States was reportedly dissatisfied that the draft did not go further in permitting zeroing, whereas other delegations objected to any authorization of zeroing at all. See International Centre for Trade and Sustainable Development, 'Divisions Persist on Anti-dumping Draft Text' (30 January 2008) 12(3) Bridges

down on this issue, it seems highly likely that it will insist on more precise, exacting language in future agreements. Given that a degree of fuzzy language is often necessary to get all parties comfortable enough to conclude an international treaty, this should be a matter of concern for other Members.

IV. The 1916 Act Case—Blurring Trade and Antitrust?

The second instance in which the Appellate Body has reached a popular result without necessarily taking into account relevant contextual considerations is its decision in the *United States—Anti-dumping Act of 1916* dispute.[46] On initial impression, this case raised few eyebrows. The law in question, which provided a private right of action (as well as the possibility of government action) for predatory international price discrimination, had not been invoked successfully in its over eighty-year history, and the US government did not particularly care whether or not it remained on the books. At the same time, the few instances where courts had left open the possibility that the right case could be successful against foreign defendants who had had anti-dumping duties levied against them in US administrative proceedings (pursuant to an entirely different statute), was enough to cause consternation amongst trading partners. Nonetheless, the Appellate Body's approach to this dispute seems again to have been somewhat outcome-driven, without fully taking into account the relevant context.

The 1916 Act (although the statute is often referred to as the Antidumping Act of 1916, its official name is 'Title VIII of the United States Revenue Act of 1916'[47] and the Act itself does not use the words 'dumping' or 'antidumping') made it illegal to 'commonly and systematically ... cause to be imported and sold ... articles within the United States at a price substantially less than the actual market price or wholesale price ... in the principal markets of the country of ... exportation ... provided, that such act ... be done with the intent of destroying or injuring an industry in the United States ... or of restraining or monopolizing any part of trade ... in such articles in the United States'.[48] The 1916 Act was a penal statute, with imprisonment a possible penalty, alongside fines. Private parties could also seek treble damages.[49]

One of the major issues in the dispute was whether the 1916 Act regulated dumping, in which case it arguably violated the mandate of GATT Article VI by providing remedies for dumping other than anti-dumping duties (the 1916 Act provided for the possibility of criminal fines and treble damages), or regulated anti-competitive behaviour in the sense of an antitrust statute. The panel and Appellate Body both

<http://www.ictsd.org/bridges-news/bridges/news/divisions-persist-on-anti-dumping-draft-text> accessed 7 March 2016; WTO, Negotiating Group on Rules, *Communication from the Chairman*, TN/RL/W/254, 21 April 2011, 6 (noting wide divide amongst members on the issue of zeroing).

[46] Appellate Body Report, *United States—Anti-dumping Act of 1916*, WT/DS136/AB/R, 28 August 2000.

[47] Revenue Act of 1916, 39 Stat 756 (1916); 15 USC s 72 (2004).

[48] Revenue Act of 1916, s 801. [49] ibid.

concluded that the Act regulated dumping. Also at issue was whether the petitioners could challenge the Act 'as such' (since it had never been successfully invoked). This issue hinged upon whether the United States Justice Department had discretion in enforcing the law or whether it was mandatory legislation. On this issue, the Appellate Body deemed the Act mandatory, and thus susceptible to an 'as such' challenge.

On the first issue, the Appellate Body seems to have discounted context in its assessment. While the international price discrimination regulated by the Act has an overlap with anti-dumping in that anti-dumping also regulates selling more cheaply in a foreign market than in the home market, the Act's predatory intent requirement is more reminiscent of an antitrust law than an anti-dumping rule. In addition, the remedies, including treble damages, were consistent with those found in the US antitrust laws. Indeed, the Act appeared[50] alongside the US antitrust laws, in Title 15 of the United States code, in a chapter immediately following a chapter entitled 'Monopolies and Combinations in Restraint of Trade'. The chapter in which the Act featured is called Federal Trade Commission; Promotion of Export Trade and Prevention of Unfair Methods of Competition. Thus the 1916 Act is not in Title 19 of the US code, which is where the US trade laws that explicitly address anti-dumping have been located, including the Anti-dumping Act of 1921 (19 USC 160 et seq) and the current law, Title VII of the Tariff Act of 1930, as amended (19 USC ch 4). Title 19 also contains the Trade Act of 1974, as amended (19 USC ch 12), which houses, inter alia, the US safeguards law and the provisions establishing the Office of the United States Trade Representative.

For most of the Act's existence, it was understood to be an antitrust statute.[51] The Act was little used because other laws existed to remedy anti-competitive, predatory conduct (for example, the Sherman Act), and it was not used to combat dumping due to the required showing of predatory intent and the availability of the Anti-dumping Act of 1921 and later Title VII of the Tariff Act of 1930, both of which addressed dumping directly and did not require a showing of predatory intent.[52]

Those who wished to use the Act to remedy anti-dumping quickly determined that the statutory requirements made it too difficult to take action. Thus there were almost immediate steps to enact an administrative mechanism to address dumping,

[50] As a result of the WTO rulings, the Act was repealed in 2004. 15 USC s 72 (2004).

[51] See e.g., Jeffrey L Kessler, 'The Antidumping Act of 1916: Antitrust Analogue or Anathema?' (1986) 56 Antitrust LJ 485, 485 (1987) ('the 1916 Act is an antitrust statute whose aim is the prevention of *predatory* international price discrimination, not the protection of domestic industries from foreign competition'. 'The 1916 Act is not a protectionist act, but an antitrust act, and … [its] purpose … is to foster competition for the benefit of the consumer'); Saxon Peters, 'The 1916 Antidumping Act After Goss: Why a More Expansive Reading of the Act's Intent Requirement Is Justified' (2004) 4 UC Davis Bus LJ 8 ('During the majority of its existence, the Antidumping Act of 1916 has largely been seen as an antitrust statute of little or no significance.'); *Zenith Radio Corp v Matsushita Elec Indus Co, Ltd*, 494 F Supp 1190, 1242 (ED Pa 1980).

[52] See also Hiroko Yamane, 'The Anti-dumping Act of 1916: A Victory at What Cost?' (2001) 7(1) Intl Trade L & Reg 12, 12–13 and n 6 (noting US Department of Justice Antitrust Enforcement guidelines describing the 1916 Act as covering 'subject matter … closely related to the antitrust rules regarding predation').

which resulted in the Anti-dumping Act of 1921.[53] The 1916 Act has been deemed 'a dead letter almost from its enactment'[54] and the efforts to bring actions under the Act were few and far between. The first courts that had occasion to interpret the Act treated it as an antitrust statute.[55] It was not until the late 1990s that two courts left open the possibility that the 1916 Act could be invoked by petitioners who had succeeded in administrative anti-dumping proceedings. It was these opinions that sparked the EC and Japan to challenge the 1916 Act as such (rather than as applied).[56] In the end, only one plaintiff ever succeeded in obtaining damages under the 1916 Act, ironically in litigation commenced *after* the initiation of the WTO proceedings.[57]

Although the panel and Appellate Body decided that the 1916 Act could be applied to remedy dumping as well as antitrust violations, it seems unlikely that this was the original legislative intent: 'it is very rare that a violation of the antidumping law also would be a violation of antitrust law'.[58]

To the extent that the Act regulated a type of dumping that rose to the level of predatory conduct, it would have better respected the separate objectives of unfair trade laws and competition laws to view the Act as addressing a type of anti-competitive conduct falling within the antitrust sphere. Reading the 1916 Act as an anti-dumping measure rather than an antitrust statute could encroach upon countries' ability to enforce aspects of their antitrust laws.[59] Deeming provisions designed to provide antitrust remedies to be contrary to the Anti-dumping Agreement effectively removes the availability of those remedies for their intended purpose.[60] As Professor Matsushita has explained, it is entirely possible based on the WTO's 1916 Act jurisprudence that WTO Members could complain about a variety of other antitrust-focused statutes, thus encroaching upon Members' ability to regulate anti-competitive conduct.[61] For example, the United States'

[53] Matthew J Marks, 'United States Antidumping Laws—A Government Overview' (1974) 43 Antitrust LJ 580, 582.

[54] See Harvey M Applebaum, 'The Antidumping Laws—Impact on the Competitive Process' (1974) 43 Antitrust LJ 590, 591.

[55] See e.g., *Zenith Radio Corporation v Matsushita Electric Industrial Co, Ltd*, 494 F Supp 1190 (ED Pa 1980).

[56] *Geneva Steel Co v Ranger Steel Supply Corp*, 980 F Supp 1209 (D Utah 1997); *Wheeling-Pittsburgh Steel Corp v Mitsui & Co*, 26 F Supp 2d 1022 (SD Ohio 1998).

[57] Goss Graphic Systems was awarded treble damages in its suit against Tokyo Kikai Seisakusho (TKS), in a trial held in the United States District Court for the Northern District of Iowa. Although this litigation was stayed for a lengthy period pending the resolution of the WTO dispute, it ultimately proceeded against TKS (other defendants settled their claims) because it did not appear that Congress would repeal the 1916 Act retrospectively, meaning this litigation would remain live (and indeed, Congress repealed the Act prospectively in 2004, during the pendency of TKS's appeal). *Goss Intern Corp v Tokyo Kikai Seisakusho, Ltd*, 294 F Supp 2d 1027 (ND Iowa 2003). The United States Court of Appeals for the Eighth Circuit affirmed the award. I was counsel to one of the other defendants in an earlier phase of the litigation and in that capacity researched the history of the 1916 Act in detail.

[58] Mitsuo Matsushita and Douglas E Rosenthal, 'Was the WTO Mistaken in Ruling on Antidumping Act of 1916?' (2001) 18 Intl Trade Reporter 1450.

[59] ibid. [60] ibid.

[61] Mitsuo Matsushita, 'Basic Principles of the WTO and the Role of Competition Policy' (2004) 3 Wash U Global Stud L Rev 363, 371.

Robinson-Patman Act[62] is an antitrust statute that regulates injurious, unjustified price discrimination and, like US antitrust laws generally, applies extraterritorially. The remedies for violating the Robinson-Patman Act, as with many US antitrust laws, include injunctive relief and the possibility of treble damages. In light of the WTO's 1916 Act findings, Professor Matsushita has noted the possibility that WTO Members could challenge the Robinson-Patman Act as well, arguing that it covers dumping in that it regulates international price discrimination, and that thus it is covered by the Anti-dumping Agreement and the only permissible remedy for a breach is the imposition of anti-dumping duties.[63]

Paul Stephan has more broadly critiqued the WTO's failure to incorporate context into its analysis of disputes with an antitrust component: 'The WTO has had little direct involvement with competition policy, but the few instances in which it has engaged these problems illustrate the shortcomings of international supervision of national competition law. In the Kodak-Fuji dispute, the WTO dispute settlement process rejected the claim that Japan's tolerance of inefficient retail distribution networks, which impeded the entry of foreign products, constituted an impermissible trade barrier.'[64] Stephan argues that the Appellate Body's condemnation of the 1916 Act as violating the Anti-dumping Agreement (ADA) further illustrates a misguided approach:

> A symmetrical dispute involving US antitrust law reinforces the point.... This statute [the 1916 Act], as interpreted by the US courts, simply recapitulated the substantive requirements of a predatory pricing violation under the Sherman Act. No criminal or civil suit under the 1916 Act had ever succeeded. But, because in form, the 1916 Act regulates dumping in a matter not authorized by the WTO agreements, the WTO condemned it as violating US obligations [under the ADA].[65]

Stephan attributes these findings as coming 'at the cost of the substantive ends that these agreements purportedly pursue'.[66]

Thus while the Appellate Body's decision was in a sense quite safe in that it addressed the 'chilling effect' concerns of the petitioners while only impacting a law that was already moribund, it was also somewhat risky to import into the WTO realm a statute that, in context, had never been successfully invoked by plaintiffs; had never been invoked by government (but was nonetheless deemed

[62] 15 USC s 13 *et seq* (1936).

[63] Matsushita, 'Basic Principles of the WTO and the Role of Competition Policy' (n 61) 371–72. Professor Matsushita also raises the possibility that private challenges to subsidies as forms of predatory pricing could lead to an argument that the remedy should be a countervailing duty rather than the remedies provided for under competition/antitrust laws. ibid 372.

[64] Paul B Stephan, 'Global Governance, Antitrust, and the Limits of International Cooperation' (2005) 38 Cornell Intl LJ 173, 200. While Stephan and Matsushita share concerns regarding the WTO's competition-law-related jurisprudence, Stephan argues against developing an international competition law regime, whereas Matsushita has advocated for incorporating antitrust to a greater degree into the WTO system: 'There will be a greater need to increase to the application of competition rules in the framework of the WTO in order to maintain market access among member states.' Mitsuo Matsushita, 'Competition Law and Policy in the Context of the WTO System' (1995) 44 DePaul L Rev 1097, 1106.

[65] Stephan (n 64) 200–01.

[66] ibid 201.

'mandatory'); and which was situated with the antitrust laws and had the hallmarks of an antitrust statute. It would have better balanced context and object and purpose to treat the 1916 Act as discretionary and not susceptible to an as such challenge. Had the Appellate Body done so and litigation never advanced beyond preliminary stages under the Act, there would have been minimal impact to deferring to the national characterization of the Act and treating it as presumptively not targeted at dumping. If, however, the Goss litigation had arisen and proceeded as it did, an 'as applied' challenge could then have been brought, with no need to grapple with whether the Act could theoretically be used to remedy dumping.

V. Safeguards

Lastly, we turn to the Appellate Body's jurisprudence in cases challenging the imposition of safeguard measures, for which it has been subject to some criticism.[67] In particular, in a series of decisions in the late 1990s and early 2000s, the Appellate Body, among other things, interpreted the Safeguards Agreement to require that the relevant increase in imports result from 'unforeseen developments' even though this language had been essentially read out of GATT Article XIX by GATT panels and does not appear in the Safeguards Agreement,[68] and appeared to conflate correlation and causation, leading to confusion as to how to demonstrate the requisite causation.[69] During this period, every safeguards measure that was challenged in WTO dispute settlement was deemed to violate WTO rules.[70] As a result, some questioned whether it would ever be possible to impose a WTO-consistent safeguard.[71]

Presumably as a result of the jurisprudence described above, the imposition of safeguards dropped significantly among WTO Members after 2003.[72] The

[67] See e.g., Alan O Sykes, 'The Safeguards Mess: A Critique of WTO Jurisprudence' (2003) U Chicago L Econ, Olin Working Paper No 187 <http://ssrn.com/abstract=415800 > accessed 7 March 2016.

[68] This interpretation was surprising given that the Safeguards Agreement had been imported in significant part from the United States safeguards law, Section 201 of the Trade Act of 1974, as amended, which does not contain an 'unforeseen developments' requirement.

[69] For a detailed critique of the Appellate Body's early safeguards jurisprudence, see Sykes (n 67).

[70] These cases included Appellate Body Report, *United States—Definitive Safeguard Measures on Imports of Wheat Gluten from the European Communities*, WT/DS166/AB/R, 22 December 2000; Appellate Body Report, *United States—Safeguard Measures on Imports of Fresh, Chilled or Frozen Lamb Meat from New Zealand and Australia*, WT/DS177, 178/AB/R, 1 May 2001; Appellate Body Report, *United States—Definitive Safeguard Measures on Imports of Circular Welded Carbon Quality Line Pipe from Korea*, WT/DS202/AB/R, 15 February 2002; and Appellate Body Report, *United States—Definitive Safeguard Measures on Imports of Certain Steel Products*, WT/DS248, 249, 251–54, 258, 259/AB/R, 10 November 2003.

[71] See e.g., Sykes (n 67) 1. My objective here is not to argue that particular safeguards decisions were incorrect, but instead to point out the systemic implications of interpreting the Safeguards Agreement quite narrowly.

[72] The number of initiations has fluctuated more dramatically over the same period. See Julien Chaisse and others, 'Mastering a Two-edged Sword: Lessons from the Rules and Litigation on Safeguards in the World Trade Organization' (2015) 13 Rich J Global L Bus 563, 572. In the case

number of safeguards measures imposed reached a peak of fifteen in 2003, and then dropped off to between five and seven between 2004 and 2008. Following the global financial crisis, there have been peaks and troughs since 2009, with as few as four safeguards imposed (in 2010) and as many as eleven (in 2011).[73] Over the period from 1 January 1996 through 30 April 2014, the primary users of safeguards were developing countries, which accounted for over ninety per cent of the measures imposed.[74] However, this figure does not entirely capture the effect the Appellate Body's jurisprudence has had on previous users of safeguards. While the United States has always imposed duties in far more anti-dumping cases than it has imposed safeguards measures, it used to impose safeguards on a regular, albeit limited, basis. From 1996 to 2002, the United States imposed a total of six safeguards, or almost one safeguard per year. Strikingly, since 2002 the United States has not imposed a single safeguard measure.[75]

The linkage between the United States' safeguards practice and the Appellate Body's safeguards jurisprudence can be inferred even more strongly when one looks at the respondents in WTO safeguards disputes. Between 1997 and 2012, forty-three WTO disputes were brought relating to the imposition of safeguard measures. Of these forty-three, the United States was the respondent in fifteen cases, or thirty-five per cent of all the disputes. However, all fifteen of the cases brought against the United States were initiated between 1997 and 2002, a period during which twenty-nine total safeguards disputes were initiated. Thus the United States went from being the respondent in over half of the safeguards cases brought between 1997 and 2002, to not imposing any safeguard measures and thus not being the subject of any further safeguards disputes from 2003 through to the present.[76]

The dramatic change in United States and other developed-country practice could be viewed as a positive. Safeguards are highly controversial because they entail a government imposing trade barriers on imports in the absence of any allegations of unfairness on the part of the importers.[77]

However, one must keep in mind the context and object and purpose of the Agreement on Safeguards. In particular, one of the objectives of the Uruguay Round negotiators was to provide a limited framework in which it would be acceptable to provide temporary support to a domestic industry, while at the same

of the United States, the latest International Trade Commission report pertaining to a global safeguards investigation was published in 2001, indicating that petitions essentially ceased after this date. See United States International Trade Commission, 'Trade Remedy Publications—Global and Special Safeguards Publications' <https://www.usitc.gov/trade_remedy/publications/safeguard_pubs.htm#201> accessed 21 April 2016.

[73] See WTO, 'Safeguard Measures by Reporting Member Period: 1 January 1995–30 April 2014' <http://www.wto.org/english/tratop_e/safeg_e/SG-Measures_By_Reporting_Member.pdf> accessed 7 September 2015.

[74] Chaisse and others (n 72) 574.

[75] See WTO (n 73). As noted above (n 72), it appears that would-be petitioners ceased filing cases in the United States after this time.

[76] Chaisse and others (n 72) 582–84.

[77] This distinguishes safeguards from the other two trade remedies, anti-dumping duties and countervailing duties, which are often described as remedying 'unfair' conduct.

time prohibiting previously used 'grey-market' measures such as voluntary restraint agreements (VRAs), orderly marketing arrangements (OMAs) and voluntary restraints on exports (VERs). The Agreement on Safeguards indeed prohibits the use of grey-market measures in Article 11(1)(b), which provides that 'a Member shall not seek, take or maintain any voluntary export restraints, orderly marketing arrangements or any similar measures on the export or import side'. While there is some uncertainty as to why this was a high priority for the negotiators,[78] logical concerns could have included the fact that grey-market arrangements are not formal treaties or agreements and as such are not transparent, and that powerful entities such as the United States and European Union could, and did, use their might to effectively impose grey-market arrangements on their trading partners.

So why allow any type of measure to protect domestic industry in the absence of 'unfair' trade practices? Grey-market measures and safeguards both serve the function of a safety valve: when political pressure becomes particularly intense to assist a domestic industry, these mechanisms provide a means to give a measure of assistance to said industry. There has long been a perceived need for such safety valves, notwithstanding their trade-distorting effects, and it seems likely that the availability of some form of safety valve was an important consideration for countries considering whether to join the WTO with its more legalistic form of dispute settlement. Thus effectively shutting the safeguards safety valve has problematic implications.

It is unlikely that Members such as the United States and others are simply withstanding the occasional intense political pressure to protect a domestic industry now that safeguards are essentially unavailable as a policy tool. Instead, they are probably reverting to the use of VRAs, VREs, and OMAs, which the Safeguards Agreement prohibits.[79] There are indicia that such measures have been used in recent years.[80] Unfortunately, it is unlikely that a WTO Member could or would police this violation of the Safeguards Agreement, because they have agreed to the breach themselves.[81]

[78] See Sykes (n 67) 12.

[79] Cf Sykes (n 67) 1, predicting that 'if the WTO continues on its present course, considerable pressure may develop for a return to "extra-legal" measures such as voluntary restraint agreements, measures that the WTO Agreement on Safeguards sought to eliminate'.

[80] One such example, albeit in the anti-dumping/countervailing duty context, is the United States—Canada Softwood Lumber Agreement of 2006, pursuant to which Canada agreed its softwood lumber industry would accept export charges or a combination of export quotas and lesser export charges, in exchange for the United States agreeing not to initiate new trade actions against the industry and to revoke retroactively various pending actions. See Softwood Lumber Agreement between the Government of Canada and the Government of the United States of America, 12 September 2006 <http://www.treaty-accord.gc.ca/text-texte.aspx?id=105072&lang=eng> accessed 7 March 2016. For a discussion of this agreement as a grey-market measure, see Yong-Shik Lee, *Safeguard Measures in World Trade: The Legal Analysis* (3rd edn, Edward Elgar 2014) 166–67.

[81] Cf Warren H Maruyama, 'The Wonderful World of VRAs: Free Trade and the Goblet of Fire' (2007) 24 Ariz J Intl Comp L 149, 154 ('the legality of VRAs was never challenged in the GATT dispute settlement process, in part because such measures were consensual and necessarily required the agreement of both parties').

Thus when we consider the Agreement on Safeguards in context and in light of its object and purpose, we can see that negotiators were agreeing to a limited safety valve, alongside an agreement to cease grey-market measures. The consequence of the Appellate Body disregarding these real-world considerations is that the permissible safety valve is now going unused by the United States and many other developed countries, and it is likely that in its stead, these Members are reverting to grey-market arrangements.

VI. Conclusion

It is important not to lose sight of the fact that the WTO is not the Free Trade Organization; it is instead a sophisticated system of *managing* trade. That system includes rules and mechanisms to remove or reduce trade barriers in many contexts. However, it also includes numerous provisions that permit various forms of government actions that are inconsistent with an unfettered free market. For example, the SPS and TBT Agreements allow Members, subject to certain conditions, to regulate to ensure the safety and healthfulness of imported foods and other products. Such regulations impede trade, because non-conforming goods will not be permitted into a regulating Member's territory. Nonetheless, the Members of the WTO, and the GATT signatories before them, determined that food and product safety were legitimate domestic objectives, and that they would therefore accept some policy space to regulate to achieve these objectives, even at the expense of some trade. The trade remedies provisions can also be seen as a form of managing trade.[82] The WTO contains entire agreements that permit, albeit with parameters, the use of trade remedies, because a number of key participants in the international trading system were not willing to commit to the GATT/WTO trade liberalization measures and limitations on national autonomy unless they could retain the right to employ certain safety valves.

While other participants would have preferred bans on such safety valves, or at least stringent limitations on their use, they recognized that some safety valves are harder to regulate than others, and as such there was some value to elaborating specified permissible safety valves, particularly if the alternative were no WTO at all. In the give-and-take of trade negotiations, these compromises were struck in the form of the Anti-dumping Agreement, Safeguards Agreement, and Agreement on Subsidies and Countervailing Measures. These agreements should be read and understood in this context. Some types of safety valves were explicitly forbidden, such as voluntary export restraints and orderly market arrangements (in the Safeguards Agreement) and the granting of remedies for dumping other

[82] For a discussion of anti-dumping as a double-edged sword, with some wishing to discipline dumping as 'unfair' and others seeking to rein in the protectionist use of antidumping measures, see Mitsuo Matsushita, 'Some International and Domestic Antidumping Issues' (2010) 5 Asian J WTO & Intl Health L & Policy 249, 250–51.

than anti-dumping duties (in the Antidumping Agreement), but in exchange, some remained.

Although there would likely be broad agreement with the proposition that the WTO's trade remedies agreements reflect a set of compromises designed to permit the use of some safety valves without issuing a blank check, it would be overly simplistic to suggest that each WTO Member had a perfect understanding of exactly what the intended meaning was of each article of every Covered Agreement. To the contrary, to reach consensus over treaty text—not just in the trade context but also in many forms of international negotiations—often necessitates using language that is vague, subject to multiple interpretations, or otherwise less than clear. In these circumstances within the WTO, dispute settlement panels and the Appellate Body may be required to determine the meaning of provisions that may have been drafted to be imprecise or unclear. Nonetheless, the panels and Appellate Body have guidance in the Dispute Settlement Understanding and VCLT. Part of the context and the object and purpose has to be to understand that the trade remedies were permitted so that Members would have agreed-to safety valves available to them if they felt it politically imperative to deviate from a hands-off, free trade approach under certain circumstances. The Appellate Body has complicated matters by disregarding the context that gave rise to the trade remedies agreements and their object and purpose.

The Appellate Body has navigated difficult terrain in its first twenty years, and is in general to be commended for positioning the WTO dispute settlement system as the 'jewel in the crown' of the WTO.[83] The Appellate Body's role is a challenging one; it is expected to refrain from judicial activism while maintaining an awareness of the systemic implications of its actions. While the Appellate Body has generally navigated these roles with only limited critiques from WTO Members and academic commentators, a subset of the anti-dumping and safeguards disputes have been more controversial. In a number of these cases, the Appellate Body has reached outcomes that Members would in the main applaud—because they would like to see more disciplines on the use of trade remedies in general—but that nonetheless raise some systemic concerns due to the substantive analysis or the flow-on implications thereof. It is probably unrealistic to expect an Appellate Body comprised of generalists, selected by a somewhat politicized process, to always be able to resolve cases involving highly technical subject matter in a manner that in the main satisfies the WTO Membership while neither adding to, nor diminishing the rights and obligations of Members provided by the covered agreements.[84] However, the Appellate Body has, particularly in some of the anti-dumping and safeguards disputes, perhaps erred too far in favour of appeasing the majority at the expense of a

[83] The dispute settlement system has been so described countless times. See e.g., Jonathan T Fried, '2013 in Dispute Settlement: Reflections from the Chair of the Dispute Settlement Body' (2013) <https://www.wto.org/english/tratop_e/dispu_e/jfried_13_e.htm> accessed 7 March 2016.

[84] DSU arts 3.2 and 19.2.

faithful VCLT analysis of what the agreements do and do not permit. While these interpretive choices may appear to be largely victimless, if nothing else, the main 'victim'—the United States—is likely to insist on more clarity and less interpretive leeway in all future trade remedies-related negotiations within the WTO. Given the gulf that already existed between the United States and many other Members on these topics, such negotiations promise to be exceedingly challenging.

10

Taming Investor–State Arbitration?

Jaemin Lee[*]

I. Introduction

As international investment arbitrations receive increasing attention from domestic constituents and as investment arbitration tribunals sometimes apply broad (or narrow) interpretation of the terms contained in investment agreements, states are contemplating various ways to limit the discretion of the tribunals. Introducing an appellate mechanism, requiring claimants to proceed to domestic courts first, and adopting lengthier and more detailed provisions in the treaty texts arguably all reflect, one way or another, such recent efforts of states.

One of the alternatives being contemplated at the moment and found in recent bilateral investment treaties (BITs) and free trade agreements (FTAs) is to expand the role of a 'Joint Committee', a consultative body composed of high-ranking officials of the contracting parties, so that it can issue a 'binding interpretation' on the terms of a BIT or an FTA, either at the request of the contracting parties or of the tribunal. As the interpretation issued by the Joint Committee binds the tribunal, this seems to be an effective way of exerting control over the investment arbitration proceeding on the part of the contracting parties. This mechanism will certainly provide peace of mind for the states. Arguably, this new attempt almost amounts to the Ministerial Council of the WTO, which is authorized to issue binding interpretation in the context of the WTO Agreements.

At the same time, this new attempt also raises new questions, both in terms of policy and legal aspects. First, with respect to the policy aspect, the new system may end up restraining the otherwise legitimate authority of the adjudicative body. It is feared that the Joint Committee issues a compromised interpretation which is not supported by the 'ordinary meaning' principle as clarified by the 1969 Vienna Convention on the Law of Treaties (VCLT). An argument can then be made about

* Professor of Law, School of Law, Seoul National University in Seoul, Korea. The basic idea of this chapter was presented at the twelfth Annual Conference of Asian Law Institute (ASLI) held at National Taiwan University in Taipei on 21–22 May 2015.

whether this will further 'politicize' the investment arbitration proceedings. As to the legal aspect, the scope and meaning of 'binding interpretation' are not entirely clear. For instance, controversies may arise as to whether the Joint Committee can issue simple interpretation of the words contained in the text or whether it can pronounce more complex interpretation loaded with legal implication—such as the term 'investor' or 'investment'—which may ultimately dispose of the legal claims at issue.

Such being the case, there are various policy and legal issues to be contemplated with regard to the expansive role of the Joint Committee in the BITs and FTA investment chapters. This chapter aims to discuss these issues in an analytical manner so that Joint Committees are tasked with proper roles and can contribute to the development of international investment law by addressing the continuing concerns of host states' governments.

II. New Suggestions to Address Structural Problems of Investment Arbitrations

Robust discussions have taken place in the international community regarding the unique nature of investment arbitrations and the rising concerns of the host states' governments that are to stand as respondents in investor–state dispute settlement (ISDS) proceedings. The unique traits and grave concerns are directly related to the current discussion of the expanded roles of Joint Committees within the context of investment agreements. As a matter of fact, investment arbitrations carry unique traits that are distinct from other forms of dispute settlement proceedings. Among the many unique characteristics, two aspects—i.e. (i) direct impact on domestic regulatory regime; and (ii) a fragmented decision-making process—stand out.

Due to these unique traits of investment arbitrations, investment chapters have now become one of the most controversial issues in FTAs.[1] This has been triggered by the realization that investment chapters pose the possibilities of eroding or usurping a host state's national sovereignty in favour of expanded rights for foreign investors.[2] The debates on ISDS proceedings tend to raise some fundamental issues in this respect,[3] including the issue of alleged infringement of the authority of the judiciary,[4] since the

[1] See, Press Release 'Response to Hankyoreh Daily's Report of "No Progress on ISDS Renegotiation"' (Ministry of Foreign Affairs and Trade of Korea, 2012), <http://www.fta.go.kr/main/info/news/data/doc/> accessed 8 March 2016; 'SSM Regulation in Seoul and U.S. Corporation COSTCO's Response' (*The Korea Herald*, 16 October 2012) (reporting on the situation in which the US retailer sues Seoul City Government over Sunday closure ordinance).

[2] ibid. See also Sang-Won Lee, 'FTA jaengjeom (2) tujaja guggasosong "pil-yo" vs "jugwonchimhae"' (*The Yonhap News Article*, 8 April 2007), <http://news.naver.com/main/ read.nhn?mode=LSD&mid=sec&sid1=101&oid=001&aid=0001599512> accessed 8 March 2016.

[3] See Free Trade Agreement Between the United States of America and the Republic of Korea (Korea–US FTA), 30 June 2007, 46 ILM 642, s B, ch 11.

[4] See Ministry of Foreign Affairs and Trade Industry and Ministry of Finance and Strategy, 'Explanatory Material on Key Issues of Korea–US FTA' (2011) 9, 15 <http://www.fta.go.kr/webmodule/_PSD_FTA/us/data/7_fta_argument.pdf> accessed 23 April 2016.

proceedings presuppose a situation where jurisprudence different from the one developed under domestic law applies to a dispute,[5] coupled with systematic circumvention of the municipal courts.[6] It is noteworthy that even in largely homogenous Europe different views on ISDS proceedings are currently being presented. For instance, countries like Germany, France, and the Czech Republic[7] have taken negative positions on ISDS proceedings, while countries like the Netherlands, Spain, and the United Kingdom remain largely positive on this issue.[8]

As such, a wide range of new alternatives has been explored in the international community to address the fundamental problems and states' concerns about (i) direct impact on domestic regulatory authority; and (ii) extremely fragmented decision-making processes that are scattered in almost 3,000 separate BITs and their respective ISDS proceedings, all operating independently and separately without visible coherence. Two ideas have been mainly explored to address these problems and concerns. They are: (i) the possible introduction of an appellate mechanism in international investment arbitrations; and (ii) the enhancement of clarity and elimination of ambiguity in the texts of investment agreements.

A. Appellate mechanism

The possibility of introducing an appellate tribunal has long been one of the priority topics in the international investment arbitration discussions.[9] At the moment,

[5] See Bahakal Yimer and others, 'Application of International Investment Agreements by Domestic Courts' (Trade and Investment Law Clinic, The Graduate Institute Geneva, 2011) 7–8 <http://graduateinstitute.ch/files/live/sites/iheid/files/sites/ctei/shared/CTEI/Law%20Clinic/Memoranda%20 2011/UNCTAD_Memo.pdf> accessed 23 April 2016.

[6] Stephan W Schill, 'Enabling Private Ordering: Function, Scope and Effect of Umbrella Clauses in International Investment Treaties' (2009) 18 (1) Minn J Intl L 1, 8.

[7] See Eliška Německá, 'The Czech Republic's Experience with Bilateral Investment Treaties' (Ministry of Finance Czech Republic, October 2013) <http://investmentpolicyhub.unctad.org/Upload/Documents/DOWNLOAD15-Czech%20Rep.-Experience%20with%20BITs.pdf> accessed 23 April 2016.

[8] With respect to the UK, cf EU Committee, *The Transatlantic Trade and Investment Partnership* (fourteenth Report of Session 2013–14, HL 179) para 169 ('We nonetheless conclude that proponents of investment protection provisions enforced by an ISDS mechanism have yet to make a compelling case for their inclusion in TTIP or to convincingly dispel public concerns'); see also Oliver Wright and Nigel Morris, 'British Sovereignty "At Risk" from EU–US Trade Deal: UK in Danger of Surrendering Judicial Independence to Multinational Corporations Warn Activists' (*The Independent*, 14 January 2014) <http://www.independent.co.uk/news/uk/politics/british-sovereignty-at-risk-from-euus-trade-deal-uk-in-danger-of-surrendering-judicial-independence-to-multinational-corporations-warn-activists-9057318.html> accessed 8 March 2016.

[9] While there are some review features contained in investment arbitrations, they are limited to specific instances requiring such reviews and do not constitute the conventional appeal mechanism where the legal issues of underlying tribunals' decisions are challenged. As for Convention on the Settlement of Investment Disputes Between States and Nationals of Other States (ICSID Convention), 18 March 1956, 575 UNTS 159, see Measures for Review Mechanism include Rectification (art 49(2)), Interpretation (art 50), Revision (art 51), and annulment (art 52). See also Jaemin Lee, 'Introduction of an Appellate Review Mechanism for International Investment Disputes' (2014) 11(1) Transnatl Disp Management, 12; Statute of the International Court of Justice, 18 April 1946, art 60 <http://www.icj-cij.org/documents/index.php?p1=4&p2=2&p3=0> accessed 8 March 2016 (stipulating no appellate procedure at the ICJ). Likewise, state-to-state arbitrations do not have

the WTO dispute settlement proceedings and some of the recent FTA dispute settlement proceedings offer rare instances of having an appellate court system in place.[10] As much as important governmental measures are challenged at investment arbitrations, states have now started to think about having another round of judicial review after the original legal proceeding.[11] At present, international investment dispute settlement proceedings, despite their paramount importance to the states and foreign investors concerned, are subject to a single, one-time decision-making formula and have no appellate review mechanism. One of the key characteristics and traits of international investment arbitration has been its promptness and simplicity, made possible, to a large extent, through the absence of an appellate review mechanism. Now, there are indications that this atmosphere is changing slowly and that a plea for the introduction of an appellate proceeding may be gathering cautious support. Some recent FTAs even specifically mention the possibility of adopting (or considering) an appellate mechanism in the future: for instance, the Korea–US FTA, which went into effect on 15 March 2012, is premised upon the general understanding between the two countries that an appellate review mechanism will be introduced in the future in a form to be negotiated between the contracting parties.[12] Likewise, the 2012 US Model BIT also envisions the ultimate introduction of an appellate mechanism, although the text has no details of it yet.[13] The Canada–EU Comprehensive Economic and Trade Agreement (CETA), whose key elements were released in October 2013 when the two sides announced their agreement to pursue the bilateral FTA, also contains in the investment chapter the possibility of an appellate mechanism.[14]

1. *Intended benefit*

Given the increasing discrepancies among the decisions rendered and approaches taken by various investment tribunals with respect to key concepts and jurisprudence

an appellate mechanism. See e.g., Permanent Court of Arbitration Optional Rules for Arbitrating Disputes Between Two States, 20 October 1992, art 32.2 <https://pca-cpa.org/wp-content/uploads/sites/175/2016/01/Optional-Rules-for-Arbitrating-Disputes-between-Two-States_1992.pdf> accessed 23 April 2016. The International Criminal Court, the International Criminal Tribunals for Former Yugoslavia, and the International Criminal Tribunals for Rwanda have appellate procedures, but these are criminal courts designed to determine personal criminal liability for certain designated international crimes. See e.g., Rome Statute of the International Criminal Court, 17 July 1998 art 81 <http://legal.un.org/icc/statute/romefra.htm> accessed 23 April 2016.

[10] See e.g., North American Free Trade Agreement (NAFTA), 17 December 1992, 32 ILM 289, ch 11; Korea–US FTA (n 3) ch 11; Free Trade Agreement Between the Republic of Korea, of the One Part, and the European Union and its Member States, of the Other Part (Korea–EU FTA), 6 October 2010, entered into force 1 July 2014, ch 14 <http://www.fta.go.kr/webmodule/_PSD_FTA/eu/doc/Full_Text.pdf> accessed 8 March 2016.

[11] The 2012 US Model Bilateral Investment Treaty (US Model BIT 2012) includes the appellate mechanism as one of the key items of the US BITs in the future. Lee (n 9) 12.

[12] See e.g., NAFTA (n 10) ch 11; Korea–US FTA (n 3) ch 11.

[13] See US Model BIT 2012, art 28, para 10.

[14] See 'Investment Provisions in the EU–Canada Free Trade Agreement (CETA)' (*European Commission*, 26 September 2014) <http://trade.ec.europa.eu/doclib/docs/2013/november/tradoc_151918.pdf> accessed 8 March 2016.

relating to investment agreements, coupled with the resulting complexities and confusion, a persuasive argument can be made that international investment arbitration might consider having an appellate mechanism in place, through which consistent and coherent legal principles and interpretations can be pronounced. Thus, it may be argued that an appellate mechanism, if properly established, will be able to address some of the key concerns harboured by stakeholders in the area of international investment arbitration. Most importantly, an appellate mechanism will be able to facilitate and foster the 'rule of law' in international investment arbitration by accumulating and spreading consistent jurisprudence in the international community.

Once coherent and reliable jurisprudence is pronounced, this will in turn assist states in their negotiations to conclude new investment agreements or amend existing ones in line with and in reflection of such jurisprudence. Over time, this process will help the global community to achieve 'multilateralization' of the global investment regime. Such coherence and clarity will certainly resolve, or at least alleviate, the chronic concerns of host states' governments in terms of investment agreements and investment arbitrations.

2. *Reality assessment*

The introduction of an appellate mechanism, however, entails complex and difficult issues in both legal and logistical terms. By way of example, how to define the nature of an appellate mechanism itself poses a difficult question. The international community may wish to create an appellate mechanism as an avenue to offer a 'second bite at the apple'—i.e., one more chance for the disputing parties to be heard before a different set of experts—to alleviate, for instance, the increasing concern of sovereign states participating in investment disputes over the possible infringement of their sovereign authority.[15] Alternatively, the international community may also wish to introduce a 'genuine' appellate proceeding, which would largely resemble appellate proceedings found in domestic courts and/or other international adjudication bodies, such as the WTO's appellate proceedings.[16] Assuming that the international community decides to introduce an appellate mechanism in the international investment dispute settlement proceedings in the future, a variety of procedural and institutional issues will then present themselves immediately. Among these are: (i) composition of an appeals tribunal; (ii) selection of a specific form of arrangements in which an appeals mechanism is established;

[15] See 'SSM Regulation in Seoul and U.S. Corporation COSTCO's at Response' (n 1) (reporting on the US retailer's suit against Seoul City Government over Sunday closure ordinance); 'One Year Anniversary of KORUS FTA: Is Seoul Ready for Changes in Global Trade Regime?' (*Yonhap News*, 14 March 2013) <http://english.yonhapnews.co.kr/news/2013/03/13/0200000000AEN20130313012800315.HTML> accessed 8 March 2016; Seung-Jun Lee, 'Minister Nominee Alludes to Revisiting Controversial ISD Clause' (*the hankyoreh*, 3 March 2013), <http://english.hani.co.kr/arti/english_edition/e_international/577175.html> accessed 8 March 2016.

[16] See Understanding on Rules and Procedures Governing the Settlement of Disputes (DSU), 15 April 1994, 1869 UNTS 401, art 17.

(iii) increase of cost and administrative burden; and (iv) an apparently discriminatory burden on developing states.[17] A variety of legal issues must be considered in connection with an appellate review mechanism in investment arbitrations. Key issues to be examined in this context include: (i) scope of appeals; (ii) initiation of appeals; (iii) remand authority of the appeals tribunal; and (iv) implications of the multiplication of the ISDS proceedings due to overlapping BITs and FTAs.

B. Detailed provisions for clarification and elaboration

Another way of addressing the current structural problems would be to set forth provisions that are as detailed as possible so as to minimize the possibility of arbitrators interpreting relevant provisions in a way that is different from what the contracting parties originally had in mind. It is evident from the recent investment agreement practice that, as states become conscious of trends in international arbitration, they tend to make treaty provisions longer and more detailed so as to ensure that their intentions prevail over the otherwise conflicting interpretations and preferences that future arbitrators may present.[18] Investment agreements and investment chapters have become thicker and more microscopic in recent years.

1. *Intended benefit*

The benefit of this approach is that it can be done with relative ease, since it does not require fundamental changes to the existing texts or regime. Rather, this approach basically involves elaboration of the existing terms and clarification of the ambiguous provisions. Enhanced clarification and reduced ambiguities would certainly help to avert unnecessary investment arbitrations. States' concerns may be adequately reflected in the course of such elaboration and clarification. In that respect, this approach may also offer a relatively easy solution to the current problems.

2. *Reality assessment*

At the same time, the downside of this approach is that it is difficult to completely overcome the ambiguities associated with the languages. This is particularly the case regarding investment agreements where the operating terms themselves are amenable to fast changes and constant evolution due to the rapid development of the global economic activities. Thus, elimination of ambiguities and enhancement of clarity of the treaty texts may only have limited effect. In addition, any effort to address the problems this way would be basically retrospective—trying

[17] See Dispute Settlement Body Special Session, *Diagnosis of the Problems Affecting the Dispute Settlement Mechanism: Some Ideas by Mexico*, TN/DS/W/90, 8, 16 (16 July 2007); see generally Gillian Reynolds, 'Promoting Imbalance: Dispute Settlement under the World Trade Organization' (2006) 7(1) Stan J Intl Relations.

[18] See examples of recent BIT contained in Chapter III, section A.

to solve the problem based on previous experiences and disputes. It may not be so effective in addressing problems and disputes that may be raised in the future, since it is difficult to tell what type of disputes will emerge before an issue is actually presented.

Furthermore, assuming that the current problems in investment agreements and arbitrations are mainly structural in nature—such as fragmented decision-making processes, the self-contained regime within the confinement of the respective BITs, and the strict application of general rules of treaty interpretation of Article 31 of the VCLT—curing these problems with mere elaboration and clarification would be subject to inherent limitations. If elaboration of terms is a cosmetic surgery, it may not be suitable or sufficient enough to address the current structural problems, which may arguably require some major overhaul.

III. Joint Committees Redefined—New Roles and Enhanced Authority

As discussed in section II, states have been exploring various methods of addressing the fundamental problems of investment agreements so as to ensure that these agreements are not used in an abusive manner. These suggestions, however, require structural changes to and significant overhaul of the existing regime and texts. Accordingly, even if the new ideas are accepted, reflecting them in the text of investment agreements may arguably take a significant amount of time and effort. Considering the ambiguities and complexities associated with investment agreements and investment disputes when devising a future mechanism, it is imperative that the new mechanism does not cause too much complication, either procedurally or substantively. Nor should it invite further legal complexities in the administration of the ISDS proceedings and the interpretation of the BITs and FTAs. The benefit of a new mechanism could easily evaporate if the new system somehow leads to *more* claims and disputes due to the introduction of the new mechanism.

It is in this context that the roles of a Joint Committee have been explored. A Joint Committee composed of the contracting parties is now mandated with the task of dealing with difficult issues arising from the implementation and interpretation of an investment agreement as seen in some of the recent investment disputes;[19] that is, (i) mobilizing collective efforts of the contracting parties to strike a balance between a state's right to regulate and the need to protect foreign investors; and (ii) interpreting the provisions of the investment agreement at issue to make sure that the parties' intention is adequately reflected.

[19] See *Vattenfall AB and others v Federal Republic of Germany*, ICSID Case No ARB/12/12, Notice of Arbitration (31 May 2012) <http://www.italaw.com/cases/documents/1655> accessed 8 March 2016. See *Philip Morris Asia Ltd v The Commonwealth of Australia*, UNCITRAL, PCA No 2012-12 <http://www.italaw.com/cases/851> accessed 23 April 2016.

A. Roles of joint committees—recent examples

Against this backdrop, the roles of Joint Committees have been expanding over the years. Various roles have been explored. Conspicuous examples of the new roles assigned to the committee are the authority (i) to make a decision on critical issues arising in arbitral proceedings; and (ii) to issue a 'binding interpretation' that will dictate the interpretation to be issued by investment tribunals. By way of example, recent investment agreements contain the following provisions regarding Joint Committees.

1. Korea–Australia FTA

Chapter 21 of the Korea–Australia FTA outlines institutional provisions of the Agreement and establishes a Joint Committee to oversee the implementation and operation of the Agreement. More specifically, pursuant to Article 21.3.2, a Joint Committee, comprised of officials of each Party, is under an obligation to supervise the implementation of the Agreement; supervise the work of committees and working groups; explore ways to enhance further trade and investment; seek to resolve disputes; and consider any other matter that may affect the operation of the Agreement.[20] The use of the word 'shall' in this particular Article, which presumably imposes strict obligatory requirement on the Joint Committee, can be manifestly contrasted with the subsequent Article, which appears to broaden the scope of the Joint Committee's role. According to Article 21.3.3, the Joint Committee 'may' consider and decide any amendment or other modification to the Agreement subject to ratification by each Party; issue interpretations of the provisions of the Agreement; and take such other action in the exercise of its functions as the Parties may agree.[21] While the two provisions contain different levels of obligations, they collectively provide the Joint Committee with a broad authority and discretion that may fundamentally affect the operation and implementation of the Agreement, either through the linkage of 'resolving disputes' or that of 'issuing interpretation'.

The role of the Joint Committee, as stipulated in Chapter 21, extends to the involvement chapter in ensuring the transparency of arbitral proceedings. For instance, with regard to the disclosure of information, Article 11.21.4(e) states that 'on request of a disputing Party, the Joint Committee shall consider issuing a decision in writing regarding a determination by the tribunal that information claimed to be protected was not properly designated'.[22] In addition, this provision goes even further to equip the Joint Committee with the significant power that can be exercised over the tribunal. Thus, the second part of the same provision elaborates that the Joint Committee's decision issued within sixty days of such a request shall

[20] Free Trade Agreement between the Government of the Republic of Korea and the Government of Australia (Korea–Australia FTA), 8 April 2014, entered into force 12 December 2014, art 21.3.2.

[21] See ibid art 21.3.3.

[22] ibid art 11.21.4(e).

be *binding on the tribunal*, and the tribunal's decision or award must be consistent with the Joint Committee's decision.[23]

The binding interpretation authority of the Joint Committee extends to other aspects of the investment chapter as well to the extent to which interpretation of substantive provisions is involved. As foreshadowed above, the Joint Committee is empowered, under Article 21.3.3(c), to issue interpretations of the provisions in the Agreement. Such an authority is reflected in Article 11.22.3 in the context of arbitral proceedings where the tribunal is obliged to be *bound* by the Joint Committee's interpretation of a provision.[24] In the same vein, Article 11.23.1 provides that the Joint Committee's interpretations of Annexes I and II are also *binding on the tribunal* and hence the tribunal's award must be consistent with the Joint Committee's decision.[25] In other words, the Joint Committee can issue its own interpretation of various key provisions in Chapter 11 that will bind reviewing investment tribunals.

2. *Japan–Australia EPA*

Similar to Chapter 21 of the Korea–Australia FTA, a Joint Committee is also established under Article 1.13 of Japan–Australia Economic Partnership Agreement (EPA), where its mandatory functions are manifestly stipulated. Pursuant to Article 1.13.2,[26] the Joint Committee, composed of representatives of the governments of the Parties, is under obligation to: review and monitor the implementation and operation of the Agreement; consider and recommend any amendments to the Agreement; supervise the work of all Sub-Committees; and adopt any necessary decisions. One of the most distinctive features that distinguishes the Joint Committee of the Japan–Australia EPA from that of the Korea–Australia FTA is the existence of the 'Sub-Committees'.[27] Although there are twelve Sub-Committees in charge of different subject matters in the Agreement, a close analysis of each Article indicates that they all share a common root in terms of obligatory functions. Take the 'Sub-Committee on Investment' as an example. Its roles are dictated in Article 14.18.2, where it is obliged to exchange information on any matters related to the Investment Chapter; review and monitor the implementation and operation of the Investment Chapter; consider any issues concerning the imposition or enforcement of performance requirements; consider any issues concerning investment agreements; report the outcome of

[23] ibid. [24] ibid art 11.22.3. [25] ibid art 11.23.1.

[26] Japan–Australia Economic Partnership Agreement (Japan–Australia EPA), 8 July 2014, entered into force 15 January 2015, art 1.13.2.

[27] Currently there are twelve Sub-Committees: on Trade in Goods (art 2.21); on Rules of Origin (art 3.28); on Customs Procedures (art 4.9); on Sanitary and Phytosanitary Cooperation (art 5.4); on Technical Regulations, Standards, and Conformity Assessment Procedures (art 6.8); on Energy and Mineral Resources (art 8.8); on Trade in Services (art 9.15); on Telecommunications (art 10.22); on Financial Services (art 11.10); on Investment (art 14.18); on Intellectual Property (art 16.21); and on Promotion of a Closer Economic Relationship (art 18.2).

discussions to the Joint Committee; and carry out other functions delegated by the Joint Committee.[28]

Unlike the Korea–Australia FTA, where the Joint Committee itself is given a wide scope of discretionary power, the Joint Committee in the Japan–Australia EPA, as indicated above, appears to have a much narrower range of power. The Joint Committee's role is further diminished by the fact that some of its functions may be delegated to the Sub-Committees. Moreover, the Joint Committee's involvement in arbitral proceedings is relatively minimal in comparison to the Korea–Australia FTA, where the Joint Committee plays a significant role in arbitral proceedings. Article 19.16.2 merely provides that the 'arbitral tribunal shall follow the Rules of Procedure adopted by the Joint Committee'.[29] Apart from this, the rest of Chapter 19 (Dispute Settlement) is silent on the role of the Joint Committee in relation to arbitral proceedings.

3. China–Canada BIT

In this regard, a provision of the recent China–Canada BIT may shed some light on the complexity of this issue in the investment dispute context. The BIT includes a provision that envisages a situation where the two parties can prepare a binding report on the validity of the prudential measure defence of a host government in an ISDS proceeding so as to bind the ISDS tribunal hearing the dispute relating to the measures at issue.[30] Put differently, the state parties in the BIT preserve the authority to issue a binding interpretation vis-à-vis an ISDS panel.[31]

4. Korea–China–Japan trilateral investment treaty (TIT)[32]

Although such an explicit provision is absent, contracting parties of the TIT have the option of resorting to the state-to-state dispute settlement proceeding[33] or to the Joint Committee[34] in order to elicit a ruling on prudential measures, which should carry significant weight for the analysis by the ISDS tribunal. A decision on the prudential measures from these other decision-making processes contained in the TIT should directly affect the outcome of an ISDS proceeding under the TIT, because the agreement explicitly carves out prudential measures from investment arbitration. Depending on how the state-to-state dispute settlement mechanism renders an opinion, jurisdictional issues may arise in the ISDS proceedings.

[28] See Japan–Australia EPA (n 26) art 14.18.2. [29] ibid art 19.16.2.

[30] See Agreement between the Government of Canada and the Government of the People's Republic of China for the Promotion and Reciprocal Protection of Investments (China–Canada BIT), 9 September 2012, arts 20 and 33, para 3.

[31] See ibid art 20, para 2.

[32] The Agreement among the Government of Japan, the Government of the Republic of Korea and the Government of the People's Republic of China for the Promotion, Facilitation and Protection of Investment (Korea–China–Japan TIT), 13 May 2012.

[33] See ibid art 17. [34] See ibid art 24.

5. *Korea–US FTA*

The Korea–US FTA establishes a Joint Committee in Article 22.2 of the Agreement. The provision also sets forth two categories of authority of the Joint Committee: the one with stringent nature using the term 'shall' and the other one with permissive nature using the term 'may'.[35] The provision stipulates in pertinent part that:

1. The Parties hereby establish a Joint Committee comprising officials of each Party, which shall be co-chaired by the United States Trade Representative and the Minister for Trade of Korea, or their respective designees.
2. The Joint Committee shall:

...

(d) seek to resolve disputes that may arise regarding the interpretation or application of this Agreement;....

3. The Joint Committee may:

...

(d) *issue interpretations of the provisions of this Agreement*, including as provided in Articles 11.22 (Governing Law) and 11.23 (Interpretation of Annexes)....

This Joint Committee is tasked with two important mandates, as in Korea–Australia FTA. The first one is the authority to make a binding decision on the appropriateness of the designation by one party as protected information so as to avoid the disclosure obligation. Article 11.21 (Transparency of Arbitral Proceedings) provides in pertinent part that:

4. Any protected information that is submitted to the tribunal shall be protected from disclosure in accordance with the following procedures:

...

(e) At the request of a disputing Party, the Joint Committee shall consider issuing a decision in writing regarding a determination by the tribunal that information claimed to be protected was not properly designated. If the Joint Committee issues a decision within 60 days of such a request, it shall be binding on the tribunal, and any decision or award issued by the tribunal must be consistent with that decision. If the Joint Committee does not issue a decision within 60 days, the tribunal's determination shall remain in effect only if the non-disputing Party submits a written statement to the Joint Committee within that period that it agrees with the tribunal's determination.

At the same time, the Joint Committee is authorized to issue an interpretation of the provisions in the investment chapter that will bind reviewing investment tribunals. In the governing law provision of Article 11.22, the Agreement provides:

3. A decision of the Joint Committee declaring its interpretation of a provision of this Agreement under Article 22.2.3(d) (Joint Committee) shall be binding on a tribunal, and any decision or award issued by a tribunal must be consistent with that decision.

As the provision above shows, it is specifically stipulated that an interpretation of the Joint Committee binds the tribunal. Furthermore, the way it is stated indicates that the Joint Committee may even override any decision of the tribunal

[35] Korea–US FTA (n 3).

insofar as there is conflict between its own interpretation and the tribunal's decision or award.

6. *Korea–Peru FTA*

The Korea-Peru FTA introduces a similar mechanism, but the entity in the Agreement is termed 'Joint Commission'.[36] Article 22.1 of the Agreement provides:

Article 22.1: Joint Commission

1. The Parties hereby establish a Joint Commission comprising the Minister of Foreign Trade and Tourism of Peru and the Minister for Trade of Korea, or their respective successors or designees.
2. The Joint Commission shall:

...

(d) seek to resolve disputes that may arise regarding the interpretation or application of this Agreement in accordance with Chapter Twenty-Three (Dispute Settlement).

3. The Joint Commission may:

...

(d) *issue interpretations of the provisions of this Agreement.*

Except for the use of a different name for the entity, basically the same role is expected of the Joint Commission so that it can issue interpretation of the provisions of the agreement including the investment chapter.

7. *Korea–Turkey FTA*

A Joint Committee is also established by the Korea–Turkey FTA.[37] This Agreement contains provisions that arguably envision a more assertive role of the Joint Committee. Article 7.1 of the Agreement provides under the title of 'Joint Committee':

1. The Parties hereby establish a Joint Committee comprising representatives of Turkey, on the one hand, and representatives of Korea, on the other.

...

3. The Joint Committee shall

...

(e) without prejudice to the rights conferred in Chapter 6 (Dispute Settlement), seek appropriate ways and methods of forestalling problems which might arise in areas covered by the Korea–Turkey FTA, or of resolving disputes that may arise regarding the interpretation or application of the Korea–Turkey FTA...

4. The Joint Committee may:

...

(d) *adopt interpretations of the provisions of the Korea–Turkey FTA* ...

The Joint Committee is thus expected to play a role in addressing problems and resolving disputes to the extent that doing so does not infringe upon the right of

[36] Free Trade Agreement between the Republic of Korea and the Republic of Peru (Korea–Peru FTA), 14 November 2010, entered into force 1 August 2011.

[37] Framework Agreement Establishing a Free Trade Area between the Republic of Korea and the Republic of Turkey, 1 August 2012, entered into force 1 May 2013.

contracting parties. Stated differently, as long as the contracting parties' rights to initiate dispute settlement proceedings and to defend themselves in the proceedings are ensured, the Joint Committee possesses a leeway to discuss problems and disputes arising from the Agreement. The term 'adopt' in paragraph 4 also apparently conveys a stronger meaning than the more frequently used 'issue'. Adoption of interpretation would be regarded as more authentic or official than mere issuance of interpretation, as the former carries the meaning of pronouncement while the latter simply provides.

8. *Korea–Canada FTA*

The Korea–Canada FTA goes one step further regarding the role of the Joint Committee.[38] Article 20.1 of the Agreement provides under the title of 'Joint Commission':

1. The Parties hereby establish a Joint Commission, composed of representatives of the Parties. The Commission shall be co-chaired by representatives of the Parties at the Ministerial level, or their designees.
2. The Commission shall

...

(f) without prejudice to the rights conferred in Chapter Twenty-One (Dispute Settlement), endeavour to resolve disputes that may arise regarding the interpretation or application of this Agreement ...

3. The Commission may:

(a) *adopt interpretive decisions* concerning this Agreement, which *shall be binding on dispute settlement panels* established under Article 21.6 (Establishment of a Panel) and on *Tribunals* established under Section B of Chapter Eight (Investor–State Dispute Settlement) ... (emphasis added).

As with the Korea–Turkey FTA, the Joint Commission will have to strive to resolve disputes arising from the interpretation and application of the Agreement as long as it does not infringe upon the contracting parties' right under the dispute settlement chapter. Again, as the parties' rights to initiate the proceeding and defend themselves in the proceedings are guaranteed, the Joint Commission can play a wide variety of roles in terms of addressing disputes arising from the interpretation and application of the Agreement, including the investment chapter (Chapter 8). Furthermore, the Joint Commission is provided with much broader authority with respect to the investment arbitration tribunals, as well as to state-to-state dispute settlement panels. Without any qualification, the Commission can 'adopt interpretative decision' that binds all types of dispute settlement tribunals, including investment arbitration tribunals. Not only is the term 'adopt' used (as in the Korea–Turkey FTA), but the term 'interpretive decision' is also chosen instead of mere interpretation. Thus, the provision arguably aims to carry the meaning of 'adoption of a binding decision' by the Joint Commission. This phrase offers by far

[38] Free Trade Agreement between the Government of the Republic of Korea and the Government of Canada (Korea–Canada FTA), 22 September 2014, entered into force 1 January 2015.

the strongest authority to the Joint Commission compared with other comparable FTAs and BITs.

The Korea–Canada FTA introduces yet another committee that can issue a binding decision on a particular topic of investment arbitration. Article 10.16 of the Agreement establishes the Financial Services Committee and it is expected to play a vital role in investment arbitrations. One of the roles it is designated to play is to issue a binding decision whether the critical exception of 'prudential measures' under Article 10.10 satisfies the requirement of the provision. This decision on the prudential measures exception is going to bind the investment arbitration tribunal. According to the relevant provisions of the Agreement:

Article 10.16: Financial Services Committee

1. The Parties hereby establish a Financial Services Committee. The principal representative of each Party shall be an official of the Party's authority responsible for financial services set out in Annex 10-C.
2. The Committee shall:

...

(c) *participate in dispute settlement procedures* pursuant to Article 10.19.

Article 10.19: Investor–State Dispute Settlement in Financial Services

1. If an investor of a Party submits a claim under Article 8.18 (Claim by an Investor of a Party on Its Own Behalf) or 8.19 (Claim by an Investor of a Party on Behalf of an Enterprise) to arbitration under Section B of Chapter Eight (Investor–State Dispute Settlement) and the disputing Party invokes an exception pursuant to Article 10.10, *the Tribunal shall, at the request of the disputing Party, refer the matter in writing to the Committee for a decision.* The Tribunal shall not proceed until it receives the decision or report under this Article.
2. In a referral pursuant to paragraph 1, the Committee *shall decide* whether and to what extent Article 10.10 is a valid defence to the claim of the investor. The Committee shall transmit a copy of its decision to the Tribunal and to the Commission. The decision shall be *binding on the Tribunal* ... (emphasis added).

The Joint Commission and the Financial Services Committee in the Korea–Canada FTA thus stand to play a critical role in the decision-making process of ISDS tribunals. Again, this Agreement envisions one of the most active roles of the contracting parties' committees to rein in the decision-making process of investment arbitration tribunals.

B. New roles—decision on specific issues

In short, one of the new functions assigned to Joint Committees is to make a decision on some of the key issues raised in specific ISDS proceedings. For instance, Joint Committees are eligible to make a decision on the status of confidential information as claimed by an information submitting party. Joint Committees also possess the authority to determine whether a particular governmental measure falls under the prudential measure exception, which basically carves out governmental measures that aim to ensure capital soundness of a financial institution from the reach of an investment agreement. These issues are closely related to policy objectives of the government at issue and are not necessarily amenable to the purely legal inquiry. It is therefore believed that having Joint Committees make decisions on these issues may better serve the interest of the parties. These decisions of the Joint Committees bind the tribunals with respect to the issues posed.

The decisions of the Joint Committees do not dictate the outcome of the investment arbitration. Nonetheless, decisions on the key intermediary issues affect the fate of the disputes significantly. What is being observed now is the tendency that the insertion of new procedural and substantive elements of the ISDS proceedings seems to prefer to solicit decisions from Joint Committees rather than investment tribunals.

C. New roles—issuance of binding interpretation

Another important role being assigned to Joint Committees is to issue a 'binding' interpretation of treaty terms that will then bind reviewing investment arbitration tribunals. Since ISDS proceedings are arguably all about treaty interpretation in accordance with Article 31 of the VCLT, Joint Committees' issuance of binding interpretations is both meaningful and critical in reaching a conclusion in a particular ISDS proceeding. This is particularly the case given that investment agreements and disputes have been suffering the ambiguities and loopholes of treaty provisions due to the gap between the conventional texts and fast-changing investment practices in the global community.

Commentators have contended that the ability of the Joint Committees to issue an interpretation of any obligation in the Agreement that is binding on an arbitral tribunal can be considered key procedural protection.[39] In the case where a party believes that particular provisions in the Agreement have been interpreted in an overly broad way by the tribunal, which the party had not anticipated, the Joint Committee may intervene, on request, to issue an interpretation that is binding on the tribunal. In this way, the parties' exposure to a relatively high degree of uncertainty that may flow from the tribunal's wide interpretation can be decreased considerably.

While some investment agreements stipulate the Joint Committees' authority to issue binding interpretations in an open-ended manner,[40] other investment agreements simply set forth the authority of Joint Committees to issue interpretation.[41] Joint Committees of the second category may not issue a 'binding' interpretation because specific stipulation to that effect is absent. Nonetheless, any interpretation issued by a Joint Committee should carry significant weight in the course of analyses and reviews by a reviewing investment tribunal as such joint declaration of interpretation by the contracting parties indicates the true intention of the parties and is eligible to be accorded significant legal weight in the course of

[39] The Parliament of the Commonwealth of Australia, 'Report 142: Treaty Tabled on 13 May 2014—Free Trade Agreement Between the Government of Australia and the Government of the Republic of Korea' (Commonwealth of Australia, September 2014) 27.

[40] See e.g., Korea–Canada FTA (n 38), art 20.1, para 3; Korea–US FTA (n 3), art 11.22, para 3.

[41] See e.g., Korea–Peru FTA (n 36), art 22.1, para 3.

interpreting the relevant terms.[42] Thus, even if an interpretation is not specifically termed as 'binding', the fact that the contracting parties have agreed to jointly issue such interpretation still carries significant weight in the tribunal's decision on the issue. So, it is arguable that both binding and ordinary interpretations of the Joint Committees play an important role in the course of ISDS proceedings.

D. Prospective consequences of expanded roles of joint committees

The newly found roles of Joint Committees arguably stand to address the complex and controversial issues of investment arbitral proceedings, most notably balancing the conflicting interests between a host state and a foreign investor. Consider a recently released EU guideline for BIT negotiations to see the spectrum of efforts by states (even developed countries such as the European Union) to strike a balance between the two conflicting interests:

- Significant clarification of the substantive protection provisions to ensure that the state's right to regulate to pursue legitimate public policy objectives is protected;
- Clarification and precise definition of the content of FET;
- Detailed language on indirect expropriation (step-by-step guidance to arbitral tribunals in finding indirect expropriation and definition of regulatory takings);
- Narrow definitions of investment (characteristics) and investor (shell companies are not to be protected);
- Detailed provisions on ISDS including transparency, procedural provisions to deal with time limits, concurrent proceedings, frivolous cases, unfounded claims by shifting costs;
- Novel features such as encouragement of ADR with a detailed mediation annex, the introduction of an appellate mechanism and a code of conduct for arbitrators.[43]

Likewise, Chapter 11 (investment chapter) of the Korea–US FTA was one of the most controversial chapters during the negotiation and ratification of the agreement.[44] Mainly, the focus of the domestic debates was about the erosion or

[42] See Vienna Convention on the Law of Treaties (Vienna Convention), 23 May 1969, entered into force 27 January 1980, 1155 UNTS 331, art 31, para 3, subpara (a).

[43] European Commission, Investment Protection and Investor-to-State Dispute Settlement in EU Agreements—Fact Sheet (November 2013) <http://trade.ec.europa.eu/doclib/docs/2013/november/tradoc_151916.pdf> accessed 23 April 2016 and European Commission, Investment Protection and Investor-to-State Dispute Settlement (ISDS) in EU Agreements—Fact Sheet, March 2014 <http://trade.ec.europa.eu/doclib/docs/2014/march/tradoc_152273.pdf> accessed 23 April 2016.

[44] See 'Response to Hankyoreh Daily's Report of "No Progress on ISDS Re-negotiation"' (n 1); 'SSM Regulation in Seoul and U.S. Corporation COSTCO's Response' (n 15); 'One Year Anniversary of KORUS FTA: Is Seoul Ready for Changes in Global Trade Regime?' (n 15); Lee (n 2).

usurpation of Korea's national sovereignty in favour of the foreign investors' expanded rights.[45] As a matter of fact, investment agreements and investment chapters are different because the interface between agreements and municipal law is more direct and closer than other agreements.[46]

On the other hand, open hearings in investment arbitration, an increasingly new phenomenon these days, also affect the treatment of confidential information. Naturally, ISDS proceedings involve a great deal of confidential information in the hearings,[47] while there are a couple of specific ways to conduct a hearing under these circumstances, such as having two different sessions (comprising a public session and a confidential session),[48] or using closed circuit transmission within a timeframe.[49] These safeguards would certainly help alleviate the concern of the information-submitting governments, but the governments would continue to face the inherent dilemma of whether, when, and how to open up its internal decision-making process and attendant documentation to foreign constituents and outside watchers.

In light of all these political sensitivities associated with investment arbitration and legal difficulties in finding equilibrium between host governments and foreign investors, as well as investment arbitral tribunals operating under the strict bounds of stipulated texts of investment agreements replete with ambiguities and vagueness,[50] Joint Committees may arguably offer a viable alternative. More than anything else, a Joint Committee may present parties' intention to investment tribunals more accurately. It may also reflect the fast-changing investment environment of the global community more appropriately and be able to consider other related similar situations and disputes pending between the two states in a comprehensive manner. More importantly, a Joint Committee may be able to take into account the policy dimension of the measure at issue more properly. The combination of all these aspects would certainly help guarantee appropriate interpretation of the terms of investment agreements. Granted, investment tribunals may also take into account all these elements in their scrutiny. But their acclaimed expertise in legal matters may not necessarily ensure the ability to see through the plethora of these non-legal, practical, and policy prisms.

Such being the case, an argument can be made that Joint Committees, when an appropriate division of labour is achieved vis-à-vis investment arbitral tribunals, would offer the most readily available alternative route to deal with political

[45] Lee (n 2).

[46] See Yimer and others (n 5); Catherine Yannaca-Smal, 'Improving the System of Investor–State Dispute Settlement: An Overview' in OECD, *International Investment Perspectives* (OECD Publishing 2006) ch 7, 189.

[47] See discussions on members of the UNCITRAL Working Group regarding UNCITRAL Transparency Rules in Treaty-based Investor–State Arbitration, 1 April 2014, art 7 <http://www.uncitral.org/pdf/english/texts/arbitration/rules-on-transparency/Rules-on-Transparency-E.pdf> accessed 23 April 2016.

[48] See Muthucumaraswamy Sornarajah, 'The Case against a Regime on International Investment Law' in Leon Trakman and Nick Ranieri (eds), *Regionalism in International Investment Law* (OUP 2013) ch 16.

[49] ibid.

[50] See Vienna Convention (n 42), art 31.

sensitivities and legal complexities associated with investment disputes. Where, as here, fundamental overhaul of the existing regime and introduction of an innovative scheme are either too elusive or illusory, at least at the moment, contemplating an enhanced role of Joint Committees or their equivalents may offer a reliable, though not perfect, alternative.

IV. Remaining Questions

While the idea and trend of expanding the roles of Joint Committees seem to offer a practical and viable way out to deal with some of the structural problems of investment agreements and arbitral proceedings, they also entail questions of their own. First of all, the wisdom of having political entities carry out interpretative functions for adjudicative bodies certainly requires careful attention. Whether this re-invigorated function of Joint Committees may run the risk of bringing the traditional de facto state-to-state dispute settlement proceedings to the main stage presents yet another question. In addition, the advent of a new breed of FTAs, such as mega-FTAs, adds yet another twist to the formation and operation of the Joint Committees composed of representatives of contracting parties. These questions and challenges are discussed below, respectively.

A. Non-judicial entities dictating terms for adjudicative bodies

The first question to be answered in this regard is whether permitting and requesting a Joint Committee, a fundamentally non-judicial consultative body, to take up the role of issuing interpretation that ultimately binds an investment tribunal, an essentially adjudicative, judicial body, would indeed be a proper course of action. If the underlying objective of establishing investment arbitration proceedings since the inception of the 1966 ICSID Convention was to legalize and de-politicize investment disputes, having the contracting parties exercise ultimate control over some of the key issues of investment disputes might not be in full compliance with this objective.

Interpretation is a critical task for any international adjudicative body. It is the interpretation of specific terms that ultimately determines the outcome of a dispute as codified in Article 31 of the VCLT. As such, allowing an outside political entity to issue (binding) interpretations would arguably amount to usurping the core authority of an international judicial entity. Whether investment arbitration requires reform in some areas and whether the parties have ultimate voices even in legal proceedings are two separate or distinct questions. At the same time, contracting parties' effort to override explicit treaty terms through political and diplomatic entities may be challenged by existing international law principles relating to treaty interpretation.[51]

[51] A contracting party is precluded from justifying its violation of a treaty provision based on its domestic statutes. See e.g., Vienna Convention (n 42), art 27. This principle has also been referred to in *Case Concerning the Factory at Chorzów (Claim for Indemnity) (The Merits) (FRG v Poland)*, 1928

On the other hand, if the contracting parties fail to agree upon a particular interpretation at a Joint Committee, it may delay or even derail an on-going investment arbitration. Should the parties agree to present a 'compromised' interpretation, which may be even more confusing than the treaty terms, the chances are that more burden is imposed on the investment tribunal. This risk relates back to the scheme of political entities dictating the terms for key issues in legal or arbitral proceedings.

B. Reverting back to state-to-state dispute settlement proceedings

Almost all international investment agreements provide for ISDS proceedings, whereby investors whose rights under the investment treaties have been violated may directly bring a claim against host states in international arbitration, rather than suing the host states in their own courts or seeking diplomatic protection from their home states.[52] This somewhat unique dispute settlement scheme has been the focal point of the discussions by the global community for the past decade.[53] What has received a relatively low level of attention is state-to-state dispute settlement proceeding that is also usually contained in investment agreements.[54] Notwithstanding the dichotomous nature of the dispute settlement proceedings of investment agreements, investment disputes have been raised and addressed mainly within the context of ISDS proceedings, while some exceptions have been spotted from time to time.[55] This trend arguably reflects the fact that

PCIJ (ser A) No 17, 4–65 (13 September); *Case Concerning Rights of Nationals of the United States in Morocco (France v US)* 1952 ICJ 176 (27 August); Appellate Body Report, *United States—Measures Relating to Zeroing and Sunset Reviews—Recourse to Article 21.5 of the DSU By Japan*, WT/DS322/AB/RW, 18 August 2009, para 182, n 463; Decision by the Arbitrator, *Canada—Export Credits and Loan Guarantees for Regional Aircraft—Recourse to Arbitration by Canada under Article 22.6 of the DSU and Article 4.11 of the SCM Agreement, Decision by the Arbitrator*, WT/DS222/ARB, 17 February 2003, paras 3.103–3.104.

[52] Efe Uzezi Azaino, 'Nationality/Treaty Shopping: Can Host Countries Sift the Wheat from the Chaff?' (2013) 16 (1) CEPMLP Ann Rev 1, 6.

[53] The fact that the ISDS proceeding has become the focal point of the entire FTA discussion is quite ironic because the proceeding has been touted as a system having been introduced to 'depoliticize' investment disputes. See Anthea Roberts, 'State-to-State Investment Treaty Arbitration: A Hybrid Theory of Interdependent Rights and Shared Interpretive Authority' (2014) 55 (1) Harv Intl LJ 1, 25.

[54] See e.g., Korea–US FTA (n 3) ch 22, s B.

[55] For instance, a recent arbitration tribunal hearing a state-to-state dispute between the United States and Ecuador under the two countries' BIT held that it does not have jurisdiction to issue a binding interpretation that will hold future ISDS panels. See Luke Eric Peterson, 'United States Defeats Ecuador's State-to-State Arbitration: Will Outcome Dissuade Argentine Copycat Case?' [2012] <https://www.iareporter.com/articles/united-states-defeats-ecuadors-state-to-state-arbitration-will-outcome-dissuade-argentine-copycat-case/> accessed 23 April 2016. But the Expert Opinion of Professor Michael Reisman submitted on 24 April 2012 to the *United States v Ecuador* panel indicates that depending upon the specific languages contained in the provision of state-to-state dispute settlement mechanism, binding force on the subsequent ISDS panels may be recognized. *Republic of Ecuador v United States of America*, PCA Case No 2012-5, Expert Opinion with Respect to Jurisdiction in the Interstate Arbitration Initiated by Ecuador Against the United States, 24 April 2012.

investment agreements have been devised to detach investment disputes from the traditional 'right of diplomatic protection', which is by nature a state-to-state dispute. The consensus has been that the states' direct intervention in individual investment disputes may heighten the political and diplomatic sensitivities for the states, which may not serve the interests of individual investors either. Noting such historic backgrounds of setting state-to-state dispute settlement (SSDS) proceedings aside, it would indeed be awkward for the two interested states to find a new way, utilizing the vehicle of a Joint Committee, to engage in an individual investment dispute directly. It is true that Joint Committees are distinguished from the SSDS proceedings, another kind of international legal proceeding. But devising Joint Committees wherein the contracting parties gather, consult, and issue (binding) interpretations arguably carries the traits of de facto SSDS or self-ruled SSDS in essence. As a matter of fact, an official interpretation adopted or issued by contracting parties of the BIT or FTA may arguably carry an important weight in the ISDS proceeding involving the same provision, even if such interpretation is not legally binding:[56] regardless of an official binding force subsequent ISDS tribunals would put a significant weight on the interpretation adopted by the parties themselves.

In other words, the expanded role of Joint Committees may amount to a tacit recognition that the approach hitherto of putting emphasis on ISDS proceedings while sidelining SSDS proceedings may now have to be recalibrated. This recognition would caution against unregulated expansion of the role of Joint Committees merely to alleviate the concern of host state governments.

C. Overlapping investment agreements and surge of mega-FTAs

On a separate note, the continuing surge of overlapping investment agreements and various FTAs, particularly mega-FTAs, also raises an additional layer of complexity in this regard. What is being observed at the moment is the situation where multiple and overlapping BITs and FTAs exist between the same parties. Consider Korea and the United States, for example. Should the Trans-Pacific Partnership (TPP) be materialized with the participation of the United States and Korea, then there will be two sets of investment rules between the two countries—the Korea–US FTA investment chapter and the TPP investment chapter.[57] Between Korea and Japan, there will be as many as three sets of rules at that point; the two countries have already concluded two BITs on their own—the 2003 Korea–Japan BIT and the 2012 Korea–Japan–China TIT, both of which are designed to remain effective at the same time.[58]

[56] See e.g., Korea–US FTA (n 3) ch 22, s B.

[57] See Korea–China–Japan TIT (n 32), art 25.

[58] See e.g., Agreement Between the Government of the People's Republic of China and the Government of the Republic of Korea on the Promotion and Protection of Investments, 7 September 2007, entered into force 1 December 2007, art 9; Agreement Between the Government of the People's Republic of China and the Government of the Republic of Latvia on the Promotion and Protection of Investments, 15 April 2004, entered into force 1 February 2006, art 9.

In these multiple, overlapping BITs and FTAs, even for the same contracting parties the roles of Joint Committees are not entirely identical or consistent among each other. Under these circumstances, exploration of expanding the roles of Joint Committees may add further complexity for the conduct and administration of the ISDS proceedings. Unless and until all BITs and FTAs are amended or somehow co-ordinated with respect to Joint Committees, it is not entirely clear how respective Joint Committees would operate between the same contracting parties. The surge of mega-FTAs increases the likelihood of overlapping existence of Joint Committees with different scopes of roles and functions, even for the same contracting parties, simply because different investment agreements co-exist at the same time.[59] It is not entirely impossible that, for various reasons, the interpretative decisions of Joint Committees of overlapping BITs may not dovetail with each other or maintain internal consistency all the time, which may then lead to the creation of further confusion.

A decision-making process of Joint Committees may go through new dynamics. In mega-FTAs, Joint Committees are composed of representatives from all contracting parties, hence twelve states in the context of TPP. In contemplating the interpretation of terms under this formula, the position of contracting parties other than the two disputing parties could sometimes carry a significant weight.[60] Interpretation thus issued is now ready to bind investment arbitration tribunals. In other words, the interpretation supported by the majority of contracting parties may sway the outcome of the ISDS proceedings as well. This is certainly a unique development that has hardly been seen in previous investment agreements and disputes.

In sum, the interpretation to be adopted by the contracting parties at a Joint Committee stands to be affected by the position of the majority of parties that may or may not share the view of the disputing contracting parties. This interpretation, in turn, may affect or bind the decision of an ISDS tribunal in an ISDS proceeding. Thus Joint Committees in mega-FTAs would formalize a collective decision-making process, which may then be imposed on the two disputing contracting parties and subsequently on their investors and government agencies participating in ISDS proceedings.

[59] For the BITs, see Ministry of Foreign Affairs, Republic of Korea, 'Status of Bilateral Treaties in Force' <http://www.mofat.go.kr/trade/treatylaw/treatyinformation/bilateral/index.jsp?mofat=001&menu=m_30_50_40> accessed 8 March 2016 (data compiled by the author from the treaties information in Korean). Six more BITs (including the Korea–China–Japan TIT (n 32)) have been recently signed and their entry into force is currently pending. See UNCTAD, Full list of Bilateral Investment Agreements concluded, (*International Investment Agreement Database*, 2013) <http://investmentpolicyhub.unctad.org/IIA> accessed 8 August 2015. For the FTAs, see Ministry of Foreign Affairs, Republic of Korea, 'FTA Status of ROK' <http://www.mofat.go.kr/ENG/policy/fta/status/overview/index.jsp?menu=m_20_80_10> accessed 8 March 2016.

[60] See ibid art 17, para 6. This mechanism is also found in the NAFTA (n 10), which is also a trilateral agreement between the United States, Canada, and Mexico. The same phenomenon could also be found in the 2012 Korea–China–Japan TIT (n 32), yet another trilateral investment treaty.

V. Conclusion

The level of attention being directed at investment arbitration is increasing continuously and rapidly on a global basis. Legal complexities and political sensitivities associated with investment arbitration have given both foreign investors and sovereign states acute difficulties in dealing with this particular proceeding. While the ISDS proceeding has become a fixture of BITs or FTAs, its potential to penetrate the sanctity of national regulatory authority makes host states' governments fret about this particular international dispute settlement mechanism. Furthermore, the fact that investment arbitration is conducted according to a bilateral treaty, concluded a long time ago using ambiguous terms through a single-adjudication process, has further caused concern for the governments of host states. The fragmented nature of investment arbitration awards provides a less-than-optimal clarity in terms of jurisprudence and guidelines for the governments.

It is against this backdrop that discussions on expanding the role of Joint Committees have been raised. Joint Committees to be established by BITs and FTAs may take up a role of making interpretative decisions regarding key terms of investment agreements so that the concerns of the host states' governments could be alleviated or addressed. This scheme may indeed offer an effective tool to rein in decisions of investment arbitral tribunals, which may look unpredictable or inconsistent in the eyes of the host states. But at the same time, the expanded role of Joint Committees, if not properly introduced or managed, may run the risk of re-politicizing or further politicizing the already controversial investment disputes by having a non-judicial, political entity issue a decision on a critical legal issue—treaty interpretation. As such, this scheme may end up resurrecting the traditional inter-state confrontation over the 'right of diplomatic protection' under public international law coupled with state-to-state dispute settlement proceedings. As the current system of investment agreements and the conspicuous ISDS proceedings have been an outcome of deliberate choices in order to move away from state-to-state dispute settlement proceedings and inter-state confrontation, questions stand to be raised if the newly found roles of Joint Committees operate as a de facto revival of the old system or dynamics.

It is true that Joint Committees will play an important role in investment disputes for now and the future. These committees are equipped with the functions that may address some of the structural problems in investment arbitrations at the moment. But at the same time, it should be borne in mind that Joint Committees should not be devised in a way that undermines the 'rule of law' of international dispute settlement proceedings in general and the core spirit of ISDS proceedings in particular.

11

The Limits of Legalization in Asia-Pacific Investment Treaty Arbitration?*

*Luke Nottage***

Bilateral investment treaties (BITs), and more recently investment chapters in free trade agreements (FTAs), are increasingly controversial—especially investor–state arbitration (ISA) options provided for foreign investors. Against this backdrop, some arbitral tribunals are interpreting older treaties in ways more favourable to host states. Some countries are also renegotiating those treaties or negotiating new ones based on new templates including features closer to those found in World Trade Organization (WTO) dispute resolution. But others are eschewing ISA completely, leaving only inter-state arbitration to resolve disputes arising under investment treaties, which may re-politicize such disputes. This chapter explores such 'limits of legalization' in an Asia-Pacific context.

In particular, Indonesia announced in 2014 that it would review its sixty-seven BITs.[1] Shortly beforehand, it had unsuccessfully challenged the jurisdiction of an International Centre for Settlement of Investment Disputes (ICSID) arbitral tribunal in a claim for expropriation and other violations brought by the Australian subsidiary of a UK coal mining company (*Planet Mining v Indonesia*). The tribunal's decision found that consent to jurisdiction existed under the coal mining licences given by Indonesian authorities, but not under the wording of the 1992 Australia–Indonesia BIT. It found that the countries had only given a 'promise

* This chapter updates and elaborates, with permission, my article entitled: 'Do Many of Australia's Bilateral Treaties Really Not Provide Full Advance Consent to Investor–State Arbitration? Analysis of *Planet Mining v Indonesia* and Regional Implications' (2015) 1 TDM <http://www.transnational-dispute-management.com/article.asp?key=2177> accessed 8 March 2016. For helpful feedback on the original paper or an earlier version of this chapter, I am also grateful to Chester Brown, Antony Crockett, Mark Feldman, Sam Luttrell, and Romesh Weeramantry. Errors or misconceptions remain my own. Research was supported by the (federal government's) Australian Research Council, for a Discovery Project (DP140102526) awarded over 2014–2016 jointly with Dr Shiro Armstrong and Professors Jurgen Kurtz and Leon Trakman.

** Professor of Comparative and Transnational Business Law, University of Sydney Law School.

[1] See e.g., Ben Bland and Shawn Donnan, 'Indonesia to Terminate More Than 60 Bilateral Investment Treaties' (*Financial Times*, 26 March 2014), <http://www.ft.com/intl/cms/s/0/3755c1b2-b4e2-11e3-af92-00144feabdc0.html#axzz3jEV2fsjh > accessed 23 March 2016.

to consent' rather than full advance consent to ICSID jurisdiction, meaning that Indonesia could still refuse consent subject to potential review through an inter-state arbitration procedure separately provided under the treaty. Further, as both countries remained party to the framework 1965 ICSID Convention facilitating enforcement of arbitral awards, another BIT provision for ad hoc ISA was also unavailable to investors.

This chapter critically assesses the arguments developed by the tribunal to reach this surprising interpretation of the Australia–Indonesia BIT. It also considers the potentially wide-ranging implications of the tribunal's reasoning given similar wording contained in many other treaties concluded by Australia, and (to a lesser extent) some other countries in the region such as Japan. Fortunately for investors, some of those treaties (including the Australia–Indonesia BIT) are now complemented by ISA rights contained in bilateral or regional FTAs, or may soon be. However, in light of the tribunal's decision, Australia should clarify the scope of its other BITs, especially with countries in Eastern Europe and the Middle East. Other nations, legal advisors, and arbitrators will also need to examine treaty wording and practice more broadly, which risks adding to growing costs and delays in ISA proceedings.

I. Re-Politicization of International Treaty Dispute Resolution

Investment chapters in bilateral and regional FTAs are increasingly superseding BITs. FTA chapters promote and liberalize cross-border investments, going beyond the services sectors or commitments that may be opened up by some Member States of the WTO; but also typically including a BIT-like panoply of protections for foreign investments once those are made. Yet investment chapters and BITs have become increasingly controversial, especially provisions on investor–state dispute settlement (ISDS), which have become a common procedural mechanism for foreign investors to invoke in order to enforce the substantive protections offered by host states. Concerns about ISDS, especially ISA generating binding decisions by international tribunals, have spread from some developing countries in South America to parts of Asia. Public policy debates and political controversy have also emerged in developed countries, as some find themselves on the receiving end of ISA claims, including in the context of the Trans-Atlantic Trade and Investment Partnership (TTIP) being negotiated between the European Union and the United States.

Such concerns have already generated various responses. Some arbitral tribunals seem to be interpreting existing treaties in ways more deferential to host states, as indicated by the claim against Indonesia analysed in section II below.[2] Some

[2] Another recent example from the Asia-Pacific region may be a claim related to a further mining investment, brought by a Singaporean investor, although the tribunal (Gary Born presiding, Michael Pryles nominated by the claimant, and Duncan Kerr nominated by Papua New Guinea) declined jurisdiction based on a narrow interpretation of an alleged consent contained in legislation enacted by

countries, such as Australia under the Gillard Government over 2011–2013, have declared that they will not enter into any future investment treaties containing ISDS provisions. Others, notably in South America, have denounced the framework 1965 Convention on the Settlement of Investment Disputes Between States and Nationals of Other States (ICSID Convention) that facilitates the creation and enforcement of ISA awards. Venezuela further declared in 2012 that it will seek to renegotiate its existing BITs. Other ICSID Convention member states, such as Indonesia in 2014, have only indicated that BITs will not be automatically renewed when their current terms expire, but will be reassessed against a new Model BIT as a negotiating template. EU institutions are also actively considering new features for future investment treaties, especially TTIP, now that the European Union (rather than individual Member States) has exclusive competence to conclude treaties with third parties dealing with foreign direct investment (FDI).[3]

Some of these new guidelines for (re)-negotiating international investment treaty provisions include proposals to set up some sort of appellate review mechanism. In May 2015, for example, following an extensive public consultation in 2014, the European Commission released a 'Concept Paper: Investment in TTIP and Beyond—The Path for Reform', subtitled 'Enhancing the right to regulate and moving from current ad hoc arbitration towards an Investment Court'. As well as proposing that arbitrators should only be chosen from a roster pre-established by the states party, it argued that the European Union's proposal for TTIP should include an appellate mechanism to review 'errors of law and manifest errors in the assessment of facts', which furthermore:[4]

> could be modelled largely on the institutional set-up of the WTO Appellate Body, with some adaptations both to make it specific for ISDS, and in light of experience in the WTO. There could be 7 permanent members (2 from each Party, 3 non-nationals) whose qualifications could be broadly similar to those of the WTO Appellate Body and/or the International Court of Justice.

This and other recent templates, and indeed already the treaty practice of several major countries (such as the United States), also often provide for other WTO-like

the host state (rather an investment treaty): *PNG Sustainable Development Program Ltd v Independent State of Papua New Guinea*, ICSID Case No ARB/13/33, Award (5 May 2015), <http://www.italaw.com/sites/default/files/case-documents/italaw4257.pdf> accessed 23 April 2016.

[3] See Jürgen Kurtz and Luke R Nottage, 'Investment Treaty Arbitration "Down Under": Policy and Politics in Australia' (2015) 30(2) ICSID Rev-FILJ 465, with a longer version at <http://ssrn.com/abstract=2561147> accessed 8 March 2016, with further references.

[4] European Commission, 'Investment in TTIP and Beyond—the Path for Reform' 9 <http://trade.ec.europa.eu/doclib/docs/2015/may/tradoc_153408.PDF> accessed 23 April 2016. Cf also Anna Joubin-Bret, 'Why We Need a Global Appellate Mechanism for International Investment Law' (2015) 146 Columbia FDI Perspectives <http://ccsi.columbia.edu/files/2013/10/No-146-Joubin-Bret-FINAL.pdf> accessed 23 April 2016; Debra P Steger, 'Enhancing the Legitimacy of International Investment Law by Establishing an Appellate Mechanism' in Armand de Mestral and Céline Lévesque (eds), *Improving International Investment Agreements* (Routledge 2012) 257–64 <http://ssrn.com/abstract=2223714> accessed 8 March 2016; Frieder Roessler, chapter 4 in this volume.

features such as enhanced transparency and opportunities for non-party involvement in proceedings, and general exceptions clauses.[5]

Nonetheless, such 'juridification' of ISA provisions and procedures may not be enough to assuage public concerns. Even with these sorts of innovations, it is conceivable that more countries will simply baulk at including any form of ISDS, even developed countries (like Australia) that are now significant capital exporters. This would leave only inter-state arbitration procedures, almost always included in investment treaties but eclipsed by the rise of ISDS over the past two decades, for foreign investors to enforce their treaty rights.[6] The system for enforcing substantive protections for foreign investors then would become even more similar to WTO dispute resolution,[7] especially if the decline of ISDS made it more feasible for the WTO or another international organization (like the Organisation for Economic Co-operation and Development) to revive and achieve the idea of a multilateral or plurilateral investment treaty.[8] Yet this would mean a significant re-politicization of international investment dispute resolution.[9]

Against this complex backdrop, this chapter explores in a specific context some of these 'limits of legalization' or brakes on the future development of Asia-Pacific treaty-based ISA, which may also be relevant to the evolving WTO system as well as this book's general theme—a critical assessment of international economic law and governance. In particular, this chapter analyses an ICSID tribunal's 2014 decision on jurisdiction in a protracted mining investment dispute between Indonesia and investors from Australia and the UK. It sketches potentially far-reaching implications for similarly worded ISA provisions in other early BITs concluded by Australia, and potentially other Asia-Pacific countries such as Japan. The chapter

[5] See e.g., Martin Weiss and others, 'International Investment Agreements (IAAs): Frequently Asked Questions' (2015) USCRS 19–24 <http://fas.org/sgp/crs/misc/R44015.pdf> accessed 23 April 2016; Jurgen Kurtz, *The WTO and International Investment Law: Converging Systems* (CUP 2016); Yasuhei Taniguchi and Tomoko Ishikawa, chapter 7 in this volume.

[6] Another possibility is to make such rights justiciable in national courts for foreign investors: Daniel Kalderimis, 'Back to the Future: Contemplating a Return to the Exhaustion Rule' (2014) 1 TDM <http://www.transnational-dispute-management.com/article.asp?key=2055> accessed 8 March 2016, also in Jean Kalicki and Anna Joubin-Bret (eds), *Reshaping the Investor–State Dispute Settlement System: Journeys for the 21st Century* (Brill 2015). Yet, even if politically acceptable, it will be less attractive than an international arbitral tribunal if the domestic court system is inexperienced, inefficient, or corrupt. Such problems generated calls for ISDS in the first place, in addition to substantive protections for investors under domestic law possibly being unavailable for foreign investors or otherwise lower than internationally accepted standards. A further possibility would be to revert to a system whereby foreign investors would have to negotiate and include ISDS rights in individually negotiated contracts with host states: M Sornarajah, 'Revolution or Evolution in International Investment Law: The Descent into Normlessness' in Chester Brown and Kate Miles (eds), *Evolution in Investment Treaty Law and Arbitration* (CUP 2012) 631–58. But this would reinstate very high transaction costs, disproportionately favouring larger investors.

[7] See generally William J Davey, chapter 2 in this volume.

[8] See generally e.g., Gary Hufbauer and Sherry Stephenson, 'The Case for a Framework Agreement on Investment' (2014) 116 Columbia FDI Perspectives <http://ccsi.columbia.edu/files/2013/10/No_116_-_Hufbauer_and_Stephenson_-_FINAL.pdf> accessed 23 April 2016. On the potential for better integration of existing investment treaties with the WTO system; cf also Tsai-yu Lin, chapter 18 in this volume.

[9] Cf also Jaemin Lee, chapter 10 in this volume.

also discusses Indonesia's controversial subsequent declaration that it would be reviewing its many existing BITs.

Specifically, on 13 March 2014, the Dutch Embassy in Jakarta announced that Indonesia had informed the Netherlands that it had decided to terminate their BIT as of 1 July 2015, with that agreement's protections to foreign investors only continuing to apply (pursuant to a sunset clause) for another fifteen years. The Embassy added that the 'Indonesian Government has mentioned it intends to terminate all of its 67 bilateral investment treaties', and that the Netherlands was 'discussing the matter with the Indonesian authorities'.[10]

As reported by the *Financial Times* on 26 March 2014, in an article headed 'Indonesia to Terminate More than 60 Bilateral Investment Treaties', a particular concern seems to be ISA mechanisms included in such treaties (and indeed FTA investment chapters, which were not referred to in the Dutch Embassy's announcement):

> Business groups argue the arbitration mechanisms are vital to encouraging foreign direct investment and needed to protect investors from government expropriations and other rogue decisions against which they would otherwise have little protection. But that argument appears to hold diminishing sway with many governments. Indonesia is facing a billion-dollar lawsuit from UK-listed Churchill Mining under the terms of one such treaty, in addition to several unrelated threats of costly litigation from international companies unhappy with a new mining law. Susilo Bambang Yudhoyono, Indonesia's president, has spoken out against the Churchill case, saying he does not want multinational companies to 'pressure developing countries like Indonesia'.[11]

Some commentators have subsequently pointed out that 'usage of the word "terminate" does not adequately capture the nuanced process that Indonesia is going through to review its ... BITs ... by letting the old ones lapse so that new and better ones can be renegotiated'.[12] Another commentator has described the new Indonesian policy as not extending BITs due to expire but also not creating new ones—lauding this as 'a brave policy' taken by (then) President Yudhoyono,[13]

[10] 'Termination Bilateral Investment Treaty' <http://indonesia.nlembassy.org/organization/departments/economic-affairs/termination-bilateral-investment-treaty.html > accessed 8 March 2016.

[11] Ben Blend and Shawn Donnan, 'Indonesia to Terminate More Than 60 Bilateral Investment Treaties' (*Financial Times*, 26 March 2014) <http://www.ft.com/cms/s/0/3755c1b2-b4e2-11e3-af92-00144feabdc0.html#ixzz2yofgwQTO> accessed 8 March 2016, citing to the President's statements at Ben Blend, 'Yudhoyono: Getting Involved in a Little Indo–UK Mining Difficulty' (*Financial Times*, 29 June 2012) <http://blogs.ft.com/beyond-brics/2012/06/29/766251/> accessed 8 March 2016.

[12] Michael Ewing-Chow and Junianto James Losari, 'Indonesia is Letting Its Bilateral Treaties Lapse So As To Renegotiate Better Ones' (*Financial Times*, 15 April 2014) <http://www.ft.com/intl/cms/s/0/20c6c518-c16c-11e3-97b2-00144feabdc0.html#axzz30LCEBA2T> accessed 8 March 2016. See also Leon Trakman and Kunal Sharma, 'Indonesia's Termination of the Netherlands–Indonesia BIT: Broader Implications in the Asia-Pacific?' (*Financial Times*, 21 August 2014) <http://kluwerarbitrationblog.com/blog/2014/08/21/indonesias-termination-of-the-netherlands-indonesia-bit-broader-implications-in-the-asia-pacific/> accessed 8 March 2016.

[13] Hikmahanto Juwana, 'Indonesia Should Withdraw From the ICSID!' (*The Jakarta Post*, 2 April 2014) <http://www.thejakartapost.com/news/2014/04/02/indonesia-should-withdraw-icsid.html> accessed 8 March 2016.

and even—more radically and controversially[14]—urging Indonesia to withdraw from the ICSID Convention.[15] The *Financial Times* itself reported the chairman of Indonesia's investment co-ordination agency (BKPM) as indicating that the government was drafting 'a new template for [BITs] so we can introduce it to our counterparts soon, hopefully this year'.[16] Some commentators subsequently speculated as to its likely contours, for example in light of issues that had arisen in the claim brought by Churchill and at least five other known ICSID arbitrations involving Indonesia.[17] Others analysed these developments against the backdrop of presidential and parliamentary elections in 2014 in Indonesia, and—perhaps more importantly—broader nationalist or protectionist tendencies especially with respect to natural resources.[18] On 12 May 2015, the *Jakarta Post* reported new twists in this protracted saga:[19]

> The latest BIT to have been terminated was signed with the Netherlands in 1994, while Switzerland was the first country to request [new] President Joko 'Jokowi' Widodo's government to review its existing treaty with Indonesia, according to Azhar Lubis, deputy director for investment monitoring and implementation at the Investment Coordinating Board (BKPM).

[14] Cf e.g., Michael Ewing-Chow and Junianto James Losari, 'Indonesia Should Not Withdraw from the ICSID' (*The Jakarta Post*, 24 April 2014) <http://mbox.thejakartapost.com/news/2014/04/24/indonesia-should-not-withdraw-icsid.html> accessed 8 March 2016.

[15] 'Convention on the Settlement of Disputes Between States and Nationals of Other States' (ICSID) <https://icsid.worldbank.org/ICSID/StaticFiles/basicdoc/partA.htm> accessed 8 March 2016.

[16] 'Indonesia to Terminate More Than 60 Bilateral Investment Treaties' (n 11), also cited in Luke Eric Peterson, 'As Indonesia Reconsiders Its Investment Treaties, Arbitrators Don't Want to Slow Down Mining Case by Separating Liability and Damages Phases' (*Investment Arbitration Reporter*, 28 April 2014) <http://www.iareporter.com/articles/20140428> accessed 8 March 2016.

[17] Junianto James Losari and Michael Ewing-Chow, 'Pacific Rim Investment Treaty Practice: Regional Considerations—Reflective or Reactionary? Indonesia's Approaches to International Investment Agreements and Recommendations for the Future' (2015) 1 TDM 4–9 <www.transnational-dispute-management.com/article.asp?key=2179> accessed 8 March 2016 (discussing e.g., direct and indirect expropriation, as well as provisions to dispose quickly of possibly frivolous claims). In addition, a Japanese consortium in 2013 notified a dispute over valuation of the Asahan aluminium joint venture project with the Indonesian government, based on a contract containing consent to ICSID arbitration, but the matter was subsequently settled: Mark Smith and Louise Browning, 'Indonesia and Nippon Asahan Aluminium Consortium Reach Settlement' (*ashurst*, February 2014) <https://www.ashurst.com/publication-item.aspx?id_Content=10053> accessed 23 April 2016.

[18] See generally Luke R Nottage and Simon Butt, 'Recent International Commercial Arbitration and Investor–State Arbitration Developments Impacting on Australia's Investments in the Resources Sector' in Gabriël A Moens and Philip Evans (eds), *Arbitration and Dispute Resolution in the Resources Sector: An Australian Perspective* (Springer 2016) 153–79 (with manuscript version at <http://ssrn.com/abstract=2340810>); Anthony Crockett, 'Indonesia's Bilateral Investment Treaties: Between Generations?' (2015) ICSID Rev-FILJ 437–48. On WTO disputes over natural resources recently, see also Thomas J Schoenbaum, chapter 17 in this volume.

[19] Grace D Amianti, 'Government Revises Investment Treaties' (*The Jakarta Post*, 12 May 2015) <http://www.thejakartapost.com/news/2015/05/12/govt-revises-investment-treaties.html#sthash.Hxl6wGDv.dpuf> accessed 8 March 2016. Cf the measured response by an international law academic: John Lumbantobing, 'Renegotiating the Bite of Our BITs' (*The Jakarta Post*, 18 May 2015) <http://www.thejakartapost.com/news/2015/05/18/renegotiating-bite-our-bits.html> accessed 8 March 2016.

In an official statement on its website, the Netherlands Embassy in Indonesia said that the European country was resuming discussions with Indonesian authorities regarding the previous government's decision to terminate its 1995 BIT signed with Indonesia. 'We will review the existing treaties step by step and focus only on those that expire soon, so we will hold the next meeting with the Law and Human Rights Ministry as well as the state secretary on May 20 to ask for their approval', Azhar said.

In addition, Azhar said the revision would be in line with the 2007 Direct Investment Law, which stipulated that international arbitration lawsuits should be filed based on an agreement between both parties. Existing BITs only require one party to file a lawsuit to international arbitration, he added.

The rest of this chapter turns its focus onto the related ICSID arbitration proceedings brought by Churchill's Australian subsidiary, *Planet Mining Pty Ltd v Republic of Indonesia*.[20] An experienced tribunal (Professors G Kaufmann-Kohler and A van den Berg, and Mr M Hwang SC) rendered a positive Decision on Jurisdiction (24 February 2014), opening a path for the investor to proceed to full hearings on the merits of the dispute,[21] but only on the basis of mining licences issued from 2005 by regional Indonesian authorities. Surprisingly, the tribunal accepted Indonesia's alternative argument that the state had not fully consented in advance to ISA under the auspices of ICSID, pursuant to Article XI(2)(b) of the 1992 Australia–Indonesia BIT.[22] Rights to ad hoc ISA under Article XI(3) were also held to be precluded, as long as Australia and Indonesia remained among around 150 Member States which have currently ratified the 1965 Convention.

With all due respect, this aspect of the tribunal's reasoning is quite questionable, as explained in section II below. Meanwhile, however, section III explains how the reasoning leaves significant ramifications, especially for many other BITs concluded by Australia that contain more or less similar wording (extracted in an online Appendix).[23] In particular, if the tribunal is correct, Australia's outbound

[20] *Planet Mining Pty Ltd v Republic of Indonesia*, ICSID Case No ARB/12/14 and 12/40, Decision on Jurisdiction (24 February 2014) <https://icsid.worldbank.org/ICSID/FrontServlet?requestType=CasesRH&actionVal=showDoc&docId=DC4193_En&caseId=C2723> accessed 23 April 2016.

[21] In a Procedural Order (No 8) subsequently issued on 22 April 2014, to avoid further delays the tribunal rejected a request by Indonesia to bifurcate proceedings to resolve issues concerning liability before proceedings assessing damages: see Peterson (n 16) and '*Churchill Mining PLC and Planet Mining Pty Ltd v Republic of Indonesia*, ICSID Case No ARB/12/14 and 12/40' (*italaw*) <http://www.italaw.com/cases/1479> accessed 8 March 2016 (also providing subsequent orders and developments in this on-going proceeding).

[22] 'Agreement between the Government of Australia and the Government of the Republic of Indonesia concerning the Promotion and Protection of Investment' <http://investmentpolicyhub.unctad.org/Download/TreatyFile/155> accessed 23 April 2016. For a general introduction to aspects of this 1992 treaty, see Chester Brown, 'Investor–State Arbitration: Getting More Bite Out of Your BIT' [2014] AMPLA Yearbook 204–20.

[23] Available via Luke R Nottage, 'Do Many of Australia's Bilateral Treaties Really Not Provide Full Advance Consent to Investor–State Arbitration? Analysis of Planet Mining v Indonesia and Regional Implications' (2015) 1 TDM <http://ssrn.com/abstract=2424987> accessed 8 March 2016. The full text of all Australia's BITs can be found via 'The Australian Treaties Database' <http://www.info.dfat.gov.au/Info/Treaties/treaties.nsf/> accessed 8 March 2016.

investors into Poland, Hungary, Romania, the Czech Republic, Lithuania, Peru, Pakistan, Egypt, and perhaps Papua New Guinea (PNG)—and vice versa—will have only highly circumscribed rights to ISA in claims under those further nine BITs. However, the purported limitation on consent in the Australia–Peru BIT may be removed if and when an expanded Trans-Pacific Partnership (TPP) FTA is ratified and enters into force,[24] including clear rights to ICSID and/or other ISA protections. Meanwhile, Australia and these nine countries (as well as Indonesia) should negotiate to clarify the scope of consent to ISA in their respective BITs.

Australia's investors into Indonesia, Vietnam, Laos, and the Philippines—and vice versa—will also have problems under the wording of those four BITs. However, they can instead bring BIT arbitration claims under the ICSID Convention (if and when Vietnam or Laos accedes) or specified non-ICSID arbitration, pursuant to the differently worded 2009 ASEAN–Australia–New Zealand Free Trade Agreement (AANZFTA), even in relation to pre-existing investments, although that only applies to disputes arising after its full entry into force (10 January 2012).[25] In addition, the BITs with India (also not yet party to the ICSID Convention), Sri Lanka, and Uruguay provide at least for non-ICSID ISA. The first five of these seven nations are also presently negotiating with Australia a Regional Comprehensive Economic Partnership (RECP or 'ASEAN+6') FTA, Vietnam has signed with Australia and ten others the expanded TPP agreement, and Australia is also negotiating bilateral FTAs with Indonesia and India. All these treaties provide further opportunities to clarify the scope of consent to ISA, albeit for future disputes.

More broadly, as sketched in section IV, the surprising conclusion that many of Australia's existing BITs arguably do not provide full ISA rights may encourage some other states negotiating the TPP or other regional agreements such as RCEP to press for similarly watered-down ISA protections, or indeed the complete omission of ISA from such new agreements. The same may occur with Australia's on-going bilateral FTA negotiations with, respectively, Indonesia itself and India. After all, a

[24] The full text of Australia's existing FTAs and descriptions of those still under negotiation can be found via 'Australian Government Department of Foreign Affairs and Trade' <http://www.dfat.gov.au/fta/> accessed 8 March 2016. On the TPP, see also e.g., Julien Chaisse, 'The Regulation of Investment in the TPP' in Jansen Calamita (ed), *The Regionalization of Investment Treaty Arrangements: Developments and Implications* (British Institute of International and Comparative Law 2014) 270–319; Leon Trakman and Kunal Sharma, 'Locating Australia on the Pacific Rim: Trade, Investment and the Asian Century' (2015) 1 TDM <www.transnational-dispute-management.com/article.asp?key=2178> accessed 8 March 2016; Christopher Hunt and Colin Trehearne, 'Japan in the Pacific Century: Opportunities and Challenges Arising From the TPP' (2015) 1 TDM <http://www.transnational-dispute-management.com/article.asp?key=2171> accessed 8 March 2016; Luke Nottage, 'The TPP Investment Chapter and Investor–State Arbitration in Asia and Oceania: Assessing Prospects for Ratification', paper presented at the GELN Biennial Symposium, 'The Age of Mega-Regionals: TPP and Regulatory Autonomy in IEL', University of Melbourne, 19 May 2016.

[25] On AANZFTA, see generally Vivienne Bath and Luke Nottage, 'The ASEAN Comprehensive Investment Agreement and "ASEAN Plus"—The Australia–New Zealand Free Trade Area (AANZFTA) and the PRC–ASEAN Investment Agreement' in Marc Bundenberg, Joern Griebel, Stephan Hobe, and August Reinisch (eds), *International Investment Law* (Nomos/Beck/Hart 2015) 283.

year before Indonesia's recent declaration, India had already announced it would be 'reviewing' its BITs providing for ISA rights.[26] In April 2015, India released a draft Model BIT for public consultation, including many provisions strongly favouring the host state. Indeed, for example, one commentary pointed out that:[27]

> [Article] 14.4(ii) provides that a claim may be submitted only if a 'written consent for the submission of the claim to arbitration by the Parties' exists, thereby implying that the BIT does not form the basis for such written consent. The preamble defines the 'Parties' as the Contracting Parties.

In addition, India (like Laos, Myanmar, Thailand, and Vietnam in Asia) has still not ratified the ICSID Convention. Similar complications may emerge for other countries in the region, such as Japan, with BITs containing similar wording to some of Australia's treaties. Delays and costs are therefore likely to escalate both in treaty negotiations and dispute resolution involving ISA. These problems are already significant, as with international commercial arbitration,[28] exacerbating concerns about ISDS and investment treaties in general.

II. The Dispute and the Tribunal's Analysis in *Planet Mining v Indonesia*

The dispute in *Planet Mining v Indonesia* involved the East Kutai mining project in Kalimantan, hosting the world's seventh largest coal deposit with an estimated pre-tax net present value of US$1.8 billion (paras 7–9 of the Decision). Mining rights and licences ended up being held by a company owned by UK mining company, Churchill (ninety-five per cent), and its Australian subsidiary, Planet (five per cent) (para 16). These were eventually revoked in 2010 by the central government, and the foreign investors failed in administrative and judicial review proceedings culminating in a judgment of the Supreme Court of Indonesia on 21 May 2012 (paras 40–42).

[26] See 'Investment Pacts Can't be Subject to Foreign Laws: FM P Chidambaram' (*The Economic Times*, 17 April 2013) <http://articles.economictimes.indiatimes.com/2013-04-17/news/38616367_1_canada-india-business-council-indian-high-commissioner-protection-agreement> accessed 8 March 2016; Prabhash Ranjan, 'India and Bilateral Investment Treaties—A Changing Landscape' (2014) 29(2) ICSID Rev-FILJ 419.

[27] Bhushan Satish and Shreyas Jayasimha, 'From Ford to Ferrari? A Brief Look at the Changes Introduced in the Draft Model Indian BIT' (*Kluwer Arbitration Blog*, 29 April 2015) <http://kluwerarbitrationblog.com/blog/2015/04/29/from-ford-to-ferrari-a-brief-look-at-the-changes-introduced-in-the-draft-model-indian-bit/> accessed 8 March 2016. The draft BIT was available, with various public comments, via Government of India: MyGov, 'Draft Indian Model Bilateral Investment Treaty Text' <https://mygov.in/group-issue/draft-indian-model-bilateral-investment-treaty-text/> accessed 23 April 2016.

[28] Luke Nottage, 'Informalization and Globalization of International Commercial Arbitration and Investment Treaty Arbitration in Asia' in Joachim Zekoll, Moritz Baelz, and Iwo Amelung (eds), *Formalisation and Flexibilisation in Dispute Resolution* (Martinus Nijhoff/Brill) 211–49, with further extensive references and data.

Each investor then filed for ICSID arbitration, invoking the 1976 UK–Indonesia BIT and 1992 Australia–Indonesia BIT respectively, and both cases were consolidated before the same tribunal subject to the issuance of two separate rulings on jurisdiction. In its Decision on Jurisdiction in *Churchill Mining PLC v Republic of Indonesia* (ICSID Case No ARB/12/14 and 12/40, 24 February 2014),[29] the tribunal upheld jurisdiction to ICSID arbitration based primarily on *travaux preparatoires*, indicating that Indonesia and the UK had provided advance consent. Churchill released a media statement repeating its preliminary estimate of damages claimable (by itself and Planet) amounting to over US$1 billion.[30] On 28 February 2014, a government official declared that Indonesia planned to seek an annulment of this Decision through ICSID.[31]

In the *Planet Mining v Indonesia* proceedings, in contrast, no such *travaux* existed or were adduced, leaving treaty wording in Article XI of the Australia–Indonesia BIT that 'does not contain Indonesia's advance consent to ICSID proceedings', according to the tribunal (para 173). It emphasized a tension between Article XI(2), stating that '*the investor … may submit the dispute for settlement*' to ICSID for arbitration or conciliation; and Article XI(4), stating that 'where a dispute is [so] referred … (a) [the host state] *shall consent in writing to the submission to the Centre within forty-five days of receiving such a request from the investor*' (emphasis added). Planet argued that the former provision and the requirement that the host state 'shall consent' amounted to its immediate and advance consent to jurisdiction. Indonesia retorted that the latter provision indicated a two-step process or a mere 'promise to consent', if it decided that other jurisdictional requirements for ICSID arbitration were made out—albeit with such a decision being subject to review in any inter-state arbitration proceedings that might be separately initiated under the BIT (paras 154–55). The tribunal essentially agreed with Indonesia's argument, interpreting the 'ordinary meaning' of Article XI as being insufficient to 'express Indonesia's advance consent to ICSID proceedings' and finding that 'it would be doing violence to the clear terms of Article XI(4)(a) to reduce this clause to a mere administrative formality for ICSID' (para 167), as had been asserted by Planet (para 166).

At first blush, this seems a surprising result. If a party to a commercial contract, for example, states that it 'shall consent to arbitration' within a certain time after receiving formal notice of the dispute, this would surely imply advance consent to the arbitration procedure. It would strain the ordinary meaning of the wording to substitute some two-step process whereby the party can later decide whether or not to proceed to arbitration, subject perhaps to some court review of its grounds

[29] *Churchill Mining Plc v Republic of Indonesia*, ICSID Case No ARB/12/14 and 12/40, Decision on Jurisdiction (24 February 2014), <https://icsid.worldbank.org/ICSID/FrontServlet?requestType=CasesRH&actionVal=showDoc&docId=DC4194_En&caseId=C2261> accessed 23 April 2016.

[30] 'Churchill Mining PLC' <http://www.churchillmining.com/> accessed 8 March 2016.

[31] Fidel Ali, 'Indonesia to File Objection to Arbitration Ruling in Favor of Churchill Mining' (*Jakarta Globe*, 28 February 2014) <http://www.thejakartaglobe.com/business/indonesia-to-file-objection-to-arbitration-ruling-in-favor-of-churchill-mining/?doing_wp_cron=1397197624.3556709289550781250000> accessed 8 March 2016. Cf section III below.

for refusing not to proceed, given that the main purpose of arbitration is to avoid having to go to court. A more usual inference from the wording would be that, after the expiry of the agreed time limit from notification, the parties intended for arbitration nonetheless to commence. Typically, nowadays, the arbitral tribunal would then have some opportunity to rule on its own jurisdiction, subject to court review at the agreed seat of the arbitration and/or later in the enforcing country.

Of course, treaty-based ISA differs in that the arbitration agreement derives from a treaty obligation assumed by host state and the foreign investor's home state. Specifically, the host state offers ISA to the foreign investor, which the latter accepts by filing for ISA under the treaty.[32] Yet the basic concept of an 'offer' is the offeror's willingness to be bound if and when the offeree accepts,[33] thus envisaging some future conduct expressing assent. Accordingly, it is not odd for the treaty to contain language using or implying the future tense, such as whereby the host state 'will consent' or 'shall consent' to ISA. The host state is thereby indicating its future willingness to be bound when the investor initiates arbitration, just as much as in situations where the wording provides, for example, that the host state 'hereby consents' to ISA.[34]

Such arguments from ordinary meaning gain force from the fact that the very purpose of providing for ISA, as under Article XI of the Australia–Indonesia BIT, is to allow an *extra* avenue to claim against the host state. Such a procedure is in addition to an inter-state arbitration process (found in almost all investment treaties, not just the Australia–Indonesia BIT in Article XII) which can be stymied by the home state deciding not to espouse its investor's claim due to diplomatic or domestic political considerations after a dispute arises. By contrast, the highly impractical implication of the decision in *Planet Mining v Indonesia* is that the foreign investor will need to clear that extra hurdle in its home state, if the host state decides to contest ICSID jurisdiction. The tribunal did consider generally the 'object and purpose' of the Australia–Indonesia BIT, but it focused only on the wording of the preamble and found that to be neutral, as it 'refers to both the private interests of the investor as well as the public interests' of the host state (para 172).

The tribunal also considered the 'context' of the wording contained in Articles XI(2) and (4). It first rejected an argument by Planet based on the insertion of the disjunctive 'or' separating Article XI(4)(a) from Article XI(4)(b). The tribunal pointed out that all other BITs concluded by Australia used instead 'and', and concluded that 'or' was 'the result of infelicitous drafting rather than a deliberate choice entailing specific consequences' (para 168). This approach differs sharply from the tribunal's later imputation to Australia of careful consideration being

[32] See e.g., Rudolph Dolzer and Christoph Schreuer, *Principles of International Investment Law* (OUP 2008) 243.

[33] See e.g., UNIDROIT Principles of International Commercial Contracts (2013), art 2.12.

[34] See also e.g., *Millicom International Operations BV and Sentel GSM SA v The Republic of Senegal*, ICSID Case No ARB/08/20, Decision on Jurisdiction (16 July 2010) para 63 <http://www.italaw.com/sites/default/files/case-documents/italaw1247.pdf> accessed 23 April 2016 (upholding jurisdiction under the Netherlands–Senegal BIT, which provided that the host state 'shall assent' to ISA).

given to the words agreed to in its treaties and the tribunal's emphasis otherwise on 'ordinary meaning', although Article XI(4)(b) anyway deals with the investor's right to choose between ICSID arbitration or mediation.

Indeed, the tribunal went on to agree that although Article XI(3) also led to 'a surprising and unsatisfactory result', on a further argument from treaty context made by Planet, 'it is the result that derives from the text of the Treaty and the tribunal cannot change the text, especially not in the absence of *travaux* that would shed a different light on the words' (para 169). Planet had argued that 'it would be absurd to allow the investor access to UNCITRAL [arbitration] under Article XI(3) as long as one or both Contracting States are not ICSID members, but to deny the investor access both to UNCITRAL and ICSID when the Contracting States are ICSID members' (para 169).[35] As the tribunal noted, both Australia and Indonesia were already ICSID members when their BIT was concluded, so UNCITRAL arbitration provided under Article XI(3) 'could only come into play if one of them were to denounce the ICSID Convention' (para 169). Given that the purpose of the ICSID Convention is to enhance ISA, not to undermine it, this is certainly a bizarre outcome that follows from the interpretation of Article XI as asserted by Indonesia.[36]

Nonetheless, the tribunal accepted that interpretation based on its 'ordinary meaning' in light of the treaty's context and overall purpose, pursuant to Article 31 of the 1969 Vienna Convention on the Law of Treaties (VCLT) (para 149). The tribunal then found this to be confirmed by 'supplementary means of interpretation under Article 32 ... *i.e.* doctrinal writings and treaty practice' (para 173).[37]

However, the tribunal acknowledged that all authors invoked by Indonesia in support of its view, that treaty wording along the lines of 'shall consent' implies

[35] As mentioned in the Appendix, art XI(3) provides (emphasis added):

> *If both Parties are not at the time the dispute arises party to the [ICSID] Convention*, the dispute may be submitted to such procedures for settlement as may be agreed between the parties to the dispute. If no such procedures have been agreed within a three month period from written notification of the claim, the parties to the dispute shall be bound to submit it to arbitration under the Arbitration Rules of the United Nations Commission on International Trade Law as then in force ....

[36] Indeed, it has been argued that:

> Article 11(3) would seem to have been intended to reassure investors as to the availability of a dispute resolution mechanism if either State subsequently denounces the ICSID Convention, thereby removing access to ICSID arbitration. The Tribunal [at para 169] seemed to accept this contextual reading of the provision. It seems arguable, therefore, that the true intent of Article 11(3) is not to restrict the investor's access to UNCITRAL arbitration, but rather to provide investors with additional protection where ICSID arbitration is unavailable. The question then becomes whether the host state's refusal to consent to ICSID arbitration renders the ICSID mechanism unavailable for the purposes of this reading of the clause.

Sam Luttrell and Isuru Devendra, 'Planet Mining Pty Ltd v Republic of Indonesia' (2014) 10(2) Asian Intl Arb J 195, 202.

[37] For applications of other aspects of art 31 in international economic law, see Chin Leng Lim, chapter 8 in this volume.

a two-step process, ultimately all refer back to early work by Aron Broches (para 176). By contrast, others who have recently considered his initial argument or derivative works, including Shotaro Hamamoto and Luke Nottage, considering similar wording in several of Japan's BITs (for example, with Egypt in 1977 and Sri Lanka in 1982), have expressed reservations about taking such a literal interpretation too far.[38]

The tribunal also observed that some authors commenting especially on Australia's relevant BITs 'do provide support for Indonesia's interpretation' (para 177). It cited Michael Pryles and Richard Garnett, for example, who had suggested that without consent in writing 'an ICSID arbitral tribunal would not have jurisdiction'.[39] However, in a subsequent volume co-edited by Luke Nottage and Richard Garnett and not cited by the tribunal, in the chapter by Mark Mangan focusing on Australia's investment treaties, the point is not taken.[40]

Anyway, the tribunal stated that it 'reached its decision irrespective of these [cited] writings, which merely rely on the authors' reasoning without reference to extrinsic materials' (para 181). Instead, it emphasized other treaty practice. The tribunal noted that 'in at least 60 out of 64 BITs, Indonesia has given advance consent' (para 186). Of the others, the 1974 Indonesia–Switzerland BIT omits ISA altogether, the 1973 Indonesia–France BIT requires consent to be included in investment approval documentation, the 1976 Indonesia–UK BIT requires that the host state 'shall assent to any request' for ICSID arbitration (but with *travaux* indicating advance consent, as noted above), and the fourth was the 1992 Australia–Indonesia BIT.

This pattern strongly suggests that Indonesia was prepared to give full advance consent to ICSID arbitration, not a mere 'promise to consent', especially since the early 1990s. Yet the tribunal instead focused mainly on Australia's treaty practice. It inferred that the wording in the 1992 Australia–Indonesia BIT 'must have been proposed by the Australian negotiators' (para 188). Reviewing then other BITs, especially the 1991 Australia–Vietnam BIT and the 2002 Australia–Sri Lanka BIT, the tribunal concluded (para 195):

> These last two treaties show that Australia deliberately entertains the distinction between advance consent and promise to consent. The foregoing review also demonstrates that Australia concluded BITs with unequivocal expressions of advance consent and thus knows how to express such an intent when it wishes to do so.

In particular, the tribunal highlighted that in the BIT with Vietnam (concluded shortly before the one with Indonesia), Article 12(2)(c) provides for the investor

[38] Shotaro Hamamoto and Luke R Nottage, 'Foreign Investment In and Out of Japan: Economic Backdrop, Domestic Law, and International Treaty-based Investor–State Dispute Resolution' (2011) 5 TDM <http://ssrn.com/abstract=1724999> accessed 8 March 2016; 'Japan' in Chester Brown (ed), *Commentaries on Selected Model Investment Treaties* (OUP 2013) 382.

[39] Michael Pryles, *Dispute Resolution in Asia* (3rd edn, Kluwer 2006) 82.

[40] Mark Mangan, 'Australia's Investment Treaty Program and Investor–State Arbitration' in Luke Nottage and Richard Garnett (eds), *International Arbitration in Australia* (Federation Press 2010) 191–221.

to invoke 'Annex B' or other agreed arbitration, if (i) both countries are not party to the ICSID Convention; or (ii) 'one party to the dispute [the host state] has not consented to [the investor] referring the dispute' to ICSID (paras 191–92).

However, it is possible that the latter wording in (ii), which is not found in the otherwise quite similar Article 14 of the 1990 Australia–Papua New Guinea BIT, was proposed either by Vietnamese negotiators or, more likely,[41] by Australian negotiators out of an abundance of caution given that Vietnam was not then (and still is not) party to the ICSID Convention—or even having in mind the possibility that an Australian investor might propose ICSID Additional Facility arbitration to Vietnam. In any event, Annex B or other agreed arbitration was left as an option for the investor, which suggests that Australia wanted to provide for *some* access to full-blown ISA (contrary to the interpretation ultimately given by the tribunal to the Australia–Indonesia and several subsequent BITs). Interestingly, Australia's 1995 BIT with Laos (also not yet party to the Convention), does not include the wording in (ii), but only the wording in (i), which is seemingly derived from the 1990 BIT with PNG. This suggests that Australia's negotiators placed little significance on the extra wording in (ii).

The tribunal also highlighted the 2002 Australia–Sri Lanka BIT, particularly two additions compared to the wording of the BIT with Indonesia (paras 193–94): the host state's consent to ICSID arbitration within thirty days of an investor's request 'shall not be unreasonably withheld' (Article 13((3)(a)), and if not given within that period it 'shall be deemed to have consented' instead to 'Annex B' ad hoc arbitration (provided in Article 13((2)(c)). Yet this point reinforces the argument made above, from ordinary meaning, that if consent is not given, it should be deemed to have been given so that some form of arbitration can proceed.

It should also not be forgotten that when Australia signed its BIT with Indonesia, it had only signed five others: one with China in 1998 (limiting ISA claims to ad hoc arbitration of the amount of compensation for expropriation, as was common with China's BITs in that era, and to ICSID arbitration if and when both states joined that Convention), the 1990 BIT with PNG, the 1991 BIT with Vietnam, and then two more in 1991 with Poland and Hungary. It strains credulity that Australia's negotiators at the time understood the fine distinction between advance consent to arbitration and a mere promise to consent, and then carefully crafted wording to obtain only the latter for the BIT with Indonesia—with such wording then also deliberately carried over into many subsequent BITs concluded by Australia. This is especially so given the 'surprising' result that, on the interpretation given by Indonesia and adopted by the tribunal, the investor is left with no effective access to ISA at all (even ad hoc UNCITRAL Rules arbitration).[42]

Furthermore, for example, the next (seventh) BIT signed by Australia was with Hong Kong, on 17 November 1993. Article 10 quite clearly gives full advance

[41] Earlier or contemporaneous BITs concluded by Vietnam with Belgium, Italy, and Indonesia have very different clauses (and the one with Thailand omits ISA altogether).

[42] In theory, it might make sense nowadays for a host state to offer more restricted access to ICSID Rules arbitration, given its more delocalized review and enforcement process. However, this applies especially to developing countries and/or net capital importers (like Indonesia, rather than Australia,

consent, even though it states that the 'parties to the dispute *shall be bound* to submit' to UNCITRAL Rules arbitration (emphasis added). Indeed, a claim by Philip Morris Asia proceeded against Australia on this basis in relation to tobacco plain packaging laws.[43] It is counterintuitive that Australia would deliberately seek (for the benefit of its outbound investors) full advance consent to ISA in a BIT with Hong Kong, a jurisdiction with a much more developed domestic legal system protecting investors' rights, but a mere 'promise to consent' in a BIT with Indonesia—which, moreover, otherwise had almost always clearly agreed to full advance consent since the 1980s.

Another difficulty with the tribunal's analysis of treaties like the Australia–Indonesia BIT is that the Australian government has never publically declared that it considers its consent to have been thus limited in such treaties. On the contrary, particularly since 2010, government agencies, officials, and politicians from various political parties have made many statements highlighting that Australia's investment treaties have intended to provide full consent to ISA, except for some exceptions including a few FTAs (such as those with the United States or New Zealand).

The Productivity Commission's *Trade Policy Review* final report (December 2010) proceeds on this basis, as did Submissions to the Commission (including DR98 from Australia's Department of Foreign Affairs and Trade),[44] before recommending that Australia no longer seek to incorporate ISA protections in future investment treaties due to greater perceived costs and risks involved. The *Gillard Government Trade Policy Statement* (April 2011) adopted the Commission's recommendation,[45] resulting in the 2012 Malaysia–Australia FTA excluding ISA altogether (although such protections remain anyway under AANZFTA). The Coalition Government elected on 7 September 2013 reverted to a 'case-by-case assessment' about the need for ISA, including provisions in the FTAs concluded respectively with Korea in December 2013 and China in November 2014, but not the FTA concluded with Japan in April 2014.[46] Meanwhile, a minority Greens Party senator from Tasmania

back in 1992), and anyway assumes that non-ICSID arbitration is also offered as an alternative to foreign investors (which the tribunal interpreted not to have been given in the Australia–Indonesia BIT).

[43] Australian Government Attorney-General's Department, 'Tobacco Plain Packaging—Investor–State Arbitration' <http://www.ag.gov.au/internationalrelations/internationallaw/pages/tobaccoplainpackaging.aspx> accessed 8 March 2016. Australia's Response to the Notice of Arbitration (21 December 2011), contesting jurisdiction primarily on the basis that there is no covered 'investment', does not argue that the italicized words from the Hong Kong BIT indicate a two-stage process or promise to consent, although it notes that the Response's 'jurisdictional objections ... are not intended to be exhaustive' (para 36). On parallel WTO claims, see also Ernst-Ulrich Petersmann, chapter 5 in this volume.

[44] See especially DFAT's paras 50–61, via Australian Government Productivity Commission, 'Bilateral and Regional Trade Agreements: Commissioned Study' <http://www.pc.gov.au/projects/study/trade-agreements> accessed 8 March 2016.

[45] Luke R Nottage, 'Investor–State Dispute Settlement Back for Australia's Free Trade Agreements' (*The University of Sydney: Japanese Law in Asia-Pacific Socio-Economic Context Blog*) <http://blogs.usyd.edu.au/japaneselaw/2013/12/isds_back.html> accessed 8 March 2016.

[46] Luke R Nottage, 'Investor–State Arbitration: Not in the Australia–Japan Free Trade Agreement, and Not Ever for Australia?' (2014) 38 J Japan L 37; Trakman and Sharma (n 24). The current Trade Minister also stated publically on 8 April 2014 that Australia has treaties containing ISA provisions with

has moved the *Trade and Foreign Investment (Protecting the Public Interest) Bill*, which would legislatively preclude Australia from including ISA in future treaties, although in July 2014 the majority reports of the relevant Senate Committee recommended against enacting this Bill.[47] If indeed the Australia–Indonesia BIT and similarly worded treaties only provided extremely limited consent to ISA, one would have expected politicians, officials, and government agencies to emphasize that this was achieved—deliberately, as suggested by the tribunal in *Planet Mining v Indonesia*, or otherwise—in order to deflect contemporary concerns about ISA. The silence on this point is deafening, including during the hearings on the Australian Senate's 'anti-ISDS Bill', at which government officials provided a submission and gave oral evidence at public hearings.[48]

The tribunal instead considered various National Interest Analysis reports prepared since 1996 by the Australian government in conjunction with new BITs, but concluded that these did not help Planet's counter-argument. The tribunal did not rely on these reports because (i) they stated only generally that the government may be at risk of assuming costs from ICSID arbitrations; and (ii) 'all post-date the entry into force of the Australia-Indonesia BIT' (para 197). The first reason is understandable, as even qualified consent (as asserted by Indonesia in this case) does involve some risk for Australia in the face of potential claims from foreign investors—although very much reduced. However, the second reason is unconvincing. As 'supplementary means of interpretation' under Vienna Convention Article 32, there seems no reason why a tribunal need only consider the text of subsequent treaties.[49] The state's (consistent) statements or conduct with respect to such treaties arguably should also be relevant, even if accorded less evidential value.[50]

Korea and '28 other countries' [sic: including Hong Kong] (Minister for Trade and Investment: The Hon Andrew Robb AO MP, 'ABC Radio National Breakfast, Interview with Fran Kelly' (8 April 2014) <http://www.trademinister.gov.au/transcripts/Pages/2014/ar_tr_140408.aspx> accessed 8 March 2016), still without indicating that many may give only limited consent to ISA (if the tribunal in *Planet Mining v Indonesia* is correct).

[47] Luke R Nottage, 'The "Anti-ISDS Bill" Before the Senate: What Future for Investor–State Arbitration in Australia?' (2015) XVIII Intl Trade & Bus L Rev 245–93 (with a longer version at <http://ssrn.com/abstract=2483610> accessed 8 March 2016).

[48] Parliament of Australia, 'Inquiry into the Trade and Foreign Investment (Protecting the Public Interest) Bill 2014' <http://www.aph.gov.au/Parliamentary_Business/Committees/Senate/Foreign_Affairs_Defence_and_Trade/Trade_and_Foreign_Investment_Protecting_the_Public_Interest_Bill_2014> accessed 8 March 2016. DFAT also did the same during an inquiry in 2015 into Australia's treaty-making process, again without suggesting that ISDS provisions in many of Australia's treaties may be highly limited in the way suggested by the tribunal in *Planet Mining v Indonesia*, despite many other submissions again raising concerns about ISDS: see Parliament of Australia, 'The Commonwealth's Treaty-making Process' <http://www.aph.gov.au/Parliamentary_Business/Committees/Senate/Foreign_Affairs_Defence_and_Trade/Treaty-making_process> accessed 8 March 2016.

[49] Art 32 specifically refers to 'preparatory work of the treaty and the circumstances of its conclusion' but it 'gives only examples of the principal supplementary means of interpretation. One may also look at other treaties on the same subject matter adopted either before or after the one in question which use the same or similar terms.' See Anthony Aust, *Modern Treaty Law and Practice* (2nd edn, CUP 2007) 248, and other cited works listing further supplementary means of interpretation that have evolved over many years.

[50] Admittedly, this possibility does not appear to be specifically mentioned in standard textbooks, such as ibid; Ulf Linderfalk (ed), *On the Interpretation of Treaties* (Springer 2007); Richard

However, a differently constituted ICSID tribunal recently declined to refer to past treaty practice, as urged by the Canadian claimant in proceedings under a BIT with Venezuela:[51]

> [T]he Claimant [NSPI] has argued that the prior treaty making practice of both Canada and Venezuela supports its reading of the term investment because in other instances these two States have excluded certain types of commercial activity from the definition of investment. Because this has not occurred in the BIT, it should be presumed that NSPI's alleged investment is included. The Tribunal does not find this argument persuasive. Whilst it is accepted that other tribunals have had recourse to prior treaty making practice, the Tribunal is not convinced that this avenue is open based on the interpretive framework provided for in the [VCLT], and thus whether it is appropriate.

Another recent ICSID tribunal, albeit in declining jurisdiction based on its interpretation of national legislation enacted by Papua New Guinea, further remarked that:[52]

> In this case, the reference to the various BITs does not advance the discussion on whether [the legislation] constitutes the Respondent's 'consent in writing', other than to illustrate the examples of possible language in which the Respondent's consent may be expressed. The language of the various BITs is irrelevant either for establishing the Respondent's consent, or, conversely, for disproving its existence.

For completeness, it should also be noted that when interpreting 'ordinary meaning', Article 31(3) requires consideration of '(a) any subsequent agreement between the parties regarding the interpretation of *the treaty* or the application of its provisions'; and '(b) any subsequent practice in the application of

Gardiner, *Treaty Interpretation* (OUP 2008). By the same token, however, there may also be doubts about referring to the text of subsequent treaties themselves.

[51] *Nova Scotia Power Incorporated v Bolivarian Republic of Venezuela*, ICSID Case No ARB(AF)/11/1, Award, para 83 (30 April 2014), <https://icsid.worldbank.org/ICSID/FrontServlet?requestType=CasesRH&actionVal=showDoc&docId=DC4774_En&caseId=C1380> accessed 23 April 2016, omitting footnote 137 at the end of this quotation, which further explains: '*I.e.* the prior treaty making practice of two States does not fit within the "context" outlined in Article 31(2) of the [VCLT], and, in the event that supplementary means of interpretation under Article 32 of the [VCLT] are to be employed, nor does it fit within those enumerated.' Leaving the door somewhat ajar, however:

> The Tribunal notes that were prior treaty making practice to be examined as a factual matter [fn 138: *I.e.* not as a supplementary means of interpretation (… Article 32) or as a contextual matter (… Article 31).], there would need to be substantial prior treaty practice and complete symmetry with regard to the particular treaty provision between Canada and Venezuela's practice, sufficient to evidence a 'meeting of the minds' and a common and continuous understanding. This *may* justifiably shed light on a bilateral investment treaty. The Tribunal has not been presented with the kind of comprehensive review of Canada and Venezuela's prior substantial treaty-making practice which would enable it to discern such symmetry. In fact, very few treaties were referred to. The Tribunal further notes that even were such symmetry established looking at prior treaty-making practice requires caution. Each treaty or international agreement is a different bargain struck and based on different sets of circumstances.

[52] *PNGSDP Ltd v Papua New Guinea* (n 2), para 332 (omitting n 641 referring to the *SPP v Egypt* decision).

the treaty which establishes the agreement of the parties regarding its interpretation' (emphasis added). It might be argued that Australia's recent public statements, assuming full advance consent to ISA in almost all its investment treaties, logically incorporate a similar assumption with respect to a *specific treaty* such as the 1992 Australia–Indonesia BIT. However, particularly if a broader interpretation is taken of Article 32 regarding general treaty practice, a more natural reading of these provisions of Article 31(3) is that they require subsequent agreement or mutual conduct relating to the particular treaty in question. Anyway, invoking them would require evidence of Indonesia's reciprocal assent to the notion that it had provided full advance to consent to almost all its own investment treaties.

III. Implications of *Planet Mining v Indonesia* for Other Australian and Regional Investment Treaties

In sum, the tribunal's adoption of Indonesia's view of the highly limited scope of consent to ISA, in its BIT with Australia, is certainly arguable but ultimately unpersuasive. This aspect of the ruling may have sought to provide some comfort to the Indonesian government in this case, having anyway found full advance consent to have been given to Planet under its licences, in the context of broader contemporary concerns about ISA in Indonesia (and indeed elsewhere) as well as some re-emergent 'resource nationalism'.[53] However, as indicated in section I above, this has not prevented Indonesia from subsequently announcing a review of all its BITs.

In addition, the tribunal's reasoning has further wide-ranging and potentially long-lasting ramifications. Its approach to interpreting the wording of the Australia–Indonesia BIT may well survive, and then be followed by tribunals ruling on similar wording used in treaties concluded by other states.[54] This could occur if, for example, Indonesia goes on to succeed on the merits (i.e. successfully defends the claim), with Planet then possibly seeking annulment only of that aspect of the final award (under the limited grounds provided in ICSID Convention Article 52).[55] Alternatively, if Indonesia loses on the merits, it may seek annulment also with respect to the Decision on Jurisdiction (incorporated into the final award) but presumably only the part that found consent to ICSID arbitration, namely the tribunal's interpretation of the mining licences. If so, Planet might then seek annulment as well, with

[53] Nottage and Butt (n 18).

[54] Indeed, one of the members of this tribunal has earlier emphasized the growing role of 'precedent' in investment treaty arbitration: Gabrielle Kaufmann-Kohler, 'Arbitral Precedent: Dream, Necessity or Excuse?' (2007) 23(3) Arb Intl 357 <http://www.arbitration-icca.org/media/0/12319143087130/00950001.pdf> accessed 23 April 2016.

[55] As noted by Dolzer and Schreuer (n 32) 279: 'Only awards are subject to annulment. There is no annulment in respect of other decisions, such as decisions on jurisdiction.... A decision by a tribunal declining jurisdiction is an award and therefore subject to annulment. Requests for partial annulment and annulment of parts of awards are possible.'

respect to the other part of the Decision which had declined jurisdiction, namely the tribunal's interpretation of the Australia–Indonesia BIT. But Planet might give up due to costs and delays involved, relative to the potential benefits of success (bearing in mind that it only has a five per cent shareholding), or settle the dispute at that stage. Then the tribunal's approach to interpreting the Australia–Indonesia BIT will stand as a type of precedent as well.

Already, the tribunal's reasoning calls into question the scope for ICSID and/or other ISA in Australia's other BITs. Treaties concluded (in chronological order) with the respective states highlighted below in **bold**, especially those also **<u>underlined</u>**, become particularly problematic for investors (as summarized further below):

- China (1988): this BIT with Australia anyway only provides for ISA concerning the amount of compensation for expropriation (as noted above). Full-scale rights may be added under RCEP, being negotiated with Australia an addition to a recent bilateral FTA.
- **PNG (1990)**: under Article 14(3)(a), the host state 'shall consent' to ICSID arbitration if sought by the investor, although the tribunal notes (at para 190) that this BIT does not set a time limit or writing requirement. That might make a difference regarding ICSID jurisdiction, although the same tribunal in *Churchill v Indonesia* had doubts about the wording 'shall assent' in the UK–Indonesia BIT. If such wording does not mean advance consent, then the same problem arises as under the BIT with Indonesia: as long as both Australia and PNG remain ICSID members, ISA under 'Annex B' of this treaty is not available either.
- **Vietnam (1991)**: as emphasized by the tribunal (para 192), this treaty does state that if the host state 'has not consented in writing' to ICSID jurisdiction, the treaty instead provides for Annex B or other agreed arbitration. Fortunately for investors, if and when Vietnam accedes to the ICSID Convention, ICSID arbitration is anyway available under AANZFTA (signed in 2009) for violations of that treaty's investment chapter. Article 21(2) provides that a 'claim shall be deemed submitted to arbitration … when the disputing investor's notice of or request for arbitration … is received'.
- **<u>Poland</u> (1991), <u>Hungary</u> (1991)**: these BITs may be suspect too as they use similar wording to the 1992 BIT with Indonesia, except that 'the time limit was included in the same paragraph as the one providing for ICSID proceedings' (para 190).
- **Indonesia (1992)**: even if the tribunal's analysis of this BIT is correct, AANZFTA (2009) again provides clear advance consent to ICSID arbitration anyway.
- Hong Kong (1993): under Article 10 the host state 'shall be bound to submit' to UNCITRAL Rules arbitration. This should be sufficient to establish advance consent (as noted above) and the treaty is not listed by the tribunal as having similar wording to the BIT with Indonesia.

- **Romania (1993)** and **Czech Republic (1994)**: the former has almost identical wording on this point compared with the BIT with Indonesia, while the latter has almost identical wording with the BITs with Poland and Hungary.
- **Laos (1994)**: this also has almost identical wording to the Indonesia BIT. However, if and when Laos adopts the ICSID Convention, ICSID arbitration will be available instead under AANZFTA. Meanwhile, that also provides for UNCITRAL or other arbitration at the request of the investor.
- **Philippines (1994)**: this also has almost identical wording to the Indonesia BIT. However, under AANZFTA there is arguably only advance consent to non-ICSID arbitration, as its footnote 14 to Article 21 provides that: 'In the case of the Philippines, the submission of a claim under the ICSID Convention and the *ICSID Rules of Procedure for Arbitration Proceedings* shall be subject to a written agreement between the disputing parties in the event that an investment dispute arises.'
- Argentina (1995): the tribunal itself remarks that this is one of 'three BITs [containing] an unequivocal expression of consent to ICSID proceedings' (para 188). Article 13(4) provides that the host state 'hereby consents' to submission to ICSID jurisdiction.
- **Peru (1995)**: this has almost identical wording to the BIT with Indonesia. Unfortunately for investors, moreover, it was automatically renewed on 2 February 2012 without changing the provisions on ISA (despite the Gillard Government Trade Policy Statement being in operation). However, when ISA provisions included in the expanded TPP agreement come into force, advance consent to ICSID arbitration will apply between Australia and Peru under that treaty instead.
- **Pakistan (1998)**: this also has almost identical wording to the BIT with Indonesia. Unfortunately for investors, the Australia–Pakistan BIT was automatically renewed on 14 October 2013, with the same problematic wording. The tribunal noted that an ICSID arbitration commenced by an Australian investor is pending (*Tethyan Copper v Pakistan*, ICSID Case No ARB/12/1), with interim measures ordered by a different tribunal after determining that it had prima facie jurisdiction. But it states that as well as this being 'a *prima facie* determination, it appears that Pakistan did not object to jurisdiction … on the grounds of lack of consent [under the BIT with Australia], and it had not known whether it provided its consent within the 45 days or whether another expression of consent applies' (para 196). The ruling in *Planet Mining v Indonesia* therefore may well still impede this pending claim against Pakistan.
- Chile (1996): the tribunal mentions this as the second of three BITs with full advance consent, citing to the Spanish version (para 188). The English version also provides that the host state 'hereby consents' to ICSID arbitration. Anyway, this BIT is no longer in force, having been superseded by the

Australia–Chile FTA (2008), which provides clear consent in Chapter 10 Article 10.17.

- **Lithuania (1998)**: this also has almost identical wording to the BIT with Indonesia.
- **India (1999)**: by inference, the tribunal did not consider this treaty to clearly provide for advance consent. Article 12(3)(a) provides for referral to ICSID if both states accede to the ICSID Convention (and India still has not), *and* if 'both Parties to the dispute consent in writing to submit the dispute' to ICSID. Arguably this wording creates more doubt about full advance consent compared even to the BIT with PNG. Fortunately for investors, however, Article 12(3)(c) provides for the investor to commence UNCITRAL Rules arbitration. In fact, an Australian investor (White Industries) has successfully pursued such a claim against India. Anyway, Australia is presently negotiating an FTA with India, as well as RCEP including both countries, which could clarify the scope of consent especially to ICSID arbitration.
- **Egypt (2001)**: this also has almost identical wording to Australia's BIT with Indonesia.
- **Uruguay (2001)**: this has quite similar wording too; but, under Article 13(2)(c), 'adopts another structure giving an investor access to the alternative [Annex B] arbitration mechanism even when both Contracting States are ICSID members' (para 190).
- **Sri Lanka (2002)**: this also has quite similar wording to Australia's BIT with Indonesia. However, as noted above and by the tribunal (para 194), consent to ICSID arbitration must not be 'unreasonably withheld' and if not given within the time limit, the host state is 'deemed to consent' to arbitration instead under Annex B of the treaty.
- Turkey (2005): this BIT is the third treaty identified by the tribunal as containing an unequivocal expression of consent to ICSID proceedings (para 188). Article 13(5)(a) provides that the host state, 'shall, for the purposes of the Centre's Rules, be deemed to have given its consent' to ICSID procedures.
- Mexico (2005): Article 13(5)(a) of this BIT has similar wording, and therefore clearly provides advance consent too although, curiously, it is not mentioned by the tribunal.

For the sake of completeness, it should be added that there are no problems with consent in Australia's remaining FTAs containing ISA provisions that have been ratified since 2003, including:

- Singapore (2003): each state 'hereby consents' to ICSID or other arbitration under Chapter 8 Article 16(3).
- Thailand (2004): under Article 917(2) the investor may choose UNCITRAL Rules arbitration or, under Article 917(3), other means provided by the

host state in subsequent treaties with other states. The latter would include AANZFTA, thus incorporating consent to ICSID procedures if and when Thailand ratifies (having already signed) the ICSID Convention.

- Korea (2014): Article 11.17 contains almost identical wording to Article 10.17 of the FTA with Chile (2008), outlined above.

Grouping together the partner states reviewed above, if the *Planet Mining v Indonesia* tribunal's reasoning is correct, to ensure advance consent exists for *any* effective ISA procedure (ICSID or otherwise) Australia also needs urgently to reassess its BITs with **Poland, Hungary, Romania, the Czech Republic, Peru, Pakistan, Lithuania, Egypt,** and possibly **PNG**. However, Australia is anyway negotiating a new investment treaty with **Peru**—via the expanded TPP, which includes full ISA rights. Especially for the others, Australia should seek mutual agreement to amend these BITs if it wishes to provide unambiguously for advance consent to ISA.[56] To assist in this process, it is time for Australia to develop a Model BIT, or at least some model provisions, including the scope of consent and other matters recently subject to parliamentary and public debate.[57] At least the Australian government could issue a public statement indicating any disagreement with the tribunal's interpretation of wording used in its BIT with Indonesia and the similarly worded treaties with the above-mentioned states. That might assist future tribunals (and legal advisors) with regard to disputes arising under those treaties (and investment transaction planning involving those jurisdictions).[58]

It would be inappropriate for Australia instead to solve problems in the drafting of these nine BITs by instead withdrawing from the ICSID Convention. That would leave investors unexpectedly (and unusually, nowadays) with the sole option of non-ICSID arbitration, also with respect to other investment treaties concluded by Australia providing for ICSID arbitration. Denunciation of the ICSID Convention, especially by a developed country, would also significantly undermine the broader international investment treaty system at a delicate stage of its historical development.[59] Not even the previous Gillard Government had ever suggested

[56] See generally Tania Voon, 'Parting Ways: The Impact of Mutual Termination of Investment Treaties on Investor Rights' (2014) 29 ICSID Rev-FILJ 451–73.

[57] See Nottage, 'The Anti-ISDS Bill' (n 47), and his Submission (No 44) and oral evidence for a subsequent Senate inquiry into Australia's treaty-making process, via Parliament of Australia, 'The Commonwealth's Treaty-making Process' <http://www.aph.gov.au/Parliamentary_Business/Committees/Senate/Foreign_Affairs_Defence_and_Trade/Treaty-making_process> accessed 8 March 2016; Trakman and Sharma (n 24).

[58] In October 2013, for example, Switzerland made such a statement in response to what it saw as an overly narrow interpretation of the umbrella clause contained in its BIT with Pakistan, taken by a different ICSID tribunal. See Luke Peterson, 'Updates on Progress of Philip Morris Arbitrations Against Australia and Uruguay' Inv Arb Rep (28 April 2014) <http://www.iareporter.com/articles/20140428_1> accessed 8 March 2016.

[59] See e.g., Ewing-Chow and Losari (n 14), with respect to recent calls for Indonesia to withdraw from the ICSID regime; and more generally Christian Campbell and others, 'Assessing Treaty-based Investor–State Dispute Settlement: Abandon, Retain or Reform?' (2013) Sydney Law School Research Paper No 13/40 <http://ssrn.com/abstract=2280182> accessed 8 March 2016 (updated for a special issue at Transnat'l Disp Mgmt vol 1 (2014) <http://www.transnational-dispute-management.com/article.asp?key=2092> accessed 8 March 2016).

that Australia should withdraw from the ICSID Convention regime, and that was certainly not proposed or conceivable under the Coalition Government (in power from 7 September 2013).[60]

Apart from these nine bilateral treaties, the BITs with **Indonesia, Laos, and the Philippines** become problematic too. However, AANZFTA (signed in 2009) now provides alternative advance consent to ICSID Convention arbitration for Indonesia and Laos (if it accedes to that Convention) as well as non-ICSID ISA protections (also available for the Philippines). For **Vietnam**, the BIT has the problematic wording regarding consent to ICSID arbitration but provides anyway for non-ICSID arbitration; and AANZFTA provides for the former (if Vietnam accedes) and the latter. In addition, the BITs with **India, Sri Lanka, and Uruguay** provide at least for non-ICSID arbitration. Clarification regarding advance consent to ICSID arbitration can also be sought in negotiations for RCEP, for the first five of these seven nations, if that FTA ends up including ISA like other ASEAN treaties; as well as in the bilateral FTA being negotiated between Indonesia and Australia.

There is also a group of nine less problematic bilateral treaties with China, Hong Kong, Argentina, Turkey, Chile, Mexico, Singapore, Thailand, and Korea. The BIT with China provides consent at least for ad hoc ISA for 'the dispute' concerning the amount of compensation for expropriation, and may provide for ICSID arbitration of 'a dispute' (more broadly) now that both countries are party to the ICSID Convention. But advance consent is added for ISA of National Treatment claims under a bilateral FTA, and potentially more broadly under RCEP. Australia's BIT with Hong Kong, which does not accede to the Convention, already provides for ad hoc UNCITRAL Rules arbitration. Australia's treaties with the other seven nations already provide advance consent to ICSID arbitration and/or non-ICSID ISA, with the last five nations furthermore involved in RCEP negotiations and/or TPP with Australia.

In addition, full advance consent to ISA is already provided via AANZFTA with respect to the other ASEAN states (Myanmar, Cambodia, Brunei, and Malaysia), despite the omission of ISA rights in the Australia–Malaysia FTA of 2012, and these countries are now negotiating RCEP as well. Australia and Korea are also involved in that FTA negotiation, and anyway provide advance consent in their new bilateral FTA.

Thus, if the tribunal in *Planet Mining v Indonesia* is correct, the scope of ISA protection is highly constrained in at least nine treaties that Australia has negotiated since 1988, out of a network of treaties in effect with twenty-nine economies which presently refer to ISA.[61] Fortunately for investors, other treaties provide ISA rights,

[60] For further background, see Leon Trakman, 'Investor–State Arbitration: Evaluating Australia's Evolving Position' (2014) 15 J World Inv & Trade 152.

[61] As indicated in the online Appendix (see Luke R Nottage, 'Do Many of Australia's Bilateral Treaties Really Not Provide Full Advance Consent to Investor–State Arbitration? Analysis of *Planet Mining v Indonesia* and Regional Implications' (2014) Sydney Law School Research Paper No 14/39 <http://ssrn.com/abstract=2424987> accessed 8 March 2016), as of September 2014 Australia

but only in some situations (such as disputes arising after 10 January 2012 in the Australia–Indonesia context, under AANZFTA). Australia's on-going regional and bilateral FTA negotiations may provide scope to clarify consent to ISA, but also no doubt only for disputes after those enter into force and there is no guarantee that ISA will be accepted with respect to all these countries, even under a Coalition Government. In fact, negotiating partners (such as Indonesia or India) may well point to the tribunal's reasoning to urge Australia to greatly curb ISA provisions in the same way, or simply omit them altogether. That will probably seriously delay negotiations and perhaps even result in Australia not agreeing to future FTAs. However, it might conceivably open up some scope for other compromises to re-balance public and private interests. One example is AANZFTA's mechanism allowing for ISA to proceed, but subject to the possibility of joint interpretations by the home and host states determining that no substantive treaty right has been violated.[62]

Other countries, such as Japan, will also need to reassess their investment treaty provisions on ISA in light of *Planet Mining v Indonesia* and may well encounter similar challenges in renegotiating problematic BITs or concluding future treaties. In the meantime, advisors to investors and host governments as well as arbitral tribunals dealing with ISA claims will need to analyse carefully the broader treaty practice of all states party to the relevant treaty, as supplementary means of interpretation.[63] Unfortunately, this will further add to the costs and delays that appear to be escalating with respect to treaty-based investment arbitration.[64]

IV. Conclusion

This perspective may be overly pessimistic. After all, the tribunal's Decision is the first and only one to rule along such lines with respect to Australia, in a

had concluded twenty-two such BITs (including one with Hong Kong) and five FTAs (but with one FTA, with Chile, superseding an earlier BIT), including AANZFTA, which extends ISA protections to four other ASEAN states where no bilateral treaty exists (namely Brunei, Cambodia, Malaysia, and Myanmar). Australia subsequently ratified a further bilateral FTA with China (albeit with their BIT remaining in force) and signed the regional TPP agreement, both including ISDS provisions.

[62] Micah Burch and others, 'Appropriate Treaty-based Dispute Resolution for Asia-Pacific Commerce in the 21st Century' (2012) 35(3) U New South Wales LJ 1013–40, Sydney Law School Research Paper No 12/37 <http://ssrn.com/abstract=2065636> accessed 8 March 2016; Jaemin Lee, chapter 10 in this volume.

[63] Those other treaties may need to be analysed anyway, if the relevant treaty provides for most-favoured-nation (MFN) treatment. Luttrell and Devendra (n 36) 203 suggest that the MFN clause in the Australia–Indonesia BIT might bring in art 8 of the Indonesia–Singapore BIT (providing for UNCITRAL arbitration as an unconditional alternative for the investor), while conceding that there is 'considerable opposition' in case law commentaries to such broad use of MFN commitments.

[64] See generally Nottage, 'Informalization and Globalization of International Commercial Arbitration' (n 28); Luke R Nottage, 'A Weather Map for International Arbitration: Mainly Sunny, Some Cloud, Possible Thunderstorms' (2015) 26 Am Rev Intl Arb 495–516. The commentaries in the volume by Brown (n 38) should provide a helpful starting point for such comprehensive analyses of the treaty practice and drafting for the relevant states, but those commentaries only cover nineteen key jurisdictions (excluding Australia, unfortunately for the *Planet v Indonesia* proceedings).

decentralized international investment treaty system that moreover has no binding system of precedent.[65] Anyway, arbitrators in prior proceedings have taken a different view of similar treaty language used by other countries.[66] The Decision in *Planet Mining v Indonesia* has also already been criticized by other commentators.[67]

However, the growing transparency associated with ISA proceedings and decisions enhances the tendency for tribunals to follow reasoning adopted by well-known arbitrators. Indeed, one member of the tribunal in *Planet Mining v Indonesia* (Professor G Kaufmann-Kohler) had earlier presented cogent arguments for the observed emergence of a de facto system of precedent in fields such as ISA that implicate greater public interests than international commercial arbitration.[68] Furthermore, another member (Professor A van den Berg) joins her as one of the 'elite fifteen' arbitrators who have collectively decided a very significant proportion of known ISA cases.[69] The third member (M Hwang SC) is also very well known in international arbitration circles. Their direct and indirect influence, through a Decision like this, is therefore likely to be considerable—despite a different approach to treaty interpretation taken in a subsequent decision by another high-powered ICSID tribunal.[70] All the more so, given that there is growing concern about the encroachment of ISA proceedings on host state sovereignty, as evidenced most recently by Indonesia's declaration that it would anyway begin reviewing its approach to investment treaties.[71]

In short, the *Planet Mining* Decision is much more than a storm in a teacup. It may well be the precursor to a typhoon in the Timor Sea between Australia and Indonesia, spreading into the neighbouring Indian Ocean and then well beyond. Recall, for example, the media commentary in May 2015 suggesting that Indonesia's new Model BIT for treaty (re)-negotiations will require a separate further consent by the host state, for ISA to proceed.[72] Indeed, recall also that India's

[65] See generally Joost Paulewyn, 'At the Edge of Chaos? Foreign Investment Law as A Complex Adaptive System, How It Emerged and How It Can Be Reformed' (2014) 29 ICSID Rev-FILJ 372–418.

[66] *Millicom International Operations BV and Sentel GSM SA v The Republic of Senegal* (n 34).

[67] Luttrell and Devendra (n 36).

[68] Kaufmann-Kohler (n 54).

[69] Around 6% each, out of 450 known ISA cases: see Pia Eberhardt and Cecilia Olivet, 'Profiting from Injustice: How Law Firms, Arbitrators and Financiers Are Fuelling an Investment Arbitration Boom' (Corporate Europe Observatory and the Transnational Institute 2012) 39 <http://corporateeurope.org/sites/default/files/publications/profiting-from-injustice.pdf> accessed 23 April 2016. See also Sergio Puig, 'Social Capital in the Arbitration Market' (2014) 25(2) Eur J Intl L 387–424.

[70] *Nova Scotia Power Incorporated v Bolivarian Republic of Venezuela* (n 51). In particular, David Williams QC (appointed by the claimant in that case) is another one of the most highly connected ICSID arbitrators: Puig (n 69). So is Judge Charles Brower, who expressed doubts about invoking subsequent treaty practice in the *Daimler v Argentina* case (discussed generally by Jarrod Hepburn and Luke Eric Peterson, 'More Divergence on MFN and Dispute Settlement as One Arbitrator Sticks to His Guns in New ICSID Ruling, While Another Has A "Change of Heart"' Inv Arb Rep (27 August 2012) <http://www.iareporter.com/articles/analysis-more-divergence-on-mfn-and-dispute-settlement-as-one-arbitrator-sticks-to-his-guns-in-new-icsid-ruling-while-another-has-a-change-of-heart/ > accessed 8 March 2016.

[71] Section I; cf *generally* Campbell and others (n 59).

[72] See n 19. Luttrell and Devendra (n 36) also suggest that Indonesia's new Model BIT might add language to restrict the possibility of such consent being found in mining licences or other

draft Model BIT of April 2015 seemed to require the host state *and* the foreign investor's home state to provide a separate consent to ISA for the foreign investor to be able to proceed.[73] Although ultimately not included in the revised Model BIT finalized by India in January 2016, which hems in ISDS in other ways,[74] such a provision would have limited options for an investor even beyond the tribunal's interpretation of the Australia–Indonesia BIT (and other earlier BITs concluded by Australia). On the latter view, at least the investor can seek the further consent directly from the host state—and, if the host state refuses, the investor may be able to entreat its home state to initiate an inter-state arbitration. Elsewhere in the region, other states may decide to eschew ISDS altogether, as Australia did in 2011–2013 when negotiating treaties under the Gillard Government Trade Policy Statement.[75]

Even if ISA remains in much attenuated forms, investors themselves may decide to focus more on treaty-based or informal investor–state negotiations or mediation,[76] or turn to their home states to initiate inter-state investment treaty arbitration.[77] The international investment dispute resolution could become considerably more politicized or less legalistic, a phenomenon already noted by others.[78] Indeed, this is perhaps the point for some states and other groups that have become increasingly concerned about the ISA system. They can also point to the way in which the WTO's inter-state dispute resolution mechanism settled down, after some initial delays and other teething problems, and indeed emerged as a major stabilizing force in the broader WTO system.[79] Yet WTO dispute resolution is also far from perfect,[80] and anyway has benefitted from features not found yet in international investment law. Appellate review mechanisms have still not been implemented in investment treaties, for example, and anyway they remain overwhelmingly bilateral instruments containing sometimes significantly different wording.

Nonetheless, contemporary pressures to move towards more inter-state arbitration of investment disputes may provide a long-term benefit for foreign investors. It makes more politically feasible a multilateral investment treaty, as the focus can turn to substantive rather than procedural rights. Indeed, the surge in ISA

documentation provided by government authorities, which allowed the tribunal in the *Planet Mining* case to establish ICSID jurisdiction.

[73] See n 27.

[74] See Article 14 of the 'Model Text for the Indian Bilateral Investment Treaty' <https://mygov.in/sites/default/files/master_image/Model%20Text%20for%20the%20Indian%20Bilateral%20Investment%20Treaty.pdf> accessed 13 April 2016.

[75] More broadly, see also Nottage (n 24) and Lauge Poulsen, *Bounded Rationality and Economic Diplomacy: The Politics of Investment Treaties and Developing Countries* (CUP 2015).

[76] See generally Burch and others (n 62).

[77] See generally Anthea Roberts, 'State-to-State Investment Treaty Arbitration: A Hybrid Theory of Interdependent Rights and Shared Interpretive Authority' (2014) 55 Harv Intl LJ 1 <http://ssrn.com/abstract=2315078> accessed 8 March 2016.

[78] See e.g., Catherine Titi, 'Are Investment Tribunals Adjudicating Political Disputes?' (2015) 32(2) J Intl Arb 261–88.

[79] See generally e.g., Yasuhei Taniguchi, 'The WTO Dispute Settlement System as Seen by a Proceduralist' (2009) 42 Cornell Intl LJ 1–21.

[80] See again William J Davey, chapter 2 in this volume.

decisions particularly over the last decade has triggered much helpful analysis and treaty redrafting. Furthermore, an historical divide between developed and developing countries continues to diminish. In 2014, for example, transnational corporations from developing countries invested almost half a trillion dollars abroad (up thirty per cent from 2013), reaching a record proportion of global FDI (thirty-six per cent, up from twelve per cent in 2007). In particular, for the first time the developing countries in Asia (especially China) became the world's largest investor region (with US$440b in investments, compared to North American with $390b and Europe with US$286b).[81] Times are certainly changing.

[81] UNCTAD, Global Investment Trends Monitor No 19 (2015) <http://unctad.org/en/PublicationsLibrary/webdiaeia2015d2_en.pdf> accessed 23 April 2016.

PART II

NORMATIVE INFLUENCES TO AND FROM WTO LAW

12

The Interplay between the G20 and the WTO: Informal Law-making in Action

*Jan Wouters and Ines Willemyns**

I. Introduction

The Group of 20 (G20) brings together leaders of the twenty systemically most important economies to discuss global issues in an informal setting. As a network it does not have the formal decision-making procedures and rules of procedure that characterize traditional international organizations, and its output takes shape in the form of communiqués and declarations, generating interesting forms of 'informal law-making'.[1] What is more, the G20 interacts in a number of ways with other, formal international organizations, like the World Trade Organization (WTO), whose Director-General is typically present at all G20 summits.

The present contribution, written in honour and friendship for Professor Matsushita, looks into the interplay between the G20 and the WTO. Professor Matsushita has himself recently written about one aspect of their co-operation, namely the semi-annual trade reports that are compiled by the WTO, the

* Respectively, Full Professor of International Law and International Organizations, Jean Monnet Chair *ad personam* EU and Global Governance and Director, Leuven Centre for Global Governance Studies and Institute for International Law, University of Leuven; Doctoral Researcher and Junior Member, Leuven Centre for Global Governance Studies and Institute for International Law, University of Leuven. The present contribution builds and expands considerably upon Jan Wouters and Dylan Geraets, 'The G20 and Informal International Lawmaking' in Ayelet Berman and others (eds), *Informal International Lawmaking: Case Studies* (Torkel Opsahl Academic EPublisher 2013) 19–54.

[1] In our earlier work the term 'informal international law-making' has been defined as follows:

> Cross-border cooperation between public authorities, with or without the participation of private actors and/or international organizations, in a forum other than a traditional international organization (process informality), and/or as between actors other than traditional diplomatic actors (such as regulators or agencies) (actor informality), and/or which does not result in a formal treaty or other traditional source of international law (output informality).

See Joost Pauwelyn, 'Informal International Lawmaking: Framing the Concept and Research Questions' in Joost Pauwelyn and others (eds), *Informal International Lawmaking* 13 (OUP 2012) 22.

Organization for Economic Co-operation and Development (OECD), and the United Nations Conference on Trade and Development (UNCTAD), which monitor the compliance of G20 members with their commitments to resist protectionism.[2] But the G20 dynamics are also said to have a complementary effect upon the WTO, in the sense that they generate political support for the decision-making process in the latter and pressurize it to accelerate its initiatives, including the Doha Development Agenda (DDA). Moreover, it has been observed that the G20's activities have a 'rebalancing effect' on global governance and international organizations, in that they bring emerging economies into agenda-setting, and co-ordination discussions serve as a possible catalyst for reform of formal international organizations like the WTO.

This contribution takes stock of these many interactions. It will first recall the nature and evolution of the G20 (section II) and explore its functioning and decision-making mode (section III) and interactions with formal international organizations generally (section IV). The interplay between the G20 and the WTO will then be explored specifically and will be assessed critically (section V). Concluding remarks will wrap up this contribution (section VI).

II. Nature and Evolution of the G20

The G20 can best be characterized as a 'network'.[3] Members depend on each other when they try to reach agreements by diplomatic means in a culture of reciprocity.[4] Unlike 'traditional' international organizations, which are typically made up of sovereign States and which usually have permanent headquarters (such as the United Nations (UN) and the WTO), the G20 is an informal forum or 'club'. Moreover, not being a traditional international organization with conferred powers, the G20 can focus on activities such as agenda-setting, policy co-ordination, consensus-building, and the distribution of tasks across existing

[2] See Mitsuo Matsushita, 'A View on Future Roles of the WTO: Should There Be More Soft Law in the WTO?' (2014) 17(3) J Intl Econ L 701; Julien Chaisse and Mitsuo Matsushita, 'Maintaining the WTO's Supremacy in the International Trade Order: A Proposal to Refine and Revise the Role of the Trade Policy Review Mechanism' (2013) 16(1) J Intl Econ L 9.

[3] Leonardo Martinez-Diaz and Ngaire Woods, 'The G20—the Perils and Opportunities of network Governance for Developing Countries' (Global Economic Programme briefing paper, University of Oxford 2009) 1 <http://www.globaleconomicgovernance.org/sites/geg/files/Woods%20Martinez%20Diaz%20Networks%20PB.pdf> accessed 23 April 2016. Martinez-Diaz and Woods characterize a network as a forum where participants are involved in repeated and enduring relations. There is no delegation of authority to the network to make decisions. There is also no dispute settlement mechanism that can solve disputes when they arise. Networks can be distinguished from formal organizations in that they have no formal rules of membership, or structure of representation. There are no formal decision-making rules, and there is no authority to make, implement, or enforce rules. Networks are typically used for agenda setting, consensus building, policy co-ordination, knowledge production, and exchange and norm-setting and diffusion.

[4] Anne Mette Kjær, *Governance (Key Concepts)* (Polity Press 2004) 41; Kjær compares markets, hierarchies, and networks as systems of governance and notes that networks are based on reciprocity and trust.

institutions.[5] Its history starts in 1999, when finance ministers and central bank governors met for the first time in response to the Asian financial crisis of the late 1990s. Until 2008 the G20 kept meeting regularly in this constellation, despite repeated calls that there should be meetings at leaders' level.[6] These calls were mostly fuelled by a wish to see the G8 meetings replaced by meetings with more representative participation.[7] Again, spurred by a moment of crisis in late 2008, the United States convened the 'Group of 20 Summit on Financial Markets and the World Economy' on 14–15 November 2008, in Washington DC, in response to the global financial crisis. It was attended by the leaders of the members of the G20 Finance Ministers and Central Bank Governors Meetings. Since the third G20 summit in Pittsburgh in 2009, the leaders have designated the G20 as 'the premier forum for international economic cooperation'.[8]

The G20 is currently made up of seven advanced economies, twelve emerging economies, and the European Union.[9] The membership comprises five continents, two-thirds of the world's population, roughly eighty-five per cent of global GDP and approximately eighty per cent of world trade. Unlike many traditional organizations, the G20 does not have any formal criteria for membership, which already highlights a substantial degree of informality. It is said that countries and regions that are of 'significance' to the international financial system were deemed important to be included in the membership.[10] However, as Jokela has demonstrated, 'economic weight does not automatically translate into a seat in the G20'.[11]

At the first five summit meetings some important agreements were reached between the members. In Washington, the G20 decided on the implementation of economic stimulus measures. Its members also agreed not to pursue protectionist policies by way of creating new barriers to investment or trade in goods and

[5] Ngaire Woods, 'The Impact of the G20 on Global Governance: A History and Prospective' in Colin I Bradford and Lim Wonhyuk (eds), *Global Leadership in Transition—Making the G-20 More Effective and Responsive* (Korea Development Institute and the Brookings Institution 2011) 37.

[6] One of the main proponents of this idea was Paul Martin, the Canadian Finance Minister at the time. For his views on the matter, consult Paul Martin, *Hell or High Water: My Life in and Out of Politics* (McLelland and Stewart 2008).

[7] Mark Beeson and Stephen Bell, 'The G-20 and International Economic Governance: Hegemony, Collectivism, or Both?' (2009) 15(1) Global Governance 67, 77; John Kirton, 'Toward Multilateral Reform: The G20's Contribution' in John English and others (eds), *Reforming from the Top: A Leaders' 20 Summit* (United Nations University Press 2005) 143. For a more elaborate discussion on the history see Gordon S Smith, 'G7 to G8 to G20: Evolution in Global Governance' (2011) CIGI G20 Papers No 6 <http://www.cigionline.org/sites/default/files/G20No6.pdf> accessed 23 April 2016.

[8] G20, 'Leaders' Statement, The Pittsburgh Summit, 24–25 September 2009' (2009) para 19 <http://www.g20.org/English/Documents/PastPresidency/201512/P020151225615583055801.pdf> accessed 23 April 2016.

[9] The nineteen countries are (alphabetically): Argentina, Australia, Brazil, Canada, China, France, Germany, India, Indonesia, Italy, Japan, the Republic of Korea, Mexico, Russia, Saudi Arabia, South Africa, Turkey, the United Kingdom, and the United States.

[10] See Stephanie Lee, 'The Group of 20' (Council on Foreign Relations 2009) <http://www.cfr.org/world/group-20/p18975> accessed 23 April 2016.

[11] Juha Jokela, 'The G-20: A Pathway to Effective Multilateralism?' (2011) European Union, Institute for Security Studies (ISS) Chaillot Papers No 125, 20 <http://www.iss.europa.eu/uploads/media/The_G20_-_a_pathway_to_effective_multilateralism.pdf> accessed 23 April 2016.

services.[12] Furthermore, they agreed to refrain from imposing new export restrictions for the coming twelve months. In the second meeting in London on 2 April 2009, further expansionary fiscal measures were agreed upon.[13] Additionally, a declaration was issued on strengthening the financial system and the upgrading of the Financial Stability Forum to a Financial Stability Board (FSB).[14] In hindsight, the second G20 summit in London can be seen as the point at which the most effective co-operation materialized.[15] In Pittsburgh, during the third meeting on 24–25 September 2009, members agreed to hold the meeting annually. Agreement was reached on the need for strengthening international co-ordination in macroeconomic policies while preparing for eventual exit strategies from the emergency fiscal measures. Again, the need for strengthened financial regulations and the importance of discouraging protectionism were emphasized.[16] However, it is now recognized that at this point diverging views on financial regulation had started to become clear.[17] The fourth meeting in Toronto on 26–27 June 2010 was characterized by an agreement on a set of principles for fiscal consolidation in the context of 'The Framework for Strong, Sustainable and Balanced Growth'.[18] G20 leaders also agreed to speed up the process of international monetary fund (IMF) reform.[19] This reform was agreed upon during the Meeting of the Finance Ministers and Central Bank Governors held on 23 October in Gyeongju, Republic of Korea, which preceded the fifth G20 Meeting in Seoul on 11–12 November 2010.[20] The Seoul Summit Document re-emphasized the need to resist protectionist policies expressed the strong wish to bring the DDA in the WTO

[12] G20, 'Declaration—Summit on Financial Markets and the World Economy' (2008) paras 5, 13 <https://g20.org/wp-content/uploads/2014/12/Washington_Declaration.pdf> accessed 23 April 2016.

[13] G20, 'London Summit: Leaders' Statement' (2009) <http://www.g20.org/English/Documents/PastPresidency/201512/P020151225614495419410.pdf> accessed 23 April 2016. Paragraph 5 of the statement states:

> The agreements we have reached today, to treble resources available to the IMF to $750 billion, to support a new SDR allocation of $250 billion, to support at least $100 billion of additional lending by the MDBs, to ensure $250 billion of support for trade finance, and to use the additional resources from agreed IMF gold sales for concessional finance for the poorest countries, constitute an additional $1.1 trillion programme of support to restore credit, growth and jobs in the world economy.

[14] G20, 'Declaration on Strengthening the Financial System' (2009) <http://www.g20.utoronto.ca/2009/2009ifi.html> accessed 23 April 2016.

[15] Woods (n 5) 40.

[16] G20, 'Leaders' Statement, The Pittsburgh Summit, 24–25 September 2009' (n 8) paras 19, 48, 50.

[17] 'Biden Asks G20 Protestors: "Give Us a Chance"' (*EuroNews*, 29 March 2009) <http://www.euronews.com/2009/03/29/biden-asks-g20-protestors-give-us-a-chance/> accessed 23 April 2016; and 'Indonesia Warns on Over-regulation' (*Financial Times*, 4 March 2009) <http://www.ft.com/cms/s/0/b70cddee-08e6-11de-b8b0-0000779fd2ac.html#axzz45boCoA13/> accessed 23 April 2016.

[18] G20, 'G20 Toronto Summit Declaration' (2010) Annex 1, 10 <http://www.g20.org/English/Documents/PastPresidency/201512/P020151225621431044503.pdf> accessed 23 April 2016.

[19] ibid para 29.

[20] G20, 'Communiqué Meeting of Finance Ministers and Central Bank Governors' (2010) para 5 <http://www.g20.org/English/Documents/PastPresidency201512/P020151225618364102289.pdf> accessed 23 April 2016.

to a successful conclusion.[21] In the run-up to the sixth G20 summit held in Cannes on 3–4 November 2011, the French presidency presented six priorities, which included the combating of commodity price volatility and the 'strengthening of the social dimension of globalization'.[22] Other items on the agenda were the phasing out of fossil fuel subsidies, anti-corruption, and innovative financing for development.[23] Very little was achieved on these topics, as growing fears concerning the European sovereign debt crisis and a possible default of Greece overshadowed most other agenda items of the sixth summit. However, this does not mean that the Cannes summit was a complete failure, as some commentators have suggested.[24] One of the decisions agreed upon was the strengthening of the resources and governance of the FSB. To this end, G20 leaders equipped the FSB with a stronger political mandate, greater financial autonomy, and legal personality.[25] In itself, this decision can be seen as an example of the formalization of processes and structures that had many informal characteristics themselves. It appears that, after a number of summits with an increasingly broad agenda, the G20 has managed to reposition itself as 'a concentrated crisis committee in global affairs'.[26]

In 2012, under the Mexican presidency, the leaders of the G20 members convened in Los Cabos and agreed on the 'Los Cabos Growth and Jobs Action Plan'. As part of this plan, the G20 established an Accountability Assessment Framework, which creates the framework to assess the members' progress on the commitments undertaken.[27] Admittedly, the establishment of this framework had already been agreed upon in Cannes.[28] Several actions were agreed upon in the context of the Action Plan to promote stability and proper functioning of financial systems.[29]

[21] G20, 'G20 Seoul Summit Leaders' Declaration' (2010) paras 8–10 <http://www.g20.org/English/Documents/PastPresidency/201512/P020151225621107614573.pdf> accessed 23 April 2016; see also G20, 'Seoul Summit Document' (2010) <http://www.g20.org/English/Documents/PastPresidency/201512/P020151225619908599180.pdf> accessed 23 April 2016.

[22] The other priorities were 'reforming the international monetary system (IMS)', 'strengthening financial regulation', 'fighting corruption', and 'working on behalf of development'. See 'French G20 and G8 Presidency Priorities' (France in the United States 2011) <http://ambafrance-us.org/spip.php?article2111> accessed 9 March 2016.

[23] G20, 'Cannes Summit Final Declaration: Building Our Common Future: The Renewed Collective Action for the Benefit of All' (2011) <http://www.g20.org/English/Documents/PastPresidency/201512/P020151225635490988746.pdf> accessed 23 April 2016.

[24] 'Markets Hit by G20 Failure To Tackle Crisis' (*Financial Times*, 4 November 2011). See also David Frum, 'For World Leaders, G-20 an Enormous Waste of Time' (*CNN*, 7 November 2011).

[25] G20, 'Cannes Summit Final Declaration: Building our Common Future' (n 23) para 38.

[26] Andrew F Cooper, 'The G20 Returns to Crisis Committee—With Positive and Negative Implications' (*CIGI*, 2011) <https://www.cigionline.org/publications/g20-returns-crisis-committee-positive-and-negative-implications> accessed 9 March 2016. John Kirton, 'Cannes 2011: A Summit of Substantial Success' (University of Toronto, the G20 Research Group 2011) <http://www.g20.utoronto.ca/analysis/111104-kirton-cannes-perf.html> accessed 9 March 2016.

[27] G20, 'The Los Cabos Growth and Jobs Action Plan' (2012) <http://www.g20.org/English/Documents/PastPresidency/201512/P020151225645777085470.pdf> accessed 23 April 2016.

[28] ibid.

[29] i.e. the focus of fiscal policies on the strengthening and sustaining of the recovery; the focus of monetary policies on maintaining price stability and sustaining the global economic recovery; and commitments on adequate supply of oil.

With regard to strengthening the medium-term foundations for growth, the G20 members equally agreed to several actions.[30] However, none of these actions translated into concrete commitments with set deadlines.[31] Most progress was achieved on dealing with the Eurozone's sovereign debt crisis, which hit Europe with full force at the time of the summit and led to deep disagreements between the G20 members. The Mexican summit therefore did not achieve any new, concrete measures to address outstanding issues.

Under the Russian presidency in 2013, two main reforms were agreed upon by the G20 members during the St Petersburg summit: reforms on enhancing fiscal sustainability, and structural reforms for strong, sustainable, and balanced growth.[32] The former require advanced economies to put forth their (concrete) strategies to maintain or lower their debt-to-GDP ratio, while it required emerging economies to lay out their strategies to promote fiscal sustainability. The latter require members to identify their concrete reforms regarding several aims: promoting investment to foster growth and enhance productivity and competition; encouraging labour force participation and human capital development; increasing resilience of national financial systems; and rebalancing of global demand.[33] Annex Three to the St Petersburg Action Plan contained a detailed description of every country's commitments. These elements reflect the need that existed at that moment to move from post-crisis stabilization to economic growth. Additionally, the Action Plan repeated the existing commitment of all members to open trade and investment, stating that this is a necessity for balanced growth.[34] One of the main achievements identified by commentators after the St Petersburg summit can be found in the endorsement of the OECD's Action Plan on Base Erosion and Profit Shifting (BEPS) in the Leaders' Declaration.[35] This Action Plan aims to combat tax avoidance, harmful practices, and aggressive tax planning by multinational corporations, and stimulates tax transparency.[36]

The November 2014 Brisbane summit under the Australian presidency focused almost completely on creating a strategy to foster growth.[37] By refocusing mainly on the fostering of economic growth, the G20 reorganized its 'modus operandi'.[38] In

[30] The members agreed to: require advanced economies to focus their fiscal finances on sustainability; rebalance global demand, where there are countries with a current account surplus increase their domestic demand; reform labour and product markets to respectively increase employment and boost competition; reaffirm commitments on the effective implementation of financial reforms; and reaffirm commitments to resist protectionism and promote open trade.

[31] Gabriel Goodliffe and Stéphan Sberro, 'The G20 after Los Cabos: Illusions of Global Economic Governance' (2012) 47(4) Intl Spectator 6.

[32] G20, 'St Petersburg Action Plan' (2013) <http://www.g20.org/Engish/Documents/PastPresidency/201512/P020151225707389026904.pdf> accessed 23 April 2016.

[33] ibid. [34] ibid 10.

[35] e.g. Michael Switow, 'Reflections From the 2013 Russian G20 Summit' (2013) 17 G20 Update E-newsletter 13 <https://www.boell.de/sites/default/files/g20_update_17_1.pdf> accessed 23 April 2016.

[36] G20, 'G20 Leaders' Declaration' (2013) para 50 <http://www.g20.org/English/Documents/PastPresidency/201512/P020151225709417239707.pdf> accessed 23 April 2016.

[37] Angel Gurria, 'Strengthening Global Growth: The G20 Brisbane Summit's Challenges and Contributions' (OECD 2014) <http://www.oecd.org/g20/meetings/brisbane/strengthening-global-growth-the-g20-brisbane-summit-challenges-and-contributions.htm> accessed 9 March 2016.

[38] ibid.

their Communiqué, released during the Brisbane summit, the G20 leaders set the (ambitious) goal to boost the G20's GDP by a minimum of two per cent by 2018.[39] The commitments undertaken by the members to reach this goal are described in the Brisbane Action Plan. Each country's specific commitments in this regard can be found in its own comprehensive 'Growth Strategy 2014' documents. Additionally, the leaders confirmed the importance of trade and investment for economic growth. To foster growth, the G20's strategy therefore include reforms to facilitate trade. The Leaders' Communiqué state that they are working to ensure that bilateral, regional, and plurilateral agreements complement each other and contribute to a stronger multilateral trading system under WTO rules.[40] Three other important commitments made during the Brisbane summit concerned investment (the Global Infrastructure Initiative), battling corruption (the G20 Anti-corruption Action Plan), and energy efficiency and affordable and reliable energy for all (G20 Energy Efficiency Action Plan and G20 Principles for Energy Collaboration). Regarding tax, the leaders approved the first seven of fifteen actions in the BEPS framework.[41] The two per cent growth goal that was formulated as a result of the Brisbane summit was applauded for being so specific, quantitative, well defined, and focused on the medium term. This re-emphasized the potential of the G20 as the forum that plays an important role in economic co-operation and that succeeds at setting ambitious goals regarding economic growth.

On 15–16 November 2015, the G20 leaders' summit was held in Antalya, Turkey. The theme of the Turkish G20 presidency was: 'collective action for inclusive and robust growth'. Interestingly, under the Turkish presidency, the G20 ministers of agriculture have convened for the first time since 2011.[42] In their meeting on 7–8 May 2015, these ministers have called for a G20 Action Plan on Food Security and Sustainable Food Systems.

The objectives of the G20 have changed and continue to change over time. During the peak of the financial crisis of 2008–2009, emphasis was placed on economic stimulus, whereas later strategies were configured to exit from the fiscal stimulus without crippling the weak economic growth in some countries. The need to abstain from adopting protectionist measures appears to have been, and continues to be, an important objective of the G20.[43] After ten G20 summits in

[39] G20, 'G20 Leaders' Communiqué, Brisbane Summit' (2014) para 3 <http://www.g20australia.org/sites/default/files/g20_resources/library/brisbane_g20_leaders_summit_communique.pdf> accessed 23 April 2016.

[40] ibid.

[41] OECD Secretary, 'General Report to the G20 Finance Ministers and Central Bank Governors' (OECD 2015), 6 <https://www.oecd.org/tax/oecd-secretary-general-tax-report-g20-finance-ministers-february-2015.pdf > accessed 23 April 2016.

[42] G20, 'Progress to Date: The Turkey's G20 Presidency' (2015) 1 <http://www.un.org/esa/ffd/wp-content/uploads/sites/2/2015/10/Progress-to-Date-G20-Turkey-2015.pdf> accessed 23 April 2016.

[43] 'Report on G-20 Trade Measures (May to Mid-October 2011)' (WTO OMC 2011) <http://www.unctad.org/en/docs/unctad_oecd2011d6_report_en.pdf> accessed 23 April 2016. Nevertheless, the report notes:

> disappointingly weak growth in some G-20 countries and continuing macroeconomic imbalances globally are testing the political resolve of many governments to abide by the

seven years, the role of the G20 appears to have evolved from providing a forum for immediate international response to the global financial crisis to a forum for international co-operation in multiple policy areas.[44] The European sovereign debt crisis forced G20 leaders to return to their core objective of being 'the premier forum for international economic cooperation'. This crisis not only caused the Los Cabos summit to focus on the stability of financial systems, but the disagreement between the members of the G20 on how to adequately respond to the crisis overshadowed the other outstanding topics.[45] The focus changed again under the Australian presidency, where it was decided to focus entirely on the fostering of economic growth. During the Turkish presidency in 2015, the focus was on enhancing resilience, strengthening recovery, and lifting potential and buttressing sustainability.[46] The G20 is therefore continuing on the line of providing a forum for international economic co-operation, going further than mere crisis management.

III. Functioning of the G20

Compared to international organizations such as the UN, the OECD, the IMF, the World Bank, or WTO the G20 does not have a permanently staffed secretariat of its own.[47] Rather, it is an informal club without permanent representatives of its members that was designed to provide a forum for debate and consensus-seeking.[48] Its chair rotates between members, and is selected from a different regional grouping of countries each year.[49] The chair is part of a revolving three-member management Troika of past, present, and future chairs. The incumbent chair establishes a temporary secretariat for the duration of its term, which co-ordinates the group's work and organizes its meetings.[50] The role of the Troika is

> G-20 commitment to resist protectionism, as reaffirmed by the G-20 Leaders at their last Summit Meeting in Seoul. Over the period under review, there is no indication that recourse to new trade restricting measures by the G-20 as a group has slackened nor that efforts have been stepped up to remove existing restrictions, particularly those introduced since the onset of the financial crisis.

[44] This change was noted by the organizers of the G20 Seoul International Symposium 'Toward the Consolidation of G20 Summits: From Crisis Committee to Global Steering Committee' which was held in Seoul, 27–29 September 2010. For a report on the symposium, see Colin I Bradford and Wonhyuk Lim (eds), *Toward the Consolidation of G20—From Crisis Committee to Global Steering Committee* (Korea Development Institute and the Brookings Institution 2010).

[45] Goodliffe and Sberro (n 31) 11.

[46] G20, 'Turkish G20 Presidency: Priorities for 2015' (2014) <http://g20.org.tr/wp-content/uploads/2014/12/2015-TURKEY-G-20-PRESIDENCY-FINAL.pdf> accessed 23 April 2016.

[47] The French presidency proposed the establishment of a permanent G20 Secretariat as it would 'strengthen the expertise of G20 and ensure the internal consistency and continuity of action'. See 'French G20 and G8 Presidency Priorities' (n 22). However, as will be seen, this idea was rejected at the Cannes summit.

[48] Jokela (n 11) 23.

[49] The Republic of Korea was chair in 2010; in 2011 and 2012 it was France and Mexico, respectively.

[50] Tom Lansford (ed), *Political Handbook of the World 2014* (CQ Press 2014) 1686.

to ensure continuity in the G20's work and management across host years. The final declaration of the G20 summit in Cannes notes that the G20 'is a leader-led and informal group and it should remain so'.[51] Nevertheless, the declaration also notes that the Troika will be formalized in order to better co-ordinate the work of the G20.[52] Part of this formalization lies in the fact that as of 2015 the annual presidencies will rotate between a number of regional groups. [53] As the G20 meets in different locations, funding of those meetings is arranged by the host state. With regard to the use of experts from private institutions and non-governmental organizations (NGOs), the G20 provides the possibility to invite them on an ad hoc basis to meetings 'in order to exploit synergies in analyzing selected topics and avoid overlap'.[54]

The G20 members themselves play the biggest role in the agenda-setting process, with a particular role for the chair of the meeting. The chair will usually host an 'agenda-setting meeting' a couple of months in advance of the actual meeting of the G20 finance ministers and the central bank governors.[55] During this meeting, deputy finance ministers and senior central bank officials will discuss what the most prominent issues are that need to be on the agenda for the meeting at ministerial level.[56] The G20 leaders' summits are further prepared by the finance ministers and central bank governors under the leadership of the chair. [57] A significant role is played by the 'Sherpas', the political advisors of the Heads of State or Government, in the preparatory process which takes place in advance of a G20 leaders' summit. Multiple Sherpa conferences are held where agenda topics and other matters are developed and possible agreements are discussed.[58] The importance of the Sherpa network is underlined by David Cameron's call for an effective use of this network to evaluate a summit's achievements and to inform and maintain the focus of the G20.[59]

[51] G20, 'Cannes Summit Final Declaration: Building Our Common Future' (n 23) para 91.

[52] ibid para 92. [53] ibid para 94.

[54] About G20, 'What is the G20: Interaction with Other International Organizations' (*China Daily*, 2010) <http://www.chinadaily.com.cn/china/2010g20canada/2010-06/10/content_9962169.htm> accessed 23 April 2016. The French presidency of the Cannes G20 summit invited Bill Gates to the summit, to 'report on financing for development'. See Bill Gates, 'Innovation with Impact: Financing 21st Century Development' (Bill & Melinda Gates Foundation 2011) <http://www.gatesfoundation.org/What-We-Do/Global-Policy/G20-Report> accessed 9 March 2016.

[55] Jan Wouters and Thomas Ramopoulos, 'The G20 and Global Economic Governance: Lessons from Multilevel European Governance?' (2012) 15(3) J Intl Econ L 751.

[56] See Se-jeong Kim, 'Meeting Shows Hassle in G-20 Agenda Setting' (*The Korea Times*, 2010) <http://www.koreatimes.co.kr/www/news/special/2010/08/176_66750.html> accessed 9 March 2016 for an insightful look into the agenda-setting process for the G20 summit in Seoul, Korea in November 2010; and 'Deputy Finance Ministers of G-20 Conclude Agenda-setting Meeting' (Yonhap News Agency 2010) <http://english.yonhapnews.co.kr/national/2010/09/05/8/0301000000AEN20100905001600320F.HTML> accessed 9 March 2016.

[57] Wouters and Ramopoulos (n 55) 16.

[58] See the website of G20 Watch of the Melbourne School of Government, Hilary Blackman, 'What is a Sherpa?' (*G20 Watch*, 2014) <http://g20watch.edu.au/what-sherpa> accessed 9 March 2016.

[59] David Cameron, 'Governance for Growth: Building Consensus for the Future' (Prime Minister's Office of the United Kingdom 2011) 16 <http://webarchive.nationalarchives.gov.uk/20130109092234/http://www.number10.gov.uk/wp-content/uploads/2011/11/GovernanceForGrowth_acc.pdf> accessed 23 April 2016.

The chair will have the final say in the adoption of the agenda, although pressure will be exerted from all delegations to get desired topics on the agenda. NGOs are absent from these meetings and thus have no direct influence on the agenda-setting process. However, they will try to influence the chair. NGOs organize amongst themselves from time to time in order to have a stronger voice.[60] Details of the G20's meetings and its work programme are posted on a dedicated website by the country currently chairing the G20.[61]

IV. Interactions of the G20 with International Organizations

Another important aspect of the G20's functioning lies in the way it interacts with formal international organizations. Co-operation is close with a number of international organizations, such as the IMF, the WTO, and the OECD, 'as the potential to develop common positions on complex issues among G20 members can add political momentum to decision-making in other bodies'.[62] Director-Generals and heads of traditional organizations take part in G20 summits: this is in particular the case for the Managing Directors of the IMF and World Bank, the Director-General of the WTO, and the Secretary-General of the OECD. UN Secretary-General Ban Ki-moon has also been present at every G20 summit, except for the one in Washington.

A prominent example of co-operation between international organizations upon request of the G20 are the semi-annual trade reports that are compiled by the WTO, the OECD, and UNCTAD, and which monitor the compliance of G20 members with their commitments to resist protectionism.[63] Reference can also be made to the report on price volatility in food and agricultural markets that was compiled by the Food and Agriculture Organization (FAO) and the OECD upon request of the G20 leaders.[64] Other international groups and organizations the G20 works with include the FSB and the Basel Committee on Banking Supervision.

[60] See e.g., Irene Khan and others, 'NGO Leaders Challenge G20 Summit to Expand Scope' (*The World Post*, 2009) <http://www.huffingtonpost.com/2009/04/02/ngo-leaders-challenge-g-2_n_182381.html> accessed 9 March 2016; Amnesty International, Greenpeace, Oxfam, Care International, and Save the Children joined forces to focus G20 leaders attention on issues such as poverty and climate change.

[61] About G20, 'What is the G20' (n 54):

> Although participation in the meetings is reserved for members, the public is informed about what was discussed and agreed immediately after the meeting of ministers and governors has ended. After each meeting of ministers and governors, the G20 publishes a communiqué which records the agreements reached and measures outlined.

[62] About G20, 'What is the G20' (n 54).

[63] 'Report on G-20 Trade Measures (May to Mid-October 2011)' (n 43). In G20, 'Seoul Summit Document' (n 21), G20 leaders reaffirmed the extension of their standstill commitments until the end of 2013 as agreed in Toronto, committed to roll back any new protectionist measures that may have risen, including export restrictions and WTO-inconsistent measures to stimulate exports, and asked the WTO, OECD, and UNCTAD to continue monitoring the situation and to report publicly on a semi-annual basis.

[64] FAO and others, 'Price Volatility in Food and Agricultural Markets: Policy Responses' (2011) <http://www.oecd.org/tad/agricultural-trade/48152638.pdf> accessed 23 April 2016. The introduction notes:

The linkages between these traditional international organizations and the G20 are not undisputed. Woods puts forward that the 2010 Toronto summit saw a much wider participation of non-G20 countries (including Algeria, Colombia, Egypt, Ethiopia (NEPAD), Malawi (African Union), the Netherlands, Nigeria, Spain, and Vietnam (ASEAN)) in response to the growing concerns that the G20 would start to conclude agreements with these organizations without consulting non-G20 countries. These concerns became particularly pressing as the G20 started to give direct instructions to international organizations, such as the IMF, 'thereby bypassing the properly constituted decision-making process of those organizations'.[65] This attitude is also prevalent within the OECD, where non-G20 members have voiced concern about the fact that, as a substantial part of its work is now carried out upon request of the G20, some of the OECD's output has bypassed the formal decision-making process. Moreover, the assignments conducted for the G20 take up a considerable part of the resources of the OECD, which also include contributions of non-G20 members.[66]

It has been suggested that the G20 will have three distinct effects on international organizations.[67] First, a 'complementary effect' will generate political support for the decision-making process in international organizations, thereby pressurizing them to accelerate their initiatives. Second, there is a 'competitive effect', whereby certain formal bodies such as the International Monetary and Finance Committee (IMFC) of the IMF and the Development Committee of the World Bank now compete with the G20 as the latter tries to gain authority on these matters.[68] Third, the G20 may have a 'rebalancing effect' in global governance and international organizations. It brings emerging economies into agenda-setting and co-ordination discussions. Furthermore, it may serve 'as a catalyst for reform of formal international organizations'.[69] This has been highlighted by the decision on IMF reform that was taken during the Seoul summit in November 2010.[70] In addition to these

> The preparation of this report, coordinated by the FAO and the OECD, has been undertaken in a truly collaborative manner by FAO, IFAD, IMF, OECD, UNCTAD, WFP, the World Bank, the WTO, IFPRI and the UN HLTF. We, the international organisations, are honoured to provide you with this joint report and look forward to continuing collaboration within the G20 framework to further elaborate and, as appropriate, implement the recommendations of the international organisations that it contains.

[65] Woods (n 5) 42–43.

[66] Jan Wouters and Sven Van Kerckhoven, 'The OECD and the G20: An Ever Closer Relationship?' (2011) 43(2) Geo Wash Intl L Rev 345, 373. The authors note that the G20 benefits from this collaboration, since the OECD has an enormous pool of knowledge and expertise in many different issue areas and the G20, as a global playmaker, increasingly taps from this pool:

> Currently, the OECD supports the G20 on matters related to bribery, development, employment, environment and energy, financial sector reform, green growth, international monetary system, investment and trade, taxation, and consumer protection. Accordingly, G20 communiqués and declarations increasingly refer to, and call upon, the OECD.

[67] Martinez-Diaz and Woods (n 3) 1.

[68] Prior to the fifth G20 summit in Seoul, November 2010, a G20 High-level Development Conference was organized on 13 October 2010 in Seoul. The Seoul Summit Document included a paragraph entitled 'The Seoul Development Consensus for Shared Growth', which included a 'Multi-year Action Plan on Development'.

[69] Martinez-Diaz and Woods (n 3) 3.

[70] See case study on IMF reform (n 71).

three effects, highlighted by Martinez-Diaz and Woods, it seems there might be a potential fourth effect, which could be called the 'replacement effect'. Now that G20 includes emerging economies such as China, India, and Brazil, it has, for instance, been put forward that the IMFC should be replaced by the Ministers of Finance of the G20.[71] In reality, however, it appears that these proposals have not acquired sufficient support and that one cannot (yet) speak of any formalized or institutionalized linking of the G20 to the IMF.

V. Interplay between the G20 and the WTO

A. Complementary effect

Has the G20 generated political support for decision-making process in the WTO and pressurized it to accelerate its initiatives? Only to some extent. A sound that until a few years ago was often heard in the corridors of the WTO was that for the DDA to be completed; what was really needed was the political will to reach an agreement. The required technical work itself has often been completed years ago. In theory, the complementary effect of the G20 should help the decision-making process move forward. In reality, however, G20 leaders have not been able to provide the political backing for an agreement. On the contrary, at the Cannes summit, G20 leaders for the first time acknowledged that the DDA negotiations, as they have been conducted to this point, would not bring the desired results.[72]

Apart from this general observation, a complementary effect is identifiable in specific instances. Since the start of the 2008 financial crisis, several countries, including G20 members, have resorted to protectionist measures.[73] In response to this, Pascal Lamy, Director General of the WTO, used the Trade Policy Review Mechanism (TPRM) to collect data on several G20 members regarding new protectionist measures and used this information to urge the G20 to address the issue.[74] The G20 members took this plea into consideration and decided on a

[71] A report authored by former IMF managing directors Michel Camdessus and Hoerst Koehler as well as former US Federal Reserve Chairman Paul Volcker and commissioned by French President Nicolas Sarkozy, puts forward recommendations for G20 reform. Those include a major overhaul to bring G20 more in line with how the IMF operates. Most importantly, the report proposes that G20 finance ministers form a council that would take strategic decisions concerning the international monetary system, replacing the International Monetary and Financial Committee. Palais-Royal Initiative, 'Reform of the International Monetary System: A Cooperative Approach for the 21st Century' (2011) <http://global-currencies.org/smi/gb/telechar/news/Rapport_Camdessus-integral.pdf> accessed 23 April 2016. See also Peggy Hollinger, 'Reform Blueprint Gives G20 Authority over IMF' *(Financial Times*, 8 February 2011) <http://www.ft.com/intl/cms/s/0/02dfb954-33af-11e0-b1ed-00144feabdc0.html#axzz45boClA3> accessed 23 April 2016.

[72] G20, 'Cannes Summit Final Declaration: Building our Common Future: The Renewed Collective Action for the Benefit of All' (n 23).

[73] Chaisse and Matsushita (n 2) 11–12.

[74] See the message of Pascal Lamy in his speech at the Lowy Institute on 2 March 2009, 'Protectionism Cannot be "Smart", Lamy tells Australian Think-tank' (WTO 2009) <https://www.wto.org/english/news_e/sppl_e/sppl117_e.htm> accessed 9 March 2016.

standstill commitment regarding protectionist measures, promising not to further raise the level of protectionism.[75] In the Declaration following the Summit on Financial Markets and the World Economy of 15 November 2008, the leaders of the G20 committed to 'refrain from raising new barriers to investment or to trade in goods and services, imposing new export restrictions, or implementing WTO inconsistent measures to stimulate exports' for the next twelve months.[76] Following this co-operation, the G20 asked the WTO to report on the monitoring of trade-restrictive measures taken by G20 members.[77] Chaisse and Matsushita argue that this 'new' role of the WTO, with its TPRM, enables it to retain influence in the international trade order.[78] The effectiveness of this co-operation is illustrated by the WTO's June 2015 monitoring report on G20 trade measures, which shows that there is a slight deceleration in the application of new trade-restrictive measures by G20 economies. At the same time, the report cautions that: 'it is not yet clear that the deceleration in the number of measures introduced will continue [...]. Therefore, continued vigilance and reinforced determination towards eliminating existing trade restrictions remains an important priority.'[79] In the report, the WTO calls upon the G20 to 'continue to show leadership in eliminating remaining trade-restrictive measures and in the pursuit of further multilateral trade liberalization'.[80] This illustrates that constructive co-operation between the WTO and the G20 is possible and expected from both sides, in order to resolve international trade issues.

But the complementary effect has also failed in a number of instances. An example in this respect concerns the taking up of the issue of food security by the G20. In 2011, France, hosting the G20 that year, organized the first G20 Meeting of Agricultural Ministers. It was expected that the G20, as a forum for the twenty biggest economic actors in the world, would be able to find an adequate, co-ordinated solution to the food price volatility problem. Even though the Ministers agreed to an Action Plan on Food Price Volatility and Agriculture, the Action Plan failed to address the structural economic issues in a meaningful way and did not address the responsibility of the G20's own members' economic policies in accelerating the crisis.[81] Based upon this Action Plan, several G20 members and third countries formulated a proposal on food export barriers and humanitarian

[75] Chaisse and Matsushita (n 2) 12.

[76] G20, 'Declaration—Summit on Financial Markets and the World Economy' (n 12) para 13.

[77] G20, 'London Summit: Leaders' Statement' (n 13) para 22.

[78] Considering that the traditional ways of dealing with governance in international trade law, e.g. the DDA negotiations in the WTO, are currently in a deadlock. Chaisse and Matsushita (n 2) 12. Excellent examples of such trade policy reviews are: Trade Policy Review Body, *Overview of Developments in the International Trading Environment: Annual Report of the Director-General*, WT/TPR/OV/13, 24 November 2010; and Trade Policy Review Body, *Report to the TPRB from the Director-General on Trade-related Developments*, WT/TPR/OV/W/3, 14 June 2010.

[79] 'Report on G-20 Trade Measures (Mid-October 2014 to Mid-May 2015)' (WTO 2015) <https://www.wto.org/english/news_e/news15_e/g20_wto_report_june15_e.pdf> accessed 23 April 2016.

[80] ibid.

[81] Jennifer Clapp and Sophia Murphy, 'The G20 and Food Security: A Mismatch in Global Governance?' (2013) 4(2) Global Policy 129, 133.

food aid by the WFP (World Food Programme). This proposal was presented at the meeting of the General Council on 30 November 2011, but eventually did not become part of the deliberations in the following Ministerial Conference.[82] Moreover, it seemed that 'the G20 declaration apparently had become an obstacle, rather than a facilitator, to a positive decision at the WTO'.[83] In May 2015, the Ministers of Agriculture convened again under the Turkey presidency and reaffirmed their commitments to meeting the challenges of global food security and nutrition. In their final communiqué, they referred to the 2014 G20 Food Security and Nutrition Framework and the current efforts on the draft of the implementation plan for this framework. Additionally, the communiqué mentioned the 'commitment to the fundamental role of the multilateral trading system in global food security and to the on-going WTO negotiations with a view to promptly concluding the DDA and to the success of the Tenth Ministerial Conference in Nairobi'.[84] The 2014 G20 Food Security and Nutrition Framework gives priority to three objectives: (i) increasing responsible investment in food systems; (ii) increasing incomes and quality employment in food systems; and (iii) increasing productivity sustainably to expand the food supply. Interestingly, one of the questions asked by the G20 in the implementation process of this framework states: 'Are there other organisations or fora that are better placed than the G20 to address this issue and/or to undertake the proposed action?'[85] It remains to be seen whether the implementation plan will make reference to the WTO as such an alternative forum.

Nevertheless, the intentions of the G20 in supporting WTO negotiations and the multilateral trading system seem genuine. The 2015 Turkish presidency mentioned among its priorities:

> [...] continuing to follow-up our commitment to resist protectionism and supporting the multilateral trading system will be important priorities of the Turkish Presidency. The World Trade Organization (WTO) rules remain the backbone of the global trading system. The Turkish Presidency will support the work to canvass the vast number of bilateral, regional and plurilateral agreements to have a better understanding of whether, as intended, they complement one another and act as building blocks to the multilateral system.[86]

[82] General Council, *Minutes of Meeting held in the Centre William Rappard on 30 September 2011*, WT/GC/M/134, 21 March 2012.

[83] Giovanni Anania, 'Agricultural Export Restrictions and the WTO: What Options do Policy-Makers Have for Promoting Food Security?' (2013) ICTSD Programme on Agricultural Trade and Sustainable Development Issue Paper No 50 <https://www.ictsd.org/downloads/2013/11/agricultural-export-restrictions-and-the-wto-what-options-do-policy-makers.pdf> accessed 23 April 2016.

[84] G20, 'Agriculture Ministers Meeting', Istanbul, 7–8 May 2015, Final Communiqué, para 8 <http://www.g20.org/English/Documents/PastPresidency/201512/P020151228315892536897.pdf> accessed 23 April 2016.

[85] G20, 'G20 Food Security and Nutrition Framework' (2014) 8 <htpp://www.g20australia.org/sites/default/files/g20/_resources/library/g20_food_security_nutrition_framework.pdf> accessed 23 April 2016.

[86] G20, 'Turkish G20 Presidency: Priorities for 2015' (n 46) 7–8.

B. Competitive effect

To what extent can the G20 be seen as being in 'competition' with the WTO? Does the G20 effectively take away some of the WTO's authority regarding international economic co-operation?

Even though there seems to be some competitive effect at play in the relationship of the G20 and other institutions, in particular the IMF,[87] the same cannot be said about the relationship between the G20 and the WTO. Why are the in-roads of the G20 on the WTO less pronounced? An important element in the answer to this question lies in the fact that the WTO is a 'Member-driven organization', with decisions being made on the basis of consensus.[88] Therefore, even where one of the members of the G20, or the G20 as a whole, proposes to put a topic on the agenda of a WTO meeting, non-G20 countries can still influence the outcome, as a consensus will be required for all decisions made within the WTO. This is different from the IMF (where consensus can be substituted by formal voting and with the G20 members accumulating a voting share of 78.63 per cent) and the International Bank for Reconstruction and Development (where formal voting happens upon request and the G20 members possess 76.71 per cent of the voting rights).[89]

As indicated above, G20 leaders' statements, since the Pittsburg summit in 2009, have designated the G20 as their 'premier forum for international economic co-operation'.[90] Similarly, in its priorities document, the Turkish presidency referred to the G20 as 'the premier platform for global economic and financial issues', pointing to the group's supremacy in international economic co-operation.[91] Even though the same document goes on to state that '[the G20 members] will focus on ways to make the G20 more relevant to the rest of the world, including the low-income developing countries (LIDCs)',[92] one is left to wonder what the legitimacy of this claim is, taking into account the existence of the WTO. Where the G20 only consists of twenty members, all of them developed or emerging economies,

[87] Examples of such decisions are the SDR allocation in the IMF and the upgrading of the Financial Stability Forum to the Financial Stability Board. See Martinez-Diaz and Woods (n 3).

[88] On its webpage regarding decision making, the WTO itself also points out the difference in decision policy between the WTO and other international organizations such as the World Bank and the IMF. 'Understanding the WTO: The Organization: Whose WTO Is It Anyway?' (WTO) <https://www.wto.org/english/thewto_e/whatis_e/tif_e/org1_e.htm> accessed 9 March 2016.

[89] These calculations are based on the voting shares of the G20's 19 member countries, together with the voting shares of the 24 EU member states that are not represented in the G20 in their own capacity. 'How the IMF Makes Decisions' (IMF 2015) <http://www.imf.org/external/np/exr/facts/govern.htm> accessed 9 March 2016; 'Illustration of Proposed Quota and Voting Shares' (IMF) <http://www.imf.org/external/np/sec/memdir/members.aspx> accessed 12 April 2016; 'Rules of Procedure for Meetings of the Executive Directors' (World Bank 1992) art 4 <http://www-wds.worldbank.org/external/default/WDSContentServer/WDSP/IB/2014/12/19/000470435_20141219094512/Rendered/PDF/933400BR0Box3800Proceedure00PUBLIC0.pdf> accessed 23 September 2015; 'International Bank for Reconstruction and Development Subscriptions and Voting Power of Member Countries' (World Bank) <http://sitesources.worldbank.org/BODINT/Resources/278027-1215524804501/IBRDCountryVotingTable.pdf> accessed 11 April 2016.

[90] G20, 'Leaders' Statement, The Pittsburgh Summit, 24–25 September 2009' (n 8) para 19.

[91] G20, 'Turkish G20 Presidency: Priorities for 2015' (n 46).

[92] ibid 2.

161 countries are Members of the WTO, including over one hundred developing and least-developed countries. How can the G20 constitute the premier forum for international economic co-operation if it only represents approximately twelve per cent of the WTO Membership?

Where the Doha Development Round is stalled, should the G20 take over to develop multilateral rules and deal with existing systematic challenges, such as global value chains?[93] Cooper and Pouilot point to the fact that the G20 is 'probably the first forum to demonstrate a (limited) capacity to accommodate this new pluralism'.[94] They propose that, as the WTO is currently in a deadlock, the G20 takes up its role as a forum for functional dialogue. In reality, what one sees happening appears to boil down much more to the aforementioned complementary effect. In line with this a WTO statement published on 17 September 2015 regarding the upcoming Ministerial Conference in Nairobi indicates that the Director-General of the WTO, Roberto Azevêdo, would be having meetings with inter alia G20 ministers with the object of successfully agreeing on a package of issues in Nairobi.[95] In October 2015 the Director-General conducted a two-day series of meetings in Turkey to brief G20 trade ministers on the state of play of negotiations in Geneva. In his concluding speech, Azevêdo welcomed the ministers' support for a significant outcome in the Nairobi Ministerial Conference in December 2015.[96]

C. Rebalancing effect

Has the G20 led to a rebalancing in the WTO? Yes and no. Even though the G20 can be said to be a successful forum for the integration of emerging countries in global agenda setting, this claim does not hold regarding the developing countries that are not members of the G20.[97] On the contrary, developing countries are at a risk of being further marginalized and excluded from decision-making dynamics. However they may portray themselves, emerging countries represented in the G20 are furthering their own interests; they are not necessarily advocating the interests of the world's poorest countries.[98] Andrew Cooper has highlighted the explicit bias towards big members of the G20 at the expense of other (smaller and poorer) countries.[99] This does not diminish the fact that the G20 generates a

[93] Peter Draper, 'The Shifting Geography of Global Value Chains: Implications for Developing Countries, Trade Policy and the G20' (2013) 1 Global Summitry, 8.

[94] Andrew F Cooper and Vincent Pouilot, 'How Much is Global Governance Changing? The G20 as International Practice' (2015) 50(3) Cooperation Conflict 334, 342.

[95] 'DG Azevêdo: A Package of Issues for Nairobi May Be within Reach' (WTO 2015) <https://www.wto.org/english/news_e/news15_e/hod_17sep15_e.htm> accessed 9 March 2016.

[96] 'Azevêdo Welcomes G-20 Ministers' Support for Significant Nairobi Outcome' (WTO 2015) <https://www.wto.org/english/news_e/news15_e/dgra_06oct15_e.htm> accessed 9 March 2016.

[97] For more information on the successful integration of emerging economies see Martinez-Diaz and Woods (n 3).

[98] Martinez-Diaz and Woods (n 3) 3.

[99] Andrew F Cooper, 'The G20 as an Improvised Crisis Committee and/or a Contested "Steering Committee" For the World' (2010) 86(3) Intl Aff 741, 742.

new concentration of power through its inclusion of the emerging countries and its cross-regional reach.[100] Additionally, some commentators do see the G20 as a facilitator for developing countries to extend their participation in 'key institutions of global governance', including in the WTO.[101]

D. Replacement effect

Is the G20 replacing the multilateral dynamics of the WTO? No such effect seems to be identifiable.

Interestingly, Jennifer Hillman proposed to transform the G20 into a 'Council of governors' as an answer to the crisis in global economic governance.[102] With regard to its relation with the WTO, this Council would focus on three tasks: (i) setting the WTO's strategic direction; (ii) infusing the WTO with direction and support from a smaller group of higher-level officials; and (iii) holding the WTO accountable for implementing the directives that come from the G20 summits and providing a forum for holding the G20 leaders accountable for their commitments to the WTO.[103] However, such a replacement effect currently only seems to exist in the proposals of commentators.

VI. Concluding Remarks

As 'premier forum for international economic cooperation', the G20 interacts on a regular basis with several international organizations, the WTO being one of them. However, due to the specific structure and decision-making process of the WTO, the influence of the G20 on the latter's agenda setting and decision-making dynamics has been relatively limited.

This contribution has looked at the interaction between the G20 and the WTO through a four-faceted lens. One can conclude that some forms of interplay have been realized more prominently than others. With regard to the complementary effect, there is a clear interaction between the G20 and the WTO. The best example of complementary acting between both institutions can be found in the practice of the reports on the G20 trade measures and the call by the WTO to the G20 members to take an active position in the DDA negotiations. Even though the involvement of the G20 in WTO negotiations does not necessarily pay off—a telling example is the food security dossier—both parties seem hopeful that a profitable co-operation on global trade issues is feasible in the coming years. The

[100] ibid 743.

[101] David Held, *Cosmopolitanism: Ideals, Realities and Deficiencies* (Polity Press 2010); Cooper and Pouilot (n 94) 335.

[102] Jennifer Hillman, 'Saving Multilateralism: Renovating the House of Global Economic Governance for the 21st Century' (March 2010) Brussels Forum Paper Series: The German Marshall Fund of the United States.

[103] ibid 28.

existing co-operation is limited in its extent and should therefore not spark concerns regarding informal law-making through the G20 without consulting non-G20 countries.

Regarding the competitive effect, reference was made to several considerations that should be taken into account when assessing this effect between the WTO and the G20. This includes the power of non-G20 members in WTO decision making and the inadequate reflection of the existing situation in world trade in the G20's membership. To the extent that the G20 supplies a forum for functional dialogue on outstanding issues in international trade, one should rather see this as complementary, not competitive, to the WTO.

There seems to be a rebalancing effect to some extent, as the G20 did give its emerging economy members a stronger voice within the WTO and more generally in international economic co-operation. This effect is somewhat limited by the under-representation of developing and least-developed countries in the G20.

Finally, a replacement effect of the G20 vis-à-vis the WTO seems non-existent, in spite of the visionary ideas of certain commentators.

In view of the above, it can be concluded that the interplay between the G20 and the WTO is limited, but that it certainly exists. Both fora do take the opinion of one another into account and both seem to want to strive towards a closer co-operation in the future. If the G20 succeeds at taking up an active role in a possible breakthrough in the DDA at future WTO Ministerial Conferences, the complementary potential could be realized more fully.

13

Unfinished Business: Competition Law and the WTO

*Rolf H Weber**

Professor Mitsuo Matsushita is very well known and highly acknowledged as an expert and judge in the field of international trade law, particularly WTO law. In addition to these merits, however, Professor Matsushita is also an eminent scholar in competition law, as evidenced by a large number of publications.[1] In addition, his professional University description starts with competition law, followed by international trade law. Therefore, this contribution to the jubilee takes up his early thoughts on 'Competition Law and Policy in the Context of the WTO System'[2] and, twenty years after its publication, attempts to outline some forward-looking ideas about the not-yet-reached reconciliation between competition law principles and the WTO legal regime.

* Professor, University of Zurich/Hong Kong University.

[1] Amongst others, the following books and articles of Mitsuo Matsushita are noteworthy in the competition law field: Mitsuo Matsushita, *International Trade and Competition Law in Japan* (OUP 1993); Mitsuo Matsushita, 'Trade and Competition Policy' in Daniel Bethlehem and others (eds), *The Oxford Handbook of International Trade Law* (OUP 2009) 646; Mitsuo Matsushita, 'Reforming the Enforcement of Japanese Antimonopoly Law' (2010) 41 Loy U Chi LJ 521; Mitsuo Matsushita, 'Basic Principles of the WTO and the Role of Competition Policy' (2004) 3 Wash U Global Stud L Rev 363; Mitsuo Matsushita, 'Competition Policy in the Framework of WTO, European Integration and International Coordination' in Armin Bogdandy and others (eds), *Studies in Transnational Law in Honour of Claus-Dieter Ehlermann* (Kluwer 2002) 305; Mitsuo Matsushita, 'Application of the Japanese Antimonopoly Law to International Transactions' in Marco Bronckers and Reinhard Quick (eds), *New Directions in International Economic Law: Essays in Honour of John H Jackson* (Kluwer 2000) 560; Mitsuo Matsushita, 'Reflections on Competition Policy/Law in the Framework of the WTO' in Barry Hawk (ed), *International Antitrust Law & Policy: Fordham Corporate Law 1997* (Juris Publishing 1998) 31; Mitsuo Matsushita, 'The Intersection of Industrial Policy and Competition: The Japanese Experience' (1996) 72 Chi-Kent L Rev 477; Mitsuo Matsushita, 'Harmonization of Competition Laws Through Bilateral Trade Negotiations: The Japanese Experience' in *New Dimensions of Market Access in a Globalising World Economy* (OECD 1995) 129. See also Julien Chaisse and Mitsuo Matsushita, 'Maintaining the WTO's Supremacy in the International Trade Order: A Proposal to Refine and Revise the Role of the Trade Policy Review Mechanism' (2013) 16 J Intl Econ L 9, in which Professor Mitsuo Matsushita recommends the adoption of typical competition soft law instruments in the realm of international trade law.

[2] Mitsuo Matsushita, 'Competition Law and Policy in the Context of the WTO System' (1995) 44 DePaul L Rev 1097.

I. Competition Law and the GATT/WTO in the Past

A. Loss of the 'restricted business practices'

After the Second World War, when the comprehensive Charter with regard to trade, the 'ITO Charter' (also called the 'Havana Charter'), was proposed, competition law was still a part of the international trade regime.[3] Chapter V of the ITO Charter contained comprehensive provisions dealing with 'restrictive business practices'.[4] The main issue has been the control over price-fixing but other forms of anti-competitive behaviour should also be covered. As convincingly outlined by Professor Matsushita, the framers of the Charter realized that the effect of trade liberalization to be achieved through the reduction of tariffs and the removal of import restrictions would risk being offset by the restrictive effects of anti-competitive practices of private enterprises[5] Therefore, competition law and policy were an integral part of the ITO Charter.

However, the ITO Charter was never ratified; only some portions have been adopted as 'General Agreement on Tariffs and Trade' (GATT) in the form of 'provisional' trade rules. Chapter V on the anti-competitive practices of private enterprises has not been incorporated into the GATT, since the political climate has changed in many countries and, therefore, the ratifying states were only prepared to agree on a minimum set of cross-border rules.[6]

B. Failure of the WTO working group on trade and competition

The fact that competition law has not become part of the GATT did not mean that the issue completely disappeared from the agenda. International competition law and policy was taken up by the GATT in the late 1950s; however, the efforts did not result in a concrete proposal.[7] During the Uruguay Round, competition law was not in the centre of the negotiations but the (new) WTO Agreements contain a number of competitive elements not only in the context of the trade-related aspects of intellectual property rights and the trade in services, but also in the abolition of voluntary export restraints, the limitation of admissible subsidies, and the rules on anti-dumping.[8] These principles and mechanisms are necessary

[3] For further details, see David J Gerber, *Global Competition: Law, Markets, and Globalization* (OUP 2012) 43ff, 48ff; Hugh M Hollman and William E Kovacic, 'The International Competition Network: Its Past, Current, and Future Role' (2011) 20 Minn J Intl L 274, 316–17.

[4] For a general historical overview see Gerber (n 3) 21ff; Claire Wilcox, *A Charter for World Trade* (Macmillan 1949) 3ff.

[5] Matsushita, 'Competition Law and Policy in the Context of the WTO System' (n 2) 1102.

[6] See also Claus-Dieter Ehlermann, 'The International Dimension of Competition Policy' (1994) 17 Fordham Intl LJ 833, 839; Hollman and Kovacic (n 3) 317–18.

[7] John H Jackson, *World Trade and the Law of GATT: A Legal Analysis of the General Agreement on Tariffs and Trade* (Bobbs-Merill 1969) 51–53.

[8] See also Matsushita, 'Composition Law and Policy in the Context of the WTO System' (n 2) 1102–03.

to promote the liberalization of cross-border trade and the improvement of market access. Furthermore, the general obligations under the WTO Agreements, in particular the national treatment and the most-favoured-nation (MFN) principles, at least partly reflect competition policies.

At the Singapore Ministerial Conference in December 1996, the WTO Members created the Working Group on the Interaction between Trade and Competition Policy.[9] This Working Group was to study possible competitive matters to be incorporated into the WTO framework. Subsequently, several reports have been published.[10] The idea of developing an international antitrust framework was later taken up at the Seattle Ministerial Conference in 1999, the Doha Ministerial Conference in 2001, and the Cancun Ministerial Conference in 2003.[11]

However, after the political problems in Seattle and the new orientation towards development issues in Doha, the competition law project has lost ground in the negotiations of the WTO Members and many countries were afraid of being forced to waive part of their sovereignty if antitrust competences would be granted to the WTO. As a consequence, the Working Group was disbanded in July 2004.[12] Further efforts, including an EU initiative that was supported by the Competition Commissioner Karel van Miert and a report of a group of 'Wiseman', published in 2005, remained without success.

C. Left-overs of competition law in WTO law

As mentioned, notwithstanding the failure of including antitrust provisions into the WTO framework, it cannot be said that competition law does not play any role whatsoever in WTO law. The national treatment (NT) and the MFN principles require Member States to observe a non-discrimination obligation. The WTO rules also provide a basis against export cartels.

The TRIPS Agreement contains provisions on licence agreements, even if it can be argued with Professor Matsushita that insufficient attention was paid to competition law issues.[13] Furthermore, the Anti-dumping Agreement plays a role in case of market distortions caused by state interventions into the cost-price mechanisms.[14] A similar assessment applies in view of the Subsidies Agreement attempting to

[9] Stefan Tsakanakis, *Efficient Antitrust Enforcement in Developed and Emerging Jurisdictions* (Schulthess 2014) 158.

[10] See Gerber (n 3) 103–04.

[11] See also Hollman and Kovacic (n 3) 300; Anu Bradford, 'Antitrust Law in Global Markets' in Einer Elhauge (ed), *Research Handbook on the Economics of Antitrust Law* (Edward Elgar 2012) 283, 313–14; Eleanor M Fox and Amedeo Arena, 'The International Institutions of Competition Law: The Systems' Norms' in Eleanor M Fox and Michael J Trebilcock (eds), *The Design of Competition Law Institutions: Global Norms, Local Choices* (OUP 2013) 444, 446; Gary Clyde Hufbauer and Jisun Kim, 'International Competition Policy and the WTO' (2009) 54 Antitrust Bull 327, 327–29.

[12] General Council, *Doha Work Programme (July Package)*, WT/L/579, 1 August 2004.

[13] Matsushita, 'Competition Law and Policy in the Context of the WTO System' (n 2) 1116–17.

[14] ibid 1116.

prevent a WTO Member from favouring the domestic producers through financial means. But general competition law principles are still not enshrined in the WTO legal framework.[15]

Nevertheless, as a principle WTO law is addressed to states; in other words, only governmental rules can be challenged under the WTO legal framework. In case of restrictive business practices between enterprises (for example, through price-fixing) the WTO regime is not the appropriate legal body, i.e. efforts have to be undertaken to develop an additional regulatory framework governing private businesses' relations.

II. Regulatory Approaches and Substantive Topics

A. Harmonization vs decentralization

1. Why harmonization?

The creation of internationally harmonized norms attempts to establish a level playing field between different jurisdictions. Contrary to the model of regulatory competition leading to decentralization or substantive divergence, the co-ordination approach between different legal regimes is founded on standardization.[16] Regulatory harmonization is a legal model for institutionalizing co-operation by confining actors and policies into a normatively standardized corset of rights and obligations.

The harmonization objective encouraging convergence consists in the attempt to avoid the risk that similar activities are treated differently due to geographical borders. National competition policies cause negative international externalities;[17] furthermore, non-co-ordinated competition laws inevitably lead to multiple procedures and administrative ineffectiveness.[18] In contrast, the concept of co-ordination enables reaching substantive convergence.[19]

In practice, harmonization or co-ordination, respectively, occurs between standard-setters or standardization organizations trying to introduce harmonized provisions in certain markets. The co-operation can cause many benefits:[20] if the market participants through their professional organizations agree on certain standards, the standards are more likely to be complied with by the market

[15] For further details of competition law efforts at the WTO and the related issues, see Martin Taylor, *International Competition Law: A New Dimension for the WTO* (CUP 2006); Philip Marsden, *A Competition Policy for the WTO* (Cameron May 2003); Kevin C Kennedy, *Competition Law and the World Trade Organization: The Limits of Multilateralism* (Sweet and Maxwell 2001).

[16] For further details, see Rolf H Weber, 'Regulatory Competition and Coordination as Policy Instruments' (2015) 30 J Intl Banking L Rev 617ff.

[17] Oliver Budzinski, 'International Antitrust Institutions' (2012) Ilmenau Economics Discussion Papers 17(72), 4–5 <http://ssrn.com/abstract=2100576> accessed 9 March 2016.

[18] ibid 7.

[19] Weber, 'Regulatory Competition and Coordination as Policy Instruments' (n 16) 609–10.

[20] ibid 611–13.

participants thereafter. Furthermore, co-operation often leads to information sharing that reduces enforcement costs.[21]

WTO law defines the term 'standard' in Annex I, para 2, of the Agreement on Technical Barriers to Trade (TBT) as 'document approved by a recognized body, that provides for common and repeated use, rules, guidelines or characteristics ... with which compliance is not mandatory'.[22] The TBT itself does not offer an exact specification of the term 'recognized body'; however, Annex I suggests that the term encompasses bodies 'whose membership is open to relevant bodies of at least all members' (para 4) which have the 'legal power to enforce a technical regulation' (para 8). Usually, legal standards express or stand for a general direction or a behavioural value, expected by the state of the average human or commercial entity.[23]

2. *Preconditions for harmonization*

In order to be optimal, harmonization and co-ordination require the establishment of an international institution that develops, interprets, and implements the harmonized rules, since this model depicts the process of unification of law. Such kind of international institution exists in the field of international trade law, namely in the form of the WTO. In contrast, similar organizations do not exist, for example, in the application of competition law, nor do they exist in the field of international financial regulation.[24]

The establishment of an international institution with competences for releasing binding decisions must be based on a multilateral agreement adopted by a substantial number of countries; unavoidably, the competences of the created body lead to the consequence that a certain shift from sovereign tasks previously held by nation states will shift to such a body.[25] However, harmonization does not necessarily define the type of national law being concerned; the best-suited regulatory technique remains to be decided by decentralized bodies.[26]

If a shift of sovereignty is not politically feasible, the harmonizing international institution can only be built on the basis of an informal understanding. The guidelines of the informal organization would then not be binding but would only have a moral or recreational force. In such a case, the harmonization level is likely to be relatively low or quite general (effect of the 'highest denominator'), leaving a lot of room for creative and individual interpretation and compliance, which, in turn, leads to legal uncertainty.[27]

[21] Tsakanakis (n 9) 154–55.

[22] Agreement on Technical Barriers to Trade, 14 April 1994, 1868 UNTS 120, annex I, para 2.

[23] Rolf H Weber, 'Mapping and Structuring International Financial Regulation—a Theoretical Approach' (2009) 20 Eur Bus L R 651, 660.

[24] Rolf H Weber, 'Multilayered Governance in International Financial Regulation and Supervision' (2010) 13 J Intl Econ L 683, 686–87.

[25] Tsakanakis (n 9) 164; for a detailed discussion of the extension of sovereignty in the field of competition law see also Gerber (n 3) 60ff.

[26] Weber, 'Mapping and Structuring International Financial Regulation' (n 23) 659.

[27] ibid.

B. Objectives of regulatory convergence in competition and trade law

1. Avoidance of incoherent (heterogeneous) antitrust norms

Heterogeneous rules make international business difficult since the providers of goods and services need to comply with different legal regimes. Such a situation increases transactional costs due to the need for compliance with multiple jurisdictions' rules and procedures.[28] In contrast, convergent rules based on broadly accepted standards lead to comparable policies and enforcement mechanisms.[29] This assessment becomes particularly relevant if the complexity of international competition policy increases.[30]

Furthermore, an internationally operating business usually has the option to select from a wide variety of business practices. The respective choice regularly depends on the available legal environment. Nation states can try to become attractive by 'offering' a not-too-strict legal regime that easily attracts business entities.[31] This situation is theoretically described as regulatory competition; in this model rule setting is implemented in a way that a preferable regulatory environment is created for businesses; however, as mentioned, such an approach leads to legal fragmentation that can cause follow-up problems for businesses in compliance matters.[32]

As Professor Matsushita pointed out more than twenty years ago, harmonization and co-ordination also help to overcome the extraterritorial application of competition rules.[33] Professor Gerber refers to the principle of 'unilateral jurisdictionalism' in case of application of the extraterritoriality principle.[34] If each state is trying to apply its own antitrust provisions outside its territory (at least under certain conditions), collisions in the application of legal rules occur and legal fragmentation is *increasing and thereby diminishing the development of* transnational legal systems.

2. Avoidance of market access barriers and discrimination

WTO law attempts to avoid the discrimination of foreign companies, mainly through the national treatment principle. In addition, however, it may well be the case that market-dominant businesses have the possibility of not only discriminating foreign but also domestic companies. Such kind of misuse of market power does not fall within the scope of WTO law but can only be combated by antitrust rules, preferably harmonized in a cross-border context in order to

[28] See above section II.A.1.
[29] Hollman and Kovacic (n 3) 278; as to the convergence principle see also Gerber (n 3) 9.
[30] Hollman and Kovacic (n 3) 280.
[31] Weber, 'Regulatory Competition and Coordination as Policy Instruments' (n 16) 611.
[32] ibid 617.
[33] Matsushita, 'Competition Law and Policy in the Context of the WTO System' (n 2) 1108–10. See also Budzinski, 'International Antitrust Institutions' (n 17) 8–9.
[34] Gerber (n 3) 5, 271.

prevent that discrimination from occurring in some countries but not in other countries.

As far as market access barriers and discrimination are concerned it must be kept in mind that competition restraints can accrue from two sides, namely from national (governmental) regulations stating the market access barriers or discriminating foreign suppliers, or from the private side based on restrictive trade practices executed by the market participants. The two sets of rules stem from completely different sources but their effects can be rather similar.

III. Alternatives for a Reconciliation of Competition Law and WTO Law

Several international organizations and not formally (multilaterally) established institutions have tried to contribute to an improvement of a harmonized (convergent) international competition law framework.[35]

A. Efforts of other international organizations

1. United Nations Conference on Trade and Development

The United Nations Conference on Trade and Development (UNCTAD) has the objective to improve trade, investment, and development, with a particular focus on ensuring that domestic policies and international actions are mutually supportive in bringing out 'sustainable development'.[36] UNCTAD has 194 members and is mainly involved in data collection, research, and policy analysis, apart from the provision of technical assistance.[37]

UNCTAD is carrying out its work through branches. In connection with competition law, the Competition Consumer Policies Branch (CCPB) is the most important branch. The CCPB is doing awareness raising and capacity building, apart from organizing conferences and sponsoring peer reviews. Amongst others, the CCPB also helps developing jurisdictions to adopt and modernize antitrust laws. In order to promote this objective, the Model Law on Competition has been drafted.[38] However, since UNCTAD does not have the competence to release binding guidelines, compliance with the Model Law is not mandatory and, as a consequence, the respective provisions have not been adopted by many (developing) countries.

[35] See also the diagram in Hollman and Kovacic (n 3) 288.

[36] 'Who We Are' (United Nations Conference on Trade and Development) <unctad.org/en/Pages/AboutUs.aspx> accessed 9 March 2016.

[37] For further details see Gerber (n 3) 113–15; Hollman and Kovacic (n 3) 295–301.

[38] 'The Model Law on Competition' (United Nations Conference on Trade and Development) <unctad.org/en/Pages/DITC/CompetitionLaw/The-Model-Law-on-Competition.aspx> accessed 9 March 2016.

Nevertheless, UNCTAD keeps its merits insofar as the organization is collecting information of national competition law developments through experts' analyses. These documents are a valuable source for those who are interested in being updated in the respective regulatory regimes.

2. *Organization for Economic Cooperation and Development*

The Organization for Economic Cooperation and Development (OECD) is an international organization that has thirty-nine members, mainly from developed countries. Similar to UNCTAD, the OECD is collecting data, doing research, organizing conferences, and conducting peer reviews.[39] The OECD has established a Competition Committee bringing together top officials of national antitrust authorities, policymakers and observers from non-member jurisdictions. Outside experts may also contribute to the discussions within the Competition Committee.[40]

Notwithstanding the theoretical competence, the OECD's activities in the field of competition law remained relatively vague. No specific recommendations have been adopted. In addition, the number of countries having joined the OECD is limited, i.e. this organization does not encompass a global reach.

B. Activities of informal international networks

1. *International Competition Network (ICN)*

The International Competition Network (ICN) has been established by antitrust authorities in order to enable their members to have regular contacts and addressing practical issues. The ICN can be described as a specialized and informal forum that fosters the dialogue and helps to build consensus and harmonization across the global competition law community.

The general goal of the ICN consists of facilitating convergence in competition law related to substance, procedure, and administration. In order to achieve this aim, the ICN engages in activities that seek (i) to increase the understanding of competition systems, including similarities and differences among them; (ii) to identify and build conscience about the practices in competition law; and (iii) to encourage the different jurisdictions to opt into better techniques.[41] Thereby, the coordination efforts strive for the legal impacts on competition policy implications.[42]

[39] 'The Organization for Economic Co-operation and Development (OECD)' (OECD) www.oecd.org/about accessed 9 March 2016.

[40] For further details see Gerber (n 3) 112–13; Hollman and Kovacic (n 3) 289–95; Marie-Laure Djelic and Thibaut Kleiner, 'The international Competition Network—Moving towards Transnational Governance' in Marie-Laure Djelic and Kerstin Sahlin-Andersson (eds), *Transnational Governance. Institutional Dynamics of Regulation* (CUP 2006) 287, 289, 295–96.

[41] See Hollman and Kovacic (n 3) 275–76.

[42] According to Hollman and Kovacic (n 3) 276, the following questions need to be asked: 'Can the ICN be effective if it continues to exist in its current form as a purely virtual network, or will the institution acquire more of the attributes—e.g. a formal, stand-alone secretariat—that one associates with older, intergovernmental organizations such as OECD and UNCTAD? How can the ICN best serve a large, diverse membership that features extensive variation with respect to

The ICN is an open virtual network attempting to stimulate interaction with a wider community, including non-governmental advisors.[43] The ICN is led by a steering group that consists of leading officials from member agencies, with the board positions rotating amongst the members.[44] The ICN neither employs a permanent staff nor owns facilities to perform its managerial and organizational tasks.[45] Apart from the annual conferences, most discussions within the working groups take place by teleconference and/or email.[46] The most important working groups (WG) are (i) the WG on the Multi-jurisdictional Merger Review; (ii) the WG on Competition Policy Implementation; (iii) the WG on Antitrust Enforcement in Regulated Sectors; and (iv) the WG on Cartels.[47]

In the meantime, the ICN has become a rather vibrant forum for convergence and cross-fertilization, not least due to the fact that so far the ICN has remained the only international body dedicated exclusively to the application of antitrust law. The ICN has managed to achieve consensual best practice recommendations in guidelines being mostly complied with by the national antitrust authorities. Furthermore, the ICN has been successful in (i) promoting the implementation of competition regimes in developing and transitory countries; (ii) publishing compilations of coherent practices in member jurisdictions; and (iii) producing handbooks, manuals, and toolkits on policy practices.[48] The work outcomes of the ICN are usually developed in three stages, namely the identification of an issue that merits further research and discussions, the establishment of a study, and finally the presentation of the findings, often in the form of recommendations or suggested practices.[49]

The (potential) success of the activities of the ICN has been assessed by several theoretical and empirical economic research papers. The result has been that even though the efforts are based on voluntary co-operation, the recommendations and proposed practices have created peer pressure due to the consensual character and public availability; in other words, the combination of published best practices recommendations and peer pressure sets strong incentives to actually comply with the ICN suggestions on the national level.[50] In addition, according to behavioural economic thinking the promotion of

national circumstances and experience with competition law? Could the ICN perhaps serve as the platform for the development of regional or multinational agreements? How should the ICN interact with the OECD, UNCTAD, and other multinational bodies involved in competition policy? And perhaps most ambitiously, can the ICN facilitate progress toward the establishment of a mechanism for the application of international competition law, including dispute resolution?'

[43] Djelic and Kleiner (n 40) 299; Gerber (n 3) 115–16.

[44] Budzinski, 'International Antitrst Institutions' (n 17) 14–15.

[45] Hollman and Kovacic (n 3) 305.

[46] See also Budzinski, 'International Antitrust Institutions' (n 17) 15.

[47] Oliver Budzinski, 'The International Competition Network: Prospects and Limits on the Road Towards International Competition Governance' (2004) 8 Competition Change 223, 229.

[48] Budzinski, 'International Antitrust Institutions' (n 17) 16–17.

[49] Hollman and Kovacic (n 3) 306.

[50] Budzinski, 'International Antitrust Institutions' (n 17) 15–16.

the targeted common competition culture incentivizes proceeding with harmonization and convergence efforts.[51] Since, however, the ICN is an informal venue and in view of the fact that it cannot exercise any rule-making function, the overall influence on competition policy in the different countries seems to remain limited and makes it sensible to look for additional co-ordination measures.

2. *Other networks and mutual cooperation*

Apart from the ICN, other existing informal bodies are supporting co-operative (but not necessarily harmonizing) efforts in the competition law field. Examples of such judicial networks are the Association of European Competition Law Judges, the International Association of Judges, and the American Judges Association. Similar to the ICN, judicial networks can facilitate the exchange of experiences and carry out educational projects.[52]

The 'weakest' form of convergence in competition policy consists in the realization of mutual co-operation. This model can include mutual notification and consultation efforts between the antitrust authorities: notification includes information about on-going antitrust procedures and exchange of general information about competition policy; consultation encompasses the exchange of more detailed information regarding technical issues (market definition, case facts, etc.) on a voluntary and/or discretionary basis.[53] If a bilateral agreement between two states has been concluded, mutual assistance would allow the co-operation in respect of information gathering and/or sanctioning in order to overcome the problems of extraterritorial investigation and enforcement, particularly if each antitrust authority agrees to respect serious interests and the sovereignty of other jurisdictions (so-called negative comity).[54]

Through mutual co-operation, a minimum degree of harmonization can be achieved if governmental officials or judges are working together to overcome the challenges of interdependence. Examples concern the co-ordination of competition policies, the regulation of markets through elaborate informal intergovernmental channels, or the parallel enforcement of laws. If such kind of mutual co-operation reaches a certain level, the activity of regulators, officers, and judges might lead to harmonization.

C. Implementation of a private antitrust code

The private sector, mainly the competition law professors in many jurisdictions, has not remained silent in view of the fact that harmonization of antitrust law by governmental actions has failed. The most comprehensive proposal for harmonization of competition law is the Draft International Antitrust Code (DIAC) that

[51] ibid 16. [52] Tsakanakis (n 9) 160–61.
[53] Budzinski, 'International Antitrust Institutions' (n 17) 10. [54] ibid.

has been developed and proposed by a group of competition law scholars led by Professor Fikentscher, Munich ('the Munich Group').[55] The DIAC proposes the establishment of an international antitrust agency sharing the responsibility of enforcement of an international antitrust code with the national governments.[56] As mentioned by Professor Matsushita, the comprehensive antitrust code intends to cover the major areas of competition law, namely horizontal agreements, vertical restraints (distribution strategies), mergers, and acquisitions, as well as the relationship between competition law and industrial policies.[57] Shorter provisions address the abuse of a dominant position, the remedies, and the public undertakings.

Another model code has been developed by the American Bar Association (ABA) proposing an agreement among states with regard to some basic antitrust principles, i.e. the unlawfulness of cartels and the unification of the filing requirements under the merger laws of various states.[58] But the ABA model would only lead to a partial harmonization regarding its key principles though the establishment of a comprehensive international authority to enforce international rules is not foreseen. Similarly, Professor Fox, New York University Law School, proposed a scheme in which the states would agree on 'a few fundamental world-linking principles' of competition policy such as the prohibition of cartels and positive comity.[59]

From a substantive prospective these private initiatives are noteworthy; however, the political impact has remained very low, mainly because the WTO Ministerial Conferences did not take up the respective regulatory proposals.

IV. Lessons from the Alternative Approaches for WTO Law

A. Present status

Summarizing the aforementioned considerations, the strengths and weaknesses of the past efforts of the formal/informal activities lead to Table 13.1 below:[60]

[55] International Antitrust Code Working Group, 'Draft International Antitrust Code—as a GATT–MTO–Plurilateral Trade Agreement' (1993) 5(5) World Trade Arb Materials 126; for further details, see Wolfgang Fikentscher, 'The Draft International Antitrust Code (DIAC) in the Context of International Technological Integration' in Frederick M Abbott and David J Gerber (eds), *Public Policy and Global Technological Integration* (Kluwer 1997) 211–20; the DIAC with commentaries of the authors is also included in this book, ibid 285–335.

[56] According to Gerber (n 3) 101, the DIAC 'was a conceptually well-developed and audacious effort to define a workable international competition law framework'.

[57] Matsushita, 'Competition Law and Policy in the Context of the WTO System' (n 2) 1111.

[58] See Barry E Hawk, 'Antitrust in a Global Environment: Conflicts and Resolutions' (1991) 60 Antitrust LJ 525, 526.

[59] See Matsushita, 'Competition Law and Policy in the Context of the WTO System' (n 2) 1111, with further references.

[60] This table is taken from Djelic and Kleiner (n 40) 304.

Table 13.1 Lessons from the alternative approaches for WTO law

	'Experts' (OECD)	'Statist' (WTO)	'Community' (ICN)
Rule-makers vs rule-followers	Separate	Separate	Combined
'Product' of governance process	Standards	Binding rules (close to laws)	Beliefs
Mode, logic of rule-monitoring	Expert-driven	Political negotiation with expert input	Negotiation with expert input and with a view to create 'communion'
Mode, logic of rule-monitoring	'Expert awe'	Coercion, constraints	Socialization
Pluses and minuses	Will not work without a very strong legitimacy of the expert body—not really the case in our story	Efficient; strong and hard rules will be likely to come though with exceptions and 'decoupling'	Easy to start; potentially leads to stronger and more stable homogenization; not very constraining in the first place

Table 13.1 and the above considerations show that notwithstanding some strengths of the present legal framework the weaknesses prevail, since a stable normative order is missing and legal certainty cannot be achieved to a satisfactory degree.[61] Therefore, new efforts to reach an adequate level of convergence are worthwhile to be undertaken.

B. Realization of a higher degree of harmonization

As mentioned, the need for a higher degree of convergence is practically uncontested in scholarship. In this sense, already more than twenty years ago Professor Matsushita has formulated a set of principles for competition policy establishing the minimum standards of competition law to be observed by the WTO Member States. This list of principles encompasses the following practically important issues:[62]

- horizontal agreements;
- exemptions of cartels;
- vertical agreements;
- mergers and acquisitions;
- predatory pricing.

[61] For an extensive overview of many internationally relevant competition laws see Gerber (n 3) 121ff, 205ff; Harry First, 'Evolving Toward What? The Development of International Antitrust' in Josef Drexl (ed), *The Future of Transnational Antitrust: From Comparative to Common Competition Law* (Staempfli and Kluwer 2003) 23.

[62] See Matsushita, 'Competition Law and the Policy in the Context of the WTO System' (n 2) 1112–14.

Looking from the present perspective, a few additional key principles could be added, particularly the issue of misuse of a dominant position being of practical importance mainly in the information technology markets. The more important task, however, consists in developing the objective of convergence as a concept or as a strategy.[63] In view of the globalization of businesses and the rising importance of transnational corporations, the mechanisms of convergence need to be analysed and the consequences of global competition law convergence are to be assessed.[64]

Convergence implies a comparison of the major characteristics of competition law regimes; based on the respective analysis, the objects and dimensions of convergence are to be concretized.[65] In addition, the gap between the 'law on the books' and the 'law in action' must be overcome. The best legal framework is only as good as it is applied in practice.

The success of the convergence strategy also depends on the availability and general acceptance of a 'convergence driver';[66] as long as a global multilateral agreement similar to the WTO framework is not likely to be realized, the 'convergence driver' function could be assumed by an international organization (such as the UNCTAD or the OECD) or by the ICN; looking at the present situation, the ICN might be the most suitable 'convergence driver'. The scope and extent of convergence is further tied to the geographical circumstances; the closer the jurisdictions are located, the more important the convergence of competition rules becomes.

In a nutshell, the 'overall prospects for convergence depend in a large measure on developing similar perceptions of global competition and similar assessments of the potential shape and consequences of global competition law development'.[67] In view of the given fragmentation of competition law, it would be worthwhile to put more efforts in the attempt of achieving increased convergence.

V. Outlook

Apart from a few scattered provisions in the WTO legal framework, the multilateral cross-border trade legislation has failed to thoroughly address the key principles of competition law. The attempts of including competition law topics into the international trade regime were not successful twice, namely at the time of conclusion of the GATT due to the refusal of the ITO by the negotiating parties, and again in the first years of existence of the WTO due to a change of the perspective to development issues (Doha). Other international organizations did not achieve much better results. Voluntary networks such as the ICN were successful

[63] See Gerber (n 3) 273ff.

[64] A basic theoretical approach can be found in Eleanor M Fox, 'Toward World Antitrust and Market Access' (1997) 91 Am J Intl L 1; William E Kovacic, 'Achieving Better Practices in the Design of Competition Policy Institutions' (2005) 50 Antitrust Bull 511.

[65] Gerber (n 3) 282–83. [66] See also ibid 287. [67] ibid 289.

in introducing some basic convergence strategies; however, these efforts will not suffice to eliminate transnational conflicts. Even in the case of jurisdictions with similar competition regimes such as shared analytical methods and consistent procedures, different outcomes owing to variations in application are still likely.[68]

Since a higher degree of convergence in competition law is desirable, the existing soft law should somehow evolve into hard law in view of the fact that global problems also require global solutions.[69] Without a higher level of harmonized rules, the interests of states are unlikely to align sufficiently in order to avoid jurisdictional conflicts and/or to resolve conflicts that arise.[70]

Possibly it could now be said that the earlier attempts to develop a multilateral competition law agreement have failed, since they were premature as many countries (particularly the United States) heavily relied on market-based economic systems.[71] In the meantime, however, not at least due to the activities of the ICN, the developing countries' suspicion that competition law is another means for developed countries to achieve their own global economic aims may have been dissipated; transition economies appear to have even greater confidence in competition agencies' ability to identify, adopt, and apply competitive policies in a way to promote economic development.[72] Therefore, the time for the development of global competition law might have become ripe.[73]

Economic literature has developed different concepts that justify the implementation of international antitrust institutions. The first concept is the idea for a lead jurisdiction model that would allocate competence and responsibility for multi-jurisdictional competition cases to the most affected regime.[74] Such a model is already realized in the banking and the insurance markets providing for regulations that require the implementation of a lead regulator for globally acting financial intermediaries.[75] The second concept is the idea of multilevel (multilayer) governance in which regimes on different vertical levels (regional, national, supranational) are interconnected with each other.[76] Both concepts appear to be suitable to adapt competition law to deep globalization.[77]

Without any doubt, further efforts to align international trade and competition policy are needed; the respective key message of Professor Matsushita remains as valid today as it was more than twenty years ago.[78] A scenario of transnational

[68] Hollman and Kovacic (n 3) 311.

[69] See Elianor M Fox, 'Antitrust and Regulatory Federalism: Races Up, Down, and Sideways' (2000) 75 NYU L Rev 1781, 1785–86.

[70] See Andrew Guzman, 'Is International Antitrust Possible?' (1998) 73 NYU L Rev 1501.

[71] Hollman and Kovacic (n 3) 319. [72] ibid. [73] See also Gerber (n 3) 384ff.

[74] Budzinski, 'International Antitrust Institutions' (n 17) 21.

[75] See Rolf H Weber and Valérie Menoud, 'Systemic Risks as a Topic of Financial Conglomerates' Prudential Supervision' (2007) 22 Banking Fin L Rev 377, 377ff.

[76] Weber, 'Multilayered Governance in International Financial Regulation and Supervision' (n 24) 689–90; Budzinski, 'International Antitrust Institutions' (n 17) 21; Wolfgang Kerber, 'International Multi-Level System of Competition Laws: Federalism in Antitrust' in Josef Drexl (ed), *The Future of Transnational Antitrust: From Comparative to Common Competition Law* (Staempfli and Kluwer 2003) 269.

[77] Gerber (n 3) 339–40.

[78] Matsushita, 'Competition Law and Policy in the Context of the WTO System' (n 2) 1111ff. See also the contributions of Matsushita in Bogdandy and others (n 1) and Bethlehem and others (n 1).

governance in competition law overcoming the type of rule-making and rule-monitoring characteristics of Westphalian states must be realized.[79] Or in the words of Professor Matsushita: 'Since the globalisation of economics has progressed to a very far extent, the attachment to the national jurisdiction is becoming outdated.'[80]

Even if the WTO is confronted with policy problems in the field of agriculture and development issues, the time appears to be ripe for new efforts in the direction of better-aligned antitrust provisions. The WTO could convene an expert group tackling the issues related to the development of a more convergent competition law framework; and in contrast to the project of the DIAC, the objective should not consist in the preparation of a multilateral agreement but in the implementation of some substantive key principles being applicable in a multilevel (multilayer) setting.

[79] Djelic and Kleiner (n 40) 304.

[80] Matsushita, 'Competition Law and Policy in the Context of the WTO System' (n 2) 1118.

14

Competition Law in Emerging Markets: The Virtue of Regulatory Diversity

*Frederick M Abbott**

I. Introduction

Mitsuo Matsushita has taken a strong interest in competition law and policy.[1] It is fitting to address this subject matter in this volume assembled in his honour.

As middle-income countries, including those often referred to as 'emerging market' countries, have recently taken a more assertive posture in the enforcement of competition law, lobbying groups representing multinational enterprises based in OECD countries are raising questions about the rules and practices being followed by enforcement authorities, notably with respect to China. Such questions implicitly presume that there are international competition law standards from which emerging market authorities may be deviating. While there may be certain basic principles common to legal systems, such as due process, reflecting international standards, there is no multilateral agreement broadly regulating the implementation and enforcement of competition law. Tracing as far back as the International Trade Organization Charter, multinational business groups have opposed the negotiation of multilateral competition rules. Multinational business groups did not support the incorporation of competition rules into the WTO framework as proposed by the Singapore Agenda.

* Edward Ball Eminent Scholar Professor of International Law, Florida State University College of Law, USA.

[1] See Mitsuo Matsushita, 'Cartel Control in Japan' (2008) 4(2) Comp L Intl 23–29 (with Yuki Nakamura); Mitsuo Matsushita, 'International Cooperation in the Enforcement of Competition Policy' (2002) 1 Washington U Global Stud L Rev 463–76; Mitsuo Matsushita, 'Competition Law and Policy in the Context of the WTO System' (1994–1995) 44 DePaul L Rev 1097–118; Mitsuo Matsushita, 'Export Controls and Export Cartels in Japan' (1979) 20 Harv Int LJ 103–26; Mitsuo Matsushita, 'Maintaining the WTO's Supremacy in the International Trade Order: A Proposal to Refine and Revise the Role of the Trade Policy Review Mechanism' (2013) 16 J Int Econ Law 9–36 (with Julien Chaisse); Mitsuo Matsushita, 'The Intersection of Industrial Policy and Competition: The Japanese Experience' in F M Abbott and D J Gerber (eds), *Public Policy and Global Technological Integration* (Kluwer 1997) 141–61.

OECD-based multinational business groups may now be re-assessing whether the risks of being targeted by multilateral competition rules are outweighed by possible gains from imposing limitations on emerging market competition authorities. If a tipping point in favour of negotiations has been reached—and there is insufficient evidence to draw such a conclusion at this stage—we might see a renewed effort to bring multilateral competition law disciplines into a forum like the WTO, this time with the backing of multinational businesses.

Assuming that there is a change in the perceived value of multilateral competition rules, would this be likely to result in the successful conclusion of an agreement? From the standpoint of the emerging market countries, and developing countries more generally, would this be beneficial?

There are important competition law doctrines that are not necessarily shared even among the higher income countries, such as doctrines addressing excessive pricing and essential facilities. To the extent that multilateral business groups would seek to constrain the use of such doctrines, this would not be in the best interests of emerging market (and other developing) countries. It would not be in the interests of consumers more generally, including those in the high-income countries.

The more prudent course may be to preserve regulatory diversity in the field of competition law. Opening up negotiation on shared substantive disciplines would present meaningful risks to the global public interest. There is no evident reason to take on such risks.

II. Trade and Competition

It is a basic premise of market economics that competition among producers and suppliers promotes public welfare.[2] Competition places continuous pressure on producers to reduce costs.[3] Competition promotes innovation, as producers seek to gain advantage by introducing new and useful product and service enhancements, and seek to improve production and distribution processes and practices. In a competitive market, reduced costs are passed on to consumers. Consumers also benefit from competition through expanded choice among goods and services; the opportunity to express preferences and to shape future production through their choices.

Trade liberalization is intended to promote competition by allowing imported goods to compete without unnecessary impediment with domestically produced goods, extending the field of competition from the national market to the international market. The global economy is encouraged to reach its production possibility frontier.[4] The benefits of productivity gains and lower input costs should be shared with consumers, enhancing public welfare.

[2] Paul A Samuelson and William D Nordhaus, *Economics* (19th edn, McGraw-Hill 2010) 35.

[3] Costs can be reduced in a number of ways, including by increasing worker productivity and by acquiring inputs at lower prices.

[4] Samuelson and Nordhaus (n 2) 347. Frederick M Abbott, 'Trade and Democratic Values' (1992) 1(1) Minn J Global Trade 9, 15–16.

For the producer, the ultimate objective is profit. Selling at a price above the costs of production and distribution, and returning the difference to the owner of the business. The government sits between the producer and the consumer, collecting taxes to fund its operation.

For the producer, competition is a mixed blessing.[5] The successful efficient producer uses competition to secure a greater market share than its competitors, with expectations of increasing its profits. But capturing market share may require reducing prices, reducing per-unit profits, leaving the producer no better off even with a higher volume of sales. There may come a point at which competition reduces profits to the extent that investors will seek to move their capital elsewhere. Competition may become 'ruinous', with enterprises forced out of business. In these circumstances, business managers may see advantages in entering into 'mutually beneficial' arrangements with competitors designed to preserve or enhance a margin of profit. One function of competition law is to preclude such arrangements.

There is another side to competition law that is directed towards dominant market actors.[6] These dominant market actors have succeeded in shutting out competition. In some cases, this is through the exercise of ordinary business acumen, in other cases this is through predatory practices, i.e. bad acts. Competition law is tolerant of the former, and is designed to prevent and redress the latter.

III. Government Limits on Competition

Governments may decide to limit competition as a matter of policy choice. In areas with high investment cost and infrastructure requirements, it can be economically inefficient to construct and operate more than a single facility to service a particular geographic area. Traditionally, areas like energy and water supply were constituted as single supplier 'public utilities' and subject to close government regulation in terms of pricing and service requirements. In recent years, many governments have shifted such traditionally regulated industries towards private-sector competition. The results from privatization of the traditional utilities have been mixed.

Governments also limit competition through grants of intellectual property rights (IPRs) that allow innovators to prevent third-party production and sale of protected products for a limited time as an encouragement to create and commercialize new products.[7] The introduction of innovative products has a tendency

[5] Frederick M Abbott, 'Anti-competitive Behaviours and the Remedies Available for Redress' in Frederick M Abbott and others (eds), *Using Competition Law to Promote Access to Health Technologies: A Guidebook for Low- and Middle-income Countries* (UNDP 2014) 60 (*UNDP Guidebook*).

[6] ibid 76–77.

[7] See generally Frederick M Abbott and others, *International Intellectual Property in An Integrated World Economy* (3rd edn, Aspen/Kluwer 2015) 133–83.

to disrupt the market status quo, creating a new source of competition. There is a trade-off between the market exclusion aspect of IPRs and the disruptive competitive aspect of innovation that presents something of a conundrum for competition law.

IV. The United States and Europe

Competition law is the product of United States legislation and jurisprudence of the late 1800s, starting with the Sherman Antitrust Act of 1890.[8] Although dealing with combinations and conspiracies in restraint of trade, the main thrust of the initial policy was to address monopolies in the petroleum and railroad sectors that took the legal form of 'trusts', giving rise to the name 'antitrust' law. The legal form of the 'trust' is no longer prevalent in the business community in the United States, and while the term 'antitrust' is still used in US jurisprudence, it is slowly giving way to the term used more commonly in other countries, 'competition law'.

Following the Second World War and formation of the European Economic Community, competition law became a part of European law.[9] The European Commission was given a prominent role in the enforcement of European competition law, with the European Court of Justice overseeing its jurisprudential development. The EU member states continue to maintain their own competition law and jurisprudence, and continue to apply it.

It should not be surprising that with 125 years of jurisprudential development, US government authorities tend to think of competition law in American terms. And, while European authorities may have only half as long a period of implementation and jurisprudential experience, it is perhaps not surprising that European government authorities also tend to view European competition law as an 'international standard'.

The United States in particular has been resistant to negotiation of multilateral competition norms going back as far as negotiation of the International Trade Organization in the mid-1940s.[10] The ITO objections were based on pushback from the US business community, which was not anxious to see its freedom to operate abroad constrained. More recent resistance to multilateral negotiating efforts from the Department of Justice no doubt reflects continuing objections from the US business community, but also reflects the Department's unwillingness to see its ability to maintain flexible application of doctrine restricted.

[8] See Sean Flynn, 'Introduction—the Interface Between Intellectual Property and Competition in Low- and Middle-income Countries' in *UNDP Guidebook* (n 5) 24–25.

[9] Eleanor M Fox, *Competition Law of the European Union in Comparative Perspective: Cases and Materials* (West 2009).

[10] See Frederick M Abbott, 'Public Policy and Global Technological Integration: An Introduction' in F M Abbott and D Gerber (eds), *Public Policy and Global Technological Integration* (Kluwer Law International 1997) 3, 9–10.

V. Competition as a Singapore Issue

The European Union pressed WTO Members to negotiate a set of competition law disciplines as part of the 1996 Singapore Agenda.[11] A Working Group on Trade and Competition was established, reports were prepared by the Secretariat, meetings were convened, and some proposals were floated. But a combination of resistance from the United States and developing countries doomed the competition agenda at the WTO. Developing countries were particularly concerned that competition law would be used to restrict their industrial policy programmes favouring local industry; a national treatment-related concern. The United States did not wish to surrender autonomy in the development and implementation of competition law.

That leaves WTO law where it has been.[12] There are routes that might be taken to challenge the implementation of competition law depending, of course, on the context. Article III:4 might be used with respect to imported products treated in a discriminatory way by the application of competition law. This would not provide relief where competition law is applied to local production, even if by foreign-owned enterprises. Article XI has similarly been mentioned in the context of disguised quotas; but again, is mainly relevant to imported products. Article X can be invoked on the question of transparency, such as involved in the provision of explanations (or lack thereof), but Article X is fairly narrowly drafted in its application to trade regulations, appearing mainly directed to customs regulations. Article XVII rules regarding state trading enterprises may be relevant. Non-violation nullification or impairment under Article XXIII(1)(b) is a possibility in certain contexts, though this is perhaps remote. The Telecommunications Annex to the WTO Services Agreement (GATS) embodies competition law elements that have already been applied in dispute settlement.[13]

The WTO Agreement on Trade-Related Aspects of International Property Rights (TRIPS) includes explicit reference to competition in Articles 8(2), 31(k), and 40.[14] While these provisions recognize the right of governments to implement competition law in the context of IPRs, they do not impose meaningful 'disciplines'. Nonetheless, to the extent that the TRIPS Agreement incorporates national treatment and transparency, it would appear to create obligations on the part of WTO Members to implement competition law within those parameters.[15]

[11] See WTO, 'Interaction Between Trade and Competition Policy' <www.wto.org/english/tratop_e/comp_e/comp_e.htm> accessed 10 March 2016; see also generally, Frederick M Abbott, 'Are the Competition Rules in the WTO TRIPS Agreement Adequate?' (2004) 7(3) J Intl Econ L 687.

[12] See e.g., Carlos M Correa, 'Intellectual Property and Competition—Room to Legislate Under International Law' in *UNDP Guidebook* (n 5) 35.

[13] Panel Report, *Mexico—Measures Affecting Telecommunications Services*, WT/DS204/R, 2 April 2004.

[14] Abbott, 'Public Policy and Global Technological Integration' (n 10).

[15] The language of the body of the national treatment provision of TRIPS, art 3, is not so direct on this issue, but footnote 3 would appear to encompass application of competition law to IPRs.

VI. Implementation in Developing Countries

Developing countries are being encouraged to implement and enforce competition law for the same reasons competition law has traditionally been enforced in the United States and Europe.[16] Concentrations of economic power have a tendency to encourage anti-competitive behaviour at the expense of the consumers.

UNDP, for example, has recently published a Guidebook on the use by low- and middle-income countries of competition law to facilitate affordable access to medicines.[17] The Guidebook takes note of the active use of competition law by legislative and executive authorities in the United States and Europe to maintain competitive markets, and illustrates with examples of enforcement action brought against pharmaceutical companies seeking to forestall price competition at the expense of consumers.

A. China and the anti-monopoly law

The United States Chamber of Commerce has been particularly critical of China's implementation of its Anti-monopoly Law of 2007 (AML).[18] The Chamber represents the interests of the multinational business community in the United States whose members prefer not to individually assert themselves on matters of China policy. China is a very profitable market for many of these companies. They are not anxious to fall out of favour with the Chinese government.

1. Regulatory authorities

The Chamber complains that investigation and enforcement authority under the AML is divided among three agencies: the Ministry of Commerce (MOFCOM), the National Development and Reform Commission (NDRC), and the State Administration for Industry and Commerce (SAIC). This leads to uncertainty regarding enforcement policy. The Chamber states that China is unusual in dividing authority among several agencies, yet notes that the United States divides authority among the Department of Justice and Federal Trade Commission, which it describes as an anomaly based on historical factors. This is a less than robust critique and/or explanation. If there was a real conceptual problem with dividing competition investigation and enforcement authority, the United States has had plenty of time to integrate the authority of the Department of Justice and Federal

[16] See e.g., Natasha Nyak, 'Advancing Competition Frameworks in the Low- and Middle-income Country Context' in *UNDP Guidebook* (n 5) 123.

[17] *UNDP Guidebook* (n 5) .

[18] US Chamber of Commerce, 'Competing Interests in China's Competition Law Enforcement: China's Anti-monopoly Law Application and the Role of Industrial Policy' (2014), <https://www.uschamber.com/report/competing-interests-chinas-competition-law-enforcement-chinas-anti-monopoly-law-application> accessed 10 March 2016.

Trade Commission (FTC). This is not to say that even experts in competition law in the United States are not confronted with some uncertainty because of the divided authority. But the United States system seems to work sufficiently well that there is no clamour for consolidation of authority.

Another critique is that China has not joined the International Competition Network (ICN) as many countries have. The ICN provides a framework for discussion and co-operation among competition authorities, but it is not an intergovernmental organization. As it describes itself, the ICN provides competition authorities with 'a specialised yet informal venue for maintaining regular contacts and addressing practical competition concerns'.[19] While China and other countries might benefit from closer interaction among competition authorities in terms of promoting mutual understanding, it is hardly a critique of a national competition authority to say that it has refrained from joining an informal network of colleagues. It might be that language barriers are perceived by Chinese authorities to reduce the benefits that might accrue to participants in ICN.

This is not a critique of the ICN, nor is it intended to suggest that China's competition authorities should not join. It is only to say that China's decision up until now not to join this informal network of competition authorities does not raise any issues regarding China's implementation or enforcement policies with respect to the AML.

That said, the Chamber does make some significant substantive critique of China's implementation of the AML. These are basically threefold: (i) discrimination among investors; (ii) lack of transparency, and; (iii) failure of due process (for example, preclusion of counsel participation).

It should be noted at the outset that the terms of China's accession to the WTO do not appear to materially affect the general application of WTO law in respect to the issues discussed below.[20] China's accession preceded the adoption of the AML, the prospect for which was foreshadowed in the Working Party Report.[21]

2. *Foreign investment controls*

The Chamber argues that China is using competition law as a means to bolster its domestic 'champions' at the expense of foreign-based/multinational competitors. So, for example, Chinese competition authorities may block mergers and acquisitions by foreign multinationals of domestically operating companies (whether foreign or domestically owned), while turning a blind eye toward similar acquisitions by locally owned, domestically operated companies. The objective, it is contended, is establishment of more powerful Chinese-owned champions, with

[19] International Competition Network, 'About' <http://www.internationalcompetitionnetwork.org/about.aspx> accessed 10 March 2016.

[20] Working Party on the Accession of China, *Report of the Working Party on the Accession of China*, WT/ACC/CHN/49, 1 October 2001.

[21] ibid para 65.

enhanced market power, and a corollary reduction in the power of foreign-owned enterprises.

Chinese government officials have rejected the allegation that they are discriminating against foreign investors in the application of competition law.[22] This chapter does not attempt to analyse the factual basis for the claims by the Chamber of Commerce. The concern here is whether there are international rules that preclude the use of competition law to control foreign investment.

Countries may negotiate international agreements establishing the conditions of foreign investment, including, for example, national treatment. Such agreements may expressly exclude limitations on ownership by foreign investors. Investment chapters establishing national treatment obligations are a common feature of preferential trade agreements today, sometimes incorporating sectoral rules controlling percentage of ownership by foreign investors. WTO rules do not establish conditions of foreign investment in the sense of requiring a country, such as China, to allow acquisition of domestic enterprises by foreign investors.

Competition policy implements a government's industrial policy preferences. There is no general rule of competition law that says a government must allow concentrations of ownership by foreign investors. Nor in principle is there a reason why a government may not use competition law with respect to mergers and acquisitions to implement targets with respect to levels of foreign control of the domestic economy.

More typically, governments have taken a more direct legislative or administrative route to control foreign investor penetration of the local market. Until fairly recently, for example, India established limits on acquisition by foreign investors of domestic pharmaceutical companies. Prior to the NAFTA, Mexico regulated the potential penetration of foreign investors in many of its business sectors, including banking, energy, and telecommunications. OECD governments spent a good deal of time in the 1990s negotiating a multilateral agreement on investment (MAI) intended to establish a set of rules that might limit restrictions on foreign investment, with a long-term view of bringing in developing countries. They were ultimately unsuccessful in bringing an agreement into force.

It is a difficult question whether a country gains or loses from certain types of foreign investment.[23] Having removed controls, India is watching as its home-grown

[22] Jet Deng and Ken Dai, 'Public Enforcement of Antitrust Law in China: Perspective of Procedural Fairness' (*Competition Policy International (CPI)*, 4 August 2015) <https://www.competitionpolicyinternational.com/public-enforcement-of-antitrust-law-in-china-perspective-of-procedural-fairness> accessed 10 March 2016.

[23] The Andean Community, through its Decision 24 in the early 1970s, attempted to transfer control of local business activity to local ownership and failed. See Frederick M Abbott, 'Bargaining Power and Strategy in the Foreign Investment Process: A Current Andean Code Analysis' (1975) 3 Syracuse J Intl L & Com 319. The question for the Andean Community was whether it had the political and economic power to enforce the types of demands that it made. As it turned out, foreign-owned companies refused to play by the newly dictated rules, and Andean Community members themselves sought to benefit at the expense of one another in terms of offering special concessions. China is not the Andean Community from a political and economic standpoint. We can count on one finger the companies that have been willing to stand up to the Chinese government (i.e. Google).

pharmaceutical industry is gradually being taken over by foreign investors, with increasing concern.

While members of the US Chamber of Commerce may well consider that Chinese efforts to control the level of foreign penetration of its market are contrary to US interests (and they may be), this does not mean that Chinese authorities are contravening some international standards with respect to enforcement of competition law. Moreover, as noted above, Chinese officials contend that they are not engaging in the conduct alleged by the Chamber.

It may be that Chinese authorities are choosing to use competition law to limit foreign investment and promote local champions, rather than using legislative limitations on foreign investment because they are concerned with reciprocal legislation being adopted by the United States, the European Union, Japan, and others. This could affect Chinese investments in those countries, and it might indeed affect inflows of foreign investment into China. Competition law is a somewhat disguised mechanism for accomplishing similar ends.

While the US Chamber of Commerce may consider China's use of competition law to limit foreign acquisitions of domestic companies as reflecting poor public policy, it is not apparent that there is some international legal rule or standard that Chinese authorities are contravening. If this is correct, it may suggest a reason why multinational business groups would shift their stance regarding negotiation of multilateral competition rules. It may not suggest a reason why China would think such negotiations a good idea.

3. *Transparency*

The Chamber complains that Chinese competition authorities are acting without providing explanation of the legal basis of their actions. This gives rise to perceptions, at least, of arbitrariness.

Interestingly, the question whether 'transparency' is a customary rule of international law with respect to treatment of foreign investors has proven controversial in the context of NAFTA dispute settlement. In *Mexico v Metalclad*, the Supreme Court of British Columbia, hearing an appeal of an arbitration award, held that the NAFTA arbitration panel had mistakenly concluded that there was an obligation of transparency under customary international law with respect to treatment of foreign investors.[24]

As noted above, the GATT in Article X establishes obligations of transparency with respect to laws and judicial/administrative decisions, but it is a narrowly drafted provision that would be difficult to extend to enforcement of competition law.

With that said, a government's failure to provide explanation for its conduct may give rise to a perception of arbitrariness, and this could rise to the level of a deprivation of property contrary to international standards under customary international

[24] *United Mexican States v Metalclad Corp* [2001] BCSC 664 (2 May 2001) (Vancouver).

law. The application of such a general principle would be dependent on the circumstances of the individual case. It is indeed doubtful that the Chinese government would seek to promote an understanding of international trade and investment rules that countenanced arbitrary and unexplained actions by government authorities. Chinese companies are significant foreign investors, and depend on fair treatment by foreign authorities.

Chinese authorities have given indication that they intend to improve their communications with respect to actions taken under the AML.[25]

4. *Due process*

The Chamber indicates complaints from its members that Chinese competition authorities have engaged in threatening behaviour, and have barred foreign counsel from attending meetings with their clients.

It should be recalled that investigative and prosecutorial authorities in OECD countries may advise targets that they are subject to criminal prosecution and potentially imprisonment under the competition laws. So, for example, in the vitamins conspiracy case (Hoffman-La Roche) in the United States, a Swiss executive was imprisoned in the United States as a consequence of misconduct, and certainly the threat of further prosecutions encouraged settlement by the target company in that case.[26]

As to 'foreign counsel', this depends on rules of legal representation applicable within the country. Foreign counsel may not have the same rights of representation in China as does the local bar, and the practice of limiting legal representation to certain categories of licensed practitioners is not uncommon in OECD countries.

Chinese competition law experts have argued that in cases complained of by the Chamber the Chinese authorities acted in accordance with applicable Chinese laws and regulations.[27] Indeed, acknowledging that Chinese investigative practices may in some cases seem harsh by US or EU standards. Yet it should also be noted that European and US investigating authorities may well appear unannounced at the offices of companies under investigation, and act to seize relevant records. It is likely that the subjects under investigation in the European Union and the United States consider these harsh investigative practices.

Assuming, for the sake of argument, that the Chamber's allegations are at least to some extent based on facts, while legal representation may be limited to those qualified to practice in the subject proceedings, it is contrary to basic concepts of due process to preclude legal representation altogether. In addition, depending upon the type of tactics that are used by investigative or prosecutorial authorities, there is a line between the types of ordinary pressure placed on targets of

25 Deng and Dai (n 22).
26 See Abbott, 'Anti-competitive Behaviours' (n 5), Box 3.2.
27 Deng and Dai (n 22).

investigation to acknowledge wrongdoing and accept remedial action, on the one hand, and abuse of power, on the other. The latter should not be countenanced.

Again, Chinese competition authorities appear to be taking account of the concerns that have been expressed, and some guidelines have been adopted in this area.[28]

B. The case for multilateral competition rules

The allegations by the US Chamber of Commerce regarding implementation and enforcement of China's AML illustrate why the multinational business community might today view more favourably the negotiation of multilateral competition rules. Assuming, for the sake of argument, that the Chamber's complaints on behalf of its members accurately describe the facts, there is minimal basis in international law for redressing the complaints. There is not a multilateral forum where alleged violations might be adjudicated and enforced.

This does not mean that the multinational business community is without recourse. Trade and economic relations are a two-way street, and Chinese enterprises are potentially subject to the same type of treatment in other countries. Perhaps unfortunately from the standpoint of the US and European businesses communities, it may be somewhat more difficult for business to make use of the levers of administrative power in the United States and Europe than it is for the Chinese government to act.

Are the Chamber's complaints sufficiently serious from the standpoint of the multinational business community to change the equation and motivate the pursuit of a new agenda at the WTO? Perhaps they are. This, however, brings us to the perspective of a wider group of countries, and the global public interest.

VII. The Virtues of Diversity

Beginning in the mid-1980s in the United States, and under the influence of the so-called 'Chicago School', government regulation of business activity began to be considered inherently suspect, and antitrust policy moved towards laissez-faire. The marketplace would sort out distortions on its own. This shift toward a 'light touch' by antitrust authorities was reflected in policy documents developed by the Department of Justice and Federal Trade Commission in the early 1990s.[29]

[28] ibid.

[29] See US Dep't of Justice/Federal Trade Comm'n, Horizontal Merger Guidelines (1992) (superseded, 2010) <http://www.justice.gov/atr/horizontal-merger-guidelines> accessed 16 March 2016; US Dep't of Justice/Federal Trade Comm'n, Antitrust Guidelines for the Licensing of Intellectual Property (1995) <http://www.justice.gov/atr/antitrust-guidelines-licensing-intellectual-property> accessed 16 March 2016; US Dep't of Justice/federal Trade Comm'n, Antitrust Enforcement Guidelines for International Operations (1995) <http://www.justice.gov/atr/antitrust-enforcement-guidelines-international-operations> accessed 16 March 2016.

The United States has not developed jurisprudence to control 'excessive pricing' as a category of anticompetitive conduct. The general theory is that excessive pricing is inconsistent with open market competition, and is effectively unsustainable. If an enterprise attempts to charge a price substantially above its marginal cost of production, competitors will enter the market and eliminate the pricing excess. On the flip side, if an enterprise is able to charge and sustain a price substantially above that of potential competitors, this must be reflective of some product advantage that cannot be replicated, and an enterprise may be rewarded for its unique contribution.

The 'essential facilities' doctrine addresses at least one of the obvious flaws in the laissez-faire approach.[30] There are circumstances in which consumers do not reasonably have a choice regarding the purchase of goods or services, and in which potential competitors cannot reasonably enter the market on the supply side.[31] Yet courts in the United States have yet to adopt an 'essential facilities' doctrine within the antitrust law. The issue was notably raised in the context of the Microsoft case in the early 1990s, with the argument that a dominant computer operating system constituted an essential facility as a consequence of 'network effects'. The Court of Appeals for the District of Columbia Circuit said that there were economic arguments on different sides with respect to the impact of networks on competition, and that it was unnecessary to adopt a new doctrine to resolve the dispute.[32] It

[30] See Flynn (n 8) 26–28; Abbott, 'Anti-competitive Behaviours' (n 5) 83; Jonathan Berger, 'Market Definition' in *UNDP Guidebook* (n 5) 119–21.

[31] As noted earlier in the text, a typical example is the local electricity supply company, sometimes a 'public utility'. Because of infrastructure requirements, it may be impractical for there to be more than a single supplier. Consumers must acquire electricity; it is not an optional good or service. In principle, because of the characteristics of the electricity supply market, the supplier could charge an excessive price and the consumer would have no choice but to pay it. In the United States, this circumstance has generally been accounted for by the establishment of energy regulatory authorities within the states and municipal jurisdictions that exercise control over pricing and access. The market is controlled.

[32] *United States v Microsoft*, 253 F.3d 34 (DC Cir 2001). The Court said:

> The second matter of note is more theoretical in nature. We decide this case against a backdrop of significant debate amongst academics and practitioners over the extent to which 'old economy' § 2 monopolization doctrines should apply to firms competing in dynamic technological markets characterized by network effects. In markets characterized by network effects, one product or standard tends towards dominance, because 'the utility that a user derives from consumption of the good increases with the number of other agents consuming the good.' …
>
> In technologically dynamic markets, however, such entrenchment may be temporary, because innovation may alter the field altogether. See Joseph A. Schumpter, *Capitalism, Socialism and Democracy* 81–90 (Harper Perennial 1976) (1942). Rapid technological change leads to markets in which 'firms compete through innovation for temporary market dominance, from which they may be displaced by the next wave of product advancements.' Shelanski & Sidak, at 11–12 (discussing Schumpeterian competition, which proceeds 'sequentially over time rather than simultaneously across a market'). Microsoft argues that the operating system market is just such a market….
>
> Whether or not Microsoft's characterization of the operating system market is correct does not appreciably alter our mission in assessing the alleged antitrust violations in the present case. As an initial matter, we note that there is no consensus among commentators on the question of whether, and to what extent, current monopolization doctrine should

would appear that the courts have left it to legislative bodies to step in where there may be distortions arising from the provision of 'necessities' to a captive public as in the case of electricity supply.

It is debatable whether the European Court of Justice has adopted an essential facilities doctrine. There is a line of thought that the *IMS Health* decision effectively embodies an essential facilities doctrine, though the court refrained from labelling it as such.[33] That decision stands at least for the proposition that where a dominant market actor controls access by differentiated downstream products it has some obligation to provide access to its dominant product.

The question of essential facilities is becoming increasingly important in respect to health goods and services; but also in the context of climate change mitigation and alternative energy technologies. In both of these areas, the key underlying issue concerns the relationship between intellectual property and regulatory exclusivity, on one side, and competition policy on the other.

Some of the more interesting issues in respect to competition law doctrine are raised in the relationship between patents used to protect innovator interests in new drugs, and the ability of consumers to have access to those drugs.[34] Patents by definition give their owners a right to block competition. The effects of an individual patent are dependent upon the structure of the market into which it is introduced, including the extent to which there are reasonable substitute products in the market. In the pharmaceuticals sector, market structure tends to be defined by 'therapeutic class' (or 'ATC'). When there are a number of existing drugs in a particular therapeutic class, it is more difficult for a newly patented entry to enforce prices substantially in excess of existing treatments. But there are exceptions, particularly for breakthrough therapies. And, where existing treatments are uniformly patented, price competition may play a small role in the market.

Recent jurisprudence from the US Supreme Court has confirmed for the United States that patents are subject to competition law disciplines. The fact that a patent confers a right to exclude others from making and selling a protected product does

be amended to account for competition in technologically dynamic markets characterized by network effects….

Moreover, it should be clear that Microsoft makes no claim that anticompetitive conduct should be assessed differently in technologically dynamic markets. It claims only that the measure of monopoly power should be different. For reasons fully discussed below, we reject Microsoft's monopoly power argument. (253 F.3d at 49–50).

[33] *IMS Health GmbH & Co OHG v NDC Health GmbH & Co KG* (2004) Landgericht Frankfurt am Main—Germany, Case C-418/01.

[34] The basic theory of antitrust law is that market participants are expected to charge competitive market prices for their products, which results in market efficiencies, and which benefits consumers. A legislated market exclusivity, such as a patent or regulatory exclusivity period, allows the owner to charge a price above a competitive market price. It does not insulate the owner from competition insofar as that competition comes from differentiated products. So, for example, a new drug therapy may be a 'breakthrough' that is uniquely capable of treating a disease, or it may be one of several drugs in the same therapeutic class with a similar effect to existing treatments. A breakthrough treatment is more likely to give its owner more significant pricing power, although even in more competitive therapeutic areas pricing may be high.

not insulate the patent owner from claims of abusive conduct, including with respect to activities within the zone of patent protection.

The particular case, *FTC v Actavis*,[35] involved the pharmaceutical patent owner practice of buying out patent challenges under the Hatch-Waxman paragraph iv mechanism. Several Courts of Appeal had ruled that because patent owners have the right to exclude third parties from the market, paying third parties during the life of the patent not to pursue a challenge was within the legitimate zone of patent protection, and effectively insulated from antitrust challenge. The Supreme Court rejected this approach, holding that conduct designed to inhibit patent challenges may represent an unwarranted attempt to stifle competition when, for example, a large unexplained payment flows from the patent owner to the challenger. Such a payment raises suspicion regarding anti-competitive motivation, and subjects the patent owner to competition law assessment under the rule of reason. For example, the patent owner may lack a good faith belief in the validity of its patent, and may be seeking to maintain a spurious patent that would be invalidated if tested in court.[36]

Yet perhaps a more serious question affecting the US pharmaceuticals market involves the charging of excessive prices by originator companies for new drug treatments. Does the fact that an originator holds a position of patent-based or regulatory-based market exclusivity justify the charging of whatever price the originator decides to charge?

The United States has a split personality with respect to pharmaceutical pricing. On one hand, it largely allows originator patent owners to charge whatever price the market will bear. This is becoming an increasingly controversial approach, as pharmaceutical companies are charging prices for new cancer therapies, among others, that are astronomical. Insurance benefit providers, physician groups, and public interest groups are pushing back, but so far with little effect on pricing practices.

At the same time, US policy and law take a very aggressive approach towards the introduction of generic versions of patented drugs, providing strong incentives for generic producers willing to challenge patent owners.[37] Most US states mandate generic substitution by pharmacists. At the end of the day, the United States has some of the lowest generic drug prices in the world.

There are a good number of recent instances in which developers of breakthrough therapies have decided to charge prices that physicians, insurance providers, and consumers consider 'excessive', or out of line with reasonable expectations. The 'poster child' for this decision making is sofosbuvir (generic),

[35] *FTC v Actavis, Inc*, 133 S.Ct 2223 (2013). See discussion in Abbott (n 5) 66–67.

[36] The Supreme Court did not put an end to questions about patent challenge buyouts because it used the circumstance of a large unexplained payment to describe circumstances in which the patent would be subject to rule of reason assessment. This created uncertainty in the lower courts regarding to what extent other circumstances might subject the patent to scrutiny.

[37] Frederick M Abbott, 'The Generics Pathway in the USA: The American Experience, a Model for the World?' (2015) FSU College of Law Public Law Research Paper No 743, <http://ssrn.com/abstract=2570922> accessed 16 March 2016.

or 'Sovaldi' (Gilead branded), a breakthrough treatment for hepatitis C. In this case, the excessive price is $84,000 for a twelve-week course of treatment. The cost of manufacturing the twelve-week course of treatment is no more than several hundred dollars.[38] Because there are many millions of sufferers of hepatitis C infection (170 million worldwide according to the US Centers for Disease Control), the aggregate revenues earned by Gilead are extraordinary, exceeding $14 billion per year.[39] There are a substantial number of oncology drugs with pricing in the hundreds of thousands per year, and while the patient base may be smaller, this pricing places an enormous strain on patients and insurance providers.[40]

As members of the US Congress have called for investigation of the pricing practices of the originator companies, requesting information regarding the cost of development and how the pricing is arrived at, the companies have taken a new approach to explaining their pricing practices.[41] Drug companies are arguing that they should be able to charge very high prices because drugs are cheaper than hospitalization.[42] Consumers and investigators should not be concerned with their R&D costs, or production costs.

This is a highly problematic approach to rationalizing healthcare prices. There are many goods and services essential to maintaining life, such as water, which are not typically scarce and for which the suppliers do not maintain life-or-death pricing power. Prices are low. Pharmaceutical companies are able to charge very high prices only because of government-adopted industrial policy mechanisms; patents and regulatory marketing exclusivity, combined with the threat of progressive disease and/or death. Without the government exclusivity mechanisms, the newest drugs would not be scarce because they are fairly readily reverse engineered (even biologics). Drug company pricing is an artificial construct effectively supported by the government. The analogy to the cost of hospitalization is a fiction built on a regulatory foundation. Yes, hospitalization is expensive, but it has nothing to do with the pricing of drugs.

[38] A preferentially licensed generic version of the course of treatment is sold in India for about US$1000.

[39] On the mathematics, see Frederick M Abbott, 'Rethinking Patents: From "Intellectual Property" to "Private Taxation Scheme"' in P Drahos and others (eds), *Kritika: Essays on Intellectual Property* (Edward Elgar 2015) 1, 7–8. Gilead did not develop Sovaldi. It was developed by a small biotechnology company, Pharmasset, which was purchased by Gilead for $11 billion. Pharmasset's internal planning was to sell the drug for less than half the price charged by Gilead.

[40] Andrew Pollack, 'Drug Prices Soar, Prompting Calls for Justification' (*New York Times*, 23 July 2015) <http://www.nytimes.com/2015/07/23/business/drug-companies-pushed-from-far-and-wide-to-explain-high-prices.html?_r=0> accessed 16 March 2016.

[41] e.g. Peter Loftus, 'Senate Committee Is Investigating Pricing of Hepatitis C Drug' (*Wall Street Journal*, 11 July 2014) <http://www.wsj.com/articles/senate-finance-committee-is-investigating-pricing-of-hepatitis-c-drug-1405109206> accessed 16 March 2016.

[42] It can be applied with equal alacrity to all of life's necessities. Since access to drinking water is a life-or-death matter, perhaps water should be priced at several thousand dollars per day. A taxi to the airport may mean the difference between attending an important business meeting or not. Perhaps taxi drivers should stop en route and negotiate prices based on the business that will be concluded at the other end of the trip.

The question for present purposes is whether competition law doctrine is suitable for addressing excessive pharmaceutical prices. The answer is 'yes'.

One factor is whether the owner of a drug patent or regulatory exclusivity has a dominant position on the market such that it is able to dictate a higher-than-competitive market price. A patent *ipso facto* grants market exclusivity, as does regulatory marketing exclusivity, but as discussed above this does not necessarily confer a dominant market position. An assessment of the market position of the exclusivity holder can be undertaken by looking at the competitors in the therapeutic class, and the extent to which the holder of exclusivity faces competition from alternative treatments. It may also be useful to look at the extent to which the drug company is providing inducements to physicians to prescribe the drug, so as to bolster its position. If all of the potential alternate treatments are patented and/or subject to regulatory exclusivity, price competition may nevertheless be limited. This factor needs to be taken into account.

It is important to look at the relationship between the cost of drug development and the price that is being charged. This is where the companies have balked at providing information even to government authorities on grounds that such information is confidential commercial information. It would not appear that such a position can be sustained throughout the course of an antitrust investigation. The drug companies argue that it is not reasonable to look at the development costs of a single drug in isolation, since failures outweigh successes, and account must be had for the overall R&D picture of the company. This is fair enough, but that does not mean it is not possible to determine the R&D costs of a drug by looking at it within the costs of the overall portfolio of the company. There are different approaches that could be taken. Most drug companies segregate their R&D activities among disease classes, and the R&D costs of a particular corporate sector can be isolated, with the successes and failures given appropriate weights.

The investigating authority can determine what would be a reasonable profit margin. In respect to the originator pharmaceutical industry, this may present a challenge because a substantial percentage of the prices charged for patented drug products are disassociated from a reasonable approximation of development and production costs. With that said, it is notable that a substantial number of countries control the prices of pharmaceutical products, including products protected by patent and regulatory exclusivity.[43] This includes most of the countries of Europe. While many of these countries use reference price formulas that essentially compare prices within the country with prices in other countries, there are circumstances in which cost-plus and pharmaco-economic assessment methodologies are used, and these formulas should provide reasonable precedent for determining reasonable prices with respect to drugs protected by patents and market exclusivity.

[43] OECD Health Policy Studies, 'Pharmaceutical Pricing Policies in A Global Market' (2008) <http://apps.who.int/medicinedocs/documents/s19834en/s19834en.pdf> accessed 23 April 2016.

The notion that the cost of developing a new drug is 'incalculable' is promoted by the pharmaceutical industry as a means to inhibit government and third-party assessment of pricing practices. But it is doubtful that investments would be made in an industry that is unable to determine its costs, even retrospectively. Moreover, pharmaceutical companies acquire new treatments in the course of development through a variety of means, including acquisition of enterprises, acquisition of portfolios, and acquisition of specific drug candidates. In acquiring a product in development, it is necessary to establish a price. Both the acquirer and the target establish their prices, and negotiate to an endpoint. This is concrete evidence that the cost of developing a new drug is not incalculable.

No doubt there is economic risk involved in new drug development. Outcomes are uncertain. But, there are economic risks inherent in virtually all business enterprises, and this does not insulate businesses from competition law scrutiny.

Competition law doctrines addressing essential facilities and excessive pricing are potentially important to developing country competition authorities, and to the protection of the public interest. These doctrines have not been given great attention by competition authorities or jurisprudence in the United States, although they have been given attention elsewhere. They are subject to additional elaboration. There is no manifest reason for curtailing their development.

VIII. The Virtue of Diversity

Developing countries, as well as high-income countries, enjoy significant flexibility in the development, implementation, and enforcement of competition law today. This includes flexibility in adopting remedies. In addition to fines and imprisonment, courts and administrative authorities may issue injunctive orders requiring that certain behaviours be stopped, and/or that certain affirmative actions be undertaken.

As emerging market and other developing countries increase attention to competition law enforcement, multinational businesses based in the OECD countries may become more interested in negotiating rules to limit flexibility.

It is difficult to see the advantage to emerging market and other developing countries from trading away their flexibility to implement and enforce competition law. It is likewise difficult to see the advantage to the public in the OECD countries. Competition law is an important tool of industrial policy, and should be tailored to the circumstances of each country. The prospects that OECD country negotiators would agree to establish robust multilateral doctrines promoting access to essential facilities, controlling excessive pricing, and developing other formula of particular relevance to developing countries are remote. This argues in favour of maintaining the status quo and its tolerance of regulatory diversity.

15

Untangling the Triangle: Issues for State-controlled Entities in Trade, Investment, and Competition Law

*Julien Chaisse**

I. Introduction

I have known Professor Mitsuo Matsushita for many years though his writings on international economic law. The breadth of his expertise always impressed me and I was even more impressed when I met him in person. Over the years, we have met in different places and I hold a great memory of the summer 2011 when I was a Visiting Professor in Yokohama National University in Japan. During this period, I had the pleasure to meet almost every week with Professor Matsushita, who was advisor at Nagashima Ohno & Tsunematsu in Tokyo. While his days were very busy in the law firm, he always found a way to spend time with me to discuss a project on the trade policy review mechanism we were developing. However, our discussions were so rich and lively that we could not only focus on this project. When I remember this wonderful time and many exchanges, what comes to my mind is Professor Matsushita's fantastic knowledge of various fields of law. In particular, I recall our discussion on the issue of the treatment of state-controlled entities, which was already pretty important at this time. Professor Matsushita drew my attention to the limits of analysing the state-controlled entities (SCEs) from the pure World Trade Organization (WTO) law perspective or investment policy angle. This chapter is a tribute to his early understanding of the problem and an attempt to explain how SCEs' operations should be read in the context of trade, investment, and also competition rules.

The increasing trend towards market liberalization and privatization in international economic law is well illustrated by a number of regulatory changes

* Professor, Faculty of Law and Director of the Centre for Financial Regulation and Economic Development (CFRED), The Chinese University of Hong Kong. PhD in Law, University of Aix-Marseille, France; LLM in European Law, University of Rennes; MPhil, University of Tübingen; LLB, University of Aix-Marseille.

at the national, regional, and international levels. However, although free trade agreements (FTAs) have emerged as a structuring facet of current international economic governance,[1] the role of the state has arguably grown in importance in the sphere of national and transnational business activities.[2] Notably, investments from emerging economies have increased, a large proportion of which was executed by state-owned enterprises (SOEs)[3] and by sovereign wealth funds (SWFs).[4] This trend has recently been further reinforced by the fact that despite the fears and turbulence that spread all over the world in the wake of the global economic and financial crisis, these investors have gradually strengthened their influence.[5]

[1] The recent economic crisis is, however, underlining the role to be played by the national governments in no uncertain terms. See generally Ian Bremmer, 'State Capitalism Comes of Age: The End of the Free Market?' (2009) 88(3) Foreign Aff 40. See also Niall Ferguson, 'We Are All State Capitalist Now' (*Foreign Policy*, February 2012) <http://foreignpolicy.com/2012/02/09/were-all-state-capitalists-now/> accessed 4 March 2016; Larry Catá Backer, 'Sovereign Investing in Times of Crisis: Global Regulation of Sovereign Wealth Funds, State-owned Enterprises, and the Chinese Experience' (2010) 19(1) Transnatl L Contemp Probs 3.

[2] See generally Aldo Musacchio and Sergio G Lazzarini, 'Leviathan in Business: Varieties of State Capitalism and Their Implications for Economic Performance' (2012) Harvard Business School Working Paper No 12-101 <http://papers.ssrn.com/sol3/papers.cfm?abstract_id=2070942> accessed 23 April 2016. See also Joseph L Bower and others, 'Global Capitalism at Risk: What Are You Doing about It?' (2011) 89 Harv Bus Rev 104, 105. See also Adrian Wooldridge, 'State Capitalism's Global Reach: New Masters of the Universe' in *State Capitalism: The Visible Hand* (Special Report, The Economist 2012); Christopher A McNally, 'Sino-capitalism: China's Re-emergence and the International Political Economy' (2012) 64 World Pol 741, 765.

[3] Wooldridge (n 2). See also United States–China Economic and Security Review Commission, '2011 Report to Congress' (United States Government Printing Office 2011) 40. The definition of SOEs is controversial. Official statistics from the Chinese Ministry of Finance define SOEs as including only wholly state-owned companies. In this chapter, SOEs are defined more broadly to include wholly state-owned SOEs and companies whose majority shares are owned by the Chinese government at various levels (including the central, provincial, and municipal levels). Jie Wu, 'Scrutinizing China's Fortune Global 500 Companies [ShenShi ZhongGuoDe ShiJie WuBai Jiang]' (*Guo Qi* 14 August, 2013) <http://news.xinhuanet.com/fortune/2013-08/14/c_125166671.htm> accessed 4 March 2016, and Tian Liang Bai, 'The New State-owned Enterprises of China [GuoQi XinZi ZhongGuo JiLiang JianJiang TingLi]' (*People's Daily Online*, 15 April 2015) <http://www.sasac.gov.cn/n1180/n1271/n20515/n2697206/15243512.html> accessed 23 April 2016. International tribunals have had to define SOEs and the *Salini v Morocco* Decision on Jurisdiction notes that generally any commercial company dominated or predominantly controlled by the state or by state institutions, whether it has a legal personality or not, is considered to be a state-owned company. See *Salini Costruttori SPA and Italstrade SPA v Kingdom of Morocco*, ICSID Case No ARB/00/4, Decision on Jurisdiction, 16 July 2001, 31. Also the *Al-Kharafi v Libya* Final Arbitral Award notes that, in certain circumstances, the separate personality of an entity fully controlled by a state can be discarded and the state is considered to be bound by the terms of a contract entered into by such an entity; accordingly, the tribunal decides that the arbitration clause set out in the contract may be invoked against various state organs/entities. See *Mohamed Abdulmohsen Al-Kharafi & Sons Co v the Republic of Libya and others*, Final Arbitral Award, 22 March 2013, 263, 266, and 268.

[4] Both forms of investments originate from state ownership and state activity, and are thus regularly referred to as investments by SCEs. See Ronald J Gilson and Curtis J Milhaupt, 'Sovereign Wealth Funds and Corporate Governance: A Minimalist Response to the New Mercantilism' (2008) 60 Stan L Rev 1346. See also Musacchio and Lazzarini (n 2) 2; see Julien Chaisse and others, 'Emerging Sovereign Wealth Funds in the Making: Assessing the Economic Feasibility and Regulatory Strategies' (2011) 45 J World Trade 837.

[5] See Thilo Hanemann and Adam Lysenko, 'Chinese FDI in the United States: Q1 2013 Update' (*Rhodium Group*, 30 April 2013) <http://rhg.com/notes/chinese-fdi-in-the-united-states-q1-2013-update> accessed 4 March 2016 ('In the past 15 months private Chinese firms spent more on US deals than in the 11 years before combined. In the same period they accounted for 80% of

The increasingly free movement of capital and the dominance of multinational corporations in cross-border trade and investment have brought with them increased suspicion about the motives of SOEs when they invest, allocate scarce resources, procure goods and services, and move goods and services across national borders. The increased suspicion includes concerns by countries about threats to their national security and to the competitive interests of producers and consumers based in their respective territories, among other concerns. When SOEs and SWFs become involved, either as the perceived 'transgressor' or as the 'defender' in the face of rules or administrative actions targeted towards such entities, the debate becomes increasingly tense.

The rise of SCEs is more than the addition of a new asset class.[6] The SCEs' growth prowess is a reflection of the new role of developing economies, and this illustrates a shift in emphasis in the global economy.[7] Just as the norm in recent decades was for Western companies and portfolio investors to invest in emerging and developing countries—meaning that capital flowed from North to South—it is now observed that the present capital surpluses in the South will seek out investment opportunities in the North.[8] In some cases, this is achieved through private-sector investment, but because many emerging and developing countries do not (for various reasons) have privately owned companies of sufficient size to invest significantly in industrialized countries, this is increasingly done by SCEs, and this makes state capitalism a key feature of contemporary global economy. Lawyers will always agree to disagree on the issue of whether trade with or investment from super-competitive and cashed-up SWFs/SOEs should be welcomed or not. However, in an increasingly interconnected world, simply discriminating on a political basis is no longer acceptable. Legal rules now apply, whether they are generated domestically or arise as a result of international agreements. Our chapter deals with the laws and policies that attempt to regulate the activities of SOEs and SWFs in trade, competition, and investment.

This chapter will consider how the principles of competition law and of trade and investment law apply where states, acting through SOEs and SWFs, involve themselves in cross-border business and investment: what are the rules; how are

transactions and 50% of total transaction value, a dramatic change compared to previous years when state-owned firms dominated Chinese capital flows to the US.'). A representative media account of this report is David Welch and others, 'Smithfield Stoking U.S. Unease Belies Benefit of China Deals' (*Bloomberg Business*, 8 June 2013) <http://www.bloomberg.com/news/2013-06-06/smithfield-stoking-u-s-unease-belies-benefit-of-chinese-deals.html> accessed 4 March 2016 (noting that '[p]rivate companies are also freer of government influence').

[6] In the plain meaning of the term, SCEs are entities of any kind controlled by a state such as SOEs and SWFs. See Karl P Sauvant and Jonathan Strauss, 'State-controlled Entities Are Important Outward Direct Investors' (2012) 4(3) Transnatl Corp Rev 1 (discussing that developing country SWFs are players in the world foreign direct investment (FDI) market which have received considerable attention, while SOEs, another class of SCEs, are serious players in the world FDI market).

[7] See *Chinese State-owned and State-controlled Enterprises: Policy Options for Addressing Chinese State-owned Enterprises before the US–China Economic and Security Review Commission* (testimony of Elizabeth J Drake, Stewart and Stewart 2012); OECD, 'State-owned Enterprises: Trade Effects and Policy Implications—an Interim Report', DAF/CA/PRIV(2010), 18 October 2010, 1.

[8] Joël Ruet, 'The Reshaping of Global Capitalism by MNEs from Emerging Countries' in Julien Chaisse and Philippe Gugler (eds), *Expansion of Trade and FDI in Emerging Asia: Strategic and Policy Challenges* (Routledge 2009) 84.

they applied; are they logical, defensible, and even-handed; and are there any gaps in the existing rules that ought to be filled? Although a number of different norms may apply to the SCEs' activities, in this chapter we will use a red line and explore this controversial issue, increasingly faced by countries and by private firms, of competing against SOEs and SWFs.

II. Legal and Economic Issues Raised by State-controlled Entities

The increasing presence of SWF investment in the European Union, as much as in the United States, has given rise to various concerns regarding sovereign investment in the EU market. Protectionist tendencies, already an area of concern in the European Union, could be further provoked by this rise in SWF and SOE activity. Owing to the geography and historical rivalry on the European continent, however, EU governments are perhaps more concentrated on Russia.[9] At the same time, the US market has remained a more attractive destination for foreign investors during the global financial crisis.[10]

These two variables explain to some extent the different perceptions on the two sides of the Atlantic and the differences in terms of regulatory approach.[11] The important difference lies in the fact that the European Union, in terms of both regulation and policy, declares, as a principle, that all restrictions on the movement of capital between Member States and between Member States and third countries are prohibited.[12] It thus extends the liberalization of capital movements to and from third countries whatever the investor class. This traditional positive perception of foreign investments explains to a large extent why the European Union has expressed a general trust with few concerns and has largely welcomed SOE and SWF investments over the past few years. Concerns, however, exist and they have contributed to generate tensions between national governments and the supranational level.

A. Defining the state-controlled entities

What definition should be used to identify whether or not a company is an SOE/SWF ... and what does that mean? Should it be an ownership test, or a 'control' test, or a 'sources of finance' test, or a 'Board of Directors' test, or any other test?

[9] Stephen Jen and Oliver Weeks, 'Celebrating the Birth of Russia's SWF' (Morgan Stanley Global Research 2008).

[10] The most vivid example is the flow of Chinese savings to finance the US' current account deficit. Backer (n 1).

[11] See Heike Schweitzer, 'Sovereign Wealth Funds: Market Investors or "Imperialist Capitalists"? The European Response to Direct Investment by Non-EU State-controlled Entities' (2011) 2 Eur YB Intl Econ L 79.

[12] This principle of free movement of capital between member states and between member states and third countries is subject to limited exceptions.

Should the threshold for determining whether a state owns or controls an enterprise be lower than the threshold applied in other contexts to determine whether one entity controls another? Should these concerns be raised if the SOE/SWF merely 'influence' an enterprise? How does one assess whether the motivations of a company are likely to be political rather than commercial?

Ownership and control can be extremely difficult to evaluate. The United States has grappled with, and continues to grapple with, these concepts in the context of pre-acquisition reviews of foreign investment from a national security perspective (under the Committee on Foreign Investment in the United States (CFIUS) regime). A question that received substantial debate when new rules for national security reviews were being debated in 2007–2008 was whether 'negative rights' should be viewed as conferring control. That is, if a given party (for example, the state) has a minority stake in a company but can block it from making certain key decisions,[13] should that party be viewed as having 'control' of the company (in the sense that it can force its will on the company by withholding consent to decisions viewed as critical by management)? If the state holds warrants or other contingent interests in a company that have not yet been exercised, does the state nevertheless have 'control'?

What exactly is an SWF is an essential question.[14] Paradoxically there are various definitions, ranging from a very broad definition (simply sovereign-owned and managed) to some which are more precise. One definition is 'a government investment vehicle which is funded by foreign exchange assets, and which manages those assets separately from official reserves'.[15] This would exclude Singapore's Temasek, because it is not funded by foreign exchange assets. Another decision, and one which has wider support, is that offered by the International Monetary Fund (IMF) in October 2008. In this definition there are three key elements: ownership (SWFs are owned by governments); investments in foreign financial assets; and objectives (wide range of investment strategies). This definition is authoritative, and strikes a good balance between precision and breadth.

How does one assess 'motivations'? Many would agree that the operations of SWFs are often obscure, with disclosure limited to regulatory compliance obligations imposed by host states. One can observe significant inconsistencies in SWF disclosures. The Norwegian SWF provides perhaps one of the few exceptions to this practice of limited disclosure. But overall, SWFs usually lack transparent structures and management processes that are domestically and internationally accountable. They operate in an opaque way, publishing neither statistics on their composition nor on their investments and strategies. For this reason, even the IMF has had to rely on a collection of estimates by private financial institutions to assess the size of these funds. But what information would be required

[13] e.g. acquiring or disposing of assets; entering into major contracts; issuing new capital.

[14] See Matthew Saxon, 'It's Just Business, or Is It?: How Business and Politics Collide with Sovereign Wealth Fund' (2009) 32 Hastings Intl & Comp L Rev 693.

[15] Press Release, US Department of the Treasury, Remarks by Acting under Secretary for International Affairs Clay Lowery on Sovereign Wealth Funds and the International Financial System (21 June 2007) <http://www.treasury.gov/press-center/press-releases/Pages/hp471.aspx> accessed 4 March 2016.

from SWFs? What level of details and, equally important, what is their frequency? What would governments do with this information? Have the Santiago Principles adopted in October 2008 had a noticeable impact on the transparency of SWF operations? A useful addition to future FTAs and bilateral investment treaties (BITs) agreements would be the requirement that the authorities collect company-level data of the sort gathered by the authors, and make it available for statistical analysis.

Moreover, is it possible to distinguish between the political rather than the commercial motivations of a company? One could think of some sectors, such as the armaments industry. In 2008, Dubai International Capital invested in Mauser (a German arms manufacturer) simply because it was a very profitable sector. Even the IMF principles stop short of requiring an explicit pledge not to invest for political ends. The principles include a call for funds to abide by local rules and regulations and to base their investments on financial and economic grounds. They simply call on funds to disclose any investment decisions 'subject to other than economic and financial considerations'.

The work done by the IMF and the release in October 2008 of the Generally Accepted Principles and Practices (GAPP) should also be mentioned. The GAPP seeks to establish a framework for SWFs that promotes operational independence in investment decisions, transparency, and accountability. They were designed largely to appease recipient country regulators, and they largely focus on state-level concerns: accountability, transparency, and economic investment purpose. The GAPP is not binding, but the shift to soft law may indicate that new rules, especially in a context of crisis, are difficult to adopt.

B. State capitalism and potential market distortions

The term 'state capitalism' means an economic system in which the state controls a substantial part of, or even all of capital, industry, and business.[16] It is therefore a command system where all or part of the means of production are legally the property of the state, or subject to its guidelines. Sometimes the means of production are in fact held, whether private or controlled, by the privileged class of the population that monopolizes political power. This expression appeared in the late nineteenth century, in the anti-capitalist movement, being presented as a negative perspective.[17] Its use has expanded during the twentieth century. There are differences, especially in terms of political affinity, as the plans are, or have been, state-capitalist. Among the schemes often analysed as such are: Germany in the First World War; the Soviet Union; and now

[16] There is growing literature on state capitalism and its implications for legal changes in China. See e.g., Li-wen Lin and Curtis J Milhaupt, 'We are the (National) Champions: Understanding the Mechanisms of State Capitalism in China' (2013) 65 Stan L Rev 697; Ming Du, 'China's State Capitalism and World Trade Law' (2014) 63 Intl Comp LQ 409. For a discourse on state capitalism in general, see e.g., Ian Bremmer, *The End of the Free Market: Who Wins the War Between States and Corporations?* (Portfolio 2010).

[17] See e.g., Mariana Pargendler and others, 'In Strange Company: The Puzzle of Private Investment in State-controlled Firms' (2013) 46 Cornell Intl LJ 569.

China, Cuba, and Algeria, from Houari Boumedienne.[18] There is no single definition of 'state capitalism'.[19] State capitalism is similar to state socialism (i.e. mostly adopted in some socialist states, for example China and Cuba). It is a form of capitalism in which the state owns and controls most of the means of production and capital. 'State capitalism' is usually described as an economic system in which commercial economic activity is undertaken by the state in the form of SOEs. Also, the management and organization of those SOEs' means of production are conducted in a capitalist manner. Ming Du stated that state capitalism is the Chinese economy system, which is fundamentally different from Western liberal market capitalism. Also, the substantial reason that state capitalism has been developed in China is because the Chinese government has transformed the country's economy from a command economy to a market economy (i.e. socialism with Chinese characteristics). The way that the Chinese government exercised 'state capitalism' is that they directly or indirectly controlled a large number of powerful SOEs, especially in strategic and key sectors (for example, China Sinopec).[20] Kratsas and Truby stated that the state direct capitalism is that the interests of sovereign and private investors clash, and they accept Keynes' maxim that 'international cash flows are always political', and many authors see this as problematic.[21]

Some of the writing about the rise of SCEs expresses a generic concern that because of state influence, these entities may be motivated by other than commercial interests, which may harm enterprises that compete with, buy from, or sell to them, or which may be generally more harmful to the public interest. However, a more detailed articulation of particular concerns is lacking, partly because there is an informational problem, due to a lack of transparency and clear communication on the part of the funds themselves. There are no exhaustive figures of foreign SCE activities in the United States or the EU common market.

In probing the adequacy or inadequacy of existing rules to address the perceived competitive distortions or other harms that SOEs/SWFs may cause, it is useful first to identify at the outset what those potential distortions and harms might be. Some that come to mind include:

- threats to national security as a result of the acquisition of critical assets by foreign SOEs or SWFs, because of a concern that the assets could be used to further foreign policy goals;
- a threat to cultural identity, to the extent that assets that are iconic or otherwise closely identified with national culture are owned by an enterprise that in turn is owned or controlled by a foreign sovereign;
- whether the SOE would become empowered to distribute scarce resources (for example, energy) in a country and use its power to 'pick favourites';

[18] Jinshan Hu, *Feizhoude Zhongguo Xingxiang* [African Images of China] (Renmin Chubanshe 2010) 197.

[19] Musacchio and Lazzarini (n 2) 2. See also Catherine P Mulder, 'State Capitalism vis-à-vis Private Communism' (2015) 27 Rethinking Marxism: J Econ Culture Soc 258.

[20] Du (n 16).

[21] Georges Kratsas and Jon Truby, 'Regulating Sovereign Wealth Funds to Avoid Investment Protectionism' (2015) 1 J Fin Reg 95.

- whether the SOE has privileged access to scarce resources (for example, land, water, energy) for its own use: the suspicion or concern that has been expressed about SWFs/SOEs is the risk that they would hoard resources and not exploit them in a manner consistent with usual commercial expectations;
- if an SOE obtains cheaper credit than a non-state-owned enterprise in like circumstances, and cheaper credit amounts to an implicit subsidy, the SOE might have an advantage both at home and abroad;
- whether the incoming SOE is exempt from tax, disclosure, and other regulatory requirements;
- where the SOE or SWF makes strategic investments to prop up national champions or others;
- whether an SOE has preferential access to the public procurement market;
- a concern that the fact of state ownership may cause an enterprise to be considered not 'in like circumstances' with other enterprises for the purposes of a national treatment (NT) analysis under investment treaties (see *UPS v Canada*).[22]

III. World Trade Organization Law Issues

In the sphere of international trade, there is a general presumption that trading enterprises will act on the basis of commercial considerations, and that, based on the theories of comparative advantage, they will expand their international trade in order to reap the benefits. However, a private firm, if it has significant power in a given market, may exercise this power in a way that distorts trade and thus causes economic detriment rather than benefit. Furthermore, governments can act in indirect ways to influence world trade in an uneconomic direction; for example, by acting through firms or enterprises to provide protection against imports or to advance exports, to the detriment of foreign producers.[23] Thus, the drafters of the General Agreement sought to place the state trading enterprise in the same competitive position—with regard to governmental support or protection—as the private firm. In other words, they sought to make state traders behave as private competitive traders, and thus to remove the potential for trade distortion offered by government involvement in an enterprise's decisions and activities.[24]

The results of the Uruguay Round of multilateral trade negotiations include the Understanding on the Interpretation of Article XVII of GATT 1994. One of

[22] *United Parcel Service of America Inc v Government of Canada*, UNCITRAL, 22 November 2002.

[23] See David M Blumental, 'Applying GATT to Marketizing Economies: The Dilemma of WTO Accession and Reform of China's State-owned Enterprises' (1999) 2 J Intl Econ L 113.

[24] See Julia Y Qin, 'WTO Regulation of Subsidies to State-owned Enterprises (SOEs)—A Critical Appraisal of the China Accession Protocol' (2004) 7 J Intl Econ L 843.

the main features of the Understanding is the 'working definition of State trading enterprise' contained in paragraph 2 of the text, which reads:

governmental and non-governmental enterprises, including marketing boards, which have been granted exclusive or special rights or privileges, including statutory or constitutional powers, in the exercise of which they influence through their purchases or sales the level or direction of imports or exports.[25]

A. The 'non-market economy' notion

In the particular situation of economies where the government has a complete or substantially complete monopoly of its trade and where all domestic prices are fixed by the state, GATT 1994 and the Agreement recognize that a strict comparison with home market prices may not be appropriate. Importing countries have thus exercised significant discretion in the calculation of normal value of products exported from non-market economies.[26]

In the trade law field, the classic 'non-market economy' (NME) obstacle used against China is well known. But are there other work-arounds emanating from the Anti-dumping or Subsidies and Countervailing Measures (SCM) Agreements? Already some countries have given China diplomatic/legal recognition as a market economy. Australia, New Zealand, and Chile are probably the only OECD Member countries to have done so, and we have seen, a number of work-arounds are employed there. They may be replicated elsewhere, and they will come more into focus given that the expiry of Article 15 of China's Accession Protocol is in 2016. And we must remember that China is not the only focus of NME rules in anti-dumping, with the Indian investigating authority having recently rejected Saudi Arabian prices in a petrochemical industry case on the basis of the state-regulated pricing of feedstocks.[27]

If the investigating authorities are no longer able to treat China as an NME, they will be more prone to using methodologies that mimic the NME methodology. Investigating authorities can, and frequently do, disregard transactions

[25] Three fundamental elements are identified in this 'working definition': (i) a governmental or non-governmental entity, including marketing boards; (ii) the granting to the enterprise of exclusive or special rights or privileges; and (iii) a resulting influence, through the enterprise's purchases or sales, on the level or direction of imports or exports. Particularly important in this definition is the phrase: 'in the exercise of which they influence through their purchases or sales the level or direction of imports or exports', because this goes to the heart of what the regulation of state trading in the WTO is aimed at: that is, the potentially distorting effects of the operations of STEs on trade. However, although this text provides considerable clarification of Article XVII, it still leaves room for differing interpretations of what is intended. Once again, it must be emphasized that an enterprise need not be state-owned, nor need it have a monopoly position, in order to be covered by art XVII and subject to WTO rules on STEs. The important criteria are that it enjoys exclusive or special rights or privileges, and that in the exercise of these rights and privileges it influences imports or exports by buying and selling activities.

[26] See Qin (n 24). See also Mitsuo Matsushita and others, *The World Trade Organization: Law, Practice, and Policy* (2nd edn, OUP 2006).

[27] See Mitsuo Matsushita, 'Some International and Domestic Antidumping Issues' (2010) 5(2) Asian J WTO & Intl Health L & Policy 249.

between affiliated parties in calculating anti-dumping duty margins. Thus, sales by an exporter in the home market to an affiliate in the target market are typically disregarded in favour of sales to the first unaffiliated party. Similarly, where a manufacturer in the home market purchases input materials from an affiliated party, the price(s) of those materials is (are) often disregarded in favour of some other metric.[28] Disregarding affiliated party transactions resembles the NME methodology, under which the nominal values of input materials and other cost elements are replaced by 'surrogate' values in deriving the benchmark prices ('normal value') to be compared to export sales prices. Thus, to the extent that an investigating authority treats China as a market economy, the result (as compared with NME treatment) might be diminished or negated altogether by treating various enterprises as 'affiliated' due to their common ownership by the state.

Other mechanisms have been used to override a perceived unfairness, or a perceived lack of commerciality, in the input prices paid by manufacturers/exporters. Although not limited to the SOE situation, to the extent that the presence of SOEs in a market is said to create a market distortion, these mechanisms impact mostly on them. Two examples come to mind: the 'particular market situation' wording of Article 2.2 of the Anti-dumping Agreement, and the requirement that financial accounts 'reasonably reflect' costs under Article 2.2.1.1.[29]

B. The notion of 'public body' construed by the DSB

Also in the trade field, the Appellate Body's decision in DS379 about the need to establish that an SOE carries out a public function before being able to label it as a 'public body', has opened up a whole new area of complication.[30] For example, if an SOE does not carry out a public function, but is nevertheless 'favoured' in some way or other because of the position of the government as its major or controlling shareholder, does it have a competitive advantage which is not 'market-oriented'? To what degree should trade competitors tolerate differences in the commercial settings of different economies with different political, cultural, and social systems?

It can be queried whether the Appellate Body's findings in DS379 really do complicate things much. It is important to distinguish between the situation in

[28] i.e., the prices of similar inputs purchased from unaffiliated parties, etc.

[29] See Julien Chaisse and Debashis Chakraborty, 'Normative Obsolescence of WTO Anti-Dumping Agreement—Topography of the Global Use and Misuse of Anti-dumping Measures' (2015) 5(1) Asian J Intl Law 3.

[30] Appellate Body Report, *United States—Definitive Anti-dumping and Countervailing Duties on Certain Products from China*, WT/DS379/AB/R, adopted 25 March 2011. This dispute concerned countervailing and anti-dumping duties simultaneously imposed by the United States on four products originating in China following concurrent countervailing duty and anti-dumping investigations. The United States began applying its countervailing duty legislation to imports from China in 2007, after the United States Department of Commerce (USDOC) determined that China's economy, albeit still not a market economy, had undergone sufficient economic reform as to enable the USDOC to identify and countervail subsidies granted by the Chinese government. In the four anti-dumping investigations, the USDOC treated China as an NME and it determined normal value by using prices in a surrogate country rather than Chinese domestic prices. China appealed

which the SOE is the allegedly subsidized entity and the situation in which the SOE is alleged to be the granter of subsidies. It is only in the latter context that the Appellate Body's findings in DS379 really come into play. In the former context, if the SOE has received a subsidy—i.e. it has been favoured in some way that amounts to a 'financial contribution' within the meaning of Article 1 of the SCM Agreement—and if the subsidy is 'specific' within the meaning of Article 2 of the SCM Agreement, presumably its exports will be subject to countervailing measures, just like exports of any other subsidised entity, or the subsidy will be vulnerable to challenge under Part III of the SCM Agreement.

Where the SOE is the granter of a financial contribution, the question is whether it is a 'public body' within the meaning of the SCM Agreement. But even if it is not a public body (for the reasons indicated by the Appellate Body in DS379),[31] a financial contribution it makes may still constitute a subsidy if the SOE has been entrusted or directed by a government to make the contribution. Perhaps the complication arises in the situation where an SOE is neither a public body nor a private body that is entrusted or directed to take particular action. Rather, it is simply providing to another entity what amounts to a 'financial contribution', and it is able to provide that contribution to the recipient at a relatively low cost by virtue of state ownership (for example, passing on its low cost of funds to the recipient).

IV. Competition Law Issues

While international trade has increased dramatically since 1990, the enforcement of competition law has remained primarily a domestic exercise. The increasingly cross-border dimension of business activities, together with the increase in the number of competition authorities, creates an additional complexity for cases with a multi-jurisdictional element. This complexity creates challenges for the effective and consistent enforcement of competition law.[32]

Competition law enforcement exists to preserve the integrity of free markets, undistorted by anti-competitive conduct. More vigorous competition has two main benefits. First, it protects consumers from companies that may, at times, seek or

certain of the panel's findings regarding the USDOC's determinations on 'public body', 'specificity', 'benefit benchmarks', and 'double remedies'.

[31] The Appellate Body upheld the panel's interpretation of art 14(d) of the SCM Agreement as allowing an investigating authority to reject in-country private prices if these are distorted due to the government's predominant role in the market, and it found that the panel properly concluded that, given the evidence of the Chinese government's predominant role as a supplier of hot-rolled steel, and having considered evidence of other factors, the USDOC could determine that private prices in China were distorted and could not be used as benchmarks for calculating the amount of the benefit. See ibid.

[32] See Mitsuo Matsushita and Julien Chaisse, 'Maintaining the WTO's Supremacy in the International Trade Order: A Proposal to Refine and Revise the Role of the Trade Policy Review Mechanism' (2013) 16(1) J Intl Econ L 9.

use market power to raise prices or reduce outputs. Second, it promotes productivity growth, largely by imposing stronger rivalry between companies to succeed in gaining the business of customers, which in turn leads to faster economic growth. The past decades have witnessed a rapid globalization of economic activity which has significantly changed the outlook of the world economy.[33] Globalization results in large economic benefits, but also raises challenges for competition authorities, who must respond to anti-competitive conduct and mergers whose effects are increasingly cross-border.

SOEs, also known as public enterprises, are owned by governments rather than by private investors. SOEs compete directly with private, profit-maximizing enterprises in many important markets. SOEs can have strong incentives to engage in anti-competitive activities that serve to expand the scale and scope of their operations. Competition law for SOEs, however, is a body of jurisprudence to which the US courts and legislators have made little direct contribution. In contrast, the European Commission's Deutsche Post decision in 2001 is an important step in the development of a competition law for SOEs.[34] In the purely competition sense, is government ownership of a foreign corporation of any relevance whatsoever? Do special rules and mechanisms exist in merger control laws that are either directly or tangentially referable to the set-up or behaviour of an SWF/SOE?

In this context we can look at how SOEs are treated by national competition authorities in jurisdictions such as the European Union, China, Russia, and Brazil. This is very important, for example, when ascertaining the extent to which an organization is subject to public procurement rules;[35] the demarcation between an organization performing an essential societal function and operating on a market for the purposes of state aid; and the turnover (revenues) of an organization for the purpose of assessing jurisdiction under merger control.[36]

[33] See Mitsuo Matsushita, 'Basic Principles of the WTO and the Role of Competition Policy' (2002) 3(4) J World Inv 565.

[34] Commission Decision of 25 July 2001 relating to a proceeding under Article 82 of the EC Treaty (COMP/C-1/36.915—Deutsche Post AG—Interception of cross-border mail), 2001 OJ (L 331) 40. The Commission found that Deutsche Post abused its dominant position in the German market for the delivery of international mail—thereby infringing art 82 of the EC Treaty—in four ways. Deutsche Post discriminated between different customers and refused to supply its delivery service unless an unjustified surcharge was paid. The price charged for the service was excessive and the behaviour of Deutsche Post limited the development of the German market for the delivery of international mail and of the UK market for international mail bound for Germany. In substance, the Decision concerning Deutsche Post AG established a yardstick for predatory prices in postal markets open to competition. This yardstick applies to all undertakings that have at their disposal resources from the statutory monopoly. See Mats Bergman, 'A Prohibition Against Losses? The Commission's Deutsche Post Decision' (2001) 22(8) Eur Comp L Rev 351. See also Phedon Nicolaides, 'Effective Competition in Network Industries: An Assessment of the Commission Decision 2001/354 Imposing a Fine on Deutsche Post for Abusing its Dominant Position in Parcel Delivery' (2001) 22(9) Eur Comp L Rev 390.

[35] See Mitsuo Matsushita, 'Major WTO Dispute Cases Concerning Government Procurement' (2006) 1 Asian J WTO & Intl Health L & Policy 299.

[36] Florian Stork, 'A Practical Approach to the New German Foreign Investment Regime—Lessons To Be Learned from Merger Control' (2010) 11 Ger LJ 260.

A. The merger control—getting the deal through

With regard to merger control, it is interesting to consider the clashes that some EU Member States have had with the European Commission when the former have sought to protect 'national champions', in particular because some 'national champions' in the utilities sector have been state-owned. The policy statements made by both sides of the argument in this context are helpful in considering the extent to which SOEs should be able to acquire actually or potentially competing businesses in other jurisdictions.

The railway industry in the European Union is a good example of how SOEs become involved in major infrastructure projects, some of which involve merger control review and clearance (for example, Eurostar trains between London and Paris/Brussels) and how the demarcation can be made between providing an infrastructure and operating a competitive market which uses that infrastructure (First Railway Package). This also raises the question of when state aid becomes anti-competitive.

A prototypical case was decided by the EU Court of Justice (ECJ) in the judgment C-274/06,[37] concerning a piece of Spanish legislation in the energy field known as Additional Provision 27 (also known as the 'anti-EDF' provision).[38] According to this, in the case of acquisition of control by a state-owned entity of a significant stake (i.e. more than three per cent) in a company operating in the Spanish energy market, the Council of Ministers had to authorize the exercise of the corresponding voting rights. Lacking the authorization, voting and other political rights could be exercised only up to, precisely, three per cent. The excuse for this piece of legislation was, in a nutshell, the security of energy supply in Spain. The ECJ declared this provision null and void on the basis of the EU rules governing the free movement of capital.[39]

B. The application of antitrust law to state-controlled entities

Antitrust laws are essentially a series of highly interpretable and ever-changing guidelines meant to encourage stable competition between businesses; in essence they are laws to protect against anti-competitive monopolists and conspiracies. However, it can probably be argued that the SCE nature of an investor is less relevant for the purposes of substantive antitrust analysis (i.e. whether the transaction will substantially lessen or prevent competition).[40] Where the SOE/SWF nature of

[37] Case C-274/06, *Comm'n v Kingdom of Spain*, 2008 E.R I-26.

[38] Supplementary Provision No 27 to Law 55/1999 of 29 December 1999 on fiscal, administrative, and social measures, in the version of that provision laid down in art 94 of Law 62/2003 of 30 December 2003. This law provides that in cases of direct or indirect acquisition or control by state companies of more than 3% of the equity or the voting rights in Spanish energy companies, voting rights attached to shares above that limit are subject to the prior authorization of Spain's Council of Ministers. The Commission considered these provisions incompatible with the Treaty and on 9 July 2003 sent Spain a reasoned opinion.

[39] *Comm'n v Kingdom of Spain* (n 37).

[40] See Angela Huyue Zhang, 'The Single-entity Theory: An Antitrust Time Bomb for Chinese State-owned Enterprises' (2012) 8 J Comp L & Econ 805.

an investor would 'bite' on the substantive side is that the investor (say, a Chinese SOE) would have attributed to it the market share and market presence of all other SOEs of that state. In the case of China (particularly in the natural resources area), for example, this could be material. SOEs from the same state may act independently in fact; however, such independence might be viewed with a degree of scepticism by antitrust regulators.

Using Canada as an example, there is no obvious competition theory or policy that the commercial orientation of an SOE is a factor in the antitrust analysis when evaluating a merger/take-over. Given the breadth of the Investment Canada Act (ICA)[41] and the ability of the Canadian Minister of Industry to step in and review and block an SOE transaction if it is not of net benefit to Canada (or threatens national security), the Canadian Commissioner of Competition is more likely than not to perform a traditional antitrust review (based on the classic principles of market power, market share, substantial lessening or prevention of competition, etc.) and defer to the Minister of Industry as to matters that relate to the commercial/political orientation of the investor.

Nevertheless, principles and concerns that could be taken into account in competition law merger control analysis include:

- Does its SCE status make it more likely that it would not lower or raise prices in circumstances where a non-SCE would?
- Do direct or indirect subsidies give the SCE an unfair advantage?
- Might the objective or intention of a foreign-owned SCE give rise to anti-competitive or disruptive effects (for example, hoarding, flooding the market, output restriction, discriminatory selling, etc.)?

The SCE nature of an investor also has procedural implications in Canada, for example; this is because the relationship to the state often results in a higher likelihood that formal competition notifications must be made because all of the other SOEs emanating from the same state are deemed to be 'affiliates', thereby usually resulting in one of the key applicable turnover/asset thresholds being met.

V. International Investment Law Issues

Such an evolution is generating a number of political and economic problems that the law has to address. The SCEs' transnational economy raises concerns because it highlights the importance of state activity in the global economy, which is perceived as being detrimental to the role of market forces.[42] The legal analysis has

[41] Investment Canada Act, RSC 1985, c 28 (1st Supp) (Canada). Non-Canadians who acquire control of an existing Canadian business or who wish to establish a new unrelated Canadian business are subject to this Act, and they must submit either a Notification or an Application for Review.

[42] See generally Adrian Wooldridge, 'The Visible Hand' (2012) *The Economist* 4.

already explored the ramifications in the trade world.[43] The issue is far more serious when one looks at the international capital trends and prospects. SCEs make significant investment across borders, which allows them to control local assets. The reality of foreign investment, and the idea that foreigners may control national assets, has given rise to a number of 'protectionist reactions'.[44] There are fears that SCEs may not make investment decisions based on economic reasons, but instead they may choose to invest for political purposes.[45] Further, most countries that have set up SCEs are located in the developing world, which ultimately may result in a politicization of capital flows vis-à-vis the SCEs.[46] The legal problems raised by the SCEs' investments will become more acute because, as a result of the financial crisis and the ensuing recession, the need for international investment in the United States or the European Union will also continue to grow, and this will inevitably increase the probability that SCEs will face obstacles on foreign markets and hence will resort to international dispute settlement to resolve this new kind of dispute.

However, the legal situation is complex. Although foreign direct investment (FDI) has increased significantly over the past two decades, outpacing the already significant expansion of trade during the same period, the current international legal framework for SCE investments is highly fragmented.[47] The current framework consists of a wide variety of national and international rules and principles that differ in form, strength, and coverage.[48] The result is an increasingly complex international setting for international investment in which foreign investors can benefit from rights that ensure their investments a great protection. Along with an increase in the number of international investment agreements (IIAs), the past

[43] See the excellent analysis by Du (n 16) (analysing how China's practice of state capitalism challenges the world trading system and how WTO law, as interpreted by WTO panels and the WTO Appellate Body, addresses these challenges).

[44] Maurizia De Bellis, 'Global Standards for Sovereign Wealth Funds: The Quest for Transparency' (2011) 1 Asian J Intl L 349.

[45] Ronald J Gilson and Curtis J Milhaupt, 'Economically Benevolent Dictators: Lessons for Developing Democracies' (2011) 59 Am J Comp L 227.

[46] See Michael C Jensen, 'Agency Costs of Free Cash Flow, Corporate Finance, and Takeovers' (1986) 76 Am Econ Rev 323, 323. For discussions of the empire-building incentives of China's SOE managers, see Angela Huyue Zhang, 'Foreign Direct Investment from China: Sense and Sensibility' (2014) 34 Nw J Intl L Bus 395.

[47] See Julien Chaisse and Christian Bellak, 'Navigating the Expanding Universe of International Treaties on Foreign Investment: Creation and Use of a Critical Index' (2015) 18 J Intl Econ L 79.

[48] The North American Free Trade Agreement (NAFTA) is a prime example of an agreement with a wide scope covering investment, since it includes three members. The Trans-Pacific Partnership (TPP) is another example of an ambitious trade pact including investment matters with twelve members. On the TPP, see Julien Chaisse, 'The Regulation of Investment in the Transpacific Partnership—Towards a Defining International Agreement for the Asia-Pacific Region' in N Jansen Calamita and Mavluda Sattorova (eds), *The Regionalization of Investment Treaty Arrangements* (British Institute of International 2015) 270. These separate investment chapters in preferential trade agreements (PTAs) are comparable, on average, to self-standing BITs. They can include both rules on investment liberalization (non-discrimination safeguards) and investment protection (substantive standards of treatment afforded by the host state to the foreign investor or investment). United Nations Conference on Trade and Development, 'World Investment Report 2014—Investing in the SDGs: An Action Plan' (United Nations 2014) 22–5.

decade has also witnessed an exponential surge in investment disputes between foreign investors and host country governments,[49] and one can anticipate a growing number of cases brought by SCEs before international investment arbitration. It is precisely this legal scenario that the present chapter wants to explore.

A. Foreign investment in services—the role of the GATS

Governments and stakeholders are sounding the alarm regarding SCEs, claiming that the existing rules are not adequate to address the harm that SCEs are uniquely capable of doing because of their state ownership and control. Are they right? How do WTO rules impact on countries that seek to set up obstacles to trade and investment by SCEs? If there are WTO rules that interfere in this, are there 'work-arounds' that countries are using to bypass the rules? How important are NT obligations in preventing discrimination against SCEs? Does the fact that a supplier or investor is state-owned defeat 'likeness' for purposes of a NT analysis?

Taking the perspective that SOEs/SWFs are unique actors that must be governed by special rules, one might consider the role of Article XVII of the GATT 1994 (together with the Understanding on Interpretation of Article XVII), which is meant to police certain conduct of state trading enterprises. Does it work? Do the panel and Appellate Body reports in *Canada—Wheat* (DS276)[50] point out gaps in Article XVII?

In the investment field, there not being a 'multilateral agreement on investment' in place, one might think that the WTO is powerless. Is that a correct perception? How can the WTO Agreements be employed in an investment context, with what implications for countries seeking to resist SOE/SWF investment? Do BITs and FTAs have a role to play, and can we see any evidence of their intrusion into business undertaken by SOEs and SWFs up to now? The patchwork of rules or principles (WTO, IMF, BITs, PTAs (preferential trade agreements)) is not satisfactory. Is the development of new rules inevitable, to ensure greater coherence? Policymakers will have to

[49] Arbitral panels are charged with the task of applying the rules of IIAs in specific cases, an often-complex process given the broad and sometimes ambiguous terms of these arrangements. See generally Kenneth J Vandevelde, 'A Brief History of International Investment Agreements' (2005) 12 UC Davis J Intl L Poly 157, 173–5 (noting that foreign investors are increasingly resorting to the mechanism of international arbitration for resolving their disputes with the government of a host country). On the emerging issue of sovereign debt restructure by international tribunals, see Julien Chaisse, '*Greek Debt Restructuring, Abaclat v. Argentina and Investment Treaty Commitments*: the Impact of International Investment Agreements on The Greek' in Chin Leng Lim and Bryan Mercurio (eds), *International Economic Law after the Global Crisis—A Tale of Fragmented Discipline* (CUP 2015) 306–28.

[50] According to the United States, the actions of Canada and the Canadian Wheat Board (an entity enjoying exclusive rights to purchase and sell Western Canadian wheat for human consumption) related to export of wheat were inconsistent with paragraphs 1(a) and 1(b) of art XVII of GATT 1994. However, the panel found that the United States failed to establish its claim that Canada had breached its obligations under art XVII:1 of the GATT 1994 with respect to the Canadian Wheat Board. The Appellate Body upheld the panel's conclusion in this regard. See Penal Report, *Canada—Measures Relating to Exports of Wheat and Treatment of Imported Grain*, WT/DS276/R, 6 April 2004 and Appellate Body Report, *Canada—Measures Relating to Exports of Wheat and Treatment of Imported Grain*, WT/DS276/AB/R, 30 August 2004.

re-work all these in order to ensure the security of market access for SWFs and a set of conditions that investors would need to satisfy in order to benefit from the said access.[51]

It should be borne in mind that the disciplines on investment are not completely foreign to the WTO regime. There is little doubt that WTO GATS deals mostly with the investment issues of all the existing WTO agreements. Although GATS does not deal officially with investment, it covers FDI through its commercial presence mode of supply. The establishment of a commercial presence relates substantially and directly to investment. As long as an SWF decides to invest in a WTO country Member and if it is in the services sector, GATS is a relevant legal instrument.

The GATS does not set out any operational conditions directly. The host countries continue regulating foreign investment through their domestic legislation and not by directly imposing obligations on foreign investors in BITs and FTAs. Nevertheless, there are some general obligations within GATS that certainly affect the investment operational conditions. Such obligations are domestic regulation, recognition, monopolies and exclusive service suppliers, and business practice obligations.

But it is only by reference to a country's schedule, and (where relevant) its most-favoured-nation (MFN) exemption list, that it can be seen to which services sectors and under what conditions the basic principles of the GATS (market access, NT, and MFN treatment) apply within that country's jurisdiction.

Under the GATS, countries negotiate schedules of commitments, which are in effect legally binding promises to allow foreign investment in specific sectors subject to specific conditions. Can SCEs use these commitments to force countries to remain open to any FDI? This raises two issues. First, can a WTO Member prohibit in their commitments Mode 3 foreign investments made by public entities, specifically? It would require further investigation but it seems that the United States and Canada (at least) did indicate in their Mode 3 commitments that some foreign public investments would be restricted. Second, it should be recognized that GATS provides only for state-to-state dispute settlement without access to compensation. This is probably another limit to the possibility of controlling national protectionism on the basis of the GATS.

National investment legislation based on national security, which may block, impede, undo, or in some other way adversely affect investments made by SWFs, might be difficult to challenge before the WTO dispute settlement body (DSB). Such domestic action would not be in itself a violation of its GATS Mode 3 commitments. The country may indeed rely on GATS Article XIVbis in order to benefit from the 'security exception'. GATS Article XIVbis is designed to preserve Members' freedom of action in areas relating to national defence and security. It seems from WTO case law that trade liberalization and international regulation do not prevail over Members' vital interests in maintaining the core of sovereignty

[51] See Julien Chaisse and others, 'Deconstructing Service and Investment Negotiating Stance: A Case Study of India at WTO GATS and Investment Fora' (2013) 14 J World Inv & Trade 44.

and they cannot restrain Members' freedom to preserve and defend their very existence.

Another relevant WTO agreement might be the Agreement on Trade-related Investment Measures (TRIMS). Manufacturing investment is covered at least to some extent by that Agreement, but this coverage is relatively limited.

B. Treaties on foreign investment

BITs and FTAs may have a role to play to the extent that they impose obligations at the 'pre-establishment' phase of investment—that is, to the extent they commit the parties not to engage in nationality-based discrimination at the stage where a foreign investor is seeking to make an investment. In the absence of pre-establishment coverage, a host state might keep a would-be investor out for any reason at all, including the perceived risk of foreign state ownership of particular assets. But, even to the extent that a BIT/FTA contains pre-establishment obligations, is it still possible for a host state to discriminate against an SCE on the grounds that state ownership or control renders the SCE not 'in like circumstances' with the domestic investors that might be considered comparable in all other respects?

On the distinction between the admission clause model and pre-establishment rights under BITs, the latter is clearly the model that is more likely to give rights to SWFs. However one should not exclude admission disputes. For example, most BITs concluded by UAE follow this model. Denial of admission disputes[52] could be submitted to international arbitration. This would give the SWFs a chance to challenge domestic restrictions before international arbitrators.

The 'like circumstances' issue also may be considered from the opposite perspective. Consider the situation where a foreign investor seeks to make or has made an investment in a host state in a sector where it is competing with an SOE of the host state. To the extent that the SOE may be accorded more favourable treatment than the foreign investor, would the fact of state ownership defeat a claim of breach of the NT obligation due to the foreign investor not being 'in like circumstances' with the would-be comparator?

The scope of the 'essential security' provision that typically is included in BITs and FTAs should also be considered. Could it be used to justify virtually any act discriminating against conduct by a SCE? In this regard, there is a trend in the United States to 'strengthen' the 'self-judging' character of the essential security provision.[53]

It might be argued that BITs and FTAs can be applied, but that they suffer from the same shortcoming as the WTO: namely, the national security exception. As it is broadly defined, governments remain free to screen SWF investments. Basically, the lack of clear international definition of national security shifts the problem to

[52] See *Generation Ukraine, Inc v Ukraine*, ICSID Case No ARB/00/9, 16 September 2003.

[53] See e.g., the United States–Peru Trade Promotion Agreement, 12 April 2006, art 22.2(b) and footnote 2, stating that if the essential security provision is invoked in either state–state or investor–state dispute settlement, the panel or tribunal 'shall find that the exception applies'.

the domestic level. BITs and FTAs have a role to play, but they probably favour governments and not investors. If we look at the US example, since 1988, foreign companies have sent the CFIUS several thousand notifications of intent to purchase US companies, but CFIUS has only investigated a few, and, of these, it has blocked only a minority.[54] However, the small number of CFIUS notifications that led to investigation, formal withdrawal, or presidential decision is actually misleading. This is because there are an unknown number of decisions made by notifiers and by prospective notifiers not to proceed, after informal consultation or before investigation, given the conditions imposed or the likely outcome.

C. The domestic regulatory layer: the national regimes

Canada's International Compliance Association (ICA) is very exceptional in that it is designed specifically to deal with the regulation of foreign investment.[55] Australia's FIRB regime is similar, but most states do not have a similar law. The ICA also now has a national security review mechanism (similar to the United States' CFIUS regime),[56] which is in addition to the pre-existing foreign investment review rules.[57] The ICA gives the Canadian government the power to review, approve, and block acquisitions of control by non-Canadians, including SOEs and SWFs. The national security review component of the ICA was added in 2009. The ICA therefore now has two different review regimes: a net benefit review, and a national security review. Under the ICA, the Canadian Minister of Industry has specifically published guidelines as to how SOEs/SWFs will be dealt with ('Guidelines—Investment by State-owned Enterprises—Net Benefit Assessment' or 'the Canadian SOE Guidelines').[58] The Canadian SOE Guidelines provide for a very broad definition of an SOE; namely, an enterprise that is owned or controlled directly or indirectly by a foreign government. The

[54] See Committee on Foreign Investment in the United States, CY 2013, Annual Report to Congress (2015).

[55] Investment Canada Act.

[56] The national security review process in the United States—often referred to as the Exon–Florio or CFIUS review process, after the relevant authorizing statute and enforcement agency, respectively—has existed for decades. It originally focused, at least in practice, on the acquisition by foreign companies of US businesses directly or indirectly supplying the US Department of Defense, but especially after the 9/11 terrorist attacks, the concept of national security—and therefore the types of transactions subject to review under the regime—was broadened by statute and in practice. Today, the national security review process can be an important part of many transactions, even though it remains voluntary. Examples of industries in which notifications under the regime have been submitted include computers; network security; cyber systems; energy (development and transport); semiconductors; aerospace; telecommunications; optics; robotics; mining and natural resources; plastics and rubber; automotive; financial services; coatings and adhesives; and chemicals and steel.

[57] See Joel Slawotsky, 'The Regulation of Sovereign Wealth Fund Investments in the United States' (2010) 29(10) Bank Fin Serv Poly Rep 1.

[58] These following guidelines were issued by the Minister responsible for the administration of the Investment Canada Act (the 'Act'), under the authority of section 38 of the Act, to inform investors of certain procedures that will be followed in the administration of the review and monitoring provisions of the Act where the investors are state-owned enterprises (SOEs).

definitions that trigger whether the net benefit review or the national security review apply are technical, but once the Canadian government has jurisdiction under the ICA, the level of discretion that can be exercised is extensive and the broad definition cited above would probably catch any SOE or SWF. Note that under the 'net benefit test', in Canada, the definition of a non-Canadian is a *de jure* test, generally focused on the 'voting shares' of the entity. Accordingly, once an entity is non-Canadian as a matter of law, the officials have jurisdiction. Under the national security regime the officials would also have the power to declare a *de jure* 'Canadian' entity to be non-Canadian 'if after consideration any information and evidence submitted by or on behalf of the entity or otherwise made available to the Minister ..., the Minister is satisfied that the entity is controlled in fact by one or more non-Canadians'.[59] Therefore, the approach in Canada to foreign investment is one of wide discretion on the part of the officials; they have significant latitude in their approach.

In the UK, corporate mergers and acquisitions (M&As) can, in principle, be reviewed for the purpose of protecting investors and ensuring fair competition through the Enterprise Act of 2002.[60] A merger situation can be considered under the competition legislation if either or both of the following tests are satisfied: (i) an acquisition of a UK enterprise valued in excess of £70 million; or (ii) the resulting combined business that will account for more than twenty-five per cent of a supply market within the UK or a substantial part of it. The substantive test applied to the merger is whether it may be expected to result in a substantial lessening of competition as a result of the transaction.[61] The government can intervene in M&As in areas of national security and the media if the acquisition is deemed to be against the public interest.[62] Among many other things,[63] the Enterprise Act 2002 makes the UK Competition Commission determinative in merger cases and in market investigations—which replace the complex monopoly investigations established under the Fair Trading Act 1973—and it changes the substantive question for these investigations. While

[59] See Investment Canada Act s 26 (2.11).

[60] Enterprise Act 2002. For a commentary, see Cosmo Graham, 'The Enterprise Act 2002 and Competition Law' (2004) 67 Mod L Rev 273.

[61] See Graham (n 60) 274.

[62] Enterprise Act 2002 (The statutory provisions for the UK's merger regime are set out in Part 3, Section 58). The Act allows for the Government to amend this list of public interest considerations, to add further categories. This was done in October 2008, when Lloyds' takeover bid for Halifax Bank of Scotland (HBOS) raised controversies in the UK. See Steve Slater and Myles Neligan, 'Doubts Raised Over Lloyds Offer to Acquire HBOS' (*New York Times*, 18 September 2008). The Government presented an Order to add the category in 'the interest of maintaining the stability of the UK financial system'. See Enterprise Act 2002 (Specification of Additional Section 58 Consideration) Order 2008, SI 2008/2645, which added this category to the list in s 58 of the 2002 Act. Under s 42(3) of the Act, the Government issued an 'intervention notice', confirming its intention to amend the Act in this way, and empowering it to instruct the Office of Fair Trading to report on its assessment of the merger to the Secretary of State (Press Notice Department for Business, Enterprise & Regulatory Reform, 18 September 2008).

[63] Daniel Prentice, 'Bargaining in the Shadow of the Enterprise Act of 2002' (2004) 5 Eur Bus Org LR 153, 153–58.

the inquiry used to be whether particular matters operate or might operate against the public interest,[64] the Enterprise Act of 2002 changes the inquiry to turn on one of four tests. The first is a *qualified public interest test*, which applies in cases that raise specific public interest issues (for example, national security or medial public interest).[65] The second is a *test of prejudice in the context of water enterprises*; this applies to the Office of Water Supply's ability to make comparisons between water enterprises in the context of mergers between water companies.[66] The third test is a *substantial lessening of competition test*, and it applies to all the other mergers that are not covered by the first two tests.[67] The final test is an *adverse effects on competition test*, and it applies in market investigations where it is believed that market features have an adverse effect on competition.[68] Even if traditionally more liberal than continental Europe, the UK, through its Chancellor, Alistair Darling at the time of writing this chapter, supported the pursuit of the G7 to toughen its stands towards SWFs.[69] Darling warned foreign governments that the UK would not tolerate politically motivated investments in key UK companies. These comments were intended as a warning to Russia that the UK would not tolerate Russia's state-owned energy company taking a stake in Centrica, the majority shareholder of British Gas.[70] The Russian state-owned gas and oil conglomerate, GazProm, that already supplies around a quarter of EU gas demand and has re-acquired most of the pipelines running from Central Asia to Europe, would not be a welcome bidder for the UK gas grid operator Centrica.

In 2004, France modified its Monetary and Financial Code.[71] The Article L 151-3 strictly limits the field of control to the reasons expressly indicated in Article 346 of the TFEU (national defence)[72] and Article 65-1 (public order and public security). Following the 2005 rumour of a takeover of Danone by American company PepsiCo,[73] the French Economy Minister announced the publication

[64] Enterprise Act 2002 (Specification of Additional Section 58 Consideration) Order 2008.

[65] Enterprise Act 2002, s 58(A)–(C).

[66] ibid s 89(1).

[67] ibid ss 47, 63.

[68] ibid.

[69] Elliot Larry, 'Chancellor Backs G7 Move to Get Tough on Sovereign Wealth Funds' (*Guardian*, 20 October 2007) <http://www.theguardian.com/politics/2007/oct/20/1> accessed 4 March 2016.

[70] Michael Harrison, 'Could Russia's Gazprom Go to National Grid? It's Not Quite as Far-Fetched as It May Seem' (*The Independent*, 26 January 2007) <http://www.independent.co.uk/news/business/comment/michael-harrisons-outlook-could-russias-gazprom-go-for-national-grid-its-not-quite-as-farfetched-as-it-may-seem-433748.html> accessed 4 March 2016.

[71] Loi 2004-1343 du 9 décembre 2004 de simplification du droit [Law 2004-1343 of 9 December 2004 on the Simplification of the Law], Journal Officiel de la République Française [JO] [Official Gazette of France], 10 December 2004, 20875.

[72] Consolidated Versions of the Treaty on European Union and the Treaty on the Functioning of the European Union (TFEU), 9 May 2008, 2008 OJ (C115) 47, art 346 stipulating that:

> [A]ny Member State may take such measures as it considers necessary for the protection of the essential interests of its security which are connected with the production of or trade in arms, munitions and war material; such measures shall not adversely affect the conditions of competition in the internal market regarding products which are not intended for specifically military purposes.

[73] Carol Matlack, 'Could PepsiCO Digest Danone?' (*Bloomberg Business*, 21 July 2005) <http://www.bloomberg.com/bw/stories/2005-07-20/could-pepsico-digest-danone> accessed 10 March 2016.

of a Decree allowing French authorities to control foreign inward investments in France. Decree 2005-1739 delimits the sectors concerned and ensures full respect for the EU principle of proportionality.[74] For the purposes of the Decree, an *investment* is defined as: (i) acquiring control, within the meaning of Article L 233-3 of the Commercial Code, a company whose headquarters is in France; (ii) to either directly or indirectly acquire all or part of an industry of a company whose headquarters is in France; and (iii) or crosses the threshold of 33.33 per cent of direct or indirect ownership of the capital or voting rights of a company whose headquarters is based in France.[75] Decree 2005-1739 introduces the disparate treatment of investments on the basis of the origin of the investment—i.e. investments of member states versus third-country investments. The scope of this authorization procedure is more extensive for investments originating from third countries—this is possible under Article 64 of the Treaty—as this measure existed prior to 31 November 1993, when the Maastricht Treaty came into force.[76] However, because indirect investments are also subject to authorization, the procedure foreseen for third-country investments could also create a restriction on investments by companies which are legally established in the European Union, but which have shareholders established in third countries. This difference in treatment, which is permitted by the rules of the WTO and TFEU Article 64, leads to a continuation of the previously applicable regime for operations originating in third countries, but with greater precision in the field of application.[77] For EU investors, on the other hand, only those operations leading to the effective transfer of a sensitive activity will be concerned. The objective is clear: France can oppose the relocation of activities or product stocks (for example, vaccines needed in case of a bio-terrorist attack) essential to its security or defence. Moreover, Decree 2005-1739 sets out in Article R 153-1 a clear list of eleven sectors which are considered strategic, and in which investment can be subject to authorization.[78] The national security rationale for this list is quite clear, although the Decree has not been formally applied so

[74] Décret 2005-1739 du 30 décembre 2005 réglementant les relations financières avec l'étranger et portant application de l'article L 151-3 (V) du code monétaire et financier [Decree 2005-1739 of 30 December 2005 Regulating Financial Relations with Foreign Countries and Implementing Article L 151-3 (V) of the Monetary and Financial Code], Journal Officiel de la République Française [JO] [Official Gazette of France], 31 December 2005, 20779. For discussion, see Backer (n 1).

[75] ibid chs 1–3.

[76] Treaty Establishing the European Economic Community (EEC Treaty), 25 March 1957, 298 UNTS 3, 4 Eur YB 412.

[77] See Simon Lester and others, *World Trade Law: Text, Materials and Commentary* (Hart Publishing 2008) 633–35.

[78] The decree lists a total of twelve strategic sectors: money gambling and casino activities; private security services; research, development, or production of pathogens or toxic substances for unlawful use or terrorist activities; wire tapping and mail interception equipment; testing and certification of the security of information technology products and systems; goods or services related to the information security systems of companies managing critical infrastructure; dual-use (civil and military) items and technologies; cryptology services; activities of firms entrusted with national defence secrets; research, produce, or trade in weapons; munitions, and explosive substances intended for military purposes; any business supplying the French defence ministry with any of the goods or services described above.

far.[79] After an initial warning,[80] the Commission has formally requested that France amend the Decree to bring it in line with the governing EU treaties as they apply to authorization procedures for foreign investments in delineated sectors and activities that could affect public policy, public security, or national defence.[81] The Commission considers Decree 2005-1739's restriction on investment as 'incompatible with the free movement of capital and the freedom of establishment'.[82] The formal request sent in October 2006 signalled the start of an infringement procedure[83] that has not been continued by the Commission. In substance, the Commission questioned whether the decree respected the free circulation of capital and the freedom of establishment within the European Union because it subjects non-EU investors to a more restrictive approval regime. More precisely, the European Commission expressed concerns,[84] which have been ignored by the French government until now, that some of the provisions of this Decree could discourage investment from other Member States, in contravention of EU Treaty rules on the free movement of capital (Article 63) and the right of establishment (Article 42). These additional requirements on European companies owned or controlled by third-country investors would also contravene the principle of Article 47 (formerly Article 48) that companies established in Member States should be treated as nationals of such Member States.

The ownership structure of corporations in the Deutscher Aktien IndeX (DAX)—a blue chip stock market index comprised of thirty major German corporations that trade on the Frankfurt Stock Exchange—demonstrates Germany's openness to foreign investments, including those by SWFs. Foreign investors are involved in many DAX companies, and sovereign funds from Kuwait and Dubai are shareholders in leading DAX companies like Daimler and Deutsche Bank.[85]

[79] In 2010, the US Danaher made a bid to acquire the French company Ingenico. Ingenico generally provides payment-processing systems but also works in biometrics data encryption for Safran, which is a French conglomerate involved in defence, aerospace propulsion and equipment, and security. In 2010, the company Ingenico was said to be strategic by the French Government, who did not apply, but threatened to make use of the 2005 Decree. Ultimately, Ingenico turned down the €1.44 billion Danaher bid. See Ben Hall, 'Danaher Move for Ingenico Blocked' (*Financial Times*, 19 December 2010) <http://www.ft.com/cms/s/2/0bfaefbe-0bc7-11e0-a313-00144feabdc0.html> accessed 4 March 2016.

[80] Press Release, European Commission, Free Movement of Capital: Commission Scrutinises French Law Establishing Authorisation Procedure for Foreign Investments in Certain Sectors (4 April 2006) (Press Release No IP/06/438).

[81] Press Release, European Commission, Free Movement of Capital: Commission Calls on France to Modify its Legislation Establishing an Authorisation Procedure for Foreign Investments in Certain Sectors of Activity (21 October 2006) (Press Release No IP/06/1353).

[82] ibid.

[83] Infringement actions are provided for under Article 258 of the TFEU. They may be applied by the Commission against a Member State whenever the Commission is of the opinion that the Member State is in breach of its obligations under Union law. For further elaboration, see Jan-Krysztof Dunin-Wasowicz, 'The Transparency Regulation in Context: A Proxy for Legitimacy or an Instrument of Regulatory Practice?' (2010) 16 Colum J Eur L 465, 489–90.

[84] See Press Release, European Commission (n 81).

[85] Jochen Möebert and Patrick Tydeck, 'Power and Ownership Structures among German Companies—a Network Analysis of Financial Linkages' (Darmstadt Discussion Papers in Economics No 35974, Darmstadt Technical University, Institute of Economics (VWL) 2007), 7 and Figure no 10.

However, in Germany there is a growing concern that a foreign SCE could decide to purchase a large German company such as Deutsche Telecom, Deutsche Bank, or Deutsche Bahn.[86] Although the above attest to the recognition of the importance of national security in the economic realm, this has not led to further protectionist measures. Stork reports as of mid-2010 that German government officials appear troubled by a number of diverse issues and recent developments including: (i) the ability of SWFs to leverage cash to make large acquisitions; (ii) a potential indirect takeover of one of Germany's largest banks by a foreign government; (iii) state-controlled investors buying small engineering companies to siphon off intellectual property; and (iv) national security concerns that may arise if parts of the German infrastructure are acquired by political investors rather than investors driven by commercial imperatives. In 2008, the Cabinet of Germany's Bundesministerium fur Wirtschaft und Technologie [Federal Ministry of Economics and Technology] (BMWi) issued a proposed amendment to the Außenwirtschaftsgesetzes und der Außenwirtschaftsverordnung [Foreign Trade Act and Foreign Trade Regulation] (FTA). The amendment, which was subsequently accepted by the German Parliament,[87] is aimed at protecting strategic national industries from unwanted foreign takeovers. As amended in 2009, the FTA vests Germany's federal government with the power to veto any investment from non-EU or European Free Trade Association countries[88] amounting to twenty-five per cent or more of a company's stakes if it deems that 'public security' or 'public order' is at risk.[89] Based on the US model, Germany's plans could lead to further attempts across the Member States aimed at blocking foreign investment incursions into sensitive industries. The US inspiration is obvious in the German pre-notification procedure. Foreign investors can pre-notify the German administration, on a voluntary basis, before an intended acquisition. The administration can then clear the acquisition and provide a level of legal certainty to the investor. Under Germany's proposals, 'public order and security' are the principal criteria for triggering a review of foreign groups' investment plans. Within Germany there seems to be a slight contradiction between private and public interests. German business associations—Deutscher Industrie- und Handelskammertag (Germany's International Chamber of Commerce) as well

[86] 'Chinesen wollen die Deutsche Bahn [Chinese Want the German Railways]' (*Die Zeit*, 4 September 2008) <http://www.zeit.de/2008/37/Macher-und-Maerkte/seite-2> accessed 4 March 2016.

[87] For the law, see Dreizehntes Gesetz zur Änderung des Außenwirtschaftsgesetzes und der Außenwirtschaftsverordnung vom [Thirteenth Law Amending the Foreign Trade and Payments Act], 18 April 2009, BGBL I at 1150 (Germany), <http://www.hohmann-partner.com/rechtsvorschriften/2010/awg_englisch-2009.pdf> accessed 23 April 2016. For a statement from the Ministry of Economy and Technology, see Press Release, Bundesministerium fur Wirtschaft und Technologie [Federal Ministry of Economic and Technology (Germany)], 'Kabinett beschließt 13 Gesetz zur Änderung des Außenwirtschaftsgesetzes und der Außenwirtschaftsverordnung [Cabinet Approves Thirteenth Act Amending the Foreign Trade Act and Foreign Trade Regulation]' (*Bundesministerium für Wirtschaft und Energie*, 8 August 2008) <http://www.bmwi.de/BMWi/Navigation/Presse/pressemitteilungen,did=266018.html> accessed 4 March 2016. For analysis of the Act, see generally Stork (n 36).

[88] The European Fair Trade Association (EFTA) is comprised of Iceland, Liechtenstein, Norway, and Switzerland.

[89] Thirteenth Law Amending the Foreign Trade and Payments Act, s 7 sub-s 1 art 4.

as the Bundesverband der Deutschen Industrie [Federation of German Industries] (BDI)—did not support the government decision, and they expressed doubts that the decision is alleged to go against EU rules on the free movement of capital.[90] The BDI insists that the law is in breach of EU Treaty rules on the free movement of capital (Article 63) and the right of establishment (Article 42), which it interprets as being necessarily applied equally to EU and non-EU investors. The BDI further argues that the FTA's definition of national security is too broad.[91] In 2014, the Economy Minister insisted that the mechanism would be used only in 'extremely rare' cases and that 'the majority of foreign investments won't be affected'.[92] Germany is and 'remains open to foreign investment'.[93] The government further argues that the law merely brings Germany in line with existing legislation in France, the UK, and the United States.[94] In other words, just as other countries have already done, Germany is creating governmental means of oversight for the few exceptional cases, and to rule out a possible threat to national security interests. Investment protectionism or an overall rejection of investments by sovereign funds, now and in the future, will not and cannot occur in Germany.

VI. Conclusion

The present chapter did not intend to provide definite answers but, rather, to shed light on a number of specific legal questions which should constitute the backbone of an emerging international law and policy for SCEs. First, some BITs and FTAs contain exceptions to the investment NT obligation for (i) government procurement; and (ii) subsidies or grants.[95] Thus, a government may favour domestic investors over foreign investors in its procurement, or give subsidies to domestic investors but not foreign investors without breaching its obligation to accord NT to investors of the other party under a BIT or FTA. Given the growing prominence of SOEs, is this a loophole that should be closed? What about preferential tax treatment for SOEs (which may avoid NT scrutiny due to the tax exception under many BITs and FTAs[96])? Second, FTAs often contain separate chapters devoted to government procurement. Like the WTO Agreement on Government Procurement, these agreements often take a 'positive list' approach, such that a

[90] Germany's International Chamber of Commerce (ICC) defended the view that 'Foreign investment brings many advantages such as economic growth, employment and as a result rising living standards', as reported by *Deutsche Welle*. The Federation of German Industry (BDI) said that German law would send 'the wrong signal for Germany as a place to invest'. 'Germany Moves to Protect Companies From Foreign Takeovers' (*Deutsche Welle*, 20 August 2014) <http://www.dw.com/en/germany-moves-to-protect-companies-from-foreign-takeovers/a-3580978> accessed 4 March 2015.

[91] ibid.

[92] Bertrand Benoit, 'Berlin Foreign Investors' Bill Clears Hurdle' (*Financial Times*, 20 August 2014) <http://www.ft.com/intl/cms/s/0/ac2762d6-6eff-11dd-a80a-0000779fd18c.html> accessed 4 March 2015.

[93] ibid. [94] ibid.

[95] See e.g., 2012 US Model Bilateral Investment Treaty, art 14.5.

[96] See e.g., ibid art 21.1.

procuring entity's obligation to treat suppliers, goods, and services of the other party in a non-discriminatory manner applies only to the extent that the procuring entity is covered by a party's schedule attached to the agreement. Isn't this the way to deal with procurement by SOEs? To the extent that a party did not negotiate to have procurement by a given SOE subject to a NT obligation, should that SOE not be allowed to discriminate in favour of domestic suppliers over their foreign-born competitors? Third, there may be circumstances in which a state delegates certain regulatory responsibilities to an SOE. What does that mean for the purposes of a NT analysis? Even if the mere fact of state ownership would not undermine 'like circumstances' for purposes of NT, would a delegation of regulatory responsibility undermine like circumstances? Where a state has a special relationship with an enterprise but not majority ownership—for example, a minority stake with an important influence on how the enterprise operates and possibly even the power to block certain decisions—should the enterprise be treated as state-owned for the purposes of a national security review of a proposed acquisition by the enterprise (as by the CFIUS)? Fourth, in order to identify the protected investor under the ICSID Convention, international tribunals rely on a criterion which is not the form but whether the company acted as agent of the government or is discharging governmental functions. Do they look at ownership or control? Fifth, as regard the GATS law, there is the issue of national investment legislation based on national security, which may block, impede, undo, or in some other way adversely affect investments made by SWFs. Would such a domestic action be in itself a violation of GATS Mode 3 commitments? Can the country rely on GATS Article XIVbis in order to benefit from the 'security exception'? Should governments clarify which sectors should be protected from foreign takeovers, going well beyond the vague criteria of public order and public security?

The current patchwork of international economic rules addressing SCEs operations ('trade and investment') is mainly made of competition, trade, and investment law and policy, each of the three being developed by specific institutions and formulated by distinct instruments. As such, it offers a considerable risk of incoherence for SCEs' operations that is a major concern for policymakers in international economic law. Indeed, the recent emergence of SCEs as active and important players in international financial markets has raised a host of questions, which are focused in the current analysis and should be answered in the future. As the current financial turmoil demonstrates, financial liquidity is vital for Western economies. SCEs as a class of trader and investor would considerably grow in importance over the next decade, both by number and by volume.

16

In Search of Coherence: Navigating the WTO in the Universe of International Law

Chien-huei Wu

I. Introduction

Over the twenty-year history of the WTO, it has been gradually expanding its policy spheres dealing with the environment, labour, public health, and human rights, leading to conflicts, and the possibility of conflicts, between the WTO and other international law regimes. These inconsistencies have attracted attention from both academics and practitioners.[1] Indeed, Uruguay Round negotiators anticipated and considered the possibility of legal conflicts and policy incoherencies between trade and policy areas of other regimes. Thus, when concluding the Marrakesh Agreement establishing the WTO, ministers adopted the Coherence Decision instructing the WTO, in co-operation with the Bretton Woods institutions, to seek greater coherence in global economic policymaking. However, the danger of incoherence does not emerge only from potential conflicts between global economic policymaking in the WTO and the Bretton Woods institutions. Indeed, the main sources of incoherence are to be found in the overlapping policy spheres of the WTO and other public international organizations, such as the International Labour Organization (ILO), the World Health Organization (the WHO), and multilateral environmental agencies (MEAs).

The potential legal conflicts and policy incoherence between trade and other policy sectors are exacerbated by three driving forces. First, the strong dispute settlement mechanism provided in the WTO raises concerns that the WTO will attempt to extend its reach beyond trade and thereby encroach into other policy

[1] On the trade linkage debates, see e.g., Mitsuo Matsushita, 'Governance of International Trade Under WTO Agreements—Relationships Between WTO Agreements and Other Trade Agreements' (2004) 38(2) J World Trade 185, 185–210; Gabrielle Marceau, 'A Call for Coherence in International Law: Praises for the Prohibition Against "Clinical Isolation" in WTO Dispute Settlement' (1999) 33(5) J World Trade 87, 87–152; Gabrielle Marceau, 'Conflicts of Norms and Conflicts of Jurisdictions: The Relationship Between the WTO Agreement and MEAs and Other Treaties' (2001) 35(6) J World Trade 1081, 1081–131; Joost Pauwelyn, 'Bridging Fragmentation and Unity: International Law as a Universe of Inter-connected Islands' 25 Mich J Intl L 903, 903–16.

sectors, as evidenced by such controversial disputes such as *US—Shrimp/Turtle*, *Brazil—Tyres*, and *Australia—Plain Packaging*. At the same time, the success of the WTO dispute settlement mechanism lends strength to the argument for the WTO acting as a 'self-contained' regime capable of carving out a sphere for itself in the broader context of public international law.[2] Second, the bourgeoning international treaty regimes and issue-specific international tribunals give rise to the threat of the fragmentation of international law.[3] The relevance of this fragmentation debate to the WTO lies in the role of public international law, whether general public international law or international treaty rules, in the WTO dispute settlement mechanism: are they part of the applicable law in the WTO?[4] Third, the race to conclude regional trade agreements (RTAs),[5] which contain various trade-related rules, WTO plus or WTO minus, may substantially reshape the rights and obligations enjoyed by Members under the WTO Agreement. The interaction between the WTO and RTA is two-dimensional. On the one hand, whether the rights and obligations arising from the RTAs may be enforced through the WTO is an issue worthy of exploration. On the other hand, there is a recent trend under which WTO rules are incorporated into RTAs, which raises a question as to whether the uniformity of WTO law is subject to challenge when these rules are interpreted by regional state-to-state dispute settlement mechanisms or investor–state arbitral tribunals as set out in the RTAs.

The proper positioning of the WTO in the broader context of various international treaty regimes is becoming an even more complicated issue. This chapter aims to navigate the WTO through the universe of public international law, and attempts to address coherence problems. The chapter is organized as follows: after this introductory note, the chapter provides an overview of the debates on 'self-contained' regimes and the fragmentation of international law, and clarifies the concept of coherence. On the basis of this background, there is an examination of those international instruments incorporated into, or explicitly referenced, in the WTO Agreement. This chapter, in section III, will then explore built-in

[2] On self-contained regimes, see e.g., Bruno Simma, 'Self-contained Regimes' (1985) 16 Neth YB Intl L 111, 111–36; Pieter Jan Kuyper, 'The Law of GATT as a Special Field of International Law: Ignorance, Further Refinement or Self-contained System of International Law' (1994) 25 Neth YB Intl L 227, 227–57; Bruno Simma and Dirk Pulkowski, 'Of Planet and the Universe: Self-contained Regimes in the International Law' (2006) 17 Eur J Intl L 483, 483–529; Andreas Fischer-Lescano and Gunther Teubner, 'Regime-collisions: The Vain Search for Legal Unity in the Fragmentation of Global Law' (2004) 25(4) Mich J Intl L 999, 999–1046.

[3] On the fragmentation of international law, see e.g., Fragmentation of International Law: Difficulties Arising from the Diversification and Expansion of International Law, Report of the Study Group of the International Law Commission, A/CN.4/L.682, 13 April 2006 (ILC Report); Martti Koskenniemi and Päivi Leino, 'Fragmentation of International Law? Postmodern Anxieties' (2002) 15(3) Leiden J Intl L 553, 553–79; Joel Trachtman, 'Fragmentation, Coherence and Synergy in International Law' (2011) 2(4) Transnatl Legal Theory 505, 505–36.

[4] See e.g., Lorand Bartels, 'Applicable Law in WTO Dispute Settlement Proceedings' (2001) 35(3) J World Trade 499, 499–519.

[5] On the WTO and RTA, see e.g., Lorand Bartels and Federico Ortino (eds), *Regional Trade Agreements and the WTO Legal System* (OUP 2006).

institutional linkage between the WTO and other specific areas of international law by way of two legislative techniques: incorporation and explicit reference. In section IV, the chapter investigates how the WTO relates to public international law by looking at two key subjects of general international law—customary rules of interpretation and state responsibility—in addition to other international treaty regimes. Section V will explore the relationship between the WTO and RTAs, which may strengthen or restrict the rights and obligations of Members under the WTO Agreement. Section VI concludes.

II. Setting the Scene: Fragmentation, Coherence, and Self-contained Regimes

The fragmentation of international law has attracted a tremendous amount of attention from scholars over the past few decades, particularly since the publication of the International Law Commission report on fragmentation of international law (ILC Report). Fragmentation is by no means a new phenomenon in international law, given its decentralized nature and lack of a central international legislator. States are the main actors with respect to international law-making processes and, by their consent, can modify existent international treaties or establish new international treaty regimes creating conflicting international legal obligations.[6] The ILC Report, by referring to an article published by Wilfried Jenks in 1953, underlines two driving forces that contribute to fragmentation. The first relates to the fact that countries tend to conclude treaties with those sharing historical, functional, or geographic similarities. Therefore, treaty rules tend to differ from one group of countries to another. A set of rules governing conflicting laws in ways analogous to the domestic context is seen as an antidote to this type of fragmentation.

The second driving force of fragmentation stems from the diversification and specialization of international law, which tends to result in less attention being paid to general principles and practices of international law[7] and to result in 'conflicts between rules or rule-systems, deviating institutional practices and, possibly, the loss of an overall perspective on the law'.[8] As Fischer-Lescano and Teubner observe, there is a trend toward 'polycentric globalisation', meaning 'an accelerated differentiation of society into autonomous social systems, each of which springs territorial confines and constitutes itself globally'.[9] This 'polycentric globalisation'

[6] Joost Pauwelyn, 'The Role of Public International Law in the WTO: How Far Can We Go?' (2001) 95 Am J Intl L 535, 535–36.

[7] ILC Report, paras 5–8.

[8] ILC Report, para 8. Scholars nonetheless have divergent views as to the impact of fragmentation of international law. Some see it as the erosion of general international law, emergence of conflicting jurisprudence, forum shopping, and loss of legal security, while others view it as a natural consequence of the increase of international activities, which can be redressed by technical streamlining and coordination. ibid.

[9] Fischer-Lescano and Teubner (n 2) 1006–07.

gives rise to a 'clash of rationalities' due to the maximization of rationality by different global functional systems in a process of functional differentiation. The root of such problems stems from the 'fragmented and operationally closed functional systems of a global society, which, in their expansionist fervour, create the real problems of the global society, and at the same time make use of global law in order to normatively secure their own highly refined sphere logics'.[10]

The second driving force of the fragmentation phenomenon is indeed closely related to the 'self-contained' regimes. These functionally differentiated and specialized regimes appear autonomous, and thus isolated, from general public international law. Similarly to the long history of fragmentation of international law, even in 1980, the International Court of Justice (ICJ) in Tehran Hostages opined that the rules of diplomatic law constitute a 'self-contained' regime.[11] This concept was further elaborated and examined in the Reports of the International Law Commission Study Group on State Responsibility (ILC Report on State Responsibility). Based on the analysis of the ILC Reports on State Responsibility, Bruno Simma, in 1985, argued against the concept of 'self-contained' regime by using diplomatic immunities, EU law, and human rights treaties as case studies.[12] Sharing the same philosophy, Pieter Jan Kuyper rejected GATT law as a 'self-contained' regime and argued for the applicability of relevant rules of state responsibility in 1994.[13]

The ILC Report identifies two types of 'self-contained' regime. In a narrow sense, the term refers to a set of special secondary rules addressing state responsibility in case of infringement of international obligations. In a broader sense, it refers to a set of interrelated primary and secondary rules, also known as 'systems' or 'subsystems', which demonstrate specific characteristics other than general international law.[14] The narrow definition focuses on the rule of state responsibility, whereas the broad definition covers the pertinent special genre of international law as a whole.

Simma and Pulkowski, with the aid of the *lex specialis* rule, employ a relativistic approach in defining 'self-contained' regimes, which can be understood from the two extremes of a spectrum. At one end of the spectrum is a regime that contracts out some rules of state responsibility and replaces them with its own *lex specialis*; at the other end of this spectrum, then, lies a regime which is unique in that its *lex specialis* excludes the application of the whole set of general rules of state

[10] ibid 1007.

[11] According to ICJ, 'The rules of diplomatic law, in short, constitute a self-contained regime which, on the one hand, lays down the receiving State's obligations regarding the facilities, privileges and immunities to be accorded to the diplomatic missions and, on the other, foresees their possible abuse by Members of the mission and specifies the means at the disposal of the receiving State to counter any such abuse. These means are by their nature, entirely efficacious.' States Diplomatic and Consular Staff in Tehran, ICJ Reports (1980) 38.

[12] Simma (n 2) 118–35.

[13] Kuyper (n 2) 251–52. Kuyper focuses on the principle of exhaustion of local remedies in anti-dumping cases. By contrast, Simma and Pulkowski argue for the applicability of countermeasures in the WTO context. Simma and Pulkowski (n 2) 519–23.

[14] ILC Report, para 128.

responsibility; thus, the latter regimes are referred to as 'self-contained' regimes.[15] The main feature of a 'self-contained' regime is its intention to exclude the applicability of rules of state responsibility, the interpretation of which depends on 'whether international law is conceived as a unified legal order or as the sum total of loosely interrelated subsystems'.[16] As they explain, the former, and universalistic approach is favoured by general public international lawyers who take their departure point from general international law. The deviation and derogation from general rules of state responsibility are accepted only to the extent that the contacting parties explicitly spell out such exclusionary intension. As a consequence, the former approach tends to deny the existence of 'self-contained' regimes. By contrast, the second and particularistic approach focuses on the sociological analysis of the particular characteristics of a given specific regime, and the analysis is generally conducted from a perspective within such a regime. This approach is supported by scholars working in special fields of international law and tends to cast special regimes as 'self-contained'. They thus conclude that 'the claim of self-containment is intrinsically linked to a particular outlook on the international legal order'.[17]

Therefore, universalistic general international lawyers pursue legal unity and try to avoid the fragmentation of international law arising from the multiplication of specialized or 'self-contained' regimes. By contrast, particularistic international lawyers tend to guard their special realms jealously, and accept possible pitfalls of a fragmented international legal order. Regardless of whether they adopt a universalistic or particularistic approach, all scholars of international law have to address potential legal conflicts and policy incoherence between treaty regimes. The functional differentiation of global society introduces a paradox: on the one hand, functionally differentiated regimes compete for jurisdiction and discursive power through the definition of the subject matter; in particular, via the language they choose to use in characterizing it.[18] On the other hand, this competition does not transform the multifaceted and interfacing nature of global challenges facing us into a single-dimensional subject. Decisions made by a given regime inevitably affect other regimes. Such concerns are especially acute in the WTO context, given the compulsory jurisdiction of its dispute settlement mechanism. Human rights and environmental lawyers strive to enforce labour and environmental standards through the WTO dispute settlement mechanism, while trade lawyers remain cautious about this approach. Moreover, trade disciplines may limit the domestic

[15] Simma and Pulkowski (n 2) 490–91. This definition corresponds to the narrow definition of 'self-contained' regime advanced by the ILC Report. However, while the definition proposed by Simma and Pulkowski focuses on the relationship between a given regime and general public international law, the same observation may be extended to its relationship with other regimes of international law, namely, disconnected from other fields of international law. This then constitutes what the ILC Report calls 'self-contained' regimes in a broad sense.

[16] ibid 495. [17] ibid.

[18] See generally, Martti Koskenniemi, 'The Politics of International Law—20 Years Later' (2009) 20(1) Eur J Intl L 1, 1–19; Martti Koskenniemi, 'International Law and Hegemony: A Reconfiguration' (2004) 17(2) Cambridge Rev Intl Aff 197, 197–218.

regulatory policy space, which leads human rights and environmental lawyers to contend that the WTO constitutes a threat to these objectives.[19]

The tension between one regime and another leads to another fundamental question: when can we ascertain the existence of a conflict between international regimes? The ILC Report observes two possible approaches—the subject matter that is governed by the rules of international law and the subjects that are bound by these international obligations—and opines that Article 30 of the Vienna Convention on the Law of Treaties (VCLT) opts for the former approach. The ILC Report goes on to elaborate on the definition of legal conflicts. In a strict sense, a conflict exists 'if it is possible for a party to two treaties to comply with one rule only by thereby failing to comply with another rule'.[20] This strict notion of legal conflict refers to a situation of incompatibility between two international rules: the fulfilment of one being possible only with the failure to comply with the other. The ILC Report nonetheless finds such a definition too narrow to include the frustration of the objective and purpose of a treaty, even in the absence of incompatibility, to which the ILC Report refers as policy conflicts. Such policy conflicts or policy incoherence are also relevant in the context of the fragmentation of international law.[21] The defragmentizing efforts in international law are intended to avoid having the contradictory policy objectives of different international laws cancel out one another and to promote positive synergies among sector-specific international rules and thus achieve greater coherence in international policymaking.

Bearing this in mind, it would be helpful to note that there is a strong presumption against normative conflicts in international law. This is actually the departure point of the ILC Report, which argues that when creating new obligations, states are assumed not to derogate from their existent international obligations.[22] Efforts should be made to interpret away normative conflicts and ensure harmony. In this interpretative exercise, the ILC Report underlines the pivotal role of Article 31(3)(c) of the VCLT,[23] the principle of systemic integration, which instructs the treaty interpreters to pay due regard to the normative environment (system) of international obligations.[24] The rationale for this is that '[a]ll treaty provisions receive their force and validity from general law, and establish rights and obligations that exist alongside the rights and obligations established by other treaty provisions, and the rules of customary international law'.[25] Since there is no intrinsic legal priority established between differing sets of treaty rules, the task for treaty interpreters is to

[19] See Economic and Social Council, Economic, Social and Cultural Rights, Liberalization of Trade in Services and Human Rights, Report of the High Commissioner, Executive Summary, 25 June 2002, E/CN.4/Sub.2/2002/9. See also Ernst-Ulrich Petersmann, 'Time for a United Nations "Global Compact" for Integrating Human Rights into the Law of Worldwide Organizations: Lessons from European Integration' (2002) 13(3) Eur J Intl L 621, 621–50; Gabrielle Marceau, 'WTO Dispute Settlement and Human Rights' (2002) 13(4) Eur J Intl L 753, 753–814.

[20] ILC Report, para 24. [21] ibid. [22] ibid 37–38.

[23] Article 31(3)(c) of the VCLT [Any relevant rules of international law applicable in the relations between the parties]. The critical point here is what the term of 'the parties' refers to. As will be shown below, this issue constitutes a decisive point in the WTO jurisprudence.

[24] ILC Report, para 413. [25] ibid 414.

approach them with care through legal reasoning and to make of them a coherent and meaningful whole.[26]

III. Built-in Linkage between WTO and Organizations and Conventions

The WTO is designated an international organization with legal personality. Its relationships with existent GATT rules, other international organizations, or conventions have to be defined clearly. Thus, some WTO provisions address institutional linkages. Two legislative techniques, incorporation and explicit reference, are employed to satisfy this regulatory need.

A. Incorporation

The incorporation of other international agreements is a novel and unique feature in WTO law, perhaps in international law in general. Two types of international agreements are incorporated into, and thus constitute, an integral part of the WTO Agreement: pre-WTO rules, and World Intellectual Property Organization (WIPO) provisions. The most illustrative pre-WTO rules incorporated into the WTO Agreement are the GATT 1947 and the subsequent protocols of accession, decisions, understandings of interpretation, which, subject to some modification, became GATT 1994, which constitutes part of the Annex 1A Agreement, Multilateral Agreements on Trade in Goods, to the WTO Agreement. By way of incorporation, the WTO inherits the whole set of GATT *aquis*. This type of incorporation addresses the mainly temporal dimension of the WTO law and clarifies its relationship with its predecessor and itself.[27]

The relationship between the WTO Agreement and the pre-WTO GATT rules may not be as simple as it appears. This issue may eventually touch upon the most controversial issues of the jurisdiction and applicable law before the WTO panel and Appellate Body. In *EC—Poultry*, the WTO judiciary was called upon to examine the WTO relevance of the Oilseeds Agreement, an agreement concluded between the European Union and Brazil and other countries, after the adoption of the GATT panel report on *EEC—Oilseeds*.[28] The task before the WTO judiciary was to clarify the relationship between the European Union's market access commitments under Schedule LXXX, which is annexed to the Marrakesh Protocol to the General Agreement on Tariffs and Trade 1994 (the 'Marrakesh Protocol') and the Oilseeds Agreement. According to the Appellate Body, while Schedule LXXX, by virtue of being annexed to the Marrakesh Protocol, constitutes an integral part

[26] ibid. [27] Pauwelyn (n 6) 543–44.

[28] Panel Report, EEC—Payments and Subsidies Paid to Processors and Producers of Oilseeds and Related Animal-feed Proteins, GATT Doc L/6627-37S/86, adopted 25 January 1990; Panel Report, Follow-up on the Panel Report 'EEC—Payments and Subsidies Paid to Processors and Producers of Oilseeds and Related Animal-feed Proteins', GATT Doc DS28/R, 31 March 1992.

of the WTO Agreement, the Oilseeds Agreement is not part of the covered agreements subject to the jurisdiction of the WTO judiciary under Articles 1 and 2 of the Dispute Settlement Understanding (DSU). Admittedly, the motivation to conclude the Oilseeds Agreement stems from a decision of the GATT panel report and the substantial content of such agreement having been written into the European Union's Schedule. Nonetheless, the Oilseeds Agreement does not constitute part of the covered agreement and thus does not fall under the jurisdiction of the WTO.[29] That being said, the interpretative value of the Oilseeds Agreement may not be denied. As the Appellate Body noted, the Oilseeds Agreement was negotiated with the framework of Article XXVIII of the GATT 1947, with the authorization of the GATT Contracting Parties, of which the substance relating a 15,500 tonne tariff-free quota for frozen poultry meat formed the basis of the European Union's market access commitment under Schedule LXXX. Therefore, 'the Oilseeds Agreement may serve as a *supplementary means* of interpretation of Schedule LXXX pursuant to Article 32 of the *Vienna Convention*, as it is part of the historical background of the concessions of the European Communities for frozen poultry meat'.[30]

In *EC—Bananas*, the WTO judiciary was called upon the examine the relevance of the Lomé Convention as the subject matter before it related to a Lomé waiver, a decision first made by the GATT Contracting Parties in 1994[31] and subsequently extended by the WTO General Council in 1996.[32] In its appeal, the European Union argued that the panel erred in examining the requirements of the Lomé Convention and requested the WTO judiciary to refer to the common views expressed by the European Union and African, Caribbean, and Pacific countries. The Appellate Body, in affirming the reasoning of the panel, held that it had no alternative but to examine the substance of the Lomé Convention to the extent necessary to interpret the Lomé waiver, given that when the GATT Contracting Parties 'incorporated a reference to the Lomé Convention into the Lomé waiver, the meaning of the Lomé Convention became a GATT/WTO issue'.[33] Whereas the Appellate Body did not clarify the legal basis for it to examine the legal obligations arising from the Lomé Convention, in the view of this author, the Lomé

[29] Appellate Body Report, *EC—Measures Affecting the Importation of Certain Poultry Products*, WT/DS69/AB/R, 13 July 1998, para 79.

[30] ibid, para 83 (*emphasis original*). It should be also noted that in *US—Countervailing Duties (China)*, where the Appellate Body was called upon the rule the WTO compatibility of concurrent anti-dumping and countervailing duties, it was held that the Tokyo Anti-dumping Code, a predecessor of the WTO Anti-dumping Agreement, was not incorporated into the WTO Agreement, and does not constitute the context of the treaty provisions in question. Further, given that the subject was clear before the Appellate Body, it was not necessary to refer to *supplementary means* of interpretation. Appellate Body Report, *US—Definitive Anti-dumping and Countervailing Duties on Certain Products from China*, WT/DS379/AB/R, 11 March 2011, paras 545–91.

[31] Contracting Parties, The Fourth ACP–EEC Convention of Lomé, Decision of 9 December 1994, GATT Doc L/7604, 19 December 1994.

[32] General Council, The Fourth ACP–EC Convention of Lomé, Extension of Waiver, Decision of 14 October 1996, WT/L/186, 18 October 1996.

[33] Appellate Body Report, *EC—Regime for the Importation, Sale and Distribution of Bananas*, WT/DS27/AB/R, 9 September 1997, para 167.

Convention constitutes the context of the Lomé waiver that enabled the Appellate Body to look into it.

The second type of incorporation relates to the WIPO obligations, which are brought under the auspices of WTO law through the Agreement on Trade-related Aspects of International Property Rights (TRIPS Agreement). These international treaties cover the Paris Convention (1967), the Berne Convention (1971), the Rome Convention (1961), and the Treaty on Intellectual Property in Respect of Integrated Circuits (1989). Relevant provisions of these treaties have been examined by the WTO judiciary in a number of disputes, such as *US—Section 211 Appropriations Act* and *EC—Trademark and Geographic Indications*.[34] Given that these treaty obligations are incorporated into the TRIPS Agreement and constitute an integral part of the WTO Agreement, the interpretation of such treaty provisions are carried out in accordance with the customary rules of the interpretation of public international law.

B. Explicit reference

Regarding explicit reference to other international treaty rules, two types of references are of note. The first relates to Bretton Woods institutions, in particular the International Monetary Fund (IMF). This type of relationship has been written into the treaty rules since the GATT era. The second type relates to standard-setting organizations, such as the Food and Agriculture Organization (FAO)/WHO Codex Alimentarius Commission, which are of great relevance in the context of the Agreement on the Application of Sanitary and Phytosanitary Measures (SPS Agreement) and the Technical Barriers to Trade (TBT) Agreement.

1. WTO and Bretton Woods institutions

The relationship between the WTO and Bretton Woods institutions dates back to the post-World War II global economic architecture. The GATT maintained some provisions delimiting the jurisdiction and co-operative relationship of the ill-fated International Trade Organization and the IMF. Members are instructed not to frustrate the intent of the GATT by exchange action, nor the intent of the IMF Agreement by trade action;[35] at the same time, the Coherence Declaration directs the WTO to work with Bretton Woods institutions to achieve greater coherence in global economic policymaking. Furthermore, when the GATT is called upon to consider or deal with problems concerning monetary reserves, balances of payments, or foreign exchange arrangements, the WTO should accept statistical

[34] In this case, the Appellate Body determined, inter alia, whether trade names are covered by the TRIPs Agreement. For a thorough analysis of the *US—Section 211 Appropriations Act*, see Julien Chaisse and Puneeth Nagaraj, 'Changing Lanes—Trade, Investment and Intellectual Property Rights' (2014) 36(1) Hastings Intl & Comp L Rev 223–70, 238.

[35] GATT art XV:4.

findings and other facts presented by the IMF and the IMF's determinations on the consistency of a Member's exchange action with the IMF Agreement.[36]

In the context of the WTO–IMF relationship, several issues are of critical importance. First, the WTO and IMF have to clarify what constitutes a trade action and an exchange action so as to avoid jurisdictional conflicts. Second, the WTO judiciary has to address whether it is bound by the determination of IMF in terms of statistical and factual findings, and the IMF findings regarding the consistency of an exchange action with the IMF Agreement. Third, what is the legal relevance of an IMF lending or structural adjustment agreement in the WTO context? Finally, cross-conditionalities or conflicting conditionalities should be avoided with a view to achieving coherent global economic policymaking.[37]

Regarding jurisdictional delimitation, in 1960, the IMF Executive Board, after examining various approaches such as intent, effect, and technique, adopted the technique test and defined a measure restricting payments and transfers for the current transaction as 'a direct governmental limitation of the availability or use of exchange as such'.[38] This definition was respected by the panel in *Dominican Republic—Cigarettes* on the grounds that neither the complaining nor defending parties were opposed to such a guiding principle advanced by the IMF.[39] Second, when dealing with a complaint relating to monetary reserves, balances of payments, or foreign exchange arrangements, the WTO panel and Appellate Body have evidenced a shift in their attitudes on the role of the IMF from a resistant approach to a more open approach, as can be seen in the case laws ranging from *India—Quantitative Restrictions*, through *Argentina—Textiles*, to *Dominican Republic—Cigarettes*. That being said, so far the WTO judiciary has taken a critical approach in appreciating the IMF's determinations on statistical and factual findings, and the IMF consistency of an exchange action, instead of accepting them without reservation.[40] Regarding the third issue, the Appellate Body addressed this in *Argentina—Textiles* by defining the legal nature of a statistical tax that Argentina argued it was obliged to impose under its Memorandum of Understanding, and the IMF, and by clarifying the relevance of the Coherence Declaration and WTO–IMF Agreement. The Appellate Body noted that it was unable to ascertain the legal nature of the Memorandum of Understanding from

[36] GATT art XV:2.

[37] On these different issues, see further, Deborah E Siegel, 'Legal Aspects of the IMF/WTO Relationship: The Fund's Articles of Agreement and the WTO Agreements' (2002) 96 Am J Intl L 561, 561–621; Dukgeun Ahn, 'Linkage Between International Financial and Trade Institutions: IMF, World Bank and WTO' (2000) 34(4) J World Trade 1, 1–36; Chien-huei Wu, 'Greater Coherence in Global Economic Policymaking: Progress and Prospect' (2013) 5 Eur YB Intl Econ L 67, 67–92.

[38] IMF, 'Decision No 1034-(60/27), June 1, 1960' (2013) 37 Selected Decisions and Selected Documents of the International Monetary Fund 622.

[39] Panel Report, Dominican Republic—Measures Affecting the Importation and Internal Sales of Cigarettes, WT/DS302/R, 26 November 2004, para 7.132.

[40] Chien-huei Wu, 'Legal Aspects of WTO–IMF Relationship Revisited' in Ernst-Ulrich Petersmann, Marise Cremona, Peter Hilpold, and Nikos Lavranos (eds), *Reflections on the Constitutionalisation of International Economic Law: Liber Amicorum for Ernst-Ulrich Petersmann* (Martinus Nijhoff Publishers 2013) 277–90.

the panel record.[41] Even assuming the statistical tax was obligatory as dictated by the IMF, such obligation was not irreconcilable with Argentina's obligations under the WTO Agreement. Moreover, the Appellate Body sees the WTO–IMF Agreement more as an administrative co-operation agreement than one containing substantial obligations. The Coherence Declaration speaks of the Ministers' intent in pursuing greater coherence in global economic policymaking, which corresponds with the objective spelled out in Article III:5 of the WTO Agreement. Again, this Coherence Declaration does not put forward substantial obligations. The Appellate Body thus concluded that neither the WTO–IMF Agreement nor the Coherence Declaration modifies Members' obligations under the WTO Agreement, and affirmed the panel's ruling that these two instruments cannot justify the conclusion that a Member's commitment should prevail over obligations arising from the WTO Agreement.[42] This ruling nonetheless makes the fourth question much more difficult to answer. If the WTO judiciary insists on the priority of WTO obligations, a WTO Member will be between a rock and hard place if caught between conflicting WTO and IMF obligations. Such a dilemma informs the fundamental question this chapter attempts to resolve. Admittedly, the major part of conflict avoidance lies in the negotiation processes wherein the IMF should take great care to not impose WTO-incompatible obligations. Nonetheless, serious efforts must be made by the WTO judiciary to interpret away treaty conflicts and ensure coherence. Scholars have argued that whereas non-WTO law cannot give rise to claims before the WTO, it can nonetheless be relied upon by the defending Member in its defence.[43]

2. *Standard-setting organizations and SPS/TBT agreements*

The second type of explicit reference relates to international standard-setting organizations. Such a reference is apparent in Article 3 of Annex 1 to the SPS Agreement, including the Codex Alimentarius Commission, the International Office of Epizootics, and the International Plant Protection Convention. The legal value of the standards, recommendations, and guidelines set out in such standard setting is clarified in Article 3.2 of the SPS Agreement[44] and Article 2.5 of TBT Agreement,[45] with a trade measure made in accordance with these standards

[41] In fact, the third party, the EC, argued that the statistic tax was only mentioned by Argentina's unilateral Memorandum of Economic Policy to the IMF but was not written into the lending agreement and did not constitute a part of IMF obligation. Appellate Body Report, *Argentina—Measures Affecting Imports of Footwear, Textiles, Apparel and Other Items*, WT/DS56/AB/R, 27 March 1998, para 33.

[42] ibid paras 70–73. [43] Pauwelyn (n 6) 569.

[44] SPS Agreement art 3.2 [Sanitary or phytosanitary measures which conform to international standards, guidelines or recommendations shall be deemed to be necessary to protect human, animal or plant life or health, and presumed to be consistent with the relevant provisions of this Agreement and of GATT 1994.]

[45] TBT Agreement art 2.5 [Whenever a technical regulation is prepared, adopted or applied for one of the legitimate objectives explicitly mentioned in paragraph 2, and is in accordance with relevant international standards, it shall be presumed not to create an unnecessary obstacle to international trade.]

presumed to be consistent with the SPS Agreement or the GATT 1994, and presumed not to create unnecessary obstacles to international trade. This special legal status has been confirmed by the WTO jurisprudence. For example, the Appellate Body in *US/Canada—Continued Suspension* reaffirmed the GATT/SPS consistency presumption of a measure conforming to international standards.[46] Moreover, even in the absence of such standards, the statements of expert witnesses from such international organizations—namely the International Office of Epizootics—before the panel are also given 'appropriate weight' in view of their repeated references in the SPS Agreement and the general objective of harmonization spelled out in the SPS Agreement.[47]

The scope and coverage of such international standard-setting organizations needs to be clarified. In addition to those explicitly referenced in the SPS and TBT Agreements, does any other international organization or treaty regime fall within the scope of such standard-setting organizations? This question is a key issue in the *Australia—Plain Packaging* dispute. While Australia may refer to the guidelines adopted by the WHO Framework Tobacco Control Convention, which recommends the implementation of a plain packaging policy as an international standard, the complaining Members do not necessarily share this view. Moreover, when the international standards are adopted by voting system, and when not all WTO Members are participating in these standard-setting organizations or treaty regimes, the legitimacy of such consistency presumption may be challenged. In fact, this issue mirrors the debate relating to Article 31(3)(c) of the VCLT: whether the term 'the parties' should be interpreted as 'all the parties'. This issue will be dealt with in section IV.

IV. The WTO and Public International Law

Regarding the role of the WTO in relation to public international law, this section addresses two issues: general international law and other international treaty law. In the context of general international law, this section will focus on customary rules of interpretation of public international law and the rules of state responsibility. International treaty law will concentrate on how other international treaty conventions relate to the WTO, notably via Article 31(3)(c) of the VCLT. Before that, it is worth citing *Korea—Measure Affecting Government Procurement*, where the panel clarified the relationship between WTO and customary international law, as this will provide a broader context for the discussion of specific issues. According to the panel:

> Customary international law applies generally to the economic relations between the WTO Members. Such international law applies to the extent that the WTO treaty agreements

[46] See e.g., Appellate Body Report, *US/Canada—Continued Suspension of Obligations in the EC—Hormones Dispute*, WT/DS320, 321/AB/R, 16 October 2008, para 694.

[47] Panel Report, *Australia—Measures Affecting Importation of Salmon*, WT/DS18/R, 12 June 1998, para 8.180.

do not 'contract out' from it. To put it another way, to the extent there is no conflict or inconsistency, or an expression in a covered WTO agreement that implies differently, we are of the view that the customary rules of international law apply to the WTO treaties and to the process of treaty formation under the WTO.

This passage explains the relationship between the WTO Agreement and customary international law and reaffirms that WTO law does not exist in clinical isolation from public international law.

A. General international law

1. Customary rules of interpretation of public international law

The relevance of customary rules of interpretation of public international law to the WTO is clear, since Article 3(2) of the DSU instructs the WTO panel and Appellate Body to clarify the provisions of the covered agreements 'in accordance with customary rules of interpretation of public international law'. According to the Appellate Body, the general rule of interpretation, as codified by the VCLT, in particular, Article 31, 'has attained the status of a rule of customary or general international law. As such, it forms part of the "customary rules of interpretation of public international law" which the Appellate Body has been directed, by Article 3(2) of the DSU, to apply in seeking to clarify the provisions of the General Agreement and other covered agreements.'[48] By virtue of this provision, the Appellate Body continued to note that 'the General Agreement is not to be read in clinical isolation from public international law'.[49] Relying upon this passage, Marceau, a WTO lawyer, argues that the Appellate Body has acknowledged that the WTO 'is not a hermetically closed regime, impermeable to the other rules of international law'[50] and attempted to connect the GATT/WTO sub-system of law to the rest of international legal order. In the same passage, Francioni, a public international lawyer, argues that the WTO Appellate Body makes it clear that the WTO does not constitute a 'self-contained' regime, but rather situates itself in the broader context of public international law.[51]

While recognition of the relevance of customary rules of interpretation of public international law to WTO law is only a small step forward, its influence is nevertheless fundamental. As Kuyper observes, the GATT diplomatic jurisprudence relied heavily on legislative history and demonstrated ignorance of the public

[48] Appellate Body Report, *US—Standards for Refomulated and Conventional Gasoline*, WT/DS2/AB/R, 29 April 1996, at 17.

[49] ibid.

[50] Marceau (n 1) 95. It should be note that Marceau distinguishes what she calls 'hermetically closed regimes' from 'self-contained regimes'. Nonetheless, she does not elaborate in great detail what the difference is.

[51] Francesco Francioni, 'WTO Law in Context: The Integration of International Human Rights and Environmental Law in the Dispute Settlement Process' in Giorgio Sacerdoti and others (eds), *The WTO at Ten: The Contribution of the Dispute Settlement System* (CUP 2006) 143–54.

international law. Recognition of the relevance of customary rules of interpretation of public international law to the WTO will help to put an end to such ignorance.[52] Besides, Pauwelyn developed the idea that the applicable law before panels and the Appellate Body extends to all international law. This theory allows adjudication of WTO disputes on the basis of other international agreements as well as general principles of law and custom. Based on this, Pauwelyn argues that recognition of the fact that the provisions of covered agreements have to be interpreted in accordance with customary rules of interpretation of public international law proves that WTO law is also a part of public international law.[53] What is more important, the recognition of the relevance of customary rules of interpretation of public international law as codified by the VCLT to the WTO law opens up a door for the WTO law to be connected with other systems of public international law. The critical bridging element here is Article 31(3)(c) of the VCLT, or the principle of systemic integration.

2. *State responsibility*

The relevance of the rules of state responsibility to the WTO may be viewed from two perspectives: the role of such rules in the WTO dispute settlement mechanism, and the possibility of rights and obligations arising from the WTO Agreement falling back to such rules.

Within the WTO dispute settlement mechanism, the panel and Appellate Body have repeatedly referred to rules of state responsibility in its case law that touches upon WTO rules as *lex specialis* as opposed to the rules of state responsibility as *lex generalis*. Such general rules of state responsibilities include the attribution of a wrongful act to a state and the proportionality of countermeasures. Basically, the WTO judiciary tends to regard some part of the ILC Articles as reflective customary international law or general principles of law.[54] However, the WTO judiciary does not seem to have a clear answer as to which part reflects customary international law or general principles of law. The ruling of the panel and Appellate Body in *US—Anti-dumping and Countervailing Duties (China)* best illustrates this ambiguity.

In response to China's argument that the ILC Articles on State Responsibility constitute 'relevant rules of international law applicable in the relations between the parties', which the panel must take into account, the panel first opined that there is no panel or Appellate Body report confirming China's contention. The various references to the ILC Articles as conceptual guidance were merely to supplement, or confirm, but not to replace, the covered agreements; the interpretative exercise of the panel should rely upon customary rules of interpretation

[52] Kuyper (n 2) 229–32. [53] Pauwelyn (n 6) 559–71.

[54] Appellate Body Report, *US—Definitive Anti-dumping and Countervailing Duties on Certain Products from China* (*US—AD/CVD*, Appellate Body Report), WT/DS379/AB/R, 11 March 2011, para 308.

of public international law as codified by the VCLT, in particular, Article 31.[55] Moreover, the rules provided in the Agreement on Subsidies and Countervailing Measures (SCM Agreement) on the definition of 'public body' constitutes *lex specialis* as opposed to the rule of attribution as set out in the ILC Articles, and thus rules out the application of the ILC Articles in the context of the SCM Agreement.[56] In characterizing the rules of the SCM Agreement as *lex specialis* and ruling out the application of the ILC Articles on State Responsibility, it can be argued that the panel viewed WTO law as a 'self-contained' regime in the narrow sense.

On appeal, the Appellate Body took a different position and considered three elements for 'any relevant rules of international law applicable in the relations between the parties': relevance; rules of international law; and applicability in the relations between the parties. The Appellate Body made it clear that the ILC Articles on State Responsibility are not binding by virtue of being an international treaty; nonetheless, 'insofar as they reflect customary international law or general principles of law, these Articles are applicable in the relations between the parties'.[57] The question to be resolved is not whether rules of the SCM Agreement on attribution constitute *lex specialis*, since the rules to be applied are the SCM Agreement and not the ILC Articles, but whether the WTO judiciary under customary rules of interpretation of public international law should take account such ILC Articles.[58] In taking account 'any relevant rules of international law applicable in the relations between the parties', which in this case refers to the ILC Articles, the Appellate Body opened a channel to connect the WTO law to general international law.

Regarding the specific issue of attribution, in *Turkey—Textile*, the panel was called upon to examine whether Turkey's quantitative restrictions—measures implementing decisions taken within the ambit of the EU–Turkey Customs Union—were measures instigated by Turkey. The panel referred to the ILC Commentaries on Article II of the Articles on State Responsibility, citing the following passage:

> the conduct of the common organ cannot be considered otherwise than as an act of each of the States whose common organ it is. If that conduct is not in conformity with an international obligation, then the two or more States will concurrently have committed separate, although identical, internationally wrongful acts.[59]

Based on the principles set out in the Articles on State Responsibility, the panel held that Turkey was responsible for the quantitative restrictions, meaning that the measures in question were Turkey's own measures.[60]

[55] Panel Report, *US—Definitive Anti-dumping and Countervailing Duties on Certain Products from China*, WT/DS379/R, para 8.87.

[56] ibid para 8.90.

[57] *US—AD/CVD*, Appellate Body Report (n 54) para 308.

[58] ibid para 316.

[59] International Law Commission, United Nations, Yearbook of the International Law Commission, 1978, Vol II, Part Two, at 99, citing from Panel Report, *Turkey—Restrictions on Imports of Textile and Clothing Product*, WT/DS34/R, 31 May 1999, para 9.43.

[60] ibid para 9.44.

Regarding the countermeasures, the Arbitrators in *US—Cotton Subsidies (Article 22.6)* addressed the interpretative meaning of the ILC Article on State Responsibility regarding the term 'countermeasures' as set out in the SCM Agreement in terms of its nature and extent. From the outset, the arbitrators note that the term 'countermeasures' as understood in public international law, may be helpful in understanding usage of the same term in the SCM Agreement. The arbitrators continued to note that 'the term "countermeasures", in the SCM Agreement describes measures that are in the nature of countermeasures as defined in the ILC's Articles on State Responsibility'.[61] Based on this understanding, the arbitrators defined 'countermeasures' as temporarily authorized measures that would otherwise infringe WTO obligations, taken in response to a breach of the obligations set forth in the SCM Agreement. The arbitrators held that such a definition was also consistent with the ILC's Articles on State Responsibility.[62] The arbitrators again referred to the ILC's Articles on State Responsibility to clarify that the only legitimate objective of countermeasures is to induce compliance to an extent commensurate with the degree and nature of the adverse effects determined to exist, which can be reflected in the principle of proportionality as codified in Article 51 of the ILC Articles.[63]

With regard to the possibility of the WTO law falling back on the general rules of state responsibility, two possible avenues have been advanced. In the earlier days of the WTO, Kuyper argues that the rule of exhaustion of local remedies should have been applied in cases of anti-dumping and countervailing duties measures and the protection of intellectual property rights (IPRs), since these are mainly the private rights of individuals and first resort should be to domestic judicial review.[64] This proposal, however, was soon proven impracticable by WTO case law.

Simma and Pulkowski compared the compensation and the suspension of concessions (or retaliation) as contained in Article 22 of the DSU, and reparation and countermeasures in the ILC Articles on State Responsibility from systemic and functional perspectives. From a systemic perspective, compensation and retaliation are intended to restore contractual reciprocity in the rights and obligations of WTO Members. Such a designation is in line with the general rules of state responsibility. From a functional perspective, the objective of a suspension of concessions is to induce compliance—an objective that differs from the restoration of equality of treaty obligations. In this sense, the suspension of concessions can be

[61] Arbitral Panel Report, *US—Subsidies on Upland Cotton: Recourse to Arbitration by the US Under Article 22.6 of the DSU and Article 7.10 of the SCM Agreement*, WT/DS267/ARB/2, 31 August 2009, para 4.31.

[62] ibid para 4.32.

[63] ibid para 4.61; see also Appellate Body Report, *US/Canada—Continued Suspension of Obligations in the EC—Hormones Dispute*, WT/DS320, 321/AB/R, 16 October 2008, para 382; Appellate Body Report, *US—Definitive Safeguard Measures on Imports of Circular Welded Carbon Quality Line Pipe from Korea*, WT/DS202/AB/R, 15 February 2002, para 259; Appellate Body Report, *US—Transitional Safeguard Measure on Combed Cotton Yarn from Pakistan*, WT/DS192/AB/R, 8 October 2001, para 120.

[64] Kuyper (n 2) 237–38.

viewed as *lex specialis* in terms of countermeasures as contained in the ILC Articles on State Responsibility. The contentious question Simma and Pulkowski ask is whether it is possible to fall back on the general rules of international law on state responsibility in case of continuous non-compliance, where only unilateral countermeasures will induce compliance.[65]

B. International treaty law

Voluminous academic literature has been devoted to the relationship between WTO law and other international treaty law. This chapter is not intended to repeat such scholarship, but to focus on one contentious issue: the application of Article 31(3)(c) of the VCLT, the principle of systemic integration. As noted above, the WTO judiciary has put forward three criteria for 'any relevant rules of international law applicable in the relations between the parties': relevance; rules of international law; and applicability in the relations between the parties.

In order to be 'relevant', the rules in question must concern the same subject matter as the treaty provision of the covered agreements being interpreted.[66] Regarding 'rules of international law', the WTO judiciary refers to Article 38(1) of the Statute of the International Court of Justice[67] and opines that such rules cover international treaties and conventions, customary international law, and general principles of law.[68]

Finally, the criterion of 'applicability in the relations between the parties' related to the scope of 'the parties', on which the WTO case laws diverge. The panel in *EC—Approval and Marketing of Biotech Products* observed that the wording of the term was not 'the parties to a dispute', which led to the conclusion that 'the rules of international law to be taken into account in interpreting the WTO agreements at issue in this dispute are those which are applicable in the relations between the WTO Members'.[69] Given the wide and diverse WTO Membership, such a strict interpretation effectively excludes the applicability of Article 31(3)(c) of the VCLT. As the ILC Report succinctly puts it, 'the panel buys what it calls the "consistency" of its interpretation of the WTO Treaty at the cost of the consistency of the multilateral treaty system as a whole'.[70] The Appellate Body in *EC—Large Civil Aircraft* took a more balanced approach, though in the

[65] Simma and Pulkowski (n 2) 521–22. In addition to the context of public international law, countermeasures may also be referred to in the context of regional trade agreements (RTAs), which authorize the use of countermeasures in case of infringement of RTAs obligations. These countermeasures adopted in the RTAs context may constitute in turn a breach of the WTO obligations. How to assess the legality in accordance with which applicable law turns out to be a thorny question for international lawyers. See Gabrielle Marceau and Julian Wyatt, 'Dispute Settlement Mechanisms Intermingled: Regional Trade Agreements and the WTO' 1 JIDS 67, 67–95.

[66] *US—AD/CVD*, Appellate Body Report, para 308. [67] ibid.

[68] Panel Report, *EC—Measures Affecting the Approval and Marketing of Biotech Products*, WT/DS291, 292, 293/R, 29 September 2006, para 7.67.

[69] ibid para 7.68. [70] ILC Report, para 450.

conclusion it found the bilateral agreement between the European Union and the United States in question was not relevant to the provision to be interpreted. The Appellate Body held:

> An interpretation of 'the parties' in Article 31(3)(c) should be guided by the Appellate Body's statement that 'the purpose of treaty interpretation is to establish the common intention of the parties to the treaty.' This suggests that one must exercise caution in drawing from an international agreement to which not all WTO Members are party. At the same time, we recognize that a proper interpretation of the term 'the parties' must also take account of the fact that Article 31(3)(c) of the Vienna Convention is considered an expression of the 'principle of systemic integration' which, in the words of the ILC, seeks to ensure that 'international obligations are interpreted by reference to their normative environment' in a manner that gives 'coherence and meaningfulness' to the process of legal interpretation. In a multilateral context such as the WTO, when recourse is had to a non-WTO rule for the purposes of interpreting provisions of the WTO agreements, a delicate balance must be struck between, on the one hand, taking due account of an individual WTO Member's international obligations and, on the other hand, ensuring a consistent and harmonious approach to the interpretation of WTO law among all WTO Members.[71]

Although the Appellate Body did not take a clear position as to whether 'the parties' can only be 'parties to the dispute', it nonetheless took a balanced approach in holding the obligations of WTO Members intact and ensuring the consistency of WTO law with non-WTO rules.

V. WTO and Regional Trade Agreements

In the context of the fragmentation of international law, the ILC Report identifies regionalism as a technique for international law-making, as well as the pursuit for geographic exceptions to universal international laws.[72] In the trade dimension, the former can be seen in a large number of WTO-plus obligations, such as environmental standards and labour standards; the best example for the latter is the recognition of China as a market economy, and consequently the disapplication of Article 15 of China's Accession Protocol relating to price comparability in determining subsidies and dumping. In this section, I address two specific issues. The first relates to the role of the WTO judiciary in interpreting WTO-plus provisions in RTAs and thus contributing to the defragmentation of international trade law. The second issue relates to a recent trend incorporating WTO rules into RTAs and the potential threat to the coherence of WTO law arising from reversal interpretation of such rules by state-to-state dispute settlement mechanisms in RTAs or investor–state arbitration.

[71] Appellate Body Report, EC and Certain Member States—Measures Affecting Trade in Large Civil Aircraft, WT/DS316/AB/R, 18 May 2011, para 845.

[72] ILC Report, paras 199–210.

A. The role of WTO judiciary in defragmentizing international trade law

Article XXIV of the GATT 1994 and Article V of the General Agreement of Trade in Services (GATS) set out the criteria to be fulfilled for a RTA to be WTO-compatible. These criteria are mainly concerned with the openness of trade liberalization in the RTAs, and do not address the potential legal fragmentation arising from conflicting rule-making or deliberate deviation from, or modification of, multilateral trade rules.[73] Moreover, the proliferation of dispute settlement mechanisms as set out in the RTAs may also give rise to the problem of jurisdictional overlapping, forum-shopping,[74] and conflicting judicial decisions.[75]

The proposal put forth in this section is to strengthen the role of the WTO dispute settlement mechanism in resolving disputes arising from the RTAs.[76] Availing Members of the WTO dispute settlement mechanism in resolving trade disputes arising from RTAs will not only contribute to the coherence of international trade law, but will also help those Members with fewer legal resources and less capacity to overcome their institutional limits. To achieve this goal, some obstacles have to be overcome, from applicable law to claims based on non-WTO law. As I argued above, the applicable law in the WTO dispute settlement mechanism is not limited to the WTO law; non-WTO law may come into law through a number of avenues, notably, through Article 31(3)(c) of the VCLT. By contrast, even those WTO lawyers who are enthusiastic about embracing public international law take a cautious position with regard to the legal basis that gives rise to a claim.

However, such a proposal is not impossible. The DSU, in fact, provides possible avenues for WTO Members, upon the mutual consent of the disputing parties and in accordance with Article 7.3, to deviate from the standard terms of reference, or to refer a dispute to an arbitral panel pursuant to Article 25 of the DSU.[77] By doing so, the WTO dispute settlement mechanism may assume the responsibility entrusted by the RTAs to their regional dispute settlement mechanisms and hear the disputes arising from such RTAs. Such a judicial defragmentation approach may enhance the coherence of international trade law between the multilateral WTO system and those trade rules as set out for in the RTAs.

[73] Sungjoon Cho, 'Defragmenting World Trade' (2006) 27(1) Nw J Intl L & Bus 39, 84–86.

[74] See, e.g., Jennifer Hillman, 'Conflicts Between Dispute Settlement Mechanisms in Regional Trade Agreements and the WTO—What Should WTO Do?' (2009) 42(2) Cornell Intl L J 194, 194–208; Kyung Kwak and Gabrielle Marceau, 'Overlaps and Conflicts of Jurisdiction Between the World Trade Organization and Regional Trade Agreements' (2003) 41 Can YB Intl L 83, 83–152.

[75] See e.g., Julia Ya Qin, 'Managing Conflicts Between Rulings of WTO and Regional Trade Tribunals: Reflections on the *Brazil-Tyres* Case' in Pieter H F Bekker, Rudolf Dolzer, and Michael Waibel (eds), *Making Transnational Law Work in the Global Economy: Essays in Honour of Detlev Vagts* (CUP 2010) 601–29.

[76] A similar proposal has also been made by Gao and Lim. However, they take a more reserved approach with regards to the applicable law. They also consider it necessary to amend the DSU so as to make the WTO judiciary competent to hear disputes arising from RTAs. Henry Gao and C L Lim, 'Saving the WTO from the Risk of Irrelevance: The WTO Dispute Settlement Mechanism as A "Common Good" for RTA Disputes' (2008) 11(4) J Intl Econ L 899, 899–925.

[77] Pauwelyn (n 6) 554.

B. The threat to coherence of WTO law arising from reversal interpretation by regional tribunals or investor–state arbitral tribunal

As mentioned above, regionalism can be employed as a technique for international law-making and in pursuit of geographic exceptions to universal WTO rules. As a consequence, the interpretation of WTO law, in conjunction with the rules in RTAs by state-to-state regional dispute settlement mechanisms inevitably presents great challenges to the coherence of WTO law. In addition, there is an increasing trend to rely upon WTO rules, in particular the TRIPS Agreement, to pursue investor–state arbitration claims, which further exacerbates the fragmentation of WTO law.

1. *State-to-state regional tribunals*

The challenges posed by regional dispute settlement mechanisms are manifold and have been documented in a wide range of academic writings. The first of such challenges is jurisdictional conflicts, the root of which is the question whether the WTO judiciary can decline its jurisdiction due to the existence of the choice-of-forum clause in the RTAs. In *Mexico—Soft Drinks*, the challenged measures were tax and other restrictive measures on soft drinks originating from the United States, which were adopted in response to the infringement of market access commitments of sugar cane under the North America Free Trade Agreement (NAFTA). Mexico pleaded before the panel and Appellate Body that the measures in question involved a broader dispute between the United States and Mexico, and urged the WTO judiciary to refrain from exercising its jurisdiction. According to Mexico, the appropriate forum to address this dispute was arbitral procedure under Chapter 20 of NAFTA.[78] However, this plea was accepted by neither the panel, nor the Appellate Body. Whereas the Appellate Body did agree with Mexico that the WTO judiciary had implied jurisdictional power by virtue of its nature of adjudicatory body, such power cannot modify substantive provisions of the DSU. In declining the jurisdiction, as suggested by Mexico, the WTO panel and Appellate Body would diminish the right of a complaining Member to seek the redress of a violation of obligations under Article 23 of the DSU and to bring a dispute in the WTO dispute settlement mechanism under Article 3.3 of the DSU.[79] Such a move runs counter to Article 3.2 of the DSU.

It should nevertheless be noted that the Appellate Body further added that, given a lack of legal impediments applicable in the case before it, such as identical subject matter and relevant provisions, or the NAFTA arbitral tribunal's examination of

[78] Such argument may be termed as a 'comity approach', which is advocated by some scholars. See e.g., Caroline Henckels, 'Overcoming Jurisdictional Isolationism at the WTO FTA Nexus: A Potential Approach for the WTO' (2008) 19 Eur J Intl L 571, 571–99.

[79] Appellate Body Report, *Mexico—Tax Measures on Soft Drinks and Other Beverages*, WT/DS308/AB/R, adopted 24 March 2006, paras 46 and 53.

the broad dispute or the exercise of exclusionary clauses, it chose not to express its view on the effect of such impediments on the exercise of the panel's jurisdiction.[80] It is thus worth exploring possible effects when such legal impediments are present. Pauwelyn and Salles try to draw lessons from domestic legal systems and apply the doctrines of *res judicata* and *lis pendens* to international courts.[81] However, the relevance of *res judicata* and *lis pendens* is limited, since the subject matter and legal bases tend not to be identical. The legal force of choice-of-forum clauses before the WTO judiciary remains to be tested. Possible arguments to give priority to such clauses over the exclusivity of the WTO jurisdiction lie in the assumption that the RTAs constitute exceptions to general WTO rules. However, Gao and Lim are sceptical as to whether parties to RTAs can exclude the jurisdiction of WTO forum by such choice-of-forum clauses in light of the WTO jurisprudence in *Mexico—Soft Drinks*,[82] since by giving the legal force to such clauses the WTO judiciary may diminish the right of the complaining party. This thus brings us to the second issue, which relates to deviation or modification of rights and obligations in the covered agreement by the RTAs: should the WTO judiciary respect such deviations and modifications?

In *Peru—Agricultural Products*, the panel was called upon to examine Guatemala's challenge of the WTO-consistency of the Peruvian price range system, comprising two components of floor price and ceiling price and reference price for different products reflecting international markets. Nonetheless, such a price range system is permitted under the Peru–Guatemala FTA.[83] Peru thus contended that Guatemala acted inconsistently with the principle of good faith by bringing a challenge before the WTO dispute settlement mechanism. The panel took an easy way out by finding that the Peru–Guatemala FTA has not yet entered into force.[84] Hard cases remain where there is a valid RTA limiting the rights enjoyed by WTO Members under the covered agreements. Such an RTA would constitute 'any relevant rules of international law applicable in the relations between the parties' as set out for in Article 31(3)(c) of VCLT, which the WTO judiciary has to take into account. The strength of such obligation to take into account is subject to debate; nonetheless, it is clear that the WTO judiciary cannot ignore relevant rights and obligations arising from the RTAs. As a consequence, the interpretation of rights and obligations of Members under the covered agreement has to be adjusted accordingly. The Appellate Body seemed to support this position. Although

[80] Appellate Body Report, *Mexico—Tax Measures on Soft Drinks and Other Beverages*, WT/DS308/AB/R, 6 March 2006, para 54.

[81] Joost Pauwelyn and Luiz Eduardo Salles, 'Forum Shopping Before International Tribunals: (Real) Concerns, (Im) Possible Solutions' (2009) 42(1) Cornell Intl LJ 77, 77–118.

[82] Gao and Lim (n 76) 910–11.

[83] Paragraph of Annex 2.3 of the Peru–Guatemala FTA provides 'Peru may maintain its Price Range System, established in Supreme Decree No 1152001EF and the amendments thereto, with regard to the products subject to the application of the system marked with an asterisk (*) in column 4 of Peru's Schedule as set out in this Annex.' Citing from Panel Report, *Peru—Additional Duty on Imports of Certain Agricultural Products*, WT/DS457/R, 27 November 2014, para 7.40.

[84] ibid para 7.88.

the Appellate Body, in hearing the appeal in *Peru—Agricultural Products*, held that, irrespective of the status of the Peru–Guatemala FTA as not being ratified by both parties, no 'clear stipulation of a relinquishment of Guatemala's right to have recourse to the WTO dispute settlement system exists in this case in relation to, or within the context of, the DSU'; [85] the Appellate Body nonetheless did not 'exclude the possibility of articulating the relinquishment of the right to initiate WTO dispute settlement proceedings'[86] subject to the qualification that 'any such relinquishment must be made clearly'.[87]

Finally, the third challenge presented by dispute settlement mechanisms in RTAs is the danger of divergent or conflicting judicial decision, which is best illustrated in *Brazil—Tyres*.[88] This dispute resulted from import restrictions on retreaded tyres, undertaken with the aim of containing tropical diseases such as dengue fever and yellow fever. However, due to a judicial decision by the arbitral tribunal of Mercosur (Mercado Común del Sur, Southern Common Market), Brazil exempted products from Mercosur member countries from such restrictive measures, which led to a sharp decrease in market share for EU products. The European Union thus challenged the import restrictions in the WTO dispute settlement mechanism. The panel and the Appellate Body had different views on whether an exemption based on the ruling of Mercosur arbitral tribunal can be defined as arbitrary and unjustifiable within the meaning of the chapeau of Article XX of the GATT 1994. The panel held that the Mercosur exemption was to implement the ruling of Mercosur arbitral tribunal, and taking into account that Article XXIV recognizes preferential treatment between contracting parties to an RTA, exempting the import restrictions from Mercosur member countries is not arbitrary and unjustifiable.[89] By contrast, the Appellate Body, relying heavily on *US—Shrimp/Turtle*, held that the discrimination between Mercosur tyres and non-Mercosur tyres defeated the public health objectives that Brazil wished to pursue. The motivation to implement a ruling by Mercosur arbitral tribunal was not 'an acceptable rationale for the discrimination, because it bears no relationship to the legitimate objective pursued by [import restrictions]'.[90]

The decision of the Appellate Body put Brazil in a legal dilemma in choosing to honour the WTO obligations and thus infringing its Mercosur obligations, and vice versa. This WTO-centric approach fails to appreciate the special relationship between the WTO and RTAs. In response to what she calls 'WTO superiority',

[85] Appellate Body Report, *Peru—Additional Duty on Imports of Certain Agricultural Products*, WT/DS457/AB/R, 20 July 2015, para 5.28.

[86] ibid para 5.25. [87] ibid.

[88] *Brazil—Tyres* also illustrates the *limited* relevance of *res judicata* in relieving jurisdictional conflicts given that the parties to the dispute in the Mercosur arbitral tribunal are Brazil and Uruguay, whereas the parties to the dispute in the WTO dispute settlement mechanism are Brazil and the European Union.

[89] Panel Report, *Brazil—Measures Affecting Imports of Retreaded Tyres*, WT/DS332/R, 12 June 2007, paras 273–74, 280.

[90] Appellate Body Report, *Brazil—Measures Affecting Imports of Retreaded Tyres*, WT/DS332/AB/R, 3 December 2007, para 228.

Qin argues that at the systemic level, the WTO judiciary has to acknowledge that 'RTA laws—including RTA treaties, internal decisions and tribunal rulings—are part of public international law, from which the WTO agreements cannot be read in "clinical isolation"'.[91] Moreover, in accordance with the presumption against conflicts and in reliance with Article 31(3)(c) of VCLT, Qin argues that 'under the interpretive principles of international law, WTO judges have a legal duty to avoid conflicts with a prior RTA decision'.[92]

2. *Investor–state arbitration*

An emergent challenge to the integrity and coherence of international trade law comes from investor–state arbitration. Creative investors incorporate the WTO covered agreements, in particular the TRIPS Agreement, into their investor claims, arguing that the host state infringes the fair and equitable treatment (FET) obligation by frustrating their legitimate expectations or violating international law; namely the WTO law, which can be best illustrated in the Philip Morris Asia's claim against Australia's plain packing measures.[93]

Views on this emergent trend of using investor–state arbitration as a venue to assert IPRs are divergent. On the one hand, IPRs, by their nature, are private rights to be enjoyed and asserted by private individuals. The reliance on investor–state arbitration of IPRs protection may help to strengthen the protection of IPRs. On the other hand, investor–state arbitration is a hybrid dispute settlement mechanism, a different genre from inter-governmental WTO dispute settlement mechanism or state-to-state dispute settlement mechanisms in the RTAs. Moreover, the rights and obligations of Members under the WTO covered agreement are intergovernmental in nature and owed by states. This also brings about a thorny question as regards the exclusivity of the WTO dispute settlement mechanism in resolving disputes arising from the covered agreements. Does this exclusivity extend to nationals of WTO Members? To be more specific, Article 23.1 of the DSU dictates WTO Members to 'have recourse to, and abide by, the rules and procedures' of the DSU, when Members 'seek the redress of a violation of obligations or other nullification or impairment of benefits under the covered agreements or an impediment to the attainment of any objective of the covered agreements'. This is generally referred to as the primacy or exclusivity of the jurisdiction of the WTO dispute settlement mechanism. However, this is an international obligation owed by WTO Members, which poses the question as to its applicability to private individuals. Similar controversies arise in the context of EU law, where the Court of Justice of the European Union (the CJEU) assumes exclusive jurisdiction on the interpretation of EU law. A controversy arose when a Belgian investor brought a claim before the International Centre for

[91] Qin (n 75) 627. [92] ibid 624.

[93] See e.g., Tsai-Yu Lin, 'Inter-mingling TRIPS Agreement with An FET Standard in Investor-State Arbitration: An Emergent Challenge for the WTO' 50 J World Trade, 71–91. See also Julien Chaisse, 'Exploring the Confines of International Investment and Domestic Health Protections—General Exceptions Clause as a Forced Perspective' (2013) 39(2/3) Am J L & Med 332–61.

the Settlement of Investor Disputes (ICSID) arbitral tribunal due to Hungary's termination of power purchase agreement.[94] Hungary and the intervening European Commission argued that the arbitral tribunal is not competent to hear the dispute, due to the exclusive jurisdiction of the interpretation of the European Union as enshrined in Article 292 of the Treaty on the Functioning of the European Union (TFEU). The arbitral tribunal was not impressed by this argument, holding that such obligation binds only EU Member States and does not extend to their nationals.[95] I share the view advanced by the arbitral tribunal on the ground that such international obligation to refer to the CJEU or WTO dispute settlement mechanism is binding only on states. This view gives rise to new challenges to the fragmentation of international trade law, this time from the investment regime rather than the trade regime. With the tendency to include investment chapter and investor–state arbitration in RTAs, it evidences a promise for the convergence of trade and investment regimes. Nonetheless, incorporating IPRs of the TRIPS Agreement into an investment claim reminds us of the perils that accompany such convergence.

VI. Conclusion

This chapter examined the relationship between the WTO and public international law in the context of the fragmentation of international law. It points to two driving forces for the fragmentation of international law: the tendency of states to enter into international agreements with historical or geographic proximity: diversification and specialization of international law. With the trend of 'polycentric globalisation', functionally differentiated and specialized regimes tend to appear autonomous and isolate themselves from general public international law, and thus view themselves as 'self-contained' regimes. However, the claim of self-containment depends largely on how one perceives international legal order: universalistic or particularistic. Universalistic general international lawyers pursue legal unity and try to avoid fragmentation of international law, while particularistic international lawyers tend to cherish their special realm.

Relying on the presumption against conflicts and the principle of systemic integration, this chapter explored possible ways to defragmentize international law and pursue coherence. It identified three main reasons for the fragmentation of international trade law: the exclusive and compulsory WTO dispute settlement mechanism; the bourgeoning subject-specific international regimes; and the proliferation of RTAs. This chapter thus examined built-in institutional linkage between the WTO and other international organizations, the relationship between WTO law and public international law, and RTAs.

The chapter argues that built-in institutional linkages between the WTO and other international organizations, established by way of incorporation and explicit

[94] *Electrabel S A v The Republic of Hungary*, ICSID Case No ARB/07/19 (30 November 2012).
[95] ibid paras 4.147–4.166.

reference, contributes to the co-ordination and coherence between WTO law and other subject areas of international law, notably IMF and the WHO/FAO Codex Alimentarius Commission. However, which international organizations or conventions can be qualified as international standard setting bodies is debatable, particularly when not all WTO Members are contracting parties to such international organizations or conventions. The critical question here is whether the term 'the parties' in Article 31(3)(c) the VCLT should be interpreted as 'all the parties'.

With regard to general international law, while it is widely acknowledged that WTO law is not to be read in clinical isolation from public international law, what it entails is not entirely clear. Such ambiguity can be seen in the legal status of the ILC Articles on State Responsibility in the WTO dispute settlement mechanism, as well as the possibility for WTO law to fall back on general international law in referring the concept of countermeasure in case of persistent incompliance. Regarding international treaty law, the most controversial issue relates to the application of Article 31(3)(c) of the VCLT. The panel in *EC—Approval and Marketing of Biotech Products* took a restrictive approach, holding that the term 'the parties' in Article 31(3)(c) of the VCLT must be 'all the parties', i.e. all WTO Members. While the Appellate Body in *EC—Large Civil Aircraft* took a balanced approach, the Appellate Body did not clarify whether 'the parties' should be limited to 'all the parties'. The controversy persists.

Finally, this chapter argued that the WTO dispute settlement mechanism should be made available to WTO Members in resolving disputes arising from their RTAs. In this context, these RTAs constitute 'any relevant rules of international law applicable in the relations between the parties' within the meaning of Article 31(3)(c) of the VCLT. Moreover, the WTO dispute settlement mechanism should pay due regard to the choice-of-forum clauses in these RTAs and judicial decisions in regional tribunals. The WTO centrality or superiority as shown in the *Brazil—Tyres* should be renounced. Above all, the most important challenge to the coherence of international trade law comes not from international trade law regime but from international investment law regime, when investors bring their investment claims before investor–state arbitral tribunal, arguing that the impairment of their IPRs frustrates their legitimate expectation or infringes international law, and thus violates the FET obligation. While the WTO judiciary should not guard its jurisdiction jealously, the same respect or judicial comity should be shown by investor–state arbitral tribunal so as to ensure the coherence of international economic law.

17

Natural Resources and the Rules of the Multilateral Trading System: A Sustainable Development Perspective

*Thomas J Schoenbaum**

I. Introduction

It is a distinct honour and a privilege to be asked to contribute to this *Liber Amicorum* to honour my esteemed colleague and good friend, Mitsuo Matsushita, who contributed so much to the development of international trade law and policy as a Member of the Appellate Body of the World Trade Organization (WTO) and as a professor and scholar of the law. As a Member of the Appellate Body and now as a frequent panel member, Professor Matsushita has participated in many landmark trade law decisions, some of which I will discuss in this chapter.

As Professor Matsushita has pointed out,[1] international trade in natural resources poses special problems for the multilateral trading system. Natural resources are commonly classified as renewable and non-renewable resources. They are derived directly from the living and non-living components of the Earth's ecosystems. Natural resources in international trade include 'raw materials' of various sorts, as well as products such as oil, natural gas, coal, water, and those derived from animals and plants, most importantly wood products. Such products historically have not been at the forefront of concern, but this has changed in recent years. With the rise of human populations and the development of emerging economies around the world, demand for most types of natural resources has rocketed, and this trend is expected to continue. Thus, trade in natural resources is bound to increase.

International trade in natural resources raises unique concerns. On the one hand, natural resources provide raw materials that are necessary for a wide variety of important consumer products, as well as for the generation of energy.

* Harold S Shefelman Distinguished Professor, University of Washington.

[1] Mitsuo Matsushita, 'Export Control of Natural Resources: WTO Panel Ruling on the Chinese Export Restrictions of Natural Resources' (2011) 3 Trade, L & Dev 267.

International trade in natural resources is vital because they are distributed unequally around the world. Resource-poor nations depend upon steady supplies of natural resources as the basis of their economies. On the other hand, what we call natural resources are vital components of functioning ecosystems. Deriving natural resources products inevitably causes some disruption of these ecosystems. Moreover, most natural resources are exhaustible or, if renewable, replaced only with great difficulty.

How may we reconcile these two facets of natural resources with respect to the law of international trade? This chapter adopts the standard commonly used to take into account both aspects of natural resources: the concept of *sustainable development*. Sustainable development means that 'the right to development does not exist in the absolute sense, but is relative always to its tolerance by the environment'.[2] The principle of sustainable development has been in the forefront of international law since the 1992 United Nations Conference on Environment and Development and was recently affirmed at the 2012 United Nations Conference on Sustainable Development held in Rio de Janeiro.[3]

Despite the unique and important character of natural resources, with the exception of Article XX(g) of the General Agreement on Tariffs and Trade (GATT), the multilateral trading system makes no specific allowance for sustainable development of natural resources.[4] Yet outside the framework of international economic law, the field of public international law creates important treaty regimes and policies with respect to sustainable development of many kinds of natural resources. For example, the Convention on International Trade in Endangered Species of Wild Fauna and Flora (CITES) (1973, in force 1975)[5] creates an important international law regime that restricts international trade in many types of animal and plant products. The United Nations Convention on Biological Diversity (1992)[6] sets out standards for the preservation of habitat and biological diversity. The United Nations Forest Principles (1992)[7] reflect a non-binding world consensus on conservation of world forests. The Berlin Rules on Water Resources (2004)[8]

[2] *Case Concerning the Gabcikovo-Nagymaros Project (Hung v Slovak)* [1997] ICJ Rep 7, 88 (separate opinion of Judge Weeramantry).

[3] 'Report of the United Nations Conference on Sustainable Development' United Nations Conference on Sustainable Development (Rio de Janeiro 20–22 June 2012) (20 June 2012) UN Doc A/CONF.216/16.

[4] As pointed out below, however, the Preamble of the Marrakesh Agreement Establishing the World Trade Organization (1994) incorporates sustainable development as a policy.

[5] Text and information available at 'Convention on International Trade in Endangered Species of Wild Fauna and Flora' <http://www.cites.org/> accessed 23 April 2016. This international regime currently has 181 parties.

[6] Text and information available at 'Convention on Biological Diversity' <http://www.cbd.int> accessed 11 March 2016. This regime currently has 196 parties.

[7] , 'Report of the United Nations Conference on Environment and Development' United Nations Conference on Environment and Development (Rio de Janeiro 3–14 June 1992) (14 August 1992) UN Doc A/CONF.151.26/Rev.1 (Vol III) Annex III.

[8] Text and information available at 'Berlin Conference (2004) Water Resources Law' (International Law Association) <http://internationalwaterlaw.org/documents/intldocs/ILA_Berlin_Rules-2004.pdf> accessed 23 April 2016.

establish customary international law rules for the use and protection of freshwater resources; and the United Nations Convention on the Law of the Sea (1982)[9] adopts environmental protection criteria for the exploitation of the living and non-living resources of the world's oceans.

The overarching question this chapter explores is to what extent the norms and criteria adopted in these and other international environmental regimes concerning natural resources may be adopted by WTO dispute settlement bodies that deal with trade disputes concerning natural resources. Of course, WTO panels and the Appellate Body are not allowed to base any decision on these agreements as such. Articles I and III of the WTO Dispute Settlement Understanding (DSU) limit the application of the WTO dispute settlement regime to the 'covered agreements', the WTO agreements themselves. However, the thesis of this chapter is that WTO panels and the Appellate Body may use the principles of interpretation of treaties contained in the Vienna Convention on the Law of Treaties (VCLT) to interpret provisions of the GATT and other WTO agreements to be consistent with the law and policies expressed in international environmental treaties. In this regard, Article 31.3 of the VCLT specifies as a matter of interpretation of treaties that 'there shall be taken into account, together with the context: (a) any subsequent agreement between the parties ...; (b) any subsequent practice ...; and (c) any relevant rules of international law applicable in the relations between the parties'. This chapter will show how this has already been done—albeit implicitly—in two very important and well-known WTO dispute settlement cases, one of which was co-authored by Mitsuo Matsushita as panel member. What is more, interpreting the rules of the multilateral trade agreements to be consistent with international environmental treaties will also benefit and uphold legitimate national policies on the preservation and conservation of natural resources insofar as they are based upon the widely accepted international regimes applicable to natural resources.

It is particularly important that WTO dispute settlement bodies take into account international environmental agreements, since it is increasingly evident that WTO Members themselves will not come to any binding comprehensive solution to the problem of the relationship between international trade rules and international environmental rules. The WTO's Committee on Trade and Environment is moribund, and the Doha Development Agenda, which specified as a negotiation topic[10] the relationship between international trade rules and the rules of multilateral environmental agreements, has failed. Thus, the burden of reconciling trade law rules with environmental rules is firmly on the WTO dispute settlement bodies.

[9] Text and information available at 'United Nations Convention on the Law of the Sea' (16 November 1994) <http://www.un.org/depts/los/convention_agreements/texts/unclos/unclos_e.pdf> accessed 23 April 2016.

[10] Agenda item 31 of the Doha Development Agenda, adopted at the Fourth Ministerial Conference of the WTO at Doha in November, 2001. See 'The Doha Round' (*World Trade Organization*) <https://www.wto.org/english/tratop_e/dda_e/dda_e.htm> accessed 11 March 2016.

Despite failure to agree on some aspects of the relationship between environment and trade by WTO Members, it should not be forgotten that the Preamble to the founding document of the WTO, the Marrakesh Agreement for the Establishment of the World Trade Organization (1994), states that the purpose of the WTO is to facilitate the 'optimal use of the world's resources in accordance with the objective of sustainable development seeking both to protect and preserve the environment and to enhance the means for doing so …' The purpose of this chapter is to explore how this objective of sustainable development is implemented under existing WTO rules and to suggest improvements to enhance this objective.

Before detailing the specific ways the WTO dispute settlement bodies have reconciled trade rules with environmental rules, this chapter will briefly summarize the principal rules of the multilateral trading system that apply to natural resources.

II. Import Rules

The import side of trade is the home of most of the rules of the multilateral trading system. The basic thrust of the GATT and associated WTO agreements is to open markets and to improve market access for foreign products. Thus, import barriers are traditionally associated with and imposed for the purpose of protectionism. However, import barriers, as we shall see, can be imposed for environmental reasons and to implement sustainable development. The question is whether a particular import barrier that a government says is for environmental purposes is really disguised protectionism. The rules of the multilateral trading system are designed to carefully distinguish between true environmental measures and disguised protectionism.

On the import side, natural resources are subject to bound tariffs under GATT Article II[11] for each Member of the WTO; each Member has its own individual bound tariff schedule, and the import tariffs vary, but are generally quite low, even for developing countries.[12] GATT Article XI forbids (with insignificant exceptions) measures such as quotas that impede imports. GATT Article III permits domestic taxes on imported natural resources, but the tax must be no more than the corresponding tax on domestically produced like products.

Therefore, on the import side, conservation measures taken for environmental reasons must meet the legal tests of GATT Article XX, the General Exceptions article. Conceptually, an import measure aimed at conservation is relatively rare. The purpose of a conservation import measure would be to conserve or preserve natural resources located outside the territory of the trade-restricting Member. For

[11] General Agreement on Tariffs and Trade (4 April 1994) 1867 UNTS 187.

[12] An exception to this statement is tariffs for imported fish products. A Food and Agriculture Organization study in 2006 found that tariffs on fish products range from 0 to 30% among WTO Members, with the median tariff at 14%. Moreover, 60% of fish tariffs are unbound. FAO 'Tariffs in World Seafood Trade' (2006) FAO Fisheries Circular No 1016 (by Arne Melchior).

a WTO Member to take such action requires a political will to force conservation of natural resources in other countries.

The most important import measures other than tariffs on natural resources are certain fauna and flora products. Two important WTO Appellate Body decisions set the standards for whether such import measures are consistent with GATT Article XX. In the famous *Shrimp/Turtle* case[13], the Appellate Body ruled that a ban on imports of shrimp from countries that did not require fishers to employ turtle excluder devices met the requirements of GATT Article XX(g) in that this measure was adopted for the purpose of conserving exhaustible natural resources (the turtles) and was accompanied by domestic conservation measures because US fishers are required to employ turtle excluder devices. But the Appellate Body ruled that the US import measure was discriminatory in violation of the Article XX 'chapeau'. After the United States revised its regulations, however, the Appellate Body[14] upheld the US import measure, ruling that the revision cured the discrimination problem. At the present time the United States still maintains a ban on imports of shrimp and prawns from certain countries.

A second celebrated case is the *EC—Seal Products* case,[15] in which the Appellate Body considered the consistency with Article XX of an EU measure that prohibited the sale of seal products in the European Union with exceptions only for indigenous hunts, travellers, and products of sustainable management hunts. The Appellate Body approved the application Article XX(a)—that the trade restriction was necessary to safeguard public morals in the European Union, although the Appellate Body ruled that, as applied, the trade restriction was discriminatory and inconsistent with the chapeau of Article XX. Nevertheless, this ruling was a victory for the European Union, which, like the United States in the *Shrimp/Turtle* case, may move to remove the discrimination and validate the seal import ban.

A third subsection of Article XX that may be employed to validate natural resource conservation measures is Article XX(b), the general exception for measures necessary to protect plant, animal, and human life and health. This provision is mainly useful as the basis for approving import measures that ban imports of products coming from endangered species and listed in one of the Appendices of CITES. No CITES ban as such has been litigated in the WTO, although the seven species of sea turtles involved in the *Shrimp/Turtle* case were listed as endangered under CITES. It seems evident that if a CITES case is litigated at the WTO, Article XX(b) as well as Article XX(g) might be used to justify the ban.[16]

[13] Appellate Body Report, *United States—Import Prohibition of Certain Shrimp and Shrimp Products* (*US—Shrimps/Turtle*), WT/DS58/AB/R, 12 October 1998.

[14] Appellate Body Report, *United States—Import Prohibitions of Certain Shrimp and Shrimp Products, Recourse to Article 21.5 of the DSU by Malaysia*, WT/DS58/AB/RW, 22 October 2001.

[15] Appellate Body Report, *European Communities—Measures Prohibiting the Importation and Marketing of Seal Products*, WT/DS400/AB/R, 22 May 2014.

[16] For the leading case interpreting the requirements of Article XX(b), see Appellate Body Report, *European Communities—Measures Affecting Asbestos and Asbestos-containing Products* (*EC—Asbestos*), WT/DS135/AB/R, 12 March 2001.

Article XX(b) would seem to justify, for example, the US Lacey Act,[17] which is used by authorities in the United States to block the import of illegally taken animals, fish, trees, and plants. The Lacey Act has been used to block imports of tropical woods listed under CITES, including ebony and mahogany.[18]

Thus, on the import side, three legal tools exist—three subsections of GATT Article XX—as primary operative provisions to implement the sustainable development policy of the Preamble of the Marrakesh Agreement Establishing the World Trade Organization. All three legal tools have strict requirements as interpreted by decisions of the WTO Appellate Body, but these three methods nevertheless are clear and important. Members employing these methods to natural resources must, however, keep in mind the non-discrimination standards of the Article XX chapeau.

Two subsidiary legal tools are available under WTO rules that bear upon the conservation of natural resources and the objective of sustainable development. A WTO Member may (i) adopt and implement sanitary and phytosanitary (SPS) measures to safeguard the environment; and (ii) adopt and enforce technical standards to secure environmental objectives.

For example, the Canadian Food Import Agency Regulation D-02-12[19] applies to imports of all raw logs, plants, tropical and non-tropical timber, and all non-processed wood products. The purpose of this requirement is to allow screening of imported natural resources that may be infested with pests or tainted by disease. Canada also enforces strict regulations applicable to live animals, insects, and amphibians and reptiles for similar reasons. These SPS measures are justified as long as they meet the standards of the WTO Agreement on Sanitary and Phytosanitary Measures (1994), which establishes criteria for SPS measures, requiring them to be based on scientific standards and objective risk assessment, as well as administered in a transparent and non-discriminatory manner.

Technical measures may be applied to require environmentally protective standards for imported natural resources products under the authority and the criteria set out in the WTO Agreement on Technical Barriers to Trade (TBT Agreement) (1994). Nevertheless, such technical requirements must comply with the exacting criteria of the TBT Agreement. For example, the United States Dolphin Protection Consumer Information Act[20] adopts criteria for labelling tuna sold in the United States as 'dolphin safe'.[21] Under WTO law, such a labelling requirement is a technical

[17] Lacey Act, 16 USC ss 3371–78 (2005).

[18] 'Animal and Plant Health Inspection Service' (United States Department of Agriculture) <http://www.aphis.usda.gov/wps/portal/ourfocus/planthealth?.html> accessed 23 April 2016.

[19] 'D-02-12: Import requirements for non-processed wood and other non-propagative wood products, except solid wood packaging material, from all areas other than the continental United States' (Canadian Food Inspection Agency, 18 July 2011) <http://www.inspection.gc.ca/plants/plant-protection/directives/forestry/d-02-12/eng/1312383927173/1312384324372> accessed 11 March 2016.

[20] Dolphin Protection Consumer Information Act, 16 USC s 1385 (1990).

[21] Dolphin-safe labeling standards, 50 CFR ss 216.91–216.92 (2009). See also *Earth Island Institute v Hogarth* 494 F3d 757 (9th Cir 2007).

standard subject to the requirements of the TBT Agreement.[22] Mexico challenged the consistency of the labelling regulations with the TBT Agreement at the WTO; the Appellate Body ruled that the US regulations were inconsistent with Article 2.1 of the TBT Agreement, which specifies that the criterion of national treatment applies to such labelling requirements. The United States then revised its 'dolphin-safe' labelling regulations to comply with the WTO ruling, but the WTO panel in a subsequent challenge brought to the WTO by Mexico ruled that the revised regulation was inconsistent with Article 2.1 with respect to certification and record-keeping requirements. Nevertheless, if the strict TBT Agreement criteria are met, WTO Members may adopt labelling and other safeguard requirements for imported natural resources.

The foregoing summary of WTO import requirements applicable to natural resources is provided with a view to evaluating whether such requirements are sufficient to meet the objective of sustainable development. The answer seems to be that, while WTO rules have made a substantial start, more needs to be done to accommodate the principle of sustainable development with respect to natural resources into the law of the multilateral trading system.

The biggest failing of WTO import rules with respect to sustainable development is the uncertainty surrounding the rules of Article XX and their possible restrictiveness compared with national policy measures to tighten natural resource import standards, for example, the US administers quotas with respect to imports of certain types of tuna in order to implement obligations under international fishing agreements.[23] In 2008, the United States strengthened the Lacey Act by amendments that prohibit the importation of any plant which has been harvested in violation of any law of a state, the United States, or any foreign state.[24] The United States also applies the Lacey Act to many species, such as ceiba wood, that are not listed as endangered under CITES.[25] In 2005, the European Union adopted FLEGT (Forest Law Enforcement, Governance and Trade) Action Plan[26] which blocks imports into the European Union of wood products derived from illegal logging and unsustainably managed forests. Non-governmental organizations, such as the Forest Stewardship Council,[27] have carried out extensive surveys of forests around the world and have compiled an inventory of forests totalling 388.7 million acres in eighty countries that are sustainably managed. Many developing countries have adopted laws to require sustainably managed forests and to curb abuses of wildlife, but they have difficulty controlling illegal wildlife trade and illegal logging activities.[28] Import restrictions are necessary in developed

[22] Agreement on Technical Barriers to Trade (15 April 1994) 1868 UNTS.120 Annex I para 1.

[23] <http://www.nmfs.noaa.gov/pr/dophinsafe/tunaHTScodes.htm> accessed 11 March 2016.

[24] See Pervase A Sheikh, 'The Lacey Act: Compliance Issues Related to the Import of Plants and Plant Products' (Congressional Research Service 2012).

[25] ibid.

[26] Council Regulation (EC) 2173/2005 on the establishment of a FLEGT licensing scheme for imports of timber into the European Community [2005] OJ L347/1.

[27] See <http://www.rainforests.mongabay.com/1010.htm> accessed 23 April 2016.

[28] e.g. Michael J Miller, 'Persistent Illegal Logging in Costa Rica: The Role of Corruption Among Forest Regulators' [2011] 20 J Envt Dev 50.

countries to discourage illegal harvesting of forests and wildlife, even if the species concerned are not listed as endangered under CITES. None of the new import conservation laws discussed above have so far been challenged at the WTO, but if such a challenge develops, the WTO dispute settlement bodies should look to international criteria adopted under multilateral environmental agreements to interpret the GATT Article XX general exceptions, especially subsections (b) and (g). For example, the 1992 Non-legally Binding Authoritative Statement of Principles for a Global Consensus on the Management, Conservation, and Sustainable Development of All Types of Forests adopts sustainable development as international policy and calls for the enactment of national laws fostering 'the protection of ecologically viable representative or unique examples of forests, including primary/old-growth forests, cultural, spiritual, historical, religious and other unique and valued forests of national importance'.

The World Bank and other development assistance organizations are taking great efforts to promote sustainable development forestry in developing countries.[29] Many developing countries have adopted new sustainable development laws,[30] and developed countries that are the consumer countries have developed import control policies[31] designed to work in tandem with these international efforts. The WTO Appellate Body and panels that may examine these import laws to judge their consistency with WTO rules should look to multilateral environmental policies in interpreting the rules of GATT Article XX to uphold these new laws, employing the principles of treaty interpretation of the VCLT outlined above.

III. Export Rules

On the export side several important recent cases have brought the issue of conservation of natural resources through export restrictions to centre stage. Let us begin, however, with the basic rules on export restrictions. Governments impose export restrictions for a variety of reasons. Developing countries may depend upon export taxes as a source of revenue. Export restrictions may also be imposed in order to diversify exports and to promote domestic processing industries, rather than exporting raw materials. Export controls may also be employed for security reasons, to relieve domestic shortages, to control a rise in domestic prices, or to reserve supplies of a raw material to domestic industry. Finally, exports may be restricted to promote environmental quality and to preserve the environment.

The rules of the multilateral trading system on the export side, in contrast to the import side of trade, are relatively flexible and undeveloped. The basic rule is Article XI:1 of the GATT, which prohibits both with respect to exports and

[29] See The World Bank, 'Strengthening Forest Law Enforcement and Governance' (2006) Report No 36638-GLB.

[30] ibid.

[31] e.g. Japan Guidelines for Verification of Logging and Sustainable Development of Wood and Wood Products, ibid 25.

imports, all restrictions of trade other than 'duties, taxes, or other charges'—in other words, *tariffs*. But while on the import side of trade most tariffs are 'bound' as a result of trade negotiations, relatively few tariffs are bound on the export side. Thus most WTO Members have complete freedom to impose high or low export taxes on exports of natural resources. However, some WTO Members, such as China,[32] have largely given up this freedom to impose export taxes in their agreements of accession to the WTO. What is more, these agreements of accession vary widely. Thus, insofar as export taxes—export tariffs—are concerned, the WTO operated a multi-tiered system of rules.[33] Most WTO Members have complete freedom, while some have very little freedom, and some Members enjoy in-between status. Some WTO Members have 'bound' export tariffs on certain categories of products as well.[34]

Moreover, the rule against all export restrictions except tariffs is subject to certain specific exceptions: GATT Article XI:2 states that the rule in XI:1 does not apply to (i) export restrictions temporarily applied to prevent or relieve critical shortages; or (ii) export measures necessary to the application of regulations for classification, grading, or marketing of commodities. GATT Article XIII adds that export restrictions, when they are permitted, must be imposed on a non-discriminatory basis. Article XII of the WTO Agreement on Agriculture, recognizing that some export restrictions on agricultural products are permitted, cautions that Members imposing such controls, must 'give due consideration to the effects of such prohibitions or restrictions on importing Members' food security'.

The GATT Article XX general exceptions also create several exceptions to the prohibition of Article XI:1. Export control measures are allowed pursuant to Article XX(c) relating to gold or silver; Article XX(f) to protect against the export of national treasures of artistic, historic, or archaeological value; Article XX(g) relating to the conservation of exhaustible natural resources; Article XX(i) involving restrictions necessary to ensure essential qualities of such materials to a domestic processing industry; and Article XX(j) essential to the acquisition or distribution of productions in general or local short supply. Finally, GATT Article XXI permits export controls to protect national security.

With respect to natural resources, the most relevant exception is Article XX(g), which specifically makes allowance for conservation of natural resources. The Appellate Body has recently decided two important cases that have extensively interpreted the requirements of Article XX(g): the *China—Raw Materials* case[35]

[32] See Appellate Body Report, *China—Measures Related to the Exportation of Various Raw Materials* (*China—Raw Materials*), WT/DS394, 395, 398/AB/R, 30 January 2012.

[33] See Julia Ya Qin, 'Reforming WTO Disciplines on Export Duties: Sovereignty over Natural Resources, Economic Development, and Environmental Protection' (2012) No 2012-04 Wayne State University Law School Research Paper <http://www.ssrn.com/abstract=2030477> accessed 23 April 2016.

[34] ibid 7.

[35] Panel and Appellate Body Report, *China—Measures Related to the Exportation of Various Raw Materials*, WT/DS394, 395, 398/AB/R, 5 July 2011 and 30 January 2012.

and the *China—Rare Earths* case.[36] The *China—Raw Materials* case concerned Chinese export restrictions in the form of export duties, export licensing, export quotas, and minimum export price requirements on a wide variety of natural resources, including forms of bauxite, coke, fluorspar, magnesium, manganese, silicon carbide, silicon metal, yellow phosphorus, and zinc. The United States, the European Union, and Mexico complained against these restrictions, charging that they were designed to keep prices low in China, but high in the rest of the world, creating comparative advantage for China. The WTO panel and the Appellate Body ruled that China, under the terms of its Accession Protocol, may only place export tariffs on eighty-four listed items; therefore export duties on most of the raw materials must be removed. In addition, GATT Article XI:1 forbids other forms of export restrictions, and the Chinese measures did not meet the requirements for any GATT exception.

In the *China—Rare Earths* case, the WTO panel and the Appellate Body similarly ruled that Chinese export duties, quotas, and other export restrictions of rare earths, tungsten, and molybdenum, as well as the administration of such restrictions were inconsistent with China's Accession Protocol, GATT Article XI:1, and were not justified under any GATT exception.

The panel and Appellate Body reports in these two cases were especially noteworthy for their interpretations of the requirements of GATT Article XX(g) in the context of export measures. Article XX(g) requires that the measure in question must satisfy the elements stated in subsection (g) as well as the requirements stated in the Article XX chapeau. The Appellate Body in the *China—Rare Earths* case emphasized that Article XX(g) presents a 'holistic' test, and that a Member invoking this exception must show that it meets all the requirements of this provision.[37] There are two separate 'prongs' of Article XX(g): first, the export measure must 'relate to the conservation of exhaustible natural resources', and second, the measure must be 'made effective in conjunction with restrictions on domestic production or consumption'. The latter requirement, the Appellate Body has stated, is a requirement of 'even-handedness', which is not a separate test from that stated and does not suggest that the burden of conservation must be evenly distributed, but does require that a measure should not impose 'a significantly more onerous burden on foreign consumers or producers' than on domestic consumers and producers.[38]

As to the two prongs of Article XX(g), the Appellate Body interpreted the first prong to mean that the export measure in question must relate to conservation, which is to say its 'design and structure' must exhibit 'a close and genuine relationship of ends and means'—between the export measure and the conservation objective, and WTO panels 'are not precluded from considering evidence relating to the actual operation or the impact of the measure at issue'.[39] The term 'conservation'

[36] Panel and Appellate Body Report, *China—Measures Related to the Export of Rare Earths, Tungsten, and Molybdenum* (*China—Rare Earths*), WT/DS431, 432, 433/AB/R, 26 March 2014 and 7 August 2014.

[37] ibid para 5.94.

[38] ibid paras 5.127–5.134.

[39] ibid paras 5.90; 5.111–5.112; 5.114.

may encompass limiting or halting exploitation or facilitating the replenishment of the resource.[40] Conservation must be flexibly interpreted in the particular context involved.[41] Similarly, the meaning of the term 'exhaustible natural resource' is not fixed or static, but is 'by definition, evolutionary'.[42]

The second prong of Article XX(g) is, perhaps, the most difficult to satisfy. Although there is no requirement that the trade-restricting measure be primarily aimed at or have as its main purpose the effectiveness of the domestic restrictions, the trade restrictions and the domestic measures are expected to 'work together' for the purposes of conservation.[43] The restriction on domestic consumption and/or production must reinforce and complement the restriction on international trade.[44]

Thus, after the panel and Appellate Body decisions in the *China—Raw Materials* and *China—Rare Earths* cases, WTO Members that wish to adopt trade measures to conserve natural resources must either employ export taxes, if they are permitted, or use the exception in Article XX(g). In the wake of the two cases involving China, however, there is no example of a successful export conservation measure gaining approval at the WTO. The strict requirements that the Appellate Body approved in the *China—Raw Materials* and the *China—Rare Earths* cases may deter WTO Members from taking trade measures to conserve natural resources and to protect the environment.

A solution would be for the WTO panels and Appellate Body in subsequent cases to consult multilateral environmental regimes and their adopted policies in interpreting the two prongs of GATT Article XX(g). International 'regimes' have been adopted for a wide variety of natural resources, and as a complementary legal analysis to the requirements of Article XX(g), WTO panels and the Appellate Body might profit from testing trade measures that purport to be for conservation purposes against the policies and criteria adopted for the resource in question in the applicable multilateral environmental agreement. As on the import side, this consultation would be permitted under WTO rules through application of the VCLT and its provisions on interpreting treaties.

IV. Natural Resources Subsidies

An area of the law of the multilateral trading system that might be profitably employed to conserve natural resources is the rules concerning subsidies. WTO law concerning subsidies is principally embodied in the WTO Agreement on Subsidies and Countervailing Measures (ASCM). As is well known and documented by economists, subsidies have a distorting effect on both the demand and supply of the subsidized product. Two varieties of natural resources where subsidies have a particularly pernicious effect are (i) subsidies of fossil fuels; and

[40] ibid para 5.89. [41] ibid. [42] ibid.
[43] *China—Raw Materials* (n 32) para 356. [44] *China—Rare Earths* (n 36) para 5.92.

(ii) fishing subsidies. According to the Organization for Economic Cooperation and Development (OECD), in the thirty-four OECD member countries alone, subsidies for fossil fuel production or use had an overall value of USD 55–90 billion per year in the period between 2005 and 2011.[45] Developing countries also heavily subsidize fossil fuel production and use. The Natural Resources Defense Council (NRDC) estimates that total consumer subsidies of fossil fuels in developing countries amounted to USD 630 billion in 2012.[46] Fishing subsidies are also widespread, particularly in developing countries. The WTO group known as 'Friends of Fish' (Argentina, Chile, Columbia, New Zealand, Norway, Iceland, Pakistan, Peru, and the United States) estimates that direct subsidies for fishing range from USD 14 to 20 billion per year.[47] These fishing subsidies make it easier and cheaper to fish when, according to the United Nations Food and Agriculture Organization, over eighty per cent of the world's fish stocks are either fully exploited or over-exploited.[48]

Natural resource subsidies are economically inefficient and environmentally destructive. Subsidies have a distorting impact on international trade and encourage over-exploitation of natural resources. Nevertheless, no complaints involving natural resources subsidies have been brought to the WTO under the ASCM. The reason seems to be that the rules of the ASCM do not reach most natural resources subsidies programs. A complete analysis of the rules of the ASCM is beyond the scope of this chapter; but some obvious reasons are apparent. First, in order to be countervailable under the ASCM, a subsidy must be specific to a particular firm or industry;[49] but most fossil-fuel subsidies are to consumers and are not specific. Second, prohibited subsidies under the ASCM are export subsidies;[50] neither fossil-fuel nor fishing subsidies are export subsidies. Third, natural resources subsidies, such as those for fuels and fishing, are purely domestic subsidies; the rules of the multilateral trading system and the ASCM reach domestic subsidies only rarely, when a WTO Member can shoe adverse effects and serious prejudice.[51] Fourth, since subsidization is so widespread, no WTO Member wishes to bring a challenge to a subsidy that it may also be using in some fashion.

In the 2001 Doha Declaration, which began the Doha Development Agenda, a round of trade negotiations among WTO Members, fishing subsidies were an

[45] 'An OECD-wide Inventory of Support to Fossil-fuel Production or Use' (OECD, 2012) 1 <http://www.oecd.org/site/tadffss/Fossil%20Fuels%20Inventory_Policy_Brief.pdf> accessed 23 April 2016.

[46] 'Governments Should Phase Out Fossil Fuel Subsidies or Risk Lower Economic Growth, Delayed Investment in Clean Energy and Unnecessary Climate Change Pollution' (NRDC, 2012) <http://www.nrdc.org/energy/files/fossilfuel4.pdf> accessed 23 April 2016.

[47] 'Introduction to Fisheries Subsidies in the WTO' <http://wto.org/english/tratop_e/rulesneg_e/fish_e/fish_intro_e.htm> accessed 11 March 2016.

[48] 'General Facts Regarding World Fisheries' (United Nations Resumed Review Conference on the Agreement Relating to the Conservation and Management of Straddling Fish Stocks and Highly Migratory Fish Stocks, 2010), <http://www.un.org/depts/los/convention_agreements/reviewconf/FishStocks_EN_A.pd> accessed 23 April 2016.

[49] Agreement on Subsidies and Countervailing Measures (ASCM), art 2.

[50] ibid art 3.

[51] ibid arts 5–6.

agenda item. In this negotiation, the group 'Friends of Fish' proposed a new Annex VIII to be added to the ASCM that would make deep cuts in fishing subsidies by prohibiting subsidies to vessels and direct costs of fishing with exceptions contingent on the adoption of a fisheries management programme that includes conservation. But the Doha Development Agenda negotiation has been suspended indefinitely, and this constructive proposal seems destined to fail.[52] Nevertheless, the issue of natural resources subsidies should be brought before future Ministerial Conferences of the WTO, and the work of fashioning international trade law rules against subsidies of natural resources should continue. Reducing or eliminating natural resources subsidies is one of the most important means that may be used by the multilateral trade system to enhance sustainable development.

V. Using Multilateral Environmental Agreements in WTO Trade Disputes over Natural Resources

This chapter has advocated that WTO panels and the Appellate Body explicitly consult multilateral environmental agreements when relevant to interpreting the provisions of WTO agreements in trade disputes over measures concerning natural resources. In two well-known decisions, WTO dispute resolution bodies have done just that—they have consulted, relied upon, and implemented the legal standards and policies of multilateral environmental agreements.

In the *Brazil—Tyres* case[53], a WTO panel, which included Mitsuo Matsushita, decided the question of whether various measures taken by Brazil to ban the import of retreaded and used tyres was consistent with the rules of GATT 1994. The panel, after ruling that the import ban was inconsistent with GATT Article XI:1, considered the applicability of the general exception in Article XX(b): measures to protect human, animal or plant life or health. In deciding this issue, the panel first considered the preliminary issue of whether Brazil's claim to protect the *environment* comes within Article XX(b)'s ambit of protecting human, animal, or plant life and health. In an important (and largely overlooked) ruling, the panel ruled that a claim of an exception for a measure designed to protect the environment can be considered under subsection (b) under the more specific rubric of protection of human, animal, or plant life or health.[54] The panel thus established a link between protection of the environment and the specific language of subsection (b).[55] Second, the panel then, after consideration of the evidence presented, concluded that, since the accumulation of waste tyres creates risks of toxic fires and mosquito-borne

[52] 'Introduction to Fisheries Subsidies in the WTO' (n 47).

[53] Panel Report, *Brazil—Measures Affecting Imports of Retreaded Tyres* (*Brazil—Tyres*), WT/DS332/R, 12 June 2007.

[54] ibid paras 7.47–7.50.

[55] When subsection (b) was drafted in the 1940s, the word 'environment' did not have the meaning the word has today; the term 'environment' referred to indoor areas, or only the immediate surroundings of a person in the out-of-doors.

diseases, Brazil's policy of reducing exposure to such risks through the reduction of accumulations of waste tyres came within the ambit of Article XX(b).[56] Third, the panel, applying the balancing test mandated by the Appellate Body,[57] concluded that Brazil's import ban on retreaded tyres can be considered 'necessary' within the meaning Article XX(b).

The panel in the *Brazil—Tyres* case then turned to the chapeau of Article XX, making a ruling that is as brilliant as it is important for the purposes of conservation of natural resources. Although Brazil had also banned the import of used tyres,[58] court decisions in Brazil had ruled that the import of used tyres had to be permitted under Brazilian law. The panel, considering the importance of this fact, ruled that permitting the import of *used* tyres to the benefit of the Brazilian retreading industry (enabling them to manufacture retreads from imported casings) seriously undermines Brazil's effort to reduce the accumulation of waste tyres and constitutes unjustifiable discrimination and a disguised restriction on international trade in violation of the chapeau of Article XX.[59]

Thus, the panel, in a brilliant ruling, held that conservation and sustainable development principles permit—indeed require—Brazil to block the import of *used* tyres in connection with its decision to block imports of *retreaded* tyres. The chapeau was used in this case not to say that Brazil should *reduce* its trade-restrictive measures, but rather to tell Brazil that for the purposes of sustainable development and to protect the environment it should impose *additional* trade-restricting measures.

In making this ruling, the panel aligned WTO law with the law and policy of the principal multilateral environmental treaty on hazardous waste—the Basel Convention on the Control of Transboundary Movements of Hazardous Wastes and Their Disposal (1989).[60] The Basel Convention authorizes trade bans on hazardous wastes, particularly between developed and developing countries. This Convention adopts as policy (i) waste minimization; (ii) waste recycling; (iii) local disposal of waste; and (iv) proper treatment of wastes.[61] These are exactly the policies mandated by the panel in the *Brazil—Tyres* case. This decision is remarkable in that it shows that not only is there no conflict between international trade law and international environmental law, but the rules of the multilateral trading system can be complementary and supportive of international environmental rules.[62]

[56] *Brazil—Tyres* (n 53) para 7-102. [57] *EC—Asbestos* (n 16).

[58] Used tyres are to be distinguished from waste tyres; the latter term refers to tyres that have reached the end of their useful lives.

[59] *Brazil—Tyres* (n 53) paras 7.355–7.357.

[60] Text available at <http://www.basel.int/TheConvention/Overview/TextoftheConvention/tabid/1275/Default.aspx> accessed 11 March 2016. Although the panel did not cite the Convention, in private conversations with Mitsuo Matsushita the author ascertained that the panel consulted the Convention in coming to its decision.

[61] See Julia Ya Qin, 'WTO Panel Decision in *Brazil—Tyres* Supports Safeguarding Environmental Values' (2007) 11(23) ASIL Insight <http://www.asil.org/insights/volume/11/issue/23/wto-panel-decision-brazil-tyres-supports-safeguarding-environmental> accessed 11 March 2016.

[62] The panel's decision was modified slightly by the Appellate Body. Appellate Body Report, *Brazil—Measures Affecting Imports of Retreaded Tyres*, WT/DS332/AB/R, 3 December 2007.

A second natural resources case in which the WTO dispute resolution cited and aligned its interpretation of the rules of the multilateral trading system with relevant multilateral environmental treaties is the *US—Shrimp/Turtle* case. In this case, as discussed above, the Appellate Body interpreted GATT Article XX(g) to apply to a US measure that required turtle-safe methods of harvesting shrimp as a condition of importation. In interpreting the term, 'conservation of natural resources', the Appellate Body stated that the words of Article XX(g) must be interpreted in the light of 'contemporary concerns' of the community of nations about the preservation and conservation of the environment.[63] The Appellate Body justified this statement by referring to the Preamble of the Marrakesh Agreement Establishing the WTO, which incorporates sustainable development into the law of international trade. In order to interpret the term 'exhaustible natural resources' in subsection (g), the Appellate Body found confirmation for its ruling that sea turtles are exhaustible natural resources in that all seven of the recognized species of sea turtles are listed in Appendix I of the CITES.[64]

Thus, two leading WTO cases involving the intersection between international trade rules and environmental concerns were resolved consistently with the rules and policies of relevant multinational environmental agreements and the principle of sustainable development. Although neither case explicitly cited the VCLT, this chapter propounds the argument that international law as expressed by Article 31 of the VCLT permits WTO dispute resolution bodies to adopt interpretations of the norms of the WTO agreements by referring to the norms and principles in relevant multinational environmental agreements.

VI. Conclusions

The WTO and dispute settlement concerning the relationship between trade and environment have come a long way since the early 1990s when the environmental community was up in arms about the *Tuna/Dolphin* cases,[65] GATT panel rulings that a US trade ban on imports of dolphin-unsafe tuna was inconsistent with provisions of the GATT. These controversial decisions led directly to the 'Battle of Seattle', the violent demonstrations that caused disruption of the WTO Ministerial Conference held in Seattle in 1999. The WTO, since its creation in 1995 has consistently taken the premise that international co-operation is the best strategy to preserve both the values of international trade and protection of the environment. In fact, the *Tuna/Dolphin* GATT rulings were overturned by the WTO employing new interpretations of the GATT Article XX general exceptions. Mitsuo Matsushita, an original member of the WTO Appellate Body, was in the

[63] *US—Shrimps/Turtle* (n 13) paras 128–31. [64] ibid para 132.

[65] GATT Dispute Panel Report, *United States—Restrictions on Imports of Tuna*, GATT BISD (39th Supp), circulated on 3 September, 3, at 155; GATT Dispute Panel Report, *US Restrictions on Import of Tuna*, 16 June 1994, 33 ILM 839, DS29/R. Neither decision was adopted by the GATT contracting parties.

forefront of those who changed WTO law from confronting environmental norms to co-operating and supporting legitimate national and international environmental policies and principles.[66]

Scholars have long argued that WTO law is not a 'self-contained regime'.[67] This chapter, in agreement with this proposition, has sought to make the case for better co-ordination of WTO law with public international law norms through explicit reference by WTO panels and the Appellate Body to relevant multilateral environmental treaties that address sustainable development of natural resources. The VCLT, Article 31, provides the best vehicle for the better integration of the law of the multilateral trading system and multilateral environmental agreements. Through the efforts of Mitsuo Matsushita this process has begun, but the WTO dispute resolution bodies have, on the whole, been too reticent in citing the norms contained in multilateral environmental agreements in their interpretation of the provisions of the WTO agreements.

The confrontation and conflict between trade and the environment[68] has been largely overcome, not by decisions taken at WTO Ministerial Conferences or by the WTO Committee on Trade and Environment, but by decisions of the WTO panels and the Appellate Body in particular disputes brought to the WTO by Members. These dispute resolution decisions have established the WTO as a co-operative player in the struggle to implement the goal of sustainable development. In the important field of international trade in natural resources, the WTO can become fully supportive and complementary to multilateral environmental regimes addressing natural resources and sustainable development.

[66] In this regard, see Appellate Body Report, *United States—Standards for Reformulated and Conventional Gasoline*, WT/DS2/AB/R, 29 April 1996. This was the first report issued by the Appellate Body, and Mitsuo Matsushita was one of the three Appellate Body members who decided this case. This decision significantly reformed the interpretation of GATT Article XX(g) and made possible the interpretation handed down by the Appellate Body in the *US—Shrimps/Turtle* cases.

[67] e.g. Anja Lindroos and Michael Mehling, 'Dispelling the Chimera of "Self-contained Regime" International Law and the WTO' (2005) 16(5) Eur J Intl L 857.

[68] Thomas J Schoenbaum, 'Free International Trade and Protection of the Environment: Irreconcilable Conflict?' (1992) 86 Am J Intl L 700.

18

Facilitating Coherent Application of WTO Law Within and Outside the Organization: Investment Regime as an Example

*Tsai-yu Lin**

I. Introduction

As the central international trade organization, the World Trade Organization (WTO) bears a highly important role in the governance of the multilateral trading system. In parallel with the WTO, free trade agreements (FTAs) and various investment treaties, including bilateral investment treaties (BITs), have been proliferating and playing an important part in the contemporary international economy.

Although developed on a separate track, the WTO and other trade or investment agreements are not mutually exclusive. Instead, the WTO agreements, the core basis underlying the WTO system, have been incorporated directly or by reference into many FTAs or BITs. For instance, on trade matters, it is common practice that Parties to FTAs explicitly affirm or repeat their existing rights and obligations under WTO agreements, or specifically refer to them within FTAs.[1] In investment matters, specific WTO agreements are also incorporated into BITs or the investment chapters of FTAs. Further, certain investors have strategically challenged the host states' breaches of the WTO agreements in light of relevant BIT standards, which arguably might bring more WTO claims into the reach of investor–state arbitration.

From the WTO's perspective, WTO-incorporated provisions located in various agreements outside the WTO (for example, FTAs/BITs) constitute part of the broader 'WTO law network'. Thus, the application or interpretation of the WTO Agreements does not only take place within the WTO. Instead, the WTO

* Professor, National Taiwan University College of Law. The first draft was presented at the 2014 Asia WTO Research Network Annual Conference in Taipei.

[1] For instance, art 301 of NAFTA explicitly refers to Article III of GATT.

provisions can be referred to various dispute settlement fora. Among these, the potential that more WTO claims may be subject to investment arbitral proceedings is likely to create a major challenge for the WTO in the future.[2] Investor–state arbitration has been prominently used to challenge host states' regulatory measures, without the involvement of the investor's home countries.

Clearly, a coherent application of WTO agreements in different contexts would be in the interests of the WTO and its Members. But to date, the WTO has been silent on this point. FTAs and BITs are fragmentary in nature. The lack of coordinated operation between the WTO and external dispute settlement bodies might increase legal uncertainty and be detrimental to the integrity of the WTO legal system.

In light of the above, this chapter argues that it is systemically important to facilitate greater coherence in the application or interpretation of the WTO agreements, both within and outside the WTO. Using BITs as the illustrative example, this chapter first takes a general view of WTO-incorporated clauses in the investment regime. It then articulates the importance for the WTO to facilitate greater coherence in the application and interpretation of WTO law throughout various investment treaties. The chapter also suggests that the WTO should play a more active role in assisting investment arbitral tribunals in applying or interpreting WTO agreements.

II. WTO-incorporated Clauses in BITs: Some Examples

Certain BITs explicitly make WTO law part of the agreements. For example, in the areas of intellectual property rights, transparency, performance requirements, and exceptions regarding other societal polices, specific WTO agreements have been embodied and have thus become relevant to the application of investment protection. Alternatively, in the absence of explicit incorporation clauses, WTO agreements are often claimed by investors to be incorporated into the BIT standards by reference (for example, fair and equitable treatment (FET), the umbrella clause, and indirect expropriation).

A. Explicit incorporation of WTO law

BITs sometimes include certain provisions incorporating the Agreement on Trade-related Aspects of Intellectual Property Rights (TRIPS Agreement). For instance, Article 6.5 of the US Model BIT states that the expropriation provision 'does not apply to the issuance of compulsory licenses granted in relation to intellectual property rights in accordance with *the TRIPS Agreement*, or to the revocation, limitation, or creation of intellectual property rights, to the extent that such issuance,

[2] See Tsai-yu Lin, 'Inter-Mingling TRIPS Obligations with an FET Standard in Investor–State Arbitration: An Emerging Challenge for WTO Law?' (2016) 5(1) J World Trade 71–91.

revocation, limitation, or creation is consistent with *the TRIPS Agreement*' (emphasis added). An expropriation provision of this kind explicitly rules out compulsory licences granted in relation to intellectual property rights; or the issuance, revocation, limitation, or creation of intellectual property rights from being considered as an expropriation, as long as they comply with the TRIPS Agreement. This TRIPS-consistent exception thus provides a legitimate safeguard for certain government measures in relation to intellectual property rights. Article 10.7.5 of the US–Peru Trade Promotion Agreement contains the same provision.

In addition, Article 8.3(b) of the US Model BIT states that paragraphs 1(f) and (h) do not apply 'when a Party authorizes use of an intellectual property right in accordance with *Article 31 of the TRIPS Agreement,* or to measures requiring the disclosure of proprietary information that fall within the scope of, and are consistent with, *Article 39 of the TRIPS Agreement*' (emphasis added). Notably, Article 8.3(b)1(f) concerns a ban on imposing the transfer of a technology as a requirement to an investment; and Article 8.3(b)1(h) concerns a ban on purchase, use, or accord a preference to technology. Regarding non-conforming measures, Article 14 of US Model BIT, states in paragraph 4 that 'Articles 3 [National Treatment] and 4 [Most-Favoured-Nation Treatment] do not apply to any measure covered by an exception to, or derogation from, the obligations under *Article 3 or 4 of the TRIPS Agreement,* as specifically provided in those Articles and in *Article 5 of the TRIPS Agreement*' (emphasis added).

The WTO Agreement on the Application of Sanitary and Phytosanitary Measures (SPS Agreement) is also relevant in the US Model BIT Article 11.8 (transparency), as regards standards-setting. Under Article 11.8, each Party shall allow persons of the other Party to participate in the development of standards and technical regulations by its central government bodies. Also, each Party shall recommend that non-governmental standardizing bodies in their respective territories allow persons of the other Party to participate in the development of standards. However, these transparency provisions do not apply to *sanitary and phytosanitary measures as defined in Annex A of the SPS Agreement.*

Some provisions incorporate the existing WTO obligations under the Agreement on Trade-related Investment Measures (TRIMS Agreement). For instance, Article 96 (prohibition of performance requirements) of the Switzerland–Japan Agreement on Free Trade and Economic Partnership reads: '[for] the purposes of this Chapter, the Annex to *the Agreement on Trade Related Investment Measures* in Annex 1A to the WTO Agreement is hereby incorporated into and made part of this Agreement, *mutatis mutandis*' (emphasis added).

Another example can be found in the WTO general exception clause. Under Article 16.2 of Chapter 16 in the Taiwan–Singapore Agreement on Economic Partnership, it is stated that subparagraphs (a), (b), and (c) of *Article XIV of GATS* are incorporated into and made part of this Agreement, for the purposes of Chapter 9 (Investment). A similar provision is also applied in the Taiwan–New Zealand Agreement on Economic Cooperation. According to Article 1 of Chapter 24 (general exceptions), 'for the purposes of this Agreement, *Article XX of GATT 1994* and its interpretive notes and *Article XIV of GATS* are incorporated into and made part of this Agreement'. Article 2 on Security Exceptions states that '*Article XXI of GATT 1994* and its interpretative notes and *Article XIV bis of GATS* are incorporated into and made part of this Agreement'[3] (emphasis added).

B. Implicit incorporation of WTO law by reference to BIT standards?

In arbitral practice, certain investors have used the relevant BIT standards to challenge potential WTO violations by the host state. As alleged, a host state's breach of WTO law might constitute a violation of the relevant BIT standards, such as the FET standard and the umbrella clause. In contrast with an explicit reference to WTO law through the incorporation clause as discussed above, the issue that arises here is whether 'the relevant BIT standards' themselves would extend to a host state's international obligations under the WTO agreements. If this was the case, a breach of WTO law would automatically establish a breach of the BIT standards.

Recent investment disputes might serve as illustrative examples. For instance, in its investment arbitration against Australia regarding tobacco plain packaging legislation,[4] Philip Morris Asia (PMA) makes an assertion that Australia has breached its obligations under the BIT and international trade treaty. According to PMA, WTO Members are subject to international obligations under the TRIPS Agreement, the Agreement on Technical Barriers to Trade (TBT Agreement), and the Paris Convention for the Protection of Industrial Property (Paris Convention). Plain packaging legislation is inconsistent with Australia's obligations under these treaties.[5] More specifically, plain packaging legislation is alleged to contravene Article 20 of the TRIPS Agreement, since it encumbers PMA's trademarks in an unjustifiable way, which causes significant detriment to the capability of its trademarks to distinguish its tobacco products from other products.[6] With respect to the TBT Agreement, it is claimed that plain packaging legislation is not necessary to achieve the objective of protecting public health as required by Article 2(2), because it lacks credible evidence that such packaging results in the reduction of smoking prevalence.[7] Given this, PMA argues that plain packaging legislation has frustrated its 'legitimate interests and expectations' and violates 'international law';

[3] See also art 95 (General and Security Exceptions) in Switzerland–Japan FTA.

[4] *Philip Morris Asia Limited v The Commonwealth of Australia*, UNCITRAL, PCA Case No 2012-12 (*PMA Notice*). Another example is the case of *FTR Holdings SA (Switzerland), Philip Morris Products SA (Switzerland) and Abal Hermanos SA (Uruguay) v Oriental Republic of Uruguay*, ICSID Case No ARB/10/7.

[5] *PMA Notice*, ibid para 6.6.

[6] Article 20 of the TRIPS Agreement states: '[t]he use of a trademark in the course of trade shall not be unjustifiably encumbered by special requirements, such as use with another trademark, use in a special form or use in a manner detrimental to its capability to distinguish the goods or services of one undertaking from those of other undertakings. This will not preclude a requirement prescribing the use of the trademark identifying the undertaking producing the goods or services along with, but without linking it to, the trademark distinguishing the specific goods or services in question of that undertaking.' *PMA Notice* (n 4) paras 6.7–6.8; 6.11.

[7] *PMA Notice* (n 4) para 6.9.

it contravenes Article 2(2) of the Hong Kong–Australia BIT regarding fair and equitable treatment to be accorded to investments.[8]

In addition, PMA raises a concern based on the umbrella clause. In the relevant part, Article 2(2) of the Hong Kong–Australia BIT provides that '[e]ach Contracting Party shall observe any obligation it may have entered into with regard to investments of investors of the other Contracting Party'. In the view of PMA, the obligations referred to in Article 2(2) are broadly formulated[9] to encompass 'other international obligations' imposed on the host state, such as the TRIPS Agreement, the Paris Convention, and the TBT Agreement. By implementing plain packaging legislation, Australia has failed to observe those obligations.

A similar assertion can be found in the investment dispute between Eli Lilly and Canada. In its Notice of Intent to Submit Investment Arbitration, Eli Lilly, the fifth-largest US-based pharmaceutical company, argues that the Canadian court's invalidation of the pharmaceutical patents previously granted to it (such as its drugs Strattera, Zyprexa, and Evista) has contravened Canada's obligations pursuant to other international treaties, including the TRIPS Agreement.[10] More specifically, Eli Lilly argues that the 'promise doctrine'[11] used by the Canadian court imposes a utility standard inconsistent with Article 27(1) of the TRIPS Agreement. It further argues that the judicial decisions amount to a de facto discrimination of biopharmaceutical patents against the same Article 27(1), which requires Members not to discriminate among different fields of technology.[12] For its investment claims, Eli Lilly challenges that breaches of intellectual property treaties would be contrary to provisions on expropriation and fair and equitable treatment under the BIT. In the case of indirect expropriation, for instance, Eli Lilly argues that '[t]he judicial decisions invalidating the Strattera patent are illegal from the perspective of international law and therefore constitute an expropriation....The Government of Canada has a positive obligation to ensure Canadian law complies with Canada's international

[8] In relevant parts, art 2(2) of the Hong Kong–Australia BIT provides: '[i]nvestments and returns of investors of each Contracting Party shall at all times be accorded fair and equitable treatment ... in the area of the other Contracting Party'. *PMA Notice* (n 4) para 7.7.

[9] The umbrella clause of this kind speaks of 'any obligation', rather than 'specific commitments' or a 'particular commitment'. They concern 'investments' in general, rather than 'specific investments'. These features may arguably leave room for different interpretations regarding the scope of application.

[10] The other IP treaties mentioned are NAFTA Chapter Seventeen on IPRs, the Patent Cooperation Treaty, and the Paris Convention for the Protection of Industrial Property. See *Eli Lilly and Company v The Government of Canada*, Notice of Intent to Submit Claim to Arbitration under NAFTA Chapter Eleven (*Lilly Note*), paras 25–26.

[11] The promise doctrine is a standard whereby the courts can determine whether a patent has achieved the utility requirement to be patentable. Such a standard has its origin in the 2005 Canadian case law. Eli Lilly described the promise of a patent as follows: 'In a series of decisions issued since 2005, the Federal Court of Canada and the Federal Court of Appeal have created a new judicial doctrine whereby *utility is assessed not by reference to the requirement in the Patent Act that an invention be "useful", but rather against the "promise" that the courts derive from the patent specification*' (emphasis added). *Lilly Note*, at ibid para 37.

[12] *Lilly Note* (n 10) paras 90–96.

treaty obligations, as well as the reasonable investment-backed expectations of the investor.'[13]

As demonstrated above, BIT provisions on the FET standard, umbrella clauses, and expropriation have been invoked by investors as the grounds for challenging WTO-conformity. Arguably, whether a violation of WTO law would establish a host state's liability under the BIT might remain open.[14] Despite this, if the relevant BIT standards can be understood as including or referring to obligations established under other treaty obligations, there is a possibility that WTO law can be interpreted as being covered by BITs.[15] Under such a situation, by implication, all WTO agreements are likely to be included in relevant BIT standards and act as the subject matter for investment disputes.

In sum, WTO agreements can serve as applicable law in certain areas of BITs through explicit or implied incorporation clauses. In certain cases, compliance with a specific WTO agreement is used as the basis for exempting investor's claims or as a legal safeguard for a host state's measure. It can also be the case that the WTO agreement is explicitly incorporated, or can be understood to be incorporated by reference to other BIT standards, as part of a host state's investment obligations. In the face of a challenge, an investment arbitral tribunal would need to determine or assess whether a measure at issue is consistent with WTO agreements. In such a case, it would be left to the investment arbitral tribunals, not the dispute settlement bodies within the WTO, to interpret or apply the WTO agreements.[16]

III. The Systemic Importance of Coherent Application of WTO Agreements Under Investment Regime: A WTO Perspective

There is a possibility that the fragmentary decisions of various investment arbitral tribunals might undermine the implementation and operation of WTO

[13] ibid para 41.

[14] See Gaetan Verhoosel, 'The Use of Investor–State Arbitration Under Bilateral Investment Treaties to Seek Relief for Breaches of WTO Law' (2003) 6(2) J Intl Econ L 496–503.

[15] Lin (n 2), 79. In this paper, I have the following opinions: 'In sum, a breach of WTO law may not itself necessarily suffice to establish a host state's liability under the general FET clauses. Despite this, considering intellectual property rights protection, there exist possible interpretations that the consistency of the TRIPS Agreement might constitute an investor's legitimate expectation underlying the FET standard. As the relevant applicable law or the interpretative context, the TRIPS Agreement would be of important relevance in the construction of the FET standard. Following this, the possibility that a host state's non-compliance with TRIPS obligations would result in a breach of the FET standard cannot be excluded.'

[16] Notably, WTO DSU art 23 only excludes the unilateral action of Members to determine WTO breaches. Members have the right to conclude other treaties with dispute settlement processes in which relevant rules overlap with WTO law. See Kyung Kwak and Gabrielle Marceau, 'Overlaps and Conflicts of Jurisdiction between the World Trade Organization and Regional Trade Agreements' in Lorand Bartels and Federico Ortino (eds), *Regional Trade Agreements and the WTO Legal System* (OUP 2006) 48.

agreements as a whole. In this section, this chapter argues that greater coherence in the application and interpretation of WTO agreements in investment agreements would be in the interests of the WTO and its Members, and also in the interests regarding resolution of investment disputes. Ultimately, it would be beneficial to harmonize the relationship between the WTO and investment regime.

A. Maintenance of the integrity of the WTO legal order

The WTO operates as the primary international organization reinforcing the rule of law in multilateral trading system. WTO agreements, as the core of the WTO system, are binding on all Members. The primary function of the WTO includes facilitating the 'implementation, administration and operation' of WTO agreements and furthering the objectives of these agreements, as required by the Marrakesh Agreement Establishing the World Trade Organization.[17] WTO agreements can also be enforced through WTO dispute settlement processes. The WTO dispute settlement mechanism has secured practical importance and made a great contribution to the WTO system's security and predictability.

In my view, the WTO has the responsibility to facilitate the 'implementation, administration and operation' of the WTO agreements, no matter whether such agreements occur within or outside the WTO. In order to maintain the legitimacy and coherence of WTO law, the WTO has sufficient justification to assist or facilitate the application of WTO agreements in other trade and economic agreements.

In cases where WTO law can act as the applicable law under BITs, investment arbitral tribunals should replace the dispute settlement body (i.e. the panel, the Appellate Body) to determine the WTO-conformity of the measure under challenge. Although WTO jurisprudence has been referenced in several investor–state disputes,[18] legally speaking, investment arbitral tribunals are not bound by such prior WTO findings. As an independent dispute settlement body, there remains a possibility that an investment arbitral tribunal might have its own reading of the same or similar provisions of the WTO agreements, which might not be consistent with the WTO's interpretation. Indeed, many arbitrators might not be very familiar with the WTO agreements. This could result in investment arbitral awards that are unable to consistently or correctly reflect the substance of WTO law.

Further to this, in the absence of relevant WTO jurisprudence, an investment arbitral tribunal would be left with more discretion to interpret or apply WTO law. For instance, within the WTO there has been no case law regarding the application

[17] Art III.1 of Marrakesh Agreement Establishing the World Trade Organization.

[18] See generally, Greg Tereposky and Morgan Maguire, 'Utilizing WTO Law in Investor–State Arbitration' in Arthur W Rovine (ed), *Contemporary Issues in International Arbitration and Mediation: The Fordham Papers* (Brill 2010) 247–83. Gabrielle Marceau, Arnau Izaguerri, and Vladyslav Lanovoy, 'The WTO's Influence on Other Dispute Settlement Mechanisms: A Lighthouse in the Storm of Fragmentation' (2013) 47(3) J World Trade 481–574.

of Article 20 of the TRIPS Agreement, an important but unexplored issue in Philip Morris's tobacco disputes.[19] It is possible that the earlier interpretation of WTO law made by an investment arbitral tribunal would be unable to secure support from other WTO Members or the subsequent WTO dispute settlement bodies. For concurrent on-going disputes brought under the WTO and the BIT, respectively, if an earlier investment award is decided, that decision is also likely to immediately impact on the processing of an on-going WTO case. As a result, the WTO law system might face the risk of fragmentation. There also exists a potential tension between the WTO and investment regimes.

Additionally, from my perspective, compared to state-to-state dispute settlement procedures, there is a greater risk that various investment arbitrations might bring in more diverse readings of the WTO agreements. This is because investment arbitrations by their very nature can be directly filed by private investors, without the involvement of their home states. It is likely that investors and their home states (WTO Members) do not have similar positions on the interpretation of a specific WTO provision. This would influence the arguments or the outcome regarding the application of WTO law. As a result, diverse arbitral awards will not only create more incoherent jurisprudence, but also undermine the stability and predictability of the WTO law system.

B. Preservation of WTO Members' legitimate interests through appropriate interpretations

Coherent application or interpretation of WTO law within and outside the WTO constitutes a common interest among WTO Members. In the majority of cases, BITs are concluded by states that are concurrently WTO Members. Arguably, the fact that Parties to a BIT directly incorporate their obligations under the WTO agreements implies that they do not intend to apply different rules. Moreover, BITs usually do not contain provisions regarding how WTO agreements should be interpreted. However, Parties to such BITs should have legitimate expectations to benefit from a consistent application of WTO law to each other, as is the case within the WTO. This is particularly important from the perspective of the respondent host state, whose measure is under challenge by the investors.

Note that, in any given case, certain provisions of the WTO Understanding on Rules and Procedures Governing the Settlement of Disputes (DSU) may be equally important for a respondent host state to defend itself. For instance, the DSU provides that the dispute settlement system serves to preserve the rights and

[19] Note that Australia's plain packaging measure has also been challenged at the WTO by several countries. See WTO *Australia—Tobacco Plain Packaging* dispute: WT/DS434 (complaint by Ukraine), WT/DS435 (complaint by Honduras), WT/DS441 (complaint by the Dominican Republic), WT/DS458 (complaint by Cuba), and WT/DS467 (complaint by Indonesia). The relevant WTO Agreements include the General Agreement on Tariffs and Trade, the TRIPS Agreement, and the TBT Agreement.

obligations of Members under the WTO agreements. Rulings of the panel or the Appellate Body cannot add to or diminish the rights and obligations provided in the WTO agreements (Articles 3.2 and 19.2 of the DSU). In other words, regarding the interpretation of WTO agreements, the rights and obligations of Members should be preserved without change. To that extent, a host state's interest could be legally protected with certainty.

One question to be asked is whether an investment arbitral tribunal should be subject to the provisions of the DSU while interpreting the WTO agreements. It is stated in Article 31(3)(c) of the VCLT that 'any relevant rules of international law applicable in the relations between the parties' shall be taken into account for the purposes of treaty interpretation. Generally, WTO agreements, as the external international law applicable between BIT Parties, could provide references for the interpretation of BIT standards. However, it is not clear as to whether an investment arbitral tribunal should refer to other 'WTO agreements' for the purposes of interpreting 'the specific WTO agreement' within the BIT context. In my view, preserving the rights and obligations of WTO Members, as required in DSU Article 3.2, serves as the fundamental rule of interpretation for all WTO agreements. Therefore it should also be relevant to the interpretation of the specific provisions of the WTO agreement, such as the TRIPS agreement. It seems sensible that an arbitral tribunal takes rules, such as the DSU, into account when interpreting specific provisions of the WTO agreement.

In addition, one might question whether WTO jurisprudence would be 'a relevant rule of international law applicable in the relations between parties' and should be taken into account for investment disputes under VCLT Article 31.3(c). In my view, legally speaking, the answer might not be definitive. Previous rulings of panels and the Appellate Body are not binding precedents for other disputes, which should include investment disputes adjudicated by an investment arbitral tribunal outside the WTO. Despite this, WTO practices have established that the previous rulings of a panel and the Appellate Body 'create legitimate expectations among WTO Members, and therefore, should be taken into account where they are relevant to any dispute'.[20] Thus, from the perspective of WTO Members, it is valid if an investment arbitral tribunal follows WTO jurisprudence when interpreting WTO law. In this regard, notably, appellate review is not available for arbitral awards in international arbitration proceedings. Making reference to the established interpretations developed by WTO practices would reduce the significant deviations from WTO law, and reflect the legitimate expectations of Parties to the BIT (as WTO Members). Therefore if future BITs contained provisions where investment arbitral tribunals are required to take WTO jurisprudence into account when interpreting or applying WTO agreements, this would clearly increase the legal certainty and coherent application of WTO law.

[20] Appellate Body Report, *Japan–Alcoholic Beverages* II, DSR 1996: I, 97 at 107–08.

C. Promotion of efficient resolution of WTO law issues in investment disputes

In investor–state arbitration, arbitrators appointed by parties tend to be practicing lawyers or academics with expertise in commercial or investment arbitration matters and in the conduct of international arbitration proceedings.[21] Unlike the legal services that the WTO Secretariat would provide to a panel or the Appellate Body, arbitrators are required to draft the awards themselves without institutional support from professional staff. Since some will have different training backgrounds and experiences, it is possible that many arbitrators might have limited understanding of the WTO's treaty clauses, rules, and jurisprudence. However, interpreting WTO law in itself will never be an easy task. Legal provisions of the WTO agreement are often compromise formulations arising from negotiations, which are drafted in general terms and tend to lack clarity.[22] For instance, Philip Morris has claimed that Australia's plain packaging measure is unnecessary for protecting public health, thus violating Article 2(2) of the TBT Agreement. This point might relate to a number of things: the interpretation of the term 'more trade-restrictive than necessary' in the text; the assessment of the reasonable connection of scientific evidence in relation to the protection of public health; or even the status of the World Health Organization (WHO) Framework of Tobacco Control (FCTC). In an absence of WTO jurisprudence, there will be no guidance from the WTO given to an investment arbitral tribunal, which would likely result in different interpretations with the WTO. Thus, if an investment arbitral tribunal can benefit from the legal assistance of the WTO, it will increase the efficient resolution of the WTO law issue, and also make a more credible arbitral award, which is accepted by other WTO Members.

IV. Assisting Investment Arbitral Tribunals with the Coherent Application and Interpretation of WTO Agreements: A New Role for the WTO

As discussed above, if the WTO agreements can be applied or interpreted in a coherent way in other external investment agreements, it is systemically important to the WTO. Therefore, it is suggested that the WTO should play a new role, maintaining its relevance to investment arbitral proceedings through participation and co-operation. More specifically, in order to assist investment arbitral tribunals, the WTO can submit its professional opinions as *amicus curiae* in investment arbitral proceedings. It can also provide guidance to the investment arbitral tribunal by

[21] Jorge A Huerta-Goldman, Antoine Romanetti, and Franz X Stirnimann, 'Cross-cutting Observations on Composition of Tribunals' in Jorge A Huerta-Goldman and others (eds), *WTO Litigation, Investment Arbitration, and Commercial Arbitration* (Kluwer 2013) 130.

[22] WTO, *A Handbook on the WTO Dispute Settlement* (CUP 2004) 3.

giving a preliminary ruling on the interpretation of the WTO agreement under the new system.

A. Submission of *amicus curiae* briefs in investment arbitral proceedings

How a non-disputing party can gain access to an investment arbitral proceeding has recently gained practical importance, due to public implications of the arbitral award rendered. Generally, under relevant investment arbitration rules, non-disputing parties are allowed to participate in an investment arbitral proceeding by filing a written submission with the tribunal as *amicus curiae*.

Take, for example, the ICSID (the International Centre for Settlement of Investment Disputes) Arbitration Rules. As stated in Rule 37(2) of the ICSID Arbitration Rules, after consulting both parties, the tribunal may allow a non-disputing party (including a person or entity) to file a written submission concerning a matter within the scope of the dispute. In determining whether to accept such an *amicus curiae* submission, the tribunal shall consider the extent to which:

(a) the non-disputing party submission would assist the Tribunal in the determination of a factual or legal issue related to the proceeding by bringing a perspective, particular knowledge or insight that is different from that of the disputing parties;
(b) the non-disputing party submission would address a matter within the scope of the dispute; [and]
(c) the non-disputing party has a significant interest in the proceeding.

The tribunal is also instructed to ensure that the *amicus curiae* submission 'does not disrupt the proceeding or unduly burden or unfairly prejudice either party, and that both parties are given an opportunity to present their observations on the non-disputing party submission'. Thus, the ICSID tribunal is authorized to consider *amicus curiae* submissions from non-disputing parties at its own initiative, even if no prior approval of the disputing parties has been obtained. Such external submissions may contribute to establishing a more credible system of investment arbitration and a higher quality of arbitral awards.

Here I propose that the WTO might consider participating in investment arbitral proceedings as *amicus curiae*, where the WTO agreement is of importance to the resolution of a dispute. First, the WTO can assist the arbitral tribunal in the determination of factual and legal issues of WTO agreements by bringing a knowledgeable perspective or insight. Second, the WTO, as the primary organization governing and monitoring the implementation of its agreements, has a significant interest in becoming involved in such proceedings, especially since WTO legal questions might implicate the WTO and its Members in the future. It is especially true that if WTO law is interpreted as a part of BITs standards, it might potentially increase more investment claims (mostly regarding breaches of WTO law). Despite this, one might question whether the WTO, as an international organization, can be a 'qualified entity' to submit *amicus curiae* briefs to the tribunal. As seen in arbitral practice, the European Commission, as the guardian of European Law, was granted permission by the ICSID tribunal to make *amicus curiae* brief in *AES Summit Generation Limited v The Republic of Hungary*.[23] More recently, a written submission jointly filed by the WHO and the FCTC's Secretariat for the case of *Philip Morris v Uruguay* concerning tobacco packaging measures have also been accepted by the ICSID tribunal. In its decision accepting the submission, the ICSID tribunal particularly recognized the unique position of the WHO as the world authority on public health matters in providing information on tobacco control.[24] Thus, it is indisputable that the WTO would be a qualified entity as *amicus curiae* for WTO-related matters.

Nevertheless, one may further question who should represent the WTO as *amicus curiae* in investment arbitration disputes, given that the WTO is a Member-driven organization. It seems to me that the Appellate Body might be a more appropriate entity to safeguard and promote the greater coherence of WTO agreements in investment arbitration. Different from a panel, the Appellate Body is a standing international tribunal.[25] The Appellate Body Members are persons of recognized authority in law and international trade, and are tasked to resolve 'issues of law covered in the panel report and legal interpretations developed by the panel'.[26] Therefore, the Body might be in a uniquely qualified position to explain the provisions of particular WTO agreements and their legal relationship with the BIT, which could certainly assist the arbitral tribunal. However, the submission of *amicus curiae* briefs by the WTO alone would not ensure that an investment arbitral tribunal will show complete deference to the WTO's opinions. What points would become relevant in its deliberation would still be left in the hands of the arbitral tribunals.

In addition, as a supportive mechanism for facilitating the WTO's participation in investment arbitral proceedings, a system of notification could be established. More specifically, WTO Members—including parties to the BITs and non-disputing party in the FTA—should be encouraged to notify the WTO if the application or interpretation of WTO agreements would be of importance to an investment dispute. Through such a systemic notification, the WTO would be kept informed and be given an opportunity to become involved in an investment dispute, including making *amicus curiae* briefs. In this regard, it is proposed that a notification can also be made by the ICSID, the World Bank's arbitration forum. Note that Article III:5 of the Marrakesh Agreement Establishing the World Trade

[23] *AES Summit Generation Limited and AES–Tisza Eromu Kft v The Republic of Hungary*, ICSID Case No ARB/07/22 (23 September 2010). In this case, the European Commission argues that the power purchase agreements between Hungary and foreign investors are against European Community law. Also see *Electrabel SA v Republic of Hungary*, ICSID Case No ARN/07/19, (30 November 2012). Christina Knahr, 'New Rules on Participation of Non-disputing Parties in ICSID Arbitration: Blessing or Curse?' in Chester Brown and Kate Miles (eds), *Evolution in Investment Treaty Law and Arbitration* (CUP 2011) 330–33.

[24] *Philip Morris Brand Sàrl (Switzerland), Philip Morris Products SA (Switzerland), and Abal Hermanos SA (Uruguay) v Oriental Republic of Uruguay*, ICSID Case No ARB/10/7, Procedural Order No 3 (17 February 2015), paras 24, 25(c).

[25] DSU art 17.1. [26] DSU arts 17.3, 17.6.

Organization specifically refers to co-operation between the WTO and the World Bank. The WTO has concluded agreements with the World Bank for mutually supportive policies.[27]

B. Provisions of legal guidance through preliminary rulings

Neither the WTO nor the BITs address the issue of mutual overlap. From my perspective, if the WTO can provide systematic guidance to investment arbitral tribunals regarding the interpretation of WTO agreements, this would greatly foster a coherent application of WTO law.

Ultimately, there should be procedural co-operation between the WTO and investment arbitral tribunals on the application or interpretation of WTO agreements. This chapter suggests that a good model to follow could come from the European Union, where Member national courts are asked to refer their difficulties in interpreting EU law to the EU Court of Justice for a preliminary ruling.[28] That is, an arbitral tribunal, as the only and final resort for an investment dispute, would be required to submit a preliminary question to the WTO Appellate Body in cases where doubts regarding the application or interpretation of WTO agreements have been formed. The Appellate Body would then issue its advisory opinions on the questions raised,[29] which would be binding upon the investment arbitral tribunal. Meanwhile, the arbitral proceeding would be stayed until the Appellate Body's opinions are given. Under this system, arbitral tribunals would not interpret WTO law completely on its own. Instead, they would have an obligation to seek the assistance of the WTO when dealing with interpretative difficulties before applying WTO law, a legal order that may be quite unfamiliar to them. In my opinion, judicial co-operation of this kind would facilitate the coherent application and legal certainty of WTO law in BITs. In effect, the Appellate Body's preliminary rulings could also be considered as guidance for other WTO Members.

V. Concluding Remarks

WTO agreements are commonly referred to or incorporated in trade and investment agreements. A greater coherence in the application of WTO agreements within the WTO and throughout the external investment regime would be in the interests of the WTO and its Members, and also in the interests of resolving investment disputes. With a view to achieving such coherence, the WTO should play a new role as an active facilitator. A core concern might arise as to how to provide assistance or guidance to the investment arbitral tribunals in the application and

[27] Peter Van den Bossche and Werner Zdouc, *The Law and Policy of the World Trade Organization* (CUP 2013) 97.

[28] See <http://eur-lex.europa.eu/legal-content/EN/TXT/?uri=URISERV:l14552> accessed 11 March 2016.

[29] It is proposed that the Appellate Body may convene a special session for this sole purpose.

interpretation of WTO agreements. In this respect, making *amicus curiae* briefs or issuing preliminary rulings regarding the interpretation of the WTO agreement by the WTO Appellate Body might be helpful.

In the face of the increased importance that FTAs and other investment agreements have in the international economic system, perhaps it is the right time for the WTO to ask itself whether it would like to guide and influence the 'WTO law network' into coherence and consistency, rather than having interpretations of WTO agreements scattered and incorporated into various agreements outside the WTO.

19

Reinterpretation of the National Treatment Principle: Making International Economic Law a Friend of Global Governance of Environmental Protection

*Won-mog Choi**

I. Introduction

It is true that in recent technical barriers to trade (TBT) cases there is a series of unusual rulings by the Appellate Body of the World Trade Organization (WTO) that marks a significant departure from the past interpretation of the non-discrimination principle of trade. This novel and distinct trend makes one wonder about the background and ultimate goal that the highest trade tribunal intends to achieve through this departure.

The past twenty years have seen an increasing debate over the linkages between trade liberalization and environmental regulations. Although supporters of the international trading system have argued that WTO rules merely attempt to balance state autonomy in such areas with a desire to eliminate policies restricting trade and protecting domestic industry, international trade rules have come under increasing attack based on a perception that they significantly constrain governments' ability to implement non-economic policies.[1]

Free traders mostly in developed countries have expressed their concerns that the competitive position of advanced economies would be eroded by environmental regulations that induce pollution-intensive industries to move to countries with lower

* Professor, Ewha Law School, Ewha Womans University at Seoul, SJD (Georgetown), Attorney-at-law (New York).

[1] For a discussion of these debates, see e.g., Michael Trebilcock and Robert Howse, *The Regulation of International Trade* (3rd edn, Routledge 2005); Robert Howse and Elizabeth Tuerk, 'The WTO Impact on Internal Regulations—a Case Study of the Canada–EC Asbestos Dispute' in Grainne de Burca and Joanne Scott (eds), *The EU and the WTO: Legal and Constitutional Issues* (Hart Publishing 2001) 327; Alan Sykes, 'Domestic Regulation, Sovereignty, and Scientific Evidence Requirements: A Pessimistic View' (2002) 3(2) Chinese J Intl L 353; and Andrew Green, 'Climate Change, Regulatory Policy and the WTO—How Constraining Are Trade Rules?' (2005) 8(1) J Intl Econ L 143.

standards. Global environmentalists, on the other hand, fear that increasing trade integration and the competition for investment and jobs may lead to a 'race to the bottom' on environmental regulations, as national governments find it more difficult to internalize environmental and social costs into prices. To these critics, the current WTO rules either internationally or in effect reduce the ability of countries to set their own environmental protection policies. Hence, trade unions and environmentalists usually demand binding international environmental standards, preferably within the framework of the WTO to ensure a 'level playing field' for all exporters.[2]

With these debates and concerns, it became obvious that the global governance of environmental protection demands more flexible interpretation of the non-discrimination principle of the WTO. In other words, more trade measures instituting regulatory distinctions need to be legitimized if they are based on global environmental concerns. Although GATT Article XX is the primary tool to legitimize such distinctions, it is no secret that the general exception provision is neither delicately drafted nor comprehensive enough to deal with contemporary issues for global environmental protection because it was drafted in the 1940s, where there arose no serious environmental concerns, as opposed to today. As a matter of fact, the relationship of trade and human rights is much broader and by far exceeds the bounds of Article XX of the GATT 1994.[3]

Having said this, it is timely and worth the effort to reinterpret the non-discrimination principle—the golden rule of multilateralism—in accordance with changed reality and contemporary necessity. Of course, any attempt at such reinterpretation should be made in due consideration for prevention of the possible clash between the two inalienable values, free trade and global environmental protection.

The recent trend in WTO Appellate Body rulings regarding the national treatment principles of the WTO Agreement bears this consideration out, even though it is not fully satisfactory. Proper analysis of this trend and observations of its implications with some suggestions will shed more light on this process of judicial activism for the future.

II. Reinterpretation of the 'Less Favourable Treatment' Standard

In several recent cases involving obligations of the TBT Agreement, the Appellate Body has elaborated on the issue of interpretation of the 'less favorable treatment'

[2] See generally Grether Jean-Marie and Jaime de Melo, 'Globalization and Dirty Industries: Do Pollution Haven Matter?' (2003) NBER Working Paper Series 9776 <http://www.nber.org/papers/w9776.pdf> accessed 23 April 2016.

[3] Julien Chaisse, 'Exploring the Confines of International Investment and Domestic Health Protections—General Exceptions Clause as a Forced Perspective' (2013) 39(2/3) Am J L & Med 332–61, at 350 (explaining that Article XX of the GATT 1994 contemplates a two-tiered analysis of a measure that a Member seeks to justify under that provision. If it is relatively easy to demonstrate that the challenged measure falls within the scope of one of the subparagraphs of Article XX, it is more difficult to further establish that the measure at issue satisfies the requirements of the chapeau of Article XX.)

standard arising under Article 2.1 of the TBT Agreement. The Appellate Body declared in the first of these cases, *US—Clove Cigarettes*[4] as follows:

> [W]here the technical regulation at issue does not *de jure* discriminate against imports, the existence of a detrimental impact on competitive opportunities for the group of imported *vis-a-vis* the group of domestic like products is not dispositive of less favourable treatment under Article 2.1. Instead, a panel must further analyze whether the detrimental impact on imports stems exclusively from a legitimate regulatory distinction rather than reflecting discrimination against the group of imported products.[5]

Thus, the Appellate Body has established two elements for an analysis of whether de facto 'less favorable treatment' exists: (i) whether the measure has a 'detrimental impact' on imported goods; and (ii), if so, whether any such impact stems exclusively from a legitimate regulatory distinction and thus reflects 'discrimination'. This means that some technical regulations that have a de facto detrimental impact on imports may not be inconsistent with Article 2.1 where a regulatory distinction is designed and applied in an even-handed manner. In assessing even-handedness, a panel must carefully scrutinize the particular circumstances of the case; that is, 'the design, architecture, revealing structure, operation, and application of the technical regulation at issue'.[6]

With regard to the issue of burden of proof under Article 2.1, the Body explained that 'it is for the complaining party to show that the treatment accorded to imported products is less favourable than that accorded to like domestic products'. Then, '[w]here the complaining party has met the burden of making its *prima facie* case, it is ... for the responding party to rebut that showing'. For example, it explained,

> [i]f ... the complainant adduces evidence and arguments showing that the measure is designed and/or applied in a manner that constitutes a means of arbitrary or unjustifiable discrimination of the group of imported products and thus is not even-handed, this would suggest that the measure is inconsistent with Article 2.1.

If, however, the respondent 'shows that the detrimental impact on imported products stems exclusively from a legitimate regulatory distinction, it follows that the challenged measure is not inconsistent with Article 2.1'.[7]

Although the Appellate Body indicated Article 2.2 and the second, fifth, and sixth recitals of the TBT Agreement preamble as its basis of such interpretation,[8]

[4] *United States—Measures Affecting the Production and Sale of Clove Cigarettes* (*US—Clove Cigarettes*), WT/DS406, 7 April 2010.

[5] *United States—Measures Affecting the Production and Sale of Clove Cigarettes*, WT/DS406/AB/R, 4 April 2012, para 182.

[6] ibid para 271. [7] ibid para 272.

[8] Article 2.2 of Agreement on Technical Barriers to Trade (TBT Agreement), 1868 UNTS 120, prescribes among others that 'technical regulations shall not be more trade-restrictive than necessary to fulfil a legitimate objective'. Second, fifth, and sixth recitals of the preamble read, respectively: '*Desiring* to further the objectives of GATT 1994', '*Desiring* however to ensure that technical regulations ... not create unnecessary obstacles to international trade', and '*Recognizing* that no country should be prevented from taking measures necessary to ensure the quality of its exports, or for the protection of human, animal or plant life or health, of the environment, or for the prevention of deceptive practices,

this interpretation of the term 'less favourable treatment' is based far beyond its ordinary meaning. Given that the non-discrimination principle in the WTO Agreement is a fundamental basis of protecting competitive opportunities of an imported product, and because the 'no-less-favourable-treatment' standard of GATT Article III.4 prohibits WTO Members from modifying the conditions of competition in the market place to the detriment of the group of imported products vis-à-vis the group of domestic products, a panel examining a claim of violation under Article 2.1 of TBT Agreement should seek to ascertain whether the technical regulation at issue modifies the conditions of competition in the market of the regulating Member to the detriment of the group of imported products vis-à-vis the group of like domestic products; in other words, whether or not there is detrimental impact on imported products ought to be determinant of less favourable treatment, and there seems to exist no room for the consideration of regulatory legitimacy in determining 'less favourable treatment'. Notwithstanding this natural understanding, the Appellate Body is intentionally endeavouring to create a new interpretation of 'less favourable treatment' based not only on the detrimental effect, but also on regulatory legitimacy of the measure.

Clearly, this interpretation draws a new borderline in a battle of interpretation of the non-discrimination principle between free trade proponents and regulatory autonomy supporters, where the 'less favourable treatment' element has traditionally been understood predominantly by the detrimental effect test. Prior to this new approach, it is clear that the element has been interpreted based on the effect-only test. In *US— Gasoline*,[9] the panel, in a finding not addressed by the Appellate Body, found that the measure in question afforded to imported products less favourable treatment than that afforded to domestic products. It was because sellers of domestic gasoline were authorized to use an individual baseline, while sellers of imported gasoline had to use the more onerous statutory baseline, as the following paragraph shows:

> The Panel observed that domestic gasoline benefited in general from the fact that the seller who is a refiner used an individual baseline, while imported gasoline did not. This resulted in less favourable treatment to the imported product. Moreover, the Panel recalled an earlier panel report which stated that 'the words "treatment no less favourable" in paragraph 4 call for effective equality of opportunities for imported products in respect of laws, regulations and requirements affecting the internal sale, offering for sale, purchase, transportation, distribution or use of products.' (*US—Section 337*, para. 5.11) The Panel found therefore that since, under the baseline establishment methods, imported gasoline was effectively prevented from benefitting from as favourable sales conditions as were afforded domestic gasoline by an individual baseline tied to the

at the levels it considers appropriate, subject to the requirement that they are not applied in a manner which would constitute a means of arbitrary or unjustifiable discrimination between countries where the same conditions prevail or a disguised restriction on international trade'.

[9] *United States—Standards for Reformulated and Conventional Gasoline* (*US—Gasoline*), WT/DS2, 24 January 1995.

producer of a product, imported gasoline was treated less favourably than domestic gasoline.[10]

In *Japan—Film*,[11] the panel reiterated the standard of equality of competitive conditions as a benchmark for establishing 'no less favourable treatment', as below:

> [W]e consider that this standard of effective equality of competitive conditions on the internal market is the standard of national treatment that is required, not only with regard to Article III generally, but also more particularly with regard to the 'no less favourable treatment' standard in Article III:4. We note in this regard that the interpretation of equal treatment in terms of effective equality of competitive opportunities, first clearly enunciated by the panel on *US—Section 337 (US—Section 337, para. 5.11)*, has been followed consistently in subsequent GATT and WTO panel reports. (*See e.g. Panel Report, Canada—Provincial Liquor Boards, paras 5.12–5.14 and 5.30–5.31; and Panel Report, US—Malt Beverages, para. 5.30; Panel Report, US—Gasoline, para. 6.10; Panel Report, Canada—Periodicals, p. 75; and Panel Report, EC—Bananas III, paras 7.179—7.180*)[12]

In *Korea—Beef*,[13] the measure at issue established a dual retail distribution system for the sale of beef. The Appellate Body first held that such different treatment of imported products did not necessarily lead to less favourable treatment. However, the Body continued to take the position that less favourable treatment is to be assessed by examining whether a measure modifies the *conditions of competition* in the relevant market to the detriment of imported products, as below:

> A formal difference in treatment between imported and like domestic products is thus neither necessary, nor sufficient, to show a violation of Article III:4. Whether or not imported products are treated 'less favourably' than like domestic products should be assessed instead by examining whether a measure modifies the *conditions of competition* in the relevant market to the detriment of imported products.[14]

A delicate signal of departure from this effect-only test was shown in *EC—Asbestos*,[15] where the panel, in examining the less favourable treatment element in Article III.4 of GATT, considered whether an identical ban was placed on domestic like products as placed on imported asbestos and asbestos-containing products. In other words, the panel's test was only centred on the detrimental effect. This interpretation by the panel was not appealed, and thus, the Appellate Body could not examine it. Despite this, the Appellate Body hinted that such an effect-only interpretation is a careless approach that does not take into account the general

[10] Panel Report, *United States—Standards for Reformulated and Conventional Gasoline*, WT/DS2/R, 29 January 1996, para 6.10.

[11] *Japan—Measures Affecting Consumer Photographic Film and Paper* (*Japan—Film*), WT/DS44, 13 June 1996.

[12] Panel Report, *Japan—Measures Affecting Consumer Photographic Film and Paper*, WT/DS44/R, 31 March 1998, para 10.379.

[13] *Korea—Measures Affecting Imports of Fresh, Chilled and Frozen Beef* (*Korea—Beef*), WT/DS161, 1 February 1999.

[14] Appellate Body Report, *Korea—Measures Affecting Imports of Fresh, Chilled and Frozen Beef*, WT/DS161/AB/R, 11 December 2000, paras 135–37.

[15] *European Communities—Measures Affecting Asbestos and Products Containing Asbestos* (*EC—Asbestos*), WT/DS135, 28 May 1998.

principle of national treatment rule as expressed in Article III.1 of GATT. The following statement by the Body bears this out:

> A complaining Member must still establish that the measure accords to the group of 'like' *imported* products 'less favourable treatment' than it accords to the group of 'like' *domestic* products. The term 'less favourable treatment' expresses the general principle, in Article III:1, that internal regulations 'should not be applied ... so as to afford protection to domestic production'. If there is 'less favourable treatment' of the group of 'like' imported products, there is, conversely, 'protection' of the group of 'like' domestic products. However, a Member may draw distinctions between products which have been found to be 'like', without, for this reason alone, according to the group of 'like' *imported* products 'less favourable treatment' than that accorded to the group of 'like' *domestic* products. In this case, we do not examine further the interpretation of the term 'treatment no less favourable' in Article III:4, as the Panel's findings on this issue have not been appealed or, indeed, argued before us.[16]

In *EC—Biotech Products*[17] the panel started to pay attention to this signal. In this case, Argentina argued that the European Communities failed to consider for final approval various applications concerning certain specified biotech products for which the European Communities had already begun approval procedures. In examining whether this violates Article III.4 of GATT, the panel first focused on the less-favourable-treatment element. The panel noted that Argentina had not alleged origin-based discrimination, and concluded that Argentina had not established that the alleged less favourable treatment of imported biotech products was explained by the products' foreign origin rather than other factors, as the following excerpt shows:

> as a result of the measures challenged by Argentina, the relevant imported biotech products cannot be marketed, while corresponding domestic non-biotech products can be marketed, in accordance with the aforementioned statements by the Appellate Body this would not be sufficient, in and of itself, to raise a presumption that the European Communities accorded less favourable treatment to the group of like *imported* products than to the group of like *domestic* products.[18]

It was in *US—Clove Cigarettes*[19] that the Appellate Body finally materialized this signal into concrete holdings by adding the regulatory legitimacy element into the less-favourable-treatment determination. It should be noted that this addition is confined only to de facto discrimination cases in the TBT context. As a consequence, a set of different conditions has been created to ascertain 'less favourable

[16] Appellate Body Report, *European Communities—Measures Affecting Asbestos and Products Containing Asbestos*, WT/DS135/AB/R, 12 March 2001, para 100.

[17] *European Communities—Measures Affecting the Approval and Marketing of Biotech Products* (*EC—Biotech Products*), WT/DS291, 13 May 2003.

[18] Panel Report, *European Communities—Measures Affecting the Approval and Marketing of Biotech Products*, WT/DS291/R, 29 September 2006, paras 7.2513–7.2516. These signals, however, might be understood in another way: what the Appellate Body meant was simply that a formally different measure may not necessarily be a less favourable treatment, and a key element that needs to be proven is the detrimental effect arising from such a different measure.

[19] *US—Clove Cigarettes* (n 4).

treatment' between GATT Article III.4 and TBT Article 2.1, despite the use of identical language.

In the face of this obvious problem, the Appellate Body seeks to blur this bifurcated approach in the *US—COOL* case,[20] and this seems intentional. The Appellate Body in the case held that, in the context of both GATT Article III.4 and TBT Article 2.1,

> for a measure to be found to modify the conditions of competition in the relevant market to the detriment of imported products, there must be a genuine relationship between the measure at issue and the adverse impact on competitive opportunities for imported products.

The 'relevant question', it explained, 'is whether it is the governmental measure at issue that "affects the conditions under which like goods, domestic and imported, compete in the market within a Member's territory" '. In this regard, it noted that '[w]hile a measure may not require certain treatment of imports, it may nevertheless create incentives for market participants to behave in certain ways, and thereby treat imported products less favourably'. However, it cautioned that:

> changes in the competitive conditions in a marketplace that are '*not* imposed directly or indirectly by law or governmental regulation, but [are] rather solely the result of private entrepreneurs acting on their own calculations of comparative costs and benefits', cannot be the basis for a finding that a measure treats imported products less favourably than domestic like products.[21]

This means that the detrimental effect test should not only reflect commercial actors' views, but it ought to be also based on the regulators' view. According to the Appellate Body, this is the way to find out a 'genuine relationship' between the measure at issue and the adverse impact on competitive opportunities for imported products. This delicate change of position by the Appellate Body seems to be an effort to pave the way for more flexible interpretation of the less-favourable-treatment element in Article III.4 for future disputes: it enables future panels to consider regulatory legitimacy (by examining change of competitive conditions from 'regulator's view') in the less-favourable-treatment test under Article III.4 itself, before applying Article XX of GATT.

In other words, this subtle statement about 'genuine relationship' seems to give a signal of 'go ahead' for panels to interpret the phrase 'less favourable treatment' in GATT Article III.4 under the full guidance of general principle of GATT Article III.1.[22] As a result, panels would be required to examine regulatory legitimacy on top of any detrimental effect in de facto discrimination cases. Article III.1,

[20] *United States—Certain Country of Origin Labelling (COOL) Requirements* (*US—COOL*), WT/DS384, 1 December 2008.

[21] Appellate Body Report *United States—Certain Country of Origin Labelling (COOL) Requirements*, WT/DS384/AB/R, 29 June 2012, para 270.

[22] Article III.1 of General Agreement on Tariffs and Trade 1994 (GATT), 15 April 1994, 1867 UNTS 187, 33 ILM 1153 (1994), sets forth the anti-protectionist principle of the national treatment obligation:

which has been dormant for a long time, is now fully geared up to apply in the golden rule of trade in GATT, as well as in the TBT Agreement.

III. Reinterpretation of 'So as to Afford Protection to Domestic Production'

Will this new trend affect the interpretation of other paragraphs under Article III of GATT, notably Article III.2? As the second sentence of Article III.2 makes explicit reference to paragraph 1 of Article III, the regulatory legitimacy factor may well be examined in considering whether the measure at issue was applied to imported or domestic products 'so as to afford protection to domestic production'. In other words, if the detrimental effect on imported products, if any, was exclusively stemming from a legitimate regulatory distinction, it could be determined that the measure at issue was not applied so as to afford protection to domestic production. This will save many legitimate regulatory distinctions that do not fall under the limited scope of general exceptions in GATT Article XX.

For this purpose, it seems that the Appellate Body needs to modify its earlier interpretation of the phrase 'so as to afford protection'. In *Korea—Alcoholic Beverages*,[23] the panel had found that the Korean taxes on alcoholic beverages were applied 'so as to afford protection' to domestic production. In making this finding, the panel noted that the 'structure of the Liquor Tax Law itself is discriminatory', and that there is 'virtually no' imported soju, so the beneficiaries of the structure are almost exclusively domestic producers. Korea argued on appeal that, inter alia, the panel ignored Korea's explanation for the tax structure, and ignored Korea's explanation for the absence of imported soju.[24]

The Appellate Body rejected Korea's appeal, and upheld the panel's finding on this issue. In doing so, it first referred to its statements in *Japan—Alcoholic Beverages*[25] on the 'so-as-to-afford-protection' element, where it had said that examination of whether a tax regime affords protection to domestic production 'is an issue of how the measure in question is *applied*', and that such an

> The contracting parties recognize that internal taxes and other internal charges, and laws, regulations and requirements affecting the internal sale, offering for sale, purchase, transportation, distribution or use of products, and internal quantitative regulations requiring the mixture, processing or use of products in specified amounts or proportions, should not be applied to imported or domestic products so as to afford protection to domestic production.

WTO panels and Appellate Body have reiterated that this principle is not a legally binding obligation, but it can give general guidance on the interpretation of the rest of paragraphs of Article III.

[23] *Korea—Taxes on Alcoholic Beverages (European Communities)*, WT/DS75, 2 April 1997; *Korea—Taxes on Alcoholic Beverages (United States)*, WT/DS84, 23 May 1997 (*Korea—Alcoholic Beverages*).

[24] Appellate Body Report, *Korea—Taxes on Alcoholic Beverages (European Communities)*, WT/DS75/AB/R, WT/DS84/AB/R, 18 January 1999, paras 147–48.

[25] *Japan—Taxes on Alcoholic Beverages (European Communities)*, WT/DS8, 21 June 1995; *Japan—Taxes on Alcoholic Beverages (Canada)*, WT/DS10, 7 July 1995; *Japan—Taxes on Alcoholic Beverages (United States)*, WT/DS11, 7 July 1995 (*Japan—Alcoholic Beverages*).

examination 'requires a comprehensive and objective analysis'. Furthermore, in that case it had also noted that 'it is possible to examine objectively the underlying criteria used in a particular tax measure, its structure, and its overall application to ascertain whether it is applied in a way that affords protection to domestic products', and that the 'protective application' of a measure can most often be discerned from 'the design, the architecture, and the revealing structure of a measure'. In this way, according to the Appellate Body, 'the very magnitude of the dissimilar taxation in a particular case' may be evidence of such protective application.[26]

This imprudent holding is indeed nothing but turning a blind eye to regulatory legitimacy of WTO Members, and it needs to be overruled or modified as soon as possible by the highest tribunal itself. No matter how great the magnitude of the dissimilar taxation is, it deserves careful consideration whether or not there is legitimacy in making such regulatory distinction, particularly when such a core sovereign issue as taxation is on international trial. The principle in GATT Article III.1 ought to be reinterpreted to mean that panels must examine whether or not the measure at issue exclusively stems from a legitimate regulatory distinction. Such reinterpretation will make three equivalent rules—i.e. the second sentence of Article III.2 of GATT, Article III.4 of GATT, and Article 2.1 of TBT Agreement[27]—mutually consistent and corresponding.

IV. Reinterpretation of 'Like Products'?

Still, the remaining task is to reinterpret the first sentence of Article III.2 of GATT[28] so as to pave the way for panels to consider regulatory legitimacy. Because the sentence does not make explicit reference to Article III.1, one cannot apply the newly interpreted 'so-as-to-afford-protection' test to disputes arising under the first sentence. Moreover, the phrase 'in excess of' under the sentence does not seem to allow consideration of regulatory legitimacy, unlike the much more flexible words 'no less favourable' in Article III.4. Indeed, such quantitative expression as 'excess' cannot possibly be interpreted to require panels to consider whether or

[26] Appellate Body Report, *Japan—Taxes on Alcoholic Beverages (European Communities)*, WT/DS8/AB/R, WT/DS10/AB/R, WT/DS11/AB/R, 4 October 1996, para 149.

[27] The national treatment obligation in taxation measures is prescribed in Article III.2, while the national treatment obligation in other regulatory measures is addressed in Article III.4. Article 2.1 of TBT Agreement sets forth the national treatment obligation in TBT measures.

[28] Fiscal measures such as taxes are regulated in Article III.2. The first sentence of Article III.2 states that imported products 'shall not be subject, directly or indirectly, to internal taxes or other internal charges of any kind in excess of those applied, directly or indirectly, to like domestic products'. The second sentence of Article III.2 broadens this rule by declaring that 'moreover, no contracting party shall otherwise apply internal taxes or other internal charges to imported or domestic products in a manner contrary to the principles set forth in paragraph 1'. Accordingly, the first sentence is concerned with the treatment of 'like' products, whereas the second sentence is concerned with the treatment of 'directly competitive or substitutable' products, which is a broader category of products than like products, as the Interpretative Note *Ad* Article III.2 clarifies.

not the measure at issue stems exclusively from a legitimate regulatory distinction, even accepting that the Article III.1 principle guides interpretation of all the paragraphs of Article III.

One solution would be to consider the regulatory legitimacy in the 'like products' determination arising under the application of the first sentence. As a matter of fact, the ordinary meaning of the words 'like products' is flexible enough to consider not only consumers' views on product likeness, but also the regulators' perspective: is it not always an open question to ask 'like products from whose perspective'? This is why the panel in *US—Clove Cigarettes* held that likeness in Article 2.1 of TBT Agreement 'must be evaluated in light of that objective' of the measure; i.e. the reduction of youth smoking. Such a purpose 'must permeate and inform our likeness analysis' to play the 'accordion' of like products in a TBT context.[29]

This aim-and-effect type of understanding of likeness was rejected by the Appellate Body, who empathized that the determination of likeness under TBT Article 2.1, as well as under GATT Article III.4, is a determination about 'the nature and extent of a competitive relationship' between and among the products at issue.[30] Given the Appellate Body's consistent antagonism to the aim-and-effect approach in determining likeness, this rejection is of no surprise.[31]

Instead, the Appellate Body went on to interpret the 'less-favourable-treatment' element based on the regulatory legitimacy criteria. By doing this, the Appellate Body succeeded in considering the regulatory legitimacy anyway in resolving the

[29] Panel Report, *United States—Measures Affecting the Production and Sale of Clove Cigarettes*, WT/DS406/R, 2 September 2011, paras 7.118–7.119. The term 'like product' appears in many provisions of the GATT 1994. The Appellate Body in *Japan—Alcoholic Beverages* (n 26) indicated that the term's meaning varies from one provision to another, and the interpretation of such meanings is like the image of playing an accordion. The accordion of 'likeness' stretches and squeezes in different places as different provisions of the WTO Agreement are applied. The width of the accordion in any one of those places must be determined by the particular provision in which the term 'like' is encountered, as well as by the context and the circumstances that prevail in any given case to which that provision may apply. See section H(1)(a), WT/DS8/AB/R, WT/DS10/AB/R, WT/DS11/AB/R (1996). This 'accordion approach' has been consistently adopted by subsequent Appellate Body rulings. For the discussions on the interpretation of 'like products', see Robert E Hudec, '"Like Products": The Differences in Meaning in GATT Articles I and III' in Thomas Cottier and Petros C Mavroidis (eds), *Regulatory Barriers and the Principle of Non-discrimination in World Trade Law: Past, Present, and Future* (The University of Michigan Press 2000) 101, 104–7, 399; Won-mog Choi, *'Like Products' in International Trade Law—Towards a Consistent GATT/WTO Jurisprudence* (OUP 2003) xix–xxi.

[30] *US—Clove Cigarettes*, Appellate Body Report (n 5) para 120.

[31] From time to time, mostly in the context of art III GATT, such factor as an aim has been suggested as an element to be taken into account in order to assess whether products were 'like'. In Report of the Panel, *US—Measures Affecting Alcoholic and Malt Beverages* (*US—Malt Beverages*) GATT BISD 28S/102, adopted 11 June 1981, paras 5.25 and 5.71 and Panel Report, *United States—Taxes on Automobiles* (*US—Automobiles*), DS31/R, 11 October 1994, unadopted, para 5.9, panels considered both the 'purpose or aim' and 'effect' of the measures in question. These panel decisions seem to be the only cases in which such factors were incorporated in the 'like product' determination, as subsequent WTO tribunals such as Appellate Body Report, *European Communities—Regime for the Importation, Sale and Distribution of Bananas* (*EC—Bananas*), WT/DS27/AB/R, 9 September 1997, para 215 and *Japan—Alcoholic Beverages*, Appellate Body Report (n 26) para 18 reverted to the traditional approach, stressing that the 'aim-and-effect' approach is not a proper test.

TBT case. At the same time, however, it failed to open the door to consider the very same element in the first sentence of GATT Article III.2 in any possible disputes in the future, where the only way to consider it might be to take the aim-and-effect type of consideration in the likeness determination.

A recent decision by the Appellate Body seems to give some consolation to the aim-and-effect proponents, even though it would not be a fully satisfactory one. In *Philippines—Distilled Spirits*,[32] the Appellate Body rejected the panel's ruling that all distilled spirits are like products under the first sentence of Article III.2 because of close physical properties. According to the Appellate Body, a finding of likeness under the first sentence requires 'a degree of competition that is higher than merely significant'.[33]

This reasoning on the product likeness recalls the divided opinion on this issue in the *EC—Asbestos* case.[34] There, two members of the Appellate Body took the view that, under Article III.4, likeness is about the 'competitive relationship' between products: 'a determination of "likeness" under Article III.4 is, fundamentally, a determination about the nature and extent of a competitive relationship between and among products'.[35] By contrast, one Member of the Division was sceptical about what he referred to as a 'fundamentally economic interpretation' of 'like products', stating: 'the necessity or appropriateness of adopting a "fundamentally" economic interpretation of the "likeness" of products under Article III.4 of the GATT 1994 does not appear to me to be free from substantial doubt'.[36]

In the *Distilled Spirits* case, the Appellate Body seems to have built on the reasoning of the *EC—Asbestos* majority, applying it beyond the coverage of Article III.4.[37] Of particular importance is that it did so despite the fact that the legal provision at issue was the first sentence of Article III.2. The *EC—Asbestos* majority had emphasized the distinction between Article III.4 and Article III.2, with the latter containing separate provisions for 'like products' and 'directly competitive or substitutable products', while Article III.4 refers only to 'like products'. For the *EC—Asbestos* majority, this distinction indicated a broader scope of coverage for likeness under Article III.4 than for likeness under the first sentence of Article III.2.[38] In *Philippines—Taxes on Distilled Spirits*, however, the Appellate Body cited a key passage from the *EC—Asbestos* reasoning, and then seemed to apply this reasoning to 'likeness' under the first sentence of Article III.2:

> While in the determination of 'likeness' a panel may logically start from the physical characteristics of the products, none of the criteria that a panel considers necessarily has an

[32] *Philippines—Taxes on Distilled Spirits* (*Philippines—Distilled Spirits*), WT/DS396, 14 January 2010.

[33] Appellate Body Report, *Philippines—Taxes on Distilled Spirits*, WT/DS396/AB/R, 21 December 2011, paras 179–82.

[34] *EC—Asbestos* (n 15).

[35] *EC—Asbestos*, Appellate Body Report (n 16) para 99.

[36] ibid para 154. See 'Appellate Body Reports: *Philippines—Taxes on Distilled Spirits*' (Dispute Settlement Commentary, Worldtradelaw.net 2012) 16–17.

[37] See ibid 'Appellate Body Reports: *Philippines—Taxes on Distilled Spirits*'.

[38] *EC—Asbestos*, Appellate Body Report (n 16) paras 94–99.

overarching role in the determination of 'likeness' under Article III:2 of the GATT 1994. A panel examines these criteria in order to make a determination about the nature and extent of a competitive relationship between and among the products.

We understand that products that have very similar physical characteristics may not be 'like', within the meaning of Article III:2, if their competitiveness or substitutability is low, while products that present certain physical differences may still be considered 'like' if such physical differences have a limited impact on the competitive relationship between and among the products.[39]

With these statements, the Appellate Body seems to have issued a clear holding that, as a general matter and regardless of which provision is at issue, likeness in the context of WTO obligations is about the economic competitiveness of products in the relevant market.[40]

The full impact of this ruling is of much significance, particularly to any environmental disputes. If two certain products sharing identical physical properties are actually treated differently in the particular market, those are not determined as like products. As the public awareness of environmental problems grows, more consumers would acquire different perceptions about environmental impacts arising from various products and their manufacturing process. More people will be interested in knowing which products are using more environmentally friendly materials, which manufacturers are more contributing to global green policies, and wastes of which products are naturally disposable. The time will come when even information of non-product-characteristics-related PPMs[41] is widely shared among consumers in the market. All of these perceptions and elements are relevant and must be taken into account in determining national treatment violations, as long as they affect product competitiveness in the market that is moving in a highly eco-sensitive direction. Indeed, it seems only to be a matter of time before in certain circumstances regulatory distinctions are allowed to be drawn between eco-friendly goods and non-eco-friendly goods, regardless of their physical similarities.

Note should be taken that this may happen under this new interpretation of product likeness in a less drastic manner than under the aim-and-effect approach. In certain circumstances, governments may need to take an initiative to draw regulatory distinctions between physically similar goods because of their different environmental impacts, even though consumer perceptions of those goods

[39] ibid para 99.

[40] See 'Appellate Body Reports: *Philippines—Taxes on Distilled Spirits*' (n 36).

[41] PPMs is the acronym of Process or Production Methods. It is important to understand the distinction between product-characteristics-related PPMs (PPMs that affect the properties or qualities of the final product) and non-product-characteristics-related PPMs (PPMs that do not affect the properties or qualities of the final product), since the two are traditionally treated differently under trade law. Trade law does not question the right of countries to discriminate based on product-related PPMs. Non-product-related PPMs, on the other hand, make no difference to the commercial or practical substitutability of the products—a criterion that is increasingly being used in the WTO to determine which products are alike and, it has been generally interpreted that WTO law does not allow countries to discriminate among like products, whatever their different environmental impacts.

have not been varied yet. In such circumstances, the two products can only be determined as like products according to the *EC—Asbestos/Philippines—Taxes on Distilled Spirits* reasoning, because the economic competitiveness between the two products in the relevant market would not be different.

In any case, although not as drastic as the aim-and-effect approach, this new interpretation of product likeness by the Appellate Body will contribute to a certain degree to opening a door towards the era of peaceful co-existence between trade liberalization and global environmental governance.

V. Conclusion

In the midst of debates and controversies concerning the linkage of trade rules and global governance of environmental protection, adjudicatory bodies that have to interpret and apply international trade treaties, including the WTO covered agreements and regional trade agreements, will need to take into account many economic and non-economic considerations before deciding whether any discrimination exists. Through a comprehensive review on newly emerging issues of interpretation arising under those agreements, such bodies must suggest a better interpretive solution for many future disputes and regulatory policies.

It took about twenty years before WTO tribunals officially recognized the significance of considering regulatory legitimacy when interpreting a non-discrimination clause of a side agreement of a WTO Agreement. As a consequence, the interpretation of the non-discrimination clause of the TBT Agreement should not be approached primarily from a competition perspective in the circumstances of dealing with a technical regulation that has a legitimate public policy objective. Rather, special notice must be paid to the significance of the policy objectives and how certain features of TBT measures are designed and structured to achieve such objectives.

Still, such recognition is limited to de facto discrimination cases within the TBT context, and when interpreting the words 'no less favourable treatment'. It falls short of recognizing the regulatory legitimacy factor in interpreting such words as 'so as to afford protection to domestic production' and 'like products' in other equivalent contexts. In other words, the march of the WTO tribunal has crossed the Rubicon halfway, but is still hesitating to land on the other side.

Despite this limited scope of recognition, future implications of this new approach by the WTO tribunal are limitless. Indeed, the concept of regulatory legitimacy is diverse and sometimes a catch-all one. Once the tribunal has crossed the Rubicon, it should conquer Rome as quickly as possible and declare new governing rules. Otherwise, it might end up being conquered by 'enemies' or so-called moralists, who are poised to hide behind environment, labour, or human rights shields and who are mostly strangers to GATT drafters. Moreover, even if the tribunal does not cross, such enemies might themselves ford the river. Indeed, to Caesar, who had not been in control of Rome, time must have been the enemy's ally.[42]

While we may have made progress in the development of trade law over the past sixty years, the relationship between legal holdings and their governing correspondence with changing reality remains enigmatic in this subject area. Perhaps the system under the rule might continue to evolve in an ad hoc, reactionary fashion as the Appellate Body has done in a series of recent TBT cases. But for those who prefer a legal system consistent with the fundamental concepts justifying its existence, discomfort is then inevitable. For these diligent people, it would be preferable to adjust the rule to make it consistent with economic and policy reality all at once. Reinterpretation by the tribunal of entire elements of non-discrimination clauses in the WTO agreements needs to be followed as quickly as possible.

Its absence (or wilful blindness to it) seems to have been covered by such theoretical excuses as the unique soil of international society and the imperfection of the science of econometrics, as well as by such practical ones as the strict time-limits on panel procedures, the lack of resources for panels' fact-finding processes, and/or considerations of judicial economy.

The role of the international tribunal in the *drive to maturity* is to provide legal security and predictability with regard to the meaning of WTO law. In a sense, the tribunal, through its case law, has to lend a hand in its own demise: it must make the meaning of WTO law so predictable that litigation will not be needed.[43] This is comparable with the inventive structure of an independent judiciary that applies the same law to the same facts.[44] It is particularly important for international adjudicators, who, unlike their municipal counterparts, lack a monopoly of enforcement power and have only the power to persuade the addressees of their decisions that those decisions are correct.[45] The international judiciary acquires its legitimacy through the consistent and coherent application of law.

In this stage of the WTO's drive to maturity after twenty years of its establishment, in which the tribunal, through its transparent and consistent standard-setting efforts, has to prepare for its own mature demise, the current excuses made by the Appellate Body will continue to lose validity.

[42] Wonmog Choi, *'Like Products' in International Trade Law—Towards a Consistent GATT/WTO Jurisprudence* (OUP 2003) 156–57.

[43] See Edwin Vermulst and others, 'The Functioning of the Appellate Body After Four Years: Towards Rule Integrity' (1999) 33(2) J World Trade 1, 32–33.

[44] ibid.

[45] See Thomas M Franck, *Fairness in International Law and Institutions* (Clarendon Press 1995) 26–46.

20

The Soft Law Approach to Regulatory Harmonization: Are We Trading Away Privacy for Economic Integration?

*Shin-yi Peng**

I. Privacy Policy and Trade Regime Recent Debate

A. Possible suspension of the Safe Harbor Agreement—adequacy?

In the context of the governance of global privacy, the dispute over the 'adequacy' of the US privacy law has always been a controversial issue.[1] Under the 1995 Data Protection Directive of the European Union (EU Directive),[2] personal data of EU citizens is permitted to be transferred to another jurisdiction only if that third country provides an 'adequate level of privacy protection'.[3] It is worth noting

* Professor, Institute of Law for Science and Technology, National Tsing Hua University (NTHU), Taiwan. Please note that these remarks are made in the author's personal capacity and the views expressed in this chapter are not intended in any way to represent the views of the government of Taiwan.

[1] See e.g., Rolf H Weber, 'Regulatory Autonomy and Privacy Standards Under the GATS' (2012) 7(1) Asian J WTO & Intl Health L & Policy 25. See also Shin-yi Peng, 'Digitalization of Services, the GATS and the Protection of Personal Data' in Reto M Hilty and others (eds), *Kommunikation, Festschrift für Rolf H Weber* (Stämpfli Publishing 2011) 753–69; Rolf H Weber, *Regulatory Models for the Online World* (Springer 2002) 156.

[2] It should be stressed that the European Union has proposed a comprehensive amendment to the current data protection directive and the completion of such reform is a policy priority for 2015. For the progress on the EU data protection reform, see European Commission, *Progress on EU Data Protection Reform Now Irreversible Following European Parliament Vote*, MEMO/14/186, 12 March 2014. On 15 December 2015, the European Commission put forward its EU Data Protection Reform in 2012 to make Europe fit for the digital age. An agreement was found with the European Parliament and the Council. The new rules will become applicable two years thereafter. See European Commission, Agreement on Commission's EU data protection reform will boost Digital Single Market <http://europa.eu/rapid/press-release_IP-15-6321_en.htm> accessed 10 April 2016.

[3] Council Directive 95/46/EC of 24 October 1995 on the protection of individuals with regard to the processing of personal data and on the free movement of such data (Principles) [1995] OJ L281/31, art 25:

> ... The adequacy of the level of protection afforded by a third country shall be assessed in the light of all the circumstances surrounding a data transfer operation or set of data transfer operations; particular consideration shall be given to the nature of the data, the purpose and duration of the proposed processing operation or operations, the country of

though that the EU Directive also stipulates several exceptions that allow for international transfers of personal information where there is no adequacy determination in place for the relevant jurisdiction.[4] A key concern of the European Union is that since the United States has long stressed 'self-regulation' by the private sector, it might not provide for 'adequate' data privacy protection under the EU Directive's criteria. Thus, in order to avoid a ban on data flow to the United States, the US and EU authorities became engaged in intensive negotiations that concluded with the US–EU Understanding on Safe Harbor Principles (Safe Harbor Agreement).[5] Pursuant to the Safe Harbor Agreement, US-based firms may self-certify that they will abide by the principles. Currently, there are more than 5,000 US firms using the Safe Harbor Agreement across a variety of sectors. Such a scheme, however, is now in serious jeopardy,[6] even facing possible suspension.[7]

Following the revelations by US National Security Agency (NSA) whistleblower Edward Snowden regarding the government's mass surveillance programs, EU policymakers and privacy advocators have stepped up efforts to increase the level of protection for EU citizens, and as such, the Safe Harbor Agreement became an immediate target.[8] Because the revelations included details concerning how the NSA gathered vast amounts of personal data from companies like Google and Facebook for use by intelligence agencies, some of which had been self-certified under the Safe Harbor Agreement, one may fairly question whether US law and practices in relation to privacy protection should fall under the so-called 'adequacy' finding afforded to the US Safe Harbor scheme.[9] In other words, Snowden's revelations are considered as further evidence to demonstrate that the Safe Harbor scheme fails to provide 'adequate' protection.[10] Thus, in this post-Snowden era, we can expect wider debate in Europe over more stringent limits of transfers of personal data to third countries.[11]

As part of the EU response to the Snowden revelations, the European Court of Justice (ECJ) is also examining the proposition that the transfer undertaken by

> origin and country of final destination, the rules of law, both general and sectoral, in force in the third country in question and the professional rules and security measures which are complied with in that country....

[4] Gregory Shaffer, 'Reconciling Trade and Regulatory Goals: The Prospects and Limits of New Approaches to Transatlantic Governance through Mutual Recognition and Safe Harbor Agreements' (2002) 9 Colum J Eur L 29, 60.

[5] In July 2000, the United States Department of Commerce and European Commission formalized an agreement creating a set of 'Safe Harbor Principles' on data privacy protection. See 'US–EU Safe Harbor' (export.gov) <http://export.gov/safeharbor/eu/> accessed 10 April 2016.

[6] Devika Kornbacher and Jeffrey Han, 'The US–EU Safe Harbor Program: Is It Safe?' (*Law 360*, 5 May 2015) <http://www.law360.com/articles/642603/the-us-eu-safe-harbor-program-is-it-safe> accessed 11 March 2016.

[7] 'EU Court Of Justice Case Could Subject "Safe Harbor" To Greater Scrutiny' (*Inside US Trade*, 2015) 33(1), World Trade Online database <http://insidetrade.com> accessed 23 April 2016.

[8] ibid 2. [9] Kornbacher and Han (n 6). [10] ibid.

[11] Ralf Bendrath, 'Trading Away Privacy: TTIP, TiSA and European Data Protection' (*eurozine*, 19 December 2014) <http://www.eurozine.com/articles/2014-12-19-bendrath-en.html> accessed 11 March 2016.

Facebook of personal data from Ireland to the United States was not adequately protected and thus should not fall under the Safe Harbor Agreement.[12] The case stemmed from a lawsuit against the Irish data protection commissioner by the plaintiff, an Austrian law student and data privacy activist, for allowing Facebook Ireland to transfer EU citizens' data back to the United States, where he believes there was no adequate privacy protection as required by the EU Directive.[13] The Irish High Court ruled that the Irish data protection commissioner, which cited the Safe Harbor Agreement and rejected the challenge, had acted correctly under the law. The Irish court was of the view that because Facebook was a Safe Harbor participant, and because the European Union had determined that the Safe Harbor Agreement provided adequate data protection, the Irish commissioner had no power to re-evaluate that decision.[14]

The judgment of the ECJ on that issue could open a door for data protection authorities of the EU Member States to determine for themselves whether personal data at a Safe Harbor-certified company is adequately protected and whether the Safe Harbor scheme is sufficient to guard its citizens' privacy. Although the EU Council appears to remain firmly in support of the Safe Harbor Agreement,[15] reports from the hearings suggested that the ECJ judges showed scepticism towards it.[16] The case may result in a major uncertainty, if not threat, to the Safe Harbor Agreement—the possibility that the ECJ rules that the Safe Harbor Agreement fails to satisfy the EU Directive and thus orders a suspension.

In any event, an 'adequacy' finding by the European Union would have no value if the data protection authority of any Member State has the authority to investigate the adequacy of the Safe Harbor Agreement, scrutinize it more thoroughly, and reach an independent national verdict regarding whether self-certifying US companies are in compliance with the EU Directive.[17] That being said, changes to the Safe Harbor scheme seem almost certain to be made.

B. Privacy standards under TTIP and TPP—interoperability?

At the same time, the US Chamber of Commerce is pushing for provisions in the Transatlantic Trade and Investment Partnership (TTIP) to broaden the ways by which US firms can comply with the EU Directive.[18] Such efforts, as expected,

[12] Anthony L Gardner, 'The Mackenzie Stuart Lecture 2015: Facing Legal Challenges in US–EU Relations' (Anthony Gardner, US Ambassador to the EU, Centre for European Legal Studies, University of Cambridge 2015) <http://www.cels.law.cam.ac.uk/mackenzie-stuart-lectures/mackenzie-stuart-lecture-2015-facing-legal-challenges-us-eu-relations> accessed 16 June 2015.

[13] 'EU Court of Justice Case Could Subject "Safe Harbor" To Greater Scrutiny' (n 7). See also Kornbacher and Han (n 6) 2.

[14] 'EU Court of Justice Case Could Subject "Safe Harbor" To Greater Scrutiny' (n 7).

[15] ibid. [16] ibid.

[17] ibid. See also 'Un-Safe Harbor: Is Safe Harbor an Adequate Means of Protecting EU Personal Data Transferred to the US?' (Wragge Lawrence Graham & Co 2014) <http://www.wragge-law.com/insights/> accessed 11 March 2016.

[18] 'Chamber Wants TTIP to Ease Data Flows Without Altering EU Regime' (*Inside US Trade*, 2014) 32(10), World Trade Online database <http://insidetrade.com> accessed 23 April 2016.

have been a challenging task for the TTIP negotiating groups. In fact, at one point, the Snowden revelations led to calls from the European Parliament to suspend the negotiations, with a warning that the Parliament may reject a TTIP deal if it in any way threatens the EU Directive. These levels of public sensation have gradually declined;[19] nevertheless, the EU officials have stressed that privacy protection should not be on the negotiating table, and that anything agreed in TTIP will have to be able to accommodate the EU Directive as it exists today and in the future.[20] To be more concrete, the trade negotiators of the European Union have insisted publicly that data protection should be kept out of trade talks, as they have no mandate to negotiate over the 'loopholes' of the Safe Harbor Agreement. The EU justice commissioner Viviane Reding has warned repeatedly against data protection issues to the TTIP trade talks on the grounds that privacy is 'a fundamental right', and as such 'it is not negotiable'.[21]

On the other hand, there have been numerous attempts by the lobbying groups of the United States to advocate that the TTIP should at least provide creative and viable alternative means for US companies to be deemed in compliance with the EU Directive requirements beyond the Safe Harbor Agreement.[22] For example, the Coalition for Privacy and Free Trade[23] and the Business Coalition for Transatlantic Trade[24] have been pushing for 'interoperability' between the European Union and the United States on privacy standards.[25] The Institute of Electrical and Electronics Engineers Glossary defines 'interoperability'[26] as 'the ability of two or more systems or components to exchange information and to use the information that has been exchanged',[27] which, in legal terms, may refer to a mutual recognition of the respective regulations on both sides of the TTIP. Privacy activists have strongly criticized this with the view that there is nothing to be interoperable with from a European perspective.[28] In their opinion, the position to replace adequacy with mere interoperability is basically 'an attempt to undermine the European data protection standard'.[29] Civil society and consumer organizations have also warned that the draft provisions in the TTIP pose a threat to European data protection standards, which could radically undermine the rights to privacy.[30]

[19] ibid.

[20] 'Brussels Round Marks Re-engagement on Market Access Offers in TTIP' (*Inside US Trade*, 2015) 33(5), World Trade Online database <http://insidetrade.com> accessed 23 April 2016.

[21] Bendrath (n 11) 1.

[22] 'EPP Chief Touts Support for TTIP in Parliament; Reding Says Data Deals Key Prerequisite' (*Inside US Trade*, 2015) 33(9), World Trade Online database <http://insidetrade.com> accessed 23 April 2016.

[23] The Coalition for Privacy and Free Trade is co-ordinated by US law firm Hogan Lovells.

[24] Business Coalition for Transatlantic Trade was founded by the US Chamber of Commerce.

[25] Bendrath (n 11) 2.

[26] See Sections III and IV of this chapter for a detailed discussion on interoperability.

[27] Institute of Electrical and Electronics Engineers, *IEEE Standard Computer Dictionary: A Compilation of IEEE Standard Computer Glossaries* (Institute of Electrical and Electronics Engineers 1990).

[28] Bendrath (n 11) 2. [29] ibid.

[30] ibid. See also Susan Ariel Aaronson and Miles D Townes, 'Can Trade Policy Set Information Free?' (The George Washington University Elliott School of International Affairs Institute for

Meanwhile, a similar story is happening in the Trans-Pacific Partnership (TPP) negotiations. The United States has been facing challenges to reach a compromise with TPP partners who did not respond enthusiastically to the proposed provisions on e-commerce. Several TPP participants deemed to 'seek the necessary policy space' under what is perceived as an overly aggressive negotiating proposal of the United States on the 'free flow of data across borders'.[31] In particular, Australia and New Zealand, which maintain strong privacy protection frameworks, have expressed concerns that the negotiating texts proposed by the United States could hamper their ability to uphold existing national privacy laws in a cross-border context.[32] In recent rounds of TPP negotiations, the United States and international trade associations representing a range of industries again urged trade ministers to include meaningful provisions on cross-border data flows in TPP that will drive the digital economy;[33] nonetheless, little progress was made due to differences among chief negotiators regarding how far to go on 'guaranteeing the free flow of data'.[34]

C. E-commerce proposals in TiSA—localization?

The leaked Trade in Services Agreement (TiSA) negotiating texts on 'localisation requirements', which have caused concerns among TiSA participants during the trade negotiations, is also a highly relevant issue concerning the tension between privacy and trade. The TiSA negotiating text of the Annex on E-commerce contains provisions on localization requirements,[35] which, according to the leaked source, may read as:

> Local Presence:
>
> *Subject to any terms, conditions, limitations and qualifications* set out in its Schedule, no Party may require a service supplier of another Party, *as a condition for the cross-border supply of a service in its territory*, to establish or maintain a representative office or any form of *commercial presence*, or to be resident or domiciled in the Party's territory. (*emphasis added*)

The proposal, aimed at removing localization requirements, demonstrates that the United States is seeking, through the TiSA, to establish broad rights for private sectors to transfer information across countries, which is strongly

International Economic Policy Working Paper Series IIEP-WP-2014-9, 2014) <http://ssrn.com/abstra<=2189153> accessed 11 March 2016. Jane Kelsey and Burcu Kilic, 'Briefing on US TISA Proposal on E-Commerce, Technology Transfer, Cross-border Data Flows and Net Neutrality' (*Public Service International*, 17 December 2014) <http://www.world-psi.org/en/briefing-us-tisa-proposal-e-commerce-technology-transfer-cross-border-data-flows-and-net-neutrality> accessed 11 March 2016.

[31] 'USTR Official: US still Faces Big Challenges on TPP Data Flow Proposal' (*Inside US Trade*, 2012) 30(38), World Trade Online database <http://insidetrade.com> accessed 23 April 2016.

[32] ibid.

[33] 'US, International Groups Endorse Free Flow of Data in TPP Deal' (*Inside US Trade*, 2014) (32)42, World Trade Online database <http://insidetrade.com> accessed 23 April 2016.

[34] 'USTR Official: US still Faces Big Challenges on TPP Data Flow Proposal' (n 31).

[35] Kelsey and Kilic (n 30) 7–11.

supported by the US services industry.[36] Should such a proposal be incorporated into TiSA, it would provide certainty that a cross-border commitment to provide services is not linked to localization requirements. In other words, any TiSA participating country that has allowed cross-border services supply in a given sector could not require a service supplier's use of a local server. Neither could a country require a service supplier of another country to have a local presence in its market.[37] The Deputy United States Trade Representative (USTR) had publicly acknowledged that the US proposal to establish broad rights for services suppliers to transfer data across borders is facing big opposition in TiSA. However, the United States insisted that such rules are essential for the development of the digital economy.[38] To stress the importance of ensuring that cross-border commitments to provide services are not linked to localization requirements,[39] the USTR stated that:

> it is absolutely fundamental that the US is the global leader in these areas, to help establish a regime for future trade agreements that allows us in our industries to bring the value of our digital products and digital economy to the global stage much as we did in prior trade agreements that allowed the current digital revolution to flourish.[40]

On the other hand, the proposal has drawn a backlash in the European Union,[41] the reason being that it is almost technically impossible to effectively govern privacy protection of the services suppliers based in other jurisdictions. In other words, service suppliers who housed their servers outside a country's territory are largely out of its privacy regulatory reach. The EU TiSA chief negotiator strongly stated that the localization provision may fail to provide adequate protection for privacy,[42] and expressed that: 'it is crystal clear that we are not going to negotiate anything that jeopardizes data protection in Europe. We are not going to enter into anything jeopardizing private data in TiSA.'[43]

II. Privacy Governance and Regionalism—the 'Soft Law'

A. The need for harmonization of privacy regulation

Privacy law, by its very nature, is a reactive force and always responds to breaches of society's 'moral code'.[44] The formulation of the legal meaning of privacy

[36] 'US Tackles Restraints on Transfers of Personal Data in TISA Proposal' (*Inside US Trade*, 2014) 32(50), World Trade Online database <http://insidetrade.com> accessed 23 April 2016.

[37] ibid.

[38] 'Holleyman Says TISA Data Flow Proposal Faces Pushback, But Vows to Press On' (*Inside US Trade*, 2015) 33(7), World Trade Online database <http://insidetrade.com> accessed 23 April 2016.

[39] ibid. [40] ibid.

[41] 'US Tackles Restraints on Transfers of Personal Data in TISA Proposal' (n 36).

[42] 'Reding Says US E-Commerce Proposal in TISA Falls Short on Privacy' (*Inside US Trade*, 2015) 33(9), World Trade Online database <http://insidetrade.com> accessed 23 April 2016.

[43] 'US Tackles Restraints on Transfers of Personal Data in TISA Proposal' (n 36).

[44] Shin-yi Peng, 'Privacy and the Construction of Legal Meaning in Taiwan' (2003) 37(4) Intl Law 1037, 1037–38.

becomes even more difficult when societies are increasingly complex and the social 'moral code' is confusing.[45] The recent debates on privacy issues in trade agreements demonstrated how numerous privacy norms at national, regional, and international levels have comprised the contemporary global privacy regulatory environment.[46] Indeed, privacy is essentially a cultural matter and reflects certain traditions from all over the world; it is not necessarily an absolute right that has supremacy over other rights.[47] Hence, global governance on privacy becomes extremely complicated when you consider how individuals define the boundaries of their personal space, how people from different cultural backgrounds perceive appropriate limits on government involvement in their personal affairs,[48] how different societies value the need for individual's privacy, and what factors and criteria must be considered by policymakers in different regions when balancing those competing interests.

Having said that, privacy regimes vary considerably, and privacy laws that emerge from divergent cultures differ dramatically from country to country—running from comprehensive to non-existent.[49] As data that flows across borders is accessed simultaneously in various countries around the world, a service supplier must comply with a myriad of privacy regulations,[50] which in many situations are overlapping or conflicting. From a perspective of compliance, service suppliers confront significant challenges when attempting to comply with often conflicting requirements of diverse national and regional privacy regulations.[51] In many cases, the dynamics of global data flows make it almost impossible to tell where personal data is at any given moment and which jurisdiction's laws should be applied.[52] For example, if data is entered into a global database in China and is available in the fifty offices in which the service supplier has offices, it will be complicated to untangle the jurisdictional issues,[53] which results in legal uncertainty. The lack of consistency among national laws creates a costly and burdensome task for the service suppliers that engage in cross-border transfers of personal data, especially when such data is transferred from a service supplier operating in a country with weaker data protection regulation to one with stronger regulation.[54] Service suppliers must seek multiple

[45] ibid 1053.

[46] Paul De Hert and Vagelis Papakonstantinou, 'Three Scenarios for International Governance of Data Privacy: Towards an International Data Privacy Organization, Preferably A UN Agency?' (2013) 9(2) I/S: JL Poly Info Socy 271, 275.

[47] Peng (n 44) 1053.

[48] Paula J Bruening, 'Interoperability: Analyzing the Current Trends and Developments' (2012) 9(5) Data Protection L Poly 12.

[49] ibid. See also Miriam Wugmeister and others, 'Global Solution for Cross-border Data Transfers: Making the Case for Corporate Privacy Rules' (2007) 38 Geo J Intl L 449, 449–50.

[50] ibid 472. [51] ibid 472–73.

[52] Dennis D Hirsch, 'In Search of the Holy Grail: Achieving Global Privacy Rules Through Sector-based Codes of Conduct' (2013) 74(6) Ohio St LJ 1029, 1036.

[53] Wugmeister and others (n 49) 474, 451.

[54] Sunni Yuen, 'Exporting Trust with Data: Audited Self-regulation as a Solution to Cross-border Data Transfer Protection Concerns in the Offshore Outsourcing Industry' (2008) 9 Colum Sci Tech L Rev 41, 45.

regulatory approvals for routine cross-border transfers and must closely track the flow of their data so as to ensure which jurisdiction's rules should be applied at any given moment.[55]

From the perspective of international trade, such diversity makes compliance challenging and therefore directs resources away from more effective mechanisms.[56] Global data flows, combined with complex privacy laws, reduce flexibility of the service suppliers and inhibit them from managing operations in an efficient manner.[57] The increasingly complex burden to comply with both local and cross-border privacy rules eventually impacts the price of products or services offered to consumers.[58]

In this information age, the global flow of data is essential for innovation and economic growth. Policy initiatives, on the one hand, recognize the need for privacy protection if the benefits of an information economy are to be realized; while on the other hand, they stress the need to simplify compliance.[59] The 'regulatory jungle' of privacy laws worldwide has resulted in trade barriers. Conversely, the emergence of a more consistent streamlined system between privacy regimes would bridge the differences among jurisdictions, diffuse the threat of legal uncertainty, reduce business costs, increase compliance, and therefore provide benefits to both industry and consumers.[60] The origin and destination countries, where data is processed, would be mutually bound by a privacy standard agreed between the governments if such a less fragmented and more harmonized privacy framework can be established, which would contribute greatly to global economic growth.[61] At the core of the matter is how privacy standards can be governed in regional trade arrangements. Which regulatory models should be followed? Or, what creative methods can be formulated?

B. Hard and soft law in international governance

As globalization has created markets that cross borders,[62] there is an increasing reliance on diverse types of international legal instruments to 'legalize' international affairs.[63] An international arrangement that is designed as an instrument of global governance can be placed on a continuum from 'hard law'—precise and legally binding obligations with official sanctions for violations, to 'soft law'—imprecise and non-binding obligations with little institutionalized enforcement

[55] Hirsch (n 52) 1036–37.
[56] 'Interoperability: Analyzing the Current Trends and Developments' (n 48).
[57] Hirsch (n 52) 1036–37. [58] Wugmeister and others (n 49) 474–75.
[59] 'Interoperability: Analyzing the Current Trends and Developments' (n 48).
[60] ibid. [61] Yuen (n 54) 55.
[62] Jean Galbraith and David Zaring, 'Soft Law as Foreign Relations Law' (2014) 99 Cornell L Rev 735, 745.
[63] See generally Shin-yi Peng, 'The WTO Legalistic Approach and East Asia: From the Legal Culture Perspective' (2000) 1(2) Asian-Pac L Poly J 13. See also Julien Chaisse and Mitsuo Matsushita, 'Maintaining the WTO's Supremacy in the International Trade Order: A Proposal to Refine and Revise the Role of the Trade Policy Review Mechanism' (2013) 16 J Intl Econ L 9–36.

for non-compliant behaviour.[64] As for international 'hard law', which should not be stressed as 'hard' if not compared with the 'soft law', there are relatively accepted legal definitions, especially on the sources and the obligations imposed on states.[65] On the other hand, as for international soft law, there is a wide variety of definitions, although an emerging consensus has been emphasized on the roots of its softness—either where it came from or the way it is enforced.[66]

One major reason for the growth of global soft law in the past four decades has been the difficulties and complexities associated with concluding 'hard' international arrangements through treaties.[67] The hard law approach generally requires a significant cost in terms of the sovereignty of states, and, as such, states may exercise more caution in drafting hard law so as to avoid consequences of a subsequent violation.[68] On the contrary, the soft law approach can be pursued by international arrangements under which sub-state actors of different jurisdictions meet with each other and harmonize the regulatory rules applied at home.[69] Much existing literature has explained how soft law offers more advantages over hard law in that it affords greater flexibility and experimentation regarding policy alternatives.[70] In fact, empirical studies also show that soft law agreements have emerged into areas of law classically associated more with domestic than with international affairs, such as privacy protection.[71]

However, the dividing line between soft and hard norms is not always a clear one. The dichotomy between hard and soft law in the context of how international law is developed may be criticized as being oversimplified. As Shaffer pointed out, hard law and soft law are most likely to be used as complements in an evolutionary manner,[72] as soft-law regimes can be 'hardened' through their links to hard law regimes by losing the flexibility and informality, while hard-law regimes can be 'softened' through their links to soft law regimes by reducing legal certainty and predictability.[73] That being said, Shaffer argued that hard and soft law can build upon each other.[74] In some conditions hard law and soft law

[64] See generally Antto Vihma, 'Analyzing Soft Law and Hard Law in Climate Change' in Erkki J Hollo and others (eds), *Climate Change and the Law* (Springer 2013) 143. Brian Sheppard, 'Norm Super-compliance and the Status of Soft Law' (2014) 62(4) Buff L Rev 787. To illustrate, the term 'soft law' is theoretically unsettling to some commentators and has been criticized as a confusing normative category. Generally, 'soft law' refers to a 'law' that is either not yet or not only law. For general explanations of soft law, see Pierre Marie Dupuy, 'Soft Law and the International Law of the Environment' (1991) 12 Mich J Intl L 420. See also Gunther F Handl and others, 'A Hard Look at Soft Law' (1988) 82 Am Socy Intl L Proceedings 371. For a detailed discussion on whether 'soft law' is really law, see Jonathan Carlson, 'Hunger, Agricultural Trade Liberalization, and Soft International Law' (1985) 70 Iowa L Rev 1187.

[65] Vihma (n 64) 145.

[66] Sheppard (n 64) 798.

[67] Galbraith and Zaring (n 62) 748.

[68] Vihma (n 64) 143–45.

[69] Galbraith and Zaring (n 62) 745.

[70] Gregory Shaffer and Mark A Pollack, 'Hard Versus Soft Law in International Security' (2011) 52(4) BC L Rev 1147, 1148–49.

[71] Galbraith and Zaring (n 62) 747–48.

[72] Gregory Shaffer and Mark A Pollack, 'Hard vs Soft Law: Alternatives, Complements, and Antagonists in International Governance' (2010) 94 Minn L Rev 706, 710.

[73] ibid 709–11.

[74] ibid 707.

are operating as mutually reinforcing complements, but in other conditions they interact in international governance as alternatives.[75] Certain objectives can be effectively pursued by soft law, while other objectives would require a hard law approach.[76]

In privacy regulation spheres, it is clear that the strategic use of hard and soft law has profound implications for the international economic order. This chapter has attempted to employ the US–EU Safe Harbor model, under which hard and soft law act as complements, and the APEC Cross-border Privacy Rules model, under which hard and soft law act as alternatives, as case studies to analyse how they can interact in complementary ways, as well as how they are used as alternatives. Crafting legal arrangements is a central tool in regulatory harmonization. Different legal issues require different solutions. How, then, should international co-operation on privacy protection proceed? How should we approach soft law to balance privacy and trade? Which international model should be applied? And how should it be implemented? These are the main queries the following sections attempt to answer.

C. Soft law as a complement—the US–EU Safe Harbor model

As explained in Section I:A of this chapter, Article 25 of the EU Directive, which seeks to ensure that the protection of the data will be 'adequate' when data of European citizens is transferred outside the European Union, requires that EU Member States prohibit the transfer of personal data to any country outside the European Union that does not 'ensure an adequate level of protection'. Under the Directive, Member States are required to prohibit transfers of personal data to non-Member States unless the transferee state ensures an 'adequate level of protection';[77] such a determination must be based on considerations including the nature of the data, the purpose and duration of the proposed processing operations, and the rules of law in force in the third country in question.[78] As of to date, the European Union has recognized privacy laws of only eleven countries as 'adequate protection' for EU citizen data.[79] Although there are several exemptions that would allow Member States to permit transfers to take place where they would otherwise be prohibited, the 'adequacy' requirement under Article 25 of the EU Directive is certainly a precise and legally binding obligation with official sanctions in case of violation.

Such a hard law regime, however strict, is supplemented with a soft law mechanism—the US–EU Safe Harbor Privacy arrangement, which contains seven key principles: notice, choice, onward transfer, security, data integrity, access, and

[75] ibid 798. [76] Vihma (n 64) 143–45.

[77] Marc Rotenberg and David Jacobs, 'Updating the Law of Information Privacy: The New Framework of the European Union' (2013) 36(2) Harv JL Pub Poly 605, 636.

[78] ibid 637.

[79] 'Commission Decisions on the Adequacy of the Protection of Personal Data in Third Countries' (European Commission) <http://ec.europa.eu/justice/data-protection/international-transfers/adequacy/index_en.htm> accessed 11 March 2016.

dispute resolution.[80] The Safe Harbor Agreement was developed in 2000 by the US Department of Commerce (DOC) in collaboration with the European Union to enable them to comply with the data export requirements of the EU Directive. Under the scheme, a US company can voluntarily opt in and either perform a 'self-assessment' or hire a third party to perform an assessment to determine whether it complies with the Principles. In other words, a company can develop its own privacy policy, essentially a code of conduct, and then certify itself by submitting a declaration to the DOC on an annual basis that it complies with the Safe Harbor Principles. Otherwise, it may join a Safe Harbor self-regulatory program—i.e., TRUSTe—which guides US companies on how to comply with the Safe Harbor Principles. Either way satisfies the Safe Harbor requirements and, as such, the US company can be considered as providing 'adequate' protection for the purposes of the EU Directive.[81]

The EU model serves as an interesting case study on how hard law and soft law interact, and whether, when working together, they can cope with the challenges of regulatory fragmentation of privacy protection. The Safe Harbor mechanism is entirely different to that of the EU Directive. The former is designed to avoid framing privacy as a 'right', to rely on the market mechanisms, to lessen the government involvement, and to reduce the burden to business.[82] The latter, however, defines privacy as a fundamental right, legalizes such right into a comprehensive law, and implements such law by an independent commission. As a result, hard law (the regulation-based 'adequacy' requirements) and soft law (the self-regulation-based Safe Harbor Principles) act as complements in transatlantic governance.

As Shaffer pointed out, the Safe Harbor Agreement constitutes 'a loose form of *de facto* harmonization of social standards',[83] which goes beyond current regulatory requirements in the United States and thereby constitutes a regulatory floor which US companies must comply with if they wish to receive data from Europe. Indeed, by recognizing the implementation of the seven principles as 'equivalent' to the 'adequate level of protection' required by Article 25 of the EU Directive, the Safe Harbor Agreement in fact necessitates a minimum standard of regulatory cohesion between the United States and the European Union. The two regulatory regimes, therefore, in broad terms, can be harmonized because of the development of common regional standards which serve as a basis of recognition. But is it working well?

As discussed in Section I, the Safe Harbor Agreement is now facing a possible suspension as the compliance of the United States has come under substantial criticism.[84] In particular, reports have highlighted numerous weaknesses in the Safe

[80] 'How Will the "Safe Harbor" Arrangement for Personal Data Transfers to the US Work' (European Commission) <http://ec.europa.eu/justice/policies/privacy/thridcountries/adequacy-faq1_en.htm> accessed 11 March 2016.

[81] ibid. See also 'Un-Safe Harbor: Is Safe Harbor an Adequate Means of Protecting EU Personal Data Transferred to the US?' (n 17); Hirsch (n 54) 1037; Rotenberg and Jacobs (n 77) 605.

[82] Virginia Boyd, 'Financial Privacy in the United States and the European Union: A Path to Transatlantic Regulatory Harmonization' (2006) 24(3) Berkeley J Intl L 939; Hert and Papakonstantinou (n 46) 271.

[83] Shaffer (n 4) 32, 34, 57.

[84] Rotenberg and Jacobs (n 77) 623–29.

Harbor regime and pointed out that the self-certified US companies did not live up to the expected degree of transparency.[85] In November 2013, the European Union declared thirteen recommendations aimed at reinforcing the Safe Harbor Agreement, most of which focused on improving transparency and ensuring effective monitoring of the Principles.[86] To illustrate, the recommendations requires self-certified US companies to publish privacy conditions of any contracts they enter into with subcontractors, and asks the US Federal Trade Commission (FTC) to systematically monitor the access to information.[87] Negotiations between the United States and the European Union remain on-going since the recommendation was proposed; nonetheless, nothing has yet been finalized. The EU negotiating team thus cited these continued negotiations and missing timetable as proof that 'efforts to fix the admitted flaws in the Safe Harbor were failing'.[88] At the same time, there has been a growing concern raised by the data protection authorities in the EU Member States.[89] They are of the view that the high reliance on self-certification and self-regulation that are based on voluntary adherence by companies has resulted in a lack of enforcement. Germany's data protection commissioners, for instance, issued a decision requesting German companies transferring data to the United States to actively check 'whether the Safe Harbor certification by the importer is still valid'.[90] In March 2014, the EU Parliament overwhelmingly passed a resolution calling for the immediate suspension of the Safe Harbor Agreement, primarily due to perceived shortcomings in the self-certification process.[91] At this moment, it remains to be seen whether the European Union will eventually abolish or suspend the Safe Harbor Agreement. It is highly likely that we will be witnessing the collapse of the old paradigm—under which hard and soft law act as complements in governing cross-border privacy protection.

D. Soft law as an alternative—the APEC Cross-border Privacy Rules model

Meanwhile, policymakers in the Asia-Pacific are drawing up the shape of a new paradigm for privacy governance under international arrangements. As shown in Table 20.1, differing from the US–EU Safe Harbor model, the APEC Cross-border Privacy Rules (CBPRs) model relies purely on soft law as an alternative to facilitate cross-border privacy governance. Since its establishment in 1989, APEC has been operating on the basis of non-binding commitments. The paradigm of APEC,

[85] ibid.

[86] 'Un-Safe Harbor: Is Safe Harbor an Adequate Means of Protecting EU Personal Data Transferred to the US?' (n 17); Kornbacher and Han (n 6).

[87] Kornbacher and Han (n 6). [88] ibid.

[89] *Communication from the Commission to the European Parliament and the Council on the Functioning of the Safe Harbour from the Perspective of EU Citizens and Companies Established in the EU*, COM (2013) 0847 final, 27 November 2013.

[90] ibid.

[91] ibid. See also 'Un-Safe Harbor: Is Safe Harbor an Adequate Means of Protecting EU Personal Data Transferred to the US?' (n 17); Kornbacher and Han (n 6).

Table 20.1 EU model v APEC model

Models	Mechanism	Level of protection	Level of harmonization	Legal effects
EU model hard and soft law act as complements	Self-certified + third-party certification	Adequacy, through mutual recognition (equivalency)	de facto harmonization	Safe harbor
APEC model hard and soft law act as alternatives	Third-party certification	Interoperability, through codes of conduct	Low-level de facto minimum harmonization	'Safer' status

(Author's analysis and composition.)

essentially a mechanism based on voluntary consensus and peer pressure, is far from a regime of 'hard' law. This kind of 'soft' law, consisting of a set of commonly agreed skeletal principles stated in broad terms,[92] is the preferred way by most Asian members. In 1998, APEC declared its Blueprint for Action on Electronic Commerce to address 'the necessity of government and business cooperation in order to achieve the full potential of electronic commerce'.[93] In 2004, the APEC Privacy Framework was formally endorsed by APEC Ministers,[94] which comprises a set of nine principles that apply to privacy protection.[95] Consistent with APEC's spirit of pragmatism, the nine principles[96] (i.e. preventing harm, notice, collection limitation, uses of personal information, choice, integrity of personal information, security safeguards, access and correction, and accountability) were drafted in rather general objective terms that offer diverse interpretations.[97]

A significant initiative—(Cross Border Privacy Rules System, CBPRs)—were endorsed in November 2011 by representatives of APEC economies. CBPRs rely

[92] Kornbacher and Han (n 6).

[93] APEC, 'APEC Privacy Framework' <https://cbprs.blob.core.windows.net/files/APEC%20Privacy%20Framework.pdf> (2005) accessed 17 June 2015.

[94] APEC, 'APEC Privacy Framework Working Group' (APEC) <http://www.apec.org/Groups/Committee-on-Trade-and-Investment/Electronic-Commerce-Steering-Group/Cross-border-Privacy-Enforcement-Arrangement.aspx> accessed 11 March 2016.

[95] See generally Stuart Hargreaves, 'Inadequate: The APEC Privacy Framework and Article 25 of the European Data Protection Directive' (2010) 8(1) Can JL Tech 1. See also Chris Pounder, 'Why the APEC Privacy Framework is Unlikely to Protect Privacy' (Out-Law.com) <http://www.out-law.com/page-8550> accessed 11 March 2016.

[96] Federal Trade Commission, 'FTC Joins New Asia-Pacific Multinational Network of Privacy Enforcement Authorities' (Federal Trade Commission 2010) <https://www.ftc.gov/news-events/press-releases/2010/07/ftc-joins-new-asia-pacific-multinational-network-privacy> accessed 11 March 2016.

[97] e.g. under the heading of Preventing Harm, APEC economies agreed that:

> individuals have a legitimate expectation of privacy in their personal information, and protections should be designed to prevent harm to individuals because of the wrongful collection or misuse of that information. Remedies for privacy infringements ought to be designed to prevent further harm to individuals and should be proportionate to the likelihood and severity of the threat that exists because of the use of that information.

heavily on co-regulatory codes of conduct.[98] In practice, a participating company prepares a code of conduct that explains how the APEC Privacy Principles apply to its specific operations, submits this code to an APEC-approved third party, and gets approval from such an agent. CBPRs also establish a framework for voluntary sharing of information and assistance in enforcing information privacy.[99] In September 2012, the United States announced that it had become the first participant in the CBPRs system. And in August 2013, IBM became the first company certified under the CBPRs.[100] As stressed by the Interoperability Working Group, APEC economies need 'pragmatic ways to bridge the gaps between different legal systems and privacy regimes'.[101]

The key concept of CBPRs is 'interoperability' instead of 'adequacy'. The APEC-type 'interoperability', by technical definition, refers to the ability of diverse systems to work together.[102] In the context of privacy protection, the basic idea behind the interoperability model is that 'different privacy regimes can be made to work together through negotiated codes of conduct'.[103] It is true that the APEC model does not fully address the legal uncertainty and the business burden resulting from the lack of consistency among national laws because an APEC-approved code of conduct does not necessarily guarantee compliance with all privacy laws of APEC economies. Such a scheme, nevertheless, offers a low level de facto regulatory harmonization as it 'encompasses the protections that the different regimes already have in common, as well as any additional necessary elements mutually agreed by the parties'.[104] The position that industry-specific codes of conduct developed through multi-stakeholder processes could be used for cross-border data transfers was emphasized in the Whitehouse Report on Privacy,[105] which elaborated by claiming that, 'while voluntary, CBPRs certification will entitle participating companies to represent to consumers that they are accountable and meet regionally recognized standards, thereby facilitating the transfer of personal data throughout the APEC region'.[106]

[98] Hirsch (n 52) 1048.

[99] Federal Trade Commission, 'FTC Welcomes a New Privacy System for the Movement of Consumer Data Between the United States and Other Economies in the Asia-Pacific Region' (Federal Trade Commission) <https://www.ftc.gov/news-events/press-releases> accessed 11 March 2016.

[100] John Kropf, 'The EU and APEC: A Roadmap for Global Interoperability' (The International Association of Privacy Professionals 2013) <https://privacyassociation.org/news/a/the-eu-and-apec-a-roadmap-for-global-interoperability> accessed 23 April 2016.

[101] APEC, *APEC Privacy Framework Working Group* (2005) <http://www.apec.org/Groups> accessed 11 March 2016.

[102] APEC, 'Scoping Paper on Privacy System Interoperability' (Data Privacy Sub-Group Meeting, 2011/SOM3/ECSG/DPS/013, 2011).

[103] Markus Heyder, 'Getting Practical and Thinking Ahead: "Interoperability" Is Gaining Momentum' (The International Association of Privacy Professionals 2014) <https://privacyassociation.org/news/a/getting-practical-and-thinking-ahead-interoperability-is-gaining-momentum/> accessed 23 April 2016.

[104] ibid.

[105] Executive Office of the President of the United States, 'Consumer Privacy Data in a Networked World' (The White House 2012) <https://www.whitehouse.gov/sites/default/files/privacy-final.pdf> accessed 23 April 2016.

[106] ibid 31–33.

At this stage it is unclear how far CBPRs can go. In any event, the APEC model provides a perspective to review how international co-operation on privacy protection can proceed by the soft law approach. As privacy is fundamentally cultural, it is increasingly obvious that solutions to the challenges posed by such diversity do not lie in attempting to map one national approach to another.[107] It is evidenced by the controversy of the EU Safe Harbor model that imposing a standard of one region to mirror that of another will not work. The APEC-type 'interoperability' may be proven to be a pragmatic way forward for providing more coherent privacy protections for regional data flows,[108] which, in the long run, might ultimately lead to a higher level of regional regulatory harmonization in privacy protection. While the CBPRs are still in their early stages of implementation, they are gaining momentum among APEC stakeholders.[109] In 2015, Canada followed the addition of Japan in 2014, Mexico in 2013, and the United States in 2012, and became the latest entrant into the CBPRs. Other economies such as South Korea, the Philippines, Thailand, Vietnam, Singapore, Hong Kong, and Australia—have affirmed their interest and have taken steps towards participation. Such a move can be seen as a further step to pave the way for expansion of the system among the remaining sixteen APEC members and as moving towards its region-wide adoption.

III. Moving from Regulatory Fragmentation towards Harmonization

A. Notice and consent? Industry aspects

The explosive amount of the volume of data collected and processed today is unprecedented.[110] Technological ability to collect, aggregate, and process an ever-greater volume and variety of data continues to grow, which in fact means that we are now living in a world of ubiquitous data collection.[111] In the age of 'big fata', wearable technologies with voice and video interfaces, combined with the networked devices, are expanding capacities to collect even more information.[112] This trend towards ubiquitous collection makes the notion of 'limiting collection' challenging, if not impossible.[113] Analysing massive datasets, including, for example, meta-data from Internet searches, mobile phone location information, credit card purchases, and social media postings for emerging patterns, has the potential to

[107] Bruening, 'Interoperability: Analyzing the Current Trends and Developments' (n 48).

[108] Heyder (n 103). See also Kropf (n 100).

[109] Heyder (n 103).

[110] Executive Office of the President of the United States, 'Big Data: Seizing Opportunities, Preserving Values' (The White House 2014) <https://www.whitehouse.gov/sites/default/files/docs/big_data_privacy_report_may_1_2014.pdf> accessed 23 April 2016.

[111] Ann Cavoukian and Jeff Jonas, 'Privacy by Design in the Age of Big Data' (Privacy by Design 2012) <https://privacybydesign.ca/content/uploads/2012/06/pbd-big_data.pdf> accessed 11 March 2016.

[112] ibid.

[113] See Executive Office of the President of United States, 'Big Data' (n 110) 10.

generate enormous value to society.[114] However, the wide variety of potential uses for big data analytics raises crucial questions primarily concerning how to protect privacy in this big data world.[115]

Regulators around the world have gradually become aware that the rise of big data represents a significant challenge to established privacy regulatory frameworks.[116] In their views, the two major foundations of the existing legal tools—purpose limitation and data minimization—no longer work.[117] The complexity of the big data analytics makes it impossible to state purposes at the outset and obtain consent for the processing. These trends require policymakers to examine the notice-and-consent framework that has been a central pillar of privacy practices for decades.[118] They argue that privacy policy should emphasize how the data is used or re-used, rather than trying to control what happens at the point when the data is collected.[119] They are also of the view that focusing on controlling the collection of personal data may no longer be sufficient to protect privacy in a big data world.[120]

That being said, it has been proposed that 'the role of third parties' is becoming increasingly important under such trends in ensuring that companies carrying out big data analytics have proper regard to privacy issues.[121] The Information Commissioner's Office (ICO) in the UK, for instance, has publicly expressed that policy framework for big data will require co-operation between the public and private sectors. One policy direction for the ICO specifically for the big data context is to work with established certification bodies, which would carry out the testing on de-identification and re-identification, and award the privacy seal.[122] Does this imply that governments will pursue less formal approaches to solving increasingly globalized privacy problems? Does it also mean that a co-regulatory mechanism that utilizes industry knowledge to produce privacy rules is working? In any event, market dynamics will affect privacy regulations. As indicated in the UK report, a third-party certification system may fulfil an important role in the big data ecosystem.[123] The 'notice-and-consent' privacy framework, which has been enforced for decades in many jurisdictions by imposing legally binding obligations with official sanctions for violations, is facing a need for regulatory reform.

To summarize, one key element of the changing character of privacy protection is the significance attached to the role of the third party, especially the certification mechanism. In the context of international economic law, technological change has brought about the emergence of a multiplicity of new actors and different privacy standard-setting bodies that may also change the role of international trade

[114] Cavoukian and Jonas (n 111) 13. See also Information Commissioner's Office (ICO), 'Big Data and Data Protection' (ICO 2014) <https://ico.org.uk/media/for-organisations/documents/1541/big-data-and-data-protection.pdf> accessed 23 April 2016.

[115] Cavoukian and Jonas (n 111) 13. See also ITU, 'Big Data: Big today, normal tomorrow' (2013) ITU-T Technology Watch Report, <http://unstats.un.org/unsd/trade/events/2014/beijing/documents/other/ITU%20-%20Big%20Data%20today,%20normal%20tomorow.pdf> accessed 23 April 2016; Executive Office of the President of United States, 'Big Data' (n 110) 10.

[116] ITU (n 115). [117] ICO (n 114) 23. [118] ibid 4, 6, 19. [119] ibid 19.

[120] ibid 42. [121] ibid 42–22. [122] ibid. [123] ibid.

agreement towards one that facilities networking between public actors and private participants.[124] Considering the impact of the big data analysis on privacy regulatory regimes, regional governance on privacy protection is not merely about the relationship between governments, but also involves private companies and industry associations. That being said, the APEC model seems to hold greater promise.

B. Challenges and opportunities—political aspects

Of course, as explained earlier, CBPRs' function to harmonize regional privacy regulations is limited by its soft character. Strictly speaking, the APEC CBPRs have not reached harmonization so far. The so-called 'interoperability' under the APEC is operating in a way different from conventional regulatory harmonization. To further illustrate, an APEC-certified code of conduct does not necessarily guarantee compliance with the privacy laws of APEC members.[125] In other words, the APEC CBPRs fall short in creating a legal safe harbor. That being said, the APEC framework does not fully address the burdens that cross-border data transfers create for private sectors because companies operating under CBPRs still have to comply with the privacy laws of all different jurisdictions to meet different sets of national requirements. The mere 'incentive' for companies that follow an APEC-approved code of conduct is to 'feel more comfortable' than they otherwise would, that their behaviour complies with the regional privacy standards under APEC, and therefore 'feel more confident' to engage in cross-border transfers among APEC members.[126] Unlike the US–EU Safe Harbor model, the APEC only provides a 'safer' status for companies that engage in cross-border data transfers among APEC economies, with the 'expectation' that the APEC economies would not enforce their strict privacy laws, if any, as harshly as they otherwise would on those CBPRs-certified companies. In this context, relying on non-binding regional standards to protect privacy, essentially, has limits. Pursuing less formal approaches to solving complex problems between trade and privacy eventually faces the pressure to move further towards a higher level of harmonization.

Nevertheless, there have been an increasing number of successful examples on soft law approach in trade areas.[127] Although it is true that such a scheme has no teeth and no disciplines are imposed for non-compliance, and it is also true that a scheme without any binding power is generally not effective as compared to one with enforceable dispute settlement mechanism,[128] in many cases under free trade

[124] Martin Lodge and Kai Wegrich, *Managing Regulation: Regulatory Analysis, Politics and Policy Managing* (Palgrave Macmillan 2012) 143.

[125] Pounder (n 95). [126] Hirsch (n 52) 1049. Hargreaves (n 95) 5.

[127] See generally Mary Footer, 'The (Re)turn to "Soft Law" in Reconciling the Antinomies in WTO Law' (2012) 11 Melb J Intl L 241. See also Julien Chaisse and Mitsuo Matsushita, 'Maintaining the WTO's Supremacy in the International Trade Order: A Proposal to Refine and Revise the Role of the Trade Policy Review Mechanism' (2013) 16 J Intl Econ L 9–36; Mitsuo Matsushita, 'A View on Future Roles of The WTO: Should There be More Soft Law in The WTO?' (2014) 17(3) J Intl Econ L 701, 711.

[128] Matsushita (n 127) 701.

agreements, the tremendous success of global governance lies in its informality and flexibility.[129] As Shaffer pointed out, the hard law international trading system overlaps and interacts in complex ways with other 'softer regimes' governing social regulations.[130] In the context of IEL, the drive towards 'hard law' increases caution on what they can commit to, the result potentially being lower ambition, if not lack of progress or absence of key players.[131] In fact, soft law is becoming employed more often as a common mode of regulation for international bodies.[132] It is generally more cost effective and easier to reach a consensus than hard law.[133] In addition, since APEC CBPRs constitute a lessened form of international commitment relative to treaties, they can be negotiated and renegotiated with greater ease, and as a result have potential to contain stronger substantive provisions in the future. In other words, as soft law provides an early signal that hard law may eventually take, the APEC-type 'interoperability' provides a 'near-term' practical solution, which may ultimately lead to regional harmonization in privacy protection.

By the same token, another more practical aspect is that, under most of the constitutional designs, soft law international agreements are subject to fewer checks domestically.[134] The soft law mechanism under the APEC Privacy Framework can be further developed by lower ranking officials who are knowledgeable about privacy regulations without going through cumbersome treaty negotiating processes associated with making a binding agreement. Recent development of CBPRs further demonstrates that APEC could use its power to facilitate co-operation and invite non-state actors to participate in crafting the international arrangements. The APEC Electronic Commerce Steering Group and Data Privacy Subgroup have been working together on the APEC Privacy Recognition for Processors (PRP) as an expansion of CBPRs' scope.[135] The PRP has been finalized and was endorsed by APEC at its most recent Senior Officials Meeting in the Philippines in February 2015.[136] The softness of the framework provides a way to avoid the problems with ratification processes required for traditional treaties.[137] The control of the negotiation process, therefore, lies more within the domain of the executive branch of APEC economies as well as pragmatic privacy professionals, experts, and regulators in the areas, rather than over-politicized legislatures and diplomats. Such a soft approach naturally increases opportunities for a meaningful plan of action on the negotiating table.

[129] ibid. [130] ibid. [131] Vihma (n 64) 143–45. [132] Sheppard (n 64) 798.

[133] ibid.

[134] Andrew T Guzman, 'International Common Law: The Soft Law of International Tribunals' (2009) 9(2) Chinese J Intl L 515, 520.

[135] 'Privacy Recognition for Processors' (Cross Border Privacy Rules System) <http://www.cbprs.org/GeneralPages/LatestNews.aspx> accessed 11 March 2016. The limited scope of the CBPR System has resulted in a call by controllers for the development of a mechanism that will help them identify qualified and accountable processors with whom to contract. The PRP represents the baseline requirements a processor must meet in order to be recognized by an APEC-recognized Accountability Agent and provide assurances with respect to the processor's privacy policies and practices.

[136] 'Cross-Border Privacy Rules' (Cross Border Privacy Rules System) <http://www.cbprs.org/GeneralPages/APECCBPRSystemDocuments.aspx> accessed 11 March 2016.

[137] Matsushita (n 127) 711–14.

IV. Are We Trading Away Privacy for Economic Integration?

The author is aware that the viewpoints of this chapter may be criticized as looking at privacy issues in a narrowly economic way. However, the chapter stresses that, privacy is essentially cultural and reflects traditions; therefore, total harmonization is neither politically popular nor realistic. Different legal issues require different solutions, and crafting legal arrangements is a central tool in moving from regulatory fragmentation towards harmonization. Soft law, while not immediately legally binding, provides a useful means to affect conduct gradually. Minimum harmonization, at least in the short term, can help effectively reduce the impact of regulatory conflict.

How, then, should international co-ordination on privacy protection proceed? How should we approach soft law to balance privacy and trade? Which international model should be applied? How should it be implemented? Those are the main queries this chapter attempts to answer. As shown in Figure 20.1, global governance on privacy protection has been administered in a fragmented international system. The empirical world of global governance on privacy protection reveals that the types of norms that have been generated under negotiations over the past decades have had a wide range of legal characteristics. After employing the EU model and the APEC model as case studies on how hard and soft law can interact in complementary

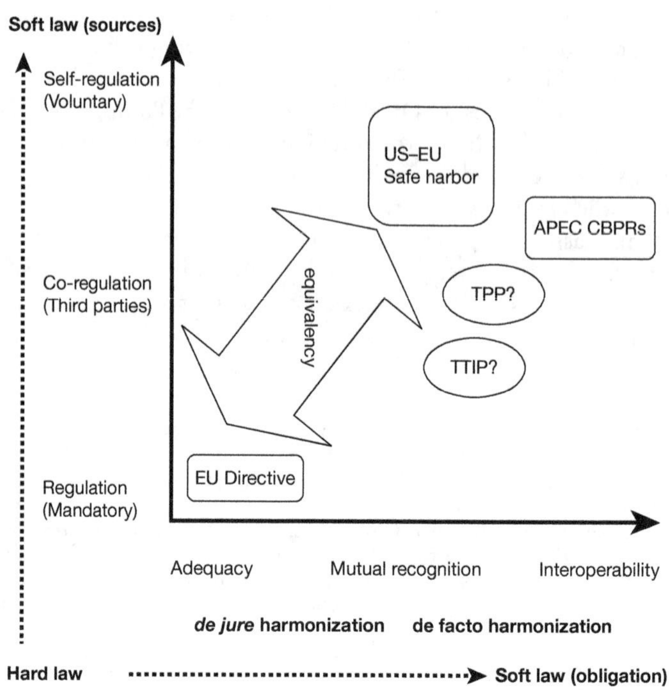

Figure 20.1 The soft law approach to privacy regulatory harmonization

ways, as well as how they can be used as alternatives, this chapter concludes that the APEC-type of 'interoperability' on privacy standards allows for national diversity and represents an idea of economic integration without deeper social integration. By reflecting a less political ambition and avoiding substantive harmonization, the APEC model might prove to be a practical way of achieving trade while sidestepping the political nightmare of deeper regulatory harmonization.

As a starting point of this chapter, the author introduced the recent controversy in TTIP, TPP, and TiSA trade negotiations and highlighted the increasing tension between privacy governance and regional economic integration. Is regionalism trading away privacy for economic integration, as feared by civil societies and privacy advocators? This chapter argues that, if the APEC model is to be incorporated into the TTIP or TPP, and if the term 'interoperability' under TTIP and TPP would have the same meaning as it has under CBPRs, the concerns that the conclusion of the trade deal would radically undermine the rights to privacy are without ground. CBPRs' function to 'harmonize' regional privacy regulations is limited to its 'softness' character, and the APEC model on privacy governance is operating in a way that differs greatly from conventional regulatory harmonization. Such a model, at least in the near term, falls short in creating a legal safe harbor, and as a result, would by no means replace the 'adequacy' standards.

However, if the term 'interoperability' under TTIP or TPP has a creative meaning and can function in an overly aggressive way—for example, FTAs parties set up a minimum privacy standard that serves as a basis of recognition among them—the necessary policy space of the participating states would be undermined and their ability to uphold existing national privacy laws in a cross-border context would be hampered. It remains to be seen whether the concept of 'interoperability' will be introduced into TTIP and TPP as a way that parties mutually recognize respective privacy regulations. In fact, there are variation and diversification in the practice of the concept of 'interoperability'. One example is the expression in the US 2012 white paper on privacy. The position that industry-specific codes of conduct developed through multi-stakeholder processes could be used for cross-border data transfers has been strongly expressed by the Obama administration as its foreign policy.[138] In its 2012 white paper on privacy, the administration explained how critical it is to create interoperability between privacy regimes for the continued growth of the digital economy. The same report also pointed out that 'mutual recognition of privacy frameworks is a means to achieve meaningful global data protection', and a starting point for mutual recognition is the embrace of 'common values surrounding privacy protection'. From such policy statement, the US position seems to be that the 'interoperability' is to be defined as the acceptance of the privacy regulatory conditions for data transfer required in one country as 'equivalent' to the conditions necessary in another country. If so, the concerns of the civil society and privacy advocators are well grounded.

[138] Executive Office of the President of the United States, 'Consumer Privacy Data in a Networked World' (n 105) 31–32.

To conclude, at this stage, it is uncertain whether the European Union will eventually abolish or suspend the Safe Harbor Agreement. Although the EU Council appears to remain firmly in support of the Safe Harbor Agreement, it is highly likely that we will be witnessing the collapse of the old paradigm—under which hard and soft law act as complements in governing cross-border privacy protection. The forthcoming judgment of the ECJ on that issue could also open a door for EU Member States' data protection authorities to determine for themselves whether personal data at a Safe Harbor-certified company is adequately protected and whether the Safe Harbor scheme is sufficient to guard its citizens' privacy. Changes to the Safe Harbor scheme will almost certainly be made. On the other hand, it is also unclear how far the APEC CBPRs can go. In any event, the APEC model offers a perspective to review how international co-operation on privacy protection can proceed by the pure soft law approach. Privacy is fundamentally cultural. It is increasingly obvious that solutions to the challenges posed by such diversity do not lie in attempting to map one national approach to another. As evident by the controversy of the Safe Harbor Agreement, exporting or imposing a privacy standard of one region to mirror that of another will not work. The APEC-type 'interoperability' may be proven to be a pragmatic way forward for providing more consistent privacy protections for regional data flows, which, in the long run, might ultimately lead to increased regional harmonization in privacy protection. In any event, as Matsushita pointed out, there have been examples of soft law approach in the governance of international economic affairs that are successfully carried out; informal activities to discuss subject matters of international trade policies seems to be a worthwhile concept to explore.[139] The strategic use of soft law has profound implications for the privacy governance and the associated international economic order.

[139] Matsushita (n 127) 714.

PART III

ISSUES IN THE POLICY- AND LAW-MAKING PROCESS

21

Members Only: Embracing Diversity in the WTO*

*Bernard M Hoekman and Petros C Mavroidis***

I. The Issue

Matsushita observes a discrepancy across the various functions of the WTO: whereas its dispute settlement consistently attracted big numbers of cases every year, the WTO did not manage to conclude even one agreement (except for one sectoral agreement, the Information Technology Agreement) since the end of the Uruguay Round.[1] His intuition is still valid almost ten years later. The WTO dispute settlement system continues to attract big numbers of cases, while not even one agreement has been added to the legislative arsenal of the WTO. The Agreement on Trade Facilitation continues to be elusive.

In this chapter, we try to respond to one of the two points made by Matsushita: why does the WTO find it so difficult to conclude agreements? What has changed since the end of the Uruguay Round? Our response is that the GATT's success has proved to be the WTO's curse. The (almost) elimination of tariff barriers has led to the painful realization that markets are now being segmented essentially through regulatory barriers. Regulatory barriers, however, are more easily addressed between homogeneous players who are prepared to commit policies in a 'deep integration' framework. 'Shallow integration' à la GATT/WTO does not work well when it comes to addressing regulatory barriers.

And here is the twist. 'Deep integration' de facto requires like-minded participants, homogeneous players. This is not the case with the WTO, which now counts 161 members with highly diverse properties. What is to be done under the circumstances? Our recipe is that the WTO must move to a WTO 2.0, where variable geometry will be a possibility, and 'clubs' of few like-minded members

* The paper was drafted before the events that opened the way to the signing of the Agreement on Trade Facilitation.

** We are grateful to Kyle Bagwell, Richard Baldwin, Jagdish Bhagwati, Paola Conconi, Henrik Horn, Gary Hufbauer, Doug Irwin, David Laborde, Phil Levy, Patrick Low, Aaditya Mattoo, Michele Ruta, Kamal Saggi, Alvaro Santos, André Sapir, Richard Steinberg, Alan Sykes, Robert Wolfe, and Stephen Woolcock for comments on different versions of this chapter.

[1] Mitsuo Matsushita, 'The 10th Anniversary of the WTO' (2006) 1 Asian J WTO & Intl Health L & Policy 1.

will be allowed to co-exist alongside the big WTO table with 161 participants. We explain.

On 8 July 2014 negotiations were launched in Geneva to liberalize trade in environmental goods. The talks span a limited number of countries, including the world's three largest trading powers: the European Union, China, and the United States. Similar to other sectoral initiatives to liberalize trade under WTO auspices, such as the 1997 Information Technology Agreement (ITA) and on-going talks to conclude an ITA-2 with broader product coverage, the aim was to get a 'critical mass' of countries to agree to liberalize trade in the chosen products. A key feature of such deals is that the benefits are extended on a non-discriminatory, most-favoured-nation (MFN) basis. Critical mass agreements (CMAs) are an important element of the multilateral trading system: if enough countries participate in a liberalization exercise, they need not worry about free riding by other countries that do not want to participate.

In July 2014, India refused to approve the adoption of a Protocol needed to incorporate a new Agreement on Trade Facilitation (TFA) into the WTO, which it had agreed to six months before at the Bali Ministerial meeting of the WTO. India took this action in an effort to increase pressure on WTO Members to address its concerns regarding the prevailing WTO rules on agricultural production support. The TFA was a carefully constructed and innovative compact that was conceived to be a stand-alone agreement in the sense that its provisions were designed to be Pareto-improving for all WTO Members.[2] The fact that standard-issue linkage tactics nonetheless led to non-adoption of the Protocol for an agreement that all WTO Ministers had signed off on was a significant setback for proponents of multilateral rules on trade facilitation.

These events point to the difficulty of achieving multilateral co-operation among 161 players. In practice, it is often easier to either pursue agreements that involve a small(er) number of countries, whether on a critical mass basis or in the context of discriminatory trade agreements, where the benefits are extended only to signatories. The proliferation of preferential trade agreements (PTAs)—some 500 have been notified to the WTO—and the willingness to pursue critical mass sectoral liberalization initiatives illustrate that governments are keen to engage in further trade liberalization and to commit to stronger trade policy disciplines 'if the price is right'. There are many more extant PTAs and on-going PTA negotiations than there are efforts to conclude critical mass-based liberalization agreements. One reason is that PTAs increasingly include a focus on regulatory co-operation, for which deals are easier to agree if they are limited to a sub-set of the WTO Membership and benefits need not be extended to non-signatories. Agreement on co-operation on regulatory matters among 161 WTO Members will in most cases be difficult, if not impossible. Even the European Union—a regime with a much more homogenous membership than the WTO—allows for

[2] Bernard Hoekman, 'The Bali Trade Facilitation Agreement and Rule-making in the WTO: Milestone, Mistake or Mirage?' (2014) Robert Schuman Centre for Advanced Studies Research Paper No RSCAS 2014/102 <http://ssrn.com/abstract=2514367> accessed 11 March 2016.

so-called Enhanced Co-operation Agreements that apply only to a sub-set of its membership.[3]

PTAs and CMAs are not the only game in town when it comes to negotiating new policy commitments among a 'club' of countries. The WTO offers another mechanism for Members to do so: conclusion of a Plurilateral Agreement (PA) under Article II.3 of the Agreement Establishing the WTO. Article II.3 permits sub-sets of the WTO Membership to agree to new disciplines applying to signatories only, subject to the approval of all WTO Members, including those that have no intention of joining. At present, there are only two Annex 4 PAs in force in the WTO: the Agreement on Government Procurement (GPA) and the Agreement on Civil Aviation.

In what follows, we distinguish between two types of agreements with less than full membership, CMAs and PAs. To date, CMAs have almost all been market access agreements of the type discussed above—agreement to remove tariffs for a set of goods on a MFN basis, with commitments to this effect incorporated into schedules of tariff concessions. There are very few instances of CMAs that extend rules in regulatory areas covered by the WTO. An example is the so-called Reference Paper, an element of the 1997 Agreement on Basic Telecommunications, which calls for signatories to have an independent regulator for this sector and to abide by certain disciplines, including requiring that interconnection fees be cost-based. To date, eighty-two WTO Members have adopted the provisions of the Reference Paper as an 'additional commitment' under Article XVIII GATS, which apply on a MFN basis to all WTO Members.[4] As we discuss below, there is no analogue to Article XVIII GATS in other WTO agreement, greatly impeding the feasibility of attaching new CMAs on regulatory policies to the WTO. This is one reason why commentators—including ourselves—focus their attention on Annex 4 PAs, as the modalities for incorporating such agreements are clearly specified in the WTO.

PTAs and PAs both permit discrimination and both involve binding policy commitments by signatories. Both define rules of the game for only a sub-set of the WTO Membership. PAs by definition go beyond prevailing WTO disciplines and commitments for the countries that join them. PTAs may also go beyond the WTO in terms of coverage of policies, but need not. In practice many PTAs simply reduce traditional market access restrictions on a preferential basis by creating a free trade area or a customs union and do not go beyond the WTO as far as trade policy disciplines are concerned. However, insofar as PTAs are used as a

[3] Article 20 Treaty on European Union—see Bernard M Hoekman and Petros C Mavroidis, 'WTO à la Carte or WTO Menu du Jour: Assessing the Case for Plurilateral Agreements' (2013) EUI Working Papers, RSCAS 2013/58 Robert Schuman Centre for Advanced Studies Global Governance Programme-57 <http://hdl.handle.net/1814/27611> accessed 11 March 2016.

[4] It is perhaps a bit of a misnomer to term the Reference Paper a CMA insofar as it is less clear what constitutes a 'critical mass' for agreements on regulatory matters among a sub-set of countries, because free-riding is much less of a concern than it will be for a market access agreement. This is a more general issue, to which we return below.

mechanism to agree to policy disciplines that go beyond the WTO, PAs could be used as an alternative mechanism to do so.

In our view, greater effort should be made by countries to pursue PAs in new policy areas for the WTO and to take action to facilitate the inclusion of new CMAs that deepen policy disciplines in areas already covered by the WTO on a MFN basis. Our premise is that it is neither necessary nor desirable to limit new rule making exclusively to PTAs. We assess the arguments for and against incorporating more PAs into the WTO and discuss what could be done to minimize downside risks of PAs from a multilateralist perspective. In our view, the status quo has negative repercussions for the multilateral trading system. Because it is too difficult to obtain approval for new PAs in the WTO and to include new CMAs under which signatories apply deeper policy disciplines on a MFN basis, governments seeking to co-operate in new areas are induced to do so through PTAs. The result is an ever increasing splintering of the trading system, generating greater discrimination and more complexity and uncertainty than would be the case if more use was made of the PA/CMA options. Enhancing the incentives for countries to pursue plurilaterals in the WTO would provide a mechanism for WTO Members to recognize and accept diversity in preferences and priorities across the Membership, while ensuring that co-operation among sub-sets of Members occurs in a manner that is more consistent with some of the key principles that underpin the multilateral trading system: transparency, openness, and inclusiveness.

In section II, we offer a discussion on the pros and cons for using PAs and/or PTAs. In section III, we address the arguments against increased use of PAs, and in section IV we explain why PAs may offer the WTO the opportunity to continue to be policy-relevant in the years to come. Section V contains our conclusions in brief.

II. PTAs and PAs: What Keeps Them Together? What Keeps Them Apart?

Consider this. The deadlock in the Doha Development Agenda (DDA) has been accompanied by steadily intensifying efforts to negotiate new PTAs by WTO Members. The pursuit of mega-regional agreements by the United States and other major players,[5] and the launch of negotiations on a trade in services agreement

[5] Examples are the Regional Comprehensive Economic Partnership (RCEP), the Trans-Pacific Partnership (TPP), and the Transatlantic Trade and Investment Partnership (TTIP). RCEP involves sixteen countries: the ten members of ASEAN (Brunei, Cambodia, Indonesia, Laos, Malaysia, Myanmar, the Philippines, Singapore, Thailand, and Vietnam) and six countries with which ASEAN has a free trade agreement (Australia, China, India, Japan, Korea, and New Zealand). The TPP spans Australia, Brunei, Canada, Chile, Japan, Malaysia, Mexico, New Zealand, Peru, Singapore, the United States, and Vietnam. TTIP is a bilateral EU–US initiative.

(TiSA) by a group of WTO Members are important illustrations.[6] Many PTAs that have been negotiated since the WTO entered into force go beyond the WTO in terms of coverage of policy areas.[7] The shift towards PTAs reflects both the heterogeneity of the WTO Membership and a desire by high-income nations to address spill-overs created by policies that are not on the table in the DDA. There are important potential downside effects of the proliferation of trade initiatives outside the WTO. Most obviously, it may lead to the balkanization of trade, especially insofar as firms are induced to invest in and source from within a bloc. Greater recourse to PAs under the auspices of the WTO can help attenuate or avoid such outcomes and support more multilateral co-operation (multilateralization) over time.

PAs and PTAs are similar in that both can be, and mostly are, applied on a non-MFN basis.[8] Thus, both are mechanisms through which signatories can prevent free-riding by non-participants. Another common element is that both instruments involve binding commitments that are enforceable. Neither Article XXIV GATT or Article V GATS, nor the various WTO provisions regulating PAs discuss this point explicitly, but if PTAs or PAs are not legally enforceable there is little point in negotiating them. Yet another commonality is that neither is a very effective instrument to address the major market access issues that have been a key source of the deadlock in the Doha Round—i.e. the fact that at the end of the day large trading powers want more liberalization of agricultural trade policies and more non-agricultural market access from each other than they are willing to give. A situation where large players all want to see more market access concessions tabled can only partially be addressed by shifting the focus to PTAs, and cannot be addressed at all through PAs. As argued by numerous commentators, what is needed is to agree on a negotiating set that has enough to interest the major powers.[9]

So what are differences between PAs and PTAs? PAs differ from PTAs in important respects. PTAs often will have as an objective the integration of the markets of the participating countries on an explicitly discriminatory basis—something that is recognized and accepted by all WTO Members as a legitimate endeavour. PTA membership will be limited to a set of countries that satisfy whatever criteria are established by the bloc. PTAs tend to be closed clubs—most PTAs do not include an accession clause. Those PTAs that do allow for accession often restrict this to countries in a specific geographic region. This helps to explain the

[6] The TiSA includes Australia, Canada, Chile, Chinese Taipei, Colombia, Costa Rica, Hong Kong China, Iceland, Israel, Japan, the Republic of Korea, Mexico, New Zealand, Norway, Panama, Paraguay, Pakistan, Peru, Switzerland, Turkey, and the United States.

[7] Henrik Horn and others, 'Beyond the WTO: An Anatomy of the EU and US Preferential Trade Agreements' (2010) 33 World Econ 1565.

[8] What follows summarizes an in-depth comparison of the WTO's rules pertaining to PAs and PTAs in Hoekman and Mavroidis (n 3).

[9] See e.g., Simon J Evenett, 'The Doha Round Impasse: A Graphical Account' (2014) 9 Rev Intl Organ 143; Bernard Hoekman, 'Sustaining Multilateral Trade Cooperation in a Multipolar World Economy' (2014) 9 Rev Intl O 241; Robert Wolfe, 'First Diagnose, then Treat: What Ails the Doha Round?' (2015) 14 World Trade Rev 7; Yvan Decreux and Lionel Fontagné, 'What Next for Multilateral Trade Talks? Quantifying the Role of Negotiation Modalities' (2015) 14 World Trade Rev 29.

proliferation of PTAs—a new agreement tends to be negotiated between members of any given PTA and non-members. PAs in contrast are 'open'—in principle no WTO Member can be excluded from a PA once it has been negotiated and accepted as an Annex 4 agreement by the WTO Membership.[10] Insofar as WTO Members can satisfy whatever conditions apply for Membership (i.e. conform to the disciplines that constitute the substantive provisions of the PA), they cannot be excluded. Indeed, a rationale for negotiating a PA in the first place is to encourage wider membership over time—that has certainly been the goal of the signatories of the Agreement on Government Procurement.

There is more. PAs also differ from PTAs in that they will be narrower in scope. A PTA will usually cover many policy areas, ranging from trade in goods and services to investment, intellectual property rights and development assistance, and other forms of 'soft law' co-operation. The condition imposed on WTO Members that PTAs cover substantially all trade (and have substantial sectoral coverage in the case of services) is intended to ensure that a PTA is not used as a mechanism to engage in selective discrimination for just a few products or a specific sector. A PA, in contrast, may deal with just one issue. The chosen issue may have many dimensions and cover many types of activities, as is the case with procurement, but it need not. This could in theory lead to PAs being used to very selectively circumvent the WTO MFN rule—which is exactly what the WTO requirement that PTAs cover substantially all trade is intended to preclude. However, WTO Members cannot use a PA to selectively violate existing WTO commitments because PAs that do so will not be approved. Thus, PAs that limit benefits to signatories can only address matters that are *not* subject to existing WTO disciplines. If they deal with matters where the MFN rule applies, benefits must be extended to all WTO Members, i.e. they must be critical mass agreements such as the ITA.

Article X.9 of the Agreement Establishing the WTO stipulates that the Ministerial Conference of the WTO may decide to add an agreement to the existing set of PAs 'exclusively by consensus'. In contrast, with the advent of the Transparency Mechanism in 2006, there is no longer any effort by WTO Members to approve new PTAs.[11] Consistency with the WTO is instead left to be determined through dispute settlement: if a WTO Member believes a PTA is inconsistent with the WTO, it can bring a claim to that effect and ask for a panel to rule on the matter, a rare occurrence as practice to date reveals that the incentives to litigate are missing. The fact that there are no provisions or criteria on what is (and should be) permitted in terms of sectors or their content/coverage implies that there is great flexibility in principle for those aspiring to establish a PA, but utilization of this flexibility is constrained by the need to obtain approval by all WTO Members to move forward, even if many or most do not intend to join.

[10] Note, however, that there is no explicit requirement in the WTO that PAs be open to any WTO Member. Article XII.3 WTO simply states that 'Accession to a Plurilateral Trade Agreement shall be governed by the provisions of that Agreement.' We return to this below.

[11] Petros C Mavroidis, 'Always Look at the Bright Side of Non-delivery: WTO and Preferential Trade Agreements, Yesterday and Today' (2011) 10 World Trade Rev 375.

It is worth keeping in mind that PAs may deal with issues that are already subject to WTO disciplines or cover matters that are not included in the WTO. The two extant PAs offer an example of each possibility. The Civil Aircraft Agreement deepened disciplines on trade policy instruments affecting trade in aircraft—removing a set of tariffs on a MFN basis (as was required, given that tariffs are covered by the WTO) and laying out more specific disciplines on the use of subsidies that prevailed at the time this PA was negotiated. The GPA addresses a policy that is explicitly excluded from the reach of Article III GATT (national treatment) and the GATS (Article XIII.1). The GPA does not undercut existing WTO commitments, as there are none. This may not be the case for PAs dealing with subjects that are already covered by the WTO but that go further. An example would be a PA on services trade. In such instances, a PA may be detrimental to non-participants if provisions are applied on a discriminatory basis, but as long as what is agreed does not violate existing specific commitments, the question non-participants should ask is what the outside option is for those that are proposing a PA and whether the outside option will be better or worse for them.

Now, in the hypothetical case of a proposed services PA, a PTA is a feasible outside option. If, however, countries want to co-operate in a regulatory area such as competition or investment policy, a PTA is not a feasible alternative, but countries might pursue co-operation outside the WTO. In assessing the implications of a potential or proposed PA, it is therefore necessary to consider what the alternative options are for those proposing a PA. The outside options may in practice be worse than accepting a PA. This is because the PA route has benefits that outside options such as PTAs do not have—including greater transparency, access to and use of the Dispute Settlement Understanding (DSU) and the possibility of eventual accession if and when countries decide to join at a future date.

The issue of transparency of PAs is ensured through the process of notification to the General Council and the need for the Council to approve any PA that is brought forward. If approved, a PA will result in the establishment of the types of WTO bodies that assist Members in the implementation of agreements, such as a Committee, with regular (annual) reporting on activities to the Council, and documentation that is open to all WTO Members. Moreover, disputes under a PA will (and must) be submitted to WTO panels (and eventually the Appellate Body). This ensures that PA-related case law will develop harmoniously with case law pertaining to the multilateral WTO agreements. Thus, PAs ensure a much closer 'connection' with day-to-day WTO activities and processes and greater coherence when it comes to case law or dispute settlement.

III. What is Wrong with PAs?

So far we have painted a rather rosy picture for PAs. There are of course, some sticking points that we examine in what follows. The fact that PAs can be adopted into the WTO exclusively by consensus (after they have been negotiated, i.e. once their content has been established) and that participation is voluntary (whatever disciplines are negotiated only apply to signatories) would appear to offer substantial assurance to WTO Members that they have nothing to fear from efforts by some countries to negotiate PAs. Why are they such a sensitive issue then?

And then, objections raised against PAs include worries that they will be used for controversial issues such as trade and labour standards; that they will erode MFN; that the rules that are negotiated will be precedent setting; that asymmetric negotiating capacity will bias disciplines towards what powerful countries want; and that PAs will reduce the prospects for issue linkages needed to conclude deals on policies that are supported by strong vested interests.

The salience of many of these concerns depends on the substance and coverage of a PA. If the PA is WTO-X (that is, deals with a new issue),[12] it may be precedent setting but there is no issue of fragmentation or undercutting MFN, as this currently does not apply. Countries that stay out may object to the PA precisely because it is precedent setting and they fear the disciplines eventually being 'imposed' on them, as was done in the Uruguay Round as a result of the creation of the WTO and the take-it-or-leave-it choice that this created,[13] but a repeat of this scenario seems very unlikely. If countries do not believe the rules of the game of a PA are in their interest they can stay out. Such a sanguine assessment also applies in the case of the so-called WTO+ PAs, i.e. agreements that deepen existing rules. WTO+ PAs that undercut existing WTO disciplines can, and presumably will, be rejected by the Membership, and can also be contested through the DSU. WTO+ PAs will be subject to the MFN rule, i.e. in principle the PAs will have to satisfy the critical mass constraint. In practice, such agreements may be discriminatory in effect, but this will be de facto and not *de jure* in that benefits may be conditional on satisfying certain technical preconditions—for example, attainment of a certain minimum regulatory performance.[14]

Having said that, PAs will define the rules of the game in a specific area for signatories. Wolfe notes that any PA will invariably include Organization of Economic Co-operation and Development (OECD) member countries that may already have achieved much of whatever level of co-operation-cum-discipline that is agreed for an issue, and that many non-OECD countries are not going to have the capacity to participate in negotiations that will set a precedent.[15] PAs

[12] Horn and others (n 7) distinguish between WTO+ and WTO-X obligations in PTAs: the former cover matters that fall under the current mandate of the WTO but where commitments in the PTA-context are more comprehensive (e.g., deeper than MFN tariff cuts); the latter refer to policy areas currently not addressed by the WTO (e.g., co-operation on macro-economic policies).

[13] See, e.g., Bernard Hoekman and Michel Kostecki, *The Political Economy of the World Trading System* (3rd edn, OUP 2009).

[14] An example would be a PA on supply chain trade under which signatories commit to specific actions that complement existing WTO agreements. This might include agreement on regulatory equivalence in different areas, under which signatories accept the regulatory process in other countries as having equivalent objectives and leading to equivalent outcomes, and thus allowing for the free circulation of goods. The result would be to improve market access conditions for signatories of the PA, but this would be conditional on regulators accepting that their respective regimes are equivalent. This can only be established on a case-by-case basis, and cannot extend to non-members unless they can demonstrate that they do satisfy whatever criteria apply.

[15] Robert Wolfe, 'The WTO Single Undertaking as Negotiating Technique and Constitutive Metaphor' (2009) 12 J Intl Econ L 835.

are likely to reflect the interests and current practices of the initial signatories, which may not be appropriate for all countries. Capacity constraints and resulting non-participation by developing countries in a negotiation makes it less likely that an agreement will address issues that are of primary concern to low-income economies. Clubs will define the rules of the game in an area that will be difficult to change subsequently if and when initial non-signatories decide to participate. Experience illustrates that it is very difficult to amend (or re-negotiate) disciplines, so that a plurilateral approach may well become analogous to the *acquis communautaire* for prospective members of the European Union, i.e. non-negotiable.

Consequently, even if countries opt out, in practice the advantage may be in favour of OECD countries and major emerging markets that have the capacity to engage effectively on the substance of the proposed rules. However, the presumption that PAs will define the rules of the game forever is not necessarily true. If large countries initially decide to stay out but subsequently become willing to join but have serious concerns regarding specific provisions, they can seek to renegotiate these. Small countries will be 'price takers' but that is the case in any event—that is not an issue that is specific to PAs. The same considerations apply regarding fears that PAs will be dominated by large OECD countries. This need not be the case. PAs also offer a mechanism that a broad set of WTO Members could use to move forward in an area where one of the large WTO Members is not willing or able to participate. A PA that centres on operationalizing 100 per cent duty-free, quota-free access for least developed countries is a possible example. This is something that is currently not feasible for the United States to agree to, but that has already been implemented by many other countries. Greater co-operation through a PA on issues like simplification, cumulation, or harmonization of rules of origin among countries offering duty-free, quota-free access could enhance the benefits for LDCs.

We submit that more intensive use of PAs may result in a long-term bifurcation in the WTO Membership, splitting 'insiders' from 'outsiders'. This was the pattern that emerged in the GATT years, with very few countries subsequently joining the Tokyo Round codes after their initial negotiation. If so, greater use of the PA approach would move the WTO towards a two-track regime with subsets of countries (clubs) playing in their own sandbox. Many developing countries have argued that this is contrary to the basic character of the WTO and conflicts with the consensus-based approach that has historically been the norm.[16] However, this argument applies even more to PTAs, which may be designed with the strategic objective of excluding specific countries. If PA club members end up agreeing to disciplines that are unacceptable to countries that are not intending to join, the question is whether a PA would be worse from

[16] Hoekman and Kostecki (n 13). This position is difficult to square with the fact that the Uruguay Round is actually an anomaly, in that the Kennedy and Tokyo Rounds, and now also the Doha Round, were not based on a single undertaking and governments concluded agreements that allowed for variable geometry.

a global welfare or systemic perspective than if countries concluded a PTA or embedded their proposed co-operation in existing PTAs. A world in which there are many PTAs that deal differently with a specific subject area could well be worse for global welfare (efficiency) than one in which the issue is addressed through a PA.[17]

It could be the case that PAs will impose additional costs on the rest of the WTO Membership by utilizing the WTO 'infrastructure'—including operation of a Committee, making use of the WTO facilities, potential invocation of the DSU, calling on the Secretariat for support, etc. The fact that the operation of a PA is centred in the WTO as opposed to occurring outside it is a positive feature but this does come with additional direct costs, as well as potential opportunity costs given limited Secretariat resources. There is a straightforward solution to this problem: signatories can be required to provide additional contributions to the WTO in order to cover the cost of implementing and administering PAs. They would need to incur these costs in any event if the PTA route was chosen instead or co-operation is pursued outside the WTO.

We should also keep in mind that moving down the PA track may imply that countries give up negotiating chips that could be used to obtain concessions in other areas in a multilateral negotiation. The fundamental premise underlying the Single Undertaking is that it permits issue linkage: country A can get something it wants by giving up something that country B wants and the trade may involve subjects that have nothing to do with each other. If PAs are negotiated for specific issues, the scope for such linkage may decline. Much depends here on the subject matter of a potential PA and contracting costs.[18] If it does not offer much in the way of negotiating leverage for the countries that are involved—i.e. nobody is inclined to 'pay' much, if anything, for a deal on the subject covered by a proposed PA—the 'linkage downside' will be small. The absence of linkage potential might, under some circumstances, act as an incentive to join the PA in the first place by lowering the opportunity cost of participation.[19]

We can sum up this discussion by stating that, as argued at greater length in Hoekman and Mavroidis (n 3), there are good reasons for preferring PAs over PTAs, and they include the following:

[17] This need not be the case, as differences in preferences and circumstances may imply that it is more efficient for sets of countries to adopt different rules of the game; i.e. 'one size fits all' is not the first best solution.

[18] See Horn and Mavroidis, for an analysis of the conditions under which separate agreements dominate a broader 'single undertaking' that encompasses a variety of issue linkages. Given uncertainty regarding the overall size of the 'cake' that is defined by an agreement that spans many issue areas, and the costs associated with negotiations, including the opportunity costs of delay, there may be good reasons for governments to pursue separate agreements as opposed to big bang package deals, where everything is conditional on everything else. Henrik Horn and Petros C Mavroidis, 'Multilateral Environmental Agreements in the WTO: Silence Speaks Volumes' (2014) 10 Intl J Econ Trade 147.

[19] There is, of course, no presumption that this will be the case, but the countries concerned will always have the option of not participating in the PA.

- PAs are Pareto-sanctioned because their content is approved by the WTO Membership. PTAs are reviewed by the WTO, but there is no sanctioning of their content; the process is limited to supply of information.[20]
- Information provision stops at the moment a PTA has been reviewed. There is no obligation to continue to supply information to WTO after that. In contrast, PAs involve regular reporting on activities to the WTO Membership as a whole.
- The plethora of PTAs results in significant dispersion in rules and approaches and thus transactions costs and trade diversion—Bhagwati's famous spaghetti bowl analogy. Multiple PTAs deal with the same subject matter, so that rules of the game for firms from a country often differ for the same issue, depending on the PTA that applies for a given trade flow. In the case of a PA, there will only be one regime regulating a given subject matter.
- PTAs are mostly closed to accession by new Members. Pas, in contrast, are required to be open.
- PTAs often have their own dispute settlement procedures. Dispute settlement is the most frequent form of 'contract completion', and as a result the WTO misses out on important information. In contrast, PAs will use WTO dispute settlement mechanisms.

IV. Increased Use of PAs Should Be Supported

In light of the heterogeneity of the WTO Membership, and for the reasons mentioned above as well, we take the view that it would be beneficial to allow for more 'variable geometry' to be pursued under the umbrella of the WTO. This is preferable to a situation where countries are pushed into ever-greater reliance on PTAs, which effectively escape multilateral disciplines, or are induced to engage in co-operation outside the WTO—as was the case in the negotiations on an Anti-counterfeiting Trade Agreement (ACTA).

We need to ask then why PAs have not proliferated so far. There are two important factors that impede the feasibility of pursuing plurilaterals under WTO auspices. The first of these was mentioned in the Introduction: there is no straightforward way for WTO Members to pursue WTO+ CMAs that involve deepening of disciplines on policies that are already subject to WTO rules and that they are willing to apply to all WTO Members on a MFN basis. The second is that incorporation of a PA into the WTO requires unanimity ('exclusively by consensus'), which in practice is a major disincentive for countries to pursue this type of co-operation.

The choice between CMAs and PAs will depend on whether governments interested in co-operating in a given area are worried about free riding and whether

[20] Petros C Mavroidis, *Trade in Goods* (2nd edn, OUP 2013).

negotiated disciplines can be applied on an MFN basis. For some issues, there may be no free rider concern. A recent example is the Bali Trade Facilitation Agreement (TFA), which involves measures that every WTO Member will benefit from implementing. Moreover, implementation will be on a MFN basis by construction: changes in customs procedures will apply to all trade, not just to signatories of the TFA. Adoption of the TFA Protocol was delayed as a result of a decision by India to link its agreement to the Protocol to additional concessions on the applicability of the Agreement on Agriculture domestic support disciplines to public stockholding of food. While this matter was eventually resolved over the course of 2014, assume for the purposes of discussion that India had maintained its blocking position. Given that the majority of the WTO Membership wanted to implement the TFA, the question is how it might have been pursued on a plurilateral basis inside the WTO. In this hypothetical situation, the PA track is not available, as presumably India would block it—after all, why accept the TFA as a PA if you do not accept the Protocol? There is no obvious way of making the TFA a CMA either. WTO Members could in theory try to use Article XXVIII GATT (Modification of Schedules) to incorporate the substantive elements of the TFA into their GATT schedules. However, this approach will not allow inclusion of the special and differential treatment elements of the TFA, which are a core part of the agreement.[21] This suggests that for the CMA path to be used to deepen disciplines in areas that are already covered by the WTO—as is the case for the TFA—the modalities of using GATT Article XXVIII need to be revisited. There is currently a disconnect in this regard between the GATS and the other WTO agreements, as Article XVIII GATS makes explicit provision for WTO Members to make 'additional commitments' that are applied on a non-discriminatory basis.[22]

With respect to the consensus requirement for new Annex 4 PAs, some are of the view that no change in the consensus rule is needed and that non-Members should be comfortable with the terms of any PA that is tabled.[23] Others argue that greater use of PAs is conditional on a relaxation of the consensus constraint.[24] Discussions in the TiSA context and the July 2014 veto by India on adoption of the protocol needed to incorporate the Bali Trade Facilitation Agreement into the WTO suggests that consensus is likely to be a binding constraint on greater use of PAs. The incentives to seek side-payments and attempt to link approval to issues that are not related to the subject matter of the PA are likely to make it too difficult to add new PAs to the WTO.

[21] See Hoekman, 'The Bali Trade Facilitation Agreement' (n 2).

[22] The relationship between different approaches to scheduling additional commitments in the WTO, including through Accession Protocols, and options to facilitate the scheduling of regulatory commitments that apply on a non-discriminatory basis is discussed further in Bernard M Hoekman and Petros C Mavroidis, 'Extending WTO Commitments: Accession Protocols and Amendment of Schedules' [2015] EUI, mimeo.

[23] Robert Z Lawrence, 'Rulemaking Amidst Growing Diversity: A Club of Clubs Approach to WTO Reform and New Issue Selection' (2006) 9 J Intl Econ L 823.

[24] Jaime Tijmes-Lhl, 'Consensus and Majority Voting in the WTO' (2009) 8 World Trade Rev 417.

We also believe that maintaining the consensus rule is arguably too strong a constraint. Consensus is not needed to ensure that PAs that raise legitimate concerns for non-participants can be blocked. Relaxing the consensus requirement—for example, through agreement that 'substantial coverage' of world trade or production is sufficient[25] or acceptance that a two-thirds majority suffices—would still ensure that proposed PAs can be rejected while removing the ability of just a few countries to block a PA that the majority of the WTO Membership finds acceptable. There is, however, very strong opposition to moving away from consensus, not just from developing countries, but also from countries like the United States, which fear being outvoted. In practice, it may not be necessary to abandon consensus if the WTO can agree in principle that more should be done to allow plurilateral co-operation to occur under WTO auspices and work together to define a code of conduct as regards new PAs.

Thus, we agree with Lawrence,[26] WEF,[27] Draper and Dube,[28] and others that a necessary condition for greater use of PAs is to address the concerns that have been expressed by WTO Members. What is needed are clear(er) *ex ante* rules which ensure that PAs are not vehicles for some countries to escape their general or specific WTO obligations and that the interests of small/poor countries are protected. One way of doing this is to launch an effort to agree on a set of principles for new PAs to be negotiated under the umbrella of the WTO. Such principles could include the following principles:

- Membership of PAs is voluntary and will always remain so.
- The subject of any PA must be clearly trade-related in the sense of involving a policy that has a direct impact on trade costs and incentives.
- The issue under negotiation should enjoy substantial support from the WTO's Membership.
- Any WTO Member may seek to join an existing PA on the same conditions that applied to original signatories.
- WTO Members opposing a PA commit to explain their substantive reasons for their opposition, and to refrain from 'tactical' opposition to extract promises (side-payments) in other areas.

[25] Gary Hufbauer and Jeffrey Schott, 'Will the World Trade Organization Enjoy a Bright Future?' (2012) Petersen Institute for International Economics, Policy Brief 12–11 <http://www.iie.com/publications/pb/pb12-11.pdf> accessed 23 April 2016. They suggest a minimum coverage of 40% of world trade as opposed to the norm of 90% that empirically has defined the feasibility of critical mass agreements in the GATT/WTO.

[26] Lawrence (n 23).

[27] World Economic Forum, 'A Plurilateral "Club-of-Clubs" Approach to World Trade Organization Reform and New Issues' (Global Agenda Council on Trade 2010) <http://www3.weforum.org/docs/GAC10/WEF_GAC_Trade_Paper_2009-10.pdf> assessed 23 April 2016.

[28] Peter Draper and Memory Dube, 'Plurilaterals and the Multilateral Trading System' (2013) E15 Expert Group on Regional Trade Agreements and Plurilateral Approaches, International Centre for Trade and Sustainable Development <http://www.ictsd.org/sites/default/files/research/E15_RTA_Draper%20Dube_FINAL.pdf> assessed 23 April 2016.

- Only parties to a PA can participate in WTO dispute settlement and retaliation in the case of non-implementation of dispute settlement recommendations limited to the policies covered by the PA (as is the case now under the GPA).
- All PAs must include mechanisms to provide assistance to countries that are not in a position to implement the provisions of the agreements but want to do so.[29]
- All PAs include transparency mechanisms to ensure that non-participants have full information on what is being and what has been achieved.

What we have stated so far are just examples of provisions that could help address concerns that have been expressed regarding PAs—no doubt others will have additional suggestions. What is needed is to launch a process to define a set of such criteria. Lawrence has suggested that one criterion for PAs should be that any new PA be open to all WTO Members in the negotiation stage, i.e. participation in the development of rules should not be limited to likely signatories.[30] This is very important, as are commitments to make discussions transparent, as this will facilitate decision making by governments who initially might not join the negotiation. An 'open-to-all' norm may be problematical, however, in that it assumes that participation will be in good faith. But what happens if countries stonewall and seek to block progress on an issue by a majority of participants? WTO Members that have no intention to participate might behave 'strategically' and try to raise the costs for those that are eager to establish new rules. Some countries engaged in the TiSA talks have indicated that they are not seeking to pull in countries that showed very limited interest in making substantial liberalization commitments in the course of the Doha negotiations. This suggests an 'open-access' criterion for the initial negotiation phase of a PA should be tempered by recognition and acceptance that at some point a PA negotiation must be limited to those countries that are serious about making commitments on a specific matter.

Open access in the sense that once negotiated any PA allows for accession by any WTO Member is not explicitly required in Article X.9 WTO. Instead, accession provisions are defined in the individual PAs. It would be desirable to agree explicitly that 'open access' *ex post* be a precondition for approval of any PA. Other criteria might be considered as well; for example, prohibiting incumbents from ratcheting up the entry price for latecomers and making this enforceable through binding arbitration if contested.

In practice not all countries will be able to engage on an equal footing in the negotiation of a PA. There are major differences in capacities to engage on regulatory matters and the ability to participate in a fully informed way. Some governments may find it difficult to determine the 'return' to applying a proposed rule (for

[29] This could build on the precedents that were negotiated in the TFA. See Hoekman, 'The Bali Trade Facilitation Agreement' (n 2) for a discussion.

[30] Lawrence (n 23).

example, the direct administrative costs or the size—and perhaps even the sign—of the net economic impact of implementing a proposed set of disciplines). LDCs are likely to be among the least able to engage in PA talks that focus on regulatory matters that are not covered by the WTO. Whatever the subject of a PA, consideration could be given to extending whatever is negotiated amongst a club of WTO Members to all LDCs on a non-reciprocal basis. Of course, the value of such action will depend on the capacity of the LDCs to benefit from (and make use of) whatever is agreed among the PA members. In practice, LDCs may not have the capacity to benefit, especially if a precondition is satisfying specific minimum standards.

In our view, this suggests that any PA should include an aid for trade component—mechanisms to assist the LDCs improve their standards, regulation, etc. to the level that is required to benefit from the PA. Such mechanisms will need to be tailored to address whatever the associated capacity-building needs are. One possibility would be to develop PA-specific 'platforms' that help LDCs, as well as other developing countries with an interest in acceding to the PA, to undertake diagnostic analysis, identify action plans, and implement needed reforms with funding and assistance from high-income PA signatories.[31] Including an operational aid for trade dimension in PAs could enhance the relevance of PAs for LDCs and other low-income countries and give them a development dimension.[32]

V. Concluding Remarks

It is commonplace that the very ambitious Doha Round is almost impossible to conclude. The inability of WTO Members 'to get to yes' in the Doha Round has led to numerous calls to revisit the Single Undertaking practice and consensus-based decision making. Moving away from these norms will not address the reasons for the Doha deadlock. The lack of progress in the Doha Round reflects the assessment of major players that what has emerged on the table is not of sufficient interest to them—it is not that a small group of small countries are holding up a deal. Trade agreements are self-enforcing treaties: if the large players do not see it in their interest to deal, no amount of fiddling with alternative institutional arrangements will make a difference.[33] Thus the role that PAs could play in moving forward on the market access issues that lie at the core of the DDA deadlock is inherently limited.

Nevertheless, PAs do offer a mechanism for sub-sets of WTO Members to cooperate and engage in rule making that goes beyond current WTO disciplines.

[31] See Hoekman and Mattoo for suggestions along these lines in the area of services trade and investment. Bernard Hoekman and Aaditya Mattoo, 'Liberalizing Trade in Services: Lessons from Regional and WTO Negotiations' (2013) 18 Intl Negot 131.

[32] Given that PTAs may be used by countries as a substitute for non-reciprocal GSP-type programmes, PAs could also be conceived to be designed to advance specific development goals. For example, a PA might aim to promote technical expertise at the micro-level in dealing with conformity assessment, customs co-operation, etc.

[33] Hoekman, 'Sustaining Multilateral Trade Cooperation in a Multipolar World Economy' (n 9).

The pursuit of co-operation on regulatory policies and administrative procedures is not likely to be very valuable from an issue linkage perspective, as most of the gains (and current costs of non-action) accrue to the countries that would join the agreement. Viewed from this perspective, PAs could be the 'regulatory hothouse' for the WTO, the forum where initial plurilateral agreements become multilateralized over time. Deeper integration will inevitably occur within clubs, and if the WTO cannot permit such clubs to form, its relevance can only decline. Deep integration is contracted now in PTAs, but can also be pursued through PAs. The WTO should build its bridges with both instruments, and do more to privilege PAs for all the reasons mentioned above.

We thus believe that the case for greater recourse to PAs as a way of allowing sub-sets of countries to move forward on an issue and permit progress to be made on rule making under the umbrella of the WTO is not new.[34] The argument has not had much traction because there is significant opposition to expanding the number of PAs in the WTO. This opposition contrasts with the general acceptance and pursuit of PTAs. Acceptance of the current situation where countries are prevented from moving forward in a PA will simply result in more and deeper PTAs, or issue-specific agreements *outside* the WTO to address regulatory policies that are not covered by existing WTO disciplines. In both scenarios, the WTO will increasingly become a set of 'minimum standards'—a global trade institution that establishes only certain baseline conditions.

The need for explicit approval of a PA for it to be incorporated into the WTO provides a strong assurance that PAs that are considered to be detrimental to the interests of non-Members can be rejected. In our view, this assurance does not require consensus. It would still be guaranteed if the WTO Membership moved towards a weaker majority rule for acceptance of new PAs. The challenge is to get the consensus required to change the consensus rule for PAs. Given that this may be impossible, a more pragmatic approach would be to focus on facilitating the incorporation of new CMAs that deepen disciplines in areas already covered by the WTO, and to allow more use to be made of the PA option. Launching a process to agree on modalities for new WTO+ CMAs and a code of conduct for the design and approval of new PAs would allow the WTO to do more to embrace rather than ignore the demand for variable geometry in the global trading system.

[34] See e.g., Lawrence (n 23); Robert Z Lawrence, 'When the Immovable Object Meets the Unstoppable Force: Multilateralism, Regionalism and Deeper Integration', E15 Expert Group on Regional Trade Agreements and Plurilateral Approaches, International Centre for Trade and Sustainable Development <http://www.ictsd.org/sites/default/files/research/E15_RTA_Lawrence_FINAL.pdf> assessed 23 April 2016; Philip I Levy, 'Do We Need an Undertaker for the Single Undertaking? Angles of Variable Geometry' in Simon J Evenett and Berrd M Hoekman (eds), *Economic Development and Multilateral Trade Cooperation* (World Bank Publications 2005) 417–37.

22

TTIP and the Post-Bali WTO: Towards a New World Trade Order?

David A Gantz and Laura Nielsen***

I. Introduction

The Transatlantic Trade and Investment Partnership (TTIP) carries the considerable allure of expanding an economic partnership that accounts for almost fifty per cent of global output, a trillion dollars in annual trade (about the same as NAFTA), $4 trillion in investment and 13 million jobs, all according to the EU Commission.[1] A new free trade agreement (FTA) between the two leading economic players in the world, with a combined population of over 800 million persons, could not help but influence the course of future WTO negotiations, even if it is many years before the WTO Members are willing to deal with issues the TTIP is expected to address (such as regulatory co-ordination and coherence, anti-competition issues, agricultural market access and investment, among others). Naturally, any FTA of a certain size will, by virtue of particularly the preferential rules of origin, move one or more type of production from a more efficient third country to one of the parties—a classical example of *trade diversion*. This happened, for example, in the NAFTA with colour television tubes from Korea that ended up being produced in Mexico. But it may also create trade, as NAFTA did in terms of Mexican consumer goods from China.

Still, the influence may also go beyond these factors—because if cases between the two superpowers are still litigated in the WTO, case law may then be influenced by the 'WTO plus' agreements between them and thus potentially pull WTO case law towards stronger obligations. This seems most likely to occur where WTO and

* Samuel M Fegtly Professor of Law and Co-Director, International Trade and Business Law Program, the University of Arizona, James E Rogers College of Law.
** Associate Professor of Law, Faculty of Law, University of Copenhagen.

[1] $3.7 trillion in two-way investment according to Shayerah Ilias Akhtar and Vivian C Jones, 'Transatlantic Trade and Investment Partnership Negotiations' (Congressional Research Service Report 2014) ii.

RTA substantive principles overlap, as is seen, for example, in NAFTA.[2] Perhaps most significantly, as a study commissioned by the EU Parliament has suggested, the TTIP 'has the potential to remake political and legal relationships between the EU and the US and pave the way to a new form of global economic governance based on international regulatory cooperation'[3]. But it may also influence the WTO dispute settlement system if the European Union and the United States chose to use the TTIP dispute settlement mechanism and thus create a competing venue to adjudicate trade disputes instead of that of the WTO; the more such a venue is used and reports are implemented, the larger degree of authority and legitimacy such a TTIP tribunal will have.[4] With the European Union and the United States directly involved in a high percentage of the WTO cases against each other, their effect on case law is naturally substantial.[5] It remains to be seen whether the TTIP parties will use the TTIP dispute resolution system extensively, but it is evident that for those cases that involve issues not regulated in the WTO Agreements, they have little other choice. For most international trade lawyers, it seems inherently unattractive to have competing jurisdictions and the considerable risk of fragmentation of international trade law jurisprudence.

This chapter concerns the TTIP and the effect, if concluded, it may have on the WTO, the post-Bali WTO agenda, and the parties' other trading partners, but it also takes on a more forward-looking approach and posits that certain global issues may not be solved multilaterally within the near future and that bilateralism (in the form of the two economic superpowers acting 'unilaterally' together) may be a more viable but also realistic eventual solution, for example, to some aspects of alternative energy and mitigation of the effects of climate change.

The TTIP negotiations are not the first instance of attempts by the United States and the European Union to bring about enhanced transatlantic regulatory co-operation. Mutual recognition agreements (MRAs) have been discussed at least since 1998 through a Transatlantic Economic Partnership action plan. Since 2005, the two have engaged in high-level regulatory fora, with the Transatlantic Council established for regulatory co-operation in 2007.[6] The MRAs have the advantage of a 'tested once' approach so that actors complying in one jurisdiction will be deemed to be complying in the other jurisdiction as well.[7] MRAs have been used in the past in such areas as telecommunications equipment, recreational craft, medical devices, and civil aircraft. The approach, which clearly requires leadership at the

[2] For example, in NAFTA, art 301 (national treatment) incorporates GATT art III and related jurisprudence by reference and NAFTA art 301 (import and export restrictions) incorporates GATT, art XI by reference.

[3] Alberto Alemanno, *The Transatlantic Trade and Investment Partnership and the Parliamentary Dimension of Regulatory Cooperation* (European Union 2014) 5.

[4] See also Joanna Jemielniak and others 'Introductory Chapter' in Joanna Jemielniak, Laura Nielsen, and Henrik Palmer Olsen (eds), *Establishing International Judicial Authority in International Economic Law* (CUP 2016) (forthcoming).

[5] See also Joost Pauwelyn, 'Minority Rules: Precedent and Participation before the WTO Appellate Body' in Joanna Jemielniak, Laura Nielsen, and Henrik Palmer Olsen (eds), *Establishing International Judicial Authority in International Economic Law* (CUP 2016) (forthcoming).

[6] Akhtar and Jones (n 1) 26.

[7] ibid 27.

political level, would be well adapted to standards for new and future technologies such as electric vehicles and nanotechnology.[8] In obvious recognition of the fact that MRAs have not gone far enough or covered sufficient sectors, the TTIP negotiators have tentatively agreed to work towards a longer-term regulatory mechanism after the negotiations are completed, depending on what is agreed upon with regard to existing regulatory barriers.[9] This would presumably go beyond attention to general regulatory coherence and improve technical barriers to trade (TBT) and sanitary and phytosanitary (SPS) processes addressed within the TTIP itself. Generally, when designing MRAs, the MRAs do not extend to trading partners with other MRAs *unless* both parties have a MRA with the third country. This is also the point raised below, in which Professor Lorand Bartels cautions against and posits that it may not be entirely WTO consistent.

The chapter is divided into four parts: section II briefly summarizes the TTIP negotiations, including their content and current status (as of February 2015). Section III addresses the issue of regulatory coherence and co-ordination issues between the European Union and the United States in greater depth. Section IV sets out the effect the TTIP could have more broadly on a post-Bali WTO, with examples as to how the WTO could in time be affected. Section V examines what we choose to call new regulatory frontiers where the European Union and the United States could (but probably will not) set new standards for such things as labour standards, environmental protection (including climate change and animal welfare protection), investment, and competition through their joint actions in the TTIP. Although much of this article constitutes a preliminary assessment of the TTIP, the negotiations conducted during mid-2016 suggest that the assessment remains basically accurate.

II. Content and Current Status of the TTIP Negotiations

The TTIP negotiations have begun slowly, and have been underway only since late 2013; they were effectively suspended in mid-2014 pending the Congressional elections in the United States and the appointment of a new EU Commission on 1 November 2014. Virtually no one expects them to be concluded before mid-2016.[10]

[8] ibid.

[9] Office of the US Trade Representative (the USTR), 'Final Report of the US High Level Working Group on Jobs and Growth' (HLWG Report) (2013) <https://ustr.gov/about-us/policy-offices/press-office/reports-and-publications/2013/final-report-us-eu-hlwg> accessed 8 April 2016 (quoting Deputy USTR Dan Mullaney).

[10] It is notable that a period of six to seven months after concluding the negotiations is required before the agreement could be signed by the President. Typically, the legal texts must be 'scrubbed' by representatives of the two parties, which commonly requires about four months. Under earlier versions of the Trade Promotion Authority (TPA) (fast track), a trade agreement could not be signed until ninety days after the text had been sent to Congress, and it can be assumed that a new version of the TPA will contain the same requirement. Although the Democratic leadership in the Senate and Congress have blocked until after the November 2014 congressional elections consideration of a bill that would give TPA to the President, it is generally anticipated that such legislation can be enacted during the first quarter of 2015. EU officials have made it clear since 1974 that they will not conclude trade agreements with the United States until the President has TPA, assuring that the Congress will not seek to amend the agreement after the fact or delay its consideration.

The authors believe that the end of 2017 is a more probable date for completing the negotiations. As of May 2014 the negotiations had not progressed far beyond the 'throat-clearing' stage,[11] the fifth, May negotiating session was said by the EU Chief Negotiator Ignacio Garcia Bercero to have addressed language in TBT, competition, state-to-state dispute settlement, and dealt with issues relating to small and medium-sized enterprises. The US chief negotiator, Dan Mullaney, emphasized that the negotiators had dealt in a preliminary manner with services, investment, and government procurement, as well as tariffs and market access for goods.[12] This was progress, albeit relatively brief, although the confidentiality of the negotiations makes it difficult to assess actual forward movement. After a long hiatus, the eighth round of formal negotiations was held in early February 2015; it was expected that a full range of issues, including SPS measures and regulatory coherence, would be discussed.[13] Still, the progress of the negotiations has been discouraging, and some have questioned whether the parties have the political will to make a 'fresh start', as the EU Commissioner Malmström and the United States Trade Representative (USTR) Ambassador Michael Froman have recently suggested.[14]

Despite the many technical complexities, as well as legal and political challenges discussed herein, the TTIP may ultimately succeed in significant part because such an agreement is one of few available alternatives to the European Union and the United States for major trade expansion between two giant economies, one of which is stagnant (the European Union) and the other (the United States) experiencing growth but without adequate employment. Notwithstanding the initial, apparent 'success' of the Bali WTO Ministerial Meeting in December 2013 in reaching agreement on trade facilitation and some food security and related agricultural trade issues, few observers believe that other pending Doha Round agreements (such as those relating to services, agricultural market access, and agricultural subsidies, among others) can be salvaged. This pessimism was confirmed by the fact that between July and November 2014 efforts to adopt the Trade Facilitation Agreement were stalled by further disputes over agricultural trade issues.[15] Officials in both the United States and the European Union are concerned about China's rising economic (as well as political and military) power and realize that their future security depends on strengthening their currently stagnant economies. Some officials in both the European Union and the United States fear that their economies may be condemned to chronic slow growth, better

[11] See Len Bracken, 'US Seeks to Move Past the "Throat-clearing" Period in TTIP Talks with EU, Punke Says' (2014) 31 Intl Trade Rep 683 (quoting Deputy USTR Michael Punke).

[12] See Len Bracken, 'US, EU Negotiators Hone Texts, Discuss Market Access in TTIP Talks' (2014) 31 Intl Trade Rep 979.

[13] See 'Regulatory Coherence, SPS in the Spotlight as TTIP Round Eight Kicks Off' (*Inside US Trade*, 2 February 2015), World Trade Online database <http://insidetrade.com> accessed 23 April 2016.

[14] See J Robert Vastine and others, 'The Transatlantic Trade and Investment Partnership: An Accident Report' (2015) 1/2015 ECIPE Policy Briefs 4.

[15] See Kartikay Mehrotra and Brian Wingfield, 'WTO Trade Talks Fail Over India's Protection of Food Subsidies' (2014) 31 Intl Trade Rep 1414.

than the twenty-year period of no growth that Japan has experienced, but sharing some of the same characteristics. Thus, for example, even though the United States achieved growth of near 2.5 per cent in 2014, the US economy appears to have shrunk at a 1 per cent annual rate in the first quarter,[16] and inflation in the European Union from March 2013 to March 2014 fell to 0.5 per cent, considered dangerously low by some observers.[17]

Despite its potential, the TTIP negotiations face mind-boggling complexities. As this chapter suggests, they will focus more on building regulatory and standards compatibility, 'regulatory coherence', with mutual recognition of regulatory procedures and on other related non-tariff barriers, what Professor Alemanno characterizes as 'the behind the borders fight against nontariff barriers (NTBs)—emerging from regulatory differences across countries—making NTBs today's most prominent obstacle to trade exchanges'.[18] In addition to differences on SPS standards, disagreements are likely to arise with regard to geographical indications and privacy, as well as the services and investment areas noted elsewhere in this chapter. For example, the names Feta, Gouda, and Edam for cheeses, native to Greece and the Netherlands, respectively, have been used routinely by US cheese producers for over a century. Privacy is a highly sensitive matter that relates directly to trade in Internet services, such as those provided by US high-tech companies such as Google, Facebook, Twitter, Microsoft, and Yahoo, where the EU and US approaches vary significantly. For example, a recent, very broad decision of the Court of Justice of the European Union held that Google (but not the newspapers or other sources that originally published the information) must upon citizen request remove links to embarrassing personal information, even if previously published, and even if true.[19] The decision is considered by many in the United States to be overly broad and to potentially erode freedom of speech and freedom of the press. It also may jeopardize the support of US high-tech enterprises for the TTIP. Finally, even if tariff reduction is not the most controversial issue, it affects powerful stakeholders on both sides of the Atlantic and thus cannot be assumed to be entirely straightforward.

Perhaps the most significant unanswered question is not whether there will eventually be a TTIP, but how 'broad and deep' it will ultimately be, with extensive coverage of agriculture; coverage of financial and other services; protection of investment; and elimination or drastic reduction of most remaining tariffs,[20] as with most other preferential trade agreements recently concluded by the United

[16] Ylan Q Mui, 'Economy Shrank in First Quarter' (Washington Post, 30 May 2014) A11.

[17] See Neil Irwin, 'Deflation Threatens Europe. Policy Makers Wait' (New York Times, 8 May 2014) (commenting on the threat of a deflationary cycle akin to Japan's).

[18] Alemanno (n 3) 27.

[19] See Craig Timberg and Michael Birnbaum, 'In Google Case, EU Court Says People are Entitled to Control Their Own Online Histories' (Washington Post, 13 May 2014) (discussing the potential impact of the decision on the Internet industry).

[20] While tariffs are already very low on both sides of the Atlantic, averaging less than 4% on a trade-weighted basis, high tariffs remain on some agricultural products, footwear, textiles, and apparel.

States and the European Union.[21] (Of course, there remains some possibility that because of the many legal and political challenges, the European Union and the United States will decide that concluding an FTA at the present time is not feasible.)

The real challenges are in such areas as encouraging regulatory coherence, equivalence, and consistency through consultation and uniform laws where appropriate, along with mutual recognition of regulatory determinations. For example, can duplicate testing in the two jurisdictions of electrical equipment, pharmaceutical products, automobiles, agricultural products, and fisheries products such as molluscs, and chemicals be reduced or eliminated, and be done so without compromising the principles of regulatory sovereignty and questions of government accountability?

Regulatory coherence and mutual recognition also imply the incorporation of improved disciplines for SPS measures and TBT, long a source of contention between the two parties—for example, using hormones to fatten cattle,[22] and GMO, even if the parties tacitly agree to disagree on these two sensitive areas. A 'wide and deep' TTIP would also address supply chain management issues and related trade facilitation requirements in a more comprehensive and obligatory manner than in the recent Bali accord on trade facilitation.

The alternative is a much more modest undertaking, with the parties settling for reduction of the already low tariffs, plus some reduction of agricultural trade barriers and non-tariff barriers, leaving more ambitious changes, including most of those related to regulatory coherence, for the future. A shallower, narrower FTA seems on the surface to be far easier to conclude, given the important political and economic groups in both jurisdictions that fear increasing competition from imports. However, such an agreement would create many fewer economic benefits for the parties, likely achieve less domestic political support in both jurisdictions, and be viewed as a failure by other WTO Members, who are closely following the TTIP negotiations, including the BRICS (Brazil, Russia, India, China, and South Africa), who would likely rejoice at the inability of the European Union and the United States to set bold new paths to trade liberalization.

At the outset, it must be recognized that there is a great deal of protectionism in both the United States and the European Union—often linked to sensitive issues which will be some of the most challenging ones on which to reach compromises. Many of these same issues, such as agricultural market access, are not confined to the TTIP, but affect global trade negotiations as well. The most difficult and sensitive for the European Union and the United States include both the traditional and the new: agriculture generally (dairy, sugar, wine, some grains, beef, and pork)

[21] See e.g., 'US–Korea Free Trade Agreement' (30 June 2007) <http://www.ustr.gov/trade-agreements/free-trade-agreements/korus-fta/final-text> accessed 8 April 2016; 'Economic Partnership Agreement Between the CARIFORUM States, of the One Part, and the European Community and Its Member States, of the Other Part' [2008] OJ L 289/I.

[22] See *European Communities—Measures Concerning Meat and Meat Products (Hormones)*, WT/DS26/AB/R, WT/DS48/AB/R, 13 February 1988.

is traditionally heavily subsidized or otherwise protected; administrative agencies (the various Commission directorate generals, SEC, FTC, and others) are resistant to change and are extremely reluctant to compromise their currently broad powers; any manufacturing groups that are not largely automated, particularly in nations with low productivity such as France, Greece, and Italy, are vulnerable (and opposed) to lower tariffs. Despite the WTO's Government Procurement Agreement, 'Buy American' and 'Buy European' legislation and regulations, and restrictions on private investment continue to exist, particularly at the state levels in the United States.[23] Among recent examples is French protectionism, whereby the French Government seeks to block foreign acquisition of French enterprises that are 'national champions', such as the online video service Dailymotion by Yahoo and the industrial company Alstom, the latter by General Electric.[24] Still, former EU Commission President José Manuel Barroso may well have been accurate when he asserted in April 2014 that an ambitious TTIP, covering not only market access for goods, services, and government procurement but the regulatory issues so important for both sides, would actually be easier to achieve 'than a less comprehensive, lower-aiming deal'.[25]

Discussions to date have addressed government procurement, labour, environment, state-owned enterprises, small and medium-sized enterprises, competition, raw materials, energy, digital trade, e-commerce, dispute settlement, rules of origin, services, and geographical indications, all apparently on a very preliminary basis.[26] The discussions of key industrial sectors such as automotive, pharmaceuticals, and chemicals are only a few of the many where the negotiations are addressing questions of regulatory compatibility, as noted in section IV, below, which are in many instances more important barriers to increased trade than tariff levels per se. Briefly explained, although tariffs remain an important area of discussion, some tariffs are already so low or have been eliminated, therefore it is not the tariffs but the NTBs that are the most important issues. But these early negotiations on regulatory coherence have not been productive.

For example, the United States and the European Union differ on the scope of financial services rules that are to be included in the TTIP under the scope of regulatory coherence. The European Union apparently favours both increased market access and 'prudential' regulations (those designed to protect depositors and other stakeholders). The United States has to date taken the position that the latter are best left for other fora where they are being addressed, as in the Trade in Services Agreement (TiSA), which would, if concluded, modify and expand the

[23] Where state participation in the Government Procurement Agreement disciplines is voluntary and currently limited to thirty-seven states. See Agreement on Government Procurement, Appendix I, US Annexes.

[24] The Editorial Board, 'Protectionism Will Only Hurt France' (New York Times, 5 May 2015).

[25] See Len Bracken, 'Ambitious TTIP Pact Easier to Achieve Than Lower-aiming Deal, Barroso Says' (International Trade Daily, 1 May 2014).

[26] All are consistent with the European Union's High Level Working Group Report on Jobs and Growth. See HLWG Report (n 9). See also Akhtar and Jones (n 1) (discussing the outstanding negotiating issues).

General Agreement on Trade and Services (GATT) for the parties to the TiSA. In the United States bureaucracy, it is the Department of the Treasury that is at least refusing to address 'prudential' regulations to date, for reasons that are not entirely clear.[27] The European Union argues, correctly in our view, that such 'operational level' regulations relate to market access as well.[28] On the other hand, the US negotiators seem more interested in ensuring the inclusion of investor–state dispute settlement (ISDS) in the TTIP than some members of the European Union (Germany, France) although publicly at least the USTR has indicated flexibility in the design of the investment mechanisms themselves.[29]

Another point that should be emphasized when discussing NTBs is that tariffs are not altogether irrelevant, although they have gradually lost their importance over the past decades for trade among developed countries. If they were completely irrelevant, they would, of course, have been eliminated on all goods, or on nearly all goods, as to avoid the administrative hassle associated with collecting the duties. The tariff reduction negotiations did not begin well; the Commission, after presenting an initial tariff offer covering ninety-five per cent of its tariff lines, was reportedly shocked when the initial US offer covered only sixty-seven per cent of its tariff lines.[30] Hopefully, these negotiations still progress, because if small and medium-sized businesses are to meet the preferential rules of origin in the TTIP and receive duty-free treatment for their goods, there should *both* be an economic advantage of a certain size *and* the preferential rules of origin should be achievable for enterprises whether large or small. At present, it almost seems as if the European Union is not negotiating that part of the agreement in good faith, as the North American market is so integrated that in many instances it does not make sense to talk about 'US origin'; 'North American origin' would make more sense. In the European Union, any EU content is counted towards EU origin, so if the negotiations were reasonably structured, the same treatment should be accorded also to any NAFTA content in determining origin for imports into any of the EU nations. In support of this argument is the recently concluded bilateral agreement with Canada (the Comprehensive Economic and Trade Partnership, or CETA), although the CETA's ultimate success remains in doubt because of the EU reservations about including ISDS.[31] For over a decade, the European Union has had a FTA with Mexico, which will almost certainly be renegotiated if both CETA and TTIP are completed.

Whilst it may be impossible for the NAFTA parties to negotiate the agreements together given that they do not have the same institutional structure nor

[27] Off-the-record discussion with a major US financial industry representative, May 2014; notes on file with author.

[28] See Len Bracken, 'Scope of Previous TTIP Text Remains Under Discussion as Round Draws to Close, Negotiators Say' (International Trade Daily, 20 December 2013).

[29] 'Froman Says ISDS Needed in TTIP to Set Standard for Other Agreements' (*Inside US Trade*, 5 May 2014), World Trade Online database <http://insidetrade.com> accessed 23 April 2016.

[30] Vastine and others (n 14) 2.

[31] Joe Kirwin, 'EU–Canada Trade Agreement in Doubt, Posing Concerns About TTIP Deal' (2014) 31 Intl Trade Rep 1770.

supranational entities as the European Union, and from a strictly legal formalistic point of view it is not necessary given NAFTA is merely an FTA and not a Customs Union (CU), it nevertheless makes sense politically to align at least the preferential rules of origin in those agreements (as has been attempted to a limited degree with regard to autos in the CETA, which anticipates a situation in which both the US and Canadian content will count towards satisfying domestic content requirements for Canadian auto exports to the European Union).[32]

However, when adding on the regulatory coherence issues where, for example, one product that is approved in the European Union would then also qualify in the United States, the next issue to tackle is whether this approval is extended also to Mexico and Canada, and if so by what legal process. Similarly, the reverse situation may exist (particularly as the CETA is likely to enter into force several years before the TTIP) where a Mexican or Canadian product may be approved also in the United States but the extent to which this applies to the European Union is uncertain. This is not normally the case, and is an issue negotiators will have to address in the future—not only because it may run afoul of the TBT Agreement of the WTO,[33] but also because it raises so many additional practical problems that the entire effectiveness of TTIP integration between the European Union and the United States could be undermined. It could even become an issue in the TPP given that the United States, Canada, and Mexico are all TPP negotiating parties.

While it can be argued that ISDS is not the optimal solution for the European Union and the United States (or the European Union and Canada under CETA), the arguments for eliminating ISDS are less than convincing for some observers. As a general rule, while the United States and the EU Member states have reliable and independent judiciary systems that cannot be expected to favour the government in a dispute with a foreign investor, there are exceptions. For example, in the 2014 Transparency International Corruptions Perception Index, seven of the EU Member states (Bulgaria, Croatia, the Czech Republic, Greece, Italy, Romania, and Slovakia) rank below fifty-two in the index, possibly suggesting a legal/court system that is less independent than those in many higher-ranking African and Middle Eastern states.[34] It is equally clear that many EU enterprises rightly or wrongly fear the costs of litigation in US courts, and are aware of the less than optimal treatment of a foreign (Canadian) investor in Mississippi courts as publicized in a famous NAFTA Chapter 11 proceeding.[35] The perception of Americans being more litigious than Europeans was, however, rebutted at a seminar at the Ministry

[32] See CETA Rules of Origin, HS 8702, note 2.

[33] This point has been raised by Professor Lorand Bartels at the mini-WTO conference 'The Post-Bali WTO in Light of the Regional and Sectoral Agreements', Ministry of Foreign Affairs, Copenhagen, Denmark (13 May 2014) (hosted by the Faculty of Law, University of Copenhagen).

[34] Transparency International, 'The 2014 Corruptions Perceptions Index' (October 2014) <http://www.transparency.org/cpi2014> accessed 12 March 2016.

[35] *See Loewen v United States*, ICSID Case No ARB(AF)/98/3 (26 June 2003) <http://www.state.gov/documents/organization/3921.pdf> accessed 9 April 2016.

of Foreign Affairs in Denmark in the spring of 2014, with figures stating that Europeans were in fact more litigious than Americans when it comes to foreign investment. Another factor that makes it less likely that such a mechanism will be excluded from the TTIP is the inclusion of ISDS in CETA. Yet what policymakers seem to focus more on is that an exclusion of an ISDS in the TTIP makes it more difficult to exclude the mechanism from future treaties that the European Union and the United States would enter into, and arguably would complicate future negotiation of bilateral investment treaties between the European Union and China and the United States and China. Interestingly, some in Germany and the EU Parliament have had second thoughts about including ISDS in the CETA (and thus in the future TTIP as well), reflecting concerns of European non-governmental organizations (NGOs), putting the final conclusion of the CETA in doubt.[36]

All that being said, however, it has been proven in numerous actions filed under NAFTA, Chapter 11 that even governments with a high level of rule of law and independence in their judiciaries occasionally take discriminatory and even arbitrary actions which may be difficult to resolve in the national court systems.[37] Moreover, some EU investors would likely welcome the option of avoiding litigation of disputes in US federal courts with their time-consuming and expensive discovery rules, and many multinational enterprises (MNEs) on both side of the Atlantic are generally more comfortable with the process of international arbitration than litigation in each other's national courts. Thus, the existence of an investor–state dispute settlement system may appeal to some potential foreign investors, even if the need for the system is not fully clear to some observers.

What perhaps is missing from the debate is a more general discussion about *which type* of dispute resolution mechanism would be most optimal—both for the trade and the investment disputes arising under the TTIP. It may in fact be time to review and rethink the entire way we perceive and understand these quasi-judicial trade tribunals. It may well be that with TTIP, the WTO Appellate Body is not the only one of its kind because the TTIP dispute resolution system may very well create a 'competing' appellate body. At a conference at the Danish Ministry of Foreign Affairs in May 2014, for example, discussions about letting the WTO Appellate Body adjudicate claims from non-WTO Agreements were raised. More radical suggestions would be to create a more permanent court. Other discourses involve issues such as who should be adjudicating the cases. With the TTIP, it could therefore also be considered whether the TTIP dispute resolution system should instead be more like a real court with 'real' judges—not holding day jobs in large law firms or universities alongside acting as arbitrator and thus creating case law one day, and in the next representing large economic

[36] See Kirwin, 'EU–Canada Trade Agreement in Doubt' (n 31).

[37] See e.g., *SD Myers Inc v Government of Canada*, UNCITRAL (13 November 2000) (interim award on merits) (where the record showed that Canadian government barred exports of hazardous materials to the United States so that the producer would be forced to use a disposal facility in Alberta instead).

interests in business life. Another issue is that in the WTO disputes neither EU nor US citizens are panellists (in the large majority of cases where one or both are parties), whereas in the TTIP it may indeed *only* be the EU and the US citizens deciding TTIP disputes. This discussion may also involve questions as to whether panellists should be picked from law firms, governments (usually the diplomats), and/or academia.

Curiously, the US negotiators have also persistently argued that the EU regulatory system should be changed so as to be more transparent, which US commentators such as Simon Lester on several occasions[38] have criticized vocally as perhaps not being the most optimal approach to reaching consensus—comparing it to how the Americans would react if the Europeans wanted the Americans to change their legislative procedures. However, from a European point of view, critique of the opaque functioning of the undemocratic EU Commission is not necessarily ill thought of, except perhaps by the increasingly large minority of anti-EU representatives in the EU Parliament. One thing that is actually missing in the debate about the TTIP is the mobilization of citizens and consumers across the Atlantic, as these probably are more in alignment on some issues than they are with their own governments.

By May 2014 the parties had agreed, with considerable encouragement from stakeholders on both sides of the Atlantic, to focus first (and try to demonstrate progress) on market opening measures, but not on an approach. The Commission favoured treating market opening for goods, services, and government procurement in a single group, while the USTR favoured addressing each area separately.[39] Still, as noted above, during the late May meeting the negotiators managed to hold fruitful discussions on both market access and some regulatory issues. It remains to be seen how the negotiations will progress now that they have been resumed as of February 2015.

III. Regulatory Coherence and Co-ordination

Regulatory coherence is understood to mean the process of co-ordinating the regulatory aspects of already existing rules that differ on each side of the Atlantic. Eliminating those differences or, for example, giving some weight to each other's approval procedures of drugs will have massive economic impact. A 2009 EU Commission study estimated that if fifty per cent of the US–EU regulatory differences and other NTBs could be aligned, EU GDP would gain $158 billion per year

[38] At the mini-WTO conference 'The Post-Bali WTO Agenda in Light of the Regional and Sectoral Agreements', Ministry of Foreign Affairs, Copenhagen, Denmark (13 May 2014) (hosted by the Faculty of Law, University of Copenhagen); the Annual WTO BIICL Conference, BMA House, London (14–15 May 2014).

[39] 'Under Pressure to Show TTIP Progress, US, EU Focus on Market Access' (*Inside US Trade*, 18 April 2014); 'Structure of Market Access Talks is Latest Sore Spot in TTIP Negotiations' (*Inside US Trade*, 25 April 2014), World Trade Online database <http://insidetrade.com> accessed 23 April 2016.

and US gains would be about $53 billion annually.[40] The focus therefore is on the process of co-ordination, rather than the substance of the regulations themselves.

Among many examples, European and US generic drug producers have called on the Commission and the USTR to include measures that would expedite release of inexpensive medicines and enhance the sustainability of health-care systems in the two jurisdictions.[41] Auto trade (vehicles and engines) would be facilitated if the European Union and the United States could agree on mutual recognition of technical regulations, an approach that is probably more promising than attempting uniform regulations. However, at a trade conference hosted by the Ministry of Foreign Affairs of Denmark in the spring of 2014, examples were mentioned of rear view mirrors where there were two centimetres in difference between the different regulations, i.e. such similar regulations can indeed be aligned 100 per cent. Similarly, with medical devices, pharmaceuticals, and cosmetics, the approach is to seek acceptance of each other's inspection of manufacturing facilities. Co-ordination of risk assessments in the chemical sector has been considered, but would apparently be complicated because of varying legal regimes and regulatory approaches. These differing approaches for distinct sectors illustrate the complexity of negotiating the reduction of what are effectively non-tariff barriers in the world's two most advanced regulatory economies. But more flexible approaches are also advanced by the industry itself. On 13 November 2014, the three leading Danish pharmaceutical companies and the Danish MEP Bendt Bendtsen organized a TTIP meeting in the European Parliament where the pharmaceutical companies pleaded for eliminating the additional clinical trials on the other side of the Atlantic, particularly for children. Often, the clinical trials must legally be repeated despite very small differences in the approaches. In addition, filing for approval in each jurisdiction appears cumbersome, and could be made a lot easier if at least filing could be in one common format. The industry is therefore often very active in formulating what they need.

An apparently authentic EU Commission paper on regulatory coherence leaked by an anti-trade NGO, the Corporate Europe Observatory, in December 2013, envisions a number of transparency measures to assist in achieving 'transatlantic regulatory co-operation', including but not limited to formal requirements for exchange of information on pending legislation in the United States and proposals by the EU Commission and efforts to encourage regulatory compatibility, while preserving each party's right to adopt new regulatory initiatives. Such regulatory compatibility could be enhanced through, inter alia, 'recognition of equivalence, mutual recognition on reliance and exchange of data and information, or other means'.[42] The EU

[40] Akhtar and Jones (n 1) 23 (citing ECORYS, 'Non-tariff Measures in EU–US Trade and Investment—An Economic Analysis: Final Report for the European Commission' [December 2009] OJ 2007/S 18-219943).

[41] Joe Kirwin, 'EU, US Generic Drug Makers Call for Regulatory Convergence in TTIP' (2014) 31 Intl Trade Rep 734.

[42] 'TPP-cross-cutting Disciplines and Institutional Procedures: Position Paper—Chapter on Regulator Coherence' <http://corporateeurope.org/sites/default/files/ttip-regulatory-coherence-2-12-2013.pdf> accessed 23 April 2016.

Commission seeks a framework for regulatory co-operation in financial services which contemplates 'an institutional framework of EU and US regulators to make sure that EU and US rules work together' and assist in preventing future crises.[43]

The parties would be required to update each other at least twice a year on principal elements of regulatory initiatives relating to transatlantic trade, and take into account comments on such from the other party. Consultation—'regulatory dialogues'—would be available on request. This would be done in part through a new 'Regulatory Cooperation Council'. Co-ordination of EU and US positions in international regulatory bodies would be encouraged, reflecting what in many respects takes place informally today. The measures would not be limited to governments; each party would facilitate consultations with stakeholders using existing frameworks (in the United States presumably including the various USTR advisory committees). Parts of this transparency process have precedents elsewhere, for example in the NAFTA.

One of the US negotiators suggested in May 2014 that 'success' with regard to establishing regulatory coherence in the TTIP would consist of four elements: (i) the establishment of horizontal mechanisms that would require regulators in each jurisdiction to communicate regularly with each other so as to make it more likely that the regulatory process would not impose unnecessary burdens on stakeholders; (ii) regulators would address areas where the approach is different on a sector-by-sector basis, focusing on those sectors where the different approach causes difficulties; (iii) a governing council, an intergovernmental entity that would supervise the co-ordination process at a very high level, perhaps by the vice-president of the United States and the Secretary-General (senior civil servant) of the EU Commission; and (iv) a mechanism for exploring new ways to open up the existing regulatory processes in both jurisdictions, whereby in the European Union more stakeholder input into the regulatory process would be solicited and in the United States a balance would be sought between the need to regulate and the need for flexibility in a context where independent, often competing, standards-developing organizations exist and the result through legislation and agency regulatory action becomes mandatory.[44]

Among the many challenges is bridging the gap between the European Union's increasingly centralized regulatory system, and the US approach, which is more decentralized despite the Commerce Clause, particularly in such areas as insurance services, legal services, and environmental protection (which are shared between the federal government and the states). In the European Union, the common commercial policy and continuing with the importance of strengthening the integration of the market (in part so that European enterprises can become more competitive in world markets) has led to this more centralized way of regulating.

[43] European Commission, 'EU–US Transatlantic Trade and Investment Partnership (TTIP): Cooperation on Financial Services Regulation' (European Commission, 27 January 2014) <http://trade.ec.europa.eu/doclib/docs/2014/january/tradoc_152101.pdf> accessed 9 April 2016.

[44] Off-the-record communications with a US TIPP negotiator in May 2014; notes on file with author.

Most standards are developed by businesses in co-operation with other stakeholders; some thirty per cent are 'adopted following a request by the Commission to support EU Legislation'. Once such standards are published, the national standards body is required to withdraw conflicting national standards.[45] Conversely, in the United States, a decentralized system predominates. As Professor Alemanno observes:

> US standardization is a *decentralized* system that is naturally partitioned into industrial sectors and supported by independent, private sector standards developing organizations (SDOs) that typically compete— unlike the European ones—among themselves. It is a *demand-driven* system in which standards are developed in response to specific concerns and needs expressed by industry, government, and consumers. And, it is a *voluntary* system in which both standards development and implementation are driven by stakeholder needs rather than mandated by government.[46]

Moreover, in the United States Congress often participates directly in the adoption of standards through legislation, which standards become mandatory for the regulatory agency, as with the Consumer Product Safety Commission and the Consumer Products Safety Improvement Act of 2008, mandating safety standards for toys made by companies regulated by the CPSC.[47] Some observers suggest that the EU process for making standards (as distinct from some other types of legislating) is arguably more transparent generally than the process in the United States, because the EU process is more centralized, with the pre-legislative process providing more opportunities for consultation with stakeholders.[48] In contrast, the US process may be generally (but not always) more flexible and predictable. Also, the EU process is typically mandatory, while the latter US standards process may be voluntary.[49] To further complicate matters, in the United States more than one domestic standard issued by different entities can exist for the same product or service, as with multiple stock exchanges (New York, NASDAQ) or differences between regulatory practices developed by the Justice Department and the Federal Trade Commission. Perhaps the most important conclusion for the TTIP is that the two processes are radically different. While collaboration between the European Standardization Organizations (European Committee for Standardization (CEN), European Committee for Electrotechnical Standardization (CENELEC), and the European Telecommunications Standards Institute (ETSI)) and the American National Standards Institute (ANSI) continues, it is evident that much work remains to be done.

The difference in approach is reflected again in areas such as foodstuffs, electromagnetic compatibility of products, recycling requirements (with many recycling standards in the United States determined by state law), and various other environmental and certification requirements, as with auto emissions. It is not so much whether one system is better or worse, but the fact that they are different, and that in some instances the differences can be used by domestic

[45] Alemanno (n 3) 16 (quoting a CENELEC position paper on technical barriers to trade).
[46] ibid. [47] ibid. [48] ibid 10. [49] ibid 17.

interests to make imports slower and more expensive. The EU Commission estimates that if such NTBs were eliminated, the EU economic output would increase by 0.5 per cent,[50] and there is no reason to believe that the gains would be any less in the United States. In addition to obvious protectionism, Professor Alemanno suggests that part of the problem is 'tunnel vision', in which national regulators simply fail to pay attention to the impact of their actions outside their own jurisdiction.[51] Whatever the actual numbers may be there seems little doubt:

> [t]hat differing EU and US approaches to regulation are a significant cause of reduced overall consumer welfare. For example, many multinational corporations cite different, and often duplicative, regulations on each side of the Atlantic as significant barriers to trade, due to the increased costs involved in modifying products to meet the different requirements of each regulatory regime.[52]

Another problem for the negotiations is perhaps best described in terms of cultural or societal preferences. There is a very broad anti-regulatory spirit in the United States, including among many members of Congress, along with a distrust of the federal government that sometimes borders on the paranoiac. This has been illustrated most recently by the initial broad support in Congress and among the public for Clive Bundy, a Nevada rancher who refused to pay $1.1 million to the federal government relating to twenty years of grazing fees for keeping his cattle on federal land. (The wide support fizzled after it became evident that in addition to owing the government large sums of money Bundy was a vicious racist.)[53]

One can speculate about whether this type of anti-regulatory spirit is manifested in some areas by a greater tolerance of potential risk, as with growth hormones or GMO, which may, however, not be the entire truth. Others argue precisely that growth hormones and GMO tolerance in the United States is the result of the industry being more powerful than US consumers, and if asked, consumers would prefer labelling. Industry, in the European Union and the United States, is generally against labelling, presumably because they know US consumers are as sceptical as the Europeans and might not purchase some items if the products were in fact labelled, and US consumers were given the right to choose. The assumption that Europe has embraced a more precautionary approach and Europeans are more sceptical than Americans might not have been the situation if consumers rather than industry and lawmakers had dominated the debate and the law-making in the United States. At the same time, when the European Union acts to allow the banning of GMO seed in crop cultivation for non-scientific (economic, social, and ethical) reasons (however defined), sceptics in the United States, including grain

50 Quoted in Alemanno (n 3) 20. 51 ibid.

52 John F Morali III, 'Determining Compatible Regulatory Regimes between the US and the EU' (US Chamber of Commerce 2012) <https://www.uschamber.com/sites/default/files/legacy/reports/Determining%20Compatible%20Regulatory%20Regimes.pdf> accessed 23 April 2016.

53 See Michelle Rindels, 'Nevada Rancher Defends Remarks, Lose Supports' (Associated Press, 25 April 2014) <http://www.ksl.com/?nid=157&sid=29614977> accessed 12 March 2016.

farmers and powerful seed companies, have pressurized US negotiators to deal with this sensitive political issue effectively in the TTIP negotiations.[54]

One of the objectives of EU and US negotiators is to improve the disciplines in the WTO Agreement on TBT and SPS measures.[55] The parties are reported to intend to achieve 'TBT-Plus' commitments, which would include an 'improved dialogue and cooperation for addressing bilateral TBT issues'. This would be brought about through 'greater openness, transparency and convergence in regulatory approaches and requirements and related standards-development development processes'. The effort would also be directed towards the reduction of 'redundant and burdensome testing and certification requirements'.[56] Among the reported concerns of the standards process in the European Union are the promotion by the EU Commission of those that meet the 'essential requirements' of EU directives within international standards bodies, a procedure which, according to some US stakeholders, prevents them from effective participation in the deliberative process.[57] This contrasts with the broader public input that characterizes the standards-creating process for US agencies that are subject to the requirements of the Administrative Procedure Act, the Freedom of Information Act, or the Sunshine Act (but not for some other regulatory processes, where standards are developed by non-government stakeholders). The Underwriters' Laboratory and the American National Standards Institute also provide for participation by interested parties.[58]

The 'SPS-Plus' would go beyond the SPS Agreement with regard to the protection of human, animal, or plant life and health in a manner that does not arbitrarily or unjustifiably discriminate between WTO Members, and require standards to be based on science. A US Working Group Report recommended in 2013 that the SPS provisions of the TTIP establish 'an ongoing mechanism for improved dialogue and cooperation' and assure that 'each side's SPS measures be based on science and on international standards or scientific risk assessments'.[59] This language, again, refers to the long-standing hormone and GMO disputes between the negotiating parties, where the wise solution is to leave those areas alone—which may prove in the end also to be the position of the US consumers who do not wish to push the agenda further on this topic, as it makes it even more difficult to call for labelling as a federal requirement, where several states already require such labelling.[60]

[54] Joe Kirwin, 'EU Members Reach Deal to Allow GM Ban in Crop Cultivation for Non-scientific Reasons' (International Trade Daily, 30 May 2014).

[55] Annex 1A of the Marrakesh Agreement Establishing the World Trade Organization, 15 April 1995.

[56] HLWG Report (n 9). [57] Akhtar and Jones (n 1) 25. [58] ibid 26.

[59] HLWG Report (n 9).

[60] See e.g., 'State Labeling Initiatives' (Center for Food Safety) <http://www.centerforfoodsafety.org/issues/976/ge-food-labeling/state-labeling-initiatives#> accessed 12 March 2016.

In this context, it is interesting to review the CETA provisions on regulatory co-ordination and coherence, including TBT and SPS, that reflect an understanding that such agreements need to create mechanisms that are process-oriented, which over time can be utilized to achieve the recognized objectives. In CETA, these include mechanisms for joint initiatives; early access to regulatory development initiatives in each party; formal procedures for requesting that each other's technical regulations be treated as equivalent; mandated further negotiations for a protocol to CETA that would provide for acceptance of each other's test results and product certifications; and an SPS Joint Management Committee to discuss issues before they become serious problems.[61] This is recognition that full achievement of regulatory coherence is an on-going process that in the view of some experts will take years or decades to achieve in the TTIP.[62]

IV. The Post-Bali WTO and the TTIP

A. Status and secrecy of the TTIP

Detailed analysis relating to the TTIP texts actually being discussed is quite sparse, for the very logical reason that the negotiations as of April 2014 have not progressed significantly and much of what has been discussed has not been made public (or leaked). Whether the increasing pressure from the European Parliament and some Member officials, such as Germany's Economics Minister and Vice-Chancellor Sigmar Gabriel, calling for more transparent negotiations and 'democracy legitimacy' will cause the EU Commission and USTR to react positively remains to be seen.[63] But the EU Commission has taken the unprecedented step of disclosing documents concerning the otherwise confidential negotiation positions on the Internet.[64] It is understood that this type of transparency by the EU Commission is happening because of fear of the European Parliament being critical and potentially turning against the entire TTIP, as they did with ACTA. In the context of the TiSA and TPP negotiations, the Chairman (ranking member as of 6 January 2015) of the Senate Finance Committee, Ron Wyden, has also emphasized the need for 'trade transparency' in place of 'trade secrecy'.[65] With

[61] 'Consolidated CETA Text' (CETA, 26 September 2014), chs 6–7, <http://trade.ec.europa.eu/doclib/docs/2014/september/tradoc_152806.pdf> accessed 9 April 2016.

[62] Remarks of Pascal Lamy (former WTO director general and EU Commissioner for Trade) at a conference at the London School of Economics, November 2014 (notes on file with author David Gantz).

[63] See Andrea Barbara Schuessler, 'Germany's Economics Minister Calls for More Transparent TTIP Negotiations' (2014) 31 Intl Trade Rep 861.

[64] 'Directives for the negotiation on the Transatlantic Trade and Investment Partnership between the European Union and the United States of America' (Council of the European Union, 9 October 2014) <http://data.consilium.europa.eu/doc/document/ST-11103-2013-DCL-1/en/pdf> accessed 9 April 2016.

[65] Daniel Pruzin, 'Concerns Over Secrecy Begin to Shadow Global Services Talks' (2014) 31 Intl Trade Rep 850 (quoting Senator Wyden).

Congressional pressure and that of the European Parliament, it is thus possible that the content of the negotiations will become clearer to the public as the discussions continue over the next year or so. One should, however, keep in mind that secrecy may be essential to moving negotiations forward, particularly at the outset, and secrecy may have been partly responsible for the negotiations moving forward as well as they did in May 2014. However, being lawyers, we of course understand that the devil may be in the detail. The final conclusion and publication of the agreement may be delayed when the government lawyers and other negotiators address possibly unclear text that masks substantive differences and accordingly requires 're-negotiation', as apparently occurred with the EU–Canada FTA, which was subject to 'numerous disputes' between the parties[66] before the negotiations were finally concluded in September 2014.

B. New World Trade Order?

In analysing the effect on the rest of the world and the WTO should the TTIP negotiations be successfully concluded and the agreement enter into force, it is important to note that the post-Bali WTO is *different* to such an extent that it seems timely to speak of a new world trade order in the sense that most significant developments in world trade law are currently taking place *outside* the WTO.[67] As of 1 February 2016, 625 regional trade agreements (RTAs or PTAs) have been notified to the WTO[68] and more are being negotiated on a regular basis, including among others the TTIP, the Transpacific Partnership[69] and the Regional Comprehensive Economic Partnership (RCEP).[70] Many of these RTAs or agreements among groups of like-minded nations such as the members of the Asia-Pacific Economic Forum, will address not only aspects of regulatory coherence, but also investment, state-owned enterprises, supply chain management, e-commerce, trade in environmental goods, and environmental protection/climate change—issues which all go far beyond the current design of the WTO and even far beyond the otherwise ambitious, but now outdated, Doha Development Agenda.

A new world order (or disorder) outside the WTO that is broader than trade rules per se may even be emerging where there is a general breakdown of faith in the multilateral systems—or where multilateralism has simply failed. If one looks at the most pressing issue of our time, climate change, it is remarkable that this goes largely unregulated except for a few instances at the national, county, or city level. While this is not the place to discuss climate change in any detail, it was anticipated that greenhouse gas emissions would be regulated internationally by

[66] Joe Kirwin, 'EU–Canada FTA Stalled Indefinitely' 31 Intl Trade Rep.

[67] David A Gantz, *Liberalizing Trade after Doha* (CUP 2013).

[68] WTO, 'Regional Trade Agreements Gateway' <https://www.wto.org/english/tratop_e/region_e/region_e.htm> accessed 9 April 2016.

[69] Australia, Brunei, Canada, Chile, Japan, Malaysia, Mexico, New Zealand, Peru, Singapore, United States, and Vietnam.

[70] The ten ASEAN nations plus Australia, China, India, Japan, Korea, and New Zealand.

the UNFCCC, under which the more tangible Kyoto Protocol and any successor agreement belong. The Kyoto Protocol was the agreement, despite considerable shortcomings, that mandated a cap over greenhouse gas emissions, which at COP15 in 2009 in Copenhagen was envisaged to be replaced by a so-called Post-Kyoto Protocol. However, in spite of high-level participation, COP15 is generally (and in particular in Denmark) thought of as a failure that ended up without an agreement to replace the expired Kyoto Protocol.

Only limited progress has been made since that time. The United States and China agreed in November 2014 that they would set long-term targets for reducing carbon emissions significantly by 2030, a development that was hailed by some as a breakthrough because even though the understanding was non-binding it committed China to reducing emissions for the first time.[71] Still, the best that can be said for the Lima and Paris Climate Change conferences in 2014 and 2015 is that they kept hopes alive for multilateral solutions, albeit they delivered minimalistic results.[72] The minimalistic results are seen by many as a further blow to faith in multilateralism, in the ability of the nations of the world to address a critical threat to future generations, at a time when we have also seen the demise of the WTO Doha Round, at least as a broad, single undertaking, and among other examples the failure of the UN Security Council to address effectively the human disaster arising from the civil war in Syria. The climate change, trade, and political/security areas each have their own explanations for the failure to conclude new multilateral deals or binding resolutions, in all instances where the costs of failure nevertheless have enormous economic and human costs to the planet.

In terms of the Doha Round, it is important to understand that the Round started immediately post-9/11 at a Ministerial Meeting hosted in an Arab state, with emphasis on the expressed resolve of Member governments to alleviate poverty (hence a 'development' round). The authors of this chapter differ in opinion as to the significance of holding the Ministerial in an Arab state—where one point of view could be simply that Doha was chosen to avoid the civil unrest experience in Seattle and because no other Members were interested in serving as hosts. Another point of view, which is not necessarily mutually exclusive, is that it had more than a symbolic value. In those months immediately after 9/11, the world was trembling and a process of self-reflection was also happening, seeking to understand why the actions of any human being could become so monstrous. Among other things, the West realized that it had to seek a better understanding of Muslim culture—so a good-faith effort in an Arab capital promising development through trade seemed

[71] Leslie A Pappas and Anthony Adragna, 'US, China Set Long-term Carbon Emission Targets in Bid to Push Global Climate Action' (2014) 37 Intl Env Rep 1589.

[72] Eric J Lyman, 'Limited Lima Agreement Leaves Major Issues Pending Before 2015 Climate Change Pact' (2014) Intl Env Rep (special report). See also e.g., Fiona Harvey, 'Paris Climate Change Deal too Weak to Help the Poor' (The Guardian, 14 December 2015) <http://www.theguardian.com/environment/2015/dec/14/paris-climate-change-deal-cop21-oxfam-actionaid> accessed 9 April 2016.

to many as a politically correct step to take—beyond merely a symbolic gesture of friendship.

However, we conclude that among the reasons the Round never delivered significant results was the lack of a real 'push' from industry, perhaps as a partial result of a highly politicized Doha Declaration, which included something for almost all WTO Members and stakeholders but little in the way of firm commitments to negotiate. Industry support in some cases was also lukewarm given that the Uruguay Round was still fairly new and had successfully addressed many of industry's most pressing issues (for example, intellectual property and services). Support was lacking for completely different reasons from the vast majority of the developing Members. Most were still trying to figure out how to implement the obligations they assumed in the Uruguay Round, particularly those under The Agreement on Trade-related Aspects of International Property Rights (TRIPS), TBT, the Customs Valuation Agreement and SPS. Such Members had also become sceptical as to whether the promised benefits, such as those under the Agreement on Textiles and Clothing, were genuine and were being implemented in good faith by the developed Members. Others now and then argue that the rounds and deals have become too comprehensive. Because the major developing countries—particularly the BRICS—now have an active, if not controlling, role in the process, it takes longer to reach consensus if consensus is even possible. The pessimists will claim that negotiations have become more like those of the UN General Assembly and are incapable of delivering hard law results in a timely fashion, if at all.

C. Unilateralism as a mechanism to solve global issues?

As a consequence, the new world trading order represents an era of sectorial and regional agreements where there is a growing preference for handling issues bilaterally, plurilaterally, or even unilaterally. In this chapter, we argue that in the short term bilateralism ought to, *de lege ferenda*, attempt to solve the most pressing global problems, or at least parts thereof. We find our role as scholars is also to outline new frontiers—knowing we are ahead of our time and some of our ideas admittedly are unrealistic. In section V below, we argue that some of the problems relating to labour rights, climate change, the environment, and perhaps even animal welfare, issues that will not be resolved multilaterally in the foreseeable future, *could* be addressed effectively by the two economic superpowers (whether or not they are actually able to do so). That being said, it seems likely that some elements relating to climate change, such as lower tariffs on alternative energy goods, fuel economy standards, co-operative measures relating to adaption, and perhaps even some discussion of carbon taxation, may be feasible. In terms of animal welfare and environmental protection of animals, it is conceivable that the parties, either in the present TTIP negotiations or in a future extension of them, could deal to some degree with trade in endangered species (given that CITES has miserably failed), possibly also with testing of products such as cosmetics on animals, although as far as we are aware these issues are not currently on the negotiating table and might well engender resistance by some stakeholders, at least in the United States.

D. The effect of the TTIP on the rest of the world

If—and it is a big if—half the world's economy—the European Union and the United States—manage to conclude an agreement that requires them to implement significant steps towards regulatory coherence, including mutual recognition of standards; address supply chain management issues and agree to strict trade facilitation obligations (likely going well beyond the Bali accord); incorporate disciplines on foreign investment (despite some doubts in the European Union when writing this chapter); improve the operation of the TBT and SPS processes; and perhaps even discuss competition law, there is likely to be an impact on other EU and US trading partners. Other members of the WTO may eventually accept the need to address some of those same issues in the course of future multilateral trade negotiations in Geneva or in other non-global trade agreements with the European Union, the United States, or both, or through such more progressive mechanisms as Asia-Pacific Economic Co-operation (APEC).

The key here for any action in Geneva is 'eventually'. It seems highly unlikely to us that the BRICS will be motivated to abandon current positions for the foreseeable future, at least five years or more, and unless they moderate their views the chances of support for addressing such issues effectively in the WTO are nil. In the shorter term, a completed TTIP may even have the opposite effect. It could reinforce BRICS' opposition to permitting the United States and the European Union to dictate the content of future WTO agreements (if any are negotiated), even if they decline to suggest alternatives of their own and remain mired in their own protectionism and slow (or slower in the case of China) or negligible economic growth. While TBT-Plus and SPS-Plus could in theory be adopted eventually by the WTO Membership, these are not among the issues that many Members consider beneficial to their interests, if only because effective administration of such regulatory processes is devilishly difficult for developed Members, let alone many in the developing world. In our view whether a WTO agreement on some form of regulatory coherence, perhaps beginning with an expanded consultation mechanism, could succeed may depend by analogy on whether the recent Trade Facilitation Agreement (TFA)[73] is effectively implemented. For developing countries the challenges of taking the necessary steps to bring about more efficient importing and exporting are likely as difficult as improving regulatory coherence and co-operation in other fields, and likely just as dependent on massive technical assistance. If this works well over the next several years, and if indeed the TFA is approved by two-thirds of the Members, this would signal to us and to many others that further steps at the multilateral level towards addressing regulatory

[73] WTO, 'Agreement on Trade Facilitation, Ministerial Decision of 7 December 2013' <http://wto.org/english/thewto_e/minist_e/mc9_e/desci36_e.htm> accessed 16 March 2016.

issues should be considered. If, instead, the developed Members fail to provide the promised technical assistance, and the developing Members show a lack of willingness to take the politically difficult steps of facilitating trade (which are opposed by protectionist stakeholders in many countries), the prospects for broader regulatory improvement are dim.

Our scepticism is based in part on the only other effort to date to expand the WTO Agreements, the adoption by the Hong Kong Ministerial Meeting of Article 31 *bis* of the Agreement on Trade-related Intellectual Property, relating to public health. After more than ten years, in 2016, only 99 Members (including the 28 of the European Union), still short of the 106 (two-thirds) required for formal adoption of the amendment, had deposited their instruments of ratification.[74] Arguably, the TRIPS amendment is far less controversial for the Membership than the TFA.

E. Implications for case law

The implications for WTO case law is the type of influence that is the most rarely discussed, but it may nevertheless be necessary to include it when we speak of the United States and the European Union. As noted earlier, these two parties are already responsible for the majority of case law in the WTO, and when not directly parties, they nearly always participate as third parties.[75] Thus, inevitably, the United States and the European Union also have a major influence on case law. By virtue of the WTO system operating with de facto *stare decisis*, the disputes between the European Union and the United States could therefore affect case law in the direction of the new and stronger obligations the parties have taken upon themselves in the TTIP. This could, for example, be an SPS-Plus obligation, which the WTO panels and Appellate Body cannot ignore when analysing WTO SPS obligations between the two parties. The world trading system may very well end up with a situation in which the panels and the Appellate Body will not apply any of the TTIP rules, but it is interpreted nevertheless in the broader context of the stronger TTIP obligations—perhaps because the parties argue that the entire case is affected by both sets of rules, or because the measure reflects much stronger obligations. Consequently, it is important for third parties to follow the discussion on which type of state-to-state dispute settlement the TTIP will incorporate. However, even in the TTIP the parties may continue to prefer WTO dispute settlement, as all three parties have in NAFTA.[76] Some disputes will have to be

[74] WTO, 'Intellectual Property: TRIPS and Public Health—Members Accepting Amendment of the TRIPS Agreement', <http://www.wto.org/english/tratop_e/trips_e/amendment_e.htm> accessed 16 March 2016.

[75] As of December 2014, 143 times by the European Union, WTO, 'The European Union and the WTO' <http://www.wto.org/english/thewto_e/countries_e/european_communities_e.htm> accessed 13 June 2015; 117 cases by the United States, WTO, 'United States and the WTO', <http://www.wto.org/english/thewto_e/countries_e/usa_e.htm> accessed 16 March 2016.

[76] It is telling that the most recent NAFTA Chapter 20 (state-to-state) dispute was decided on 6 February 2011, more than thirteen years ago, while various WTO decisions in which two or more of the NAFTA parties were claimants or respondents before the WTO are common. Panel Report, *United State—Final Anti-dumping Measures on Stainless Steel from Mexico*, WT/DS344/RW

resolved by the TTIP dispute resolution mechanism because they concern issues that are not included in the WTO Agreements. This, as we mentioned in the introduction, may prompt a new situation of fragmentation of international trade law decisions. Finally, some may wonder if cases between two close trading partners and allies are even likely to arise. The frequency of trade disputes between these two close trading partners in the WTO's dispute settlement body suggests that there will be many disputes under the TTIP, whether they are resolved under the WTO or TTIP mechanisms. The softwood–lumber dispute is probably the prime example that the best of friends (Canada and the United States) can so passionately disagree over thirty years in pursuing a dispute that has resulted in a wide range of different types of international cases brought in the WTO, NAFTA, and the LCIA.[77]

V. New Regulatory Frontiers

Discourses relating to regulatory coherence and the setting of unilateral standards are quite different to the discourses relating to the issue of regulatory coherence. Unilateral standards are different in that they relate to areas neither side has regulated—often with the excuse or explanation that it cannot be regulated domestically without being coupled with a ban on imports because otherwise cheap imports will out-compete the more expensive EU or US products (now more expensive production due to certain processes or production methods being outlawed). The consequence for the discourse is thus often that where regulatory coherence concerns standards and procedures already in place where the difference mostly serves as an extra cost for companies doing business in both the European Union and the United States, setting new standards in previously unregulated areas or heightening such standards are met with applause from the NGOs advocating higher standards, but with much scepticism from industry, which will face the extra economic burden in meeting new standards.

It is, however, very timely to investigate exactly those new frontiers and new standards, scrutinize the resistance behind them, and urge governments to seize the historic opportunities at hand. As the former Danish Minister for Trade, Nick Hækkerup, said at the opening of the Copenhagen Centre for Commercial Law (CCCL) in September 2013, the European Union and the United States are facing

(circulated 6 May 2013); Appellate Body Report, *United States—Certain Country of Origin Labelling Requirements* (Canada, Mexico), WT/DS384, 386/AB/R (adopted 23 July 2012).

[77] None of the post-1995 softwood lumber cases were referred to NAFTA's Chapter 20, but either to the DSB or to NAFTA's unique Chapter 19 (which does not exist in any subsequent US, Canada, or Mexican free trade agreement). Under the 2006 Softwood Lumber Agreement, disputes were referred to the London Court of International Arbitration, excluding both NAFTA and the WTO mechanisms. 'Softwood Lumber Agreement between the Government of Canada and the Government of the United States of America' (12 September 2006), art XIV <http://www.treaty-accord.gc.ca/text-texte.aspx?id=105072&lang=eng> accessed 16 March 2016.

a historic opportunity to make a real impact on regulating international trade. Most likely the two economic superpowers will not have that same opportunity in twenty years, or even ten years—not because they cannot reopen negotiations then, but because they may well have been surpassed economically by countries like China, if not India, Indonesia, and Brazil. This chapter thus has focused on the opportunities the European Union and the United States have *at present*—and aims to inspire both governments in thinking out of the box and being ambitious. Whilst much effort is spent on the differences in culture and approach between the European Union and the United States as in the approach to risk and new technologies in food production, quite a lot less time is spent on the common ground shared. Common ground could, for example, be the high ambitions in the environmental area where the EU and US efforts, for example, are more comparable than those of the BRIC countries, Africa, Asia, or South America. Another area could be animal welfare, where the recent *EU—Seal Products* case[78] illustrates that animal welfare is a policy that justifies trade barriers, which may give rise to more animal welfare trade barriers—often driven by consumer and NGO demands. Yet another area is climate change. In these areas, the European Union and the United States could probably raise the standards world-wide by acting together, but only if they do so soon, a development that seems unlikely given current opposition in the US Congress and business community. Without such action, it will likely be up to the BRIC countries to set such standards, or to block them, in five to ten or twenty years.

The first question is therefore; why wait? The second is whether the United States and the European Union dare to wait, because although the text book example will tell us that by raising the standard of living, the middle class will eventually raise the awareness of environmental degradation and animal welfare issues, how do we actually know it will happen (in the rest of world, where such action thus could come from—for example, from China, who is now adopting quite strong environmental regulations[79] and is perhaps less hesitant in adopting unilateral rules compared to the European Union and the United States)—and in time to prevent global environmental catastrophe? What obviously speaks *for* such developments happening outside classical 'Western societies' are the numerous examples surfacing: from the legislation on cage-free hens in egg production in Taiwan[80] (and, perhaps surprisingly in the very 'red' state of Arizona), to the increasingly rapidly rising environmental ambitions in China—perhaps catalysed by the suffocating and deadly pollution problems in China's big cities. So the real question may be whether, in a world lacking multilateral solutions for a multitude

[78] Appellate Body Reports, *European Communities—Measures Prohibiting the Importation and Marketing of Seal Products*, WT/DS400, 401/AB/R (circulated 22 May 2014).

[79] Jonathan Kaiman, 'China Strengthens Environmental Laws' (The Guardian, 25 April 2014) <http://www.theguardian.com/environment/2014/apr/25/china-strengthens-environmental-laws-polluting-factories> accessed 12 March 2016.

[80] 'Taiwan Launches New Guidelines for Welfare in Egg Production' (*Animal Welfare and Trade*) <http://animalwelfareandtrade.com/taiwan-launches-new-guidelines-for-welfare-in-egg-production> accessed 12 March 2016.

of environmental, climate, and animal welfare problems, the European Union and the United States, which are in theory at least the most capable ones, will charge ahead and essentially set the standards for the rest of the world, or whether the two jurisdictions will pass because reaching agreement is too difficult politically.

A. Types of measures

Trade measures can be designed in many ways, but if one adheres to the traditional categories of bans, product-related process and production methods (PR–PPM), and non-product-related process and production methods (NPR–PPM), then a multitude of issues can be illustrated.

If the European Union and the United States, for example, agreed to ban certain types of pesticides within their combined territories, this would be a relatively uncontroversial trade ban, not running a major risk of being inconsistent with any of the tests in Article XX of the GATT.[81] However, the next problem that arises is that, if other countries still produce fruits, vegetables, and grains with the usage of pesticides, they may have a competitive advantage in that they may yield more produce and thus have an unfair competitive advantage vis-à-vis the European Union and the United States if that type of production method is banned. The question is thus: should the internal ban of pesticides be coupled with a PPM banning imports of fruits, vegetables, and grains that are produced with the usage of pesticides? And should this ban be extended to processed foods, such as cookies, pizzas, tomato sauce, etc., which contain ingredients produced with the usage of pesticides? The point is here that if the European Union and the United States did take such steps acting jointly, the effect would be massive, as they are the largest importers in the world of consumer goods, including foodstuffs.

[81] For an analysis of a total ban in relation to art XX of the GATT, see Laura Nielsen, *The WTO, Animals and PPMs* (Brill 2007).

23

Regulatory Co-operation and Regulatory Coherence through Mega-FTAs: Possibilities and Challenges

*Junji Nakagawa**

I. Introduction

In his review of my book, International Harmonization of Economic Regulation,[1] Professor Matsushita adequately pointed out that the book lacked the analysis of international harmonization of economic regulation through free trade agreements (FTAs).[2] This chapter addresses this issue by focusing on the provisions of recent mega-FTAs on regulatory co-operation, including regulatory harmonization, and on regulatory coherence.

Regulatory co-operation and regulatory coherence are two distinct terms that refer to different types of arrangements on domestic regulation, though there are no commonly accepted definitions. So as to avoid misunderstanding, this chapter adopts the following definitions. The term 'regulatory co-operation' refers to the process of interaction *between* national regulators to deal with regulatory diversity among them. It aims to achieve a variety of goals, from something as simple as information sharing to something more substantial such as mutual recognition, equivalence arrangement, and regulatory harmonization.[3] It also takes a variety

* Professor of International Economic Law, Institute of Social Science, University of Tokyo.

[1] Junji Nakagawa, *Keizai Kisei no Kokusai Teki Chōwa [International Harmonization of Economic Regulation]* (Yuhikaku 2008). An updated and revised translation was published as Junji Nakagawa, *International Harmonization of Economic Regulation* (OUP 2011).

[2] See Mitsuo Matsushita, 'Bunken shōkai, *Keizai Kisei no Kokusai Teki Chōwa* [Book review, *International Harmonization of Economic Regulation*]' (2009) 18 Nippon kokusai keizai hō gakkai nenpō [The Japan Association of International Economic Law annual report] 211–13. More generally, Professor Matsushita also discussed the challenge to regulatory coherence raised by FTAs and suggested an increased role of the WTO Trade Policy Review Mechanism (TPRM). See Julien Chaisse and Mitsuo Matsushita, 'Maintaining the WTO's Supremacy in the International Trade Order: A Proposal to Refine and Revise the Role of the Trade Policy Review Mechanism' (2013) 16 J Intl Econ L 9–36.

[3] See US Chamber of Commerce, 'Regulatory Coherence & Cooperation in the Transatlantic Trade and Investment Partnership (TTIP)' (US Chamber of Commerce 2015) 1–2 <https://www.uschamber.

of forms, in some cases through formal intergovernmental agreements, in some cases through international organizations, and in other cases through informal networks of regulators.[4] On the other hand, the term 'regulatory coherence' refers to regulatory practices, transparency, and stakeholder engagement in a *domestic* regulatory process.[5] Accordingly, as a general rule, regulatory coherence needs no international arrangement, though, as will be shown in this chapter, there exist international arrangements that promote, or even oblige, regulatory coherence among the parties.

Trade agreements traditionally took a discreet stance towards domestic regulation of the parties, leaving little room for regulatory co-operation and regulatory coherence. Under the GATT, a contracting party enjoyed a wide range of discretionary power on its domestic regulation insofar as it was applied in a non-discriminatory manner (Article III). Even a domestic regulation that was discriminatory was allowed if it had a legitimate policy objective as enumerated in Article XX. The discreet stance of the GATT towards domestic regulation of contracting parties was modified when the Tokyo Round Agreement on Technical Barriers to Trade (the Standards Code)[6] was adopted. The Standards Code introduced elements of regulatory co-operation and regulatory coherence in the preparation, adoption, and implementation of product standards and conformity assessment. However, their legal effects were limited, still allowing much room for domestic regulation. Under the WTO, regulatory co-operation and regulatory coherence were enhanced in the field of product standards and conformity assessment, and a different set of elements for regulatory co-operation and regulatory coherence were introduced in the field of food safety standards. WTO also introduced elements of regulatory co-operation and regulatory coherence on intellectual property rights and domestic regulation of services. However, their legal effects are still limited, and WTO Members have a wide range of discretion in the exercise of their right to regulate.

While multilateral trade agreements took a discreet stance towards domestic regulation of the parties, national governments conducted regulatory co-operation and regulatory coherence outside the framework of trade agreements through multilateral/regional fora such as the Organization for Economic Co-operation and Development (OECD) and the Asia-Pacific Economic Co-operation (APEC),[7]

com/sites/default/files/regulatory_coherence_regulatory_cooperation_-chamber_ttip_paper_-_final_3-02.pdf> accessed 23 April 2016; Committee on Technical Barriers to Trade, *Regulatory Cooperation Between Members: Background Note by the Secretariat*, G/TBT/W/340, 7 September 2011, 2–3.

[4] For a comprehensive catalogue of the forms and methods of international regulatory co-operation, see OECD, *International Regulatory Co-operation: Addressing Global Challenges* (OECD 2013) 22–43.

[5] See US Chamber of Commerce (n 3) 1.

[6] The text of the Standards Code is available at 'Agreement on Technical Barriers to Trade' <https://www.wto.org/english/docs_e/legal_e/tokyo_tbt_e.pdf> accessed 23 April 2016.

[7] A notable example was APEC–OECD, 'Integrated Checklist on Regulatory Reform: A Policy Instrument for Regulatory Quality, Competition Policy and Market Openness' (APEC–OECD 2005) <http://www.oecd.org/regreform/34989455.pdf> accessed 23 April 2016.

through bilateral arrangements,[8] or even unilaterally.[9] Trade agreements and regulatory co-operation and regulatory coherence were, therefore, separate groups of international arrangements until fairly recently.

As a consequence of the substantive tariff reductions and the elimination of quantitative restrictions, however, recent FTAs address non-tariff measures (NTMs) as a focal point of trade and investment liberalization. As NTMs often take the form of domestic regulation,[10] FTAs came to address such NTMs through regulatory co-operation and regulatory coherence. This trend was intensified during the last decade, as the Doha Round of multilateral negotiations was stalled and major trading countries sought opportunities for further trade and investment liberalization/facilitation and trade- and investment-related rule making with like-minded trading partners.[11] Mega-FTAs, such as the Trans-Pacific Partnership (TPP) and the Transatlantic Trade and Investment Partnership (TTIP), are at the forefront of this trend, as they intend to achieve high-level regulatory co-operation and regulatory coherence on a broad range of subject matters.

Regulatory co-operation and regulatory coherence through FTAs, notably through mega-FTAs, have both possibilities and challenges for the parties. On the one hand, they may be effective in addressing regulatory barriers to international trade and investment. They may also be effective in making domestic regulations of the parties more effective, efficient, and transparent. On the other hand, they may impede the achievement of legitimate regulatory objectives of the parties such as environmental protection, consumer safety, or human rights protection. They may also result in the fragmentation of domestic regulations, as different elements of regulatory co-operation and regulatory coherence in different FTAs are likely to produce different regulatory outcomes among the parties.

This chapter deals with these possibilities and challenges of regulatory co-operation and regulatory coherence through mega-FTAs, and seeks effective ways to enhance such possibilities, while avoiding negative outcomes of regulatory co-operation and regulatory coherence. Section II briefly reviews regulatory co-operation and regulatory coherence under the GATT and the WTO. Section III

[8] For instance, Japan conducted a series of regular dialogues on regulatory co-operation and regulatory coherence, under various names, with the EC since 1994 and with the United States since 1997, respectively. See Junji Nakagawa, 'Regulatory/Systemic Reforms for Maintaining/Enhancing Competitiveness: The Importance of Developing a Multi-tiered Strategy' in Japan Institute of International Affairs (JIIA) (ed), *Policies Needed to Ensure Japan's International Competitiveness* 113 (JIIA 2012) 117–18.

[9] Regulatory co-operation and regulatory coherence date back to the deregulation efforts in major developed countries in the 1970s and 1980s, which were conducted by individual countries. See ibid 117.

[10] For a comprehensive review of non-tariff measures including domestic regulation, see WTO, 'World Trade Report 2012 Trade and Public Policies: A Closer Look at Non-tariff Measures in the 21st Century' (WTO 2012) 94–133 <https://www.wto.org/english/res_e/booksp_e/anrep_e/world_trade_report12_e.pdf> accessed 23 April 2016.

[11] See, for instance, Debra P Steger, 'Institutions for Regulatory Cooperation in "new Generation" Economic and Trade Agreements' (2012) 38(4) Legal Issues Econ Integration 109; Tracey Epps, 'Regulatory Cooperation and Free Trade Agreements' in Susy Frankel and Meredith Kolsky Lewis (eds), *Trade Agreements at the Crossroads* (Routledge 2014) 141–66.

analyses the elements of regulatory co-operation and regulatory coherence that are being contemplated by mega-FTAs. Section IV elucidates the possibilities and challenges of regulatory co-operation and regulatory coherence through mega-FTAs. Section V concludes.

II. Regulatory Co-operation and Regulatory Coherence Under the GATT and the WTO

A. Regulatory co-operation and regulatory coherence under the GATT

The GATT took a discreet stance towards domestic regulations of the contracting parties, leaving little room for regulatory co-operation and regulatory coherence. Under the GATT, a contracting party enjoyed a wide range of discretionary power on its domestic regulation insofar as it was applied in a non-discriminatory manner (Article III). Even a domestic regulation that was discriminatory was allowed if it had a legitimate policy objective as enumerated in Article XX. Successful rounds of trade negotiations under the GATT substantively reduced tariffs and other border barriers to trade in goods, and the diversity in domestic regulations of the contracting parties surfaced as the major non-tariff barriers to trade. This led to the conclusion of the Standards Code in 1979.

The Standards Code dealt with a specific field of domestic regulation, namely product standards (legally binding 'technical regulations' and non-legally binding 'standards') and conformity assessment. It introduced elements of regulatory co-operation by: (i) requiring parties to base technical regulations or standards on international standards where they exist or their completion is imminent (Article 2.2); (ii) requiring parties to play a full part in the preparation of international standards by international standardizing bodies (Article 2.3); and (iii) requiring parties to accept test results, certificates, or marks of conformity issued by relevant bodies of other parties even when they differ from their own (Article 5.2). It also introduced elements of regulatory coherence by: (i) requiring parties to publish/notify proposed product standards, so that other parties and/or interested parties in other parties may comment on them (Article 2.5); (ii) requiring parties to promptly publish product standards that have been adopted (Article 2.7); and (iii) requiring parties to allow a reasonable period of time between the publication of a technical regulation and its entry into force (Article 2.8). Several procedural requirements on conformity assessment (Articles 5.1.2–5.1.6) were also intended to enhance regulatory coherence on conformity assessment.

Although these provisions were intended to control the parties' right to regulate in the field of product standards and conformity assessment, their legal effects were limited and the parties could maintain a wide range of regulatory space under these provisions. First of all, the requirement of international harmonization allowed the parties to deviate therefrom for such reasons as national security requirements, the prevention of deceptive practices, protection of human health, or safety (Article 2.2). Second, regarding the degree of conformity with international standards, there was no obligation *to adhere to* international standards. Instead, the parties were required *to use them as a basis* when formulating their own technical regulations and standards (Article 2.2). Third, the requirement to play a full part in the preparation of international standards under Article 2.3 is not a legal requirement but a hortative, best-effort encouragement, conditioned by such considerations as resource limitations. Fourth, the requirement to accept the results of conformity assessment issued by relevant bodies of other parties, even when they differ from their own, is conditional on the self-assessment of equivalence by the importing parties (Article 5.2, first sentence, proviso). Fifth, the requirements on regulatory coherence under Articles 2.5 and 2.8 may be omitted where urgent problems of safety, health, environmental protection, or national security arise or threaten to arise for the party (Article 2.6). Last but not least, the Code was a plurilateral agreement and was binding only the contracting parties of the GATT who accepted it. By the end of the GATT, only thirty-four contracting parties were the parties to the Code.

B. Regulatory co-operation and regulatory coherence under the WTO

The TBT Agreement built on the elements of regulatory co-operation and regulatory coherence of the Standards Code. On regulatory co-operation, Articles 2.4 and 2.6 of the TBT Agreement succeed Articles 2.2 and 2.3 of the Standards Code, respectively, and set out basically similar requirements on technical regulations.[12] Article 2.7 of the TBT Agreement succeeds Article 5.2 of the Standards Code on technical regulations.[13] On regulatory coherence, Articles 2.9–2.12 of the TBT Agreement almost literally succeed Articles 2.5–2.8 of the Standards Code. Article 5.2 of the TBT Agreement succeeds and elaborates on procedural requirements of the Standards Code (Articles 5.1.2–5.1.6). In contrast to the Standards Code, the TBT Agreement is one of the multilateral agreements of the WTO and is applicable to all the Members of the WTO.

On sanitary and phytosanitary measures (SPS measures)[14] applied to imported products, the WTO Agreement on Sanitary and Phytosanitary Measures (the SPS Agreement) adopts elements of regulatory co-operation and regulatory coherence that are basically similar to those under the TBT Agreement. On regulatory co-operation, Article 3.1 requires Members to base their SPS measures on international standards, guidelines or recommendations, where they exist.

[12] Similar requirements are applied to standards under sections F and G of the Code of Good Practice for the Preparation, Adoption, and Application of Standards (Annex 3 to the TBT Agreement), and to conformity assessments under arts 5.4 and 5.5 of the TBT Agreement, respectively.

[13] Similar requirements are applied for conformity assessment under art 6.1 of the TBT Agreement but they are not applied for standards.

[14] For the definition of SPS measures, see WTO Agreement on the Application of Sanitary and Phytosanitary Measures (the SPS Agreement), 1867 UNTS 493, 15 April 1994, Annex A, s 1.

Article 3.3 requires Members to play a full part in the relevant international organizations for international harmonization of standards, guidelines, and recommendations. Finally, Article 4.1 requires Members to accept SPS measures of other Members as equivalent, even if these measures differ from their own, if the exporting Member objectively demonstrates to the importing Member that its measures achieve the importing Member's appropriate level of SPS protection. On regulatory coherence, Annex B of the SPS Agreement provides detailed rules for securing transparency of SPS regulations, paraphrasing the elements of regulatory coherence under Articles 2.9–2.12 of the TBT Agreement. Annex C provides for procedural requirements in the operation of control, inspection, and approval procedures, which will enhance the transparency and speediness of the procedures.

To the extent that these elements of regulatory co-operation and regulatory coherence under the TBT and SPS Agreements succeed those of the Standards Code, their legal effects are limited. In practice, however, the WTO has increasingly recognized the importance of regulatory co-operation and regulatory coherence in these fields, and has intensified its effort in elaborating on substantive and procedural requirements for these purposes. Two types of activities are worth mentioning. First, the WTO Committees on Technical Barriers to Trade (the TBT Committee) and on Sanitary and Phytosanitary Measures (the SPS Committee) have developed recommendations, decisions, and principles that are aimed at facilitating Members' implementation of the TBT and SPS Agreements. For instance, the SPS and TBT Committees have agreed that the time for comments on draft regulations should be at least sixty days.[15] A more general guidance is the 2000 Decision of the TBT Committee on Principles for the Development of International Standards, Guides, and Recommendations with Relation to Articles 2, 5, and Annex 3 of the TBT Agreement.[16] Although these are not agreed amendments to the TBT and SPS Agreements, they are adopted by consensus by WTO Members and form part of the WTO *acquis* on regulatory co-operation and regulatory coherence.[17]

Second, the TBT and SPS Committees are acting as a forum to address trade issues on account of SPS measures, product standards, and conformity assessment, referred to as 'Specific Trade Concerns' (STCs). Most STCs relate to measures that have been notified by Members as required by Article 2.9.2 of the TBT Agreement and Section 5(b) of the Annex B to the SPS Agreement, respectively. As the measures under discussion are generally in draft form, there

[15] For TBT, Committee on Technical Barriers to Trade, *Decisions and Recommendations Adopted by the Committee Since 1 January 1995*, G/TBT/1/Rev.12, 21 January 2015, 23; and for SPS, Committee on Sanitary and Phytosanitary Measures, *Recommended Procedures for Implementing the Transparency Obligations of the SPS Agreement (art 7)*, G/SPS/7/Rev.3, 20 June 2008, 3.

[16] The text of the Decision is available at Committee on Technical Barriers to Trade, *Decisions and Recommendations Adopted by the Committee Since 1 January 1995*, G/TBT/1/Rev.2, 6 November 1995, 47–49.

[17] See Eric Wijkström, 'The Third Pillar: Behind the Scenes, WTO Committee Work Delivers' (2015) E15 Task Force on Regulatory Systems Coherence Think Piece, 3 <http://e15initiative.org/wp-content/uploads/2015/07/E15-Regulatory-Wijkstrom-final.pdf> accessed 23 April 2016.

is still time for the measure to be amended prior to entry into force. Discussions offer an opportunity for peer review that helps align Members' national practices. STC procedures have, therefore, contributed to the enhancement of the elements of regulatory co-operation and regulatory coherence of the TBT and SPS Agreements.[18]

Judging from these, the requirements of regulatory co-operation and regulatory coherence under the TBT Agreement and the SPS Agreement are fairly modest, leaving each Member much room for discretionally determining the pace, extent, or the content of regulatory co-operation in standards and accreditation.[19]

Besides the TBT and SPS Agreements, the WTO expanded the subject matter of regulatory co-operation and regulatory coherence to cover intellectual property rights and domestic regulations on services.

The Agreement on Trade Related Aspects of Intellectual Property Rights (the TRIPS Agreement) advanced international harmonization of intellectual property rights through the method of setting international minimum standards (Article 1.1).[20] The Agreement incorporated several multilateral conventions for the protection of intellectual property rights as the basis of the international minimum standards, including the Paris Convention for the Protection of Industrial Property (Article 2.1) and the Berne Convention for the Protection of Literary and Artistic Works (Article 9.1). It also set international minimum standards on intellectual property rights that were not covered by existing international conventions, such as copyright protection for computer programs and compilations of data (Article 10) or geographical indications for wines and spirits (Article 23). On regulatory coherence, Part III of the TRIPS Agreement prescribed detailed legal obligations for the enforcement of intellectual property rights in Members' domestic legal systems.

The GATS introduced elements of regulatory co-operation and regulatory coherence in the field of domestic regulation on trade in services, but they were weaker than those for trade in goods. Article VII of the GATS provides that a Member may recognize education obtained, requirements met, licences, or certifications granted in a particular country for the fulfilment of its standards or criteria for the authorization, licensing, or certification of services suppliers. The

[18] See Erik Wijkström and Devin McDaniels, 'International Standards and the WTO TBT Agreement: Improving Governance for Regulatory Alignment' (2013) WTO Economic Research and Statistics Division, Staff Working Paper ERSD-2013-6, 5–10 <https://www.wto.org/english/res_e/reser_e/ersd201306_e.pdf> accessed 23 April 2016.

[19] As Joel Trachtman points out:

> WTO legal standards, including requirements to treat foreign products in a non-discriminatory way, requirements that national product standards be designed in such a way as to achieve their regulatory goal in the least trade restrictive way possible, and even including the requirement for a scientific basis as applied to sanitary and phytosanitary standards, have been carefully designed, and have been applied, only to smoke out protectionism, and to leave non-protectionist national regulation unrestricted.

Joel P Trachtman, *Trade Law, Domestic Regulation and Development* (World Scientific 2015) xiv.

[20] Art 1.1 of the TRIPS Agreement provides that members may implement in their law more extensive protection than is required by the Agreement.

legal effect of this provision is limited as it encourages, not obliges, Members to conduct such recognition. The GATS also leaves Members a lot of room for the selection of the methods for such recognition, including harmonization, agreement, or arrangement with the country concerned, or autonomous recognition (Article VII.1, second sentence).

General discipline of the GATS on domestic regulation (Article VI) contains little element of regulatory co-operation and regulatory coherence, except that Article VI.5(b) requires that, in determining whether a Member is in conformity with its obligation under Article VI.5(a), account shall be taken of international standards applied by that Member. The same article provides for a general requirement on regulatory coherence, to the effect that each Member shall ensure that all measures of general application affecting trade in services are administered 'in a reasonable, objective and impartial manner'. The legal effect of these obligations is also limited, as they are obligations only applicable to Members' specific commitments, and the application of international standards is not a requirement but solely a factor to be taken into account in determining the conformity of the Member's obligation under Article VI.5(a).[21]

On the other hand, the WTO Council for Trade in Services (the GATS Council) has developed guidelines that elaborate on the provisions of the GATS on domestic regulation in a specific sector, namely accountancy service. Article VI.4 of the GATS calls on the GATS Council to develop necessary disciplines so as to ensure that measures relating to qualification/licensing requirements do not constitute unnecessary barriers to trade in services. Pursuant to this article, the Uruguay Round Decision on Professional Services called for the establishment of a Working Party on Professional Services, setting work in the accountancy sector of professional services as a priority.[22] In May 1997, the GATS Council adopted Guidelines for Mutual Recognition Agreements or Arrangements in the Accountancy Sector[23] as a practical guidance for governments or other entities entering into mutual recognition negotiations on accountancy services. In December 1998, the GATS Council adopted Disciplines on Domestic Regulation in the Accountancy Sector,[24] elaborating on the provisions of the GATS on domestic regulation.

To sum up, the WTO built on the elements of regulatory co-operation and regulatory coherence contained in the Standards Code and introduced elements of regulatory co-operation and regulatory coherence in intellectual property rights and trade in services. Though there have been developments to enhance regulatory co-operation and regulatory coherence in the covered area of domestic regulation since the inception of the WTO, it still maintains the generally prudent stance of

[21] See Joel P Trachtman, 'Mutual Recognition of Services Regulation at the WTO' in Aik Hoe Lim and Bart de Meester (eds), *WTO Domestic Regulation and Services Trade: Putting Principles into Practice* 110 (CUP 2014) 116–19.

[22] WTO, *Decision on Professional Services*, S/L/3, 4 April 1995, s 2.

[23] Council for Trade in Services, *Guidelines for Mutual Recognition Agreements or Arrangements in the Accountancy Sector*, S/L/38, adopted 28 May 199.

[24] WTO, *Disciplines on Domestic Regulation in the Accountancy Sector*, S/L/64 adopted 14 December 1998.

its predecessor towards domestic regulation of Members, leaving still limited room for regulatory co-operation and regulatory coherence.

III. Regulatory Co-operation and Regulatory Coherence through Mega-FTAs

Recent FTAs, in particular mega-FTAs, put much emphasis on regulatory co-operation and regulatory coherence. Before analysing the possible contents of mega-FTAs on regulatory co-operation and regulatory coherence, it is appropriate to analyse the contents of regional trade agreements (RTAs) seeking a single market on regulatory co-operation, as they, by definition, need to achieve a high level of regulatory co-operation so as to form a single market. On the other hand, these RTAs put less emphasis on regulatory coherence, as the latter is not necessarily required in forming a single market.

A. Regulatory co-operation through RTAs seeking a single market

RTAs that seek a single market need to achieve a high level of regulatory co-operation. The European Union is a good example. Harmonization and mutual recognition of domestic regulations within the European Union are key elements of the single market programme for promoting the free circulation of goods, capital, people, and services within the European Union.[25] The European Union has adopted a similar method of regulatory co-operation in its trade agreements with EU membership candidate countries (the so-called Stabilization and Association Agreements (SAAs)), but they promote gradual approximation of the laws of candidate countries with those of the European Union, or *acquis communautaire*.[26] For instance, the SAA between the European Community and its Member States and the former Yugoslav Republic of Macedonia[27] provides that the latter shall endeavour to ensure that its laws will be gradually made compatible with those of the Community (Article 68.1). The coverage of the laws to be approximated is wide, extending to certain fundamental elements of *acquis communautaire*, as well

[25] See Department of Business, Information and Skills, the Government of the United Kingdom (BIS), 'Regulatory Cooperation' (2011) Trade and Investment Analytical Papers Topic 17 of 18, 6 <https://www.gov.uk/government/uploads/system/uploads/attachment_data/file/32467/12-533-regulatory-cooperation.pdf> accessed 23 April 2016.

[26] On the other hand, the European Union favours convergence towards international standards in FTAs with countries that are not affected by the EU enlargement. See Caroline Lesser, 'Do Bilateral and Regional Approaches for Reducing Technical Barriers to Trade Converge Towards the Multilateral Trading System?' (2007) OECD Trade Policy Working Paper No 58, 29 <http://www.oecd.org/tad/ntm/39711550.pdf> accessed 23 April 2016.

[27] Stabilisation and Association Agreement between the European Communities and their Member States, of the one part, and the former Yugoslav Republic of Macedonia of the other part, [2004] OJ L84/13.

as to other trade-related areas, along a programme to be defined in co-ordination with the European Commission, including competition law, intellectual property law, standards and certification law, public procurement law, and data protection law (Article 68.3).

Another example of intensive regulatory co-operation through RTAs seeking a single market is the Australia–New Zealand Closer Economic Relations Trade Agreement (ANZCERTA).[28] Originally entered into force in 1983, the ANZCERTA promoted the formation of a single market by a series of subsequent agreements that promoted intensive regulatory co-operation, including systems for joint accreditation and harmonization,[29] establishment of joint regulatory agencies,[30] and mutual recognition arrangements.[31] In contrast to regulatory co-operation under the European Union, regulatory co-operation under the ANZCERTA is limited in its coverage, focusing on product standards and accreditation. On the other hand, it is more intensive than the one under the WTO TBT and SPS Agreements, as it entails institutional arrangements for regulatory co-operation. These two examples offer one lesson for regulatory co-operation through mega-FTAs, namely that merely setting substantive and procedural rules is not enough for regulatory co-operation. Rather, the design of institutional structure is critical to the success of regulatory co-operation.[32]

B. Regulatory co-operation and regulatory coherence through mega-FTAs

While regulatory co-operation through RTAs seeking a single market is wide in its subject-matter coverage and intensive in its form and method, regulatory co-operation through FTAs has been less ambitious. First of all, the coverage of regulatory co-operation has mostly been limited to product standards and accreditation. Second, most FTAs reaffirm the rights and obligations of the parties under the WTO TBT and SPS Agreements, with no institutional arrangements

[28] Australia New Zealand Closer Economic Relations Trade Agreement (ANZCERTA), 28 March 1983, entered into force 1 January 1983 <http://dfat.gov.au/trade/agreements/anzcerta/Documents/anzcerta1.pdf> accessed 23 April 2016.

[29] In the area of food standards, the Australia–New Zealand Food Authority (ANZFA) was established as a result of the 1995 Agreement on Establishing a System for Development of Joint Food Standards, which led to the adoption of a joint Australia–New Zealand Food Standards Code in 1999. See 'Food Standards Australia New Zealand' <http://www.foodstandards.gov.au/Pages/default.aspx> accessed 12 March 2016.

[30] The Joint Accreditation System of Australia and New Zealand (JAS–ANZ), established in 1991, provides for a harmonized approach to auditing and certification of quality management systems on the basis of international standards. See 'Joint Accreditation System of Australia and New Zealand' <http://www.jas-anz.com.au/> accessed 12 March 2016.

[31] The Trans-Tasman Mutual Recognition Arrangement of 1996 (TTMRA), signed on 14 June 1996 and entered into force on 1 May 1998, provided for mutual recognition of product standards and occupational qualifications. See 'The Trans-Tasman Mutual Recognition Arrangement' (Council of Australian Governments) <https://www.coag.gov.au/the_trans-tasman_mutual_recognition_arrangement> accessed 12 March 2016.

[32] See Steger (n 11).

for regulatory co-operation other than regular information exchange and consultation.[33]

Some FTAs contain additional provisions for enhanced regulatory co-operation, such as specific provisions on mutual recognition or product-specific arrangements for regulatory co-operation. An example of the former is Chapter 6 of the Japan–Singapore Economic Partnership Agreement (EPA)[34] that provides for the mutual recognition of conformity assessments. It allows for the mutual acceptance of the results of conformity assessments conducted by a body designated by the government of the exporting country, based on the criteria and procedures of the importing country, as providing the same assurance as the conformity assessment conducted within the importing country. It applies to electronic products, communication terminal equipment, and wireless devices.[35] An example of the latter is Article 9.4 of the US–Korea FTA[36] that provides for enhanced co-operation on regulatory issues in automobiles, such as transparency, the promotion of good regulatory practices, alignment with international standards, and use of accreditation to qualify conformity assessment bodies for specific issues or sectors. An Automotive Working Group was established so as to facilitate, among other things, enhanced co-operation in developing, implementing, and enforcing relevant standards, technical regulations, and conformity assessment procedures.[37]

Mega-FTAs under negotiation, in particular the TPP and TTIP, are expected to contemplate elements of regulatory co-operation that are wider in coverage and more intensive in method than the aforementioned FTAs. These mega-FTAs are also expected to contemplate elements of regulatory coherence with wide subject-matter coverage and intensity in its form and method. Although they are under negotiation and their final texts are not available, some of the negotiating texts are publicly available, as they are either officially disclosed or leaked to the public. In this section, the following two documents are taken up so as to forecast the final result of the TPP and TTIP negotiations on regulatory co-operation and regulatory coherence: the leaked draft text of the TPP chapter on regulatory coherence, and the European Union's revised TTIP negotiating text on regulatory co-operation and regulatory coherence.

1. *TTP negotiating text on regulatory coherence*

Regulatory coherence was one of the four cross-cutting issues that the United States intended to introduce in the TPP as a model of 'trade agreement for the 21st

[33] See Lesser (n 26).

[34] The Japan–Singapore Economic Partnership Agreement (Japan–Singapore EPA), 13 January 2002, entered into force 30 November 2002 <http://www.mofa.go.jp/region/asia-paci/singapore/jsepa.html> accessed 12 March 2016.

[35] See ibid Annex III.

[36] Free Trade Agreement between the United States of America and the Republic of Korea (US–Korea FTA), 30 June 2007, revised 15 March 2012 <https://ustr.gov/trade-agreements/free-trade-agreements/korus-fta/final-text> accessed 23 April 2016.

[37] ibid Annex 9-B, art 2(b).

century'.[38] The United States submitted its draft chapter on regulatory coherence at the sixth round of the TPP negotiation in March/April 2011.[39] The draft chapter was leaked to selected media later in 2011.[40] It is reported that, after several rounds of negotiation, the parties have reached agreement on the final text of the chapter on regulatory coherence.[41] As the finalized text has not been made public, the rest of this section will forecast its content based on the leaked draft chapter.

The draft chapter on regulatory coherence consists of nine articles.[42] The two major elements of the draft chapter on regulatory coherence are the establishment of a central regulatory co-ordinating mechanism to help limit duplication and conflicting regulatory actions among domestic ministries (Article 2), and the conduct of regulatory impact assessments (RIAs) in reviewing new regulatory measures that exceed a threshold of economic impact established by the party, as among the implementation of core good regulatory practices (Article 3). The former is closely modelled on the US Office of Information and Regulatory Affairs,[43] and the provisions of the latter reflect the good regulatory practices outlined in the APEC–OECD Integrated Checklist on Regulatory Reform.[44]

Perhaps partly due to the resistance of US regulators against allowing their domestic responsibilities to be subject to increased restrictions in international trade agreements, and partly in consideration of the concern of US civil society groups and other TPP members, the legal effect of these elements of regulatory coherence is limited.[45] First, the institutional details of central co-ordinating mechanisms will be left to each TPP party. Article 2.2 admits that 'the design, scope of authority, and institutional location of national coordinating bodies or other appropriate processes or mechanisms will vary depending on their respective national

[38] See Office of the United States Trade Representative, Letters of US Trade Representative Ron Kirk to Speaker of the House Nancy Pelosi and Senate President Pro Tempore Robert Byrd, dated 14 December 2009. Trans-Pacific Partnership Announcement (Office of the United States Trade Representative 2009) <http://www.sice.oas.org/whatsnew_pending/TTP_Congress_e.pdf> accessed 23 April 2016.

[39] 'USTR Tables Text on Regulatory Coherence in Sixth TPP Round, Reports "Significant Progress"' (*Inside US Trade*, 1 April 2011), World Trade Online database <http://insidetrade.com> accessed 23 April 2016.

[40] See US Proposal for Regulatory Coherence Chapter, March 2011. Trans-Pacific Partnership (TPP) Regulatory Coherence, 4 March 2010 <http://www.citizenstrade.org/ctc/wp-content/uploads/2011/10/TransPacificRegulatoryCoherence.pdf> accessed 23 April 2016.

[41] 'Chilean Official Says Six of More Than 20 TPP Chapters Closed Thus Far' 31(35) (*Inside US Trade*, 2013), World Trade Online database <http://insidetrade.com> accessed 23 April 2016.

[42] The titles of the articles are as follows: art 1: General provisions; art 2: Establishment of central co-ordination and review processes or mechanisms, including national coordinating bodies; art 3: Implementation of core good regulatory practices; art 4: Sectoral approaches; art 5: Institutional framework; art 6: Engagement with interested persons; art 7: Definitions; art 8: Dispute settlement; art 9: Confidentiality.

[43] See Thomas A Bollyky, 'Regulatory Coherence in the TPP Talks' in C L Lim and others (eds), *The Trans-Pacific Partnership: A Quest for a Twenty-first-century Trade Agreement* 171 (CUP 2012) 181.

[44] See, in particular, APEC–OECD (n 7) 15–17, 19.

[45] See Bollyky, 'Regulatory Coherence in the TPP Talks' (n 43) 182–83.

circumstances (including differences in levels of development and political and institutional structures)'. Second, the conduct of RIAs is a best-effort encouragement for TPP parties when their domestic regulatory authorities develop new regulatory measures. Third, application of the TPP state-to-state dispute settlement procedure is limited to the obligation to have 'processes or mechanisms to facilitate central coordination and review of certain new regulatory measures' (Article 8).

While the legal effects of the elements of regulatory coherence in the TPP draft chapter are limited, the chapter establishes an institutional structure for continuous monitoring and peer review of the implementation and operation of the chapter (Article 5). The Committee on Regulatory Coherence shall convene within one year after the entry into force of the TPP, and at least once every year or every two years thereafter. It will consider issues associated with implementation and operation of the chapter and identify future priorities for co-operative activities related to regulatory coherence among the parties (Article 5.1). Through the Committee, the parties' implementation of the provisions of the chapter, including the establishment of a central co-ordinating mechanisms and the conduct of RIAs, will be continuously monitored and reviewed, so that these provisions may be implemented in incremental steps.

2. *The European Union's revised TTIP negotiating text on regulatory co-operation and regulatory coherence*

The final report of the High Level Working Group on Jobs and Growth of 11 February 2013,[46] which supported the commencement of the TTIP negotiation, refers to five basic components of TTIP provisions on regulatory issues: (i) the SPS plus component; and (ii) the TBT plus component, both of which would build on the key principles of the WTO SPS and TBT Agreements; (iii) sectoral annexes containing commitments for regulatory co-operation for specific goods and services sectors; (iv) cross-cutting disciplines on regulatory coherence; and (v) an institutional framework for regulatory co-operation.[47] According to the European Union, the first three components are contained in the respective chapters of the TTIP, namely the SPS chapter, the TBT chapter, and the sectoral annexes to chapters on trade in goods and trade in services. So as to materialize the fourth and the fifth components on regulatory co-operation and regulatory coherence, the European Union tabled its initial negotiating text on regulatory co-operation[48] in the eighth negotiating round of 2–6 February 2015,[49] and tabled the revised text

[46] 'Final Report High Level Working Group on Jobs and Growth' (2013) <http://trade.ec.europa.eu/doclib/docs/2013/february/tradoc_150519.pdf> accessed 23 April 2016.

[47] ibid 4.

[48] The European Union's initial and revised negotiating texts use the term 'regulatory co-operation' to cover both regulatory co-operation and regulatory coherence in the terminology of this chapter.

[49] The initial negotiating text was made public on 10 February 2015. 'EU–US TTIP the Eighth Negotiating Round of 2–6 February 2015' (2015) <http://trade.ec.europa.eu/doclib/docs/2015/february/tradoc_153120.pdf> accessed 23 April 2016.

in the ninth negotiating round of 20–24 April 2015.[50] The revised text adds new provisions related to regulatory co-operation at the non-central level, i.e. by US States and EU Member States.[51]

The revised text consists of three sections. Section I provides for the general objectives and principles of the chapter on regulatory cooperation (Article 1), definitions of the terms (Article 2), and the scope of the chapter (Article 3). The general objectives of the chapter are:

1. to enhance regulatory co-operation thereby facilitating trade and investment, while pursuing a high level of protection in areas such as consumer safety, health, and environment;
2. to reduce unnecessary regulatory requirements affecting trade or investment;
3. to promote an effective, pro-competitive regulatory environment; and
4. to further the development, adoption, and strengthening of international instruments for regulatory co-operation.

Section II sets out three good regulatory practices on how regulations are produced, clarifying the European Union's negotiating position on regulatory coherence. The first is the early information on the planned regulatory acts at central level (Article 5). The second is the consultation with stakeholders in the preparation of regulatory acts at central level (Article 6). The third is the conduct of an impact assessment for planned regulatory acts (RIA) at central level (Article 7).

Section III sets out institutional mechanisms for bilateral regulatory co-operation between the European Union and the United States. The parties establish a bilateral mechanism to support regulatory co-operation between their regulators and competent authorities to (i) foster information exchange; and (ii) seek increased compatibility between their respective regulatory frameworks, where appropriate (Article 8.1). So as to identify priority areas for regulatory co-operation, the parties will prepare an Annual Regulatory Co-operation Programme (Articles 8.2 and 14.2(a)). They will also designate an office to act as a focal point responsible for exchanging information about envisaged and existing regulatory acts (Article 8.3). Detailed provisions are made on information exchange on regulatory acts (Articles 9 and 11) at central and non-central level, respectively, and on the promotion of regulatory compatibility at central level (Article 10).[52] While these provisions aim to enhance *bilateral regulatory co-operation* between the European Union

[50] It was made public on 4 May 2015. 'EU–US TTIP the Ninth Negotiating Round of 20–24 April 2015' (2015) <http://trade.ec.europa.eu/doclib/docs/2015/april/tradoc_153403.pdf> accessed 23 April 2016.

[51] See European Commission, 'Explanatory Note: Publication of the Revised EU Proposal on Regulatory Cooperation in Transatlantic Trade and Investment Partnership (TTIP)' (2015) 2 <http://trade.ec.europa.eu/doclib/docs/2015/may/tradoc_153432.1.1%20Explanatory%20note%20-%20revised%20Regulatory%20cooperation%20EU%20legal%20text.pdf> accessed 23 April 2016.

[52] Promotion of regulatory compatibility at non-central level is not envisioned in the European Union's proposal.

and the United States, Article 13 provides for the promotion of *international regulatory co-operation* by the parties through such means as joint initiatives, proposals, and approaches in international bodies or fora. Finally, the parties establish a Regulatory Co-operation Body (the RCB) in order to monitor and facilitate the implementation of the above provisions of section III on regulatory co-operation (Article 14). The composition of the RCB is provided for under Article 16. Besides the functions enumerated in Article 14.2, the RCB will hold, at least once a year, a meeting open to the participation of stakeholders to exchange views on the Annual Regulatory Co-operation Programme (Article 15.1).

IV. Possibilities and Challenges of Regulatory Co-operation and Regulatory Coherence through Mega-FTAs

As was stated in section I of this chapter, regulatory co-operation and regulatory coherence through mega-FTAs have both possibilities and challenges for the parties. On the one hand, they may be effective in addressing regulatory barriers to international trade and investment. They may also be effective in making domestic regulations of the parties more effective, efficient, and transparent. On the other hand, they may impede the achievement of legitimate regulatory objectives of the parties. They may also result in the fragmentation of domestic regulations, as different elements of regulatory co-operation and regulatory coherence in different FTAs are likely to produce different regulatory outcomes. How feasible will the possibilities of the TPP and the TTIP be? How large will the negative outcomes of regulatory co-operation and regulatory coherence through the TPP and the TTIP be? How are these mega-FTAs designed so as to minimize the possible negative outcomes of regulatory co-operation and regulatory coherence through mega-FTAs?

A. Possibilities of regulatory co-operation and regulatory coherence through mega-FTAs

The first of the two possible positive outcomes of regulatory co-operation and regulatory coherence through mega-FTAs is that they may be effective in addressing regulatory barriers to international trade and investment. This outcome is more likely to result from regulatory co-operation than from regulatory coherence, as the former addresses regulatory diversity among the parties. On the other hand, regulatory coherence is more likely to address the second of the two possible outcomes, namely making domestic regulations of the parties more effective, efficient, and transparent.

In comparison with the provisions of the GATT/WTO on regulatory co-operation and regulatory coherence, provisions of the TPP and the TTIP on regulatory co-operation and regulatory coherence are likely to produce more tangible results on both of these respects. On regulatory co-operation, the European Union's revised TTIP proposal takes a sector-specific approach, as the parties will prepare an Annual Regulatory Co-operation Programme so as to identify priority areas for regulatory co-operation (Articles 8.2 and 13.2(a)). TTIP takes a similar sector-specific approach on trade in goods and services, as it will have sectoral annexes containing commitments for regulatory co-operation for specific goods and services sectors. The TPP is likely to have similar sectoral annexes on specific goods and services sectors, as the TTP negotiating text on regulatory coherence refers to 'sectoral regulatory coherence provisions in other chapters of this Agreement' (Article 4). In contrast to the general wording of the GATT/WTO on regulatory co-operation, the sector-specific approach of these mega-FTAs is intended to produce tangible outcomes on the designated areas of domestic regulation.

On regulatory coherence, the TPP and the TTIP take a different approach. The TPP draft chapter on regulatory coherence is intended to improve the quality of domestic regulatory system *as a whole* by introducing a central regulatory co-ordination mechanism and RIAs. Section II of the European Union's revised TTIP negotiating text on regulatory co-operation is also about good regulatory practices on how regulations are produced, with no subject-matter limitation. Improvement of *general* regulatory coherence in the parties' domestic regulatory system may improve regulatory coherence in *specific* goods and services sectors.

The *real* effect of these provisions depends, of course, on their substantive and procedural content, their legal force (legally binding or non-binding), and on the institutional setting for monitoring and reviewing their implementation. On account of the substantive and procedural contents, most of the provisions of the TPP and TTIP on regulatory co-operation and regulatory coherence are not intended to impose specific obligations on the parties. As most of the provisions of the TPP and the TTIP are legally non-binding, their real effect is minimal *at the outset*. Rather, they are intended to inaugurate institutional mechanisms to monitor and review implementation of the provisions and the parties' commitments on regulatory co-operation and regulatory coherence. On regulatory coherence, the TPP will inaugurate a Committee on Regulatory Coherence, consisting of the representatives of the parties, so as to monitor implementation and operation of the chapter and identify future priorities for co-operative activities related to regulatory coherence among the parties. The Committee will also identify future priorities, including potential sectoral initiatives, for co-operative activities related to regulatory coherence among the parties with respect to obligations under other chapters of the TPP (Article 5.1).

On regulatory co-operation, the European Union's TTIP proposal sets out institutional mechanisms for bilateral regulatory co-operation between the European Union and the United States. The main axis of the mechanisms is a Regulatory Cooperation Body, which will monitor and facilitate the implementation of the provisions of the TTIP on regulatory co-operation. Though little information has been disclosed as to the structure and functions of the Regulatory Cooperation Body, it is likely to build on the existing Transatlantic framework for regulatory co-operation.[53]

[53] See, for instance, Raymond J Ahearn, 'Transatlantic Regulatory Co-operation: Background and Analysis' (2009) Cong Research Serv RL34717.

It is unlikely that the TPP will inaugurate a similar institutional mechanism for regulatory co-operation, except for several sector-specific initiatives to address diversity in product standards and conformity assessment and to address specific service sectors. The challenge is that the TPP is a plurilateral agreement, consisting of twelve countries at different stages of economic development. Even when the TPP countries take a sector-specific approach in regulatory co-operation, they will find it difficult to agree on the specific products or service sectors to take up, and on the methods for regulatory co-operation that will go beyond information exchange and consultation.

To sum up, the TPP and TTIP will inaugurate institutional frameworks for regulatory co-operation and regulatory coherence. Their possible positive effects in addressing regulatory barriers to international trade and investment and in making domestic regulations of the parties more effective, efficient, and transparent will not become evident promptly. Rather, these effects will appear incrementally in the course of the operation of these institutional frameworks.

B. Tackling with possible negative outcomes of regulatory co-operation and regulatory coherence through mega-FTAs

Enhancing regulatory co-operation and regulatory coherence while securing the achievement of legitimate regulatory objectives of the parties is no easy task. The European Union's revised proposal repeatedly refers to the parties' right to regulate for the achievement of legitimate public policy objectives. In particular, Article 1.3 provides that '(t)he provisions of this Chapter do not restrict the right of each Party to maintain, adopt and apply timely measures to achieve legitimate public policy objectives, such as those mentioned in paragraph 1,[54] at the level of protection that it considers appropriate, in accordance with its regulatory framework and principles'. One way of meeting this challenge would be to inaugurate a mechanism for regulatory co-operation that is flexible and transparent enough for the parties to take such legitimate public policy objectives of domestic regulation into account. The European Union's revised proposal offers an example. Under the institutional mechanisms for bilateral regulatory co-operation as set out in section III of the proposed chapter, the parties will inaugurate an information exchange mechanism about the proposed regulatory acts at central level that are likely to have a significant impact on international trade or investment, coined as 'regulatory exchange' (Article 9). When a regulatory exchange has been initiated, a party may propose to the other party a joint examination of possible means of regulatory co-operation on the proposed regulatory act (Article 10.2). The proposal shall be duly substantiated, including the choice of

[54] Art 1.1 provides an illustrative list of legitimate public policy objectives as follows: protection of, inter alia: the environment; consumers; public health, working conditions; social protection and social security; human, animal, and plant life; animal welfare; health and safety; personal data; cybersecurity; cultural diversity; and preserving financial stability.

the method. The party receiving the proposal shall respond to the requesting party without undue delay, and the response should be substantiated (Article 10.3). This mechanism is transparent, as it is triggered by a regulatory exchange and duly substantiated exchanges of requests and responses are required for the start of the joint examination of the possible means of regulatory co-operation. It is also flexible, as the process of regulatory co-operation is conducted on a voluntary basis.

Flexibility and transparency also characterize the institutional design of the TPP negotiating text on regulatory coherence. TPP parties have wide discretion on the design, scope of authority, and institutional location of the central co-ordination bodies (Article 2). Conduct of RIAs is encouraged, not legally mandated (Article 3.1). On the other hand, TPP parties shall notify relevant information regarding their central co-ordination bodies to the Committee on Regulatory Coherence (Article 5.4). This will trigger the discussion of the adequacy of each party's decision on its central co-ordination body, including its justifiability according to the legitimate policy objectives of the party.

The risk of fragmentation of domestic regulations is more salient in regulatory co-operation through mega-FTAs than in regulatory coherence, because the latter deals with the quality of domestic regulatory process, while the former deals with the diversity of the content of domestic regulation among the parties. As there is no formal mechanism to co-ordinate different mega-FTAs so as to assimilate their contents on regulatory co-operation, the best way to minimize the risk of fragmentation would be either to achieve de facto assimilation of their contents or to base regulatory co-operation on international standards. De facto assimilation would be achieved through mutual learning among the parties to different mega-FTAs. The key players would be those countries that are parties to more than one mega-FTAs, as they can influence the negotiation of these mega-FTAs. The United States, European Union, and Japan are in the best position to be the key players, as they are negotiating three mega-FTAs among them. There is a chance that assimilations on regulatory co-operation among the TPP, TTIP, and Japan–EU EPA would produce de facto global standards on regulatory co-operation. At the same time, this would create a club of regulatory co-operators, to the exclusion of many non-members to these three mega-FTAs, most of them developing countries.[55] One way to avoid this negative outcome is to 'open the club' to outsiders, with generous support to developing country candidates. Linking mega-FTA membership with an intensive support program such as Aid-for-Trade should be worked out.[56]

[55] Trachtman, 'Mutual Recognition of Services Regulation at the WTO' (n 21) 123–24, emphasizes this negative exclusive risk adjacent to mutual recognition of services regulation, but the risk is applicable to all forms of regulatory co-operation through mega-FTAs.

[56] See Olivier Cataneo, 'Promoting Greater Regulatory Coherence and Co-operation through Aid for Trade: What Could Be Done? What Role for the Private Sector and the WTO?' (2015) E15 Task Force on Regulatory Systems Coherence, Think Piece <http://e15initiative.org/wp-content/uploads/2015/07/E15-Regulatory-Cattaneo-final.pdf> accessed 23 April 2016.

In parallel with de facto assimilation, parties to the mega-FTAs should seek regulatory co-operation based on international standards. The European Union's revised proposal addresses this by providing that:

> (t)he Parties agree to co-operate between themselves, and with third countries, with a view to strengthening, developing and promoting the implementation of international instruments *inter alia* by presenting joint initiatives, proposals and approaches in international bodies or fora, especially in areas where regulatory exchange have been initiated or concluded pursuant to this Chapter and in areas covered by [specific or sectoral provisions—to be identified] of this Agreement (Article 13.1).

Although this is a legally non-binding, best-effort requirement, it would be a pertinent means for linking the parties' regulatory co-operation activities to international regulatory co-operation.

V. Concluding Remarks

Regulatory co-operation and regulatory coherence are among the most salient characteristics of the mega-FTAs as a model for the trade agreement for the twenty-first century. They deal with regulatory diversity among the parties, as well as the quality of domestic regulatory process of the parties, so that they may streamline the regulatory environment for the globalization of supply chains, while respecting the parties' right to regulate to pursue legitimate public policy objectives. As the multilateral trading system has lost its capacity to provide an optimal forum for regulatory co-operation and regulatory coherence, mega-FTAs are the only forum practically available for these regulatory arrangements.[57] This chapter analysed their expected contents (section III) and elucidates their possibility of furthering their intended positive outcomes and minimizing their possible negative outcomes (section IV). A follow-up analysis will be needed to check the adequacy of these analyses when the negotiations of these mega-FTAs are concluded and their institutional mechanisms start their operations and produce expected outcomes.

[57] Thomas J Bollyky, 'A Role for the World Trade Organization on Regulatory Coherence' (2015) E15 Task Force on Regulatory Systems Coherence, Think Piece <http://e15initiative.org/wp-content/uploads/2015/07/E15-Regulatory-Bollyky-final.pdf> accessed 23 April 2016; Bernard Hoekman and Petros C Mavroidis, 'Regulatory Spillovers and the Trading System: From Coherence to Cooperation' (2015) E15 Task Force on Regulatory Systems Coherence, Overview Paper <http://e15initiative.org/wp-content/uploads/2015/04/E15-Regulatory-OP-Hoekman-and-Mavroidis-FINAL.pdf> accessed 23 April 2016, call for plurilateral agreement for regulatory co-operation and regulatory coherence, rather than those through mega-FTAs, as a means of multilateralizing regulatory co-operation and regulatory coherence within the framework of the WTO.

24

Rise of the Plurilaterals: Threat or Opportunity for Multilateral Trade Governance

*R V Anuradha**

I. Introduction

A key defining characteristic of trade negotiations since the beginning of the twenty-first century has been a growing shift from the World Trade Organization (WTO) to preferential trade agreements (PTAs). Several descriptive phrases have emerged in trade linguistics to describe PTAs, such as 'spaghetti bowl', 'noodle bowl', and 'termites in the trading system'.[1] The WTO acknowledges that the effects of PTAs on global trade liberalization and economic growth are not clear, given that the regional economic impact of PTAs is *ex ante* inherently ambiguous.[2] There have been at least four major studies which have dealt with the issue of PTAs: the Sutherland report in 2004,[3] the

* R V Anuradha is a Partner at the New Delhi-based law firm of Clarus Law Associates. She heads the Firm's International Trade and Investment Law and Policy practice groups. She is a member of the Asia WTO Research Network. She regularly advises the Government of India and the private sector on various matters arising under the WTO and free trade agreements, including disputes arising under such agreements. She has also undertaken studies on trade law and policy for the Centre for WTO Studies–IIFT, The World Bank, UNCTAD–India and export promotion associations in India. She also teaches at various international training sessions and capacity-building programmes on trade law and policy.

[1] See e.g., Jagdish Bhagwati, *Termites in the Trading System: How Preferential Agreements Undermine Free Trade* (OUP 2008). The term 'spaghetti bowl effect' is attributed to Professor Bhagwati in his earlier writings see Jagdish N Bhagwati, 'US Trade Policy: The Infatuation with FTAs' (Columbia University Academic Commons 1995) <http://hdl.handle.net/10022/AC:P:15619> accessed 21 April 2016. In 2013 Julien Chaisse and Mitsuo Matsushita noted that 'the proliferation of PTAs causes two problems to the WTO and the world trading system. One is that [...] PTAs may undermine the basis of multilateral international trading order [and] the other problem is that PTAs are bilateral, regional or plurilateral agreements and the trade rules, such as origin rules and trade remedies contained in a PTA, may be different from other PTAs. However, enterprise activities are becoming more and more globalized.' see Julien Chaisse and Mitsuo Matsushita, 'Maintaining the WTO's Supremacy in the International Trade Order: A Proposal to Refine and Revise the Role of the Trade Policy Review Mechanism' (2013) 16 J Intl Econ L 9–36.

[2] See e.g., WTO, 'Regional Trade Agreements: Scope of RTAs' (WTO) <http://www.wto.org/english/tratop_e/region_e/scope_rta_e.htm> accessed 13 March 2016.

[3] Peter Sutherland and others, 'The Future of the WTO: Addressing Institutional Challenges in the New Millennium' (WTO 2004) <http://www.wto.org/english/thewto_e/10anniv_e/future_wto_e.htm> accessed 13 March 2016.

report of the Warwick Commission in 2007,[4] and the WTO's World Trade Reports in 2003[5] and 2011,[6] each of which has highlighted the fact that there are several concerns regarding PTAs. In his opening speech at a conference on the subject in 2007, the then WTO Director-General Pascal Lamy said that the proliferation of PTAs has led to the '*concern about incoherence, confusion, exponential increase of costs for business, unpredictability and even unfairness in trade relations*'.[7]

The World Trade Report of 2011 presents several interesting statistics and analysis on the growth of PTAs:[8]

- From the 1950s onwards, the number of active PTAs increased more or less continuously to about seventy in 1990. Thereafter, PTA activity accelerated noticeably, and PTAs in force in 2010 were close to 300.[9]
- The surge in PTA activity is driven both by a growing number of countries taking an interest in reciprocal trade opening and by an increase in the number of PTAs per country.
- The coverage of PTAs in terms of policy areas has widened and deepened over time beyond the traditional tariff-cutting exercises and often includes policy areas such as services trade, investment, intellectual property, technical barriers to trade, and dispute settlement. About one-third of the PTAs in force contain services commitments compared to less than one-tenth in 1990.
- PTAs are not really resulting in preferential trade, since a large portion of intra-PTA trade is most-favoured-nation (MFN) duty-free. In a survey conducted of twenty largest importers from all their trading partner countries, accounting for ninety per cent of world merchandise trade in 2008, of that only sixteen per cent qualified as preferential trade, assuming full utilization of preferences. The finding was that despite the explosion of PTAs in recent years, eighty-four per cent of world merchandise trade still takes place on a non-discriminatory MFN basis. First, this is because half of world trade is already subject to zero MFN tariff rates. Second, PTAs tend to exempt high

[4] First Warwick Commission, 'The Multilateral Trade Regime: Which Way Forward?' (First Warwick Commission 2007) <https://www2.warwick.ac.uk/research/warwickcommission/worldtrade/report/uw_warcomm_tradereport_07.pdf> accessed 23 April 2016.

[5] WTO, 'World Trade Report 2003: Trade and Development' (WTO 2003) <https://www.wto.org/english/res_e/booksp_e/anrep_e/world_trade_report_2003_e.pdf> accessed 23 April 2016.

[6] WTO, 'World Trade Report 2011: The WTO and Preferential Trade Agreements: From Co-existence to Coherence' (World Trade Report 2011) (WTO 2011) <https://www.wto.org/english/res_e/booksp_e/anrep_e/world_trade_report11_e.pdf> accessed 23 April 2016.

[7] Pascal Lamy, 'Proliferation of Regional Trade Agreements "Breeding Concern"' (Address Before Conference on 'Multilateralizing Regionalism' in Geneva, Switzerland 10 September 2007) <http://www.wto.org/english/news_e/sppl_e/sppl67_e.htm> accessed 13 March 2016.

[8] World Trade Report 2011 (n 6) 7–9.

[9] As of 1 February 2016, the WTO reports that 625 notifications of RTAs (counting goods, services, and accessions separately) had been received by the GATT/WTO. Of these, 419 were in force. WTO, 'Regional Trade Agreements' (WTO) <https://www.wto.org/english/tratop_e/region_e/region_e.htm> accessed 13 March 2016.

MFN-tariff items from preferential treatment and continue to trade these products at MFN rates.

- Nevertheless, another interesting finding is that if preferences are available in a PTA, even when this may result in just one per cent difference in tariff, there is a high rate for utilization of such preferences. The report, however, cites that complications and costs involved in complying with rules of origin were cited as considerations influencing preference utilization, especially where preference margins were low. This is also reaffirmed in a survey conducted by the Asian Development Bank in 2008 covering East and South-East Asian firms.[10]

Since 2010–2011, there has been gradual emergence of a new phase in trade agreements—the development of PTAs involving a larger number of countries, as opposed to bilateral or trilateral PTAs. The Trans-Pacific Partnership Agreement (TPP), the Trans-Atlantic Trade and Investment Agreement (TTIP), and the Regional Comprehensive Economic Partnership (RCEP) Agreement, present three mega-PTAs. Simultaneously, WTO Members are attempting to replicate the model followed under the Information Technology Agreement (ITA), with ITA-II, and a similar model for liberalization of tariffs on environmental goods. A third agreement between a few WTO Members, whose exact scope is not clear as yet, is the Trade in Services Agreement.

This chapter will examine this changing landscape of trade agreements and assess the challenges it presents. The starting point for its assessment is that countries will act in their sovereign economic interests, and that various factors drive domestic economic policy goals. This chapter does not seek to question those factors. It will explore how country interests in the area of trade negotiations are being manifested in an increasing choice for moving towards plurilateral agreements. At the same time, recent developments at the WTO in facilitating concrete steps towards a new agreement on trade facilitation indicates a keen desire to keep the WTO alive and relevant.

II. The Changing Landscape of International Trade Agreements

To put the discussion in context, it is worth examining some of Professor Matsushita's early observations on the challenges for effective WTO negotiations. In 2005, at the tenth anniversary of the WTO, Professor Matsushita noted the slow pace of negotiations under the WTO, and in his inimitably clear and succinct

[10] Asian Development Bank, 'Emerging Asian Regionalism' (Asian Development Bank 2008) <http://www.aric.adb.org/emergingasianregionalism/pdfs/ear%20highlights%20080421.pdf> accessed 23 April 2016.

style explained the changes in the negotiating scenario of multilateral trade negotiations that were responsible for it:[11]

1. Increasing number of Members: he noted the emergence of developing country Members who have demonstrated that they can act together and prevent the passage of resolutions that they consider are contrary to their interests, and that this is a change from the early years of WTO negotiations, when important matters were typically decided by the United States, European Communities, Canada, and Japan in the 'Green Room' and attempts were made to 'persuade developing country Members to go along with them'. He recommended that 'it is time to establish formats for negotiations in which developing country members substantially participate'.
2. General decline of tariff rates: the considerable reduction in tariff levels for industrial goods now leaves open only certain items, on which negotiations for reductions are difficult.
3. Trade in services: the differences in levels of competitiveness between developed and developing countries presents difficulties in negotiations in this area.
4. The Singapore issues: except for trade facilitation, the differences in perspectives between WTO Members on issues relating to investment, competition, and government procurement are another stumbling block.

As anticipated by Professor Matsushita, a fledgling agreement on trade facilitation alone saw the light of day at the WTO's Bali Ministerial Conference in December 2013, and in line with the Bali decision, on 27 November 2014 WTO Members adopted a Protocol of Amendment to insert the new Trade Facilitation Agreement into Annex 1A of the Marrakesh Agreement Establishing the WTO (the WTO Agreement). This new Agreement will enter into force once two-thirds of Members have completed their domestic ratification process.[12] The Trade Facilitation Agreement contains provisions for expediting the movement, release, and clearance of goods, including goods in transit. It also sets out measures for effective co-operation between customs and other appropriate authorities on trade facilitation and customs compliance issues. It further contains provisions for technical assistance and capacity building in this area.

This modest achievement at the WTO has been foreshadowed to a large extent with more ambitious developments. These can be divided in two broad categories: (i) standalone pacts within the WTO; and (ii) other plurilateral agreements. Generally, members of a PTA provide each other more favourable treatment than they provide to non-Members, and this presents a deviation from the WTO's MFN

[11] Mitsuo Matsushita, 'The Tenth Anniversary of the WTO' (International Conference on 'Policy and Law Aspects of Asia and WTO: Challenges and Opportunities', Taipei, 8–9 July 2005).

[12] WTO, 'Members Accepting the Protocol of Amendment to Insert the WTO Trade Facilitation Agreement Into Annex 1A of the WTO Agreement' (WTO) <https://www.wto.org/english/tratop_e/tradfa_e/tradfa_agreeacc_e.htm> accessed 13 March 2016.

principle. As will be discussed below, two of the agreements in the first category of 'within WTO' pacts—the Information Technology Agreement and the proposed Environmental Goods Agreement—seek to offer all benefits of liberalization to all other WTO Members on a MFN basis.

A. Stand-alone pacts within the WTO

The flagship agreement within this category is the Information Technology Agreement (ITA). The other agreement on the anvil in this category is the Agreement on Environmental Goods.

1. Information Technology Agreement (ITA-II)

The first Information Technology Agreement (ITA) was concluded in 1996 and resulted in eighty-one WTO Members eliminating tariffs on over 150 information technology products, which has been estimated to account for ninety-seven per cent of the world trade on such products.[13] Hailed as the biggest of the 'tariff-busting deals' of the Uruguay Round,[14] the original ITA was concluded through a 'Ministerial Declaration on Trade in Information Technology Products' at the first WTO Ministerial Conference, held in Singapore. A defining concept in the context of the ITA negotiations was that of the 'critical mass', whereby the ITA negotiating parties agreed that it would only be implemented if participants accounting for at least ninety per cent of world trade in IT products joined the initiative.

The ITA concessions are included in the participants' WTO schedules of concessions, and the tariff elimination is implemented on an MFN basis. This means that even countries that have not joined the ITA can benefit from the trade opportunities generated by ITA tariff elimination.

In a second round of tariff liberalization covering an additional 201 products, twenty-four Members of the WTO (including the European Union) adopted the Ministerial Declaration on the Expansion of Trade in Information Technology Products at the Nairobi Ministerial Conference held in December 2015 ('ITA-II'). Pursuant to the Declaration, it is expected that a majority of tariffs will be eliminated on the 201 products within three years, with reductions beginning in 2016.

A majority of developing countries, including India, Indonesia, Brazil, and South Africa, were not part of the ITA-II negotiations. Although India and Indonesia are both members of the original ITA, they stayed out of the ITA-II negotiations based on the assessment that the ITA had not resulted in significant benefits for them. In India's case, the assessment was that it had undermined the

[13] WTO, 'Information Technology Agreement: An Explanation' (WTO) <https://www.wto.org/english/tratop_e/inftec_e/itaintro_e.htm> accessed 13 March 2016.

[14] WTO, '15 Years of the Information Technology Agreement' (WTO 2010) 10 <https://www.wto.org/english/res_e/publication<_e/ita15years_2012full_e.pdf> accessed 13 March 2016.

growth of India's semiconductor and other hardware industries, and had resulted in the country relying to a large extent on imports.[15]

2. *Environmental Goods Agreement (EGA)*

Inspired by the ITA model, a few countries are contemplating an Environmental Goods Agreement under the WTO. A Joint Statement[16] issued by fourteen WTO Members (Australia, Canada, China, Costa Rica, the European Union, Hong Kong, Japan, Korea, New Zealand, Norway, Singapore, Switzerland, Chinese Taipei, and the United States) at the World Economic Forum at Davos in January 2014, notes that the environmental goods agreement would reinforce the rules-based multilateral trading system and benefit all WTO Members by applying the MFN principle.

The negotiations were officially launched in July 2014, and uses a list of fifty-four environmental goods developed by the Asia-Pacific Economic Co-operation (APEC) as the basis for negotiations to reduce applied tariffs ('APEC list'). The APEC list classifies environmental goods under fifty-four products based on six-digit-level Harmonized System (HS) subheadings.[17] There have been eight rounds of negotiations so far, and the number of participating countries has increased from fourteen to seventeen, with the inclusion of Turkey, Iceland, and Israel.

Like the ITA, the Joint Statement on the EGA notes that the agreement would take effect once a critical mass of WTO Members participates. Determining the 'critical mass' is yet to be achieved. In the ITA's case, this was pegged at ninety per cent of world trade in IT products. A study estimates that the fourteen WTO original EGA participants accounted for eighty-six per cent (seventy-eight per cent of imports and ninety-three per cent of exports) of global trade of the APEC list in 2012.[18] This figure includes re-imports and re-exports, as well as intra-EU trade, the exclusion of which would result in reduction of the estimate.[19] The same study also notes that the trade in environmental goods accounts for only a small portion

[15] The minutes of the meeting of Committee of Participants on the Expansion of Trade in Information Technology Products held on 15 May 2012, notes that the Indian representative has requested that India's name as one of the beneficiaries of ITA in terms of increasing employment, IT spending, and investment should be removed: Committee of Participants on the Expansion of Trade in Information Technology Products, 'Minutes of the Meeting of 15 May 2012', G/IT/M/55, 19 October 2012.

[16] WTO, 'Joint Statement Regarding Trade in Environmental Goods' (24 January 2014) <http://trade.ec.europa.eu/doclib/docs/2014/january/tradoc_152095.pdf> accessed 23 April 2016.

[17] The HS nomenclature, developed by the World Customs Organization, is accepted by most countries to classify internationally traded products.

[18] Rene Vossenaar, 'Securing Climate Benefits in the Environmental Goods Agreement' (27 November 2014) 8(10) BIORES <http://www.ictsd.org/bridges-news/biores/news/securing-climate-benefits%E2%80%A8-in-the-environmental-goods-agreement> accessed 13 March 2016. The paper also notes that non-EGA participants with the largest value of total trade in the fifty-four subheadings of the APEC list for the period 2011–2013 are, in descending order, Mexico, Malaysia, India, Russia, Thailand, Brazil, Turkey, South Africa, Indonesia, Saudi Arabia, the Philippines, Israel, and Vietnam. Turkey and Israel have now applied to join the EGA.

[19] ibid.

of all trade and that majority of the forty-six of the fifty-four goods HS subheadings on the APEC list reflect goods that are not used primarily for environmental purposes.[20] It also notes that multiple-use products with certain environmental applications may be traded under HS subheadings not usually included in the analyses of trade in environmental goods.[21] Achieving clarity on all these aspects, therefore, remains a key challenge towards arriving at a WTO-EGA.

B. The plurilateral agreements

There are four agreements in this category that are briefly discussed below: the TPP; the TTiP; the Trade in Services Agreement, and the RCEP.

1. The Trans-Pacific Partnership Agreement (TPP)

The membership of the TPP is merely twelve countries (the United States, Australia, Brunei Darussalam, Canada, Chile, Japan, Malaysia, Mexico, New Zealand, Peru, Singapore, and Vietnam), but in terms of its scope and coverage, it is a mega-deal, with its negotiating countries comprising an estimated forty per cent of the world's GDP.[22] The TPP Agreement was signed between the twelve members in October 2015. It has been hailed as a 'high-standards' agreement that sets 'a new standard for global trade while taking up next-generation issues'.[23] The reference to 'high standards' is with regard to the elaboration and consolidation of provisions of the WTO relating to Technical Regulations and Standards and Sanitary and Phytosanitary Measures (SPS) under the TPP Agreement. In addition to this, the TPP Agreement deals in substantial detail with standards on WTO-plus areas, namely labour and the environment. It also has an elaborate chapter on Intellectual Property Rights (IPRs) that goes beyond the WTO's Agreement on Trade-related aspects of IPRs, in terms of harmonization of both IPR standards, and also enforcement mechanisms.

The overall approach of the TPP Agreement in each of these areas is to essentially consolidate and build on the provisions on these areas as can be seen in the many bilateral PTAs that the United States has concluded since 1995, including disciplines in the areas of labour and environment, which are areas that it has not been able to push through under the WTO. In fact, the United States has pre-existing PTAs with several of the TPP parties, including Australia, Chile, Canada, Mexico, Peru, and Singapore which comprise of provisions similar to those incorporated in the TPP.

[20] ibid. [21] ibid.

[22] See Office of the United States Trade Representative, 'Overview of the Transpacific Partnership' <https://ustr.gov/tpp/overview-of-the-TPP> accessed 23 April 2016.

[23] See, for example, the Press Releases on Summary of the TPP Agreement announced by the Governments of Australia, and the United States: <http://dfat.gov.au/trade/agreements/tpp/outcomes-documents/Pages/summary-of-the-tpp-agreement.aspx>; and <https://ustr.gov/about-us/policy-offices/press-office/press-releases/2015/october/summary-trans-pacific-partnership> accessed 23 April 2016.

The TPP Agreement will come into force two months after all the original signatories complete their own domestic ratification procedures. Countries such as South Korea[24] and Taiwan[25] have expressed interest in considering future accession. The inherent problem for any new countries acceding to an existing treaty is that the agreement is presented to them as a fait accompli, with little negotiating room in respect of existing obligations. What may be even more onerous is the higher price that countries seeking accession may be asked to pay by the existing members.

2. *Trans-Atlantic Trade and Investment Partnership Agreement (TTIP)*

The TTIP Agreement between the United States and the European Union is the other mega-deal that the United States is negotiating. Its aim is to eliminate tariffs on almost all the trade between the United States and the European Union, and also achieve an agreement on services, investment, competition rules, and regulatory co-operation in a wide range of areas including chemicals, pharmaceuticals, cosmetics, engineering products, textiles, cosmetics, etc. It will be interesting to see whether the US and EU will have meeting ground on all of the TPP-type provisions under the TTiP. For example, the TPP emphasizes on science-based risk assessment for SPS measures, to contain reliance on the precautionary principle. The EU on the other hand, has traditionally shown greater emphasis on precaution to deal with scientific uncertainty, especially in contentious areas such as genetically modified organisms. The negotiations are mostly shrouded in secrecy and as of now, not much is known on the extent of progress on the same.

3. *Trade in Services Agreement (TiSA)*

The TiSA agreement is a trade agreement that is currently being negotiated by twenty-five Members of the WTO: Australia, Canada, Chile, Chinese Taipei, Colombia, Costa Rica, the European Union, Hong Kong China, Iceland, Israel, Japan, Korea, Liechtenstein, Mauritius, Mexico, New Zealand, Norway, Pakistan, Panama, Paraguay, Peru, Switzerland, Turkey, the United States, and Uruguay. Along with the TPP and the TTIP, the TiSA is seen as part of the US-led triumvirate of ambitious trade agreements.

An EU report notes that together, the negotiating countries for TiSA account for seventy per cent of world trade in services.[26] It also notes that China is seeking to be part of the negotiations.

The talks started formally in March 2013, and by July 2015, the EU report notes that thirteen negotiation rounds have taken place, with the European Union,

[24] 'South Korea Reiterates Interest in Trans-Pacific Partnership', Washington State Journal (5 October 2015) <http://www.wsj.com/articles/south-korea-reiterates-interest-in-trans-pacific-partnership-1444057143> accessed 18 April 2016.

[25] 'Taiwan Trains Sights on TPP Participation' (Taiwan Today, 7 October 2015) <http://taiwantoday.tw/ct.asp?xItem=237489&ctNode=2182> accessed 18 April 2016.

[26] European Commission, 'TiSA in a Nutshell' (European Commission) <http://ec.europa.eu/trade/policy/in-focus/tisa/> accessed 13 March 2016.

Table 24.1 Multiple existing agreements between RCEP negotiating parties

ASEAN	Australia	New Zealand	Japan	Korea	India	China
Australia–New Zealand	ASEAN	ASEAN	ASEAN	ASEAN	Japan	ASEAN
Korea	Singapore	China	India	India	Korea	New Zealand
China	Malaysia	Singapore	Australia	Singapore	Singapore	Malaysia
India	China	Malaysia	Singapore	China	Malaysia	South Korea
Japan	India (under negotiations)	India (under negotiations)	Malaysia		ASEAN	Australia
			Indonesia			
			Philippines			

Australia, and the United States chairing the talks in turns. While it notes progress in the talks, it states that there is no set deadline for ending the negotiations.[27]

4. *Regional Comprehensive Economic Partnership Agreement (RCEP) Agreement*

The RCEP Agreement is between the member countries constituting the ASEAN and six others: Australia, New Zealand, South Korea, Japan, China, and India. The negotiations were launched in 2012, and as of May 2016, twelve rounds of negotiations have been held between the parties. The combined trade between the RCEP parties is estimated at thirty per cent of the world GDP,[28] and the agreement, once concluded, is expected to enhance trade opportunities on goods, services, and investment between the parties.

The interesting aspect about the RCEP is that there are multiple inter-crossing PTAs between the negotiating parties. For example, ASEAN has PTAs with each of the non-ASEAN participating countries,[29] and each of the non-ASEAN countries has entered into inter se agreements, and also agreements with individual ASEAN countries. Each of these is expected to co-exist with the RCEP Agreement. In other words, what appears to be primarily expected from the RCEP is that ASEAN will move towards its best possible position relative to its commitments with non-ASEAN countries, but it is not clear whether non-ASEAN countries will necessarily yield their most liberal commitments under RCEP, as opposed to bilateral PTAs. The presence of China as part of the agreement is also likely to have an impact on the scope and coverage of the agreement.

Table 24.1 summarizes the multiple existing agreements between RCEP negotiating parties.

[27] ibid.

[28] Department of Foreign Affairs and Trade, Australian Government, 'Regional Comprehensive Economic Partnership' (Department of Foreign Trade and Affairs, Australian Government) <http://dfat.gov.au/trade/agreements/rcep/pages/regional-comprehensive-economic-partnership.aspx> accessed 13 March 2016.

[29] Australia, New Zealand, South Korea, Japan, China, and India.

III. WTO and Other Trade Agreements

Promising as they are in terms of the depth and scope of trade coverage, the increasing proliferation of PTAs presents several challenges for the WTO system. Professor Matsushita has examined this issue and observes that while PTAs can be easy substitutes for difficult multilateral agreements, they present a serious systemic problem to the WTO regime.[30] This, he explains, is the inherent risk of imbalance in competitive conditions among trading nations, which can thereby cause unfairness and inequity in trading relations, and especially present challenges for developing countries that are outside the PTAs.[31] The position of developing countries is especially vulnerable in bilateral trade negotiations because of the difference in bargaining power between developed and developed countries, which may be exploited by developed countries to impose conditions favourable to them and unfavourable to the developing countries.[32]

He then explains that perhaps a simple way to deal with the problem is to make use of multilateral PTAs in which not only two but several parties participate and in which more than one developing country are members, which may effectively check the imposition of hard conditions that a powerful developed country may impose.[33] He concludes that it 'makes sense to emphasize the importance of multilateral rather than bilateral PTAs'.[34]

The emergence of the TPP, TTIP, RCEP, EGA, and TiSA in the recent past reaffirms the basic logic of that observation. These agreements, however, continue to present challenges of fragmentation of the rules of the trading system—both at legal and institutional levels.

A. WTO provisions on PTAs

The WTO envisages certain basic rules for conclusion of PTAs. It envisages the possibility of deviation from the MFN principle through the formation of PTAs relating to both goods and services, provided certain conditions are satisfied. The General Agreement on Tariffs and Trade (GATT) and the General Agreement on Trade in Services (GATS), two of the core agreements of the WTO, envisage PTAs as an exception. The frequent use of the PTA exceptions under the GATT and the GATS has, however, led to the observation that these are making MFN seem the exception, rather than the rule.[35]

Article XXIV.5 of the GATT recognizes that preferential arrangements can be set up as a special exception, provided that: (i) duties and other trade regulations of commerce are reduced or removed on substantially all trade in the group; and (ii) the PTA does not raise the overall level of protection vis-à-vis other WTO

[30] Mitsuo Matsushita and Yong-Shik Lee, 'Free Trade Agreements: WTO Disciplines and Developing Country Perspectives' in Yong-Shik Lee and others (eds), *Law and Development Perspective on International Trade Law* (CUP 2011) 247–48.

[31] ibid 248. [32] ibid 249. [33] ibid 249–50. [34] ibid 250.

[35] Sutherland and others (n 3), and First Warwick Commission (n 4) (suggesting use of the term 'least-favoured-nation treatment' to define the norm, as opposed to 'most-favoured-nation treatment').

Members. Similarly, Article V of the GATS provides for economic integration agreements in services, provided such an agreement has substantial sectoral coverage, in terms of number of sectors, volume of trade affected, and modes of supply. The Article also mandates that there should not be exclusion of any mode of supply of services.

Despite the GATT and GATS rules on PTAs, there continues to be lack of legal certainty on the application of these rules. Uncertainty exists on the interpretation of the phrase 'substantially all trade'. A separate Understanding on the Interpretation of Article XXIV of GATT 1994 was concluded as part of the WTO Agreements in 1994. It attempted to address the manner in which the general incidence of duties and other regulations of commerce applicable before and after the formation of a PTA would be evaluated. However, as noted in discussion papers for the WTO on this issue, the 1994 Understanding did not provide any substantive clarification or interpretation of the essential requirements contained in Article XXIV on PTAs,[36] and existing WTO rules on PTAs have proved throughout the years to be ill-equipped to deal with the realities of PTAs.[37]

As part of the WTO's Doha Round, members of the Negotiating Group on Rules are mandated to improve the rules around Article XXIV of the GATT, in particular, in relation to the phrase 'substantially all trade'. Progress on this aspect, however, has been slow. In the absence of clarity in interpreting what would constitute 'substantially all trade', there is no concrete theoretical policy or legal framework that can enable countries to assess and measure the impact of PTAs in which they enter. There are controversies on issues such as rules of origin under PTAs, arising from the absence of WTO rules on this aspect.[38]

Another relevant aspect to consider is that the overall mandate that was envisaged under Article XXIV.5 of the GATT and Article V of the GATS was clearly that PTAs can be entered into by WTO Members when they involve deeper integration of areas already covered under the WTO Agreements, such as deeper cuts in tariffs and greater liberalization of service sectors. They are silent on incursions into new areas not addressed within the WTO framework. PTAs, however, have made frequent incursions into several newer policy areas, which are often not related to trade. These are exemplified in PTAs driven by the United States and the European Union, whose scope frequently cover policy areas such as labour, environment, competition, investment, capital movement, and various TRIPS-plus[39] provisions in relation to intellectual property. One of the main concerns about this

[36] Roberto V Fiorentino and others, 'The Changing Landscape of Regional Trade Agreements: 2006 Update' (2006) WTO Discussion Paper No 12, 27 <http://www.bilaterals.org/article.php3?id_article=8744> accessed 13 March 2016.

[37] Jo-Ann Crawford and Roberto V Fiorentino, 'The Changing Landscape of Regional Trade Agreements' (2005) WTO Discussion Paper No 8, 19 <https://www.wto.org/English/res_e/booksp_e/discussion_papers8_e.pdf> accessed 13 March 2016. The authors point out that the rules, which require RTAs to be transparent and to provide for deep internal trade liberalization and neutrality vis-à-vis non-parties trade, have been subject to diverging interpretations for nearly half a century. The authors further contend that these rules thus opened the door to a situation of great ambiguity with respect to the relationship between RTAs and the multilateral trading system.

[38] ibid.

[39] This refers to the provisions over and above those prescribed under the Agreement on Trade Related Aspects of Intellectual Property Rights (TRIPS Agreement) of the WTO.

expanding scope and reach of PTAs is that the European Union and the United States are effectively using the PTA approach as a tool to export their own regulatory approaches to PTA partners,[40] especially when attempts to push similar issues at the multilateral level have not succeeded.

Questions relating to legitimacy of PTAs are, however, unlikely to get serious attention in a world where practically every WTO Member is engaged in negotiation of multiple PTAs. Each WTO Member would be hesitant to raise questions about the scope of another Member's PTA and its WTO compatibility. As pointed out in the Sutherland Report, there are too many WTO Members with interests in their own PTAs for a critical review of a PTA's provisions to take place or a consensus on their WTO conformity to be ascertained.[41]

The Nairobi Ministerial Declaration concluded at the Tenth WTO Ministerial Conference in December 2015, reaffirms that 'Regional Trade Agreements (RTAs) remain complementary to, not a substitute for, the multilateral trading system.' It has also instructed the WTO Committee on RTAs to discuss the systemic implications of RTAs for the multilateral trading system.[42] The scope and content of this review is yet to emerge.

B. Plurilateral trade agreements within the WTO

The WTO envisages the possibility of plurilateral trade agreements, and Annex 4 to the WTO Agreement lists these, the most prominent being the Agreement on Government Procurement. Any Annex 4 agreement can be introduced as part of the WTO framework only through consensus of *all* WTO Members. This is a precondition for introducing a plurilateral trade agreement into Annex 4 of the WTO Agreement. Furthermore, benefits of the plurilateral agreement may be available for the countries that are part of the closed group.

The WTO Agreement provides under Article X:9 as follows:

> The Ministerial Conference, upon the request of the Members parties to a trade agreement, may decide exclusively by consensus to add that agreement to Annex 4. The Ministerial Conference, upon the request of the Members parties to a Plurilateral Trade Agreement, may decide to delete that Agreement from Annex 4.

For adding a plurilateral agreement to the WTO, the following provisions would apply.

- Certain subsets/groups of WTO Members can propose to add a plurilateral agreement to be included to Annex 4 to the WTO Agreement.

[40] For a discussion on 'WTO-plus' and 'WTO-extra' areas covered under RTAs, see Henrik Horn and others, 'Beyond the WTO? An Anatomy of EU and US Preferential Trade Agreements' (2009) Bruegel Blueprint Series vol XII <http://bruegel.org/wp-content/uploads/imported/publications/bp_trade_jan09.pdf> accessed 13 March 2016. See also Bhagwati (n 1) 83–85 (discussing elements of coercion often used by the USTR to ensure developing countries enter into RTAs with the United States).

[41] Sutherland and others (n 3) 22.

[42] Paragraph 28, Nairobi Ministerial Declaration, WT/MIN(15)/Dec (19 December 2015).

- The decision as to whether the same should be added is subject to consensus by all WTO Members. Article X.9 does not leave any room for voting, and states that a decision on introducing a plurilateral agreement has to be made exclusively by consensus. Implicit in this requirement is an understanding that a plurilateral agreement may affect the rights, interests, and benefits of all Members.
- *It should be noted that the consensus referred to under Article X:9 is not a precondition for concluding a plurilateral agreement*; it is only a precondition for concluding a discriminatory plurilateral agreement that becomes part of the WTO treaty (i.e. part of Annex 4, but not extending its benefits to all WTO Members). The core legal effect of adding a plurilateral agreement to Annex 4 is, indeed, that it allows (but does not require) the plurilateral agreement to deviate from the MFN principle. Another legal consequence is that, as part of the WTO treaty, the Dispute Settlement Understanding (DSU) becomes available to enforce the Annex 4 plurilateral agreement.

C. The path of the ITA

The ITA is not a plurilateral agreement under Annex 4 of the WTO Agreement, nor is it incorporated as a stand-alone Annex I agreement. It can best be characterized as falling within a *sui generis* category of an agreement that can be enforced as part of its members modifying their schedules of commitments under GATT. The two legal instruments that are relevant for an understanding of the operationalization of the ITA are:

§ the *Ministerial Declaration on Trade in IT Products* concluded by fourteen WTO Members (including the European Community), concluded at the Ministerial Conference in December 1996; and

§ General Council decision entitled *Implementation of the Ministerial Declaration*, which was subsequently concluded between twenty-six Members.

The Modalities specified in the Annex to the Ministerial Declaration provide the basis for duty concessions. Its principal features are provisions that deal with: (i) incorporation into WTO Schedule of Concessions; and (ii) review of documents on consensus basis. The Implementation Procedure modifies the procedure provided under Article XXVIII, which is the core provision on modification of schedules. This amounts to an amendment of a provision of GATT, 1994. However, the same seems to have been undertaken without any recourse to Article X of the Marrakesh Agreement.

What is curiously missing in the ITA constitutional documents (the Ministerial Declaration and the Implementation Procedures) is any reference to the legal basis under the WTO framework for such an Agreement. In effect what appears to have happened is that a few Members of the WTO got together and arrived at a declaration between themselves, and modalities for tariff reduction, without any interference or objections from other Members, which thereby resulted in modification of their schedule of commitments that are reflected in their GATT schedules.

The main objective of the ITA was to achieve elimination of entry barriers on information technology products and thereby increase trade and competition by enhancing market access opportunities for such products. The Annex to the Ministerial Declaration provides for the Modalities and Product coverage in Attachments A and B. The commitments undertaken under the ITA are on an MFN basis, and therefore all benefits accrue to all WTO Members regardless of whether they are party to the ITA. This model may be replicable only in very limited circumstances, where the focus is on tariff reductions that can be effected through modification of tariff schedules. This model, however, is unlikely to work for more complex agreements comprising of multiple issues such as standards, services, non-tariff barriers.

D. EGA and TiSA: what are the options?

The EGA and the TiSA are not clear on the route they seek to follow. It is likely that the EGA would follow the same route as the ITA; i.e. get adopted through a Ministerial Decision, and modification of tariff schedules of the participating countries. However, the scope of the EGA will determine whether the ITA model is entirely replicable in its case. For instance, if it has provisions on environmental services, non-tariff barriers, technology transfer, and capacity building, etc., mere modification of schedules will not achieve the objectives. It will therefore need to be considered as an agreement within the WTO or be structured as a PTA outside the WTO.

With regard to the TiSA, the negotiations have been more secretive, and the WTO website itself does not provide any details of the on-going meetings and discussions.[43] Furthermore, while the negotiations are to be theoretically open for all WTO Members, the rules for engagement are not clear. The European Union notes, for instance, that China has 'applied' to be part of TiSA, and the European Union 'supports' its participation; but does not say whether China's participation can actually be blocked by any of the other participants.[44]

It is possible for TiSA to become an outside-WTO preferential agreement that meets the requirements of GATS Article V. Although some reports of TiSA also indicate that it will be a plurilateral agreement within the WTO, there has been no legal assessment of how this is to be achieved. At a discussion initiated by the European Parliament in 2013, one scholar observed that the constitutional DNA of the TiSA remains a 'closed shop', and then proceeded to explain that: 'If TISA is an Article V PTA, let's do it—there are no constraints on this. If, however, it is designed as a multilateral agreement that will be embedded alongside the GATS

[43] Details on the EGA as specified in this chapter are from the website of the Canadian Government, and on TiSA, from the European Union.

[44] European Commission (n 26).

in the WTO, then we have a problem. This is unchartered territory; we have never negotiated a plurilateral agreement in an area of rule-making that already commands a multilateral instrument.'[45]

IV. Concluding Thoughts

International trade relations is witnessing turmoil and rapid movement towards more ambitious deals. With progress of negotiations being slow and contentious at the WTO, it is certainly tempting and easier for countries to achieve consensus in smaller groups and have fragmented plurilateral agreements.

The rapid proliferation of multiple criss-crossing PTAs—whether in the form of bilateral agreements, or larger plurilateral agreements—presents legal and institutional considerations for the WTO. Countries negotiating such agreements, at this point of time, seem to be predominantly focused on concluding agreements rather than on nuances of interplay of agreements, and implications of fragmentation in the long run. Countries remaining outside these agreements are currently convinced that there is no real benefit to be gained from these agreements and that it is better to remain outside of them.

The main benefit that plurilateral agreements present as opposed to bilateral ones, as noted by Professor Matsushita, is that they allow for groups of countries, especially more than one developing country, to participate and negotiate together, and this could act as an effective check against imposition of hard conditions.[46] While plurilateral PTAs with more than two trading partners are certainly better than bilateral PTAs, multiple plurilateral PTAs continue to present a fragmented trading scenario, which poses institutional and administrative challenges, especially for developing countries with limited resources and negotiating capital. This is evidenced in the recently concluded TPP Agreement, where the agenda on issues, which could not progress at the WTO, owing to opposition from a large group of developing countries, has materialized in concrete provisions. As discussed earlier, these issues span labour, environment, and TRIPs-plus IPR standards, and reflect the United States' approach to these issues under its various PTAs. Six of TPP's twelve members are developing countries: Brunei, Chile, Malaysia, Mexico, Peru, and Vietnam. The outcome of the negotiations reflects how the change in format from a multilateral to a plurilateral negotiation process resulted in dilution of conflicting viewpoints, and enabled the United States to achieve agreement on areas where it has had to face opposition at the WTO.

At the practical level, fragmentation for developing countries often translates to few government officials bearing the responsibility for negotiating multiple deals. Mobilizing adequate machinery for taking on board stakeholder concerns during

[45] Pierre Sauavé, 'Proceedings of the Workshop on Trade in Services Agreement' (September 2013) <http://www.europarl.europa.eu/RegData/etudes/workshop/join/2013/433722/EXPO-INTA_AT(2013)433722_EN.pdf> accessed 23 April 2016.

[46] Matsushita and Lee (n 30).

negotiations, and translating the benefits of concluded agreements for businesses, is often sub-optimal in such a fragmented scenario.

Multiple plurilateral PTAs also do not address the issue of weak bargaining positions of countries that initially remain outside of the agreement, and seek membership over a period of time. For instance, under the TiSA and the EGA Agreement, the current approach appears to be that a small core group of like-minded countries enter into a deal, with the expectation that other countries join in future. For a non-party, the pressures and pulls of becoming a party to such agreements would depend on a variety of geo-political and economic factors. However, as seen in the process of accession of new Members into the WTO, the bargaining power for newer members could be compromised in the context of a pre-existing deal. For instance, as noted earlier, a few countries are considering eventual accession into the TPP. An acceding member will, however, not have any negotiating room as far as the text of the agreement is concerned; and on the contrary may be required to adhere to stricter conditionalities in return for entry into the TPP club.

Countries that seek to remain outside of the mega-agreements that are currently being negotiated therefore need to assess whether to take a more practical approach at the multilateral level and keep up the emphasis on a stronger WTO, which arguably offers greater safeguards for building coalitions and arriving at consensus on contentious issues. In the broader context, there is no substitute for the WTO. A significant advantage of a multilateral agreement such as the WTO is what is often rightly characterized as one of its biggest achievements—the rule-based, enforceable dispute settlement system. Any agreement within the WTO system would have the benefits of utilizing this system. A key challenge therefore is to find a way to retain agreements within the WTO system, and ensure that the balance that the multilateral system presents, is available for all. This issue assumes higher significance in view of the ongoing negotiations on the TiSA and the EGA.

Innovative approaches need to be considered to achieve progressive liberalization in a phased manner that would be adequately sensitive to concerns of specific countries. The debate on remaining within the framework of the WTO system needs to be resurrected through a deeper and clearer assessment of the ramifications of too much fragmentation, and innovating various approaches to preserve and consolidate the WTO.

25

Trade in Pharmaceuticals: Patents and Access to Medicines since TRIPS—Some Certainty and Several Lingering Questions

*Bryan Mercurio**

I. Introduction

More than twenty years have passed since intellectual property rights (IPRs) were incorporated into the global trading regime via the Agreement on Trade-Related Aspects of Intellectual Property Rights (TRIPS). The incorporation of IPRs into the World Trade Organization (WTO) was at the time controversial, and remains so today.[1] The intervening years have seen hundreds of articles written on the TRIPS Agreement, and perhaps hundreds on each of the popular IP issues of patents, copyright, and trademark. The focus of this chapter is patents, and more narrowly, pharmaceutical patents. Pharmaceutical patents gained an almost notorious reputation throughout the TRIPS negotiations and in the years following due to the complete awakening to the tragedy of the AIDS crisis and the widely held belief in some circles that pharmaceutical patents impede access to medicines. Issues involving pharmaceutical patents and access to medicines came to a head in the Doha Ministerial in 2001 and remain very much in the news and feature prominently in contemporary academic literature.

This chapter draws from over a decade of my scholarship in the area, both synthesizing and crystallizing ideas which have been at the forefront of my research. The analysis in this chapter represents, it is hoped, some of the qualities of Professor Matsushita's own work in that it recognizes and takes account of exogenous factors, whether they be seemingly separate areas of the law or political economy issues. Professor Matsushita's recognition of the importance of other areas of law, including competition law and international investment law, in the study of WTO

* Professor and Vice Chancellor's Outstanding Fellow of the Faculty of Law, The Chinese University of Hong Kong. Member of the Asian WTO Research Network since 2008, and a grateful mentee of and friend to Professor Matsushita.

[1] See generally, Mitsuo Matsushita, 'Japanese Perspective on Intellectual Property Rights and the GATT' (1992) 1992 Colum Bus L Rev 81.

law is an inspiration and model for any scholar hoping to have any influence on public policy.[2] I am honoured to call Professor Matsushita a friend and deeply grateful for his guidance over the years.

The chapter begins by reviewing the promise, expectations, and worries of and about the TRIPS Agreement, focusing on claims that TRIPS will improve protection of IPRs and decrease counterfeits, boost innovation, and result in, or even cause, a public health crisis, respectively—all of which have proven to be overblown and largely inaccurate. The reality is that while the TRIPS Agreement did significantly alter the landscape relating to pharmaceutical patents, its impact has been far less substantial than proponents hoped for or critics feared. That being the case, some significant achievements have occurred, namely the Doha Declaration on TRIPS and Public Health (2001) but perhaps as significantly the WTO panel decision in *Canada—Pharmaceutical Patents* (2000) a year earlier. Both the Doha Declaration and panel decision reinforce my longstanding position that the TRIPS Agreement is not necessarily a threat to public health.

Of course, several health-related issues remain unresolved and numerous future challenges exist which could possibly have a negative impact on public health. This chapter cannot possibly exhaustively cover all such issues, but instead focuses on a number of the more interesting and threatening ones. These include the scope and limits of jurisdictions to determine standards of patentability and perimeters of compulsory licensing, the consistency of seizing medicines in transit with the TRIPS Agreement, and the increasing presence of TRIPS-Plus provisions in bilateral and regional trade and international investment agreements. The largest challenge remains unresolved—that is, how the WTO and its Members can contribute to increasing access to medicines and improving global health throughout the developing world.

Section II discusses the promise, expectations, worries, and realities of the TRIPS Agreement, while section III focuses on the unresolved issues and challenges for the future. Section IV concludes.

II. The Promise, Expectations, Worries, and Realities of the TRIPS Agreement

This section reviews the promise, expectation, worries, and realities of the TRIPS Agreement, with the first subsection focusing on the intention of the TRIPS proponents and the initial predictions of the critics. The second part of the section explores the situation twenty years hence and finds the reality that TRIPS has neither fulfilled its promise and expectations nor is it as frightening and ill-conceived as the critics claimed.

[2] See e.g., Mitsuo Matsushita, 'Basic Principles of the WTO and the Role of Competition Policy' (2002) 3(4) J World Inv 567; Mitsuo Matsushita, 'Competition Law and Policy in the Context of the WTO System' (1994–1995) 44 DePaul L Rev 1097.

A. Improving protection, enhancing innovation, and stopping trade in counterfeits

The impetus for the inclusion of an international IP agreement in the WTO is clear—developed countries and related private interests sought to increase minimum standards and enforcement norms in developing countries.[3] By the late 1970s, most developed nations shifted from a manufacturing or agricultural base to a knowledge-based economy. With the inventive capacity and potential, as well as availability of sources of capital to fund innovative activities, these nations had attained a comparative advantage in knowledge goods.[4] At the same time, industry began pressing governments to act[5] and almost succeeded in getting the contracting parties to include a GATT agreement on counterfeiting as part of the Tokyo Round (1973–1979).[6] Efforts failed, however, mostly because of a lack of evidence demonstrating harm to industry, export interests, and the overall economy.[7] The 1982 GATT Ministerial Meeting revitalized the notion of an IP agreement within the multilateral trade regime,[8] and at the same time industry and governmental studies began to be produced showing the amount of harm and loss caused by counterfeiting and piracy of IPRs. The most notable and influential in this regard is the 1984 report of the US International Trade Commission, which through survey evidence of firms found that over seventy per cent of US production is susceptible to foreign counterfeiting at high cost to the domestic industry:

> Along with the similar unfair practices of passing off and trade dress infringements and copyright and patent infringements on similar articles, product counterfeiting is a global business that, according to industry estimates, accounted for $6 billion to $8 billion in

[3] See generally Susan K Sell and Christophe May, *Intellectual Property Rights: A Critical History* (Lynne Rienner Publishers 2005); Duncan Matthews, *Globalising Intellectual Property Rights: The TRIPs Agreement* (Routledge 2002).

[4] The World Bank defined a knowledge-based economy as 'rel[ying] primarily on the use of ideas rather than physical abilities and on the application of technology rather than the transformation of raw materials or the exploitation of cheap labor'. World Bank, *Lifelong Learning in the Global Knowledge Economy: Challenges for Developing Countries* (World Bank Publications 2003).

[5] Susan K Sell, *Private Power, Public Law: The Globalization of Intellectual Property Rights*, Cambridge Studies in International Relations No 88 (CUP 2003) 40–41:

> The push for an IP code in the GATT began in 1978, near the end of the Tokyo Round of negotiations. The Levi Strauss Corporation initiated an effort to combat foreign counterfeiting of its trademark blue jeans. Levi Strauss pressed its case with other trademark-sensitive firms (lobbying as the International Anti-Counterfeiting Coalition) and obtained the backing of the USTR for an anti-counterfeiting code. Owing in part to the eleventh-hour introduction of the proposal, the effort ultimately failed.

[6] See GATT Secretariat, Agreement on Measures to Discourage the Importation of Counterfeit Goods, GATT Doc No L/4817, 31 July 1979.

[7] Matthews (n 3) 9.

[8] See e.g., GATT Secretariat, Agreement on Measures to Discourage the Importation of Counterfeit Goods, GATT Doc No L/5382, 18 October 1982. Discussions had continued between industry and governments (notably the United States, the European Community, Canada, Japan, and Switzerland) between 1980 and 1982. For more detail on the 1982 Ministerial meeting, see Matthews (n 3) 9–10.

lost U.S. and export sales in 1982. Domestic sales lost to counterfeiting and similar trade practices and lost export sales were each estimated at $3 billion and $4 billion.[9]

A follow-up report published in 1998 found losses to US business 'higher than the loss range of $16–$20 billion'.[10] Both reports supported the efforts being taken at the GATT to address counterfeiting. These efforts were buttressed by the European Communities (EC), which stated: 'The EC and its member States consider that the problem of international trade in counterfeit goods has now become of such gravity that urgent action at international level is required.'[11] These governmental efforts were, of course, supported, if not led, since the early 1970s by industry, who viewed the trade-based mechanisms of the GATT as a more suitable forum to combat counterfeiting and piracy than the more traditional forum of the World Intellectual Property Organization (WIPO).[12] The industry support and governmental efforts culminated in an agreement which serves to expand, secure, and protect markets for the export of knowledge goods.

Proponents of the TRIPS also claim that the negotiation of the agreement and the corresponding raising of standards (and quasi-harmonization) led to greater innovation. These claims have often been made *ex post* and are essentially a floccinaucinihilipilification; innovation was simply not at the core of the TRIPS negotiations. In fact, neither the negotiating government nor the host of corporate interests pushing for a trade-based IP agreement stated or even hinted that such an agreement within the WTO would lead to increased innovation. Instead, all discussions focused on protecting innovations that, it is implied, were created for the benefit of the richer markets. The text of the TRIPS illustrates this point quite clearly—the term 'innovation' only features once in the agreement, with Article 7 ('Objectives') stating:

> The protection and enforcement of intellectual property rights should contribute to the promotion of technological innovation and to the transfer and dissemination of technology, to the mutual advantage of producers and users of technological knowledge and in a manner conducive to social and economic welfare, and to a balance of rights and obligations.

Even then, the truism that IPRs should contribute to technological innovation is not included in the substantive part of the treaty but included in 'Part I: General

[9] United States International Trade Commission, *The Effects of Foreign Product Counterfeiting on US Industry: Final Report on Investigation No 332-158 under Section 332(b) of the Tariff Act 1930* (United States International Trade Commission Publication 1984) 24.

[10] United States International Trade Commission, *Foreign Protection of Intellectual Property Rights and the Effect on US Industry and Trade Report to the United States Trade Representative, Investigation No 332-245, under Section 332(g) of the Tariff Act of 1930* (United States International Trade Commission Publication 1988) 4–2.

[11] GATT Secretariat, *International Trade in Counterfeit Goods—Communication by the European Communities*, GATT Doc No L/5512, 8 July 1983, 9.

[12] See especially Sell, *Private Power, Public Law* (n 5) 44–51, 76, 83–84, 89, and 107; Matthews (n 3) 18–28. On the perceived failures of WIPO, see Michael Blakeney, 'Intellectual Property in World Trade' (1995) 1(3) Intl Trade L Reg 76, 76.

Provisions and Basic Principles', which, as I have previously stated, 'perhaps can serve as an aid to interpreting the treaty and potentially guide domestic implementation, but certainly does not provide a justification for IPRs'.[13] Beyond this, the fifth recital of the Preamble of TRIPS is the only other place in the text with any reference to innovation, and that mention simply (and vaguely) recognizes underlying public policy objectives, including developmental and technological objectives, for the protection of IPRs. The point to make here is that if increased or enhanced innovation was truly a reason behind the negotiation of the TRIPS, one would have expected that it would have 'featured more prominently in the substantive provisions of the Agreement or at least to be better reflected within those provisions'.[14]

Simply stated, the objective of TRIPS was to increase IP standards and provide for better protection and enforcement of IPRs, not to increase or enhance innovation. It is therefore not surprising that there is little evidence that enhanced protection of IPRs (and more specifically patents) has led to an increase in innovation.[15] To the contrary, in some cases, such as where cumulative innovation occurs (i.e. where one product relies on multiple patents), there is evidence to suggest that 'the patent system may discourage innovation overall rather than encouraging it'.[16]

This is not to suggest that patents are unwanted, or even unnecessary to the pharmaceutical industry. To the contrary, the industry is capital intensive, with high costs to innovation, and low barriers to imitation. Without patent protection, firms would be hesitant to heavily invest in risky research and development (R&D) and the flow of new and life-saving medicines would halt.[17] At the same time, the fact that monopoly rights can suppress innovation is evident; competition is generally seen as a driver of innovation in itself—incentivizing the efficient use of resources, constant progress, and protecting consumers—and a necessary component of a market economy.

[13] Bryan Mercurio, 'TRIPS and Innovation: A Necessary Reappraisal?' (The E15 Initiative Strengthening: The Global Trade and Investment System for Sustainable Development, International Centre for Trade and Sustainable Development (ICTSD) and World Economic Forum 2014).

[14] ibid.

[15] There is no doubt that the number of patents granted has grown at a faster rate over the past twenty years, but this does not necessarily lead to increased R&D or innovation. See John H Barton, 'Reforming the Patent System' (2000) 287 Sci 1933, 1933–34. See also, Michele Boldrin and David K Levine, 'The Case Against Patents' (2013) 27(1) J Econ Perspectives 3; Frederic M Scherer, 'The Political Economy of Patent Policy Reform in the United States' (2009) 7(2) J Telecomm High Tech L 167; Josh Lerner, 'The Empirical Impact of Intellectual Property Rights on Innovation: Puzzles and Clues' (2009) 99(2) Am Econ Rev 343, 343–47; Nancy T Gallini, 'The Economics of Patents: Lessons From Recent US Patent Reform' (2002) 16(2) J Econ Perspectives 131; Adam B Jaffe, 'The US Patent System in Transition: Policy Innovation and the Innovation Process' (2002) NBER Working Paper No 7280 <http://www.nber.org/papers/w7280> accessed 13 March 2016.

[16] James Bessen and Eric Maskin, 'Sequential Patents, Innovation and Imitation' (2009) 40(4) RAND J Econ 611. See also Angus C Chu and others, 'Does Intellectual Monopoly Stimulate or Stifle Innovation?' (2102) 56(4) Eur Econ Rev 727.

[17] Estimates on the average cost of developing a new drug is at USD$2.558 billion. See Joseph A DiMasi, Henry G Grabowski, and Ronald W Hansen, 'Innovation in the Pharmaceutical Industry: New Estimates of R&D costs' (2016) 47 J Health Econ 20–33.

Even with pharmaceuticals, however, the current patent system is not without problems. With the boundaries of patent claims blurred, and with additional patent claims added throughout the life of a pharmaceutical product, innovation could become impeded. Moreover, with economic incentives favouring R&D into incremental advancement over proven drugs rather than R&D on potential new gains, the industry is subject to distortions. With such a playbook, pharmaceutical firms have acted in an entirely rational (and expected) manner by attempting to protect their interests and advocating even more protection.[18] In so doing, firms have diverted resources away from innovative R&D, and into safer R&D, lobbyists, and lawyers. Boldrin and Levine refer to such behaviour as the political economy effect, where the optimum range of protection and system balance is upset through the perpetual increase of protection as a result of the lobbying efforts of entrenched firms, and without regard to the system as a whole.[19] Of course, such behaviour also counters the evidence, which suggests that 'policy changes that strengthen patent protection … [do] not spur innovation'[20] and that 'the costs of stronger patent protection may exceed the benefits'.[21]

When one looks at the specifics of the pharmaceutical sector, the disconnect between greater patent protection in the developing world and increased innovation becomes even more obvious. The United States accounts for nearly forty per cent of all pharmaceutical sales, with Europe and Japan accounting for twenty-four per cent and twelve per cent, respectively. Developed countries account for the majority of the remainder. With the volume of sales in the developing world fairly small, the increase in protection and corresponding revenue raised would simply not be significant enough to spur any additional R&D. Thus, while the industry may use enhanced patent protection to increase *profits*, it will not see these profits as an incentive for increased R&D. Again, patent protection is necessary for the pharmaceutical industry—but there is no evidence that increased and more harmonized world standards have not led to increased innovation.

More surprising perhaps is that while the improved enforcement against trade in counterfeits (and to a lesser extent, piracy) were the *raison d'être* of the TRIPS, the agreement has done little to stem illicit trade. In fact, somewhat outdated estimates on the cost of counterfeiting and piracy ranging from US$250 billion (as per the OECD in 2009)[22] to over US$600 billion (as per the International

[18] William M Landes and Richard A Posner, *The Economic Structure of Intellectual Property Law* (Harvard University Press 2003) 318.

[19] Boldrin and Levine (n 15) 9–14.

[20] Josh Lerner, '150 Years of Patent Protection' (2002) 92(2) Am Econ Rev 221; United Nation Conference on Trade and Development, Using Intellectual Property Rights to Stimulate Pharmaceutical Production in Developing Countries: Reference Guide, UNCTAD/DIAE/PCB/2009/19, 2011, 72.

[21] Jaffe (n 15) 555.

[22] See Press Release, World Intellectual Property Organization, Counterfeiting and Piracy Endangers Global Economic Recovery Say Global Congress Leaders, WIPO Press Release PR/2009/621, 3 December 2009 <http://www.wipo.int/pressroom/en/articles/2009/article_0054.html> accessed 13 March 2016.

Anti-counterfeiting Coalition)[23]—regardless of the figure, the increase in counterfeiting and piracy since TRIPS is staggeringly high.[24] The biggest source of counterfeits is China, which paradoxically has significantly increased exports of IP-violating goods in the wake of the Membership in the WTO as the combination of liberalized trade policies (coupled with fewer export restrictions and the cessation of the state-trading exportation monopoly), and the rise of the Internet and e-commerce has made it far easier to sell and export infringing goods.[25]

The realization that TRIPS did not resolve the issue of counterfeiting and piracy—and that enforcement in general could be the TRIPS' 'Achilles heel'[26]—can be illustrated by the perceived need of countries in negotiating the stand-alone Anti-counterfeiting Trade Agreement (ACTA). This ill-fated treaty is the culmination of the longstanding concern among some WTO Members that the TRIPS Agreement does not go far enough in effectively enforcing the substantive norms and standards of the Agreement. For this reason, and far from a mere codification exercise, the ACTA was meant to be a substantive enforcement agreement which would expand upon the TRIPS framework. In the words of Luc Devigne from the trade division of the European Commission: 'There was no intention to duplicate TRIPS … we want to go beyond it … TRIPS is the floor, not the ceiling.'[27]

In addition, the forum shift away from the WTO and to a stand-alone format is not coincidental but represents the end of several fruitless years spent inside the corridors of the WTO lobbying Members to take action against and improve the enforcement function of the TRIPS and across the city in WIPO advocating for an enforcement treaty. With such overtures repeatedly rejected out of hand by a large contingent of developing countries, and therefore with neither the WTO's TRIPS Council nor WIPO's Advisory Committee on Enforcement willing to discuss norm-setting in the area of IP enforcement, it would seem that those countries desiring to establish a higher global standard for the enforcement of IPRs had no choice but to move to an alternative forum. As I have argued elsewhere, the negotiation of the ACTA was both a signal that the present regime was not working as contemplated and a vote of no confidence in the institution to be able to correct the perceived deficiencies.[28]

[23] See International Anti-counterfeiting Coalition, 'Counterfeiting Statistics' (International Anti-counterfeiting Coalition) <http://www.iacc.org/resources/about/statistics> accessed 13 March 2016. The coalition also estimates that counterfeiting results in a loss of US$250 billion to the US economy and 750,000 American jobs.

[24] See Peggy Chaudhry and Allen Zimmerman, *The Economics of Counterfeit Trade* (Springer 2009) 13.

[25] For background, see Daniel C K Chow, 'Why China Does Not Take Commercial Piracy Seriously' (2006) 32 Ohio NUL Rev 203.

[26] See Peter K Yu, 'TRIPS and Its Achilles' Heel' (2011) 18 J Intell Prop L 479.

[27] Monika Ermert, 'European Commission on ACTA: TRIPS is Floor Not Ceiling, Intellectual Property Watch' (*Intellectual Property Watch*, 22 April 2009) <http://www.ip-watch.org/2009/04/22/european-commission-on-acta-trips-is-floor-not-ceiling/> accessed 13 March 2016.

[28] For more discussion on the background and substance of ACTA, see Bryan Mercurio, 'Beyond the Text: The Significance of the Anti-counterfeiting Trade Agreement (ACTA)' (2012) 15(2) J Intl Econ L 361; Bryan Mercurio, 'The Anti-counterfeiting Trade Agreement: Ambitious Aims vs Political Reality' (2013) 3(2) KLRI JL Legis 315; Bryan Mercurio, 'The Anti-counterfeiting Trade Agreement, Less Harmonization, Further Fragmentation' in C L Lim and Bryan Mercurio (eds), *International Economic Law after the Global Crisis: A Tale of Fragmented Disciplines* (CUP 2015) 406–26.

Returning to the framework of ACTA, from the beginning the treaty was designed not merely to codify existing practice among developed nations in the hope that others would sign up (as was later claimed), but to deal directly with the growing scourge of counterfeiting and piracy through increased enforcement. The genesis of the ACTA was a meeting of the Group of Eight (G8) in July 2005, where Japan pushed for and the G8 published a four-paragraph statement on 'Reducing IPR Piracy and Counterfeiting Through More Effective Enforcement', which highlights the ills brought about by piracy and counterfeiting, sets out a number of steps that countries could take to 'reduc[e] substantially global trade in pirated and counterfeit goods, and efficiently combat ... the transnational networks that support it'[29] and calls for future action to implement the identified steps.[30] Japan followed up in November 2005 with a proposal for a 'Treaty on Non-proliferation of Counterfeits and Pirated Goods',[31] and shortly thereafter the G8 at a meeting in July 2006 issued a statement announcing a comprehensive IP rights enforcement strategy entitled 'Combating Intellectual Property Rights Piracy and Counterfeiting',[32] with the focus on increased co-operation among governmental agencies and international organizations.

The following year, Japan announced its intention to negotiate 'a new international legal framework to strengthen the enforcement of intellectual property rights'.[33] The initiative was quickly supported by the European Union and the United States and negotiations on a plurilateral, ACTA began in earnest.[34] The agreement, negotiated between thirty-seven countries over eleven formal rounds held and concluded in late 2010, purported to enhance international co-operation regarding both the civil and criminal enforcement of IP and to establish a *new* best practice and standard enforcement framework in order to better combat global counterfeiting and piracy. These aims were often publicly repeated during the negotiations. For example, the website of the US Trade Representative (USTR) stated that the ACTA includes 'innovative provisions to deepen international

[29] 'Reducing IPR Piracy and Counterfeiting through more Effective Enforcement' (Post-meeting Statement, G8 Gleneagles, 2005) para 3 <http://www.mofa.go.jp/policy/economy/summit/2005/piracy.pdf> accessed 18 April 2016.

[30] ibid para 4.

[31] See Tove Iren S Gerhardsen, 'Japan Proposes New IP Enforcement Treaty' (*Intellectual Property Watch*, 15 November 2013) <http://www.ip-watch.org/weblog/index.php?p=135> accessed 13 March 2016; reporting that the Japanese originally envisaged either Interpol or the World Customs Organization overseeing the treaty.

[32] 'Combating IPR Piracy and Counterfeiting' (G8 Saint Petersburg, 16 July 2006). See also Tove Iren S Gerhardsen, 'G8 Outcome Has IP Implications for Enforcement, Trade and Health' (*Intellectual Property Watch*, 19 July 2006) <http://www.ip-watch.org/2006/07/19/g8-outcome-has-ip-implications-for-enforcement-trade-and-health/> accessed 13 March 2016.

[33] Press Release, Ministry of Foreign Affairs of Japan, Framework of the Anti-Counterfeiting Trade Agreement (ACTA), 23 October 2007 <http://www.mofa.go.jp/announce/announce/2007/10/1175848_836.html> accessed 13 March 2016.

[34] See Anti-counterfeiting Trade Agreement (ACTA): Notice of Public Meeting, 73 Fed Reg 51860, 5 September 2008; Anti-counterfeiting Trade Agreement (ACTA): Request for Public Comments, 73 Fed Reg 8910, 15 February 2008; *Recommendation From the Commission to the Council to Authorize the Commission to Open Negotiations of a Plurilateral Anti-counterfeiting Trade Agreement*, SEC(2008) 255 final/2, 27 February 2008.

cooperation and to promote strong enforcement practices'.[35] Likewise, the USTR website claims the 'negotiations aim to establish a state-of-the-art international framework that provides a model for effectively combating global proliferation of commercial-scale counterfeiting and piracy in the 21st century'.[36] Another page of the USTR website reads:

> ACTA aims to establish a comprehensive international framework that will assist Parties to the agreement in their efforts to effectively combat the infringement of intellectual property rights, in particular the proliferation of counterfeiting and piracy, which undermines legitimate trade and the sustainable development of the world economy. It includes state-of-the-art provisions on the enforcement of intellectual property rights, including provisions on civil, criminal, border and digital environment enforcement measures, robust cooperation mechanisms among ACTA Parties to assist in their enforcement efforts, and establishment of best practices for effective IPR enforcement.[37]

Having agreed that counterfeiting and piracy is a large and growing problem which needs to be addressed, the negotiating parties agreed to negotiate a treaty containing 'state-of-the-art provisions' in order to curtail the problem. Such a treaty could have been useful in combating global counterfeiting and piracy. Unfortunately, the negotiations did not proceed as planned and the result was a treaty that essentially codified existing practice among the great majority of participants. Such a result is, of course, the antithesis of the very reason for the negotiations.

The points to conclude this section are simple—the aim of the treaty was to counteract the growth scourge of counterfeiting and piracy so as to better protect IPRs through trade-related measures. Nothing in the negotiating history or literature suggests that the creation of the TRIPS was primarily to increase innovation, in either the developed or developing world. Twenty years later, we can say that the treaty has failed in its primary purpose. Counterfeiting and piracy remains a problem, and is a much worse problem now than it was when the treaty was first discussed. Nor can we say that the *ex post* justification of increased innovation has been successful. We have more patents, increased filings, and far-reaching technological inventions, but there is little to suggest that the increased standards contained in the TRIPS have directly led to an increase in innovation.

B. Public health crisis

The advent of TRIPS sparked an outcry from civil society and scholars, who claimed that the agreement would benefit the developed world to the detriment of developing countries. Whether by conscious design or otherwise, the

[35] Anti-counterfeiting Trade Agreement (ACTA), (Office of the United States Trade Representative (USTR)) <http://www.ustr.gov/acta> accessed 2 September 2015. See also USTR, 'ACTA: Meeting US Objectives' (USTR October 2011) <http://www.ustr.gov/about-us/press-office/fact-sheets/2011/september/acta-meeting-us-objectives> accessed 23 April 2016.

[36] ibid.

[37] Press Release, USTR, U.S., Participants Finalize Anti-Counterfeiting Trade Agreement Text, November 2010 <https://ustr.gov/about-us/policy-offices/press-office/press-releases/2010/november/us-participants-finalize-anti-counterfeiting-trad> accessed 23 April 2016.

introduction of minimum standards and broad protection would impact upon future development strategies of the poorer, less innovative WTO Members in that these countries can no longer imitate freely, build a manufacturing base, and then transition to a regime of stronger IP laws and regulations, as happened with so many of the early economic developers (including Japan, Korea, Taiwan, and Singapore).[38] Decried as a corporate-driven agreement,[39] critics were especially pessimistic about the role of TRIPS on public health, including the ability of countries to react to and manage public health crises. TRIPS also suffered from a case of bad timing, with its creation coinciding with the height of the HIV/AIDS crisis.

There is little doubt that 'the field of international intellectual property law underwent a tectonic shift with the promulgation of the [TRIPS]';[40] or, stated more forcefully, that TRIPS 'profoundly altered the nature, scope, and economic consequences of international intellectual property regulation'.[41] But it is questionable whether TRIPS has come anywhere close to having the effect—whether positive or negative—that the early proponents and critics predicted. This is not to say that TRIPS has had no effect. Of course it has, and to suggest otherwise would be irresponsible—prior to TRIPS, patent protections varied widely. The mere fact that TRIPS more extensively regulated and added minimum standards to a number of areas within patent law would suggest that on some level the TRIPS has had some impact.

The impact of TRIPS on medicines is most often attributed to two substantive requirements.[42] First, TRIPS standardized the length of patent protection. More specifically, Article 33 requires that patent rights be granted for a minimum period of twenty years from the date a patent application is filed. Prior to TRIPS, both the basis and the length of protection varied widely—with most countries granting an average of fifteen to seventeen years' protection from the date of filing, but others only granting patent protection for five to seven years.[43] To the extent that

[38] For early analysis of likely effects, see Jerome H Reichman, 'Universal Minimum Standards of Intellectual Property Protection Under the TRIPS Component of the WTO Agreement' (1995) 29 Intl Lawyer 345; United Nation Conference on Trade and Development, *The TRIPS Agreement and Developing Countries* (United Nations 1996) 36.

[39] See generally Sell, *Private Power, Public Law* (n 5); Carolyn Deere, *The Implementation Game: The TRIPS Agreement and the Global Politics of Intellectual Property Reform in Developing Countries* (OUP 2009).

[40] Charles R McManis, 'Teaching Current Trends and Future Developments in Intellectual Property' in Yo Takagi and others (eds), *Teaching of Intellectual Property: Principles and Methods* (CUP 2008) 300.

[41] Ruth L Okediji, 'Legal Innovation in International Intellectual Property Relations: Revisiting Twenty-one Years of the TRIPS Agreement' (2014) 36(1) U Pa J Intl L 101, 101.

[42] Such requirements have led many to make sweeping accusations and statements. See United Nations Development Programme (UNDP), *Good Practice Guide: Improving Access to Treatment by Utilizing Public Health Flexibilities in the WTO TRIPS Agreement* (UNDP 2010) 4 (calling intellectual property protection 'one of the more significant' factors contributing to the high price of medicines).

[43] WHO, 'WTO and the TRIPs Agreement' (World Health Organization) <http://www.who.int/medicines/areas/policy/wto_trips/en/index.html> accessed 13 March 2016.

TRIPS raised the term of protection, it could be argued that it negatively impacted upon the price of medicines in that it extended the monopoly selling period for the branded pharmaceutical manufacturer. The extended period of monopoly rights delayed competition and therefore allowed for higher prices to be charged for a longer period of time.

Second, and more damaging, is that TRIPS requires countries to provide patent protection for both processes and products, in all fields of technology. Prior to TRIPS, as many as fifty countries provided patent protection for processes but not products.[44] The wording of Article 27.1 prevents such differentiation, instead requiring patents protecting the process or method used to manufacture the product as well as protecting the product itself—thereby providing more complete protection for the patent holder. The requirement to grant product patents is the critical requirement here, as it prohibited the common technique used by generic pharmaceutical manufacturers of 'reverse engineering' to develop a different process or method to create an equivalent product.[45] Again, it could be argued that the requirement to grant patent protection over the process as well as the product resulted in a less competitive environment and thereby lengthened the term of protection a branded drug would have otherwise had, and in so doing allowed higher prices to be charged for a longer period of time.

These requirements, however, are tempered through the inclusion of so-called 'flexibilities' within the TRIPS. Perhaps the most important of these flexibilities are found in Part IV and provide for transitional arrangements for developing and least-developed countries (LDCs) providing an additional period of time to bring national legislation and practices into conformity with the Agreement. More specifically, Article 65 contains two transitional arrangements relating to developing country Members (65.2) and Members in transition (65.3) the right to delay the application of TRIPS (other than Articles 3, 4, and 5) for four years (that is, until the year 2000). In addition, Article 65.4 extends the transitional period for an additional five years (that is, until 2005) for developing country Members to provide product patent protection in the areas of technology that had not been protected at the time of the TRIPS coming into force (including pharmaceutical and agricultural-chemicals). For some countries (notably Brazil and India), this transitional arrangement means that generic manufacturers in those countries

[44] UNDP (n 42) 5. See e.g., The Patents Act, 1970, No 39, Acts of Parliament, s 5 (India). Even though the Patents Act allowed for medically related process patents, such patents offered limited protection (five to seven years) and provided for automatic licensing after three years. For these reasons, few companies sought process patents in India. See The Patents Act, s 53(1)(a). For commentary, see Julien Chaisse and Samira Guennif, 'Present Stakes Around Patent Political Economy—Legal and Economic Lessons from the Pharmaceutical Patent Rights in India' (2007) 2(1) Asian J WTO L Policy 65.

[45] On the acquired skills of the Indian generic industry, see Sudip Chaudhuri, *The WTO and India's Pharmaceutical Industry: Patent Protection, TRIPs and Developing Countries* (OUP 2005) 52. See also Amy Kapczynski, 'Harmonization and its Discontents: A Case Study of TRIPs Implementation in India's Pharmaceutical Sector' (2009) 97 Cal L Rev 1571, 1578 fn 33.

could continue copying and producing drugs that would otherwise have required patent protection by the year 2000.[46]

The third transitional arrangement, contained in Article 66, allows LDCs to delay implementation of obligations until 2006 owing to 'the special needs and requirements of [LDCs], their economic, financial and administrative constraints, and their need for flexibility to create a viable technological base'. In November 2001, Members agreed in the Doha Declaration on the TRIPS Agreement and Public Health (Doha Declaration) to extend the transitional arrangements for LDCs until 2016 with respect to patents on pharmaceutical products and exclusive marketing rights—meaning LDCs are under no obligation to provide for, nor to enforce patents and data protection with respect to pharmaceutical products until 2016. In 2013, the Members extended the implementation period to 2021.[47]

The aforementioned Doha Declaration represented the crowning achievement of developing countries in their frustration with the TRIPS Agreement and in essence the first (and perhaps only) 'win' for developing countries in the WTO-era. While the Doha Declaration did little more than re-assert rights and flexibilities which already existed in the TRIPS Agreement, the restatement provided a useful reminder that Members can prioritize and have the right to take measures necessary to protect public health.[48]

Of course, in the longer term the Doha Declaration also led to a solution to the issue of compulsory licensing. The issue here was that Article 31(f) of the TRIPS Agreement states that compulsory licences 'shall be authorized predominantly for the supply of the domestic market of the Member authorizing such use', but of course many Members have no or insufficient manufacturing capabilities and thus technically could not make use of this important exception to patent rights. The Doha Declaration itself did not resolve the issue, but merely 'recognize[d] that WTO with insufficient or no manufacturing capacities in the pharmaceutical sector could face difficulties in making effective use of compulsory licensing under the TRIPS Agreement' and called for the TRIPS Council to come to an 'expeditious solution' to resolve the issue.[49] The issue was contentious and the solution did not come until 30 August 2003, when

46 The only caveat to this extended transitional period is that from 1995 countries were obliged to accept patent applications and keep the applications dormant in a patent 'mailbox' until 2005, when the mailbox was unlocked and the applications assessed.

47 For background and criticism, see Arno Hold and Bryan Mercurio, 'After the Second Extension of the Transition Period for LDCs: How Can the WTO Gradually Integrate the Poorest Countries into TRIPS?' in Bryan Mercurio and Kuei-Jung Ni (eds), *Science and Technology in International Economic Law: Balancing Competing Interests* (Routledge 2013) 260–90.

48 The Declaration begins by 'recogniz[ing] the gravity of the public health problems afflicting many developing and least-developed countries, especially those resulting from HIV/AIDS, tuberculosis, malaria and other epidemics'.

49 World Trade Organization, Ministerial Declaration of 14 November 2001 (Doha Declaration), WT/MIN/(01)/DEC/1, 41 ILM 746 (2002) para 6. For discussion, see Bryan Mercurio, 'TRIPs, Patents and Access to Life-saving Drugs in the Developing World' (2004) 8(2) Marq Intell Prop L Rev 211, 229–30 (recounting negotiating positions of developed and developing countries over the issue).

the Members agreed to the Decision Implementing Paragraph 6 of the Doha Declaration providing for a 'waiver' of obligations under Article 31(f) and thus allowing any Member to export pharmaceutical products made under compulsory licences to others with insufficient or no manufacturing capabilities within the terms set out in the Decision. The waiver is scheduled to be transformed into the first ever amendment of the TRIPS Agreement in due course. And while the Decision has been criticized for being too cumbersome,[50] and to date has only been utilized once,[51] it acts as a bargaining tool for countries in pricing negotiations with pharmaceutical companies and in this regard has proven to be invaluable. More abstractly, it is an important illustration of the flexibilities of the WTO system to allow for the promotion of public health interests above that of trading interests.

Another illustration of the interpretive flexibility of the TRIPS Agreement is the general exception clause contained in Article 30 allowing for undefined exceptions to patent rights so long as the exceptions meet the three-step test of being (i) limited; (ii) not unreasonably conflicting with the normal exploitation of the patent; and (iii) not unreasonably prejudicing the legitimate interests of the patent owner, taking account of the legitimate interests of third parties. In relation to public health, the panel report in *Canada—Pharmaceuticals* is the only case involving Article 30.[52] In that case, the panel held that Canada's so-called regulatory exception (also called 'Bolar'[53] and 'early working' exception) which allows generic manufacturers to use and produce test-batches of a patented product prior to the expiry of the patent in order to gain regulatory approval to market the product was a legitimate exception and consistent with Article 30. This decision is important in terms of promoting competition as it allows for a generic manufacturer to begin producing, distributing, and selling its pharmaceutical product soon after the expiry of the patent as opposed to waiting until that point in order to begin testing and seeking marketing approval.

To conclude this section, although there can be no doubt that the TRIPS Agreement had the potential to affect public health, it seems clear that in hindsight the Agreement's impact on public health has been a lot more muted than critics originally predicted. To the contrary, the twenty years since the creation of the TRIPS Agreement has seen Members strongly asserting their rights (including flexibilities) and a WTO panel interpreting the Agreement in a manner conducive to public health.

[50] See e.g., Médecins Sans Frontières (MSF), 'Neither Expeditious, nor a Solution: The WTO August 30th Decision is Unworkable' (MSF 2006).

[51] For details, see Matthew Rimmer, 'Race Against Time: The Export of Essential Medicines to Rwanda' (2008) 1(2) Pub Health Ethics 89; Matthew Rimmer, 'The Jean Chretien Pledge to Africa Act: Patent Law and Humanitarian Aid' (2005) 15(7) Expert Opinion on Therapeutic Patents 889.

[52] Panal Report, *Canada—Patent Protection of Pharmaceutical Products*, WT/DS114/R, 7 April 2000.

[53] See *Roche Products v Bolar Pharmaceutical*, 733 F2d 858 (Fed Cir 1984).

III. Unresolved Issues and Challenges for the Future

This is not to suggest that everything has been resolved and that the TRIPS Agreement is not a threat to the ability of Members to take measures to protect public health. To the contrary, several unresolved issues both within the WTO system and externally pose challenges for the future. This section will discuss some of the more important issues and challenges.

Uncertainty around the patentability standards is perhaps the greatest potential challenge for the future. While the TRIPS Agreement provides for a rather uniform approach to patents, with Article 27.1 mandating protection 'for any inventions, whether products or processes, in all fields of technology, provided that they are new, involve an inventive step and are capable of industrial application', it does not provide a definition of invention, nor does it set any perimeters for what is 'new', an 'inventive step', or 'capable of industrial application'.[54]

Thus, while Article 27.1 may seem inflexible in that it prohibits Members from excluding pharmaceutical, chemical, and process patents from patentability (as many countries did prior to the TRIPS Agreement), it leaves ample scope for Members to interpret the requirements in a manner conducive to its economic and social needs and in line with its policy priorities.[55] That being said, there must be some meaning to the text and standards of Article 27.1, meaning there are limits to the flexibility of Members to craft their own standards.

In pharmaceuticals, the standard for what is new and an inventive step plays a critical role in defining the scope of a patent. While most Members have taken a loose approach to this issue, India has, by contrast, explicitly and intentionally taken legislative steps to limit patent protection for new uses of known products in an effort to curtail the so-called 'evergreening' of patents; that is, the practice of branded pharmaceutical companies seeking to extend patent protection for pharmaceutical products (often for anti-competitive purposes) through small and incremental improvements or changes to the delivery method.[56] More specifically, Section 3(d) of the Indian Patent Act limits patent protection for pharmaceutical derivatives only if it enhances the efficacy of the known substance (i.e. new forms of existing drugs do not automatically qualify as an 'invention').[57]

[54] Owing to differences in the wording of standards in Europe and the United States/Canada, a footnote to art 27.1 states that the terms 'inventive step' and 'capable of industrial application' may be deemed by a Member to be synonymous with the terms 'non-obvious' and 'useful', respectively.

[55] It should also be noted that paragraphs 2 and 3 of art 27 allow for exclusions to patentable subject matter, including those 'necessary to protect ordre public or morality, including to protect human, animal or plant life or health or to avoid serious prejudice to the environment' and medical and surgical methods and plants and animals (other than micro-organisms).

[56] For more information on evergreening, see John R Thomas, 'Patent "Evergreening" Issues in Innovation and Competition' (2009) Cong Research Serv R40917.

[57] For discussion, see Shamnad Basheer and T Prashant Reddy, 'The "Efficacy" of Indian Patent Law: Ironing Out the Creases in Section 3(d)' (2008) 5(2) SCRIPTed 232. See also Shamnad Basheer and T Prashant Reddy, 'Ducking TRIPS in India: A Saga Involving Novartis and the Legality of Section 3(d)' (2008) 20(2) Natl L Sch India Rev 131.

Section 3(d) has attracted worldwide attention and been at the forefront of a number of high-profile disputes, the most notable being its role in the rejection of a patent for the cancer drug Glivec. In that case, the Indian Supreme Court in April 2013 upheld the initial ruling against granting a patent to Glivec in January 2006, since the drug's active ingredient, imatinib mesylate, was already known before the development of Glivec. In this regard, the patent office and Court found that Glivec did not represent an 'innovation' in accordance with the relevant sections of the Patent Act, but rather that the originality of Glivec was merely a suitable form to deliver the known drug. Thus, since the drug was not substantially different from one for which patents had already been given in the United States and Europe, Glivec did not pass the novelty test. In contrast, Novartis argued it was entitled to a patent for the amended version of Glivec because the original patented compound was never suitable for making into the beta crystal form (i.e. making the drug into a pill). The US patent granted in 1993 (no patent was granted in India) was for the synthesis of the molecule of imatinib. Without further development, Novartis asserted that this molecule could not be administered to patients safely. The later development is what made Glivec a viable treatment for cancer.

It is not only India that narrowly interprets certain aspects of the criteria for patentability. For instance, since 2005 Canada has adopted a unique interpretation whereby utility (i.e. capable of industrial application) is assessed not by reference to the requirement in the Patent Act that an invention be 'useful', but rather against the 'promise' that the courts derive from the wording of the applicant's patent specification. Under the so-called 'promise doctrine', drugs must actually do what the inventor said or implied, it would do when it applied for the patent—backed by evidence. Such a standard would seem to be inimical to the modern reality of pharmaceutical research and marketing where drugs must be patented at an early stage of development in order to maintain novelty, and in most cases before stage one, two, or three clinical trials.

Requesting detailed information and holding the patent applicant to the 'promises' made in the patent application will likely lead to the invalidation of a number of patents. In fact, this has proven to be the case, with the Federal Court invalidating a patent in Stratterra, a drug used to treat attention deficit hyperactivity disorder (ADHD), after finding a seven-week, double-blind placebo-controlled study of twenty-two patients was 'too small and too short in duration to provide anything more than interesting but inconclusive data'. In another case, the Federal Court found that the drug Zyprexa, an anti-psychotic drug used to treat schizophrenia, did not meet the implied promise that the drug is *markedly* superior to other drugs for the long-term treatment of schizophrenia. In both cases, the Federal Court held that the drugs failed the 'utility' threshold in the Patent Act, even though the drugs were being marketed and used in Canada to treat the prescribed disorders. While Canada's standard is being challenged by Eli Lilly in investor–state arbitration under NAFTA Chapter 11 it has not as yet been challenged at the WTO.[58]

[58] *Eli Lilly and Company v Government of Canada*, UNCITRAL, Notice of Arbitration, 30–31, 12 September 2013. For Canada's statement of defence, see *Eli Lilly and Company v Government of Canada*, UNCITRAL, Government of Canada Statement of Defence, 36–43, 10 June 2014.

The point of these two examples is simply to highlight that the scope and contours of patentability remain unclear under Article 27.1. While the uncertainty perhaps allows Members to craft their own standards, it also has the potential to produce a chilling effect. Following the decision in *Canada—Pharmaceuticals*, several countries (including the complainant, the European Union) adopted a similar measure, but with the consistency of India's extra requirement relating to an inventive step and Canada's enhanced utility standard unchallenged, others are hesitant to adopt similar legislation.[59]

Other challenges remain, most notably the scope of Article 31 relating to compulsory licences. Again, India has pushed the boundaries in its interpretation of Article 84(1) of the Indian Patent Act, which reads:

> At any time after the expiration of three years from the date of the [grant] of a patent, any person interested may make an application to the Controller for grant of compulsory licence on patent on any of the following grounds, namely:— (a) that the reasonable requirements of the public with respect to the patented invention have not been satisfied, or (b) that the patented invention is not available to the public at a reasonably affordable price, or (c) that the patented invention is not worked in the territory of India.

While the three-year waiting period, satisfaction of the 'reasonable requirements of the public', and that the patented invention must be made available 'at a reasonably affordable price' are fairly uncontroversial and unlikely to raise any issues in regards to WTO consistency, the requirement that the patented invention must be 'worked' in India is more controversial. This issue came to the fore in 2012 when in the case of *Bayer v Natco* the Indian Controller General issued a compulsory licence in relation to Bayer's patented anti-cancer drug Nexavar, finding that worked in the territory of India means manufactured to a reasonable extent in India. While this is undoubtedly in line with Article 83 and other relevant parts of the Indian Patent Act, the issue is whether this is in line with the requirement of Article 27 to not 'discriminate' between locally produced and imported patented products. To some, this clearly means that discriminating on the basis of whether a patented product is imported or locally produced would always amount to a violation of Article 27. To others, the case is not so clear, given the panel's comments in *Canada—Pharmaceuticals* regarding discrimination as 'unjustified differentiation'—'Is the issuance of a compulsory licence a case of justified or unjustified differentiation?'—as well as Article 5(A)(2) of the Paris Convention, which implies that 'importation' would not amount to working of a patent and is incorporated into the TRIPS Agreement via Article 2.2.[60] Through a comprehensive and holistic evaluation of the issue under the various elements of Article 31 of the Vienna Convention on the Law of Treaties I have argued that local working requirements

[59] To this author's knowledge, Argentina is the only country to model a domestic law on India's Section 3(d). No other country has a utility standard modelled on the Canadian court interpretation.

[60] The Paris Convention for the Protection of Industrial Property (Paris Convention), 14 July 1967, 21 UST 1583, art 5(a)(2) provides: 'Each country of the Union shall have the right to take legislative measures providing for the grant of compulsory licenses to prevent the abuses which might result from the exercise of the exclusive rights conferred by the patent, for example, failure to work.'

are consistent with the TRIPS Agreement, but the issue has not been heard before a WTO panel.[61]

Likewise, several other parts of the text lend themselves to interpretive uncertainty. This is especially the case in Section III on enforcement. One aspect of enforcement came to prominence in 2009 when the Netherlands and other members of the European Union began detaining generic drugs legally produced in India (and elsewhere) whilst in transit to a third country. The issue here was that while the drugs would violate a legitimate patent in the European Union, the drugs at issue were not patented in the country of destination. India and Brazil filed a complaint at the WTO, but the parties reached a negotiated solution and a panel was never formed.[62] The issue is complicated, and would undoubtedly require the panel to interpret the meaning of the phrase 'country of importation' under Article 52 of the TRIPS Agreement—in short, the question is whether a transit country is a 'country of importation' or whether that term is reserved for the country of final destination.[63]

The final challenge to be discussed is that of bilateral and regional trade agreements (also called free trade agreements or FTAs). Perhaps in part due to the success of the 'access to medicines' and constant protestations of the 'access to knowledge' movements, some developed countries have moved to increase standards and reduce flexibilities through stand-alone agreements as well as through FTAs.[64] This pushback is without question the most important challenge facing the international IP system and access to medicines. The issue has been discussed extensively in the literature,[65] but it is worth recounting that increased periods of patent protection through extensions, test data protection, linking marketing approval to patent status, limitations to the use of compulsory licences and TRIPS-consistent flexibilities and other TRIPS-Plus provisions have the potential to negatively impact access to medicines in that they serve to extend the monopoly selling period of the branded drug and in so doing keep the price of the drugs higher for a longer period of time. While the threat stemming from such clauses can be limited or curtailed through precise drafting, most agreements contain standard language and few (if any) safeguards. In this regard, while some developing countries are resisting pressure and resisting the increased standards, resistance is generally limited and lacking in success. Paradoxically, while the United States is one of the primary drivers behind the push to maximize IPRs, it

[61] Bryan Mercurio and Mitali Tyagi, 'Treaty Interpretation in WTO Dispute Settlement: The Outstanding Question of the Legality of Local Working Requirements' (2010) 19(2) Minn J Intl L 275.

[62] See Press Release, Ministry of Commerce and Industry of India, 'India EU Reach an Understanding on Issue of Seizure of Indian Generic Drugs in Transit', 28 July 2011 <http://pib.nic.in/newsite/erelease.aspx?relid=73554> accessed 13 March 2016.

[63] For detailed analysis, see Bryan Mercurio, '"Seizing" Pharmaceuticals in Transit: Analysing the WTO Dispute That Wasn't' (2012) 61(2) Intl Comp LQ 389.

[64] See Okediji (n 41) 104.

[65] See Michael Handler and Bryan Mercurio, 'Intellectual Property' in Simon Lester and Bryan Mercurio (eds), *Bilateral and Regional Trade Agreements: Analysis and Commentary* (2nd edn, CUP 2015) 324–63.

has also taken the lead in creating exceptions (whether through legislation or the courts) domestically.[66] Many of these exceptions and flexibilities do not make it into partner countries' domestic law.

IV. Conclusion

This chapter reviewed the state of the law and policy of pharmaceutical patents since the advent of the TRIPS Agreement. The Agreement has neither led to increased innovation, nor had as much impact on access to medicines, as many predicted. This is not to say that the Agreement has not had any impact on the access to medicines. Several provisions do impact the protection of pharmaceutical patents, but this chapter argues that the effect of such clauses has been muted. Several issues and future challenges remain, including several unresolved interpretive issues on TRIPS provisions and the higher levels of protection required by FTAs.

To conclude, it is worth noting that increased access to medicines and the attainment of a healthier world is not dependent upon patent status. The poorest countries in the world are under no obligation to protect patents, yet are least able to provide access to medicines or even basic health care. In this author's view, time, energy, and effort focusing on the issue of patents have diverted necessary attention away from more pressing issues such as infrastructure, training, and other measures which could better provide access to medicines and health care. In order to really make progress, sustained effort must be undertaken to address the larger issues that will facilitate the entry and distribution of medicines.[67] Until that occurs, patents are distinctly secondary and should be practically irrelevant to the debate.

[66] See Okediji (n 41) 110–11, citing Jerome H Reichman, 'Richard Lillich Memorial Lecture: Nurturing a Transnational System of Innovation' (2007) 16 J Transnl L Poly 143, 162. See also Deere (n 39) 9.

[67] Bryan Mercurio, 'Health in the Developing World: The Case for a New International Funding and Support Agency' (2009) 4(1) Asian J WTO & Intl Health L & Policy 27.

26

Trans-Pacific Partnership Intellectual Property Controversies

*Raj Bhala**

I. Secrecy, Controversy, and Scepticism

In contrast to the work of Professor Mitsuo Matsushita, there is little about the proposed Trans-Pacific Partnership (TPP) that is transparent. The World Trade Organization (WTO) Appellate Body reports he intrepidly co-authored as a founding member of that august adjudicatory tribunal are readily and freely available, with his signature line, for the world to read. That is not true of any of the twenty-nine Chapters of the TPP, which remain classified. Three have been leaked to and published by WikiLeaks—the Chapters covering the Environment, Investor–State Dispute Settlement (ISDS), and Intellectual Property (IP).

The present contribution, humbly offered in honour of the work of Professor Matsushita, relies only on publicly available sources, not leaked documents. There certainly has been no shortage of media coverage of the TPP, especially its IP provisions. Secrecy has fuelled controversy, and controversy has fuelled scepticism. Whatever benefits the lack of transparency may have provided for candour in negotiations, the costs have overwhelmed them. Doubts about the TPP are so grave that even if Congress renewed Presidential fast-track Trade Promotion Authority (TPA), its approval of the TPP is dubious.

* Associate Dean for International and Comparative Law, and Rice Distinguished Professor, The University of Kansas, School of Law, <http://en.wikipedia.org/wiki/Raj_Bhala > accessed 14 March 2016. JD, Harvard (1989); MSc, Oxford (1986); MSc, London School of Economics (1985); AB, Duke (1984). Marshall Scholar (1984–1986). Member, Council on Foreign Relations, Royal Society for Asian Affairs, and Fellowship of Catholic Scholars. Author of *Trade, Development, and Social Justice* (Carolina Academic Press 2003), *Understanding Islamic Law (Sharīʿa)* (LexisNexis 2011), *Modern GATT Law* (2nd edn, Thomson: Sweet & Maxwell 2013), *Dictionary of International Trade Law* (3rd edn, LexisNexis 2015), and *International Trade Law: An Interdisciplinary, Non-Western Textbook* (4th edn, LexisNexis 2015).

This contribution builds on a portion of an earlier article, Raj Bhala, 'Trans-Pacific Partnership or Trampling Poor Partners? A Tentative Critical Review' (2014) 11 Manchester J Intl Econ L issue 1, 2–59, and a portion of Annex A, Note A-2, in Raj Bhala, *Dictionary of International Trade Law* (LexisNexis 2015).

That is for good reason. This ambitious, twenty-first-century free trade agreement (FTA) is designed—according to the rhetoric of the United States Trade Representative (USTR) and the business interests lobbying for the TPP—to level the playing field on which American exporters compete. With a level (or more level) playing field, US workers will have more and higher-paying job opportunities in a diverse array of agricultural, industrial, and service export sectors. Underlying all those sectors, that is, a key source of their comparative advantage, is their IP: they all rely on some type of patent, trademark, or copyright, or a trade secret, to gain, maintain, or increase their appeal to foreign customers. In turn, from the perspective of its champions, central to the TPP are its strong IP protections.

That strength is precisely a fatal weakness, say detractors. The IP provisions reveal that the TPP is trade promotion for the plutocracy, specifically, plutocratic interests like the Pharmaceutical Research Manufacturers Association of America (PhRMA), which seek to extend the life of their protected monopoly interests. Which side is right, or whether both sides are to a degree, is difficult to say without inspecting the text of the TPP and thinking through the ramifications of each of its provisions. But, as the discussion below argues, there is good reason for dissension. Those controversies cover copyright, third-party pre-grant patent opposition, patent protection periods, biologics and data exclusivity, and criminal liability for trade secrets.

Indeed, all twelve TPP countries—the original four from June 2005, Brunei, Chile, New Zealand, and Singapore, plus the eight others that joined the talks between February 2008 and March 2013, Australia, Canada, Japan, Malaysia, Mexico, Peru, the United States, and Vietnam—were so concerned about so many IP issues that the Chapter governing the topic was the longest of any in the FTA, and consumed the most time to negotiate.[1] The contentious issues went beyond conventional copyright, patent, and trademark protections, geographical indications (GIs), and trade secret matters.[2] They included novel topics such as data

[1] See Len Bracken, 'Japan Engaging in Market Access Talks With More TPP Members, Froman Says' (2014) 31 Intl Trade Rep 991; Len Bracken, 'US Chamber Seeks Trade Secrets Clauses In TPP, Pinpoints Other Policy Preferences' (2013) 30 Intl Trade Rep 1364.

[2] GI matters seemed to be of greater concern in negotiations with the European Union for a Trans-Atlantic Trade and Investment Partnership (TTIP) than in TPP talks. The United States and the European Union had 'diametrically opposed positions' on GIs, said USTR Ambassador Michael Froman. Quoted in Rossella Brevetti, 'Sen Hatch Welcomes Progress in TPP Pact, Welcomes Administration Focus on TPA' (2015) 32 Intl Trade Rep 223.

A GI is a sign on a good attesting to the geographical place from which that good originates, and conveys the sense that the good has special qualities, or a special reputation, because of that origin. The WTO *Agreement on Trade-related Aspects of Intellectual Property Rights* (*TRIPs*) condones the use and protection of GIs, particularly on wines and spirits, but a broad set of rules on GIs has eluded Doha Round negotiators.

Some US politicians, such as Senator Tammy Baldwin (Democrat-Wisconsin), wanted to ensure that any FTA would not impede US producers of beer, cheese, and meat from using the common names for those goods. (All three products are ones for which her state of Wisconsin is famous.) She said US feta cheese producers lost export opportunities in Canada because of restrictions on use of the word 'feta' in the Canada–EU FTA. (The European Union was also pressing for restrictions on the common names 'asiago', 'muenster', and 'parmesan,' which she said the United States should oppose.) Likewise, EU FTAs with some Central American countries adversely affected US

needed for regulatory approvals, data exclusivity, and traditional knowledge. For the President's Export Council (PEC), the way to address all the controversies was clear: the TPP should contain IP provisions at least as strong as those in the United States' most recent FTAs, particularly the *United States—Korea FTA* (*KORUS*), and should add protections for trade secrets.[3] That position was not universally shared among TPP negotiating countries. As the bargaining ground on, fewer TPP countries seemed to agree with the United States.

II. Copyright Enforcement

Common to all IP issues was enforcement.[4] New Zealand, for instance, observed that counterfeit films cost its movie industry—which includes hits by producer Sir Peter Jackson like *The Hobbit*—over US$100 million annually.[5] But, that was not their only subject.

At the thirteenth round of negotiations in July 2012 in San Diego, California, the United States put forward its first proposal on IP.[6] It concerned copyright, and the United States said the aim of its proposal was to balance the need for strong protection of copyright interests, on the one hand, with the need for exceptions for fair use for commentary, criticism, reporting, research, and scholarship, on the other hand. Accordingly, America proposed that the TPP contain the same exceptions and limitations on copyright protection as exist under US law; for example, a fair-use exception, and the same safe harbours for Internet service providers (ISPs) that exist under the *Digital Millennium Copyright Act*, and which also are found in Article 18:4(7)(d)–(e) of *KORUS*.[7] Moreover, the United States sought an extension of copyright protection from fifty to seventy years.[8]

opportunities to export bologna to those countries. The European Union insisted in those FTAs that all 'bologna' sold in those countries must come from Italy. Senator Baldwin argued for a strong, clear negotiating objective in any fast-track trade bill that would mandate opposition to any limits on American producers using common food names. (Such language was contained in Senate Bill 1900 from the 2013–2014 Congress.) See Rossella Brevetti, 'Finance Committee Leadership Pressed on Use of Generic Names for Cheeses, Meat' (2015) 32 Intl Trade Rep 433.

[3] See Brian Flood, 'Obama Meets Export Council, Expresses Optimism for Trade Promotion Authority' (2013) 30 Intl Trade Rep 1465.

[4] See Len Bracken, 'TPP Members Grapple with Japan's Entry, Ways to Speed Talks Ahead of 17th Round' (2013) 30 Intl Trade Rep 495.

[5] ibid. The importance of copyright enforcement is not limited to developed countries. Developing countries with emerging IP sectors care about it, too. For example, 7.3 per cent of Philippine GDP is linked to creative and other industries dependent on copyrights. See Len Bracken, 'Sen. Warren, Others Voice TPP Concerns on ISDS, Market Access, Capital Controls' (2015) 32 Intl Trade Rep 40.

[6] See Len Bracken, 'USTR's Marantis Cites Progress on TPP, Says Tough Issues Remain at this Stage' (2012) 29 Intl Trade Rep 1330.

[7] See Tony Dutra and Amy Tsui, 'USTR Proposing Exceptions and Limitations on TPP Copyright Protection, Enforcement' (2012) 29 Intl Trade Rep 1330.

[8] See Monika Ermert, 'Big Trading Blocs Moving at Breakneck Pace to Raise Free Trade Standards' (*Intellectual Property Watch*, 22 May 2013) <http://www.ip-watch.org/2013/05/22/special-report-big-trading-blocs-moving-at-breakneck-pace-to-raise-free-trade-standards/> accessed 14 March 2016.

The American proposal had a three-step test on exclusive right of reproduction; namely, it is up to a country to permit reproduction of a work, without the express consent of the author:[9]

1. in special cases;
2. if the reproduction does not conflict with normal exploitation of the work; and
3. if the reproduction does not unreasonably prejudice the interests of the author.

This test was developed in 1967, and—as the United States pointed out—is manifest in and thus consistent with the WTO Agreement on Trade Related Aspects of Intellectual Property Rights (TRIP Agreement) (including Article 13), the Berne Convention for the Protection of Literary and Artistic Works (including Article 9(2)), and the World Intellectual Property Organization (WIPO) Copyright Treaty.

Some commentators queried whether this test might be construed too broadly.[10] Article 2*bis* of the Berne Convention allows for political speech to be excluded from copyright protection. These commentators said political speech should not be subject to the three-part test, but rather granted the same fair-use exception as under the Convention. In other words, the Convention does not mandate the use of the test in every possible instance of fair use. But, by referring expressly to criticism, comment, news reporting, teaching, scholarship, and research, the US proposal for the TPP seems to demand all fair-use exceptions to meet the three-step test, thus expanding rather dramatically the scope of copyright protection.

In October 2014, Wikileaks obtained a draft text of the IP Chapter dated 16 May 2014 (discussed further below). Reportedly, this text called for binding obligations to expand the liability of third parties for copyright infringement.[11] It also appeared that the United States sought higher penalties in a case of copyright or trademark infringement where the counterfeited items posed a threat to consumer health or safety.[12]

III. Third-party Pre-grant Patent Opposition

How easy ought it to be for a third party to oppose granting of a patent, before that patent is granted? In other words, should it be simple for a third party to challenge the standards under which a patent would be granted, and thereby possibly prevent

[9] See Tamlin H Bason, 'Leaked TPP Copyright Text Purportedly Expands Berne Convention's Three-Part Test' (2012) 29 Intl Trade Rep 1341.

[10] ibid.

[11] See Stephanie Cohen, 'Leaked Draft of TPP Chapter Includes US Proposal to Give Pharma Longer Patents' (2014) 31 Intl Trade Rep 1870.

[12] See Len Bracken, 'US Seeks Civil, Criminal Response in TPP for Theft of Trade Secrets, Holleyman Says' (2014) 31 Intl Trade Rep 2041.

its granting? In February 2011, the United States said 'not easy'. It argued against pre-grant opposition under the TPP. A third party ought to be able to put up only post-grant opposition.

By August 2013, the United States softened its position, saying reasonable pre-grant opposition procedures were acceptable. The US shift was in line with an August 2013 proposal by Canada, Chile, Malaysia, New Zealand, and Singapore for a provision in the TPP IPR Chapter expressly allowing for pre-grant opposition procedures. Their idea was that '[e]ach Party shall provide a procedure for third persons to oppose the grant of a patent, either before or after the grant of a patent, or both'.[13]

Why the shift? The problem with allowing third parties only post-grant opposition is that the patent owner enjoys the benefits of the patent throughout the pendency of the patent challenge litigation. Such disputes can take years to resolve, and are expensive. Third parties face these disincentives to mount post-grant challenges, whereas they do not if they are allowed to make a pre-grant challenge. In the September 2011 America Invents Act, the United States changed its domestic posture: it created pre-grant patent opposition procedures. So, its shift in the TPP talks reflected the Act.

Still, the United States faced opposition from other countries. Most other TPP countries with pre-grant opposition procedures had no exceptions to those procedures, and did not permit a patent seeker to conceal its patent application. The America Invents Act seemed to tolerate a patent seeker avoiding a pre-grant challenge by asking the US Patent and Trademark Office (PTO) to keep secret its application until a final decision on patentability.[14] Only then would a challenge be entertained.

IV. Twenty-five-year Pharmaceutical Patent Protection

Agreeing on a period for patent protection of pharmaceuticals requires a compromise between developers of medicines that incur hundreds of millions, sometimes billions, of dollars to research, test, and market a new drug and patients for whom those drugs are designed, many of whom cannot pay full price for them. The TRIPS Agreement (in Article 33) sets the period at twenty years, an increase from the traditional US period of seventeen years. Apparently not content with that increase, the United States sought in TPP negotiations an additional five years, for a total of twenty-five years.

At the nineteenth round in August 2013, it won.[15] None other than Mexico claimed that a twenty-five-year period for pharmaceutical products was a 'done

[13] Quoted in Len Bracken, 'US Supports More Flexible Approach to Patent Opposition in TPP, USTR Says' (2013) 30 Intl Trade Rep 1896.

[14] ibid.

[15] See Maja Wallengren, 'Mexican Official Says Agreement Reached To Extend Pharmaceutical Rights Protections' (2013) 30 Intl Trade Rep 1365.

deal'. However, Mexico explained that the extension from twenty to twenty-five years would not be automatic. On the contrary, twenty years would remain the baseline period. A five-year extension could be granted on a case-by-case (that is, drug-by-drug) basis, upon application. The applicant—presumably a pharmaceutical company—would have to prove the particular medicine for which it sought an extension (i) took considerably more time and money than the average of ten years; and (ii) there was a valid need to expend the extra time and funds.

Why did Mexico, a developing country, support the idea? Its pharmaceutical industry is the second most important (measured in terms of value). It accounts for sales of $14 billion (in 2012), 78,000 direct and 300,000 indirect jobs, and grew by fourteen per cent (between 2007 and 2009).[16] Its National Pharmaceutical Industries Chamber, Canifarma, represents both generic and non-generic firms. Canifarma understood that the Mexican pharmaceutical sector had developed to the point that portions of it could benefit from extended patent protection, but other parts—plus poor patients—needed access to cheap drugs. The discretionary five-year extension seemed to strike the right balance.

Conversely, certain constituencies in Australia opposed any effort through the TPP to extend the monopoly rights enjoyed by pharmaceutical companies beyond the customarily accepted limits. In March 2015, a think tank, the Center for Primary Health Care and Equity at the University of Sydney, performed a heath impact assessment of the TPP IP texts that previously had been leaked.[17] The Center warned that those provisions would increase the cost of medicines to the Australian public, which otherwise are subsidized under the Australian Pharmaceuticals Benefits Scheme (PBS). Those provisions would give foreign pharmaceutical multinational companies influence over decisions under the PBS to list a medication, and to set the price of that medication.

V. Biologics Data Exclusivity

The treatment of biological medical products was another point of major IP controversy in TPP negotiations. The broad issue is balancing incentives to innovate and develop new medicine versus ensuring wide access to medicines for underprivileged people. The specific issue is the period of protection for these products, which also are called 'bio-pharmaceutical medicines', known commonly by the short-hand term 'biologics'.[18] Biologics are created from living organisms, and the medicine is used to treat cancer, diabetes, and other diseases. They are expensive

[16] ibid.

[17] See Murray Griffin, 'Australian Think-Tank Subjects TPP to "Health Impact Assessment"' (2015) 32 Intl Trade Rep 475.

[18] See Len Bracken, 'TPP Ministers To Brief Leaders Oct 8 On Margins Of APEC Summit in Indonesia' (2013) 30 Intl Trade Rep 1561; Len Bracken, 'US Negotiating "Biologics" Proposal, Marking End to "Period of Reflection"' (2013) 30 Intl Trade Rep 1366; Bronwyn Mixter, 'Lawmakers Urge President to Protect Biologic Exclusivity in Trade Negotiations' (2012) 29 Intl Trade L 1341.

drugs because of the significant research and development (R&D) and manufacturing expenses: they cost between $20,000 and $400,000 per person annually.[19] Among the major manufacturers of brand-name biologics are Amgen and Genetech.[20] They produce data from clinical trials, which they are eager to protect from potential generic producers.

The WTO TRIPs Agreement does not mandate a so-called 'data exclusivity' regime for biologic medicines. Rather, it leaves WTO Members the policy space to adopt such a regime, or not, and to fashion its details. Those details may include a prescribed period of protection. Alternatively, instead of mandating exclusivity and thereby limiting access to medicines, Members could set rules against unfair commercial use of data.[21]

Under the 2012 health care reform law championed by President Obama (i.e. the Affordable Care Act, commonly called 'Obamacare'), a branded biologic (that is, a biological medical product that is patented) enjoyed twelve years of market exclusivity.[22] The twelve-year total is the sum of four years for data and a further eight years for marketing. (Only after all twelve years have expired can a 'biosimilar', explained below, rely on the clinical test data from the brand-name producer to prove its version is 'pure, potent and safe'.[23])

Major multinational pharmaceutical companies that make such brands are Baxter, Eli Lilly, Novartis, and Pfizer. For these name-brand companies, the twelve-year test data protection period equates to non-patent exclusivity. During those twelve years, no generic biological drug—also called a 'biosimilar'—can lawfully enter into the market in competition with the branded biologic, if the biosimilar relied on the same data as did the branded biologic. Rather, a generic producer must conduct its R&D, including clinical trials, just as did the branded drug producer. Only after the expiry of the twelve-year period can a generic manufacturer use test data from the clinical trials conducted by producers of the brand name drug as a basis for making the generic drug.

Obviously, 'biosimilar' medicine is a less expensive, follow-on, generic version of the original, expensive 'biologic' drug.[24] Generic manufacturers oppose data exclusivity for biologics. Nobel-Prize-winning Economist Joseph Stiglitz sided with the generic producers, saying he had opposed the USTR position on such

[19] See Len Bracken, 'Report Makes Case for US Biologics Law In TPP as Chief Negotiators Meet in Hawaii' (2015) 32 Intl Trade Rep 528; See Len Bracken, 'Hatch Stresses IPR, ISDS Objectives in Trans-Pacific Partnership Agreement' (2015) 32 Intl Trade Rep 304.

[20] See Len Bracken, 'Good TPP Market Access Deal Needed to Resolve Rules Issues, Brilliant Says' (2014) 31 Intl Trade Rep 1975.

[21] See Len Bracken, 'Coalition of Groups Presses Obama on TPP Provisions Concerning Medicine' (2015) 32 Intl Trade Rep 53.

[22] The specific portion of the *Act* in which the twelve-year rule is set is known as the *Biologics Price Competition and Innovation Act*, or '*BPCIA*'. Patient Protection and Affordable Care Act, Pub L 111–148, 124 Stat 119 (2010).

[23] Bracken, 'Report Makes Case for US Biologics Law in TPP as Chief Negotiators Meet in Hawaii' (n 19).

[24] See Bracken, 'TPP Members Grapple with Japan's Entry, Ways to Speed Talks Ahead of 17th Round' (n 4).

issues since 1995–1997, when he served on the White House Council of Economic Advisors (CEA).[25]

Nevertheless, US negotiators sought to vault the US legal standard of twelve-year biologics exclusivity into the TPP.[26] Predictably, the PhRMA backed the American position. Its members include Amgen, Genetech (part of the Roche Group), Pfizer, Merck, Novartis, Eli Lilly, Johnson & Johnson, and GlaxoSmithKline, each of which makes biologics.[27] If that were the TPP rule, then biosimilar producers could not avoid 'reinventing the wheel' by using data generated by the branded producer. In turn, they could not save R&D costs, and hence not price biosimilars as cheaply as they would like to.[28] Of course, other opposing interests, in the US and overseas, preferred a far shorter period of protection, such as five to ten years.[29]

That is, the nature of the twelve-year exclusivity is one of data protection. Another company, such as a generic manufacturer, cannot use the data created by the inventor (innovator) of the branded biologic for twelve years after the patent has expired—the so called 'test data'. A generic manufacturer might seek to use those data to develop a biosimilar. This twelve-year period runs subsequent to the twenty or twenty-five years of patent protection. Hence, the effective market exclusivity enjoyed by the branded biologic over the biosimilar competition is a whopping thirty-two (twenty plus twelve) or thirty-seven (twenty-five plus twelve) years. That is far above the simple twenty-year TRIPS standard.

Obviously, the longer the period of protection for branded biologics, the slower the access to the market makers of generic drugs have for their biosimilars. In turn, high monopoly prices, and consequent high health care costs and limited access for poor populations to life-saving and life-enhancing medicines, result. Defenders of this idea pointed out that significant R&D costs need to be recouped if pharmaceutical companies are going to have an incentive to innovate. Without the dilated period, global innovation would be stifled. Surely innovators need to capture the gains (or at least some of them) from their creativity. They can take their gains, and pursue yet a new generation of innovative medicines, thus yielding a 'virtuous cycle'.[30] Moreover, twelve years of protection means that clinical trial data will ensure that biologic drugs are safe and effective.[31]

[25] See Bracken, 'Hatch Stresses IPR, ISDS Objectives in Trans-Pacific Partnership Agreement' (n 19).

[26] See Griffin (n 17).

[27] See Len Bracken, 'TPP Chief Negotiators, Key Experts Gather in Salt Lake City to Advance Negotiations' (2013) 30 Intl Trade Rep 1816.

[28] See Bracken, 'US Negotiating "Biologics" Proposal, Marking End to "Period of Reflection"' (n 18).

[29] See Len Bracken, 'Road to Finalizing TPP Starts in Tokyo, Ends With Approval Votes on Capitol Hill, Outlook 2015—Trans-Pacific Partnership' (2015) 32 Intl Trade Rep 146.

[30] Bracken, 'Report Makes Case for US Biologics Law in TPP as Chief Negotiators Meet in Hawaii' (n 19) (quoting Stephen Ezell, Director of Global Innovation Policy, Information Technology & Innovation Partnership (ITIF), who authored a March 2015 report in favour of the twelve-year period, 'The Imperative of Protecting Life Sciences Innovation in the *TPP*').

[31] See Griffin (n 17).

Not surprisingly, these (and other) IP proposals contemplated for TPP attracted strong criticism. The United States stood alone in the world with a twelve-year exclusivity period for biologics. Brunei, Malaysia, Mexico, Peru, and Vietnam provide for no biologic exclusivity periods. Australia, New Zealand, and Singapore have five-year periods, as does Chile (for what Chile calls 'new chemical entities' or 'small molecule drugs'). Canada and Japan have eight-year periods.[32] Simply put, the United States wanted one-third longer protection than the next longest period.

That was another example of corporate US greed. Médecins Sans Frontières (MSF) thus expressed concern that US demands for 'aggressive' expansion of IP rights beyond those in the TRIPS Agreement would adversely affect access to affordable medicines, in rich and poor countries alike, by creating 'high-priced monopolies': 'One of the most outrageous provisions the US is pursuing is an unprecedented specially extended period of monopoly protection for medical products known as biologics, which include important treatments and vaccines.'[33] Australia, thus, was adamant that it would not change its law.[34] Similarly, Peru said it would go no further than its February 2009 Trade Promotion Agreement (TPA) with the United States in respect of IPR protection of pharmaceuticals. Under the TPA, data exclusivity for biologics is permissible, but not mandatory.

So, among the US-backed charges were the IP provisions which would impede the delivery of low-cost medicines (i.e. generics) to treat HIV/AIDS and malaria in poor countries by extending monopoly protection for old, branded drugs, and would extend copyright protection to an unreasonably long period.[35] Critics touted the concept of 'patent delinking', whereby the cost of R&D is separated from the cost of the pharmaceutical product.[36] R&D expenses are covered by grants, or other monetary incentives, so as to assure pharmaceutical countries they can profit from a new, low-priced medicine they invent.

Pharmaceutical industries in developing, and even some developed, countries participating in the TPP talks, such as Australia, Brunei, Canada, Chile, Mexico, Peru, and Vietnam, opposed US efforts to extend periods of patent protection and fix data exclusivity rules.[37] 'Data exclusivity' is 'a non-patent form' of IP protection 'for biologic medicines that prevents generic manufacturers from using previous data

[32] See Bracken, 'Report Makes Case for US Biologics Law in TPP as Chief Negotiators Meet in Hawaii' (n 19).

[33] ibid (quoting Judit Rius Sanjuan, US Manager and Legal Policy Advisor, MSF Access Campaign).

[34] See Bracken, 'Hatch Stresses IPR, ISDS Objectives in Trans-Pacific Partnership Agreement' (n 19).

[35] See Bernard K Gordon, 'Trading Up in Asia—Why the United States Needs the Trans-Pacific Partnership' (2012) 91(4) Foreign Affairs 17–22.

[36] See Lucien Chauvin, 'Stakeholders Focus on IPR, Investment at Trans-Pacific Partnership Talks in Peru' (2013) 30 Intl Trade Rep 739.

[37] See Maja Wallengren, 'TPP Partners Agree to Exempt Four Countries From Extended IP Pharmaceutical Provisions' (2013) 30 Intl Trade Rep 1738; Maja Wallengren, 'Mexico's Pharmaceutical Industry Opposes Proposed Extension of IP Protections in TPP' (2013) 30 Intl Trade Rep 501.

from clinical trials' for a specific period.[38] Protestors in Malaysia, in connection with the April 2014 visit to that country of President Barack H Obama, said that the TPP would lead to higher costs of medical supplies, and accused their own government of being bullied by the Americans—a charge the Malaysian Prime Minister Dato Sri Mohammed Najib Tun Abdul Razak rejected.[39] Underlying the US position, they said, was the greed of large, rich, country pharmaceutical companies, which would injure not only generic producers, but more poignantly poor patients in poor countries. They feared the cost of medication would rise, and generics would no longer be available if the standards for IP protection in the TPP were too high.

To be fair, the evidence was not all on their side. For instance, since the 1 February 2009 implementation of the Peru Trade Promotion Agreement (PTPA), the cost of medicines had fallen, and the supply of generics increased—and the PTPA has raised IP standards. Still, the opponents were not persuaded. Peru accepted that the PTPA had addressed new issues, including second-use patents. But, it objected to any effort by the United States to foist its Stop Online Piracy Act (SOPA) onto the TPP as a potential restriction on free speech. Peru said the TPP should go no further on IP obligations than does the PTPA.[40] Indeed, even in the United States, NGOs like the Access to Medicines Program of Public Citizen said that the TPP might 'lock in the United States to patent controls for biologicals that are still under debate at home'.[41]

Budgetary concerns within the United States mattered, too. The Office of Management and Budget (OMB), which is responsible for devising a budget to pay for drugs under Medicare and Medicaid programs, opposed a twelve-year data exclusivity period.[42] A seven-year period would accelerate the marketing of biosimilars, allowing for faster price reductions and thereby reduced health care costs. In other words, the PhRMA position pushed in the TPP negotiations by the USTR was more than a disservice to US biosimilar producers. It also was a threat to the US government budget deficit. After all, the United States was no more immune from rising drug costs than a developing country. Eleven of the last twelve cancer drugs brought to market (as of September 2013) cost over $100,000 per course of treatment.[43] That price tag was one Americans and foreigners alike could not afford.[44]

[38] Yu-Tzu Chu, 'Taiwan to Create Patent Linkage System for Drugs in Quest for TPP Membership' (2014) 31 Intl Trade Rep 1530.

[39] See Stephanie Cohen, 'Obama, Najib Reject Criticism that US is Bullying Malaysia in TPP Discussions' (2014) 31 Intl Trade Rep 813.

[40] See Lucien O Chauvin, 'Seventeenth TPP Round Starts in Peru, Official is Confident of Wrap-Up by Year's End' (2013) 30 Intl Trade Rep 738.

[41] Lucien O Chauvin, 'Progress Made as Latest Round Ends; Questions Remain on Japan's Upcoming Role' (2013) 30 Intl Trade Rep 773, 773–74 (characterizing remarks of Peter Maybarduk, Head of the Access Program).

[42] See Bracken, 'US Negotiating "Biologics" Proposal, Marking End to "Period of Reflection"' (n 18).

[43] ibid.

[44] Reportedly, in October 2013 the United States proposed that four TPP developing countries could avail themselves of temporary exemptions on extended patent rights. See Maja Wallengren, 'Mexican Minister Says TPP Negotiators Draft Final "Action Plan" For IP Chapter' (2013) 30 Intl Trade Rep 1603.

In November 2013, WikiLeaks released a draft of the IP Chapter that contained a proposal on data protection that was not as rigorous as the US regime.[45] The leaked text, spanning ninety-five pages containing 941 brackets (indicating points on which no agreement was reached), was dated 30 August 2013, and reflected contributions at the nineteenth negotiating round in Brunei. The proposal, made by Canada, Chile, New Zealand, Malaysia, and Singapore, and supported by Vietnam, essentially called for protection of data at the level of that in the TRIPS Agreement:

> Where a Party requires, as a condition of marketing, regulatory or sanitary approval for pharmaceutical products which utilize new chemical entities, the submission of undisclosed test or other data, the origination of which involves considerable effort, that Party shall protect such data against unfair commercial use. In addition, each Party shall protect such data against disclosure, except where necessary to protect the public or unless steps are taken to ensure that the data is [*sic*] protected against unfair commercial use....

Each Party may provide that the protection of data under paragraph 1, inter alia:

- is limited to undisclosed test or other data, the origination of which involves a considerable effort;
- is limited to pharmaceutical products that do not contain a new chemical entity that has been previously approved for marketing in the Party;
- is limited to pharmaceutical products which utilitze a new chemical entity;
- is available only once per pharmaceutical product;
- is not available for new uses or indications, new dosage forms, or methods of making a pharmaceutical product;
- is limited to a period of time as determined by the Party; or
- may be waived to facilitate the marketing, regulatory, or sanitary approval of a pharmaceutical product that is the subject of a voluntary or compulsory licence, or a licence otherwise issued pursuant to the TRIPS.[46]

Thus, the proposal did not include any provision or proposal for data exclusivity, in contrast to US law.

That is, the TPP did not appear to have a rule for test data exclusivity for biologics, whereas the US rule protects data for twelve years. But, the TPP did contain a placeholder—i.e. an indication of a possible specific provision on biologics—surely at the United States' insistence. Civil society groups, including the MSF Access Campaign and the Global Access to Medicines Program of the Public Citizen, explained that the United States was nearly alone in its insistence on data exclusivity, as most other TPP countries were against binding TRIPS-Plus commitments.

The leaked text also indicated that the United States, with Japan, opposed a proposal by the same five countries—Canada, Chile, New Zealand, Malaysia,

[45] See Len Bracken, 'Leaked TPP Text on IPR Includes Proposal On Data Protection from Five Countries' (2013) 30 Intl Trade Rep 1820.

[46] ibid.

and Singapore—calling for an enhancement of the role of IP in economic development.[47] Conversely, the American–Japanese proposal to make it illegal to deny a patent based on the lack of enhanced efficiency of that patented item was rejected by all other TPP countries. The proposal was designed to facilitate secondary patents.

Likewise, a US proposal on patent term adjustment, which would allow (at the request of a patent holder) for lengthening a patent as compensation for unreasonable delays in granting a patent, was opposed by Canada, New Zealand, and Japan. The proposal stated:

> For purposes of this subparagraph, an unreasonable delay at least shall include a delay in the issuance of the patent of more than four years from the date of filing of the application in the territory of the Party, or two years after a request for examination of the application has been made, whichever is later.... Periods attributable to actions of the patent applicant need not be included in the determination of such delays. Any patent term adjustment under this article shall confer all of the exclusive rights of a patent subject to the same limitations and exceptions that would otherwise apply to the patent absent any adjustment of the patent term.[48]

Given this and the above-mentioned US positions, it is difficult to escape the conclusion that the United States was driven, indeed captured, by the interests of PhRMA, with little regard to effects of those positions on economic development or poverty alleviation. In contrast, generic producers showed flexibility to compromise. The Generic Pharmaceutical Association, the members of which include Impax Laboratories, Momenta Pharmaceuticals, Mylan Pharmaceuticals, Perrigo Pharmaceuticals, and Teva Pharmaceuticals, supported a data exclusivity period of seven years under US law, but thought it premature to have any such period in the TPP.[49]

After all, the resistance of nearly all TPP countries to data exclusivity reflected their domestic legal position: for them, the US proposal would be a significant change in their laws. Some of them afforded no regulatory data protection for biologics, others granted five years, and still others gave eight years.[50] It was highly unlikely that the United States would accept less than an eight-year data exclusivity period, as that would run four years short of its domestic period.[51] It also was nearly certain that the United States would insist on five years of data exclusivity for small medicines manufactured with molecules.

In November 2013, the United States suggested it might accept a tailored approach, allowing for differences across TPP countries.[52] More flexibility could be allowed for poorer countries, but less for richer ones, as the United States had

[47] ibid. [48] ibid.

[49] See Bracken, 'TPP Chief Negotiators, Key Experts Gather in Salt Lake City to Advance Negotiations' (n 27).

[50] See Len Bracken, 'Hatch Says TPP with Committed Partners Better Than Deal Weak on IPR, Data Flows' (2013) 30 Intl Trade Rep 1869.

[51] See Bracken, 'US Seeks Civil, Criminal Response in TPP for Theft of Trade Secrets, Holleyman Says' (n 12).

[52] See Len Bracken, 'US Discussing Tailored Approach to IPR for Medicines in Trans-Pacific Partnership' (2013) 30 Intl Trade Rep 1896.

agreed in its FTAs with Peru and Korea, respectively. So that month, negotiators announced they agreed that four countries—Brunei, Chile, Peru, and Vietnam—could have an exemption from the TPP Chapter on IP, specifically the provisions mandating enhanced protection for pharmaceuticals.[53] These diverse countries would be treated as developing, and not have to provide extended patent protection for human or veterinary medicine, or for biologics.

In December 2013, WikiLeaks published two further TPP documents showing unpopular US positions on IP issues.[54] The United States insisted on a Transparency Annex on Medicines, in the context of the TPP Transparency Chapter. It sought to permit pharmaceutical companies to challenge a TPP government for subsidising medicines and medical devices. Whether that was the same proposal the United States had made in 2011 was unclear, but Australia and Japan backed the Annex idea. The United States also favoured a tax on medicine pricing boards.

The leaks concerning IP continued in 2014.[55] In October, Wikileaks obtained a draft of the IP Chapter dated 16 May 2014. Reportedly, and based on an analysis of that Chapter by Public Citizen, provisions such as extended, automatic monopolies for biotech drugs (i.e. biologics) would advantage the pharmaceutical industry, and possibly lead to delayed access to pharmaceuticals, thus undermining policies in the United States to reduce Medicare and Medicaid expenses. Yet, the draft also reduced the scope of certain other monopoly protections, and cut out a proposal for allowing patents on surgical methods.

No consensus was evident from the leaked May 2014 draft on patent term adjustments; that is, whether to permit extensions, and if so, what the length of those extensions should be. The draft indicated that an earlier draft, from November 2013 (which Wikileaks also obtained, and which Public Citizen also analysed), called for extensions, with limitations on the period of extension, on both pharmaceutical products and methods to make or use those products. The new draft dropped the idea of patent extensions for methods of making or using medicines. That distinguished the new draft from *KORUS*. The new draft also dropped any limitations on the extension period, and proposed to leave it to each TPP country to prescribe its own conditions and duration for extensions.

In brief, the new draft text on pharmaceutical data exclusivity reportedly was akin to that in the United States' FTA with Australia.[56] There would be at least:

1. five years of data exclusivity, that is, market exclusivity, for new pharmaceuticals; and

[53] See Wallengren, 'TPP Partners Agree to Exempt Four Countries From Extended IP Pharmaceutical Provisions' (n 37).

[54] See Brian Flood, 'Leaked TPP Documents Show Fault Lines Underlying Singapore Ministerial Meeting' (2013) 30 Intl Trade Rep 1943.

[55] See Cohen, 'Leaked Draft of TPP Chapter Includes US Proposal to Give Pharma Longer Patents' (n 11).

[56] ibid.

2. three years of exclusivity for previously approved drugs that contain new clinical information (other than data on bio-equivalency) or that have prior approval from a TPP country from the date of marketing approval for the drug in the relevant TPP country.

Further, in contrast to the November 2013 draft, under the May 2014 draft, the exclusivity would concern data not in the public domain; i.e. only undisclosed test data. Aside from Public Citizen, the NGO Knowledge Ecology International criticized the new draft for its provisions demanding (i) twelve years of monopoly over data to register biologic drugs and vaccines; (ii) a restrictive three-step test for compulsory licensing of pharmaceutical patents; (iii) patent extensions beyond twenty years; and (iv) that regulatory agencies investigate any allegations that a registered drug or vaccine infringes on evergreening patents.[57]

There was also no consensus on how to deal with the poorest of the TPP countries.[58] Should they be allowed a transition period, after which they would be obligated to comply fully with TPP IP rules? If so, then on what basis should that period be computed? Name-brand drug producers advocated for a fixed number of years, and for them, the fewer the better. Other proposals called for a transition period based on the *per capita* income of the country. Not until a country reached a certain level of GNP per head should it be required to assume the IP obligations.

VI. Trade Secrets and Criminal Liability

Should a thief of a trade secret face criminal liability? The United States Chamber of Commerce thought so, and urged the TPP to include such a provision.[59] The Chamber argued in August 2013 that innovation and protection of trade secrets are intimately related. It said a trade secret is 'property', and as such should be governed by laws on theft. In just over a year, the Chamber got the explicit support of the USTR. It announced in November 2014 that the United States wanted to see in the TPP both civil and criminal penalties for theft of trade secrets, and reinforced the point in April 2015.[60]

Trade secrets are property stolen to help the thief differentiate its product or price, or improve the efficiency of its supply chain. Sometimes, the thief is an employee of one company, who simply purloins the secret, joins another company,

[57] ibid.

[58] See Len Bracken, 'TPP Ministers Seek Solutions on Legal Texts, Focus on Market Access, Joint Report Says' (2014) 31 Intl Trade Rep 2005.

[59] See Bracken, 'US Chamber Seeks Trade Secrets Clauses in TPP, Pinpoints Other Policy Preferences' (n 1).

[60] See Ali Qassim, 'US Will Insist on IP Rights Protections in Any TPP Trade Deal, USTR Official Says' (2014) 32 Intl Trade Rep 738 (quoting Probir Mehta, Acting Assistant US Trade Representative for Intellectual Property and Innovation, as saying TPP would have to contain 'criminal penalties against trade secret theft'); Ian F Fergusson and others, 'The Trans-Pacific Partnership (TPP) Negotiations and Issues for Congress', Cong Research Serv R42694 33; Bracken, 'US Seeks Civil, Criminal Response in TPP for Theft of Trade Secrets, Holleyman Says' (n 12).

and shares it with that second company. Air Canada, Deutsche Bank, and DuPont have been among the many victims.[61] (In the Air Canada case, the employee gave its trade secrets to WestJet, which then protected the employee from liability.) That trade secret theft was increasing in the Asia-Pacific region, despite the existence of civil penalties in many TPP countries, was proof that criminal liability was needed as a deterrent.

VII. March 2014 UNITAID Critique of TRIPS-Plus Proposals

In April 2014, the global health initiative, UNITAID, published a stinging critique of U TPP TRIPs-Plus proposals.[62] Examining the leaked November 2013 text posted on Wikileaks, UNITAID claimed those proposals would:

1. reduce standards of patentability (for example, by allowing evergreening);
2. limit exclusions from patentability (also by permitting evergreening);
3. weaken disclosure requirements;
4. eliminate the ability to oppose a patent prior to the granting of that patent (i.e. prohibit pre-grant opposition, which is a safeguard);
5. impede (via trademark rules) the ability of generic producers to make and sell medicines by circumscribing their ability to use names, colours, or shapes that are similar to those used by the producer of the original patented medicine;
6. impede civil prosecutions in patent cases, and civil and criminal prosecutions in trademark cases, because of rebuttable presumptions that a patent or trademark is valid, and because of limits on defences raised in infringement cases.

Overall, the rules the United States advocated for the TPP would 'delay generic market entry and competition'.

To be sure, UNITAID had a bias counter to that of US pharmaceutical producers. Based at the World Health Organization (WHO), it is a facility established in 2006 by the Brazilian, British, Chilean, French, and Norwegian governments to purchase pharmaceuticals. It buys medicines to treat HIV-AIDS, malaria, and tuberculosis in bulk so as to negotiate price reductions and then provide the medicines at low cost to low-income countries. TRIPS-Plus TPP rules would be orthogonal to the efforts of UNITAID to make medicines more available and

[61] See Bracken, 'US Chamber Seeks Trade Secrets Clauses in TPP, Pinpoints Other Policy Preferences' (n 1).

[62] See UNITAID, 'The Trans-Pacific Partnership Agreement: Implications for Access to Medicines and Public Health' (UNITAID March 2014) <www.unitaid.eu/images/marketdynamics/publications/TPPA-Report_Final.pdf> accessed 23 April 2016; UNITAID, 'UNITAID Concerned That TPP Negotiations Undermine Public Health Goals' (UNITAID 13 November 2013) <www.unitaid.eu/en/resources/press-centre/statements/1289-unitaid-concerned-that-tpp-negotiations-undermine-public-health-goals> accessed 14 March 2016; Daniel Pruzin, 'Study Claims US IP Proposals for TPP Could "Seriously Hamper" Medicine Access' (2014) 31 Intl Trade Rep 670.

affordable in poor countries. Manifestly, the UNITAID critique highlighted how sophisticated IP issues in the context of a major FTA had devolved to a simple zero sum game.

VIII. Middle-class Doubts

The TPP could be the most economically and politically significant FTA in the Asia-Pacific region. Conceived in 2006 by just four small countries, it embraces twelve that account for nearly forty per cent of global GDP.[63] It promises to be a twenty-first-century accord in terms of the breadth and depth of trade barriers it identifies and disciplines.

But, with controversial provisions such as those pertaining to IP, the TPP appears to fall short of a 'free' trade accord in the Neo-Classical Economic sense. It manages trade in sensitive sectors, and IP, while not dubbed 'sensitive' in the conventional sense like beef, rice, or sugar, is treated as such.[64] This sensitivity, like all of the TPP, has been treated not with sunshine, or even shade, but darkness. Negotiated in a shamefully non-transparent manner, the TPP may well advance a US corporate agenda, with insufficient regard to the most pressing matter in the Asia-Pacific region: poverty alleviation. And, is not poverty alleviation in that region a vital national security interest of the United States?

Not surprisingly, therefore, champions of the TPP oversell the deal. They have had to do so. They cite US Department of Commerce data showing '[m]anufacturing workers who produce exports earn, on average, 18% more' than non-export related jobs, because of 'the higher productivity of competitive exporting businesses'. Further, such advocates downgrade the relative importance of industrial workers, favouring those in the service sector, and then conclude with hopes, however noble, which few if any FTAs have realized:

> In recent years, such business services as software, finance, architecture, and engineering employed 25% of American workers, more than twice as many in manufacturing. Business-service employees earned over 20% more than the average manufacturing job, and the U.S. consistently runs a trade surplus in business services.
>
> ...

[63] See John Boudreau, 'US Trade Negotiator Sees "Important Progress" in TPP Talks' (2014) 31 Intl Trade Rep 1649.

[64] Agriculture always is a case in point. Eager to boost their exports, but chary of import competition, over fifty companies (e.g., food processors like Cargill Inc, Kraft Foods Group, Smithfield Foods Inc, and Tyson Foods Inc) and organizations (e.g., the American Farm Bureau, National Chicken Council, and National Pork Producers Council) representing US agricultural interests spent more than $34 million in lobbying efforts to influence TPP rules. Those interests extended to national and state commodity groups, and biotechnology firms (e.g., DuPont). See Catherine Boudreau, 'In 2014, US Agriculture Lobbying on TPP Illustrates Importance of Exports' (2015) 32 Intl Trade Rep 376.

Just as US commerce in the nineteenth and twentieth centuries sailed with missionaries, engineers, and educators, so twenty-first-century trade, investment, and business networks will promote the causes of civil society, human rights, the environment, and gender equality.[65]

Understandably, the American middle class is sceptical of the TPP: they do not see American trade officials using FTAs as opportunities to rebuild at least a portion of the post-Second World War industrial base of the United States, or to develop a more just and affordable health care system. If those officials do not empathize with their socioeconomic fragility, then why should they support the deal?

65 Charles Boustany and Robert B Zoellick, 'An Opportunity for Obama and the New Congress' [2014] Wall Street J 11.

27

Interdependence and the WTO Agreement as a 'Contractual Constitution'

*Chios Carmody**

I. Introduction

Mitsuo Matsushita is the national of a country, Japan, famous for its prowess in supply chain manufacturing. Japanese terms such as *kanban* (カンバン) (lean production), *kaizen* (カイゼン) (continuous improvement), *mottainai* (モッタイナイ) (regret for waste), and *poka-yoke* (ポカヨケ) (zero defects) have entered the global lexicon of engineering, mass production, and sustainability because of Japan's skill in that regard. Its success is due, at least in part, to the way that its culture traditionally values interdependence.[1]

Interdependence is also a theme in international trade law. Indeed, Japan could be said to enjoy the success it has in the international trading system because the law and practice of international trade reproduce the threads of its own cultural fabric so closely. Interdependence is a feature of international trade law, however, because it goes beyond the existence of any one country and

* Associate Professor and Canadian Director of the Canada–United States Law Institute, Faculty of Law, Western University, London, Ontario, Canada. Email: ccarmody@uwo.ca.

[1] Academics and observers of Japanese culture have long noted the predisposition in Japan to group and collaborative activity emblematic of interdependence. See Chikio Hayashi and Yasumasa Kuroda, *Japanese Culture in Comparative Perspective* (Praeger 1997) 26 (noting that the Japanese concept of self 'is diffuse with ambiguous boundaries and interdependency designed to reward mutually within a group');

> The Japanese are much more likely than Westerners to operate in groups or at least to see themselves as operating in this way. Whereas Westerners may at least put on a show of independence and individuality, most Japanese will be quite content to conform in dress, conduct, style of life, and even thought to the norms of their group.

Edwin Reischauer, *The Japanese Today: Change and Continuity* (Belknap Press 1988) 128; 'The larger the factory organization [in Japan], the happier the people appear to be in their work. Working is like belonging to an orchestra or football team, a collaborative activity which gives mutual satisfaction of a high order.' Alan MacFarlane, *Japan Through the Looking Glass* (Profile Books 2007) 98.

binds all of them together as the 'guarantor of peace'.[2] In doing so, it creates community.[3]

Interdependence pervades virtually every aspect of the law of the World Trade Organization (WTO), from tariff negotiations to service commitments to the minimum level of intellectual property protection mandated in the WTO Agreement, the WTO's basic treaty.[4] WTO Member countries rarely extend tariff concessions without knowledge of reciprocal tariff concessions made by their WTO counterparts.[5] They rarely make service commitments without some sense that their closest trading partners are ready to do likewise.[6] And they agree to minimum levels of intellectual property protection because they realize that such protections are generally beneficial to themselves and others.[7]

Interdependence is also something that has been highlighted in the WTO's dispute settlement system. In *Mexico—Corn Syrup*, for example, the Appellate Body examined a claim by Mexico that the panel had failed to set out a 'basic rationale' for its decision, contrary to Article 12.7 of the WTO Dispute Settlement Understanding (DSU), the system's code of procedure. The Appellate Body dismissed the claim, but nevertheless observed that the obligation on a panel to provide a basic rationale promotes the aims of security and predictability in the multilateral trading system 'because the requirement to provide "basic" reasons

[2] Neil Richardson, 'International Trade as a Force for Peace' in Charles Kegley, Jr (ed), *Controversies In International Relations Theory: Realism and the Neoliberal Challenge* (St Martin's Press 1995) 281; Bruce Russett, 'Violence and Disease: Trade as a Suppressor of Conflict When Suppressors Matter' in Edward Mansfield and Brian Pollins (eds), *Economic Interdependence and International Conflict: New Perspectives on an Enduring Debate* (University of Michigan Press 2003) 159. For an examination, see Constance Wagner and others (eds), *Trade As Guarantor of Peace, Liberty And Security?: Critical, Empirical And Historical Perspectives* (American Society of International Law 2006).

[3] Gerard Delanty notes, 'Community, which derives from the Latin word *com* (with or together) and *unus* (the number one or singularity), is a widely used term in popular and academic discourse, but it is also contested.' Gerard Delanty, *Community* (2nd edn, Psychology Press 2010) x. 'A community arises whenever two or more persons have interests in common.' G Merle Bergman, 'The Communal Concept of Law' (1947) 57 Yale LJ 55, 61.

> A developed community ... differs from other forms of association in that each party expects an ongoing relationship to persist for as long as he or she is affiliated with the community. In addition, there may be specific relationships between some members that exclude others, but even these will be governed by secondary rules of recognition generalized, rational principles of distinction which apply all the way to the outer limits of the rule's reach and in which all have an interest.

Thomas Franck, *The Power of Legitimacy Among Nations* (OUP 1990) 197–98.

[4] Final Act Embodying the Results of the Uruguay Round of Multilateral Trade Negotiations, 1867 UNTS 14, 33 ILM 1143 (1994).

[5] See Anwarul Hoda, *Tariff Negotiations and Renegotiations under the GATT and WTO* (CUP 2001) 95.

[6] Aaditya Mattoo and Marcelo Olarreaga, 'Reciprocity Across Modes of Supply in the World Trade Organization' (2000) World Bank Policy Research Working Paper 2373, 3–4 <http://documents.worldbank.org/curated/en/2000/06/437123/reciprocity-across-modes-supply-world-trade-organization-negotiating-formula> accessed 14 March 2016.

[7] See Peter Gerhart, 'Reflections: Beyond Compliance Theory: TRIPS as a Substantive Issue' (2000) 32 Case Western Res J Intl L 357.

contributes to *other* WTO Members' understanding of the nature and scope of [*their* WTO] rights and obligations ... (emphasis added)'.[8] In other words, reliance by WTO Members on the results of each other's litigation is to be expected. It is a characteristic of their interdependence.[9]

But this still leaves open the more profound question of what interdependence means legally. What are its *substantive* implications? This is the central question that I am interested in exploring in this brief contribution. In particular, I am interested in examining how awareness of interdependence can help to explain and reconcile two competing understandings of the WTO Agreement, one as a 'contract', the other as a 'constitution'.

What I suggest here is that neither of these images is entirely accurate on its own. Instead, what is necessary is a more comprehensive understanding of the treaty that recognizes the on-going role of interdependence, the way that interdependence encourages countries to calibrate their behaviour, if not always in an identical manner, and how this results in an arrangement that is a hybrid of the two mentioned above, something that can be identified by the shorthand of a 'contractual constitution'. In a contractual constitution, the basis of legal obligation is neither right nor obligation exclusively, but a triune order of legal element imposed by virtue of membership in a community.

II. The Matrix of WTO Law

To begin to answer the question put forward above—what are the substantive implications of interdependence in WTO law?—it is important to understand the matrix underlying the WTO legal system. WTO concessions and commitments originate in the General Agreement on Tariffs and Trade of 1947 (GATT 1947),

[8] Recourse to Article 21.5 of the DSU by the United States, *Mexico—Anti-dumping Investigation of High Fructose Corn Syrup (HFCS) from the United States*, WT/DS132/AB/RW, 22 October 2001, para 107.

[9] This is distinct from the [enormous] material interdependence that WTO disciplines give rise to. In *US—Civil Aircraft (Second Complaint)*, for instance, a panel detailed the multinational list of suppliers involved in manufacturing the Boeing 787 Dreamliner:

> Completion of sub-assemblies and integration of systems takes place in Everett, Washington, with many components being pre-installed before delivery to Everett. The 787 composite wings are being manufactured by Mitsubishi Heavy Industries. The horizontal stabilizers are being manufactured by Alenia Aeronautica in Italy, and various parts of the fuselage sections are being built by Alenia in Italy, Vought in Charleston, South Carolina, Kawasaki Heavy Industries and Fuji Heavy Industries in Japan, Alenia in Italy and Spirit Aerosystems in Wichita, Kansas. The main landing gear and nose landing gear are being supplied by the French company Messier-Dowty, while passenger doors are being made by Latécoère in France, and the cargo, access and crew escape doors by Saab in Sweden.

See Panel Report, *United States—Measures Affecting Trade in Large Civil Aircraft (Second Complaint)*, WT/DS353/R, Appendix VII.F.1, 31 March 2011, para 25. For similar descriptions see Panel Report, *United States—Restrictions on Imports of Cotton and Man-made Fibre Underwear*, WT/DS24/R, 8 November 1996, para 2.1; Panel Report, *Mexico—Measures Affecting Telecommunications Services*, WT/DS204/R, 2 April 2004, para 7.38.

which was founded on reciprocal tariff concessions between countries involving goods. In brief, Country X would agree to lower its tariff on a certain good in exchange for Country Y doing the same on identical or other goods. These concessions were subsequently extended unconditionally to the entire GATT membership.[10] Over the next several decades this framework, built primarily on a bilateral matrix, came to be accompanied by a range of non-tariff disciplines undertaken for the purpose of safeguarding the original commitments. Thus, for instance, a tariff agreed to by Country X could be undermined if Country X decided to impose a tax at the point-of-sale, an anti-dumping duty, or a licensing fee, that would nullify or impair whatever tariff concession Country X had originally granted.

In the beginning it was easy to understand this arrangement as amounting to a 'contract' and to pair this with a conception of the treaty as a voluntary engagement, something Member countries were free to change at any time. A number of features of GATT oblige in this conception. For instance, the original membership was referred to as the '*Contracting* Parties' and the treaty itself was amended on a number of occasions. Later, its successor arrangement, the WTO Agreement, foresaw continuing negotiations, the possibility of re-negotiation, compensation for temporary non-compliance, and the possibility of suspending concessions as a 'last resort'.[11] The WTO Appellate Body also appeared to confirm this understanding in its observation in *Japan—Alcoholic Beverages* that:

> The WTO Agreement is a treaty—the international equivalent of a *contract*. It is self-evident that in an exercise of their sovereignty, and in pursuit of their own respective national interests, the Members of the WTO have made a bargain. In exchange for the benefits they expect to receive as Members of the WTO, they have agreed to exercise their sovereignty according to the commitments they have made in the WTO Agreement[12] (emphasis added).

[10] The term 'Members' is used loosely here to refer to governments who formally participated in GATT 1947 as 'Contracting Parties'. The designation 'Contracting Parties' was applied originally to stress the provisional nature of the treaty as an undertaking. GATT 1947 was meant to be folded into the *Havana Charter for an International Trade Organization* (United States Department of State Bulletin 1948). When the Havana Charter was 'stillborn' in 1950 due to US congressional opposition, GATT 1947 was left to function on its own and did so until 1994, when the WTO Agreement was concluded.

[11] Understanding on Rules and Procedures Governing the Settlement of Disputes art 3.7 (DSU) provides, 'The *last resort* which this Understanding provides to the Member invoking the dispute settlement procedures is the possibility of suspending the application of concessions or other obligations ...' (emphasis added).

[12] Panel Report, *Japan—Taxes on Alcoholic Beverages*, WT/DS8/AB/R, October 4 1996, 14. See also Panel Report, *United States—Definitive Safeguard Measures on Imports of Circular Welded Carbon Quality Line Pipe from Korea*, WT/DS202/R, 29 October 2001, para 7.40 ('WTO Members have *contracted* a package of rights and obligations....' (emphasis added)); Panel Report, *United States—Continued Suspension of Obligations in the EC—Hormones Dispute*, WT/DS320/R, 16 October 2008, para 7.336 ('Customary international law applies generally to the economic relations between the WTO Members. Such international law applies to the extent that the WTO agreements do not "*contract out*" from it' (emphasis added)).

The Appellate Body's statement emphasizes the limited nature of the treaty and its legal system. The WTO Agreement is a 'contract' and national sovereignty is constrained only to the extent that countries have made 'commitments' under it.

The conception of GATT, and now the WTO Agreement, as a contract has endured. It accords with history and with intuition. One popular way of referring to the treaty today is as an 'incomplete contract', something which is always in the process of being finished, always an expression of will.[13] Needless to say, contractualism is politically popular as a paradigm in the sense that it allows countries to sidestep the delicate issue of what they are bound to do.[14]

There is also something else that contractualism emphasizes. This is the idea of *rights*. Concluding a contract is an exercise of rights. Traditionally, a right is conceived of as a claim.[15] A right allows 'the right-holder to invoke the law to obtain

[13] Henrick Horn and others 'The GATT/WTO as an Incomplete Contract' preliminary draft (September 2005); Simon Schropp, *Trade Policy Flexibility and Enforcement in the WTO* (CUP 2009) (see especially 131–32, 'Theorizing about the WTO as an incomplete contract'). Similarly, George Berman and Petros Mavroidis has referred to the WTO Agreement as an 'incomplete contract'. In their view, negotiators were 'well aware that various [governmental] policies ... might have an impact on trade, and that is why they decided to discipline the exercise of these policies. They did not, however, proceed to enumerate every one of them, nor did they provide specific disciplines for each.' George Berman and Petros Mavroidis (eds), *Trade and Human Health and Safety* (CUP 2006) 2.

[14] Not surprisingly, countries have found a contractual conception of the treaty appealing and have referred to it on a number of occasions. See statement by Brazil in Appellate Body, *European Communities—Measures Affecting the Importation of Certain Poultry Products*, WT/DS69/AB/R, 13 July 1998, para 15 (describing the WTO Agreement as 'an international treaty laying down *contractual* obligations and not *erga omnes* obligations'); Argentina in Dispute Settlement Body, Minutes of Meeting, WT/DSB/M/42, 14 (referring to SPS obligations as '*contractual* international obligations'). The contractual optic was also evident in WTO, *The Future of the WTO: Addressing Institutional Challenges in the New Millennium* (World Trade Organization 2004) (The Sutherland Report). See, for instance, '*contractual* requirements of membership' (para 3), 'the *contractual* detail of the WTO' (para 200), 'an institution founded on negotiated *contractual* commitments among governments' (para 206), 'countries should have *contractual* entitlement to capacity building support' (para 306), and 'the WTO, in future, should contain provisions for a *contractual* right' (para 311). For commentators supportive of this view, see Joost Pauwelyn, *A Typology of Multilateral Treaty Obligations: Are WTO Obligations Bilateral or Collective in Nature?* (2003) 14 Eur J Intl L 907, 938 ('Put differently, the values, aspirations and priorities of close to 150 WTO Members remain far too diverse for WTO norms to be streamlined into constitutional-type obligations ...').

[15] In 1918, Wesley Hohfeld pointed out that the terms 'rights' and 'obligations' encompass a much wider array of legal relationships than their casual usage might suggest. Hohfeld's most seminal contribution to the study of jurisprudence was to maintain that there are at least four correlative relationships in law. All of Hohfeld's correlatives are identifiable in WTO law. For instance, all WTO Members have the *right* to expect equal treatment for their exports under GATT art I. Correlatively, WTO Members are under an *obligation* to accord this level of treatment to imports from all Members. Similarly, every WTO Member is allowed the *freedom* to set its own 'appropriate level of protection' (ALOP) against human, animal, or health diseases or risks under the WTO SPS Agreement. WTO Members have *no right* to challenge the appropriate level of protection selected. Furthermore, a number of WTO bodies like the Ministerial Conference, General Council, or the WTO Balance of Payments Committee have the *power* to make decisions binding on the Membership, and Members are likewise subject to a *liability* to comply with them. Finally, WTO Members are *immune* from decisions taken under parts of the WTO Agreement that they have not acceded to, like the WTO Agreement on Government Procurement (AGP), but are unable, or '*disabled*', from raising claims under the AGP against non-signatories. See Wesley Hohfeld, *Fundamental Legal Conceptions, as Applied in Judicial Reasoning and Other Essays* (Yale University Press 1920) 36. The interactions promoted by WTO generate a product both quantitatively and qualitatively distinct from the individual relationships it is composed of. The bilateralism inherent in Hohfeld's analysis is therefore at best a point of departure for the ideas founded in interdependence and put forward here.

certain willing and acting from another person'.[16] According to the paradigm of the WTO Agreement as a contract, therefore, the treaty can be regarded simply and innocuously as an exercise of rights.[17]

The transition mentioned above in GATT from tariff to non-tariff disciplines, however, involved a subtle, but significant, change in this understanding. That was because the introduction of certain supplementary provisions like anti-dumping disciplines and so forth stressed the notion of a common threshold, or floor, underlying all else in the treaty. This, in turn, generated a second, competing understanding of GATT as a 'constitution'.

A constitution is defined as '[t]he fundamental laws of a state, governing the actions of officials and the making and execution of laws. The constitution is the organisation of a government....'[18] The term 'constitution' is also employed in the law of international organizations to denote the basic instrument of an international organization.[19] In both domestic and international law, references to 'governing' and 'organization' highlight how a constitution is directive. It directs the arrangement of the organization by means of *obligation*, in the first instance, since it is through obligations that the aims of a constitution are achieved.

A constitution also involves choice, since obligations always include some choices and exclude others. And out of this inclusion and exclusion come order. A constitution directs actions that achieve the aims of the order. It does this by distributing powers, by defining the relations among powers, and by providing recourse against those powers. A constitution may also provide a mechanism for amendment and conflicts that define the relationship with powers outside the order. In all of these senses, a constitution is concerned with structure.

Given its tendency to structure, a second view of GATT and the WTO Agreement that emerged is constitutive. John Jackson and others have referred to the WTO Agreement as a 'constitution', and Gail Evans has made the observation that 'WTO law may be explained as a trade constitution having the capacity to universalize norms of substantive law'.[20] A number of features of GATT and the WTO Agreement

[16] Philip Allott, *Eunomia* (CUP 1990) 161 para 10.46.

[17] Allott notes that 'By a legal relation in the form right, society is considered to confer on the right-holder the benefit, the protection, the assurance, the individuality of the law.' ibid 160.

[18] Stephen Sheppard (ed), *The Wolters Kluwer Bouvier Law Dictionary* vol 1, (desk edn, Aspen Publishers 2012) 545.

[19] Henry Schermers and Niels Blokker, *International Institutional Law* (4th rev edn, Brill 2003) 722.

[20] Gail Evans, *Lawmaking Under the Trade Constitution: A Study in Legislating by the World Trade Organization* (Kluwer 2000) 44. For a range of constitutional views, see John Jackson, *The World Trade Organization: Constitution and Jurisprudence* (Royal Institute of International Affairs 1998); Deborah Cass, *The Constitutionalization of the World Trade Organization: Legitimacy, Democracy, and Community in the International Trading System* (OUP 2005). Also Peter Gerhart, 'Two Constitutional Visions of the World Trade Organization' (2003) 24 U Pa J Intl Econ L 1. For a critical appraisal of the constitutional view, see Jeffrey Dunoff, 'Constitutional Conceits: The WTO's Constitution and the Discipline of International Law' (2006) 17 Eur J Intl L 647. For evidence of constitutionalism in international law generally, see Nigel White, 'The United Nations System: Conference, Contract or Constitutional Order?' (2000) 4 Singapore J Intl Comp L 281, 290–91.

appear to confirm this characterization, notably the rarity of contract-type action in the form of renegotiation, compensation, and countermeasures, as well as the difficulty of amendment.[21] Still, this second view is a controversial one inasmuch as constitutions, as orders of obligations, stress 'the burden, the order, the universality of the law',[22] and in doing so 'seem to diminish the possibilities of the duty-holder, by excluding certain possibilities in the actuality of a legal relation'.[23] In other words, constitutions imply a restraint at odds with the notion of sovereign freedom.

At the very core of WTO Agreement, then, there are two fundamentally antagonistic visions, one involving contract, the other involving constitution. How can they be reconciled and what light can this unification of opposites shed on the nature of WTO law?

An important realization is that the contrasting ideas of contract and constitution outlined above are reductible to competing visions of the treaty as an order of rights *and* an order of obligations. In law the classic relationship among rights and obligations is one of correspondence. Each right is considered to be matched by a single offsetting obligation.[24] The relationship between the two elements is also one of interdependence. No right exists without a correspondent obligation (and vice versa). By the process of parallel reasoning, it is possible to suggest that competing ideas of contract and constitution are interdependent as well.

Confirmation of this point comes from the work of Gerald Fitzmaurice on the nature of treaty obligations in the 1950s. Fitzmaurice divided treaties into two types—*bilateral* and *multilateral*—and further subdivided multilateral treaties into

[21] For instance, in the WTO era the frequency of renegotiation under GATT art XXVIII has fallen steeply. The decrease is probably related to the relative decline in the importance of tariffs as an instrument of trade policy, as well as the difficulty of negotiating with almost 160 other Members. The WTO Analytical Index observes: 'As of May 2011, there had been 35 requests to enter into renegotiations under GATT Article XXVIII since 1 January 1995. Of these, 4 had been withdrawn, 11 had been concluded and formally certified, 5 had been concluded, but not certified, and 15 were in principle ongoing.' Likewise, with respect to compensation negotiated under DSU art 22.2, there have only been two instances since 1995. See *United States—Section 110(5) of the US Copyright Act*, WT/DS160, 26 January 1999; *United States—Subsidies on Upland Cotton*, WT/DS267, 27 September 2002. With respect to retaliatory countermeasures authorized under DSU art 22.6, there have only been nineteen instances of authorization among almost 500 matters reported to the WTO dispute settlement system. None were continuing in 2015.

[22] Allott (n 16) 160 para 10.43. [23] ibid.

[24] The idea of a correspondence between rights and obligations was recognized by early philosophers but developed most insightfully by Wesley Hohfeld, who postulated that there are rights and that these are distinct from privileges, powers, and immunities, and that they are matched by jural correlatives in the form of duties, no-rights, liabilities, and disabilities. See Hohfeld (n 15). Also William A Edmundson, *An Introduction to Rights* (CUP 2004) 43 (discussing Edmund Burke's contribution to the idea of right-obligation correspondence). There has been much debate about the need for a primacy of rights in global justice, something which challenges the idea of correspondence. Onora O'Neill has warned about the illusory nature of 'manifesto rights'—that is, rights for which there are no associated obligations:

> The most questionable effect of putting rights first is that those rights for which no allocation of obligations has been institutionalized may not be taken seriously. When obligations are unallocated it is indeed right that they should be met, but nobody can have an effective right—an enforceable, claimable or waivable right—to their being met. Such abstract rights are not effective entitlements. If the claimants of supposed 'rights' to food or development cannot find where to lodge their claims, these are empty 'manifesto' rights.

Onora O'Neill, *Bounds of Justice* (CUP 2000) 126.

three basic subtypes—*reciprocal, interdependent,* and *integral*—based on the consequences of their breach. For instance, in the case of a bilateral treaty the treaty can be suspended or terminated by either party because it involves a simple exchange of obligations. Subsequent inconsistent treaties are valid, subject to applicable rules concerning priority.[25] The same could be said for multilateral treaties of a *reciprocal* type. In such cases, the treaty is conceived of as a bundle of bilateral obligations. In both bilateral and multilateral reciprocal treaties the underlying arrangement is a 'contract'.

At the other extreme, multilateral treaties of an *integral* type cannot be suspended or terminated, since 'the force of the obligation is self-existent, absolute and inherent for each party'.[26] Subsequent inconsistent treaties are also void. Here, the underlying arrangement can be thought about as a 'constitution'; that is, something unconditional and unalterable.

In the residual category—multilateral treaties of an *interdependent* type:

> the obligation of each party [is] dependent on a correspondent performance by *all* the parties; and therefore, in the case of a fundamental breach by one party, the obligation of the other parties would not merely cease towards that particular party, but would be liable to cease altogether and in respect of *all* the other parties' (emphasis added).[27]

Subsequent inconsistent treaties are void.

Multilateral treaties of an interdependent type would therefore appear to have attributes of *both* contract and constitution. They allow for suspension or termination, as in the case of the treaty-contract, but are otherwise entrenched and non-derogable, as in the case of a treaty-constitution.

Does this characterization as a multilateral treaty of an interdependent type accurately explain the nature of WTO obligations? I suggest that it does. Fitzmaurice gave as examples of multilateral interdependent treaties disarmament treaties, nuclear free zone treaties, 'or any other treaty where each parties' performance is effectively conditioned upon and requires the performance *of each of the others*'.[28] To recall, he also noted that in the case of fundamental breach the obligation under the treaty would 'not merely cease towards that particular party, but would be liable to cease altogether and in respect of *all* the other parties'. One could argue that this statement is not accurately reproduced in WTO law, since WTO Members are required to continue observing their obligations towards *all other* WTO Members when they suspend concessions towards *one* breaching Member.[29]

[25] This question would be determined according to art 30 of the Vienna Convention on the Law of Treaties (VCLT), 1155 UNTS 331; 8 ILM 679 (1969) (Application of successive treaties relating to the same subject matter).

[26] VCLT art 19.

[27] Gerald Fitzmaurice, Third Report on the Law of Treaties, [1958] 2 YB Intl L Commn 20, UN Doc A/CN.4/115, para 91.

[28] ibid 44.

[29] DSU art 22.2 provides 'If no satisfactory compensation has been agreed ... any party having invoked the dispute settlement procedures may request authorization from the DSB to suspend the application *to the Member concerned* of concessions or other obligations under the covered agreements.' (emphasis added)

Nevertheless, there are at least three other considerations that work to sustain a view of the WTO Agreement as a multilateral treaty of an interdependent type, of WTO obligations themselves as likewise interdependent, and of the ensemble *in toto* as a 'contractual constitution'. First, there is the idea of a breach of a multilateral interdependent treaty leading to 'radical change', something that is reproduced in WTO law in a number of disputes where panels and the Appellate Body have referred to a breach of the treaty as potentially upsetting the 'balance' of rights and obligations among *all* Members.[30]

Second, there is the phenomenon of selective non-observance. It is well known that WTO Member countries do not fulfil their WTO obligations to the letter. Member countries' compliance with their WTO obligations is highly variable. Observance related to MFN treatment[31], subsidization[32], agricultural disciplines,[33] and intellectual property protection[34]—in other words, large swaths of the WTO Agreement—have been shown to be inconsistent. This inconsistency is often tied to non-observance by trading partners of *their* obligations. In other words, a rough symmetry of compliance *and* non-compliance is tolerated. Why? Because governments condition their observance of the treaty on the observance of the treaty *by others*. Compliance too is interdependent, even if not perfectly equalized.

Third, there is the careful way in which countries have crafted their international obligations subsequent to the conclusion of the WTO Agreement so as to avoid conflict.[35] In a number of instances, WTO Member countries have sought

[30] This idea is implicit in DSU art 21.1, which stipulates that 'prompt compliance with recommendations or rulings of the DSB is essential in order to ensure effective resolution of disputes *to the benefit of all Members*' (emphasis added). In other words, disputes are to be settled for the benefit of all Members because they are understood to *affect* all Members. See Arbitration Award, *European Communities—Regime for the Importation, Sale and Distribution of Bananas* (*EC—Bananas*), WT/DS27/15, 7 January 1998, para 18; Appellate Body Report, *Australia—Measures Affecting Importation of Salmon*, WT/DS18/AB/R, 20 October 1998, para 223.

[31] For instance, the WTO Secretariat's Report in the EU Trade Policy Review of 2007 observed that the European Union only extended MFN status to nine WTO Member countries. All other Members benefit in one way or other from preferential trade agreements with the European Union that gave them better access than the MFN tariff schedule: see Trade Policy Review Body, *Trade Policy Review European Communities*, WT/TPR/S/177, 22 January 2007, x.

[32] See Gregory Shaffer, Robert Wolfe, and Vinhcent Le, 'Informal Law's Discipline of Subsidies: Variation in Definitions, Obligations, Transparency, and Organizations' (April 2015) <http://e15initiative.org/publications/informal-laws-discipline-of-subsidies-variation-in-definitions-obligations-transparency-and-organizations/> accessed 14 March 2016.

[33] See David Orden and others (eds), *WTO Disciplines on Agricultural Support: Seeking a Fair Basis for Trade* (CUP 2011) (examining the extent of non-compliance with the WTO Agreement on Agriculture and noting that while there is still disarray in world agriculture, seeking greater discipline remains a valuable guiding principle for future negotiations).

[34] See nn 30–31.

[35] There are at least five methods of avoiding WTO inconsistency in subsequent agreements: 1. seeking of a waiver of obligations under WTO art X:3–4, as in the case of the Kimberley Process (see Council for Trade in Goods, Waiver Concerning Kimberley Process Certification Scheme For Rough Diamonds, G/C/W/432/Rev.1, 24 February 2003); 2. drafting agreements so as to avoid express conflict, as in the case of the Framework Convention on Tobacco Control, 42 ILM 515 (2003), where rules apply to domestic regulations that, if administered neutrally, would not violate the WTO Agreement (but see litigation in *Australia—Certain Measures Concerning Trademarks and Other Plain Packaging Requirements Applicable to Tobacco Products and Packaging*, WT/DS434, 13 March 2012); 3. where

waivers or 'workarounds' to avoid the spectre of subsequent inconsistent agreements. This practice would suggest that Member countries recognize the treaty's constitutive primacy within its own sphere of international economic relations and tend to confirm the fact that the WTO Agreement, as an interdependent treaty, renders subsequent inconsistent treaties void.

III. Interdependence: Substantive Implications for WTO Law

I have demonstrated that the WTO Agreement is most accurately understood as a multilateral contract of an interdependent type and that WTO obligations themselves are fundamentally interdependent. They rely upon each other, although not in an absolute or completely correspondent way, but instead in a roughly calibrated manner. Linking this to what was seen earlier, the hybridism of the arrangement infers that the treaty as an order of rights and an order of obligations is a combination of both contract and constitution. In any single moment it can be understood as a 'contractual constitution'.

Drawing on terminology adopted in international environmental law, some commentators have prefigured the characterization of the treaty I advance here by referring to the WTO Agreement as a 'constitutional contract'. A constitutional contract has been defined as 'an agreement setting forth an interlocking system of behavioral prescriptions expected to remain operative over an indefinite period'.[36] Xu Yu-Chong and Patrick Weller have borrowed the term to describe GATT as follows:

> The creation and expansion of [GATT] rules was the beginning of the process of international 'constitution' making in the post-war era. A treaty is a consensual instrument. It has no force unless the state has agreed to it. Consequently, a state is bound by a treaty, as a matter of international law, by virtue of having accepted it. In other words, the treaty

countries have not made WTO commitments in the sectors covered by a subsequent agreement, as with respect to the Convention on the Protection and Promotion of the Diversity of Cultural Expressions (2005); 4. where subsequent agreement does not apply to WTO Member countries, as in the case of the 2006 Convention on International Trade in Endangered Species (CITES) ban on international trade in certain species of caviar; 5. WTO Members agreeing *inter se* not to litigate inconsistent measures before WTO dispute settlement, as in the case of the OECD Sector Understanding on Export Credits for Civil Aircraft (2007). It is theoretically possible for this last method to be challenged by a WTO Member non-signatory to the DSU since panels and the Appellate Body have repeatedly indicated that bilateral and plurilateral agreements concluded between Members *inter se* do not, absent a waiver, alter the rights and obligations of WTO Members: Panel Report, *Turkey—Restrictions on Imports of Textile and Clothing Products*, WT/DS34/R, 31 May 1999, para 9.178; Appellate Body Report, *European Communities—Regime for the Importation, Sale and Distribution of Bananas*, WT/DS27/AB/R, 9 September 1997, paras 164–70.

36 Oran R Young and Gail Osherenko (eds), *Polar Politics: Creating International Environmental Regimes* (Cornell University Press 1993) 2, n 3. Catherine Redgwell, who has written 'constitutional contract', refers to the dynamic force of negotiated treaties, treaties that are not one-off events but dynamic instruments that evolve over time. The 'constitutional contract' is relational rather than discrete. See Catherine Redgwell, 'Multilateral Environmental Treaty-Making' in Vera Gowland-Debbas (ed), *Multilateral Treaty Making* (Martinus Nijhoff 2000) 91.

becomes valid and overlays the domestic policies and laws once it is accepted under national law as binding international obligations.[37]

Yu-Chong and Weller's description is useful as a shorthand to designate the way that the treaty arrives at a medial point—a point between extremes of bilateralism and multilateralism. I have chosen to *invert* the term here to suggest that the dominant aspect of the WTO Agreement is in fact constitutive. This is evident in the way that the treaty is qualitatively different from bilateral relations that prevailed among nations as a basis for organizing their trading relationships before the GATT/WTO era.

What implications does this sort of interdependence have for the nature of WTO law? There are several. First, the body of law is oriented *temporally* more in terms of the future than it is of the past, although an accurate description of it as interdependent would suggest that the combination is rooted in the law in the present, a present which looks to the future. This is consistent with case law and what has been said about the WTO legal order as protective of 'legitimate *expectations*' going forward.[38]

Second, WTO law as a body of law *juridically* can be deconstructed as involving individual rights and obligations at any one time, although its contractual and constitutional double aspect makes WTO law a *sui generis* legal system; that is, a distinctive regime of legal elements.[39] This dualism conditions the behaviour of actors within the system in peculiar ways. For example, WTO rules about third-party standing and compensation depart from the ordinary rules of international law.[40]

Third, I have spent the bulk of this contribution explaining how WTO law can be explained *structurally* in terms of a 'contractual constitution'. This designation is distinct from referring to the treaty simply as a 'contract' and reveals how continuing to do so is seriously under-representative, possibly even misrepresentative. The treaty has notable features that go well beyond the structure of bilateral pairings in the image of a contract. At the same time, they are in their totality neither one nor the other of the dominant images, but their combination.

[37] Xu Yu-Chong and Patrick Weller, *The Governance of World Trade: International Civil Servants and the GATT/WTO* (Edward Elgar 2004) 67–68.

[38] See Panel Report, *India—Patent Protection for Pharmaceutical and Agricultural Chemical Products*, WT/DS50/R, 5 September 1997, para 7.22 ('we recall that one of the precepts developed under GATT 1947 is that rules and disciplines governing the multilateral trading system serve to protect *legitimate expectations* of Members as to the competitive relationship between their products and those of the other Members' (emphasis added)).

[39] Gabrielle Marceau, 'WTO Dispute Settlement and Human Rights' (2002) 13 Eur J Intl L 753; see also Pieter-Jan Kuijper, 'The Law of GATT as a Special Field of International Law—Ignorance, Further Refinement or Self-contained System of International Law' (1994) 25 Neth YB Intl L 227.

[40] The traditional rule in international law is that a treaty creates no rights or obligations for third parties, a rule now formalized in VCLT art 34. This logic is questionable in a treaty like the WTO Agreement whose 'central' and 'essential' feature is a most-favoured-nation clause, a clause that multilateralizes all benefits to the WTO Membership. Thus, in WTO law a more permissive approach is contemplated, now found in DSU art 10.1. With respect to compensation, art 36 of the International Law Commission's Draft Articles on State Responsibility (DASR) appears to formulate a primarily retrospective view of this remedy ('compensation shall cover any financially assessable damage including loss of profits insofar as it is established'). The Commission has described WTO rules on compensation under DSU art 22.2 as a *lex specialis*, that is, a 'special law' departing from the ordinary consequences of international law, because it is understood to be prospective in nature: see James Crawford, *The International Law Commission's Articles on State Responsibility: Introduction, Text, and Commentaries* (CUP 2002) 307.

Fourth, the body of law *jurisprudentially* can be identified with values of equality and fairness. WTO *obligations* can be linked to equality, since they are most often applied on the basis of equality-oriented standards. This is true whenever the treaty calls for MFN, national treatment, equivalence, harmonization, or mutual recognition. It is also true when equality is employed as a default value in judicially crafted standards such as 'even-handedness', 'balance', or parallelism. Conversely, WTO *rights* can be linked to structured inequality, or what can be described as 'fairness', whenever they allow countries to discriminate for a variety of purposes that reinforce the treaty. This includes, for instance, special and differential (S&D) treatment for developing country Members, or proportionality, or appropriateness in the exercise of rights. In these instances, WTO Members are allowed to invoke flexibilities that ultimately strengthen the community of law embodied in the treaty. The combination of these two values promotes the treaty's distinctive vision of what is just.

Fifth and finally, WTO law can be understood *rationally* in terms of deductive and inductive logic. In the first instance, WTO law can be said to be characterized by deductive logic—the logic of what 'will be'—based on assumptions about the way things are.[41] This preoccupation is expressed constitutively in WTO law's heavy reliance on presumptions, notably the presumption of nullification or impairment embodied in DSU Article 3.8, and on inference.[42] In a second, contractual instance, however, WTO law can be characterized by *inductive logic*—the logic of what 'is' or 'was'—based on proof.[43] Induction is hard to sustain in a legal system like the WTO with limited fact-finding ability. Therefore, in a third instance WTO law is characterized by *abductive logic*—the logic of what 'might be'—based on the combination of presumption *and* proof.[44] Abductive logic is not watertight. Instead, it offers the 'best' or most intelligent explanation on existing evidence and provides the possibility of change as new information becomes available. Abductive reasoning is open, tentative, and provisional, and in this way, allows the WTO system a degree of adaptive flexibility as law and facts change.[45]

[41] Roger Martin, *The Opposable Mind: How Successful Leaders Win Through Integrative Thinking* (Harvard Business School Press 2007) 144–45.

[42] DSU art 3.8 provides:

> In cases where there is an infringement of the obligations assumed under a covered agreement, the action is considered prima facie to constitute a case of nullification or impairment. This means that there is normally a *presumption* that a breach of the rules has an adverse impact on other Members ... (emphasis added).

For an overview of these topics, see Michelle Grando, *Evidence, Proof and Fact-finding in WTO Dispute Settlement* (OUP 2009).

[43] Martin (n 41). [44] ibid.

[45] For examples of abductive logic in WTO law see *US—FSC*, where a compliance panel had to determine whether certain amounts 'otherwise due' were 'foregone' for the purposes of the definition of a subsidy in SCM Art 1.1(a)(1)(ii). The panel observed that determining what was 'otherwise due' was not only ascertainable 'where a purely mechanical exercise of inspection was feasible', since this would give a defendant country 'every reason to ensure that there was no automatic or explicit link to the situation of what would otherwise be due'. See *US—FSC*, WT/DS108/RW, para 8.14 (20 August 2001). Hence, the panel refused to be limited to a strictly inductive inquiry; that is, by examining what countries had done in fact. At the same time, the panel noted that a purely deductive approach would be undesirable as well. The panel concluded that it would be impossible 'simply to assert that revenue is otherwise due in the abstract. It cannot be presumed'. ibid, para 8.17. An intermediate approach 'grounded in the actual

Each of the above implications of interdependence is important in its own right. At their core, the contrasting impulses recall deconstructionist ideas of '*differance*' and '*trace*'. '*Differance*' was the term of art used by Jacques Derrida to describe the mutual dependence and differentiation of concepts. '*Trace*' is the retention of absent concepts that remain present in the understanding of other concepts.[46] Derrida's ideas of *differance* and *trace* are relevant because they describe how so many key features of the law contain elements *of their opposite* as a function of interdependence. This hybridism is an abiding characteristic of the WTO Agreement.

IV. Conclusion

This brief contribution has illustrated the way that WTO law can be understood as a 'law of interdependence'. Not only does the interaction of its basic legal elements—rights and obligations—conduce to interdependence on a material level in terms of production and consumption, but as I have shown, it also has very profound substantive consequences in terms of the law. Perhaps the most important of these is the treaty's nature as a combination of contract and constitution, a 'contractual constitution', with the emphasis being on the latter. The arrangement is one that subordinates rights to obligations, past to future, fairness to equality, induction to deduction. In the process, a *sui generis* system of law is created.

All of this remarkable development is a function of interdependence. It is noteworthy that the Japan of Mitsuo Matsushita's generation recognized the importance of engaging with this extraordinary undertaking in the form of GATT and the WTO Agreement, and in the process, of benefiting from their continuing application.

way in which the US tax regime functions' was called for, one that looked 'at the overall situation as *an integrated whole*'. ibid, para 8.23 [emphasis added]. Based on an abductive approach, the panel was able to conclude that treating the overseas income of certain US manufacturers as non-taxable led to 'the foregoing of revenue otherwise due', as prohibited under the SCM. ibid, para 8.26. For other examples of abductive logic in WTO law, see *US—Steel Safeguards*, WT/DS248/R, para 10.340 (11 July 2003). One issue in that case was whether the surge in imports complained of could be attributed to EC-originating steel, something that required the investigating authority to examine plausible alternative arguments about the surge's source. A qualitative analysis would point to deductive reasoning, whereas one that was quantitative would be more inductive and require metrification. The WTO Safeguards Agreement is silent on the exact method to be employed. The panel ultimately concluded that 'the results of … quantification may not necessarily be determinative'. Instead, 'an overall qualitative assessment that takes into account all relevant information, must always be performed'. ibid.

46 Jack Balkin, 'Nested Oppositions' (1990) 99 Yale LJ 1669, 1676.

28

Bridging Global and Regional Governance of International Trade

*Chang-fa Lo**

I. Introduction

International trade is basically governed by three layers of rules: multilateral/global rules, regional rules, and domestic rules. At the international level, the global and regional layers of governance are under the World Trade Organization (WTO) and under many free trade agreements (FTAs) or other economic integration, respectively.

Various WTO and FTA rules are widely discussed. This chapter is not to engage in the discussions of the interpretation or application of these rules, nor to debate the problem of regionalism as opposed to multilateralism. Instead, it intends to look at the governance aspects of these two layers of rules and to explore their proper interaction so as to bridge them and to enhance the governance of trade as a whole.

The discussion in this chapter will begin with briefly explaining the meaning of governance in the context of international trade and the features of international trade governance from global and regional perspectives. It will further discuss the gaps between global and regional governance and the possible ways to reduce these gaps. The chapter suggests some mutually supportive approaches for these two layers of governance so as to enhance their governance.

II. Governance in the Context of International Trade

The term governance is commonly used to refer to 'the process of decision-making and the process by which decisions are implemented (or not implemented)'.[1] There is a wide consensus that in order to be considered as performing good governance,

* Justice, Constitutional Court, Taiwan; Professor, National Taiwan University College of Law.

[1] United Nations Economic and Social Commission for Asia and the Pacific, 'What Is Good Governance?' <www.unescap.org/sites/default/files/good-governance.pdf> accessed 23 April 2016.

eight major characteristics must be seen: participation, the rule of law, transparency, responsiveness, consensus-oriented, equality and inclusiveness, effectiveness and efficiency, and accountability.[2]

Certainly the same characteristics of good governance can be applied to international trade so as to examine: (i) whether there has been appropriate participation from stakeholders in the process of domestic policymaking and in the decision making at the WTO and FTA levels; (ii) whether trade and related practices are subject and accountable to domestic, regional, and multilateral trade rules, and whether such rules are fairly applied and enforced; (iii) whether such rules are enacted and administered in a transparent manner; (iv) whether such rules and their players are responsive to the external situations; (v) whether the decision-making process under these rules is consensus-oriented; (vi) whether the stakeholders are treated with equality; (vii) whether effectiveness and efficiency are the core elements in the scheme; and (viii) whether those who fail to comply will be held accountable.

However, in this chapter, the term 'governance' is used in a narrower sense. It will not look at the quality of multilateral and regional trade rules and the decision-making process under these rules. The chapter will only look at the operation of these rules and discuss the governance thereunder. Hence most characteristics of good governance (such as participation, transparency, consensus-orientation, equality and inclusiveness, and accountability) are not the main concern of the discussion. The main concerns in this chapter are whether there are gaps between the governance of WTO rules at a global level and the governance of FTA rules at regional level, as well as whether there could be some ways of addressing or narrowing such gaps.

III. Features of Multilateral and Regional Trade Governance

A. Features of global governance

There are some key features forming the global governance of international trade under the WTO. The first key feature of global trade governance is the mandatory requirements concerning non-discrimination, trade liberalization, compliance of trade rules, and the protection of intellectual property rights to be followed by its Members. The WTO basically does not have much experience in soft law.[3] Most WTO rules are mandatory. Members are required to implement their obligations created under these rules. There are two types of obligations that Members are required to fulfil: the obligation to implement the concessions they made in their

[2] ibid.

[3] In this connection, Professor Matsushita's call for an increased role of soft law in WTO is truly important. See Julien Chaisse and Mitsuo Matsushita, 'Maintaining the WTO's Supremacy in the International Trade Order: A Proposal to Refine and Revise the Role of the Trade Policy Review Mechanism' (2013) 16 J Intl Econ L 9.

negotiations (including tariff commitments in relation to trade in goods and specific commitments in relation to trade in services), and the obligation to implement the trade rules under the WTO agreements. In this regard, it is fair to say that overall, Members are fulfilling their WTO obligations. There are still many disputes under the WTO, and the number of disputes shows that non-compliances are still identified as problems. But relative to the large number of WTO Members and the large volumes of their trade governed by the WTO rules, the disputes only reflect a small portion of non-compliances. There have not been massive violations of WTO rules by a specific WTO Member or by a particular trading bloc. Nor are there consistent, systemic and wilful violations of a particular type of WTO rule by its Members. In other words, it can be said that the mandatory rules under the WTO are properly governing international trade behaviours.

One aspect that deserves a closer look is the de facto non-mandatory rules under the most recently concluded Trade Facilitation Agreement.[4] There are quite a number of provisions in this agreement drafted in a mandatory form but which are actually providing leeway to Members in implementing the requirements. For instance, Article 2.1.1 states:

> Each Member shall, *to the extent practicable* and *in a manner consistent with its domestic law and legal system*, provide opportunities and an appropriate time period to traders and other interested parties to comment on the proposed introduction or amendment of laws and regulations of general application related to the movement, release and clearance of goods....[5]

There is room for a Member not to provide opportunities to interested parties to make comments if it is *not practical* to this Member or if providing such opportunities would *not be consistent with its domestic law and legal system*. It is yet to see the impact to the implementation of WTO rules arising from such de facto discretion given to WTO Members and the implication for the future negotiation of new WTO rules. Other than this, Members' discretion to deviate from WTO requirements is generally very limited.

The second key feature of global governance of international trade under the WTO is the mechanism to facilitate the implementation of WTO rules. The feature is basically embedded in paragraph 1 of Article III of the Agreement Establishing the World Trade Organization (WTO Establishing Agreement), which reads:

> The WTO shall facilitate the implementation, administration and operation, and further the objectives, of this Agreement and of the Multilateral Trade Agreements, and shall also provide the framework for the implementation, administration and operation of the Plurilateral Trade Agreements.

The facilitation of the implementation of WTO agreements by WTO Members provided in Article III:1 of the WTO Establishing Agreement depends largely on

[4] The text of the Trade Facilitation Agreement is available at <www.wto.org/english/thewto_e/minist_e/mc9_e/desci36_e.htm> accessed 14 March 2016.

[5] Art 2.1.1 of the Trade Facilitation Agreement (emphasis added).

the monitoring activities, which in turn depend on the transparency and notification requirements under various WTO agreements to make information available to other countries and to traders. It also depends on the councils and committees established for Members to discuss issues and adopt measures, as well as on the periodic peer review of Members' trade policies and practices under the Trade Policy Review Mechanism. In addition, the WTO Secretariat has produced regular global trade monitoring reports for overall review on Members' use of trade measures in response to the changing economic climate.[6] In this regard, the global governance under the WTO in helping its Members to implement their obligations has been operating quite well.

The third key feature of global governance of international trade is the platform provided by the WTO for its Members to engage in useful dialogues and to improve the rules so as to be responsive to the new situation as economies develop, societies evolve, and human knowledge improves. The element is basically embedded in paragraph 2 of Article III of the WTO Establishing Agreement, which reads:

> The WTO shall provide the forum for negotiations among its Members concerning their multilateral trade relations in matters dealt with under the agreements in the Annexes to this Agreement. The WTO may also provide a forum for further negotiations among its Members concerning their multilateral trade relations, and a framework for the implementation of the results of such negotiations, as may be decided by the Ministerial Conference.

The WTO providing the forum for negotiation under Article III:2 of the WTO Establishing Agreement can be further implemented by the collective decision of the Members. For instance, the Trade Negotiation Committee operating under the authority of the General Council was set up by the Doha Declaration specifically for the management of the Doha negotiations.[7] The multilateral trading system is supposed to sponsor and to launch negotiation rounds from time to time when its Members consider necessary. In the age of the General Agreement on Tariffs and Trade (GATT) 1947, the first several negotiation rounds were primarily used to deal with tariff reductions. In later years of GATT 1947, negotiation rounds were launched to reduce tariffs and establish additional trade rules. The Uruguay Round was a big success in creating the WTO and establishing many new rules. In the WTO age, there has only been one negotiation round (the Doha Round) which is still on-going. Its purposes are not only to enhance market access through tariff reduction for trade in goods and through improving specific commitments for trade in services, but also to improve other trade rules.

Notwithstanding the current stalemate in the Doha Round, the WTO negotiation forum is a very positive mechanism not only to allow its Members to engage in further concessions, but also to provide opportunities for Members to improve the existing rules (such as improving the anti-dumping rules) and even to adopt

[6] WTO, 'Implementation and Monitoring' <www.wto.org/english/tratop_e/monitor_e/monitor_e.htm> accessed 14 March 2016.

[7] WTO, 'DOHA Development Agenda: Trade Negotiations Committee' <www.wto.org/english/tratop_e/dda_e/tnc_e.htm> accessed 14 March 2016.

new rules (such as the possibility of adopting trade-related environmental rules) so as to respond to the new situations arising from economic, social, and technological developments.

The fourth key feature of global trade governance is the effective dispute settlement mechanism to ensure compliance with the established rules. The dispute settlement procedure under the WTO 'underscores the rules of law' and 'makes the trading system more secure and predictable'.[8] For this feature, there has been remarkable achievement in attracting about 500 complaints within twenty years of the WTO history since its establishment in 1995. This shows the wide reliance and trust on the WTO dispute settlement mechanism by its Members for resolving their trade disputes. Many of the complaints under the WTO dispute settlement mechanism did not come to the penal stage. This means either the disputing parties were able to find mutually satisfactory solutions for their disputes or the complaining parties considered it not necessary to further pursue their complaints due to other reasons. Basically, this shows that the WTO dispute settlement mechanism has been working towards resolving disputes even in the early stages of the process. Furthermore, there are also many disputes having come to the panel stage, the appellate stage, or even the implementation stage so as to ultimately and legally resolve their disputes. For such cases, most responding parties whose measures were found to have not been in compliance with WTO rules have been quite consistent in bringing their measures into conformity with their obligations.

It should be fair to say that the fourth feature of global governance of international trade has been the most remarkable element in effectively and efficiently ensuring that international trade is functioning properly under the governance of the WTO.

B. Features of regional governance

Different FTAs have different degrees and paces of trade liberalization. They also have different trade rules and even different scopes of WTO-plus coverages (such as different coverages in investment, competition, labour, environment, and TRIPS-Plus subjects). Hence, it is not practical to use one FTA as the basis to affirm that others are the same for the purpose of regional trade governance. However, if the features of traditional FTAs and the recently concluded FTAs are taken into account, it can be seen that the common features constituting regional trade governance are: further liberalization, binding rules, and broader subject-matter coverage. But it must also be noted that FTAs are generally weak in serving as a platform for further development of new rules and that their dispute settlement mechanisms are not often resorted to.

The first key feature of regional trade governance is the further liberalization and the binding rules for regional trade governance. The core idea of concluding

[8] WTO, *Understanding the WTO* (5th edn, WTO 2015) 55 <www.wto.org/english/thewto_e/whatis_e/tif_e/utw_chap3_e.pdf> accessed 23 April 2016.

an FTA is to have the mutual trade between the constituent parties subject to a regime that is supposed to be far more liberalized than the multilateral regime under the WTO. This is actually required by Article XXIV:8(b) of GATT 1994 to have import tariffs and other restrictive regulations of commerce eliminated for substantially all the trade between the constituent territories of the FTA, and required by Article V:1 of the General Agreement on Trade in Services (GATS) to have substantially all discrimination eliminated with respect to substantial sectoral coverage of service trade. The tariff and service commitments made by FTA parties to each other are binding. Most trade rules under FTAs are also mandatory. Hence FTA parties are subject to normative trade rules, which are supposed to be of minimal trade restrictiveness.

Most FTAs have very detailed requirements in their lengthy texts. For instance, the North American Free Trade Agreement (NAFTA) has twenty-two chapters and numerous annexes. The text and its annexes are approximately 2,000 pages in length.[9] The mandatory rules spell out the rights and obligations of the parties in a very detailed manner.

The second key feature of regional trade governance is the broader subject-matter coverage for regional trade governance. As mentioned above, most recently concluded FTAs have more or fewer WTO-Plus subject matters, such as those relating to competition policy, labour protection, and environmental protection. Many FTAs have quite advanced provisions in these fields, such as requiring their parties to follow labour protection treaties or to prioritize the application of environmental treaties. But depending on the texts of specific FTAs, some FTA rules could be voluntary. For instance, although many FTAs concluded in recent decades include mandatory provisions or chapters on competition, labour, and environment protections, there are still FTAs dealing with these matters on a voluntary basis. The European Free Trade Association (EFTA) (the members of which include Norway, Iceland, Liechtenstein, and Switzerland) has approved model provisions for integrating environmental and labour standards into its FTAs with other regions. But these are non-binding.[10]

Although some of such matters are subject to non-binding rules under some FTAs, many FTAs impose obligations on their parties concerning these trade-related subject matters. Hence regional trade governance is farther reaching in the sense that many trade-related issues are being covered and wider scope of activities are governed by normative rules provided in the respective FTAs.

The third aspect of regional trade governance is the weakness in serving as a platform for further developing new rules for regional trade governance. As opposed to the WTO, which serves as a platform and sponsors negotiation rounds for its Members to conduct trade negotiations on a continuous basis, FTAs basically do not require their parties to conduct continuous and periodic rounds of

[9] Jose Luis Siueiros, 'NAFTA Institutional Arrangements and Dispute Settlement Procedures' (1992) 23 Cal W Intl LJ 384, 384.

[10] Alliance Sud, 'FTA: Labour Provisions à la Carte' (Alliance Sud 2010) <www.alliancesud.ch/en/policy/trade/fta-and-labour-provisions> accessed 23 April 2016.

negotiations. Hence, although FTAs are more advanced in requiring their parties to remove substantially all tariffs and other restrictive regulations for trade in goods and substantially all discrimination for trade in services, they basically do not provide a mechanism to require or expect their parties to further negotiate the elimination of 'remaining' tariffs and restrictive regulations for trade in goods and the remaining discriminations for trade in services.

The fourth aspect of regional trade governance is the dispute settlement mechanisms being not constantly resorted to for regional trade disputes. Most recently concluded FTAs have detailed rule-based dispute settlement procedures in their texts. Many FTAs adopt the model of judgments by standing tribunals to resolve disputes arising from their FTAs. Many others adopt the WTO model to rely on an ad hoc panel to hear the dispute. No matter which model is adopted, the general situation of their dispute settlement mechanism being not constantly used is similar, with the exception that the dispute settlement mechanisms under NAFTA are quite frequently used.[11] Hence it can be generally said that the compliance of regional trade norms is not heavily based on the operation of dispute settlement mechanisms of FTAs. It does not mean that the detailed provisions of dispute settlement mechanisms are not relevant. In fact, the existence of rule-based detailed dispute provisions could have the effect of deterring non-compliance of FTA norms. But the fact that most FTAs' dispute settlement mechanisms are not frequently utilized could be because of any of the following reasons: their parties are more willing to comply with FTA rules so that there had been fewer regional disputes; or their parties prefer to resort to WTO dispute settlement mechanism over regional mechanism; or their parties are more reluctant in resorting to FTA dispute settlement procedures for other reasons (such as maintaining friendship); or they consider regional mechanism as ineffective.

IV. Gaps between Global and Regional Governance and the Ways to Bridge Them

A. Gap in the degree of liberalization and the way to bridge the gap

Apparently, all regional trade are governed by more liberalized trade rules than multilateral rules. Hence there is a gap between regional trade norms and multilateral trade norms in their degree of trade liberalization. It is also an apparent situation that the gap is getting narrower after many rounds of multilateral trade negotiations. If WTO trade negotiations can be continuously and successfully conducted, multilateral trade will be subject to a more liberalized trade regime,

[11] See the dispute settlement decisions and reports of the NAFTA at NAFTA Secretariat, 'Decisions and Reports' <http://www.nafta-sec-alena.org/Home/Dispute-Settlement/Decisions-and-Reports> accessed 14 March 2016.

which could be similar to regional trade regimes concerning the degrees of liberalization. However, it must be recognized that after many rounds of trade liberalization under a multilateral system, further negotiations on trade liberalization are getting more and more difficult, because such negotiations will unavoidably touch upon the removal of some minimum tariff protection for more sensitive sectors of the negotiating countries. It must also be recognized that by its nature, regional liberalization under FTAs is always supposed to be more advanced than multilateral liberalization under the WTO.

But the existence of such a gap is undesirable, for a number of reasons. First, WTO Members which are non-parties to a specific FTA could be effectively discriminated against because the FTA could provide much more advantageous treatment for their parties and hence could distort international trade. Second, different trade liberalizations and different trade rules under various FTAs could create unnecessary difficulties, confusion, and costs to traders. Third, multilateral regimes that were established to serve as the main governing body of global trade could become marginalized.

There are a couple of apparent ways to bridge the gap between global and regional governance regarding the different degree of trade liberalization. One way of bridging the gap is to fasten multilateral trade negotiations so as to make global trade subject to a more liberalized governing regime. This would require WTO Members to prioritize multilateral negotiation in their agenda. But at this stage, we do not see WTO Members prioritizing the multilateral negotiations. Another way is to widen the geographic coverage of current bilateral and regional FTAs by admitting more non-parties to enter FTAs and to make them much more plurilateral. If FTAs can be massively plurilateralized, the discriminated WTO Members will become fewer and the discriminative effect can be reduced. In order to achieve this, the accession process under FTAs should be simplified so as to make geographic expansion easier.

Another problem arising from plurilateralization of FTAs is the possible increase in conflicts among different FTAs due to the higher likelihood of the same countries becoming parties to different but overlapping FTAs. In this regard, it should be desirable to have a co-ordination mechanism to deal with the possible conflicts between overlapping FTAs. Such a co-ordination mechanism should allow parties of an FTA (which are non-parties to another overlapping FTA) to participate in the operation and the dispute settlement procedure under another overlapping FTA as third parties so as to ensure the consistency between these FTAs.

B. Gap in the subject-matter coverage and the way to bridge the gap

As mentioned above, most recently concluded FTAs have chapters or provisions addressing some important issues directly or indirectly related to international trade (such as competition policy, labour protection, and environmental protection). Their ways of dealing with such issues could be different, but their main ideas are similar: to provide better protection of certain values (for instance, the important value of protecting labour rights, and of protecting environment as an essential element of sustainable development) or to co-ordinate with other related policies (for instance, the inclusion of some competition policy provisions or chapters as a way of co-ordination between trade and competition norms).

When FTAs are negotiated, participating countries are more ambitious in forming new norms in new fields that relate to international trade. This is also because negotiating countries are encountering similar issues and hence different FTAs are using or copying each other's texts. This situation of FTAs adopting similar approaches or texts can be called a 'peer-learning process', which is one of the reasons that we can see the trend of FTAs broadening the contents in their subject-matter coverage and having certain models for dealing with such matters. Another reason for expanding FTAs' subject-matter coverage is that some main proponents of FTAs have their own model texts. For instance, the United States and the European Union have their own model FTA texts. When they negotiate with their partners, they tend to use their model texts. This makes many texts of FTAs quite similar. Yet another reason is that negotiating countries of FTAs are more able to exchange their interests in a smaller (bilateral or regional) setting than in the multilateral setting. So a country in need of accessing the market of another country would be more willing to accept the expansion of their FTA's subject-matter coverage.

In this regard, the WTO has much room to improve. The WTO has not been able to discuss or successfully negotiate the adoption of new trade-related rules, such as rules to co-ordinate trade and competition policy, the introduction of norms to better protect labour and environment, and the adoption of ways to co-ordinate the treaties governing labour protection, environmental protection, and protection of public health.[12] It has even been struggling to complete the current Doha negotiations.

It is desirable to co-ordinate this gap for the following reasons. First, it should be positive to co-ordinate between global trade regime and international norms of labour and environmental protection so as to avoid their possible inconsistencies and to make them mutually supportive. Second, it should also be positive to introduce certain fundamental human values, such as human rights (including labour protection) and environmental protection into the operation of global trade governance, so as to make global trade regime more supportive of these values.

The ways to bridge the gap between FTAs (many of which have already included chapters or provisions for labour protection and environmental protection) and the WTO (which basically lacks such rules) include engaging in multilateral negotiations to create additional multilateral trade-related norms and relying on treaty interpretation methods. Based on the experience of the Doha negotiation, where some trade-related issues (including labour protection and investment) had been excluded

[12] See e.g., Tsai-Yu Lin, 'Inter-Mingling TRIPS Agreement with an FET Standard in Investor-State Arbitration: An Emergent Challenge for the WTO' (2016) 50 J World Trade 71–91. See also Julien Chaisse, 'Exploring the Confines of International Investment and Domestic Health Protections—General Exceptions Clause as a Forced Perspective' (2013) 39(2/3) Am J L & Med 332–61.

from the negotiation agenda, it should be a reasonable assertion that the first possible way (i.e. relying on multilateral negotiation to create such norms) is not feasible in the near future. The only way left would be to rely on treaty interpretation so as to introduce values that are external to the WTO into the multilateral system.

It is the view of the author that, when possible, the interpreters of WTO agreements should choose the interpretation which is more in line with the protection of such fundamental values, such as the protection of core labour standards, environment, and public health. For instance, if the lack of protection of core labour standards in an exporting country would lead to undermining or adversely affecting the fundamental values of the importing country, and if the traded product relates to infringement of core labour standards, it should be made possible for the importing country to adopt trade measures to protect its fundamental values. This could be done through interpreting the text of WTO rules. For instance, it should be possible to incorporate the value of 'core labour standards' into the GATT and the GATS through textual interpretation of the ordinary meaning of 'public morals' under GATT Article XX(a).

C. Gap in the opportunity to improve the norms and the way to bridge the gap

Regarding the opportunity to improve the norms, we can see the advantages of global governance. As mentioned above, the WTO provides a platform for its Members to periodically negotiate the improvement of market access and existing rules and even to enact further rules. But in practice, the negotiations for further trade liberalization, improvement of existing rules, and enactment of new rules have been very slow pace. In contrast to the WTO, although FTAs generally have institutional arrangement to allow their parties to discuss FTA-related matters, and although some FTAs also provide the opportunities for their parties to incrementally enact additional rules, most FTAs are not widely expected to serve as a platform for further and continuous improvement of trade liberalization and enactment of new trade rules.

This is an operational gap between global and regional trade governance. The WTO platform is a very positive design but is operating in an inefficient way. On the other hand, most FTAs do not provide such useful platform for continuous and periodic liberalization and enactment of new norms. It should be useful for FTAs to bring the global mechanism into regional mechanism though adopting rules or establishing practices for the purpose of having FTAs' periodic 'internal negotiation rounds' in order to review and even gradually remove the residual trade barriers and/or to negotiate possible new norms.

D. Gap in the dispute settlement's functions and the way to bridge the gap

As mentioned above, the WTO has a very successful dispute settlement mechanism in its design and operation. It has been heavily relied upon by WTO Members to resolve their disputes. On the other hand, most recently concluded FTAs have detailed rule-based dispute settlement mechanisms. But most of them are not constantly relied on, for different reasons. Hence there is another operational gap between global and regional trade governance in this respect.

It has been proven by the large number of dispute settlement cases that the WTO dispute settlement mechanism is heavily relied upon as a mechanism in the global trade governance. More use of the WTO dispute settlement mechanism is desirable because of the following reasons. First, it has established professionalism in resolving trade disputes. Second, it has also established trust from its Members. Third, resorting to multilateral dispute settlement mechanism is a proper way to enhance co-ordination between multilateral and regional trade governance and to maintain the integrity of the multilateral system.

However, the multilateral dispute settlement mechanism has its limits in dealing with trade disputes. For instance, a tariff measure adopted by a country can violate its obligation under an FTA (which requires a zero tariff for a disputed product), but it might not violate its WTO commitment (which does not require a zero tariff for the same product). In such a case, the WTO dispute settlement mechanism is not useful in addressing the related tariff dispute. Also, for instance, a mandatory requirement of protecting labour is provided in an FTA but is not provided in the WTO. In such a situation, a dispute arising from the violation of an FTA provision might not become a WTO dispute because of the inexistence of WTO provision for labour protection. In other words, as between the WTO and an FTA, it is very likely that a measure adopted by a country only violates its FTA obligations, but not its WTO obligations, because of the fact that FTA obligations could be wider and stricter than obligations required by the WTO.

One way of making more use of the WTO dispute settlement mechanism is to include some provisions in the FTAs explicitly allowing its parties to resort to multilateral mechanism, or at least not to include FTA provisions discouraging its parties to resort to the multilateral mechanism for disputes that are concurrently governed by the WTO and by an FTA.

Another way is to have a broader interpretation of Article 1.1 of the Understanding on Rules and Provisions Governing the Settlement of Disputes (DSU) under the WTO, which provides in part that: 'The rules and procedures of this Understanding shall apply to *disputes brought pursuant to* the consultation and dispute settlement provisions of *the agreements listed in Appendix 1* to this Understanding (referred to in this Understanding as the "covered agreements").' The requirement of 'disputes brought pursuant to the covered agreements' could be understood to mean that all disputed issues should be directly arising from the interpretation and application of the covered agreements. It should also be possible to have broader interpretation so as to address issues arising from other multilateral treaties.

For instance, suppose there is a disputed issue arising from a covered agreement (such as GATT Article XI concerning prohibition of import restriction), and there is a preliminary issue arising from whether an established external norm is violated (such as whether a treaty for labour protection is violated), and the alleged violation of such external norm is relevant to the application of a covered agreement (such as whether the public moral exception provided in GATT Article XX(a) is applicable). The panel should be expected to separately address the preliminary issue of the challenged violation of the external norm. This is a way to narrow the gap between the FTA's wider coverage (such as covering labour protection issues) and the WTO's narrower coverage (such as non-existence of labour protection). If the violation of certain important external norms can become a separate issue to be specifically addressed in the WTO dispute settlement procedure, some external human values of key importance (such as labour protection and environmental protection) can be integrated into the operation of the WTO.

V. Some Concluding Remarks

The architects of the global trade governance envisaged high percentages of world trade volumes being fully subject to global governance. What was not expected was the immense proliferation of FTAs. The global trade governance and the regional trade governance have their gaps.

The WTO and FTAs have different approaches in the governance of global and regional trade. Their rules are both mandatory. But FTAs require deeper liberalization and their scope of subject-matter coverage is broader than the WTO rules. The WTO has a more comprehensive scheme for rounds of trade negotiations for further liberalization and for establishing new rules. But their operation is not as effective as one would expect. FTAs generally have detailed rule-based dispute settlement mechanisms. But many of them are not constantly used. Many FTA parties have relied on, or prefer to rely on, WTO dispute settlement mechanism to resolve their differences. The author argues that it is desirable to bridge the gaps between global and regional governance so that the two layers of trade governance can be more mutually supportive.

For regional trade governance, this chapter suggests widening the geographic coverage of FTAs by admitting more non-parties to the FTAs so as to make them much more plurilateralized. It also suggests adopting rules or establishing practices so that FTAs will have periodic 'internal negotiation rounds' in order to review and even gradually remove the residual trade barriers and/or to negotiate possible new norms.

For global governance, this chapter suggests relying on treaty interpretation to introduce values that are external to the WTO into the multilateral system. It also suggests allowing WTO dispute settlement mechanism to address preliminary issues arising from external norms so that some external human values of key importance (such as labour and environmental protection) can be integrated into the operation of the WTO. This could bring the two layers of trade governance more in line with each other in the sense that such external values are both respected, although through different means.

29

Decision making in the WTO: From Negotiated Law-making to Judicial Law-making

*R Rajesh Babu**

I. Introduction

The World Trade Organizations (WTO) is often viewed as one of the most democratic and Member-driven organizations of our time. The core of this perception is the democratic decision-making process that embraces all Member States, irrespective of their size, strength, or share in the annual contribution to the WTO. All decisions are reached through 'consensus', be it interpretation or amendment of the WTO Agreements, or creation of binding and enforceable international trade rules. While the practice of seeking consensus dominates the decision-making process, however, in its absence, the decisions can be taken by a majority vote, through a one-member–one-vote process. The consensus practice, at least in theory, could act as a veto, permitting any Member to block the adoption of a decision, making every Member's vote vital for decision making in the Ministerial Conference or the General Council. The system marks a significant departure from the practices of other prominent post-World-War-II organizations such as the International Monetary Fund (IMF), World Bank, or even the United Nations, where a nation's economic or military strength is reflected in its voting strength.[1]

The system of 'consensus' has worked well since the General Agreement on Tariff and Trade (GATT) 1947 and has been viewed as inclusive and empowering all Members in the decision-making process. At the same time, there has

* Associate Professor of Law, Indian Institute of Management Calcutta. Email: rajeshbabu@iimcal.ac.in.

[1] See Articles of Agreement of the International Monetary Fund, 22 July 1944, entered into force 27 December 1945, 60 Stat 1401, 2 UNTS 39, art XII; Articles of Agreement of the International Bank for Reconstruction and Development, 22 July 1944, entered into force 27 December 1945, 2 UNTS 134, art V; Charter of the United Nation, 26 June 1945, entered into force 24 October 1945, 1 UNTS XVI, art XXVII. See generally, William N Gianaris, 'Weighted Voting in the International Monetary Fund and the World Bank' (1990) 14 (4) Fordham Intl LJ 910.

been increasing concern about the effectiveness of the model in the context of the large number of WTO 'active' Members, representing diverse interests and objectives, which have complicated the WTO decision making and consensus building. Questions have been raised on the suitability and workability of the 'consensus' system, given the constant deadlocks in the decision-making and negotiating process, apart from making the entire process tedious and time consuming. The WTO witnessed a total breakdown of the 'consensus-building' process at Seattle Ministerial Conference, which has continued to inhibit the trade negotiations under the Doha Development Agenda (DDA) launched in 2001. The critics have also pointed out that the success of the democratic decision making by consensus depends on the ability of countries to voice their dissent. However, the power politics within the WTO ensure that veto or blocking of consensus is rarely exercised.

At the other extreme of the WTO decision-making apparatus is the Dispute Settlement Body (DSB), the key organ entrusted with the implementation of the Dispute Settlement Understanding (DSU).[2] The DSB decision-making process deviates significantly from the consensus rule when decisions are made connected with the establishment of the panels, adoption of panel and Appellate Body reports, and when it authorizes retaliation. These decisions are adopted by the DSB through 'negative' or 'reverse' consensus principle; i.e. the DSB shall decide in favour of the establishment, adoption, or retaliation, unless there is a consensus not to adopt the decision. In other words, under the 'negative' consensus rule, the DSB must approve the decision unless there is a *consensus against it*.[3] This deviation, influenced by historical reasons, forces the DSB decision-making process to become almost automatic. The Member States have minimal control over the outcome, including the legal interpretations and clarifications of the WTO agreements by the panels/Appellate Body. This inability of the political bodies to respond to the recommendations and rulings of the Appellate Body, specifically when such interpretations are considered improperly to 'add to or diminish the rights and obligations'[4] in the agreements, has been a matter of grave concern.

This chapter reflects on these two contrasting decision-making procedures with a view to understand its implications on the developing countries and the WTO multilateralism. The chapter argues that the judicial norm creation, on the one hand, and the inability of the political bodies to provide adequate checks and balances has resulted in a scenario where judicial law-making has superseded negotiated consent-based law-making. This development has not only undermined the rights and obligations assumed by the developing countries under the WTO covered agreements but also undermined State sovereignty and the Member-driven decision-making process. Consequently, the legitimacy of the panels/Appellate Body rulings and the credibility of the dispute settlement process are under threat. The chapter is divided as follows: section II starts with a descriptive and analytical

[2] Understanding on Rules and Procedures Governing the Settlement of Disputes, Marrakesh Agreement Establishing the World Trade Organization, Annex 2, 15 April 1994, 1896 UNTS 401 (DSU).

[3] DSU arts 6(1), 16(4), 17(14), 22(6), (7).

[4] DSU art 19(2).

study of the decision-making process in WTO Agreements, with a specific focus on the decision making under the Marrakesh Agreement and the DSU. Section III specifically examines the Ministerial Conference/General Council's power of 'authoritative interpretation' and differentiates the same with the 'clarification' function of the panels and the Appellate Body. Sections IV and V highlight the changing nature of norm creation in the WTO through the judicial process, and reflect on the impact of this trend on the developing countries, institutional legitimacy, and the WTO multilateralism.

II. The WTO Decision-making Apparatus

The organizational structure of the WTO as envisaged in the Marrakesh Agreement Establishing the WTO came into force in January 1995, replacing GATT 1947. The Agreement envisaged a hierarchy of decision-making bodies, with the Ministerial Conference at the apex. The Ministerial Conference represented by all WTO Members at the ministerial level is the highest decision-making body and is empowered to take decisions on all matters under any of the multilateral trade agreements.[5] The General Council, the next organ in the hierarchy, handles the day-to-day business and management of the WTO. Since the Ministerial Conference meets only once every two years, the General Council is in practice the key decision-maker. The General Council, also represented by all the Members, acts as the DSB as well as the Trade Policy Review Body (TPRB), depending on the terms of reference.[6] The TPRB periodically reviews the trade policies and practices of all Member States, with a view to improving adherence by the WTO parties to their obligations.[7] The DSB oversees the implementation and effectiveness of the dispute resolution process for all WTO agreements, and the implementation of the decisions on WTO disputes.[8] There are three councils; the Councils for Trade in Good, Trade in Services, and Trade-related Aspects of Intellectual Property Rights (TRIPS) are also represented by all Members and operate under the mandate of the General Council.[9]

'Consensus' is the preferred mode of decision making in all the WTO bodies. If the WTO Members are unable to arrive at a consensus, the WTO Agreement provides

[5] Marrakesh Agreement Establishing the World Trade Organization (Marrakesh Agreement), 15 April 1994, 1867 UNTS 154, art III.

[6] WTO, 'Whose WTO Is It Anyway?' (World Trade Organization) <https://www.wto.org/english/thewto_e/whatis_e/tif_e/org1_e.htm> accessed 14 March 2016.

[7] See generally Julien Chaisse and Mitsuo Matsushita, 'Maintaining the WTO's Supremacy in the International Trade Order: A Proposal to Refine and Revise the Role of the Trade Policy Review Mechanism' (2013) 16 J Intl Econ L 9–36.

[8] All WTO Members' policies are reviewed periodically. The policies of the European Union, the United States, Japan, and China are examined approximately once every two years. The next sixteen countries are reviewed every four years, and the remaining countries every six years. See WTO, 'Trade Policy Reviews: Ensuring Transparency' (World Trade Organization) <https://www.wto.org/english/thewto_e/whatis_e/tif_e/agrm11_e.htm> accessed 14 March 2016.

[9] Marrakesh Agreement (n 5), art IV.6.

for voting in certain cases, with each Member of the WTO having one vote.[10] Voting as an option is, however, never resorted to in practice. The decision making by voting at the Ministerial Conference and the General Council, if opted for, are by majority vote *cast*, which means a simple majority.[11] The quorum required is the majority of the Members in each decision-making organ.[12] There are certain exceptions to this simple majority rule, where a special majority is mandated. For instance, a decision under Article IX:2 of the Marrakesh Agreement on a 'waiver' from implementing an obligation imposed on a Member by the WTO Agreements must receive support from three-quarters of the Membership of the Ministerial Conference.[13] However, if the 'waiver' is with respect to an obligation 'subject to a transition period or a period for staged implementation' that the requesting Member has not performed by the end of the relevant period, such decisions shall be taken only by consensus.[14]

Similarly, in the context of 'amendments' to the WTO Agreement, Article X prescribes different procedures depending on the provisions proposed for amendment. With respect to the provisions of the Marrakesh Agreement, or of the multilateral trade agreements in Annexes 1A (GATT) and 1C (TRIPS), such an amendment shall 'take effect for the Members that have accepted them upon acceptance by two thirds of the Members and thereafter for each other Member upon acceptance by it'.[15] In comparison, any changes to Article X:2 of the Marrakesh Agreement shall take effect only upon acceptance by all Members.[16] Further, a decision to add a new Plurilateral Trade Agreement (PTA) to Annex 4 must be made exclusively by consensus.[17] A decision to admit a new Member requires a two-thirds majority in the Ministerial Conference or the General Council in between conferences.[18] By contrast, in the DSB all decisions are made by consensus unless otherwise provided for in the DSU.[19]

A. Decision making through consensus

The decision-making process in the WTO continues to be guided by consensus principles, one-member–one-vote, and Member-driven character.[20] As mentioned

[10] Where the European Community exercise their right to vote, they shall have a number of votes equal to the number of their Member States which are Members of the WTO.

[11] Marrakesh Agreement (n 5), art IX:1.

[12] Rules of Procedure for Sessions of the Ministerial Conference and Meetings of the General Council, WT/L/161, 25 July 1996, r 16. Rüdiger Wolfrum and others (eds), *WTO—Institutions and Dispute Settlement* (Martinus Nijhoff 2006) 112.

[13] Marrakesh Agreement (n 5), art IX:3. [14] ibid. [15] ibid art X.

[16] ibid art IX; General Agreement on Tariffs and Trade 1994 (GATT 1994); Marrakesh Agreement (n 5), Annex 1A, arts I and II; General Agreement on Trade in Services (GATS); Marrakesh Agreement (n 5), Annex 1B, art II:1; Agreement on Trade-related Aspects of Intellectual Property Rights (TRIPS); 1 Marrakesh Agreement (n 5), Annex 1C, art 4. See also art X:6.

[17] Marrakesh Agreement (n 5), art X:9. [18] ibid art XIV.

[19] See also DSU art 2.4: 'The DSB shall be deemed to have decided by consensus on a matter submitted for its consideration, if no Member, present at the meeting of the DSB when the decision is taken, formally objects to the proposed decision.' See Wolfrum and others (n 12) 112–13.

[20] Margaret Liang, 'Notes: Evolution of the WTO Decision-making Process' (2005) 9 Singapore YB Intl L Contributors 125, 125.

above, the default mode of all decision making in the Ministerial Conference, the General Council, and the DSB is through consensus.[21] There is a deemed consensus if no Member present and voting at the meeting formally objects to the proposed decision.[22] In other words, a single Member could, at least in theory, veto a consensus. Article IX:1 of the Marrakesh Agreement states that:

> The WTO shall continue the practice of decision-making by consensus followed under GATT 1947. Except as otherwise provided, where a decision cannot be arrived at by consensus, the matter at issue shall be decided by voting. At meetings of the Ministerial Conference and the General Council, each Member of the WTO shall have one vote. Where the European Communities exercise their right to vote, they shall have a number of votes equal to the number of their member States which are Members of the WTO. Decisions of the Ministerial Conference and the General Council shall be taken by a majority of the votes cast, unless otherwise provided in this Agreement or in the relevant Multilateral Trade Agreement.[23]

This provision provides primacy to the consensus process, with voting as the fallback option, to be resorted to only in the event that a consensus is not forthcoming.

This consensus practice has its origin in the consensus procedure followed by the Contracting Parties to the GATT 1947.[24] The practice is founded on the principle of sovereign equality and was considered as the best way to protect the interests of the states.[25] Even the smallest and the economically weak Members of the WTO could participate in the decision-making process, make their voice heard, and block the adoption of undesirable outcomes.[26] In other words, the consensus decision making has given even the smallest countries some measure of representation in the WTO, and 'a certain degree of say in issues and processes'.[27] The ability to veto consensus has also ensured greater bargaining power among the negotiating participants in favour of the developing countries.[28] John Jackson notes:

> The [consensus] rule forces the membership to achieve as wide an acceptance of new measures as possible, thus lending democratic legitimacy to measures that are finally adopted.

[21] The consensus decision-making modal is not unique to the WTO, but is used by many international organizations.

[22] Marrakesh Agreement (n 5), art IX.

[23] ibid art IX.1.

[24] Wolfrum and others (n 12) 109.

[25] Thomas Cottier, 'A Two-tier Approach to WTO Decision-making' in Debra P Stege (ed), *Redesigning the World Trade Organization for the Twenty-first Century* (Wilfrid Laurier University Press 2010) 57.

[26] Ilan Kapoor, 'Deliberative Democracy and the WTO' (2004) 11(3) Rev Intl Pol Econ 522; Loren King, 'Deliberation, Legitimacy, and Multilateral Democracy' (2003) 16(1) Governance 23; Robert Wolfe, 'Decision-making and Transparency in the "Medieval" WTO: Does the Sutherland Report Have the Right Prescription?' (2005) 8(3) J Intl Econ L 631.

[27] Memory Dube, 'The Way Forward for the WTO: Reforming the Decision-making Process' (Economic Diplomacy Programme Occasional Papers Number 118, South African Institute of International Affairs, July 2012) 5.

[28] Robert E Baldwin, 'Failure of the WTO Ministerial Conference at Cancun: Reasons and Remedies' (2006) 29(6) World Econ 677.

It therefore forces the richer and more powerful members of the organization to take into consideration the needs and opinions of all parts of the organization, including the poorer and less powerful governments.[29]

Since the decision making is consent-based, the general compliance level with such a decision arrived at by consensus is expected to be significantly higher than in the case of a majority-based decision, or weighted voting system, where decisions are thrust on the minority group.[30]

Indeed, if the consensus is not forthcoming, the WTO Agreement provides that the Member States could opt for the majoritarian system of voting on the basis of 'one country, one vote'. A majoritarian voting system is, however, discouraged, as it runs the risk of decisions being controlled by the majority, which may be the developing countries in the WTO context.[31] The developing countries had argued in the 1970s against the use of majority voting, which would put them in a minority position, since they are numerically less. They were willing to agree 'to accept a one-country one-vote arrangement on the assumption that voting would not be used and that the veto would only be applied with great moderation'.[32] The WTO's 'one-member–one-vote' also marks a significant departure from the practices of other organizations such as the IMF, World Bank, or even the UN.[33] The IMF and the World Bank, for instance, follow the 'weighted voting system', a practice that grants few members of the institution greater voting power and thus, more influence and control over decisions.[34] In the IMF, the United States alone has about sixteen per cent of the voting power, while the entire African countries have about three per cent in total.[35]

The inclusive nature of the decision-making process of the WTO has created a perception of the institution being the most democratic and Member-driven organization of our time. The functioning of the WTO in the past two decades has, however, created certain doubts about the effectiveness of the decision-making process, in terms of both process and outcome. Critics argue that although in principle a decision could be blocked by any Member, the ultimate outcome would depend on the power equation, meaning that the largest countries generally yield

[29] John H Jackson, *Sovereignty, the WTO and Changing Fundamentals of International Law* (CUP 2006) 114. See also Wenwei Guan, 'Consensus yet not Consented: A Critique of the WTO Decision-making' (2014) 17(1) J Intl Econ L 77.

[30] See generally Giovanni Maggi and Massimo Morelli, 'Self-enforcing Voting in International Organizations' (2006) 96(4) Am Econ Rev 1137.

[31] See Stephen Zamora, 'Voting in International Economic Organizations' (1980) 74(3) Am J Intl L 566.

[32] Patrick Low, 'WTO Decision-making for the Future' (2011) WTO Staff Working Paper ERSD-2011-05, 4 <https://www.wto.org/english/res_e/reser_e/ersd201105_e.htm> accessed 23 April 2016.

[33] An outcome based on weighted voting, for instance, casts a shadow over negotiations where states know that they will either be disadvantaged or favoured by a decision that reverts to the default rule. Richard H Steinberg, 'In the Shadow of Law or Power? Consensus-based Bargaining and Outcomes in the GATT/WTO' (2002) 56(2) Intl Org 339.

[34] Daniel J Blake and Lockwood Payton, 'Decision Making in International Organizations: An Interest Based Approach to Voting Rule Selection' (International Politics Workshop, 2009) 5.

[35] ibid 6.

more weight than small countries. For instance, Low argues that it would be 'more costly for smaller countries to challenge an outcome popular with large countries than vice-versa. Similarly, blocking a consensus with a veto is much more difficult for less powerful countries.'[36] Steinberg also calls the consensus-based WTO decision-making rules based on the sovereign equality of states as organized hypocrisy in the procedural context.[37]

According to Cottier, the consensus decision-making process in reality is an informal system of weighted voting system where powerful members can block consensus more easily while the same remedy comes at a high political cost for the small and medium-size countries.[38] Consensus decision making 'ascribes power that, in reality, does not exist for most'.[39] Narlikar points out that most developing countries may block consensus once or twice, or simply remain silent because of their fear of the consequences of expressing their objections publicly, such as finding themselves isolated in due course.[40] Further, since consensus in the WTO means the absence of objection, developing countries end up agreeing to decisions that they have problems with.[41] The democratic legitimacy of consensus is therefore merely formal and does not offer a true and transparent account of the power relations.[42] Thus, 'power' inhibits consensus decision making in the WTO.

Besides, consensus decision making also suffers from both procedural and substantive disadvantages. First and foremost, arriving at a consensus decision by itself is difficult, particularly when the membership is very large, as in the case of the WTO. Second, the 'decision outcome' of the decision-making process gets highly diluted owing to the need for getting acceptance from all Members, to arrive at a consensus. Blake and Payton note that consensus decision making hinders the ability of institutions to act swiftly and generally leads to 'shallower' co-operation. According to Zamora:

> The disadvantage of the rule of unanimity, of course, is that international agreement is impossible to obtain when any single participant can block a decision; to achieve unanimous consent, the strength of a decision must be diluted so as to please everyone.[43]

Reaching a decision by consensus in a body composed of 160 very different Members is difficult, if not an impossible task. Although consensus decisions

[36] Low (n 32). See also Steinberg, 'In the Shadow of Law or Power?' (n 33) 339.

[37] Steinberg, 'In the Shadow of Law or Power?' (n 33).

[38] Cottier (n 25) 57. Cottier recommends that a consensus-minus rule and blocking of decisions must be limited to coalitions or blocks rather than individually.

[39] ibid.

[40] Amrita Narlikar, 'WTO Decision-making and Developing Countries' (2001) Trade-related Agenda, Development and Equity (TRADE) Working Papers 11, South Centre <http://www.iatp.org/files/WTO_Decision-Making_and_Developing_Countries.htm> accessed 23 April 2016. See also Bernard Hoeckman, 'Global Trade Governance' in Thomas G Weiss and Rorden Wilkinson (eds), *International Organization and Global Governance* (Routledge 2014) 556.

[41] Narlikar (n 40).

[42] The traditional 'Green Room' process, in which a relatively small number of self-selected developed and developing countries get together to decide on divisive issues, excluded too many newly active players in WTO negotiations and thus had problems with building consensus.

[43] Zamora (n 31) 574.

have the advantage of being more acceptable to all Members, as Schott notes: 'The WTO will likely suffer from slow and cumbersome policy-making and management—an organisation with more than [160] member countries cannot be run by a "committee of the whole". Mass management simply does not lend itself to operational efficiency or serious policy discussion.'[44] This is evident from the number of decisions that the Ministerial Conference and the General Council have adopted under Articles IX and X of the WTO Agreement in the past twenty years. The Ministerial Conference or the General Council is yet to adopt a decision on the 'authoritative interpretation' of the WTO Agreements. While there have been several decisions on granting a waiver from the WTO Agreement, most of them had no substantive consequence except for the Decision on the TRIPS Agreement and Public Health.[45]

The Ministerial Conference Decision on TRIPS Agreement and Public Health has been viewed as an evidence of the flaw inherent in the consensus decision-making process. Studying the effectiveness of the decision-making process in the context of this decision, Morin and Gold observe that the procedural norm of 'consensus-seeking can also lead not only to unworkable outcomes, but to flawed processes as well'.[46] The Decision on Public Health was hailed as a significant outcome as it was expected to address the 'access to medicine' concerns of the poor countries and was considered a breakthrough that, for the first time, became a permanent amendment to the WTO TRIPs Agreement.[47] However, in practice the Decision changed little in terms of guaranteeing access by medicine to poorer countries, even after a decade.

[44] See also Elimma C Ezeani, 'Trade Decisions Devoid of Judicial Activism: "Too Much Too Soon" for the Dispute Settlement Body?' (2004) 3(2) J Intl Trade L Policy 21, 23.

[45] The waiver decision on implementation of Paragraph 6 of the Doha Declaration on the TRIPS Agreement and Public Health of 30 August 2003 Decision defined conditions under which a country could export pharmaceutical products to another under a compulsory licence. As of 30 September 2011, there have been thirty-one waiver decisions, including fourteen waivers of arts I and/or XIII of the GATT 1994 in connection with trade preferences, fourteen waivers delaying application of WTO obligations, one waiver of art XV:6 of the GATT 1994, the waiver decision on implementation of Paragraph 6 of the Doha Declaration on the TRIPS Agreement and Public Health, and the waiver decision implementing the Kimberley Process Certification Scheme for Rough Diamonds. See WTO, 'Analytical Index: Marrakesh Agreement Establishing the World Trade Organization' (World Trade Organization) <https://www.wto.org/english/res_e/booksp_e/analytic_index_e/wto_agree_03_e.htm#fntext345> accessed 14 March 2016.

[46] Jean-Frédéric Morin and E Richard Gold, 'Consensus-seeking, Distrust and Rhetorical Entrapment: The WTO Decision on Access to Medicines' (2010) 16(4) Eur J Intl Relations 563, 565.

[47] Paragraph 6 of the Doha Declaration recognized this problem in that 'WTO members with insufficient or no manufacturing capacities in the pharmaceutical sector, could face difficulties in making effective use of compulsory licensing under the TRIPS Agreement' and thus instructed the TRIPS Council to find an expeditious solution to this problem and to report to the General Council before the end of 2002. On 30 August 2003, following nearly two years of negotiations, the General Council of the WTO finally adopted the Decision on Implementation of Paragraph 6 of the Doha Declaration on the TRIPS Agreement and Public Health (the August Decision). The WTO solution is essentially a waiver of the export restriction, thereby allowing the total amount of production under a compulsory licence to be exported. See WTO, 'WTO Decision on the Implementation of Paragraph 6 of the Doha Declaration on the TRIPS Agreement and Public Health' (World Health Organization) <http://www.who.int/medicines/areas/policy/wto_impl_para6/en/> accessed 14 March 2016.

Morin and Gold note that the states compromised because they recognized that walking away as an option, with nothing in hand was worse than a mechanism that they knew was flawed. The states became 'trapped in rhetoric of consensus-seeking that made it preferable for all to agree to an unworkable agreement—a flawed mechanism'.[48]

The practical difficulties in arriving at a consensus are also manifest from the failure at the Seattle Ministerial Conference in 2000 to reach agreement on a trade negotiation agenda and the on-going deadlock in the Doha Round, which started in 2001. Indeed, the deadlock could be attributed to the change in the negotiating dynamics since the Uruguay Round, with developing countries actively participating in the process. The developing countries now have a greater stake in the world trading system and the decision-making process than before.[49] Because of the 'single undertaking' requirement at the Uruguay Round, the developing countries committed themselves to substantially greater reforms that they avoided in the GATT era by claiming special and differential treatment. With such an experience in the background, their reluctance at the Doha Round of negotiations is only understandable. Moreover, the trend of coalition building among the developing countries, such as the G20 and the African Group, has relatively strengthened their negotiating position, rendering the negotiating outcome unpredictable and difficult.[50] The larger problem has been that the developed countries have been inflexible and reluctant to accommodate the legitimate concerns of the developing countries.

To reach consensus at the Bali Ministerial Conference, they had to move away from the 'single undertaking' principle, a hallmark of the decision-making process in the negotiating context. In the WTO, consensus and single undertaking are two concepts that are mutually intertwined and serve the same institutional purpose.[51] The problems with the consensus-building process in trade negotiations are amplified by the requirement of 'single undertaking'.[52] The concept essentially means that 'nothing is agreed until everything is agreed', and as such, in the case of the Uruguay Round Final Act, the on-going negotiations under the DDA are treated as a 'package deal' and Member States must consent to all decisions under all agenda items without reservations.[53] At the Uruguay Round many developing countries accepted obligations developed without their participation, which gave

[48] Morin and Gold (n 46).

[49] Jeffrey J Schott and Jayashree Watal, 'Decision-making in the WTO' (2000) Peterson Institute for International Economics, Policy Brief 00-2 <https://piie.com/publications/pb/pb.cfm?ResearchID=63> accessed 14 March 2016.

[50] Hoeckman (n 40). [51] Guan (n 29) 85.

[52] Paragraph 47 of the Doha Ministerial Declaration provides that the conduct, conclusion, and entry into force of the outcome of the negotiations shall be treated as parts of a single undertaking. However, agreements reached at an early stage may be implemented on a provisional or definitive basis. Philip I Levy, 'Do We Need an Undertaker for the Single Undertaking? Considering the Angles of Variable Geometry' in Simon J Evenett and Bernard M Hoekman (eds), *Economic Development and Multilateral Trade Cooperation* (Palgrave Macmillan and the World Bank 2006).

[53] See Low (n 32); Dube (n 27) 15.

them great difficulty in implementing.[54] The concept recognizes neither the different levels of economic development nor the differing implementation capacities of developing countries. The developing countries' experiences with the Uruguay Round 'package deal' had compelled them to rethink and hard bargain before committing to anything new.

Thus, with single understanding in place, Members have to reach a consensus on all items on the negotiating agenda.[55] This scenario, exuberated by the hard negotiating stand taken by the developed countries, have created a permanent deadlock in the negotiations, prompting a status quo in the WTO rule-making vis-à-vis review of the existing rules and expansion into new areas. The status quo seems retrograde in the current scenario, where there is a need to expand the role of the WTO norms to capture the emerging realities of global trade. Concerns were expressed on the protracted negotiations that could encourage states to move towards regional trade arrangements, thereby undermining WTO multilateralism. Jackson cautions that:

> if the WTO fails to keep abreast of the changes in the world and to evolve as an institution, some of the major users of the institution, and particularly some of the large trading powers, may begin to turn elsewhere to solve their problems. This could mean that these countries would turn to other multilateral institutions, such as the OECD, or to regional organizations, bilateral measures, or even unilateral measures. If the major users become disillusioned, the WTO could gradually atrophy, which would then be disappointing to some of the other users of the system.[56]

The fear of a failed Doha Round and the consequent collapse of the WTO multilateralism have compelled Members to deviate from the 'single undertaking' hurdle and decide on 'early harvest' of some of the negotiation issues at the Bali Ministerial Conference. After much hard bargaining, they were able to reach a consensus in the 2013 Bali Conference referred to as the 'Bali Package'.[57] One tangible outcome was the Trade Facilitation Agreement (TFA), which will enter into force once two-thirds of Members ratify the Protocol of Amendment to insert the new Agreement into Annex 1A of the WTO Agreement adopted by the General Council on 27 November 2014.[58]

B. Decision making in the DSB

The WTO DSU is considered to be the most significant achievement of the Uruguay Round of multilateral trade negotiations.[59] The DSU established three

[54] Schott and Watal (n 49). [55] Baldwin (n 28); Dube (n 27) 15.

[56] John H Jackson, 'The WTO "Constitution" and Proposed Reforms: Seven "Mantras" Revisited' (2001) 4(1) J Intl Econ L 67, 71.

[57] World Trade Organization, Ministerial Declaration and Decisions, Ninth Session, Bali, WT/MIN(13)/DEC, 7 December 2013.

[58] General Council, *Protocol Amending the Marrakesh Agreement Establishing the World Trade Organization*, WT/L/940, 28 November 2014.

[59] R Rajesh Babu, *Remedies Under the WTO Legal System* (Martinus Nijhoff 2012) 19.

bodies—the political organ Dispute Settlement Body (DSB), and under it a hierarchy of quasi-judicial organs—an ad hoc panel and a standing Appellate Body. The DSB is entrusted to administer the rules and procedures of dispute settlement, which include establishing the panel; adopting panel and Appellate Body reports; maintaining surveillance of implementation of rulings and recommendations; and authorizing suspension of concession and other obligations under the covered agreements.[60] The Appellate Body shall hear appeals from panel cases, which is limited to issues of law and legal interpretations developed by the panel.[61]

The DSB enjoys compulsory and exclusive jurisdiction over disputes arising out of the WTO covered agreements.[62] Since the WTO Member States have given *ex ante* consent to compulsory jurisdiction under the DSU, any Member could initiate an action against another Member without awaiting consent from the other party. The departure from the consent-based jurisdiction eliminated a major obstacle in its adjudicatory process. Article 23.1 of the DSU provides that:

> When Members seek the redress of a violation of obligations or other nullification or impairment of benefits under the covered agreements or an impediment to the attainment of any objective of the covered agreements, *they shall have recourse to*, and abide by, the rules and procedures of this Understanding[63] (emphasis added).

All decisions in the DSB, as in the case of other political bodies, are adopted through 'consensus', which means that no Member present at the meeting of the DSB formally objects to the proposed decision.[64] However, the DSU departs from the regular consensus practice and provides for 'negative consensus' while deciding critical procedural matters such as the establishment of the panel, adoption of the rulings, and recommendations of the panels/Appellate Body, including the compliance review reports and authorization for retaliation.[65] This would mean that a decision will be considered adopted unless the DSB decides by consensus not to adopt the report. This was a key procedural improvement over the GATT 1947 dispute settlement system, where a single negative vote (including that of the losing party) could block the adoption of a decision by the Contracting Parties.[66] This veto power was often used to block the adoption of panel reports. The reverse consensus rules made the dispute settlement process time bound and

[60] ibid art 2. Pascal Lamy, 'The Place of the WTO and Its Law in the International Legal Order' (2007) 17(5) Eur J Intl L 969, 969.

[61] DSU art 17.4.

[62] As the Appellate Body summarized in *Brazil—Measures Affecting Desiccated Coconut*, Appellate Body Report, *Brazil—Measures Affecting Desiccated Coconut*, WT/DS22/AB/R, 21 February 1997, 11, '[t]he "covered agreements" include the WTO Agreement, the Agreements in Annexes 1 and 2, as well as any Plurilateral Trade Agreement in Annex 4 where its Committee of signatories has taken a decision to *apply the DSU*'.

[63] The WTO legal system provides a de facto mandatory jurisdiction and a Member has a de facto 'right' to a panel. Joel P Trachtman, 'The WTO Cathedral' (2007) 43 Stan J Intl L 128, 135.

[64] DSU art 2(4). [65] ibid arts 6(1), 16(4), 17(14), and 22(6), (7).

[66] WTO, 'Historic Development of the WTO Dispute Settlement System' (World Trade Organization) <https://www.wto.org/english/tratop_e/dispu_e/disp_settlement_cbt_e/c2s1p1_e.htm> accessed 14 March 2016.

automatic. Once a dispute is initiated, the procedure guaranteed the continuation of the dispute settlement process without any 'blockage' or delay until the dispute settlement process would culminate in the adoption of a legally binding decision, including a decision on countermeasures in case of non-compliance by the DSB.[67] Together with the compulsory jurisdiction, this procedural improvement has contributed to the success of the WTO dispute settlement system as we see it today.

III. Authoritative Interpretation of the WTO Agreements

In the WTO, the Ministerial Conference, the General Council, and the DSB are the three key organs responsible for interpretation and clarification of the WTO covered agreements. The nature and scope of the interpretation function, however, vary considerably. The authoritative interpretation developed by the Ministerial Conference and the General Council is binding on all Members, whereas the clarification of the DSB is case-specific and subsidiary to that of the other higher political bodies. However, in practice the difference in the decision-making procedure in these organs has resulted in a situation unforeseen during the Uruguay Round of negotiations. As we shall see in this section, the resultant consequence has been the judicial norm creation by the panels and Appellate Body through interpretation, at the expense of the political bodies' inability to react to such unauthorized interpretations.[68] This section will briefly consider and differentiate the interpretation function of the Ministerial Conference and the General Council vis-à-vis the DSB and its adjudicating bodies, and the consequences thereof.

A. Authoritative interpretation by the Ministerial Conference/General Council

The WTO Agreement vests in the highest decision-making political bodies—Ministerial Conference and the General Council of the WTO—the 'exclusive authority to adopt interpretations' of the WTO agreement.[69] The responsibility would entail ratification of the newly formed interpretations in case of conflicts or ambiguities that may arise in the implementation of the provisions of the WTO covered agreements.[70] Article IX:2 of the WTO Agreement was introduced with the intent of providing the political bodies an opportunity to refine the existing trade rules.[71] Article IX:2 WTO Agreement states:

[67] R Rajesh Babu, 'Interpretation of the WTO Agreements, Democratic Legitimacy and Developing Nations' (2010) 50 (1) Indian J Intl L 45.

[68] ibid. [69] Marrakesh Agreement (n 5), art IX:2. [70] ibid.

[71] Claus-Dieter Ehlermann and Lothar Ehring, 'The Authoritative Interpretation Under the Article IX:2 of the WTO Agreement: Current Law, Practice and Possible Improvements' (2005) 8(4) J Intl Econ L 803.

> The Ministerial Conference and the General Council shall have the exclusive authority to adopt interpretations of this Agreement and of the Multilateral Trade Agreements. In the case of an interpretation of a Multilateral Trade Agreement in Annex 1, they shall exercise their authority on the basis of a recommendation by the Council overseeing the functioning of that Agreement.... This paragraph shall not be used in a manner that would undermine the amendment provisions in Article X.

If the consensus is not forthcoming, all such 'authoritative interpretations' must have a three-quarters majority of Members voting in favour. If the matter concerns interpretation of the GATT, General Agreement on Trade in Services (GATS), or TRIPS Agreement, the Ministerial Conference and the General Council shall exercise their authority on the basis of a recommendation by the respective Council overseeing the agreement. These Councils do not provide for voting, and the decisions are taken by consensus. If the Council is unable to reach a decision by consensus, the matter must be referred to the General Council.[72] In such a situation, the Council's 'recommendation will be replaced by action of the General Council, where the prior recommendation and the authoritative interpretation itself arguably collapse into one single act'.[73]

The authoritative interpretation adopted by the Ministerial Conference and the General Council is binding on all Members. The interpretation function under Article IX goes beyond the role of the DSB to clarify the existing provisions of the covered agreements. In that sense, the power of interpretation under Article IX is not bound by the constraints imposed on the DSB's interpretation, as laid down in Article 3.2 of the DSU. [74] The only restraint on this power is that such authoritative interpretation must not undermine the amendment provisions.[75] Such interpretations are meant to clarify the meaning of existing obligations, 'not to modify their content', and shall not be used in a manner that would undermine the amendment provisions in Article X (Amendments).[76] The Appellate Body in *EC—Bananas III* (Article 21.5) noted that interpretations adopted pursuant to Article IX:2 of the WTO Agreement: 'can be likened to a subsequent agreement regarding

[72] General Council, *Rules of Procedure for Meetings of the Council for Trade in Goods*, WT/L/79, 7 August 1995, r 33.

[73] In the current practice (related to other decisions), however, the referral foreseen in Rule 33 often does not take place when consensus cannot be reached. Ehlermann and Ehring, 'The Authoritative Interpretation under the Article IX:2 of the WTO Agreement' (n 71) 806.

[74] DSU art 3.2:

> The dispute settlement system of the WTO is a central element in providing security and predictability to the multilateral trading system. The Members recognize that it serves to preserve the rights and obligations of Members under the covered agreements, and to clarify the existing provisions of those agreements in accordance with customary rules of interpretation of public international law. Recommendations and rulings of the DSB cannot add to or diminish the rights and obligations provided in the covered agreements.

[75] Marrakesh Agreement (n 5), art IX.2 last sentence: 'This paragraph shall not be used in a manner that would undermine the amendment provisions in Article X.'

[76] Appellate Body Report, *European Communities—Regime for the Importation, Sale and Distribution of Bananas Second Recourse to Article 21.5 of the DSU by Ecuador and the United States*, WT/DS27/AB/RW2/ECU, WT/DS27/AB/RW/USA, 26 November 2008, para 393.

the interpretation of the treaty or the application of its provisions pursuant to Article 31(3)(a) of the Vienna Convention, as far as the interpretation of the WTO agreements is concerned'.[77] However, the extent to which such an interpretation may change the WTO law (add or diminish the rights and obligations) as it stands is contested.[78] It can be assumed that the authority to 'interpret' falls somewhere between 'clarification' and 'amendment'.

The power of authoritative interpretation remains unused to date.[79] One key hindrance has been the procedural restraint of consensus. In practice, consensus among all the Member States is a prerequisite for any decision-making process, meaning any single country could oppose the adoption of an interpretation. Even when the voting option is exercised, the Article IX:2 process is still constrained by the requirement that substantive interpretations are binding only for those Members accepting such a proposal. In addition, the non-use of Article IX could also be due to the DSB's clarification of the WTO covered agreements, through the dispute settlement system, the adoption of which does not require a consensus or three-quarters majority. A formal request for an authoritative interpretation was once made by the EC to settle the 'sequencing' problem in the DSU. The General Council, however, did not adopt the requested interpretation, and the broad support was for reaching a negotiated solution in the discussions on the review of the DSU.[80]

Thus, the realities of procedural requirements restrict the political organ's ability to adopt an authoritative interpretation of the WTO covered agreements, and the mechanism has become an embellishment.[81] Had the Article XI:2 process been workable, it could have been used as a mechanism to provide normative guidance in the case of ambiguous rules, or to correct the interpretations developed by the panels and the Appellate Body, thereby providing a 'check and balance', or correcting jurisprudential developments. Unfortunately, the WTO Members have failed to exercise this arguably broad and very important policymaking authority. This mechanism, though constrained by the need for consent, if effectively used would reflect the legitimate process of norm making in international law.[82]

[77] ibid. See also Ehlermann and Ehring, 'The Authoritative Interpretation under the Article IX.2 of the WTO Agreement' (n 71) 806.

[78] Frank Biermann, 'The Rising Tide of Green Unilateralism in World Trade Law. Options for Reconciling the Emerging North–South Conflict' (2001) 35(3) J World Trade 421, 436; Ehlermann and Ehring, 'The Authoritative Interpretation under the Article IX.2 of the WTO Agreement' (n 71) 807.

[79] Diane Desierto, *Public Policy in International Economic Law: The ICESCR in Trade, Finance and Investment* (OUP 2015) 242.

[80] See General Council, *Request for an Authoritative Interpretation Pursuant to Article IX:2 of the Marrakesh Agreement of the WTO (Communication from the European Communities)*, WT/GC/W/133, 25 January 1999 (in relation to arts 3.7, 21.5, 22.2, 22.6, 22.7, and 23 of the DSU) broadly on the question of the sequence problem between arts 21.5 and 22 of the DSU. See WTO, 'Analytical Index' (n 45) and Ehlermann and Ehring, 'The Authoritative Interpretation under the Article IX.2 of the WTO Agreement' (n 71) 803.

[81] Thomas Cottier and Satoko Takenoshita, 'The Balance of Power in WTO Decision Making: Towards Weighted Voting in Legislative Response' (2003) 58 Aussenwirtschaft 171.

[82] Babu (n 67).

B. Interpretation and clarification by the judicial bodies

The WTO DSB and its quasi-judicial bodies, the panel and the Appellate Body are tasked to 'clarify' the existing provisions of the WTO covered agreements 'in accordance with customary rules of interpretation of public international law'.[83] A 'legal interpretation' developed by the panel in a dispute settlement process is subject to appeal and review of the Appellate Body, which is effectively the final authority on the interpretation of the WTO agreements.[84] The DSB's 'clarification' of the covered agreements is limited to cases where their implementation has resulted in a dispute. Further, such an interpretation adopted by the DSB under Article 3.9 of the DSU is without prejudice to the Members' right to seek 'authoritative interpretation' of provisions of the covered agreements under Article IX:2 of the WTO Agreement from the Ministerial Conference and the General Council. In other words, interpretation of the panel and the Appellate Body, even when adopted by the DSB, does not constitute a 'definitive interpretation' for which only the political bodies are empowered.[85]

Indeed, the institutional hierarchy of the interpretation function is without dispute and the function of 'authority to interpret' under the WTO Agreement granted to the political organs is much broader than the 'clarification' function entrusted with the panels and the Appellate Body. The legal interpretation developed by the panels and the Appellate Body is case-specific; that is, it binds only Member parties to a dispute.[86] Specifically, in the context of the function of the panel and Appellate Body in Article 11 of the DSU:

> The function of panels is to assist the DSB in discharging its responsibilities under this Understanding and the covered agreements. Accordingly, a Panel should make an objective assessment of the matter before it, including an objective assessment of the facts of the case and the applicability of and conformity with the relevant covered agreements, and make such other findings as will assist the DSB in making the recommendations or in giving the rulings provided for in the covered agreements.[87]

Further, in terms of Article 3.2 of the DSU, the rulings and recommendations of the DSB serve only 'to clarify the existing provisions of those agreements' and 'cannot add to or diminish the rights and obligations provided in the covered agreements'.[88]

The Appellate Body has openly clarified that their function does not involve law-making. The Appellate Body in *US—Wool Shirts and Blouses* emphasized that:

[83] DSU art 3.2.

[84] ibid art 17.6. See also J Patrick Kelly, 'Judicial Activism at the World Trade Organization: Developing Principles of Self-restraint' (2002) 22 Nw J Intl L Bus 353.

[85] Ehlermann and Ehring, 'The Authoritative Interpretation under the Article IX.2 of the WTO Agreement' (n 71) 805.

[86] Accordingly, the DSU mandate to clarify WTO rules is without prejudice to the rights of Members to seek authoritative interpretations under art IX:2 of the WTO Agreement (DSU art 3.9).

[87] DSU art 11.

[88] Appellate Body Report, *United States—Tax Treatment for 'Foreign Sales Corporations'*, WT/DS108/AB/R, 24 February 2000, fn 127.

Given the explicit aim of dispute settlement that permeates the DSU, we do not consider that Article 3.2 of the DSU is meant to encourage either panels or the Appellate Body to 'make law' by clarifying existing provisions of the WTO Agreement outside the context of resolving a particular dispute. A panel need only address those claims which must be addressed in order to resolve the matter in issue in the dispute.[89]

The Appellate Body has also rejected in *Japan—Alcoholic Beverages II* the precedential value of the panel/Appellate Body interpretation. The Appellate Body clarified that the panel report does not constitute 'subsequent practice' by virtue of the decision of the DSB to adopt them, noted that the fact that such an 'exclusive authority' in interpreting the treaty has been established so specifically in the Article IX:2 of the WTO Agreement is reason enough to conclude that such authority does not exist by implication or by inadvertence elsewhere.[90]

The WTO adjudicating bodies are not 'courts of general jurisdiction' competent to apply all applicable international law. They can entertain only claims based on WTO covered agreements.[91] In other words, a WTO panel has jurisdiction only to decide whether or not an obligation in the WTO treaty has been violated.[92] Thus, only disputes falling within the 'covered agreements' may be referred to the WTO for settlement.[93] This does not, however, prevent the panel and Appellate Body from liberally interpreting the 'law applicable' in a given dispute.[94] Schoenbaum argues that Article 11 of the DSU, by authorizing panels and the Appellate Body to make 'such other findings as will assist the DSB in making the recommendation or in giving the rulings provided for in the covered agreements', provides a kind of 'implied powers' allowing the panels and Appellate Body to decide all international legal issues involved in a dispute properly before them.[95] Moreover, the 'customary rules of interpretation of international law' as reflected in the Vienna Convention has provided the panels/Appellate Body enormous flexibility and unrestrained freedom to devise meaning to specific terms in the treaty text in arriving at a pre-determined conclusion. Further, the Appellate Body had stated in the *US—Gasoline* case that the General Agreement is not to be read in clinical isolation from public international law.[96]

[89] Appellate Body Report, *United States—Measures Affecting Imports of Woven Shirts and Blouses from India*, WT/DS33/AB/R, 25 April 1997, 19–20.

[90] Appellate Body Report, *Japan—Taxes on Alcoholic Beverages* (Appellate Body Report, *Japan—Alcoholic Beverages II*), WT/DS8/AB/R, WT/DS10/AB/R, WT/DS11/AB/R, 4 October 1996, 12–15.

[91] Joel P Trachtman, 'The Domain of WTO Dispute Resolution' (1990) 40 Harv Intl LJ 333, 338. Malcolm N Shaw, *International Law* (6th edn, CUP 2008) 1036.

[92] Joost Pauwelyn, 'The Jurisdiction of the World Trade Organization' (2004) 98 Am Socy Intl L 135. See also *Compétence de la compétence*, suggested by the Appellate Body Report, *United States—Anti-dumping Act of 1916*, WT/DS136/AB/R, WT/DS162/AB/R, 28 August 2000, para 54.

[93] David Palmeter and Petros C Mavroidis, 'The WTO Legal System: Sources of Law' (1998) 92(3) Am J Intl L 398, 399.

[94] Lorand Bartels, 'Applicable Law in WTO Dispute Settlement Proceedings' (2001) 35(3) J World Trade 499, 501.

[95] Thomas J Schoenbaum, 'WTO Dispute Settlement: Praise and Suggestions for Reform' (1998) 47(3) Intl Comp LQ 647, 653.

[96] Appellate Body Report, *United States—Standards for Reformulated and Conventional Gasoline*, WT/DS2/AB/R, 29 April 1996, 17.

The experience of the panel/Appellate Body interpretation for the past two decades reveals that the adjudicating bodies have exercised considerable leeway while exercising their interpreting function. The restraint imposed by Articles 3.2 and 19.2 of the DSU, which provides that the 'recommendations and rulings of the DSB cannot add to or diminish the rights and obligations provided in the covered agreements', is an ambiguous provision, the practical relevance of which is rather limited.[97] The leeway enjoyed by the adjudicating bodies is further complimented by the highly ambiguous or hortatory nature of language used in the agreements, which is susceptible to several possible interpretations allowing the adjudicating bodies to reach a conclusion of their choice.[98]

Further, while the Appellate Body has been categorical that their reports carry no precedential value and the earlier rulings are non-binding and case-specific, in practice, the previous reports are followed in support of the interpretation given to a WTO rule in subsequent cases. In other words, there is a strong tendency to follow the earlier interpretations developed in particular by the Appellate Body, thereby adhering de facto to the rules of precedent. In *US—Stainless Steel (Mexico)*, the Appellate Body added that the failure of the panel to follow previously adopted Appellate Body reports addressing the same issues undermined the development of a coherent and predictable body of jurisprudence clarifying Members' rights and obligations under the covered agreements as contemplated under the DSU. They noted:

> Clarification, as envisaged in Article 3.2 of the DSU, elucidates the scope and meaning of the provisions of the covered agreements in accordance with customary rules of interpretation of public international law. While the application of a provision may be regarded as confined to the context in which it takes place, the relevance of clarification contained in adopted Appellate Body reports is not limited to the application of a particular provision in a specific case.

Also, according to the Appellate Body, their interpretations 'create legitimate expectations' among WTO Members, and, therefore, should apply the same meaning in similar disputes.[99] In short, the virtual automaticity of adoption of these interpretations by the DSB has given rise to a body of WTO jurisprudence binding on subsequent panels, deviation from which is onerous.[100]

[97] Wolfrum and others (n 12) 302. [98] Babu (n 67).

[99] *Japan—Alcoholic Beverages II* (n 90) 107–08. See also Appellate Body Report, *United States—Import Prohibition of Certain Shrimp and Shrimp Products (Recourse to Article 21.5 of the DSU by Malaysia) (US—Shrimp/Turtle, Recourse to art 21.5 of the DSU by Malaysia)*, WT/DS58/AB/RW, 22 October 2001, para 109. Marion Panizzon, *Good Faith in the Jurisprudence of the WTO: The Protection of Legitimate Expectations, Good Faith Interpretation and Fair Dispute Settlement* (Hart Publishing 2006).

[100] Jackson argues that:

> there is quite a powerful precedent effect in the jurisprudence of the WTO, but that it is certainly not stare decisis, and it is not so powerful as to require panels or the Appellate Body considering new cases to follow prior cases, with the possible exception that once prior cases have been numerous regarding a particular issue and approach, and apparently accepted by all members of the WTO, then the language of the Vienna Convention about

IV. From Negotiated Law-making to Judicial Law-making

The combined effects of these factors (flexibility in interpretation and automaticity in adoption) have bestowed on the quasi-judicial bodies unchecked power, creating a body of law made by an organ having the least democratic legitimacy in the WTO. Over the years, the panel and Appellate Body have become the most influential organs of the WTO institutional framework, exercising considerable discretionary powers and influencing decisions not only on the consistency of the Members' domestic measures, but also attributing meaning to specific provisions of the covered agreements, thereby influencing the course of WTO jurisprudential development. Increasing numbers of scholars now perceive that the panels/Appellate Body have been misusing their discretion and improperly engaging in a process of 'judicial activism', creating new WTO rules and procedures[101] through the technique of 'filling legal gaps', 'completing the analysis', or 'clarifying ambiguity'.[102] This view transcends the developed–developing countries divide. Specifically, obligations that are neither foreseen nor negotiated during the Uruguay Round of negotiations have been read into the WTO rules. Ragosta, Joneja, and Zeldovich refer to this trend as the result of 'structural problems within the system, including the binding nature of the dispute settlement system, the unclear and ambiguous substantive provisions of the WTO agreements, the lack of democratic oversight of the Appellate Body and the panels, and the absence of procedural protections in the system'.[103]

The judicial law-making seems to affect adversely developing countries more than their developed counterparts. As the conventional wisdom would suggest, establishing binding third-party arbitration, as in the case of DSU, should favour

> 'practice under agreement,' may suggest a stronger impact. But short of that situation, it appears that the 'flavor' of the precedent effect in the WTO is still somewhat fluid, and possibly will remain fluid for the time being.

See Jackson, *Sovereignty, the WTO and Changing Fundamentals of International Law* (n 29) 177.

[101] John Ragosta and others, 'WTO Dispute Settlement: The System is Flawed and Must Be Fixed' (2003) 37(3) Intl Lawyer 697, 744–45; Daniel K Tarullo, 'The Hidden Costs of International Dispute Settlement: WTO Review of Domestic Anti-dumping Decisions' (2002) 34 Law Polcy Intl Bus 109, 112; Juscelino F Colares, 'A Theory of WTO Adjudication: From Empirical Analysis to Biased Rule Development' (2009) 42(2) Vand J Transnatl L 383; Armin von Bogdandy, 'Law and Politics in the WTO—Strategies to Cope with a Deficient Relationship' (2001) 5 Max Planck YB UN L 609, 611; Rahul Singh, 'The World Trade Organization and Legitimacy: Evolving a Framework for Bridging the Democratic Deficit' (2008) 42(2) J World Trade 347.

[102] See generally Joel P Trachtman, 'The Constitutions of the WTO' (2006) 17(3) Eur J Int L 623, 638; Claus-Dieter Ehlermann, 'Six Years on the Bench of the "World Trade Court": Some Personal Experiences as Member of the Appellate Body of the World Trade Organization' (2002) 36(4) J World Trade 605, 617. See also Robert Howse, 'The Most Dangerous Branch? WTO Appellate Body Jurisprudence on the Nature and Limits of the Judicial Power' in Thomas Cottier and Petros C Mavroidis (eds), *The Role of the Judge in International Trade Regulation: Experience and Lessons from the WTO* (University of Michigan Press 2003) 17; Richard H Steinberg, 'Judicial Lawmaking at the WTO: Discursive, Constitutional, and Political Constraints' (2004) 98(2) Am J Intl L 247, 252.

[103] Ragosta and others (n 101) 744–45.

smaller, less powerful states.[104] However, this does not seem to work in the case of the WTO. Given their inferior position, the panels and the Appellate Body have assumed greater leverage of interpretation when clarifying the rights and obligations of developing countries. Developing countries' experience in various WTO cases tends to support the contention that the WTO adjudicating bodies may be favouring leading industrial countries, the United States, and the European Union, at the expense of the rights of developing countries.[105] Hudec, in his study on the GATT 1947 dispute settlement system, concludes that the panel was more responsive to the interests of stronger countries, which, according to him, was natural in a young legal system.[106] Further, most special and differential treatment provisions have been watered down to the point of being meaningless.[107] This judicial apathy has resulted in tilting the balance of rights and obligations against developing countries.[108]

The *US—Shrimp/Turtle I* case[109] is a classic example to demonstrate the problem of ingenious interpretation.[110] The interpretation handed down by the Appellate Body had the following consequences. First, environmental standards (and possible other standards) in the form of foreign Product Process Method (PPM) (i.e. how shrimps are produced), which were consciously kept outside the framework of the WTO, was justified under GATT Article XX.[111] Second, 'exhaustible natural resource' was interpreted to include 'living beings' (sea turtles). [112] Third, to justify their conclusions, the Appellate Body selectively relied on the WTO preamble to explicitly acknowledge the broad, undefined norm of sustainable development as

[104] James Smith, 'Inequality in International Trade? Developing Countries and Institutional Change in WTO Dispute Settlement' (2004) 11(3) Rev Intl Pol Econ 542. See also James Smith, 'WTO Dispute Settlement: The Politics of Procedure in Appellate Body Rulings' (2003) 2(1) World Trade Rev 65.

[105] Nicholas Perdikis and Robert Read (eds), *The WTO and the Regulation of International Trade: Recent Trade Disputes Between the EU and the US* (Edward Elgar 2005) 41. See also Chad Bown, 'Participation in WTO Dispute Settlement: Complainants, Interested Parties and Free Riders' (2005) 19(2) World Bank Econ Rev 287; Bernard M Hoekman and Petros C Mavroidis, 'WTO Dispute Settlement, Transparency and Surveillance' (2000) 23(4) World Econ 527.

[106] Robert E Hudec, *Enforcing International Trade Law: The Evolution of the Modern GATT Legal System* (Butterworth Legal Publishers 1993) 273.

[107] Babu (n 67).

[108] Chakravarthi Raghavan, 'The World Trade Organization and its Dispute Settlement System: Tilting the Balance Against the South' (2000) Third World Network, Trade and Development Series No 9 <http://www.twn.my/title/tilting.htm> accessed 14 March 2016.

[109] Panel Report, *United States—Import Prohibition of Certain Shrimp and Shrimp Products* (*US—Shrimp/Turtle*), WT/DS58/R, 15 May 1988; and Appellate Body Report, *US—Shrimp/Turtle*, WT/DS58/AB/R, 12 October 1998.

[110] For a detailed consideration of the issue, see Babu (n 67). Gillian Reynolds, 'Promoting Imbalance Dispute Settlement Under the World Trade Organization' (2006) 7(1) Stan J Intl Relations.

[111] B S Chimni, 'WTO and Environment: *US—Shrimp/Turtle* and *EC—Hormones* Cases' (2000) 35(20) Econ Pol Weekly 1752. See also B S Chimni, 'WTO and Environment: Legitimisation of Unilateral Trade Sanctions' (2002) 37(2) Econ Pol Weekly 133.

[112] From the perspective embodied in the preamble of the WTO Agreement, we note that the generic term 'natural resources' in Article XX(g) is not 'static' in its content or reference but is rather 'by definition, evolutionary'.

one of the many objectives of the WTO regime.[113] Fourth, the Appellate Body openly used an 'evolutionary' method of interpretation that ignored the original intent of the parties, past GATT decisions, and the declared positions of the vast majority of nations.[114] Fifth, the Appellate Body interpreted GATT Article XX as justifying unilateral measures having extraterritorial application[115] and endorsed the panel finding that before taking unilateral measures a 'good-faith' effort to negotiate an international agreement would suffice, there being thus no obligation to 'conclude' a treaty. [116] Finally, the Appellate Body also interpreted DSU Article 13 to permit acceptance of *amicus curiae* briefs and thereby opened the DSB to lobbying by western non-governmental organizations and private interests.[117]

While adoption of the report at the DSB took place, several Members accused the Appellate Body of using this case as an instrument for extending its powers beyond those permitted under the DSU.[118] By giving a new interpretation to certain DSU provisions, the Appellate Body has overstepped the boundaries of its authority and undermined the balance of rights and obligations of Member States.[119] India, for instance, noted that the 'Appellate Body might have interpreted one of the important provisions of DSU loosely and wrongly, which could upset the balance of rights and obligations of Members.... It appeared that by this approach the Appellate Body had transcended the strict boundaries of law and had entered into the political domain strictly preserved for Members.'[120] However, there was no response from the General Council, and the issues remain controversial and contested.[121] Kelly notes that:

> the 'evolutionary methodology' the Appellate Body utilized is inconsistent with the structure of governance in the WTO agreements and the interpretive methodology of the VCLT required by the DSU essentially a contractual regime where nations negotiate rather specific

[113] *US—Shrimp/Turtle* (n 109) para 153.

[114] ibid paras 129–30, in J Patrick Kelly, 'International Law and the Shrinking Space for Politics in Developing Countries' (2008) Widener Law School Legal Studies Research Paper Series No 08-31, 596 <http://ssrn.com/abstract=1104694> accessed 14 March 2016.

[115] The GATT 1947, *US—Tuna (Dolphin)* cases prohibited the possibility of unilateral trade measures to protect the global environment. GATT Dispute Settlement Penal Report, *United States—Restriction on Imports of Tuna*, 30 ILM 1594, 16 August 1991 and GATT Dispute Settlement Penal Report, *United States—Restrictions on Import of Tuna*, 33 ILM 936 (1994). See Robert Howse and Donald Regan, 'The Product/Process Distinction—an Illusory Basis for Disciplining "Unilateralism" in Trade Policy' (2000) 11(2) Eur J Intl L 249, 250.

[116] *US—Shrimp/Turtle, Recourse to art 21.5 of the DSU by Malaysia* (n 99) para 48.

[117] *US—Shrimp/Turtle* (n 109) paras 107–10. See also Appellate Body Report, *United States—Imposition of Countervailing Duties on Certain Hot-rolled Lead and Bismuth Carbon Steel Products Originating in the United Kingdom*, WT/DS138/AB/R, 10 May 2000, para 42; Chimni, 'WTO and Environment' (n 111) 1755; Brigitte Stern, 'The Emergence of Non-state Actors in International Commercial Disputes through WTO Appellate Body Case-law' in Giorgio Sacerdoti and others (eds), *The WTO at Ten: The Contribution of the Dispute Settlement System* (CUP 2006) 376–78; Georg C Umbricht, 'An "*Amicus Curiae* Brief" on *Amicus Curiae* Briefs at the WTO' (2001) 4(4) J Intl Econ L 773, 785–86.

[118] Dispute Settlement Body, *Minutes of the DSB Meeting Held on 6 November 1998*, WT/DSB/M/50, 14 December 1998, 5.

[119] ibid 6. [120] ibid 7–8.

[121] See General Council, *Minutes of Meeting Held on 22 November 2000*, WT/GC/M/60, 22 November 2000.

norms and standards. As a state-centered contractual treaty regime, law-making authority properly resides in the Ministerial Council, not the Appellate Body. Second, the proper interpretation of the Article XX(g) exception does not include living creatures as 'exhaustible natural resources' rather regulation of human, animals and plants properly fall under the XX(b) exception. Article XX(b) wisely contains a 'necessary' requirement as a filter for protectionist uses of this exception. Third, neither the Article XX(b) or (g) exceptions, properly interpreted, apply to the unilateral regulation of production methods abroad.[122]

Similarly, in the *India—Quantitative Restrictions (QR)* case,[123] the Appellate Body is considered to have gone beyond the duty of interpretation by asserting that it was competent to review the justifications of BOP restriction under the Understanding on Balance of Payment (BOP) Provisions of the GATT 1994.[124] The Appellate Body is further alleged to have based their finding against India's QR measures primarily on the opinion of the IMF and refused to take account of the developmental concerns of a developing country. Hudec notes that, 'had the Appellate Body considered development policy informed by a conception of equity that includes the notion that development policy is a matter in the first instance for participation of those who are affected, it would have analyzed the legal issue quite differently'.[125] The *Brazil—Aircraft Subsidy* case[126] also presents another instance where the Appellate Body ignored the inherent disadvantage of developing countries accessing international capital, to arrive at a finding that the 'interest equalization subsidy' confers a material advantage to Brazil.[127]

The *US—Section 301*[128] is another instance where the Appellate Body came up with an innovative interpretation to save the US legislation.[129] Despite finding

[122] Kelly, 'International Law and the Shrinking Space for Politics in Developing Countries' (n 114) 597. See also Jagdish Bhagwati, 'After Seattle: Free Trade and the WTO' in Roger B Porter and others (eds), *Efficiency, Equity, and Legitimacy: The Multilateral Trading System at the Millennium* (Brookings Institution Press 2001) 60–61.

[123] Appellate Body Report, *India—Quantitative Restrictions on Imports of Agricultural, Textile and Industrial Products*, WT/DS90/AB/R, 23 August 1999, 20. See also Appellate Body Report, *Turkey—Restrictions on Imports of Textile and Clothing Products*, WT/DS34/AB/R, 22 October 1999.

[124] Frieder Roessler, 'The Institutional Balance between the Judicial and the Political Organs of the WTO' (Conference on Efficiently, Equity, and Legitimacy: The Multilateral Trading System, Millennium, 1–2 June 2000); Ezeani (n 44) 25.

[125] Robert Howse and others, 'Pursuing Sustainable Development Strategies: The Case of the Balance of Payment Rules in the WTO' (UNCTAD Sustainable Debt Conference, 2005) 19.

[126] Appellate Body Report, *Brazil—Export Financing Programme for Aircraft*, WT/DS46/AB/R, 2 August 1999 and Panel Report, *Brazil—Export Financing Programme for Aircraft*, WT/DS46/R, 14 April 1999.

[127] ibid. See also Brazil's Statement at the DSB Meeting, Dispute Settlement Body, *Minutes of the DSB Meeting Held on 20 August 1999*, WT/DSB/M/67, 30 September 1999, 2. In the '*Byrd Amendment*' case it has been argued that this case has raised some serious concerns about the power of panels and Appellate Bodies to effectively rewrite the rules painstakingly negotiated and agreed to by the WTO Members. Appellate Body Report, *United States—Continued Dumping and Offset Act of 2000*, DS217/AB/R, DS234/AB/R, 16 January 2003 in Eliza Patterson, 'World Trade Organization Ruling on US Continued Dumping and Offset Act of 2000 (CDSOA)' (2003) 8(4) Am Socy Intl L Insights.

[128] Panel Report, *United States—Sections 301–310 of the Trade Act of 1974*, WT/DS152/R, 22 December 1999.

[129] Trade Act of 1974, 19 USC ch 12, ss 301–10.

the US law inconsistent, the panel decided to accept the oral assurance of the United States that they shall refrain from making unilateral determinations of violations.[130] While the show of deference towards national law is appreciable, the adjudicating bodies refused to show similar trust and deference to the assurance of a developing country, as is evident in the *India—Pharmaceutical Patent* case.[131] Here, India had assured with *absolute certainty* that India can, when patents are due in accordance with Article 70.8(b) and (c) of TRIPs, decide to grant such patents based on the applications currently submitted.[132] The Appellate Body expressed doubts about the legal soundness of the 'administrative instructions' and considered an assurance from the Indian authorities as unreliable.[133] Finally, in several cases, the adjudicating bodies have indulged in procedural norm creation that does not rest on the provision of the treaties.[134] The procedural 'clarifications' made by the Appellate Body include burden of proof, judicial economy, completing the analysis, *stare decisis*, etc.[135]

V. Judicial Norm Creation: Implications for the Developing Countries and the WTO Multilateralism

In short, the power of interpretation has been arbitrarily used by the panels and the Appellate Body to create new WTO rules via the backdoor, most often to the detriment of the developing countries.[136] The judicial bodies are able to continue with this undemocratic, unauthorized expansion of WTO law owing to the inability and unwillingness of the political bodies, the Ministerial Conference and General Council, to serve as a check against such norm creation.[137] The failure to make authoritative interpretation, a necessary instrument of check and balance vis-à-vis the WTO's quasi-judicial bodies, has made the panel and the Appellate body the de facto authoritative interpreter of the WTO covered agreements.[138] Cottier and Takenoshita observe that the lack of legislative response not only creates an imbalance, but also prevents the law from being incrementally developed beyond the narrow bounds of the case

[130] See Babu (n 67); Raghavan (n 108).

[131] Appellate Body Report, *India—Patent Protection for Pharmaceutical and Agricultural Chemical Products*, WT/DS50/AB/R, 19 December 1997.

[132] ibid para 60.

[133] ibid para 70. Statement of Jamaica at the DSB Meeting, Dispute Settlement Body, *Minutes of Meeting Held on 27 January 2000*, WT/DSB/M/74, 22 February 2000, 18.

[134] See Donald McRae, 'Treaty Interpretation and the Development of International Trade Law by the WTO Appellate Body' in Giorgio Sacerdoti and others (eds), *The WTO at Ten: The Contribution of the Dispute Settlement System* (CUP 2006) 361–62.

[135] ibid 362–63; Babu (n 67).

[136] Chimni, 'WTO and Environment' (n 111) 138.

[137] Robert Howse and Kalypso Nicolaidis, 'Legitimacy through "Higher Law"? Why Constitutionalizing the WTO is a Step Too Far' in Thomas Cottier and Petros C Mavroidis (eds), *The Role of the Judge in International Trade Regulation* (University of Michigan Press 2003) 309.

[138] Ehlermann and Ehring, 'The Authoritative Interpretation under the Article IX.2 of the WTO Agreement' (n 71) 812.

law.[139] Many also see this attempt at indirect norm expansion through the judicial process as inherently dangerous, usurping the functions of the WTO political bodies.[140] This trend has serious implications on the future of the WTO as a multilateral institution and the rights and obligations of the developing countries in particular.

The WTO adjudicators have also shown no sign of exercising judicial restraint. The general tendency in judicial law-making has been a jurisprudence that clarifies the existing provisions of the agreements consistently in one direction, that of protecting the interests of the powerful countries. According to Reynolds:

> Politically-driven decisions made under the DSU have conferred even more power to developed nations throughout the dispute settlement process. First, the structure of dispute resolution favors developed countries, due to their ability to influence the selection of the Appellate Body, and disadvantages LDCs because they cannot use retaliation effectively because of their small market sizes. Second, recent changes in legal procedures, shaped by the Appellate Body, further undermine LDCs, which cannot benefit from private counsel, *amicus curiae* briefs, or third party involvement, because of the heavy legal and monetary burdens they entail. Last, Appellate Body reports have tended to conciliate to developed countries in order to preserve the authority of the Appellate Body.[141]

Reynolds adds that the Appellate Body rulings against the developed nations could lead to these discontented countries weakening its authority, especially when the political stake for powerful nations such as the United States or the European Union are involved.[142] Garrett and Smith confirm that 'the more powerful the defendant (i.e. the greater its economic size and political influence) … [or] the more numerous and more powerful the third-party governments that are likely to support the defendant … the more likely that the Appellate Body will conciliate'.[143] Raghavan notes that, through the steady process of interpretations 'the panels have, with single-minded purpose, eroded the rights of the developing countries, increased their obligations, and tilted the balance in the system against them'.[144] In many areas where the Uruguay Round negotiators could not agree on exact things, the panel process is now being used to give the same meaning to what the United States had sought.[145] This has the effect of the WTO dispute settlement system gradually tilting the balance against developing countries inside the WTO,

[139] Thomas Cottier and Satoka Takenoshita, 'Decision-making and the Balance of Powers in WTO Negotiations: Towards Supplementary Weighted Voting' in Stefan Griller (ed), *At the Crossroads: The World Trade System and the Doha Round* (Springer 2007) 185. See also Cottier and Takenoshita, 'Decision-making and the Balance of Powers in WTO Negotiations: Towards Weighted Voting in Legislative Response' (n 81).

[140] Babu (n 67). [141] Reynolds (n 110).

[142] Geoffrey Garrett and James McCall Smith, 'The Politics of WTO Dispute Settlement' (Annual Meeting of the American Political Science Association, Atlanta, 1999).

[143] ibid 7. [144] Raghavan (n 110).

[145] Martin Khor, 'WTO Dispute System Tilting Balance against South' (*Third World Network*, 2000) <http://www.twn.my/title/tilt.htm> accessed 23 April 2016.

increasing their obligations, through perverse interpretations of the rules, and expanding the rights of a few industrialized countries.[146]

Indeed, it has been argued that the Appellate Body has done a commendable job in clarifying ambiguities in the WTO obligations. However, creation of non-negotiated obligations under 'the guise of interpreting negotiated agreements is antithetical to the basic principle that what sovereign states have not specifically promised to do cannot be legally required of them'.[147] At the fundamental level, judicial law-making undermines sovereignty and goes against the Member-driven character of the WTO. In the current process, the panels and the Appellate Body have the least democratically unaccountable power, and therefore, their 'gap filling', which goes beyond the permissible limits of interpretation, lacks democratic legitimacy.[148] If the adjudicating bodies do not use judicial restraint, in the long run the institutional legitimacy of the panels and Appellate Body will be lost, with a large part of the Membership refraining from raising their disputes with the WTO.[149] It may be recalled that the Asian African States had developed a deep-rooted distrust and scepticism about the impartiality of the judges, which held them back from taking their cases to the International Court of Justice (ICJ).[150] Noting in this context, Professor Anand pointed out that there was a feeling among 'the underdeveloped … members of the international community that the present system of international law, developed as it was historically among the Western European countries, must now be interpreted and modified with due regard to their economic and social conditions and the present changed structure of the international society'.[151] The statement is still relevant in the context of the WTO. If the WTO adjudicating bodies choose to continue this trend, there is a strong possibility that the developing countries as a group would reject the dispute settlement system to the detriment of the cohesiveness of the WTO multilateralism.

Besides, the trend undermines the WTO institutions and institutional process. The stalemate at the Doha negotiations is a clear indication of the policymaking paralysis that inhibits any attempt to negotiate new or review existing rules. One of the prime reasons why developing countries are extremely cautious of committing themselves to new obligations during the current Doha negotiations owes to their concerns over the dispute settlement process. They do not want to add obligations to a system which is perceived to have undermined their existing commitments and worked against their interests. States have started preferring regional trade arrangements over WTO negotiations for creating new rules. Judicial norm creating through 'interpretation' do have limited roles in any judicial process; however, in

146 Babu (n 67).

147 Colares (n 101) 438.

148 Robert Howse, 'How to Begin to Think About the "Democratic Deficit" at the WTO' in Robert Howse (ed), *The WTO System: Law, Politics & Legitimacy* (Cameron May 2007) 57–76.

149 In the past twenty years not a single African country has initiated a dispute in the WTO.

150 R P Anand, 'The International Court of Justice and Impartiality between Nations' in R P Anand (ed), *Studies in International Adjudication* (Vikas Publication 1969) 74.

151 ibid 81.

an international setting where the obligations are undertaken after careful negotiation, any expansion of such obligations by a body without understanding the political constraints and concerns would undermine the DSM, which has been to a large extent effective in settling trade disputes. The current system does not offer any solution, and the panels and the Appellate Body have exercised minimal self-restraint.

VI. Towards a Transparent and Accountable Interpretation

The WTO jurisprudence once created by the panels/Appellate Body is difficult to correct through 'legislative action' by the Members.[152] The clear paralysis of the decision-making process in the political bodies, apart from undermining the institutional edifice of the WTO, has ensured that the 'interpretations' by the adjudicating bodies become part of the WTO *corpus juris*. Indeed, there have been several suggestions to check the effects of interpretation without undermining the role of the dispute settlement system. For instance, the 'Sutherland report' of 2005 recommends selecting particular findings of panels or the Appellate Body to be analysed by a special expert group of the DSB. This group would report to the DSB and perhaps propose an authoritative interpretation for the future to be adopted by the General Council.[153] Ehlermann and Ehring nevertheless wonder whether this could become another review of the panels and the Appellate Body rulings with the potential of undermining the working of the dispute settlement system.[154]

However, in the current scenario, the check and balance against judicial overreach must come from within and outside. In the interim, until a final solution is found, one way to ensure independent and impartial judicial functions is to ensure transparency and accountability in the functioning of the system. The idea is that while you are making important interpretations that have implications on wider concerns, it cannot be done behind closed doors. As Jeremy Bentham famously said, 'Where there is no publicity there is no justice. Publicity is the very soul of justice. It is the keenest spur to exertion and the surest of all guards against improbity. It keeps the judge, while trying, under trial.' Publicity automatically brings in

[152] Dispute Settlement Body Special Session, *Negotiations on Improvements and Clarifications of the Dispute Settlement Understanding on Improving Flexibility and Member Control in WTO Dispute Settlement Contribution by Chile and the US*, TN/DS/W/28, 17 December 2002. Claus-Dieter Ehlermann and Lothar Ehring, 'Decision-making in the World Trade Organization: Is the Consensus Practice of the World Trade Organization Adequate for Making, Revising and Implementing Rules on International Trade?' (2005) 8(1) J Intl Econ L 51, 71.

[153] WTO Consultative Group appointed by the Director-General in June 2003. Consultative Board, 'The Future of WTO: Addressing Institutional Challenges in the New Millennium' (World Trade Organization 2005) 57 <https://www.wto.org/english/thewto_e/10anniv_e/future_wto_e.htm> accessed 23 April 2016.

[154] Ehlermann and Ehring, 'The Authoritative Interpretation Under the Article IX.2 of the WTO Agreement' (n 71) 822.

self-accountability and the courts must not fear publicity. 'If the way courts behave cannot be hidden from the public ear and eye this provides a safeguard against judicial arbitrariness or idiosyncrasy ....' The process must be open for scrutiny by not just the WTO Members, but also the public at large. Indeed, publicity or public scrutiny of the judicial function puts additional burden on the Appellate Body, but it is the surest means of meeting the demand for transparency and accountability. It does not, however, require every aspect of the judicial process to be open. This is not new to the WTO, as a public hearing was conducted in *US—Continued Suspension (Hormones)* and *Canada—Continued Suspension (Hormones)* held on 1 August 2005.[155]

One cannot shape jurisprudence without dissenting and separate opinions, and the WTO must encourage the practice.[156] The concept is rooted in the practices of most mature legal systems, as well as that of international adjudicating bodies such as the ICJ, the International Tribunal for the Law of the Sea, etc.[157] It has been asserted that dissenting opinions act 'as a safeguard of the individual responsibility of the judges as well as of the integrity of the Court as an institution'.[158] It also serves as an 'assurance that the case was fully considered and thoroughly argued by the bench as a whole and that the opinion of the Court was not merely adopted as written by one member'.[159] Dissenting opinions do not undermine the authority of the adjudicating bodies, nor violate the principle of secrecy of deliberations. They only strengthen the judicial body's reputation and enhance transparency. The independence and impartiality of the members of the panels and Appellate Body as mandated in the DSU would be strengthened if individual dissents were permitted. After reviewing the few dissents found in the WTO reports, Lewis demonstrates that '50% of the arguments raised in dissents at the panel level were adopted in whole or in part on appeal by the Appellate Body, thus illustrating dissents can and do make a difference'.[160] Dissenting opinions would thus considerably enhance the credibility of the interpretation and the report, apart from contributing to the growth of the WTO jurisprudence. Considering that the Appellate Body is moving towards a formulation of a WTO *corpus juris* largely in line with judges

[155] *United States—Continued Suspension of Obligations in the EC—Hormones Dispute*, WT/DS320, 8 November 2004; *Canada—Continued Suspension of Obligations in the EC—Hormones Dispute*, WT/DS321, 8 November 2004. See Christiane Ahlborn and James Headen Pfitzer, 'Transparency and Public Participation in WTO Dispute Settlement' (Center for International Environmental Law 2009) 22; Yves Bonzo, *Public Participation and Legitimacy in the WTO* (CUP 2014).

[156] Only 5% of panel reports and 2% of Appellate Body reports contain separate opinions of any kind. See Meredith Kolsky Lewis, 'The Lack of Dissent in WTO Dispute Settlement' (2006) 9(4) J Intl Econ L 895, 903–16.

[157] Statute of the International Court of Justice, 59 Stat 1055, 26 June 1945, art 57.

[158] R P Anand, 'The Role of Individual and Dissenting Opinions in International Adjudication' (1965) 14(3) Intl Comp LQ 788.

[159] Manley O Hudson, 'The Twenty-eighth Year of the World Court' (1950) 44 Am J Intl L 1, 20.

[160] Lewis (n 156).

of the Anglo-American judicial process, it is imperative that option to dissent and an open court system be made integral to that process.

VII. Conclusion

To conclude, the decision-making process of the WTO's political bodies, the Ministerial Conference, and the General Council has become a challenge for adopting an authoritative interpretation of the existing provisions, as well as the expansion of the WTO law through amendments and trade negotiations. Except for the recent piecemeal success at Bali, the Doha Round continues to remain unproductive and frustrating for all the stakeholders. It is, however, also acknowledged widely that the decision-making process is not the sole reason for the failure. While in the past, the developed countries could easily push for a consensus, the strengthening of the developing countries coalition on crucial negotiating issues has resulted in more onerous decision-making. More important is the fact that the developed countries had been insensitive and inflexible towards the genuine concerns of the developing countries, demanding both with respect to present and future rules. It is their position not to make sufficient commitments, for instance, in the context of agriculture subsidies that has led to the current impasse. The developed countries could no longer dictate terms that serve their domestic interests alone. It is this change in the bargaining power that is prompting developed countries to look for a PTA route to assert their power and terms. In other words, the argument advanced to change the decision-making procedure does not hold much weight as the reasons for the deadlock are extraneous to the process. It is the strength of the consensus procedure that has made the developing countries assert their position, which is otherwise weak.

In order to function effectively, every judicial organ must enjoy a certain level of flexibility and discretion to interpret rules. That is part of their central function. However, as mentioned earlier, the apprehensions of the developing countries regarding 'judicial law-making' are real, as neither the institutional nor the judicial process has addressed their concerns. In fact, there is a systemic bias against the developing countries, where rules are selectively interpreted to advance the interests of the powerful countries—such as finding the developing countries' obligations enhanced and rights diminished. Such backdoor rule-making undermines the consent-based decision-making process which is the cornerstone of the WTO edifice. Despite concerns about judicial overreach, there is a certain reluctance among the WTO Membership as well as in the scholarship to address these issues. There is also a fear that the failure of the Doha Round would accelerate the chance of developed countries imposing new obligations *via* the WTO dispute settlement system.

If the WTO panels and the Appellate Body continue to indulge in rule-making, the institutional credibility of the WTO DSB as well as the Appellate Body would suffer, leading to the rejection of a much cherished system by a large section of the WTO Membership. Already most less-developed Members have refrained from approaching the WTO dispute settlement system. Constitutionalization of the WTO law cannot happen when the development of the law is skewed against the interests of the large majority. The DSB must take stock of the situation and conduct a reality check to restore the credibility and legitimacy lost in the process. In the interim, measures must be put in place to ensure transparency and accountability, apart from exercising judicial self-restraint. The objective must be to make the system work for all, not just for a few developed countries and larger developing countries. Otherwise, the trend would undermine not just the carefully negotiated rights and obligations, but most importantly the WTO dispute settlement system that holds the WTO multilateralism together.

30

Legal Development of WTO Trade Remedy Practices in East Asia

*Dukgeun Ahn**

I. Introduction

The East Asian countries have been at the centre of the GATT/WTO trade remedy system, conventionally as the targets but recently as more aggressive users of trade remedy actions.[1] This chapter reviews the current situation of China, Japan, and Korea in the WTO system regarding the trade remedy system. In fact, many of those measures have generated trade disputes in the WTO dispute settlement system. The decisions by panels and the Appellate Body will also be examined to draw unique features of the trade practices by the East Asian countries.

II. Trade Remedy Measures in East Asia

As shown in Figure 30.1, China and Korea have been the two most frequent targets of anti-dumping (AD) investigations. The WTO Accession Protocol of China allows investigating authorities of importing countries to use dumping margin calculation methodology for non-market economy 'if the producers under investigation cannot clearly show that market economy conditions prevail in the industry producing the like product with regard to manufacture, production and sale of that product'.[2] This arrangement has been one of the main reasons for Chinese

* Professor of International Trade Law and Policy, Graduate School of International Studies, Seoul National University. I am very grateful to excellent research assistance by Kyounghwa Kim, Ji Yeong Yoo, and Dongchul Kwak. I also acknowledge the financial support from the National Research Foundation of Korea Grant (NRF 2014S1A3A2043505), as well as Seoul National University Asia Center (SNUAC-2015-008).

[1] See the comprehensive analysis of Professor Matushita in WTO, *Trade Remedy System: East Asian Perspectives* (Cameron May 2006). See also Mitsuo Matsushita, 'Some International and Domestic Antidumping Issues' (2010) 5(2) Asian J WTO & Intl Health L & Policy 249–68; Mitsuo Matsushita and Ava Lino, 'The Blocking Legislation as a Countermeasure to the US Anti-dumping Act of 1916: A Comparative Analysis of the EC and Japanese Damage Recovery Legislation' (2006) 40(4) J World Trade 753–76.

[2] WTO, *Accession of the People's Republic of China Decision of 10 November 2001*, WT/L/432, 23 November 2001, 9.

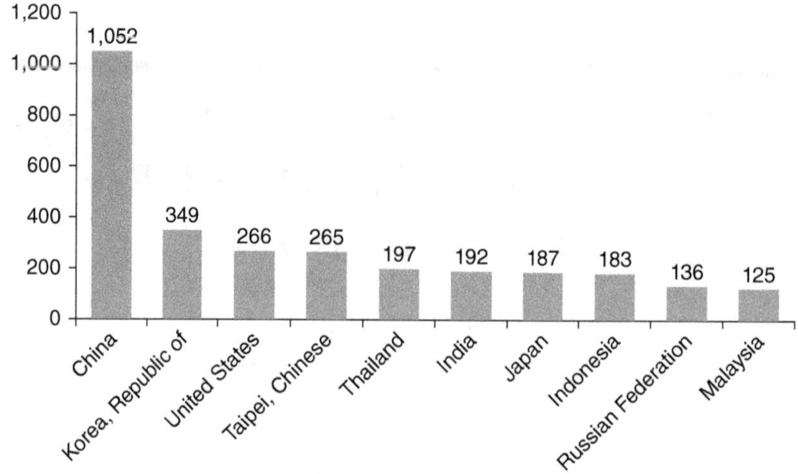

Fig. 30.1 Frequent targets of AD investigations: 1995.1.1–2014.12.31

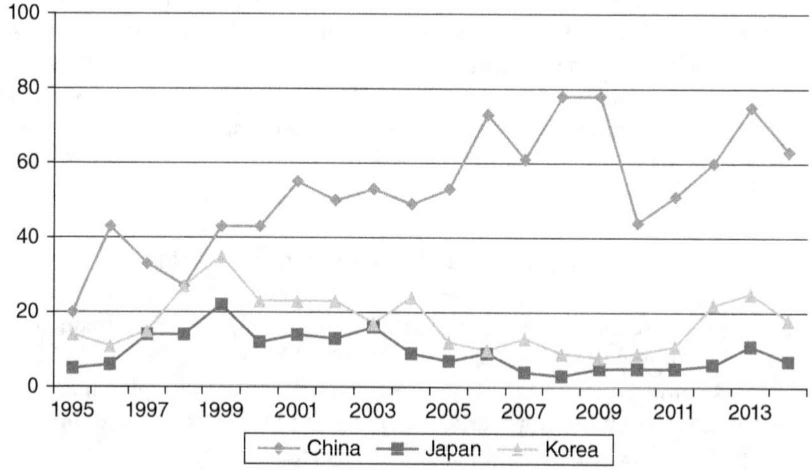

Fig. 30.2 AD initiation against China, Japan, and Korea

exportation becoming highly vulnerable to AD challenges. China tried to mitigate this problem through bilateral negotiations by which China's trading partners agree not to invoke the non-market economy provision in their AD investigations. It has been reported that more than sixty WTO Members agreed with China not to use the non-market economy provision. Although the non-market economy provision will lapse in December 2016 due to the fifteen-year expiry requirement, it remains to be seen whether that will substantially reduce AD challenges or not.

On the other hand, considering the fact that the export volume of China is on average more than four times bigger than that of Korea, exports from Korea have become relatively more frequently targeted by AD actions. Japan has also been

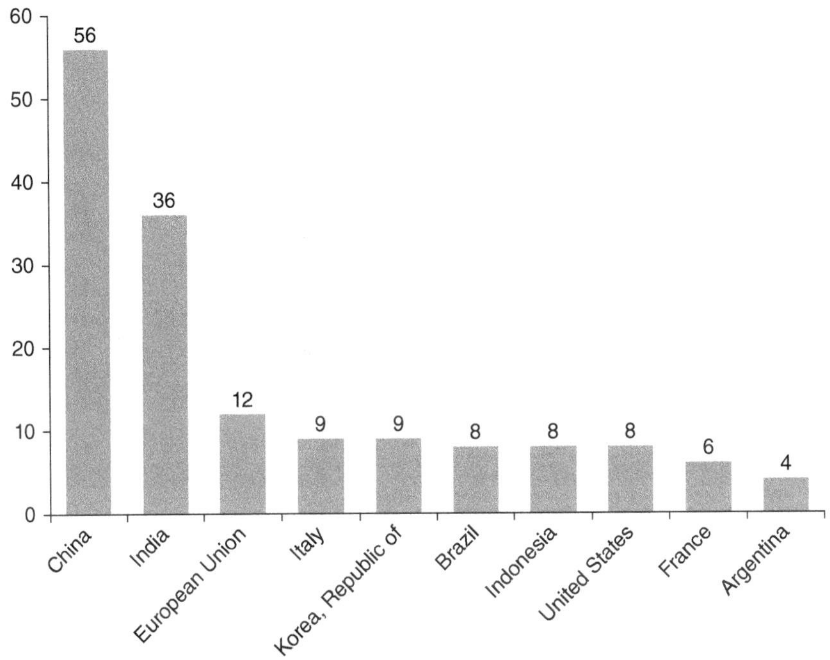

Fig. 30.3 Frequent targets of CVD investigations

among the typical targets for AD actions, along with other Asian countries such as Chinese Taipei, Thailand, and India, although the exports from Japan have been subject to many fewer AD actions in recent years.[3]

Despite such a general tendency in regard to trade remedy actions, Figure 30.2 shows some interesting characteristics of AD actions against the East Asian countries. First, China emerged as the obvious top target of AD actions in the WTO system.[4] In fact, global initiatives such as G20 commitments that were driven mainly by the global financial crisis, appear to effectively work in reducing and constraining unnecessary trade remedy actions, at least in 2010. But, as shown in Figure 30.2, the AD actions against China rapidly increased from 2011 and reached back to the level of the prior G20 commitment. It is also noted that AD actions against Japan and Korea increased in 2012 and 2013, to an even higher level than that prior to the G20 commitment.

Figure 30.3 shows frequent target economies for countervailing duty (CVD) investigations. It is noted that unlike AD investigation cases, the European Union

[3] WTO, 'Anti-dumping Initiations: By Exporter 1 January 1995–31 December 2014' (WTO) <https://www.wto.org/english/tratop_e/adp_e/AD_InitiationsByExpCty.pdf> accessed 23 April 2016.

[4] See generally Julien Chaisse and Debashis Chakraborty, 'Normative Obsolescence of WTO Anti-dumping Agreement—Topography of the Global Use and Misuse of Anti-dumping Measures' (2015) 5(1) Asian J Intl L 1–31.

Table 30.1 CVD actions against China in the WTO system

Year	2004	2005	2006	2007	2008	2009	2010	2011	2012	2013	2014	Total
Initiation	3	–	2	8	11	13	6	9	10	14	8	84
	Canada (3)		Canada (1)	Canada (1)	Australia (2)	Australia (1)	Canada (1)	Australia (2)	Australia (2)	Australia (1)	US (5)	
			US (1)	US (7)	Canada (3)	Canada (1)	EU (2)	Canada (1)	Canada (3)	Canada (4)	Canada (2)	
					South Africa (1)	India (1)	US (3)	Mexico (1)	EU (2)	EU (3)	EU (1)	
					US (5)	US (10)		EU (1)	US (3)	US (6)		
								US (4)				
Measure	–	2	–	1	10	6	10	5	8	10	1	53
		Canada (2)		Canada (1)	Canada (3)	Canada (1)	Australia (1)	US (3)	US (2)	Australia (3)	EU (1)	
					US (7)	US (5)	Canada (1)	EU (1)	Australia (2)	Canada (3)		
							US (8)	Canada (1)	Mexico (1)	EU (2)		
									Canada (3)	US (2)		

and Member countries such as Italy are among the major targets. Other than that, the major targets are China, India, and Korea, while Japan has never been targeted by CVD investigation since the inception of WTO.

In particular, it is very exceptional for China to become the target of CVD investigations since 2007. CVD actions by Canada against China actually began only in 2004 and became the major trade remedy issue between the United States and China when the US DOC decided to reverse their decision not to use CVD against non-market economies. Although the US DOC decision to impose CVD against China in 2006 was blocked due to the negative injury decision by the US International Trade Commission (ITC), it opened a path for the US DOC to explore new trade remedy actions against China. Table 30.1 shows that since 2007, the US DOC has relied heavily on CVD to deal with massive amounts of trade deficits against China.[5]

A CVD action against China itself does not necessarily raise a problem of WTO inconsistency. However, the fact that more WTO Members adopt CVD measures against China has caused a serious systemic tension in the WTO. Challenges against China tend to address various systemic issues such as when state-owned entities can be seen as a public body for the purpose of the Agreement on Subsidies and Countervailing Measures (SCM Agreement), how subsidy amounts can be calculated, and whether certain policy measures with social implications or financial transactions by state-owned banks in the Chinese economy can be regarded as WTO-inconsistent subsidies. Since many of those issues are directly related to the integrity and legitimacy of the unique economic system implemented by China under the name of state capitalism, the WTO rulings, especially in the disputes brought by the United States, have increased the tensions and conflicts at the governance level of the WTO Membership.

On the other hand, China, Japan, and Korea have used only few safeguard actions since the inception of the WTO.[6] China and Japan both initiated only one investigation in 2000 and 2002, respectively. Korea used safeguard actions relatively more often, one investigation in 1995, two in 1996, and one in 1999.[7] But after its safeguard measures caused a WTO dispute with the European Union and a trade conflict with China, Korea has not used safeguard actions since 2000.

As shown in Figure 30.4, the most distinguished point for the WTO safeguard actions is the very aggressive utilization of safeguard actions by WTO Members with limited experience in terms of trade remedy actions. It is noted that despite such trends, the East Asian countries have rarely relied on safeguard measures.[8] It

[5] For a more detailed account of the US DOC policy change and the relevant WTO disputes, see Dukgeun Ahn and Jieun Lee, 'Countervailing Duty Against China: Opening a Pandora's Box in the WTO System?' (2011) 14 J Intl Econ L 329, 329–68.

[6] See generally J Chaisse, D Chakraborty, and A Kumar, 'Mastering a Two-edged Sword—Lessons from the Rules and Litigation on Safeguards in the World Trade Organization' (2015) 13(4) Richmond J Global L B 563–92.

[7] The safeguard investigations were made for soybean oil, bicycle, dairy products, and garlic.

[8] WTO, 'Safeguard Initiations by Reporting Member Period: 1 January 1995–30 April 2015' (WTO) <https://www.wto.org/english/tratop_e/safeg_e/SG-InitiationsByRepMember.pdf> accessed 23 April 2016.

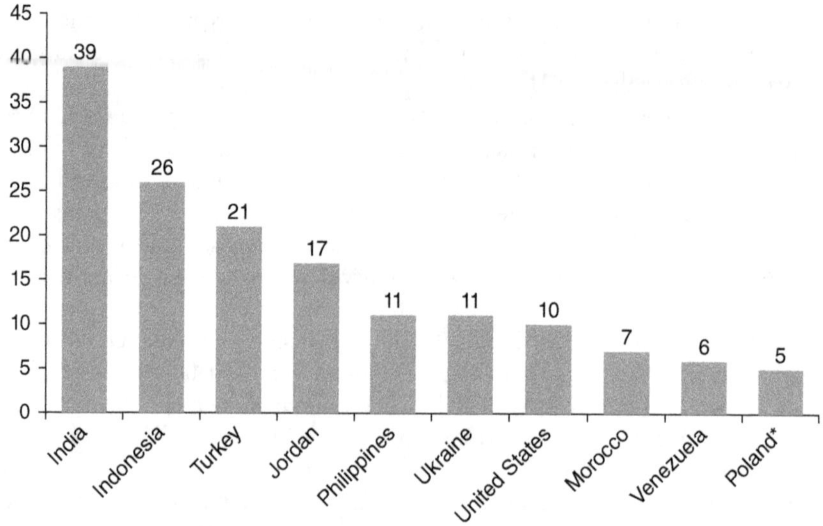

Fig. 30.4 Major safeguard users: 1995.1.1–2014.12.31

is also contrasted with the AD actions that China and Korea still use often to address domestic injuries.

III. Trade Disputes Concerning Trade Remedy Actions in East Asia

A. China

1. WTO disputes

Trade remedy issues are the main elements for disputes that China has brought to the WTO dispute settlement system. As of August 2015, out of the total of thirteen cases China brought as a complainant, ten cases are about trade remedy measures (Table 30.2). Among those ten trade remedy cases, eight cases are against the United States and two against the European Union. In particular, two cases are about safeguard measures, seven cases about AD measures, and four against CVD measures.[9]

In addition, it is noted that China brought a complaint concerning the US import ban on vehicle and light truck tyres taken under the transitional product-specific safeguard mechanism (TPSSM). This dispute is unique in the WTO jurisprudence in that the legal issues at dispute are not about the covered agreement but the accession protocol. The loose languages—thus relatively weak legal disciplines—in the

[9] Three cases involved both AD and CVD measures.

Table 30.2 WTO trade remedy disputes involving China as a complainant

DS number	Dispute name
DS252	United States—Definitive Safeguard Measures on Imports of Certain Steel Products
DS368	United States—Preliminary Anti-dumping and Countervailing Duty Determinations on Coated Free Sheet Paper from China
DS379	United States—Definitive Anti-dumping and Countervailing Duties on Certain Products from China
DS397	European Communities—Definitive Anti-dumping Measures on Certain Iron or Steel Fasteners from China
DS399	United States—Measures Affecting Imports of Certain Passenger Vehicle and Light Truck Tyres from China
DS405	European Union—Anti-dumping Measures on Certain Footwear from China
DS422	United States—Anti-dumping Measures on Certain Shrimp and Diamond Saw Blades from China
DS437	United States—Countervailing Duty Measures on Certain Products from China
DS449	United States—Countervailing and Anti-dumping Measures on Certain Products from China
DS471	United States—Certain Methodologies and their Application to Anti-dumping Proceedings Involving China

accession protocol were the reason why the panel and the Appellate Body did not find any fault from the US ITC decision. Before this measure was taken, the US ITC completed five investigations pursuant to section 421 of the US Trade Act of 1974 that incorporated the TPSSM. Four investigations produced positive injury determinations based on the legal requirements of section 421, 'market disruption', but all proposals to adopt import bans were uniformly rejected by the US President because of public interest. Thus when the US President Obama decided to take the measure under the TPSSM, it provoked much controversy among scholars as well as the WTO Members.[10]

On the other hand, Chinese trade remedy actions have also been challenged within the WTO dispute settlement system. Eight out of thirty-three cases dealt with Chinese AD and CVD actions and five cases produced the panel and/or the Appellate Body reports.

The recent WTO rulings summarized in Table 30.3 show the structural problems of the Chinese trade remedy practices. The decisions found many procedural mistakes, as well as violations of the WTO duties in basic steps of AD investigations such as the adoption of facts available, drafting the final reports, and injury determinations.

[10] S Chung, J Lee, and T Osang, 'Did China Tire Safeguard Save US Workers?' (*ERIA Discussion Paper*, March 2015) <http://www.eria.org/ERIA-DP-2015-26.pdf> accessed 23 April 2016.

Table 30.3 WTO trade remedy disputes involving China as a respondent

DS number	Dispute name	Legal issues
407	China—Provisional Anti-dumping Duties on Certain Iron and Steel Fasteners from the EU	In consultation
414	China—Countervailing and Anti-dumping Duties on Grain-oriented Flat-rolled Electrical Steel from the United States	Procedural Issues: Scope of Appeal—Relationship of ADA arts 3.1/3.2 and SCMA arts 15./15.2 Substantive Issues: MOFCOM's price effects findings; 'facts available' for unknown exporters; 'essential facts'; public notice and explanation; disclosure of data and calculation used to establish dumping margin
425	China—Definitive Anti-dumping Duties on X-Ray Security Inspection Equipment from the European Union	Procedural Issues: ADA Standard of review Substantive Issues: price effects; state of the domestic industry; causation; MOFCOM's treatment of non-confidential summaries; disclosure of 'essential facts'; public notice
427	China—Anti-dumping and Countervailing Duty Measures on Broiler Products from the United States	Procedural Issues: 'particularized' review of a general claim; relationship of consultations request to panel request; legal basis of complaint Substantive Issues: cost of production; price effects; definition of the domestic industry; 'facts available' for unknown exporters; disclosure of 'essential facts'; public notice
440	China—Anti-dumping and Countervailing Duties on Certain Automobiles from the United States	Procedural Issues: request for leave to provide additional comments; timetable issues due to delayed request for review of interim report; terminated measures Substantive Issues: price effects; causation; definition of the domestic industry; 'facts available' for unknown exporters; disclosure of 'essential facts'; non-confidential summaries
454	China—Measures Imposing Anti-dumping Duties on High-Performance Stainless Steel Seamless Tubes from the European Union (Japan)	Panel report under appeal
460	China—Measures Imposing Anti-dumping Duties on High-performance Stainless Steel Seamless Tubes from the European Union (EU)	Panel report under appeal
483	China—Anti-dumping Measures on Imports of Cellulose Pulp from Canada	Panel composed

2. *Bilateral trade disputes*

Adjacent countries became more and more concerned with agricultural imports from China, particularly Japan and Korea. When both countries resorted to safeguard measures to protect their domestic farmers, China was not yet a WTO Member. In response to those safeguard measures, China engaged in retaliatory actions against imports from these two countries. The two incidents demonstrate typical situations of trade disputes without multilateral disciplines. Since China is now a formal Member of the WTO, it will no longer resort to such unilateral actions. In that regard, the following incidents offer very interesting cases to illustrate the value and role of the WTO dispute settlement system.

'Garlic Battle' between Korea and China

On September 30, 1999, the National Agricultural Co-operative Federation (NACF) applied for safeguard measures to the Korea Trade Commission (KTC) concerning peeled garlic and frozen pickled garlic from China.[11] On 18 November, the Ministry of Finance and Economy imposed a provisional safeguard duty of 285 per cent for frozen or pickled garlics. Subsequently, the KTC made a positive injury determination on 2 February 2000 and the 315 per cent safeguard duty was imposed for three years beginning on 1 June 2000.

On 7 June 2000, in response to the Korean safeguard measure, the Chinese government retaliated with the import sanction on major export items from Korea, such as cellular phones and polyethylene, in an amount of more than 100 times the garlic export values. Since China was not yet a WTO Member, neither country could use the WTO dispute settlement system to resolve this issue in a more neutral manner.[12]

Both governments engaged in the negotiation to deal with this trade conflict during the period of 29 June to 15 July 2000. When the Chinese government agreed to repeal the import ban, the Korean government agreed to shorten the safeguard period by five months so as to terminate on 31 December 2002. Moreover, Korea agreed to increase the minimum market access and in-quota amounts under tariff rate quota systems for garlic imported from China from 1 June 2000. On 2 August 2000, the Chinese government removed the import ban on pertinent Korean products (Figure 30.5).

On 12 April 2001, the Chinese government requested the Korean government to import about 10,500 tons of garlic that were not exhausted from the minimum market access, threatening to impose an import ban again on major Korean products such as cellular phones and polyethylene. On 21 April the Korean government agreed to import the unexhausted volume of garlic that amounted to $6.7 million under the in-quota rate.

[11] NACF requested the increase of existing MFN tariffs for peeled garlic from 376% to 500% and for frozen pickled garlic from 30% to 380%. Korea Trade Commission, 'The KTC History of 20 Year' (2008), 146 <http://www.ktc.go.kr/file/db/pdf/PR/PR706_2007-G.pdf> accessed 23 April 2016.

[12] See Mitsuo Matsushita, 'Some International and Domestic Antidumping Issues' (2010) 5(2) Asian J WTO & Intl Health L & Policy 249–68.

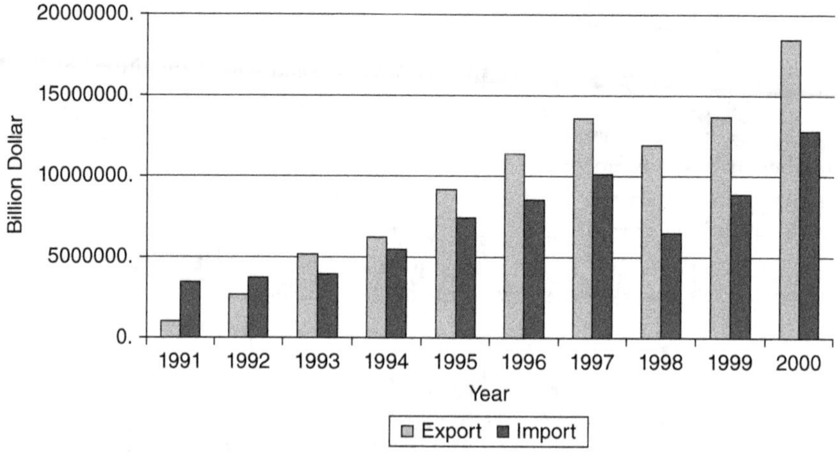

Fig. 30.5 Korea's trade with China: 1991–2000

On the other hand, the KTC self-initiated the interim review procedure on 1 February 2001 and concluded to maintain the existing safeguard measure. At that time, however, the KTC recommended agricultural policies for restructuring garlic farming as well as fiscal policies to address the unexhausted minimum market access. In fact, after Korea imported those minimum market access amounts, it exported them to Indonesia and India at a lower price than the import price from China. The costs incurred by this gap between import and export prices for garlic trade were equally shared by the Ministry of Agriculture and Forestry, the Ministry of Information and Communication, and the Ministry of Industry and Energy.

The first conflict between Korea and China in 2000 with the safeguard measure and the retaliation illustrated the importance of the WTO dispute settlement system to resolve a trade conflict in a reasonable manner. If it had thought the Korean measure was unjustified, China would have brought a case on the Korean safeguard measure to the WTO without resorting to the unilateral retaliation, and if that had happened, Korea would have corrected it pursuant to the WTO rules. The second conflict and the subsequent settlement in 2001 saliently demonstrated the consequence of the vacuum in the rule-based trading system.

The underlying economic situation shed some light on the trading politics of the 'Garlic Battle'. Korea has sustained a substantial trade surplus against China since 1993 (Figure 30.5). Thus, the Korean government had a great stake in the Chinese market, whereas China had no such economic stake in terms of trade retaliation. This trade imbalance undermined Korea's negotiating stance in the trade confrontation with China. On the other hand, the reliance of each country on the other market for pertinent products was as in Table 30.4[13]

[13] H Kim, 'Comparison of the Korean and the Japanese Response to China's Retaliation' (2001) KIEP Global Econ Rev 82, 83.

Table 30.4 Korea's trade situation concerning the Garlic Battle (1999)

Products	Import from China	Export to China	
	Garlic	Cellular phones	Polyethylene
Amount and share	\$8.98 million (99.9% of the total import)	\$41.4 million (1.2% of the total export)	\$471.3 million (40.7% of the total export)

It was reported that the Korean manufacturers of cellular phones and polyethylene suffered a serious injury to the tune of approximately \$100 million during about fifty days of the import sanction, until the Korean government agreed to remove the safeguard measure.

The 'Garlic Battle' became a big 'Garlic Scandal' in the domestic trade politics in 2002. As the due date for the original safeguard action, 31 December 2002, approached, the Korean garlic farmers tried to extend market protection. On 28 June 2002, NACF applied for extension of the existing safeguard measure. Only when the debates on the necessity or legitimacy of such extension caused huge controversy on the basis of prior experience did the Korean farmers find that the Korean government agreed not to extend the safeguard action in accordance with the agreement of 2000. This unexpected and unknown fact for the Korean farmers caused huge turmoil, which led the Economic Advisor to the President—who was the Minister of Trade during the bilateral negotiation—to resign. Despite all those political pressures, the KTC declined to initiate a review for possible extension of the safeguard measure. Subsequently, in September 2002, the NACF brought a suit against the KTC in the administrative court concerning its decision to decline the extension application. The KTC decision was upheld by the court, but the KTC never used a safeguard action against China after this case.

This case illustrates the political dynamics of the Korean government in terms of trade remedy measures. Unlike the United States, which imposes a safeguard measure only after inter-agency consultation to carry out public interest consideration, the Korean government did not have such an effective mechanism to co-ordinate different interests among different ministries. Thus a strong position by the Ministry of Agriculture and Forestry with the major jurisdiction on the issue at dispute prevailed over opposing positions by other ministries (Figure 30.6).

'Mushroom Battle' between Japan and China

On 27 March 2001, the Japanese Ministry of Agriculture, Forestry and Fisheries requested a safeguard measure on tatami-omote, welsh onions, and shiitake mushrooms to the Ministry of Finance and the Ministry of Economy, Trade and Industry. Japan imposed a provisional safeguard measure on

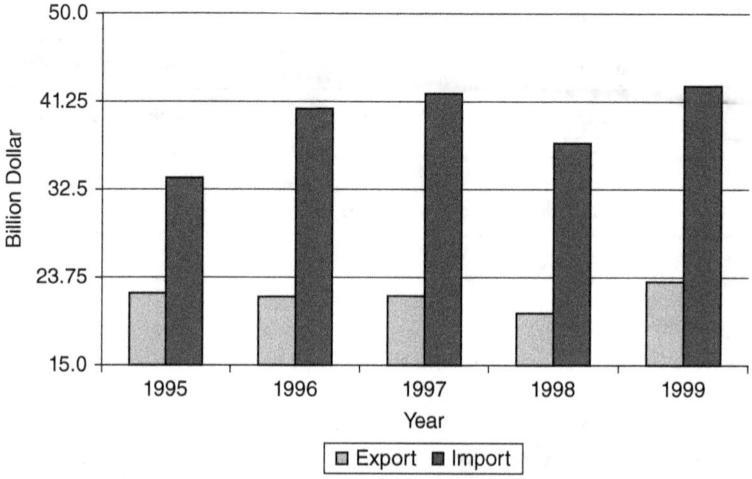

Fig. 30.6 Japan's trade with China: 1995–1999

23 April to last for 200 days.[14] The measures are tariff quotas adopted in special duties.[15]

In response to the Japanese safeguard measures, on 22 June China imposed retaliatory duties of 100 per cent on cars, cellular phones, and air-conditioners from Japan.

At a ministerial meeting[16] held in Beijing on 21 December 2001, Japan and China finally agreed to resolve their trade dispute over import sanctions. Japan agreed to terminate the safeguard investigation when China agreed to retract its retaliatory tariffs on Japanese automobiles and other industrial products.[17] Japan and China also adopted a memorandum of understanding, under which the two countries would create a private-level trade consultation panel to promote orderly trade of three farm products. Consultations at the panel are to be held mainly by private-sector groups, but government officials may participate to give advice on the planting and production of the three products, as well as on the healthy development of

[14] Committee on Safeguards, *Notification Under Article 12.4 of the Agreement on Safeguards Before Taking a Provisional Safeguards Measure Referred to in Article 6*, G/SG/N/7/JPN/1, 25 April 2001.

[15] The provisional safeguard measures are:

Products	Tariff quotas (ton)	Current rate	Additional rate
Welsh onion	5,383	3%	225 yen/kg
Shiitake mushroom	8,003	4.3%	635 yen/kg
Tatami-Omote	7,949	6%	306 yen/kg

[16] Japan was represented by the Minister of Economy, Trade and Industry (Hiranuma Takeo) and Minister of Agriculture, Forestry and Fisheries (Takebe Tsutomu), and China was represented by the Foreign Trade and Economic Co-operation Minister (Shi Guangsheng).

[17] Committee on Safeguards, *Information to be Notified to the Committee Where a Safeguard Investigation is Terminated with No Safeguard Measure Imposed*, G/SG/N/9/JPN/1, 10 January 2002.

Table 30.5 Japan's trade situation concerning the Mushroom Battle (1999)

Products	Import from China			Export to China		
	Mushroom	Onion	Tatami	Car	Cellular phone	Air conditioner
Amount and share	$11.5 million (88%)	$0.4 million (6.2%)	$0.2 million (80%)	$25.4 million (0.6%)	$4.8 million (6.2%)	$4.4 million (4.9%)

trade relations. Practically, the Japanese government would play a significant role in adjusting the production and trade volume of the three products (Table 30.5[18]).

In contrast to the Garlic Battle involving Korea, Japan settled the dispute relatively promptly with China. The contrasting background features of this incident and the 'Garlic Battle' include, inter alia, huge trade deficits of Japan in relation to China, weak dependency of targeted products on the Chinese market, and the precedent effect of the 'Garlic Battle' in which Korea was repeatedly forced to meet China's demand. (Figure 30.6)

B. Japan

Japan has not used trade remedy actions frequently. Japan initiated the AD investigations eight times until 2014, notably four times in 2007, which led to four AD measures in 2008. Japan imposed the CVD only once against Korea and initiated a safeguard investigation mainly to deal with the Chinese agricultural products without imposing the final measure.[19] The infrequent use of trade remedy actions by the Japanese government led to only one WTO dispute as a respondent.

During the GATT period, Japan was the major target of AD actions by other developed countries. For example, the AD action against the Japanese semiconductors led to the famous 'US–Japan Semiconductor Agreement'.[20] As shown in Table 30.6, the trade remedy actions have remained the major issues for Japan to bring the disputes to the WTO dispute settlement system.

Until the very recent cases against China and Ukraine, all trade remedy disputes have been against the United States. Except for two disputes on safeguard measures, all other disputes involve AD actions and regulations. Since Japan was never subject to CVD investigations after the inception of the WTO, there was no CVD-related dispute brought by Japan.

C. Korea

As shown in Table 30.7, Korea also brought many cases concerning trade remedy actions to the WTO dispute settlement system.

[18] Kim (n 13) 84.

[19] See Section A para 2(2).

[20] Mitsuo Matsushita, 'Interplay of Antidumping Remedies and Competition Laws: Tension and Compromise Between Antitrust and Antidumping' in M Matsushita, D Ahn, and T Chen (eds), *The WTO Trade Remedy System: East Asian Perspectives* (Cameron May 2006) 123–43.

Table 30.6 WTO trade remedy disputes involving Japan as a complainant

DS number	Dispute name
DS162	United States—Anti-dumping Act of 1916
DS184	United States—Anti-dumping Measures on Hot-Rolled Steel Products from Japan
DS217	United States—Continued Dumping and Subsidy Offset Act of 2000
DS244	United States—Sunset Review of Anti-dumping Duties on Corrosion-Resistant Carbon Steel Flat Products from Japan
DS249	United States—Definitive Safeguard Measures on Imports of Certain Steel Products
DS322	United States—Measures Relating to Zeroing and Sunset Reviews, Recourse to Article 21.5 of the DSU by Japan
DS454	China—Measures Imposing Anti-dumping Duties on High-Performance Stainless Steel Seamless Tubes ('HP-SSST') from the European Union and Japan
DS468	Ukraine—Definitive Safeguard Measures on Certain Passenger Cars

Table 30.7 WTO trade remedy disputes involving Korea as a complainant

DS number	Dispute name
DS89	United States—Anti-dumping Duties on Imports of Colour Television Receivers from Korea
DS99	United States—Anti-dumping Duty on Dynamic Random Access Memory Semiconductors (DRAMS) of One Megabit or Above from Korea
DS179	United States—Anti-dumping Measures on Stainless Steel Plate in Coils and Stainless Steel Sheet and Strip from Korea
DS202	United States—Definitive Safeguard Measures on Imports of Circular Welded Carbon Quality Line Pipe from Korea
DS215	Philippines—Anti-dumping Measures Regarding Polypropylene Resins from Korea
DS217	United States—Continued Dumping and Subsidy Offset Act of 2000
DS251	United States—Definitive Safeguard Measures on Imports of Certain Steel Products
DS296	United States—Countervailing Duty Investigation on Dynamic Random Access Memory Semiconductors (DRAMS) from Korea
DS299	European Communities—Countervailing Measures on Dynamic Random Access Memory Chips from Korea
DS336	Japan—Countervailing Duties on Dynamic Random Access Memories from Korea
DS402	United States—Use of Zeroing in Anti-dumping Measures Involving Products from Korea
DS420	United States—Anti-dumping Measures on Corrosion-Resistant Carbon Steel Flat Products from Korea
DS464	United States – Anti-dumping and Countervailing Measures on Large Residential Washers from Korea
DS488	United States—Anti-dumping Measures on Certain Oil Country Tubular Goods from Korea

Table 30.8 WTO trade remedy disputes involving Korea as a respondent

DS number	Dispute name
DS98	Korea—Definitive Safeguard Measure on Imports of Certain Dairy Products
DS312	Korea—Anti-dumping Duties on Imports of Certain Paper from Indonesia, Recourse to Article 21.5 of the DSU by Indonesia

Out of the total seventeen cases, fourteen cases dealt with trade remedy issues. It is also noted that nine cases addressed AD actions, while only two dealt with safeguard actions and four cases were related to CVD actions and laws.[21] In addition, except for two disputes against the European Union and Japan, twelve disputes were against the United States. This peculiar situation of predominant AD disputes against the United States in the WTO explains the reason why the Korean government tried desperately to address the AD practices of the US investigating authorities in the Korea–US free trade agreement (FTA) negotiation.

On the other hand, the Korean trade remedy actions were brought to the WTO dispute settlement system (Table 30.8).

The *Korea—Dairy Products* case, as the first litigated dispute dealing with a safeguard measure, set forth important jurisprudence for the WTO Safeguard Agreement. For example, the Appellate Body ruled that 'unforeseen development', long regarded as a meaningless expression or mere explanation for the needs of safeguard measures, must be proven as a precondition for imposing a safeguard measure.[22] Emphasizing the principle of effectiveness in the interpretation of treaties that requires a treaty interpreter to give meaning and effect to all the terms of the treaty, the Appellate Body clarified that 'unforeseen development' stipulates the prerequisite for safeguard actions.[23]

In the *Korea—Paper* case, the panel did not find WTO inconsistency in most of the Korea Trade Commission (KTC)'s practices. It found a relatively minor flaw that the KTC's lack of explanation for using inconsistent information in a constructed normal value calculation violated the duty under the WTO AD Agreement. When the KTC carried out a review pursuant to the panel ruling, it merely presented a new explanation in support of the original calculation instead of adopting a different proxy as requested by the complainant.[24] Indonesia brought

[21] Three cases involved both AD and CVD.

[22] For more serious legal discussions on safeguard jurisprudence, see Dukgeun Ahn, 'Restructuring the WTO Safeguard System' in Matsushita, Ahn, and Chen (n 20) 11–31.

[23] Appellate Body Report, *Korea—Definitive Safeguard Measure on Imports of Certain Dairy Products*, WT/DS98/AB/R, 14 December 1999, para 80.

[24] Indonesia requested the panel specifically to suggest that the KTC implement its findings by basing CMI's interest expenses on April Fine's data, in which case margins of dumping for Indah Kiat and Pindo Deli would become *de minimis*. The panel declined to make such suggestions. Panel Report, *Korea—Anti-dumping Duties on Imports of Certain Paper from Indonesia*, WT/DS312/RW, 28 September 2007, para 7.6.

the compliance panel request again to challenge the KTC explanation, which was indeed found to be inadequate.[25]

Because Korea lost the case even in the compliance panel, Indonesia could have tried to impose retaliatory measures under the WTO authorization. But this case raised a very difficult issue for calculating how much retaliation should be authorized. Although the panel repeatedly found the KTC's reasoning for adopting a certain proxy in dumping margin calculation to be inadequate, it is not clear how much such flaws can be incorporated in calculating retaliation amounts.

In fact, Indonesia brought the KTC decision to the Administrative Court that is allowed under the judicial review procedure. The Court, however, rejected the Indonesian claims.[26]

IV. Trade Remedy Systems in FTAS

A. AD/CVD system

The recent phenomena of 'rule diversity' with regard to trade remedy rules has also been observed in East Asian FTAs, especially involving Korea.[27] As shown in Table 30.9, Singapore seems to be the most active WTO Member to experiment with rule diversification in respect of trade remedy systems.

Korea, however, incorporated such an approach in its FTAs and could arrange interesting modified rules such as mandatory prohibition of zeroing, requirement to apply lesser duty rules, public policy consideration, and one-year prohibition of renewed AD action after expiry.

Generally, there is no special provision exclusively applicable to CVD action in FTAs. The intrinsic multilateral nature of subsidy rules appears to be the primary reason to avoid any arrangement disciplining subsidy policies in FTAs. In this regard, although it is not a CVD provision, Article 11.11 of the Korea–EU FTA is noteworthy in that it is an exception provision to address subsidy rules in a bilateral FTA.

B. Safeguard system

FTA safeguard systems are nowadays almost standardized, basically following the model adopted in the North American Free Trade Agreement (NAFTA), except for the provision to exclude NAFTA parties from the global safeguard measures. Thus the FTAs involving the East Asian countries also follow this model without showing any peculiar element.

[25] Despite the violation rulings on those legal issues, the KTC announced that it won the case. It indicated the practical importance of those legal points.

[26] Haeng-jeong beobwon [Admin Ct], 2004-5911, 1 September 2005 (S Kor).

[27] For a more detailed discussion of 'rule diversity' in terms of trade remedy systems, see Dukgeun Ahn, 'Foe or Friend of GATT Article XXIV: Diversity in Trade Remedy Rules' (2008) 11 J Intl Econ L 107, 107–33.

Table 30.9 FTAs with special anti-dumping rules

FTA (date of entry into force)	Special AD rules	
	Prohibition of AD action	Modification of AD rules
EFTA–Singapore FTA (1 January 2003)	No AD measure allowed (competition policy measures)	
Singapore–New Zealand FTA (1 January 2001)		• 5% of export price as *de minimis* margin for refund and review cases as well as new cases • 5% of import volume • 3-year sunset review
Singapore–Australia FTA (28 July 2003)		• Lesser duty rule
Jordan–Singapore FTA (22 August 2005)		• 5% of export price as *de minimis* margin for new case • 5% of import volume • No third-country dumping • 12-month period for injury determination • 3-year sunset review • Lesser duty rule • Prohibition of zeroing • No AD if SG imposed
Korea–Singapore FTA (1 March 2006)		• Lesser duty rule • Prohibition of zeroing
Korea–EFTA FTA (1 September 2006)		• Lesser duty rule
Korea–US FTA		• Early notification
Korea–EU FTA		• Lesser duty rule • Public interest • Early notification
Korea–Peru FTA		• Early notification • Questionnaire in English
Korea–India FTA		• Lesser duty rule • 1-year prohibition after AD expiry • Prohibition of zeroing

Since the United States always insists on such selective safeguard mechanisms, the arrangement to exclude FTA parties from a global safeguard measure is also adopted in the Korea–US FTA. The only difference from NAFTA with respect to selective application of global safeguard measures is the discretionary authority to exclude FTA parties instead of mandatory exclusion. Article 10.5 of the Korea–US FTA stipulates that 'a Party taking a global safeguard measure may exclude imports of an originating good of the other Party if such imports are not a substantial cause of serious injury or threat'. This provision is indeed a template article adopted in most of the FTAs involving the United States after NAFTA. In contrast, the European Union has never adopted such a selective safeguard system in FTAs, including the Korea–EU FTA. But both the Korea–US FTA and the Korea–EU FTA require the choice of either a bilateral FTA safeguard action or the WTO safeguard action, and do not permit concurrent application of them. Another interesting element of the Korea–US FTA is the once-only safeguard action. Practically speaking, it will be almost impossible to invoke a bilateral safeguard action more than once within an FTA context. But the Korea–US FTA is one of the very few FTAs that specifically limit a bilateral safeguard action to only once.

It is noted that the Korea–India FTA incorporated various special provisions in relation to a bilateral safeguard system, such as judicial review requirement, and prohibition of retaliation for the first two years. Considering the fact that India is currently the most active safeguarding country in the WTO[28], the new elements adopted in the Korea–India FTA may provide an important implication for future FTA or WTO rule negotiations.

V. Future Challenges

East Asian countries have always been at the centre of trade remedy actions, especially Japan and Korea during the GATT period and China and Korea during the WTO period. Trade remedy actions against Japan and Korea during the GATT period even caused foreign direct investment into the United States and the European Union to overcome those measures. Trade remedy actions against China during the WTO period have caused many controversial disputes related to systemic issues of non-market economies. In this regard, recent CVD actions against China will be a major challenge for the WTO trade remedy system.

On the other hand, East Asian countries will play a more significant role in institutional developments of trade remedy systems. Japan is still the only country among major developed countries that does not have a standing investigating authority. But if Japan joins the Trans-Pacific Partnership (TPP), the Japanese government may need to establish a standing body in charge of trade remedy investigations in order to deal with more substantial importation from FTA parties. The Chinese government's practices have been seriously disciplined by the WTO challenges in recent years. As discussed in section III, various aspects of the MOFCOM's practices will become more refined pursuant to the WTO jurisprudence. The KTC has also substantially enhanced its capacity and further considered various options to augment the system, including establishment of an independent agency by detaching it from the Ministry of Trade, Industry and Energy. Therefore, it remains to be seen how these countries develop their trade remedy practices as well as institutions, which will become more important factors

[28] From 1 January 1995 to 30 April 2015, India initiated thirty-nine safeguard investigations. WTO (n 8).

for future development of the WTO trade remedy system. The extent to which the East Asian countries contribute to the evolution of the WTO trade remedy system, however, will critically hinge on how they embrace the WTO rules and jurisprudence within their domestic system. Thus it appears a very important challenge for them to maintain their trade remedy systems in compliance with the increasingly complicated WTO trade remedy jurisprudence.

31

A Managerial Approach to Secure Compliance with the SPS Agreement

Yuka Fukunaga

I. Introduction

The Agreement on the Application of Sanitary and Phytosanitary Measures (SPS Agreement) is one of the most frequently raised agreements in the World Trade Organization (WTO) panel and Appellate Body review. As of the end of June 2015, violations of the SPS Agreement have been alleged in 43 disputes among nearly 500 disputes since 1995, and panels have been established in nineteen of the forty-three disputes. Violations of the SPS Agreement were found by panels and upheld by the Appellate Body in most of these cases. The measures that were found to violate the Agreement were normally withdrawn or modified in accordance with recommendations of the panels and the Appellate Body.[1] The SPS Agreement is no exception to the success of WTO dispute settlement in resolving trade disputes and securing compliance with the WTO Agreement.

However, disputes involving the SPS Agreement also vividly exemplify negative side effects of the success because they inevitably raise a concern that the sovereign right of WTO Members to adopt and enforce public health policy of their own choice might be unduly restricted by the panel and Appellate Body review.[2] Most famously, the Appellate Body's finding that the European Community's (EC's) ban on the import of meats and meat products treated with hormones violated the SPS Agreement and its recommendation that the EC bring the ban into conformity with its obligation under the SPS Agreement provoked criticism against

[1] Violations of the SPS Agreement were *not* found only in cases where the complainant did not pursue its complaints under the SPS Agreement, either because it brought complaints under other agreements such as the Agreement on Technical Barriers to Trade (TBT Agreement) or because it reached a mutual solution to a dispute with the respondent. See also Committee on Sanitary and Phytosanitary Measures, *Review of the Operation and Implementation of the SPS Agreement: Background Document: Note by the Secretariat* (*Fourth Review Report*), G/SPS/GEN/1312, 7 March 2014; G/SPS/GEN/1312/Corr.1, 21 March 2014, para 14.1.

[2] Thomas Cottier, 'Risk Management Experience in WTO Dispute Settlement' in David Robertson and Aynsley Kellow (eds), *Globalization and the Environment: Risk Assessment in the WTO* (Edward Elgar 2001) 41, 41–42.

WTO dispute settlement and drove home the concern regarding sovereignty.[3] The concern has never been more real than today, when pressure mounts to further liberalize trade in food, and we are surrounded by foods that are prepared in unknown countries by unknown methods. Under such circumstances, the panel and Appellate Body review may be seen as a threat to the legitimate right of people and their governments to take SPS measures necessary for the protection of human, animal, or plant life or health, as explicitly recognized by the SPS Agreement.[4]

Against this background, this chapter explores the usefulness of a managerial approach in securing compliance with the SPS Agreement as an alternative or supplement to the dispute settlement procedures.

Section II discusses what a managerial approach means and section III examines provisions in the SPS Agreement that take the managerial approach, and considers whether they are effective in paying due respect to the sovereign right of WTO Members to pursue public health policies while securing compliance with the SPS Agreement. Section IV concludes.

II. What Does a Managerial Approach Mean?

A managerial approach to secure compliance with international law rules is most famously discussed by Chayes and Chayes. They first point out that 'the principal source of non-compliance is not willful disobedience but the lack of capability or clarity or priority' and that therefore 'coercive enforcement is as misguided as it is costly'.[5] They then argue the usefulness of a 'managerial model' of compliance that 'reli[es] primarily on a cooperative, problem-solving approach instead of a coercive one'.[6] According to their arguments, activities such as ensuring transparency and capacity building are among typical examples of the managerial approach.[7] With respect to dispute settlement, they argue that while adjudicative dispute settlement procedures that produce final and binding findings and occasionally result in sanctions for violations are regarded as 'coercive enforcement', dispute settlement can also be conducted in a managerial way by using more informal and conciliatory procedures.[8]

The managerial approach is most prevalent in international environmental law. For example, Victor, Raustiala, and Skolnikoff emphasize the importance of systems for implementation review as 'a crucial aspect of practical and effective international environmental governance'.[9] According to them, systems for

[3] Cf Reinhard Quick and Andreas Blüthner, 'Has the Appellate Body Erred?: An Appraisal and Criticism of the Ruling in the WTO Hormones Case' (1999) 2 J Intl Econ L 603.

[4] The WTO Agreement on the Application of Sanitary and Phytosanitary Measures, 1867 UNTS 493 (SPS Agreement), art 2.1.

[5] Abram Chayes and Antonia Handler Chayes, *The New Sovereignty: Compliance with International Regulatory Agreements* (Harvard University Press 1995) 3.

[6] ibid 22. [7] ibid 2, 22–25. [8] ibid 24–25.

[9] David G Victor and others, 'Introduction and Overview' in David G Victor and others (eds), *The Implementation and Effectiveness of International Environmental Commitments* (The MIT Press 1998) 20.

implementation review 'operate primarily by "managing" implementation problems', such as exchanging data, sharing information on implementation, monitoring activities, assessing the adequacy of existing commitments, and handling problems of poor implementation.[10] In addition, non-compliance procedures in some international environmental conventions are praised as an alternative to traditional dispute settlement procedures that cannot effectively address issues of compliance with international environmental conventions.[11]

Following the line of the above arguments, this chapter defines a managerial approach, an approach that encourages voluntary compliance with international law rules through co-operative and conciliatory methods instead of binding and coercive ones.

In this connection, the WTO panel and Appellate Body review has clear characteristics of the '*non*-managerial' approach for the following reasons. First, panels and the Appellate Body make final and binding findings regarding consistency with the WTO Agreement. Second, when panels and the Appellate Body find violations of the WTO Agreement, the respondent Member bears an international legal obligation to bring its violating measure into conformity with the WTO Agreement. Third, although rare, the complainant Member may suspend concessions or obligations under the WTO Agreement against the respondent Member if the latter refuses to bring the violating measure into conformity with the Agreement.

Needless to say, the panel and Appellate Body review is not the only way to secure compliance with the WTO Agreement. In fact, the WTO also utilizes managerial methods to secure compliance with the WTO Agreement. A number of notification requirements in the WTO Agreement, as well as the Trade Policy Review Mechanism, are particularly important among such examples. In addition, the WTO dispute settlement system offers managerial types of dispute settlement such as good offices, conciliation, and mediation, though they have hardly been used so far. Despite the availability of managerial methods in the WTO, they have received little attention both in academic research and in practice compared to the binding and coercive approach of the panel and Appellate Body review. The disparity of interest between the binding and coercive approach and the managerial approach might be explained by the outstanding success of the former in resolving trade disputes and ensuring compliance with the WTO Agreement.

However, the lack of interest in the managerial approach does not mean its lack of importance. Rather, the usefulness of the managerial approach may be simply overshadowed by the readily availableness and glowing success of the coercive approach to dispute settlement. In fact, some argue that we should take full advantage of the managerial approach in the WTO. For example, Weiss points out that, while trade disputes are traditionally viewed as disputes between two parties and

[10] ibid 16, 19.

[11] Jan Klabbers, 'Compliance Procedures' in Daniel Bodansky and others (eds), *The Oxford Handbook of International Environmental Law* (OUP 2007) 1000–05.

bilateral in nature so that they are better addressed by judicial dispute settlement procedures, there are trade disputes that involve procedural obligations and affect not just a limited number of specific parties but all the WTO Members, and that these disputes 'might well benefit from the softer dispute resolution techniques used in environmental agreements'.[12] In a different context, Matsushita argues that 'it is time for the WTO to use a soft law approach' in addition to its traditional 'hard law' approach.[13] In particular, Matsushita proposes that the WTO Members use the trade policy review mechanism (TPRM) to 'coordinate activities of FTAs (Free Trade Agreements) and link them together'.[14] He believes that such use of the TPRM 'promotes compatibility and cooperation among FTAs and between WTO norms and FTA rules'.[15]

While the usefulness of the managerial approach varies depending on the nature of individual WTO Agreements, this author argues that the approach can be particularly useful in securing compliance with the SPS Agreement, considering the nature of non-compliance with the SPS Agreement.

In this author's view, there are three major sources of non-compliance with the SPS Agreement, and all of them can be effectively addressed by the managerial approach. The first source is ignorance of the law. SPS measures are typically drafted by a health ministry in consideration of the interests and concerns of domestic stakeholders such as producers and consumers. This drafting process may not be well suited to take into account the issue of consistency with the SPS Agreement. Making the process transparent can enable other WTO Members to check the consistency of adopted measures with the SPS Agreement. The second source of non-compliance is the lack of capacity. The adoption and administration of SPS measures require various financial and non-financial resources to which developing country Members may not have access. In such circumstances, managerial methods such as capacity-building activities and information sharing would more effectively assist developing countries in implementing the SPS Agreement than the panel and Appellate Body review. The third and most important source of non-compliance (or alleged non-compliance) is the lack of agreement concerning the scientific veracity of risks. SPS measures are adopted in order to prevent risks to human, animal, or plant life or health, and Article 5.1 of the SPS Agreement requires that SPS measures be 'based on an assessment of … the risks'. Thus, whether a risk has properly been assessed is often the key in determining the consistency of an SPS measure at issue with the SPS Agreement. However, an answer to the question is not always crystal clear, because even scientists may disagree on whether a

[12] Edith Brown Weiss, 'Strengthening National Compliance with Trade Law: Insights from Environment' in Marco Bronckers and Reinhard Quick (eds), *New Directions in International Economic Law: Essays in Honour of John H Jackson* (Kluwer Law International 2000) 468–69.

[13] Mitsuo Matsushita, 'A View on Future Roles of The WTO: Should There Be More Soft Law in The WTO?' (2014) 17 J Intl Econ L 701, 702.

[14] ibid 707.

[15] ibid 708. See also Julien Chaisse and Mitsuo Matsushita, 'Maintaining the WTO's Supremacy in the International Trade Order: A Proposal to Refine and Revise the Role of the Trade Policy Review Mechanism' (2013) 16 J Intl Econ L 9.

risk exists. In fact, many past SPS disputes arose as a result of controversy over the existence of risks. Given the difficulty, or even the inability, to determine the veracity of a risk, it may be more useful to use conciliatory procedures to manage the disagreement on a risk instead of having a panel and the Appellate Body to render a binding decision on the issue.

Section III examines managerial methods provided in the SPS Agreement. It pays particular attention to managerial dispute settlement procedures under Article 12 of the SPS Agreement and discusses their usefulness in resolving SPS disputes in a non-binding manner and in securing compliance with the SPS Agreement.

III. Managerial Methods Provided for in the SPS Agreement

This section examines the usefulness of managerial methods provided in the SPS Agreement, i.e. transparency requirements, technical assistance, clarification of the Agreement, and ad hoc consultations.[16] Special attention is paid to informal and conciliatory dispute settlement, which can be used as an alternative or supplement to the binding panel and Appellate Body review.

A. Transparency requirements

'Members shall notify changes in their sanitary or phytosanitary measures and shall provide information on their sanitary or phytosanitary measures in accordance with the provisions of Annex B.'[17]

According to the Committee on Sanitary and Phytosanitary Measures (SPS Committee), the aim of transparency requirements is 'to achieve a greater degree of clarity, predictability, and information about trade policies, rules and regulations of Members'.[18] The notification requirement under Article 7 of the SPS Agreement plays a central role in securing the transparency of SPS measures. In addition to the transparency requirements under the SPS Agreement, the Trade Facilitation (TF) Agreement that was adopted as part of the so-called Bali Package includes some 'SPS-plus' obligations regarding the transparency of SPS regulations.[19]

[16] The SPS Agreement provides for other managerial methods as well. See e.g., *Catalogue of Instruments Available to WTO Members to Manage SPS Issues: Submission by Canada and Kenya, Revision*, G/SPS/W/279/Rev.2, 4 March 2015.

[17] SPS Agreement, art 7.

[18] Committee on Sanitary and Phytosanitary Measures, *Recommended Procedures for Implementing the Transparency Obligations of the SPS Agreement (Article 7) as of 1 December 2008* (*Recommended Procedures for Transparency Obligations*), G/SPS/7/Rev.3, 20 June 2008, para 1.

[19] See, e.g., arts 1 and 2 of the Trade Facilitation Agreement (TF Agreement). See also WTO, 'The Relationship Between the Trade Facilitation Agreement and the Agreement on the Application of Sanitary and Phytosanitary Measures (SPS Agreement)' (21 March 2014) 2–3, <http://www.wto.org/english/tratop_e/sps_e/tf_sps_e.pdf> accessed 23 April 2016.

In accordance with Article 7 and Annex B of the SPS Agreement, Members are required to publish all SPS regulations that they have adopted.[20] In particular, Members shall allow a 'reasonable interval' between the publication of an SPS measure and its entry into force in order to enable exporters to adapt their products and methods of production to the requirements of the measure.[21] The publication of SPS regulations is considered a 'fundamental component of transparency under the SPS Agreement'.[22] Members shall also establish an enquiry point that is responsible for providing answers to all reasonable questions from interested Members regarding the adopted SPS regulations.[23]

When a Member seeks to introduce an SPS regulation that is not substantially the same as an international standard, guideline, or recommendation, or is not covered by an international standard, guideline, or recommendation and that may have a significant effect on the trade of other Members, the Member shall publish a notice in order to enable interested Members to become acquainted with the proposed regulation.[24] Moreover, Members are encouraged to notify all regulations that are based on, conform to, or are substantially the same as an international standard, guideline, or recommendation, if they are expected to have a significant effect on the trade of other Members.[25] The notifying Member shall allow reasonable time for other Members to make comments on the proposed regulation in writing, discuss these comments upon request, and take the comments and the results of the discussions into account.[26]

As of 15 September 2014, regular, emergency, and other notifications totaling 17,305 have been submitted in accordance with Article 7 and Annex B of the SPS Agreement and the Recommended Procedures since 1 January 1995.[27] The SPS Information Management System (SPS IMS), developed by the WTO Secretariat, includes the most recent information on notifications under the SPS Agreement as well as other SPS-related documents in order to allow users to track information regarding notified SPS regulations.[28]

The transparency requirements set forth in the SPS Agreement enable Members to be informed about SPS regulations adopted by other Members and to identify potential concerns regarding their consistency with the SPS Agreement. Members

[20] SPS Agreement, Annex B, para 1. What to notify under this paragraph can be controversial. See e.g., Appellate Body Report, *Japan—Measures Affecting Agricultural Products*, WT/DS76/AB/R, 22 February 1999, paras 102–08. See also Chris Downes, 'The Impact of WTO Transparency Rules: Is the 10,000th SPS Notification a Cause for Celebration?—a Case Study of EU Practice' (2012) 15 J Intl Econ L 503, 512–15.

[21] SPS Agreement, Annex B, para 2.

[22] *Recommended Procedures for Transparency Obligations* (n 18) para 58.

[23] SPS Agreement, Annex B, para 3.

[24] SPS Agreement, Annex B, para 5(a).

[25] *Recommended Procedures for Transparency Obligations* (n 18) para 8.

[26] SPS Agreement, Annex B, para 5(d). For more about the notification requirements, see e.g., Joanne Scott, *The WTO Agreement on Sanitary and Phytosanitary Measures: A Commentary* (1st edn, OUP 2007) 197–211.

[27] Committee on Sanitary and Phytosanitary Measures, *Overview Regarding the Level of Implementation of the Transparency Provisions of the SPS Agreement*, G/SPS/GEN/804/Rev.7, 6 October 2014, para 3.2–6.

[28] WTO, 'SPS Information Management System' <http://spsims.wto.org/> accessed 16 March 2016.

with such concerns may submit a comment to the notifying Member and put peer pressure on it to ensure that SPS regulations are adopted in compliance with the SPS Agreement. The possibility of a comment regarding a notification turning into a full dispute settlement complaint gives Members additional incentive to comply with the SPS Agreement and thereby prevents an SPS dispute from arising.[29]

That said, the current rules are limited in the sense that Members are only required to allow for a certain period of time for comments but not to take them into account. An additional requirement to oblige Members not only to give time to but also to take into consideration the received comments would enhance the chance of comments being reflected in proposed SPS measures and would encourage Members to adopt regulations consistent with the SPS Agreement.[30]

B. Technical assistance

Members agree to facilitate the provision of technical assistance to other Members, especially developing country Members, either bilaterally or through the appropriate international organisations....[31]

In furtherance of the objective of this provision, technical assistance has been provided by Members and the Secretariat.[32] Moreover, the Standards and Trade Development Facility (STDF), a global partnership and trust fund, has been established by the WTO and other relevant international organizations to support developing countries in building their capacity to implement international SPS standards, guidelines, and recommendations.[33] The operations of the STDF have been periodically reported to the SPS Committee.[34] In addition, based on a proposal made by New Zealand, the WTO Secretariat launched a 'mentoring' mechanism in 2008 to assist developing country Members in implementing and benefiting from the transparency provisions of the SPS Agreement.[35]

[29] A notifying Member that receives comments by other Members on a proposed sanitary or phytosanitary regulation may voluntarily amend the proposed regulation in response to the comments. Downes (n 20) 516–17.

[30] Cf Committee on Sanitary and Phytosanitary Measures, *Fourth Review of the Operation and Implementation of the Agreement on the Application of Sanitary and Phytosanitary Measures: Transparency Under the SPS Agreement (Article 7 and Annex B) Proposals for Actions, Submission by Chile, the European Union, Morocco and Norway*, G/SPS/W/278, 26 May 2014, para 4.

[31] SPS Agreement, art 9.1.

[32] Some of the technical assistance is set forth in a document prepared by the Secretariat. Committee on Sanitary and Phytosanitary Measures, *Overview of SPS-related Technical Assistance Reported to the WTO/OECD Trade Capacity Building Database: Note by the Secretariat*, G/SPS/GEN/726, 4 October 2006.

[33] Standards and Trade Development Facility, 'STDF Vision and Mission' <http://www.standardsfacility.org/vision-and-mission> accessed 16 March 2016.

[34] See e.g., Standards and Trade Development Facility (STDF), 'Standards and Trade Development Facility, Annual Report 2014' (2014) STDF Annual Report, paras 2.13 and 2.15 <http://www.standardsfacility.org/sites/default/files/STDF_Annual_Report_2014_FINAL.pdf> accessed 23 April 2016.

[35] Committee on Sanitary and Phytosanitary Measures, *Update on the 'Mentoring' System of Assistance Relating to the Transparency Provisions of the SPS Agreement, Note by the Secretariat*, G/SPS/GEN/1097, 24 June 2011, paras 1–2. See also Committee on Sanitary and Phytosanitary

Technical assistance in the context of the SPS Agreement principally serves two purposes. The first is to enable developing country Members to comply with SPS measures in export markets in order for them to benefit from the provisions of the SPS Agreement. Moreover, if an exporting developing country Member identifies significant difficulties with an SPS regulation notified by another Member, the notifying Member shall, upon request, enter into consultations with the purpose of finding a mutually satisfactory solution to the problem through, for example, a change in the regulation, providing technical assistance to the developing country Member, or granting special and differential treatment.[36]

The second purpose, which is more relevant to the topic of this chapter, is to assist developing countries in adopting and enforcing their own SPS measures in accordance with the SPS Agreement.[37] Given the high technicality of the SPS Agreement, it may be the case that developing country Members often fail to comply with the Agreement due to their lack of capacity in scientific and administrative matters. Technical assistance can not only improve compliance with the SPS Agreement by developing country Members but can also facilitate importing into their markets by removing unnecessary SPS measures.

C. Clarification of the agreement

'[The Committee on Sanitary and Phytosanitary Measures] shall carry out the functions necessary to implement the provisions of this Agreement and the furtherance of its objectives, in particular with respect to harmonization....'[38]

In order to facilitate the implementation of the Agreement, the SPS Committee has adopted several guidelines and procedures to clarify the meaning of the provisions of the SPS Agreement.[39]

Measures, *Technical Assistance for Operating the SPS Notification Authority and SPS Enquiry Point*, G/SPS/W/214, 1 October 2007; Committee on Sanitary and Phytosanitary Measures, *Proposal for a 'Mentoring' System of Assistance Relating to the Transparency Provisions of the SPS Agreement: Note by the Secretariat*, G/SPS/W/217, 20 February 2008.

[36] Committee on Sanitary and Phytosanitary Measures, *Procedure to Enhance Transparency of Special and Differential Treatment in Favour of Developing Country Members*, G/SPS/33/Rev.1, 18 December 2009.

[37] For the technical assistance activities by the WTO Secretariat, see e.g., Committee on Sanitary and Phytosanitary Measures, *WTO SPS Technical Assistance Activities in 2015: General Information, Selection Process and Application Form*, G/SPS/GEN/997/Rev.5, 3 March 2014; Committee on Sanitary and Phytosanitary Measures, *SPS Technical Assistance and Training Activities 1 September 1994 to 31 December 2014*, G/SPS/GEN/521/Rev.10, 24 February 2014.

[38] SPS Agreement, art 12.1.

[39] In addition to the guidelines and decisions stated below, the SPS Committee is required by art 12.7 of the SPS Agreement to 'review the operation and implementation of [the] Agreement three years after the date of entry into force of the WTO Agreement, and thereafter as the need arises'. At the Fourth Session of the Ministerial Conference, Ministers instructed the Committee to conduct a review under the provision at least once every four years. Committee on Sanitary and Phytosanitary Measures, *Review of the Operation and Implementation of the Agreement of the Application of Sanitary and Phytosanitary Measures*, G/SPS/36, 11 July 2005, para 2. So far, the SPS Committee has completed four reviews under this provision, the last of which was completed in 2014. *Fourth Review Report* (n 1).

For example, in accordance with Article 5.5 of the SPS Agreement, the SPS Committee has adopted guidelines that assist WTO Members in achieving consistency in the application of the concept of the appropriate level of SPS protection and compliance with the obligation in order to avoid arbitrary or unjustifiable distinctions in the levels considered appropriate if those distinctions result in discrimination or disguised restrictions on international trade.[40] Moreover, the Committee has adopted a decision regarding the consideration and recognition of the equivalence of SPS measures provided in Article 4 of the SPS Agreement.[41]

The Committee has also clarified procedural aspects of the Agreement. For example, the Committee has adopted a procedure to monitor the process of international harmonization and the use of international standards, guidelines, and recommendations pursuant to Articles 3.5 and 12.4 of the SPS Agreement.[42] With respect to the transparency requirements, the SPS Committee has adopted recommended procedures for the publication and notification of SPS regulations.[43] In addition, a procedural manual for the operation of Enquiry Points and National Notification Authorities is made available by the Secretariat in order to facilitate the implementation of the transparency provisions.[44]

The guidelines and decisions adopted by the SPS Committee are not binding and cannot add to or diminish the rights and obligations under the SPS Agreement. Nevertheless, the guidelines and decisions are often regarded by national authorities as norms that have to be complied with.[45]The clarification efforts are expected to facilitate the implementation of the Agreement and prevent disputes, especially those that could arise from a misunderstanding or disagreement as to the meaning of the Agreement.

D. Ad hoc consultations

'The Committee shall encourage and facilitate *ad hoc* consultations or negotiations among Members on specific sanitary or phytosanitary issues.'[46]

While Article 11 of the SPS Agreement provides that disputes involving the SPS Agreement may be brought to the binding dispute settlement under the

[40] Committee on Sanitary and Phytosanitary Measures, *Guidelines to Further the Practical Implementation of Article 5.5*, G/SPS/15, 18 July 2000.

[41] Committee on Sanitary and Phytosanitary Measures, *Decision on the Implementation of Article 4 of the Agreement on the Application of Sanitary and Phytosanitary Measures*, G/SPS/19/Rev.2, 23 July 2004.

[42] Committee on Sanitary and Phytosanitary Measures, *Revision of the Procedure to Monitor the Process of International Harmonization: Decision of the Committee: Revision*, G/SPS/11/Rev.1, 15 November 2004; Committee on Sanitary and Phytosanitary Measures, *Decision to Modify and Extend the Provisional Procedure to Monitor the Process of International Harmonization: Adopted on 28 June 2006*, G/SPS/40, 5 July 2006.

[43] *Recommended Procedures for Transparency Obligations* (n 18).

[44] WTO, 'Procedural Step-by-Step Manual for SPS National Notification Authorities and SPS National Enquiry Points' (WTO 2011), <http://www.wto.org/english/res_e/booksp_e/sps_procedure_manual_e.pdf> accessed 23 April 2016.

[45] Downes (n 20) 521.

[46] SPS Agreement, art 12.2.

Understanding on Rules and Procedures Governing the Settlement of Disputes (DSU), Article 12.2 provides that informal and conciliatory ad hoc procedures may be used to settle or avoid SPS disputes.

Although the SPS Agreement does not specify how the ad hoc consultations under the provision should be conducted, they have been held in essentially three ways: (i) through a regular agenda item on specific trade concerns; (ii) through agenda items on specific issues such as equivalence or private standards; and (iii) through the development of a mechanism for using the good offices of the SPS Chairperson.[47] Whatever option is taken, the ad hoc consultations are expected to assist Members in reaching mutually satisfactory solutions to SPS issues without recourse to formal and binding dispute settlement procedures.[48] The first and the third options are discussed below, respectively.

1. Specific trade concerns

The ad hoc consultations are most commonly held in the context of the review of 'specific trade concerns'.[49]

The review of 'specific trade concerns' began following a suggestion by Argentina in 1996. That is, Argentina suggested that 'countries with bilateral disagreements about the interpretation of their rights and obligations under the SPS Agreement [should be encouraged] to use the Committee, whenever possible, as a forum for consultation on and disclosure of these situations, rather than use the dispute settlement provisions'.[50] In response, the SPS Committee decided to add a permanent sub-item entitled 'Specific trade concerns' under the item 'Implementation of the Agreement' to encourage Members to discuss trade problems in the Committee whenever possible before initiating formal and binding dispute settlement procedures, without prejudice to their rights under that process.[51]

In practice, a specific trade concern is raised in accordance with the Rules of Procedures of the Committee.[52] In many cases, bilateral consultations are held in the margins of meetings of the SPS Committee between a Member maintaining an SPS measure and another Member raising a specific trade concern over the regulation.[53] During a meeting of the Committee, the Member raising the

[47] Committee on Sanitary and Phytosanitary Measures, *Ad Hoc Consultations and Resolution of Trade Concerns: Note by the Secretariat* (*Note on ad hoc Consultations*), G/SPS/GEN/781, 15 June 2007.
[48] Committee on Sanitary and Phytosanitary Measures, *Proposed Recommended Procedure Relating to the Implementation of Article 12.2: Revision*, G/SPS/W/259/Rev.7, 9 September 2013, 2.
[49] Cf Committee on Sanitary and Phytosanitary Measures, *Review of the Operation and Implementation of the SPS Agreement: Report Adopted by the Committee on 18 March 2010*, G/SPS/53, 3 May 2010, para 117.
[50] Committee on Sanitary and Phytosanitary Measures, *Argentina-Guidelines to Supplement the SPS Committee's 1996 Programme Work*, G/SPS/W/53, 4 April 1996.
[51] Committee on Sanitary and Phytosanitary Measures, *Summary of the Meeting Held on 29–30 May 1996*, G/SPS/R/5, 9 July 1996, para 28.
[52] *Note on ad hoc Consultations* (n 47) para 5. See also Committee on Sanitary and Phytosanitary Measures, *Working Procedures of the Committee: Adopted by the Committee at its Meeting of 29–30 March 1995* (*Working Procedures*), G/SPS/1, 4 April 1995.
[53] *Note on ad hoc Consultations* (n 47) para 8.

concern, as well as any other interested Members, may comment on the concern, and the Member maintaining the regulation is asked to reply.[54] Members are requested to inform the Committee when the concern is resolved.[55]

In addition to bilateral consultations, good offices may also be provided by the Chairperson of the SPS Committee pursuant to Paragraph 6 of the Rules of Procedure of the Committee.[56] Nevertheless, there have been only three reported cases where good offices were solicited by Members.[57] While one of the cases was only partially resolved, the remaining two were reportedly resolved.[58] It is reported that the Chairperson made non-binding suggestions regarding possible actions that the Members could take to resolve the problem.[59] However, it is not entirely clear to what extent the Chairperson was involved in the substance of the consultations.[60]

There were 382 specific trade concerns raised between 1995 and the end of 2014, and 14 among those concerns were raised in 2014.[61] The United States and the European Union are among those that most frequently raise specific trade concerns, while the European Union is also the Member that most frequently becomes the target of specific trade concerns raised by other Members.[62] In the Asia-Pacific region, Canada, China, and Australia are among the most frequent 'concern-raising' Members while Australia, Japan, and the United States are among the most frequent 'target' Members.[63] Thus far, 175 out of the 382 trade concerns have been reportedly resolved, at least partially.[64] Some of the remaining unreported concerns may also have been resolved without notification to the Committee.[65]

In July 2014, the SPS Committee adopted a procedure to encourage and facilitate the resolution of SPS issues among Members in accordance with Article 12.2 of the SPS Agreement.[66] According to the adopted procedure, any Member(s) may at any time request consultations with another Member(s) regarding any SPS

[54] ibid para 9. [55] ibid para 10. [56] *Working Procedures* (n 52).

[57] *Note on ad hoc Consultations* (n 47) paras 16–19. [58] ibid. [59] ibid para 20.

[60] For example, with respect to good offices regarding a specific trade concern on India's ban on bovine semen imports from Canada, Canada indicated that the Chairperson participated in the bilateral consultations between Canada and India, but did not specify the exact role played by the Chairperson. Committee on Sanitary and Phytosanitary Measures, *Canadian Experience Using Article 12.2 Ad Hoc Consultations to Facilitate the Resolution of an SPS Trade-related Issue: Communication from Canada*, G/SPS/GEN/1080, 25 March 2011.

[61] Committee on Sanitary and Phytosanitary Measures, *Specific Trade Concerns: Note by the Secretariat: Revision* (*Summary of 2015*), G/SPS/GEN/204/Rev.15, 24 February 2015, 5.

[62] Henrik Horn and others, 'In the Shadow of the DSU: Addressing Specific Trade Concerns in the WTO SPS and TBT Committees' [2013] IFN Working Paper No 960, 8–10 <http://entwined.ivl.se/download/18.372c2b801403903d275574f/1382610321157/In+the+Shadow+of+the+DSU+Addressing+Specific+Trade+Concerns+in+the+WTO+SPS+and+TBT+Committees.pdf> accessed 6 April 2016.

[63] ibid. [64] *Summary of 2015* (n 61) 7–8.

[65] ibid. One study suggests that the 'vast majority of "serious" SPS' specific trade concerns have been resolved. Horn and others (n 62) 24–28, 30.

[66] Committee on Sanitary and Phytosanitary Measures, *Procedure to Encourage and Facilitate the Resolution of Specific Sanitary or Phytosanitary Issues Among Members in Accordance with Article 12.2: Decision Adopted by the Committee on 9 July 2014* (Adopted Procedure), GPS/61, 8 September 2014.

measures.[67] A Member that receives a request will provide a response accepting or rejecting the request for consultations.[68] When the responding Member accepts the consultation request, the requesting and responding Members will agree on a Facilitator that is typically served by the Chairperson of the SPS Committee.[69] The Facilitator is expected 'to encourage and facilitate an exchange between the consulting Members on specific SPS issues raised in the consultations with a view to resolving the issue'.[70] If the consulting Members agree, the Facilitator may suggest possible ways to resolve the issue.[71] The Facilitator and the consulting Members may agree to allow 'input of technical expertise' as well as third-party participation.[72] Consultations shall be completed within a reasonable period of time that shall be mutually agreed upon, and normally should not exceed 180 days.[73] Upon completion of the consultation, the Facilitator shall normally 'prepare and issue a written factual report on the consultations to the consulting Members'.[74] One of the most important features of the procedure is confidentiality. All communications and other documents in the course of the consultation as well as a factual report issued by the Facilitator shall be kept confidential unless otherwise agreed by the consulting Members.[75] The confidential nature could facilitate the flexible resolution of SPS issues.

2. *Are the ad hoc consultations effective in dealing with SPS issues?*

According to the SPS Committee, the ad hoc consultations under Article 12.2 of the SPS Agreement are expected to stimulate a dialogue within the Committee to identify concerns regarding the practical implementation of the SPS Agreement and to help create a multilateral consensus on how they should be addressed.[76] In fact, the informal and conciliatory process through the ad hoc consultations may work as an alternative or at least as a supplement to the binding panel and Appellate Body review,[77] given its advantages, when compared to the panel and Appellate Body review, in the following respects.

First, the ad hoc consultations enable Members to conduct long-term monitoring of SPS measures. SPS issues often require long-term monitoring rather than immediate findings regarding consistency with the SPS Agreement because the appropriateness and consistency of SPS measures with the SPS Agreement may vary as factual situations underlying the measures change during the course of time. For example, Russia raised a specific trade concern with respect to the European Union's temperature treatment requirements for imports of processed

[67] ibid para 1.3. [68] ibid para 2.3. [69] ibid para 2.8. [70] ibid para 2.9.
[71] ibid. [72] ibid para 2.10. [73] ibid para 2.13. [74] ibid para 2.14.
[75] ibid paras 2.12 and 2.14.
[76] Committee on Sanitary and Phytosanitary Measures, *Summary of the Meeting Held on 8–9 October 1996: Note by the Secretariat*, G/SPS/R/6, 14 November 1996, para 10.
[77] Scott (n 26) 54–55, 58. See also Committee on Sanitary and Phytosanitary Measures, *Review of the Operation and Implementation of the Agreement on the Application of Sanitary and Phytosanitary Measures: Report of the Committee*, G/SPS/12, 11 March 1999, para 25.

meat products.[78] In particular, Russia contended that the European Union's certain regulation created difficulties for its ready-to-eat meat product exports from Russia, except the Kaliningrad region.[79] In response, the European Union underlined that establishments approved to export the identified products were situated exclusively in the Kaliningrad region, and that an audit from the EU authority would be required to verify satisfactory animal and public health conditions in order to approve establishments in the other regions.[80] It follows that the appropriateness of the European Union's measure may change if establishments are founded and approved in the other regions of Russia. In other words, the European Union would have to amend its measure if Russia takes appropriate steps to ensure its meat products are properly exported not only from the Kaliningrad region but also from the other regions. In addition, the appropriateness of SPS measures may also be affected by scientific and technological developments.[81] For example, while a restriction on trans fatty acids might have been found as lacking scientific basis regarding risks twenty years ago, the finding would be different today because scientific knowledge has increased regarding its long-term risks. In this regard, the panel and Appellate Body review may fail to take into account long-term risks as it examines the consistency of an SPS measure in consideration of a risk assessment (or the lack thereof) made at a certain point in time. Thus, in cases where scientific evidence on long-term risks is not firmly established, long-term monitoring by the SPS Committee may be more desirable than the panel and Appellate Body review.

Second, the ad hoc consultations facilitate collaborative interactions between interested Members to resolve SPS issues. In the panel and Appellate Body review, an examination centres on the question of whether the complainant Member proves that an SPS measure taken by the respondent Member violates the SPS Agreement. Such an unidirectional examination may reveal only half of the entire picture because the appropriateness and consistency with the SPS Agreement of an SPS measure can only be judged when consideration is given not only to the SPS measure taken by an importing country but also to sanitary conditions in exporting countries. For example, whether an import restriction on beef due to Bovine Spongiform Encephalopathy (BSE) can be justifiably imposed in accordance with the SPS Agreement depends not only on the restriction itself but also on whether proper measures to control and contain the disease are being taken by exporting countries.[82] In this regard, the ad hoc consultations are more bidirectional than the panel and Appellate Body review in the sense that interested Members may freely discuss not only the question of whether an SPS measure at issue taken by an importing country Member is inconsistent with the SPS Agreement, but also the question of what measures should be taken by exporting countries to address a relevant public health concern of the importing country Member.

[78] *Summary of 2015* (note 61) para 2.76. [79] ibid para 2.80 [80] ibid.

[81] Rosie Cooney and Andrew T F Lang, 'Taking Uncertainty Seriously: Adaptive Governance and International Trade' (2007) 18 Eur J Intl L 523, 539–42.

[82] Recall Russia's specific trade concern with respect to the European Union's temperature treatment requirements for imports of processed meat products discussed above.

Third, scientific experts can be given a more proactive role in resolving SPS issues in the ad hoc consultations than those appointed in the panel review. In the panel review, panels are required to apply deferential standard of review in the sense that they shall not make their own risk assessment and shall confine themselves to a review of the assessment made by the respondent Member.[83] This deferential standard of review could limit the degree to which opinions presented by scientific experts appointed by panels are reflected in panels' findings because the opinions may only be used to review the reasonableness of the risk assessment of the respondent Member and not to make a de novo risk assessment.[84] Moreover, the selection of scientific experts often raises a controversy between the disputing parties, as the selection itself could determine the substance of expert opinions and definitively affect panels' conclusions.[85] On the contrary, in the ad hoc consultations, interested Members may freely use scientific expert opinions and engage in a full exploration of the facts regarding an SPS measure at issue without any deference. In this regard, it is relevant to point out that scientific experts have been playing a significant role through meetings and site visits in the course of bilateral consultations between Japan and Korea with respect to Korea's import restrictions on food and feeds allegedly contaminated with radionuclides.[86] It should also be noted that the SPS Committee could assist in the exploration of scientific facts between the consulting Members by seeking advice from relevant international organizations such as the Codex Alimentarius Commission, the International Office of Epizootics, and the Secretariat of the International Plant Protection Convention pursuant to Article 12.3 of the SPS Agreement. In addition, in cases where a specific trade concern arises as a result of the absence or inappropriateness of a relevant international standard, the ad hoc consultations can take advantage of expert evidence and contribute to promoting the creation or revision of an international standard.[87]

Fourth, the ad hoc consultations are more accessible for developing countries, as evidenced by their high participation rate in the consultations. The active participation

[83] Yuka Fukunaga, 'Standard of Review and "Scientific Truths" in the WTO Dispute Settlement System and Investment Arbitration' (2012) 3 J Intl Disp Settlement 559, 561–65. See also Appellate Body Report, *United States—Continued Suspension of Obligations in the EC—Hormones Dispute*, WT/DS320/AB/R, adopted 14 November 2008, paras 59–92; Appellate Body Report, *Canada—Continued Suspension of Obligations in the EC—Hormones Dispute*, WT/DS321/AB/R, adopted 14 November 2008, paras 59–92.

[84] Yuka Fukunaga, 'Experts in WTO and Investment Litigation' in Jorge A Huerta-Goldman and others (eds), *WTO Litigation, Investment Arbitration, and Commercial Arbitration* (Wolters Kluwer Law & Business 2013) 149. See also See Julien Chaisse and Luan Xinjie, 'Preliminary Comments on the WTO Seals Products Dispute: Traditional Hunting, Public Morals and Technical Barriers to Trade' (2011) 22(1) Colorado J Intl Env L&P 79–121.

[85] Fukunaga (n 84) 143–46.

[86] See e.g., Committee on Sanitary and Phytosanitary Measures, *Summary of the Meeting of 15 and 17 October 2014, Note by the Secretariat*, G/SPS/R/76, 2 December 2014, paras 3.9–3.10; Committee on Sanitary and Phytosanitary Measures, *Summary of the Meeting of 26–27 March 2015, Note by the Secretariat*, G/SPS/R/78, 21 May 2015, paras 3.16–3.17.

[87] David J Hornsby, 'WTO Effectiveness in Resolving Transatlantic Trade–Environment Conflict' (2010) 9 J Intl Trade L 297, 300–05.

reflects the collective nature of the ad hoc consultations in the sense that not only a Member raising a specific trade concern against another Member but also other interested Members may engage in talks.[88] As specific trade concerns are discussed in multilateral settings of the SPS Committee, developing country Members that may not be aware of potential harm to them caused by a certain SPS measure may be alerted when other Members raise a specific trade concern regarding the measure.[89] In fact, a specific trade concern raised by one Member is often supported by other Members at a later stage.[90] For example, a number of developing countries raised and supported a specific trade concern regarding the European Union's regulation on novel foods, arguing that it restricts not only the import of novel foods, such as genetically modified foods, but also the import of traditional foods imported from developing countries, and that its complex approval process burdens exporters in developing countries.[91] The European Union revised its regulation in November 2015 in response to comments by Members raising and supporting the concern.[92]

Fifth, the ad hoc consultations have advantages to developing country Members even when they are the target of a specific trade concern because they often fail to comply with the obligations of the SPS Agreement due to the lack of their capacity to implement the Agreement rather than due to lack of the will to do so. The consultations can help reveal the source of non-compliance and identify what measures should be taken to deal with it. For example, Indonesia's plan to close several entry ports to imports of fruit and vegetables, including the main port of Jakarta, was raised as a specific trade concern by China, New Zealand, the United States and the European Union, and was supported by several other Members.[93] Indonesia is claiming that the closures are due to the lack of appropriate facilities at the ports in order to implement necessary quarantine measures.[94] Although the issue has not yet been resolved, talks among interested Members may facilitate providing technical assistance to Indonesia to build the necessary facilities at the ports. It should also be recalled that violation findings by the panel and Appellate Body would not produce a viable solution to SPS issues when noncompliance with the SPS Agreement is the result of lack of capacity.

Finally, but most importantly, the ad hoc consultations can be regarded as more sensitive to the sovereign right of Members to adopt and enforce public health

[88] Yoshiko Naiki, 'Accountability and Legitimacy in Global Health and Safety Governance: The World Trade Organization, the SPS Committee, and International Standard-Setting Organizations' (2009) 43 J World Trade 1255, 1266–67.

[89] Robert Wolfe, 'Regulatory Transparency, Developing Countries and the WTO' [2003] 2 World Trade Rev 157, 169–69.

[90] Developing country Members who support concerns raised by other Members outnumber developed country Members who support concerns raised by other Members, while more developed countries raise concerns than developing countries. *Summary of 2015* (n 61) para 1.3.

[91] *Summary of 2015* (n 61) paras 2.22–2.73 (Application and Modification of the EU Regulation on Novel Foods (Specific Trade Concern 238)).

[92] ibid. A proposal to amend the regulation was presented by the European Commission and is currently under review by the European Parliament and the Council. European Commission, Food Safety, Food, Novel food, 'Legislation', <http://ec.europa.eu/food/safety/novel_food/legislation/index_en.htm> accessed 17 March 2016.

[93] *Summary of 2015* (n 61) paras 2.114–2.149 (Indonesia's Port Closures (Specific Trade Concern 330)).

[94] ibid.

policies, when compared to the panel and Appellate Body review. The ad hoc consultations do not produce any binding findings or recommendations but simply facilitate discussions among interested Members. This fact alone can appease Members' fear of interference from the WTO when drafting these important public policies and makes it easier for them to engage in constructive talks with other Members to find a solution to concerns.[95] The non-binding and conciliatory nature of consultations is particularly useful when the scientific evidence regarding risks is not clear. In this regard, Japan's experience in the wake of the Fukushima nuclear power plant accident exemplifies difficulties involving the scientific uncertainty of risks. Some Asian countries introduced import restrictions on certain agricultural and fishery products from Japan after the accident for fear that the products may be contaminated with radionuclides. Japan has been raising concerns with respect to the restrictions, though bilateral consultations in the SPS Committee have not produced a satisfactory resolution.[96] Chinese Taipei, for example, insisted on the need to assuage concerns of consumers, consumer protection groups, and legislators with respect to the levels of radionuclides contained in food exported from Japan.[97] These facts suggest that governments need to address not only scientifically proven risks but also the lack of scientific evidence regarding safety. Meanwhile, the panel and Appellate Body reviews are limited to the existence of scientific evidence regarding risks, and do not extend to the lack of scientific evidence regarding safety. In this sense, the panel and Appellate Body review may not properly consider Members' sovereignty in adopting a policy to address the lack of scientific evidence regarding safety.

It is true that the advantage of the ad hoc consultations in respecting sovereignty could be a weakness in securing compliance with the SPS Agreement. Because a Member maintaining an SPS measure is not legally obliged to respond to a consultation request or to amend or revise the measure, the success of the ad hoc consultations depends on voluntary co-operation between the Member maintaining the measure and the Members raising a concern. For example, Japan filed a consultations request under the DSU with respect to Korea's import bans as well as testing and certification requirements for radionuclides,[98] arguing that it could not obtain sufficient co-operation from Korea in the context of bilateral consultations in the SPS Committee.[99]

[95] For example, in response to a specific trade concern raised against its proposed amendment to its regulation on novel foods, the European Union has been engaged in talks with interested Members and has been reviewing the amendment.

[96] *Summary of 2015* (n 61) paras 2.21–2.220. [97] ibid.

[98] Request for Consultations by Japan, *Korea—Import Bans, and Testing and Certification Requirements for Radionuclides* (*Consultations Request, Korea—Import Bans*), WT/DS495/1, G/L/1116, G/SPS/GEN/1410, 1 June 2015.

[99] *Summary of 2015* (n 61) paras 2.151–2.158. It is notable that one of Japan's principal claims is concerned with Korea's failure to comply with the transparency and publication obligations under the SPS Agreement. *Consultations Request, Korea—Import Bans* (n 98). While it is not clear how Japan will proceed with the complaint, if a panel and the Appellate Body find violations of the transparency and publication obligations, and if Korea complies with the panel and Appellate Body's recommendation by providing and publishing the required information, the ad hoc consultations between Japan and Korea may be facilitated. Put differently, the panel and Appellate Body review could function to complement (and not to replace) the ad hoc consultations.

IV. Conclusion

This chapter explores the usefulness of a managerial approach in securing compliance with the SPS Agreement as an alternative or supplement to the panel and Appellate Body review. In particular, it argues that the ad hoc consultations under Article 12 of the SPS Agreement, when compared to the panel and Appellate Body review, can more effectively deal with SPS issues and can be more sensitive to the sovereign rights of Members in adopting and enforcing SPS measures of their choice.

Needless to say, it is up to Members to decide whether to use the ad hoc consultations or to have recourse to the panel and Appellate Body review in order to secure compliance with the SPS Agreement. There may well be cases where a Member can reasonably decide, in light of the scientific basis and economic impact of a relevant SPS issue, that the issue should be brought to the panel and Appellate Body review. That said, the relatively limited number of SPS disputes under the DSU in comparison to the growing list of specific trade concerns suggests that Members have been making the decision of whether to use the ad hoc consultations or to have recourse to the panel and Appellate Body review carefully and that they often regard the ad hoc consultations as a better option to resolve SPS issues.

In order to encourage this positive trend, it is useful to discuss possible improvements to the ad hoc consultations that can solve SPS issues more effectively but without interfering with the sovereign right of Members to draft public health policies. The good offices by the Chairperson of the SPS Committee may be one such improvement, but the infrequent use of good offices thus far suggests a rough road ahead. We may have to think about repairing and surfacing an already established road by improving procedures for specific trade concerns rather than paving a new one.

32

Conclusion: Some Thoughts on the WTO's Next Twenty Years

*Julio A Lacarte Muró**

There is an element of uncertainty, if not of presumption, involved in any views expressed on the future of an important inter-governmental organization over the period following its first twenty years of existence, and I am well aware of the risk attending any pronouncement to this effect. It is on this understanding, therefore, that I take the liberty of making the commentary that follows.

The WTO encompasses any number of areas of vital interest for governments and private operators alike, and the universe of subjects is such that one must necessarily limit—albeit arbitrarily—any pronouncement on what is in store for it in the mists of times to come.

It has been said that the past is prologue, and I subscribe to these words. So very often, we discover that what is happening today has roots in what occurred before and I will follow this precept.

The first issue I would like to stress concerns the most-favoured-nation clause, which has been from the first one of the two pillars of the GATT/WTO system. The other is national treatment.

When GATT was negotiated, back in 1947, the essential purpose was to establish a level playing field in international trade, where all countries would compete on equal terms. There existed the preferences of the Ottawa Agreements, and those that were part and parcel of the arrangements established between metropolitan territories and their colonies, such as those of France, the Netherlands, or Belgium. There were some other similar schemes in application as well.

For a number of reasons—both political and economic—it was decided that these preferences would be retained but not intensified, and that they should be clearly set out in an Annex to the GATT. This is, in effect, what was done.

* Ambassador Julio A Lacarte is a Uruguayan career diplomat and internationalist with a trade and economic background. He has been negotiator in the establishment of GATT, UNCTAD, Inter-American Development Bank, River Plate Basin Treaty, World Trade Organization (particularly, the WTO Agreement and the Dispute Settlement Understanding, over which he presided), and the Global System of Trade Preferences among Developing Countries.

The GATT also contained another provision that concerned preferences, in Article XXIV, which set out the conditions under which groups of countries could set up common markets and free trade agreements (FTAs) among themselves. I believe that, originally, negotiators did not feel that there would be frequent recourse to the facilities offered by Article XXIV, and indeed this is what happened during the first years.

However, there existed many reasons why a group of European countries might very well wish to establish a common market among themselves at some time in the future. Starting with the Iron and Steel Community, the six nations that would one day become the European Common Market began to work in that direction. Their successive governments showed an extraordinary capacity to persevere, overcoming one obstacle after another, and they finally signed the Rome Treaty in 1957. According to the contents of Article XXIV of GATT, the Treaty had to be presented to the other contracting parties of GATT for its consideration and subsequent approval. This process was launched, it became very lengthy owing to a substantial degree to the complexity of the treaty's provisions and their likely derivations, and great masses of documentation were produced to satisfy the numerous requests for information made by many countries. At the same time, the European Common Market continued to be gradually implemented, while conversations were being held in GATT.

There were many reasons why the Common Market was esteemed a very necessary part of international relations. It brought together France and Germany, whose rivalry had led to bloody wars over many years. If they managed to mesh their economic and social interests deeply, the risk of further conflict would disappear. Furthermore, the Cold War was on, opposing the United States and the Soviet Union. The emergence of a third, strong group of nations in Europe, peace loving by the very nature of the Rome Treaty, would have an overall stabilizing influence on events.

It became increasingly apparent that the provisions of the Rome Treaty did not always conform to GATT. This meant that approval under the terms of Article XXIV might become very difficult, if not impossible. At the same time, a number of contracting parties were aware of the disadvantages of rejecting it. So there was no pronouncement. The exchange of information went on, the matter was kept on the agenda, and in the end and to this day, the Rome Treaty remains neither approved nor rejected.

Inevitably, this action—or lack of action—had its consequences. What was applicable to the European Common Market surely would be valid for any other group of contracting parties. As time went by, the number of free trade agreements and common markets notified to GATT—and later to the WTO—gradually increased, and today there are 612 such notifications, of which 406 are in force.

Little by little, trade has moved for years in the direction of preferences and away from the most-favoured-nation clause. This process has now begun to speed up due to the mega-FTAs that have come into the picture. In August 2014, Canada and the European Union concluded their negotiation for the Comprehensive Economic and Trade Agreement (CETA), which is being reviewed from a legal point of view before being submitted to ratification. While the full text has not yet been published, official statements made on both sides indicate the scope of the agreement, which in many respects goes much further than present WTO commitments, for example on customs duties, rules of origin, services, investment, telecommunications, intellectual property, services, energy, maritime transport, public contracts, regulatory co-operation, and sanitary regulations. The working table of contents of the treaty has forty-two chapters. Clearly, CETA is intended to establish a strong preferential system between its partners, which signifies not only a radical departure from the WTO in terms of its contents, but also the firm intention to apply new measures to improve their share in world trade.

Presently, the United States and the European Union are also negotiating along the same lines. Conversations for a Trans-Atlantic Trade and Investment Partnership remain confidential, but the information available indicates that the contents of the proposed agreement are intended to be as comprehensive as CETA, if not more so. Improved market access for goods and services, measures on regulatory coherence and operation, agreements on sectoral areas such as motor-cars, textiles, and sanitary questions, and the setting up of international standards on a very large range of subjects, are on the agenda of twenty-four negotiating groups which it is expected will conclude their work by 2016. Very clearly, this process will create pressures on other countries, if they wish to remain in this market, since they will have to conform to the requirements now being established. It is not unthinkable that Mexico and the EFTA countries would in due course adhere to the treaty.

There is little question that the US–EU negotiation has great obstacles to overcome, not only because of the need to harmonize so many different regimes, but also because of the vested interests on both sides, which will be winners or losers according to the final provisions of the treaty. At the same time, not to succeed would be such an economic and political failure that the participating countries will certainly bend every effort to avoid it.

In the meantime, the United States has pursued a similar objective in the Pacific Basin area, through the Trans-Pacific Partnership with countries both in East Asia and the west coast of Latin America, which include Canada and Japan. Members account for some forty per cent of world trade. The basic agreement was signed on 5 October 2015, and is now under legal review.

The subject matter of the agreement remains confidential, although leakages of information indicate that its contents will parallel to a large degree those of the Trans-Atlantic Trade and Investment Partnership.

Finally, we must remember that the European Union and Japan are presently negotiating an FTA.

If one surveys the picture that will emerge, it shows that if all these FTAs come into force, as seems likely, the conclusion is obvious: most world trade in goods and services will be conducted under preferential treatment, and a great number of new obligations—going beyond those contained in the present scope of the WTO—will come into force.

Under those conditions, the WTO's most-favoured-nation clause will lose a significant part of its significance, and the international standards set by the FTAs will necessarily have to be met by countries if they wish to continue to enter those markets. A change of this nature will have worldwide repercussions, and countries will necessarily have to conform to it.

Of course, when we note the great share of world trade that members of these mega-agreements represent, we must remember that these are present flows. The question is, to what degree this great emphasis on preferences will increase commerce among participants. There is no clear reply for the moment, if it isn't to conclude that there will certainly be an effect.

Preferential agreements often have the effect of disguising inefficiencies, and those that have been concluded or are on the point of doing so will be no different. Since they will apparently cover many areas of economic activity, well beyond the traditional customs duties and non-tariff barriers, their scope could be extremely wide. As we well know, private operators will endeavour to take advantage of preferences to enlarge their profits. This is a part of the picture that negotiators will surely have considered in the course of their work.

In any case, it seems reasonable to interpret that the most-favoured-nation clause contributes more than preferences to efficiency in trade, and—consequently—to the world economy.

What of the WTO in all this? It will remain the overall administrator of the rules, benefits, and obligations that are contained in its provisions. It will continue to review the economic and trade performance of all its Members. Its dispute settlement mechanism will maintain its supremacy as a model of efficiency and objectivity. And it will certainly not weaken its role as the meeting place where all countries meet to promote the benefits of trade.

It could well be that the WTO will have, in the future, a new and highly important task, in bringing harmony, coherence, and rationalization to the hundreds of FTAs and common markets presently in force. In due course, the need to do so will become apparent and a new stage in world trade relations will have been entered.

There are two other matters which seem to appear on the WTO's horizon and which deserve attention. One is the manner in which multilateral negotiations are conducted and the other is its internal functioning.

The Uruguay Round was the biggest and most successful trade negotiation ever held. It brought together some hundred countries, opened the way for many others to later join the WTO, and established a new institutional framework for world trade. The negotiations went from one crisis to another; at times they seemed to be on the point of failing, but every obstacle was surmounted in the end. There was a common will among governments to succeed; two successive GATT Directors General—Arthur Dunkel and Peter Sunderland—made an outstanding contribution to the work, and the forces of protectionism were rolled back.

The present Doha Round has been on over ten years, and it has not attained its initial aims. There has been progress here and there, but the core issues remain unsolved. Over this lengthy period, the world has changed a good deal, and so has trade.

One can no doubt find many explanations for this situation, and each one will be valid to some degree. Did governments aim too high in agreeing a programme of work that was too ambitious? Or has there not existed the determination to accept new obligations in exchange for increased benefits?

I suggest a possible cause for what has happened. In past multilateral negotiations in the GATT period, there is no question that the prime movers were the developed countries. Time after time, their final schedules of concessions basically referred to products that were part of trade among themselves. Items such as textiles, agricultural products, and leather were consistently excluded, although they were the ones of most interest to developing countries; as a consequence, they were granted few market access concessions.

In the Uruguay Round the same problem persisted, but there was enough for developing countries to participate in the work more fully than in the past, although many of them felt eventually that the balance of benefits and obligations arising from the Round was not to their advantage, and that the implementation of measures agreed had not been satisfactory.

In the Doha Round, as is well known, it has not yet been possible to reach agreement on agricultural and other products of interest to these countries.

However, much has happened over the past years, and it has had its repercussion in the Doha Round. A number of developed countries have had to surmount severe economic problems, while their rate of progress has slowed significantly. This certainly does not contribute to accepting new trade challenges from abroad. In other words, it exacerbates protectionist forces.

In the same period, a great number of developing countries, large and small, have attained high levels of yearly increases in their economic performance: and they have done so without any new WTO market access concessions. Simply, the forces of the global economy have moved in their favour.

So, while one group of countries has found it difficult to further open up their markets to foreign competition and thus to grant new Doha Round concessions, another group has found it has prospered, while not having to depend on new benefits from the Round.

As a consequence, the urge to liberalize trade has inevitably diminished.

This is, I believe, one of the main reasons for the stagnation of the Doha Round. If I am correct, it is likely that advances in the near future will not reach the dimension originally established.

Furthermore, as I commented earlier, the sharp and very important recourse to FTAs, with their attendant preferential treatment, is pointing the way to a different policy, which bypasses the Doha Round and seeks benefits elsewhere.

In these circumstances, it is difficult to conceive a broadly successful Doha Round in the immediate future. Rather, we should expect progress on specific sectors, and possibly with the participation of a limited number of Members, such as the proposed Agreement on Services.

What of the future? Certainly, the WTO must work for the liberalization of trade. That is what it's all about. And multilateral negotiations are the way to attain this end.

No doubt, the Doha Round experience is going to be much taken into account when preparing for later negotiations, and the switch towards FTAs will be a part of the picture. More than once in the past, some trade experts have advanced the view that the WTO should operate on two levels: one, with the participation of all Members, and the other with whatever countries were ready to deepen their trade concessions.

In their way, FTAs answer to this concept. When all the mega-FTAs come into force, the trade picture will probably change a good deal. In essence, this is a question that will have to be faced at the WTO when the panorama becomes clearer, and whatever is decided will have a profound effect on the future of the organization. The WTO is here to stay. It's the meeting place for all countries on trade issues. A great number of its provisions are of universal application and they commit all its Members. Whatever happens, the WTO has a very great role to play now and in the future. What that role will be precisely will give rise to debate and—almost certainly—to disagreements; but since governments have gone through similar stages in the past and finally agreed, we can expect that this will also occur when the moment comes.

A third issue that I believe is due to concern the WTO and will come up, is that of its internal functioning. In particular, I refer to the creation or otherwise of some sort of executive board with limited membership, entrusted with assuring the efficient day-to-day functioning of the organization. In the past, very strong opinions have been voiced, both for and against this idea, and one was during the Uruguay Round.

The notion of an organ of this kind is acceptable to large trading countries, which would expect to be always—or generally—Members. As the importance of other countries diminishes, so does their interest in this sort of arrangement. The WTO had for a time the Group of 18, which carried out this function. In the end, it was discontinued because too many countries were not comfortable with it.

The essence of the problem, in my view, is that it is extremely difficult, if not impossible, to separate procedure from substance on trade issues. Often, the very form in which a negotiation will take place, in one way or another is pointing to the areas in which agreement can be reached, and excluding others. Under these circumstances, everybody feels it is essential they should participate in all stages of the work, and this limits the scope and mandate of any limited membership organ.

On the other hand, it is certainly true that WTO Membership continues to grow and that there could well exist a valid reason for setting up some sort of limited membership organ.

In any case, I suspect that this matter will come up sooner or later and will surely be debated with as much vigour as in the past.

There are very many other challenges with which the WTO will need to contend in the future. In this brief commentary, I have limited myself to three of them, which I believe will surely be on the WTO's working agenda.

The push towards world globalization is strong, aided by constant progress in the field of transport and communication. It is unlikely that international trade will escape this tendency. We must therefore see the WTO as a prime actor in events that will shape our future.

One final word. I am extremely fortunate to contribute to a book that renders tribute to my friend Mitsuo Matushita, in whose company I spent so many hours settling disputes among governments. He was always wise, very well informed, and extremely positive. He very much deserves recognition as one of the group that launched the WTO Appellate Body and to which he contributed so generously. It is my privilege to be part of this enterprise.

Index

Page references to Figures or Tables will be in *italics* followed by the letters 'f' or 't', while references to footnotes will be followed by the letter 'n' and note number.

The manufacturer's authorised representative in the EU for product safety is Oxford University Press España S.A. of el Parque Empresarial San Fernando de Henares, Avenida de Castilla, 2 – 28830 Madrid (www.oup.es/en or product.safety@oup.com). OUP España S.A. also acts as importer into Spain of products made by the manufacturer.

www.ingramcontent.com/pod-product-compliance
Lightning Source LLC
LaVergne TN
LVHW011855200926
848484LV00002B/456

* 9 7 8 0 1 9 8 7 7 8 2 5 7 *